Handbook of
Marital Interventions

Handbook of Marital Interventions

Luciano L'Abate, Ph.D.
Department of Psychology
Georgia State University
Atlanta, Georgia

Sherry McHenry, Ph.D.
Co-director
The Link Counseling Center
Atlanta, Georgia

Grune & Stratton
A Subsidiary of Harcourt Brace Jovanovich, Publishers
New York   London
Paris   San Diego   San Francisco   São Paulo
Sydney   Tokyo   Toronto

Library of Congress Cataloging in Publication Data

L'Abate, Luciano, 1928–
    Handbook of marital interventions.

    Bibliography.
    Includes indexes.
    1. Marital psychotherapy. I. McHenry, Sherry.
II. Title.
RC488.5.L34   1983   616.89'156   82-24227
ISBN 0-8089-1502-9

Grune & Stratton, Inc.
111 Fifth Avenue
New York, New York 10003

Distributed in the United Kingdom by
Academic Press Inc. (London) Ltd.
24/28 Oval Road, London NW 1

Library of Congress Catalog Number 82-24227
International Standard Book Number 0-8089-1502-9
Printed in the United States of America

Contents

Acknowledgments

We could not have even attempted to review the current state of the art of marital therapies without the help of a great many friends and colleagues. We are both grateful to and appreciative of the following individuals for their help in researching the existing literature in the field of marital therapy: Marcia Weiss and the late Eugene E. Dunne for Chapter 2 on assertiveness training; Stephanie Ezust for Chapter 3 on communication; Cinda Caiella and Juan Flores for Chapter 4 on covenant contracting; James George for Chapter 5 on marriage encounter; Lyn Sommer for Chapter 6 on enhancement; Debbie Walter for Chapter 8 on conflict resolution; Shawn O'Sullivan for Chapter 9 on problem solving; Jim Kochalka and Bruce Freedman for Chapter 10 on sexuality; Jim Kochalka, Michael O'Shea, Carole Torrence, and Hillary Buzas for Chapter 11 on behavioral marital therapy; Debbie Daniels, Linda Talmadge, and David Kearns for Chapter 13 on marital therapies; Stephanie Barge and David Karan for Chapter 14 on divorce mediation; and Kay Watson and Edgar Jessee for Chapter 16 on the measurement of intervention outcome.

We thank Jim Kochalka, Debbie Daniels, and Linda Talmadge for offering numerous helpful criticisms and comments throughout the writing of the first draft of this book.

We also owe a debt of gratitude to Marie Morgan for her combination of careful typing and editing of the entire manuscript, and to Sherry Martin, who organized and crosschecked numerous references with her usual efficiency and clarity.

Foreword

As family therapists, we have reason to be worried about our field. Family therapy has too often tolerated unresearched, untested techniques and assumptions. Even successful therapists often follow the newest dramatic techniques of the charismatic "expert" passing through town or through print.

This remarkable book is a comprehensive effort to apply critically the hard data of research on marriage and marriage interventions to the theory and practice of marriage therapy. It describes each school of marital therapy, outlines its basic assumptions, practices, and techniques, and then explores the data base for it. All existing educational and behavioral approaches are examined. The chapter on psychotherapies includes a look at the currently popular schools of family therapy. L'Abate and McHenry are properly frustrated with the inadequacy of data in these fields, asking whether the theory is really related to the therapy. The section on premarital counseling demonstrates the discouraging lack of clarity and research in that vital but neglected field. By contrast the section on divorce mediation is inspiring, as the section on divorce counseling is hopeful. The section on theory and research presents a variety of promising theories and work in progress. The section on training is particularly encouraging.

This is a book that family therapists should know. We often bewail the shortage in family therapy of psychologists and the hard research they are trained to provide. Family therapy was founded by a scattering of maverick psychiatrists, a small group of experts in communication, and a daring social worker. Psychologists were not present in full force in the beginnings of family therapy. Most of the primary research that has been done seems to focus on the marital dyad rather than on the "messier" unit of the family. This research, however incomplete, constitutes the data base for our field. It should not be overlooked by family therapists, even if it seems addressed to the marginally different group of marital therapists. L'Abate and McHenry are presenting this material to both groups.

This book provides a much needed reminder that without data, our internal debate over theory and technique is bravado. Our allegiance to some approaches is an act of faith not science. We need to make ourselves uncomfortable, since we're not likely to question what we're doing otherwise.

Lou L'Abate has been a prolific writer. The driving force behind all his work is data. It is always there at the center, hard as a rock. He has been a firm teacher, determined that no one who encounters him could continue to accept anything without data. He is one of the most tough-minded researchers in our notoriously soft field.

Sherry McHenry has been running a much admired program at The Link for years. This counseling center has embodied our belief that psychotherapy can be much more than it usually is, that it can reach a population it usually doesn't, and that it can be based on fact rather than faith. She devotes herself to teaching her clients and others that life and the world can and should make sense.

This is a scholarly work—not pedantic, not just a review of the literature. It is an informed study of the field. It understands and summarizes and gets to the core of everything it tackles. It is sometimes brief, but never superficial or cursory. It tackles everything. It is comprehensive. There is nothing left out about the nuts and bolts of marriage and marital therapy and the training of marital therapists. It surely takes on every organized school, approach, or program that deals with people's marriages.

Yet this is far more than a scholarly compilation of hard data and an indictment of its lack. The authors deal directly with each approach; programs are outlined and explained as they appear to their adherents, on the basis of their theoretical assumptions and actual practice, and then on the basis of whatever data, if any, support them. Respectful of each, the text avoids supporting any specific point of view.

It is understandable that normal people are content to derive comfort from accepting things on faith without troubling themselves to find out for sure. Researchers, however, must live with doubt. Those researchers who allow themselves to get comfortable, thinking they know the answers, are no longer researchers at all, but theorists—former researchers who have lost their doubt. Perhaps L'Abate and McHenry can restore it to them. Their book is a massive achievement. For the moment it is the last word in the field, but we hope it is only the beginning.

Frank S. Pittman, III, M.D.
Psychiatrist and Family Therapist
in Private Practice
Atlanta, Georgia

1

The Field of Marital Interventions and Therapies

Marital therapies and treatment interventions are relatively recent phenomena in the history of the institution of marriage and the field of psychology. It has only been in the latter half of this century that a separate profession has developed to clinically treat couples seeking help with their relationship difficulties. What began in the 1920s as attempts to help individuals adjust to their roles and role responsibilities has evolved into a vast and often disparate array of theories and interventions for both functional and dysfunctional couples. In particular, the past decade has been an era of proliferation of psychological methods and techniques that purport to treat virtually every aspect of the marital relationship. These methods and techniques, in part or in total, address such abstract issues as intimacy, communication, growth, and marital satisfaction, as well as a number of specific and more concrete issues, such as sexual functioning, conflict resolution, negotiation, and decision-making.

Currently, the practitioner or student in the field of marital therapy is confronted with an array of literature that ranges from the practical to the innovative, from the simplistic to the overly complex, and from the cautionary to the dogmatic. Even though most marital therapists still describe themselves as eclectic, newer methods and techniques are beginning to display some integration of theory development with practice.

This book has been written for several purposes: to address the need to condense, review, and assess the literature on most methods and techniques of interventions with couples; to review current developments in theory and practice; and to offer a critical look at the current state of the art of marital therapy/intervention. It is hoped that the format of this book will help readers to understand, assess, and integrate current developments and future needs in this still rapidly growing field.

Each chapter addresses a specific method or technique. Some of the approaches reviewed are for functional marriages, while others are for dysfunctional marriages. The majority of the literature reviewed addresses itself to the more functional relationship, however. This focus reflects no bias on the part of the authors, but reflects current trends in marital therapy/intervention. Newer methods and techniques tend to focus on intimacy and growth, rarely presupposing severe dysfunction in one or both members of the couple.

Initially, the criteria for inclusion of a particular method or technique were that (1) it had emerged or been developed in the last decade; (2) it had a minimum of overlap with other methods in philosophical assumptions and theory; (3) the content and process, or the sequence of behaviors defining the therapeutic intervention, differed significantly from other treatments; and (4) it had been widely discussed in the literature. In other words, those methods/techniques were sought that would be distinguishable, both theoretically and practically, from other methods/techniques. Other initial criteria for selection were ethical and professional soundness as defined by both public and professional acceptance, demonstrated effectiveness or efficiency as evaluated by empirical research, and subjective and objective reports from consumers of the particular method or technique.

In evaluating the validity of particular methods and techniques, we concur with Patterson, Weiss, and Hops' (1976; also Weiss, Hops, & Patterson, 1973) assessment that there are ultimately at least four requirements for acceptance of effectiveness: (1) ability to replicate treatment effects for consecutive cases by the same investigator; (2) ability to replicate in other investigations, (3) comparisons of treatment effects with untreated control groups; and (4) multiple criteria assessments before, during, and after intervention. In reality, however, most methods/techniques overlap in both theory and practice, contrary to the claims of their originators and/or advocates. For example, there is now a consistent focus on communication and negotiation, as well as on the underlying goals of increased intimacy and psychological growth, in virtually all forms of marital intervention. Perhaps the only major distinctions that consistently delineate varying methods and techniques are whether they are structured or unstructured approaches and whether they are educational or problem-treatment-focused approaches.

The first major distinction among the methods and techniques presented in this book is whether they are structured or unstructured. In structured techniques and methods, a specific marital topic or issue has been selected by the therapist or client prior to intervention. Any contractual agreement with the participating couple includes consensus on the specific focus of intervention, the length of treatment, and the role of the therapist. Unstructured techniques are those that do not necessarily specify focus of intervention and length of treatment. The reader will note, however, that there is often an overlap between these two categories.

The second major distinction among the methods and techniques presented in this book

is whether they are, in fact, methods or treatment techniques. Most, but not all, structured interventions are educational methods that teach skills to participants. They are defined as methods because they can often be learned and applied by different individuals with a presumed minimum amount of deviation from practitioner to practitioner. Most of the unstructured interventions are defined as treatment techniques because they rely heavily on the training and competence of the professional and, as a whole, are much more complex and difficult to learn and master than structured methods. Their goal is usually problem alleviation and change rather than skill training and education. Most educational methods have sets or sequences or reproducible instructions or operations that can be learned within a relatively short time period and that are presumed to depend minimally on the personal or professional competence of the individual. Most techniques are operations that depend for the most part on the thinking, intuition, style, and personality of the therapist, and as such are much more difficult to duplicate and apply.

A commonality among the methods and techniques presented in this book, however, is that of origin. Some methods, such as enhancement, effectiveness, and problem-solving, and some techniques such as Behavioral Marital Therapy and Gestalt Marital Therapy did not evolve from the context of addressing the marital relationship. Instead, they evolved from initial interventions with individuals and/or parent–child relationships. As these interventions gradually defined a common set of principles and techniques, their application to marital relationships became evident as a logical extension of the treatment focus.

In our review of the current methods and techniques of marital intervention, we have found emerging praiseworthy trends as well as questionable theory and practice. As so often occurs in other mental health specialties, as the field of marital therapy becomes more popular and diverse, debate among various proponents of different and specific interventions increases. Although diversity offers a broad range of treatment choices, there must also be some critical integration of the mushrooming numbers of differing approaches to marital intervention. It is our hope, therefore, that the reader will view this book not as a manual of interventions and techniques but as an aid to the theoretical and practical integration of the current available marital therapies. We also hope that this book will help the reader to question those assumptions that are now emerging as the major foci of marital treatment. An underlying question that cannot be overlooked by the marital therapist of the 1980s is how appropriate current theories and interventions are to the evolving institution of marriage.

THE CURRENT STATUS OF MARITAL INTERVENTIONS

Broderick and Schrader (1981) cite four major influences that have contributed to the growth and present interest in marital and family therapy: the social work movement, the development of social psychiatry, the influence of early sexologists, and the family life education movement. To these four trends, we would add the growth of psychoanalysis and psychotherapeutic approaches, the rise of behaviorism as a new technology, and the growth of humanistic approaches as the "third" force in reaction to deficits in psychoanalytic and behavioral approaches. Finally, and perhaps most important, there has been an increasing consumer demand for help with relationship difficulties.

Historically, marriage therapies and interventions have gone through four distinct phases, which Broderick and Schrader divide into Phase I (1929 to 1932), a beginning pioneer stage dominated by individual practitioners such as Emily Mudd; Phase II (1934 to 1945), an establishment stage marked by the formation of the American Association of Marriage Counselors (which is now the American Association of Marriage and Family Therapists); Phase III (1946 to 1963), a construction and formalization stage ending in recognition of a new profession; and Phase IV (1964 to the present), a formative stage marked by years of intense growth and clarification of standards and competencies.

Two additional movements have been parallel contributors to the development and growth of marital therapies and interventions: first, the tremendous growth of the family therapy movement, and second, the growth of the social skills training movement. Both these movements have added specific bodies of knowledge concerning marriage, a self-definition of professionals whose major identity is concern for marital intervention and therapy, and the institutionalization of the field through specific publications and the beginnings of training programs devoted solely to marriage and marital therapy.

The lack of extensive training programs exclusively devoted to marriage and marital interventions results in part from the fact that marital therapies have been enmeshed with family therapies and have only recently become defined as different and independent from the field of family therapy. Only the future will tell whether or not such a differentiation will continue, however, as well as whether or not it will be necessary, useful, or warranted. We suspect and predict that as the fields of marital and family therapies and interventions continue to become more differentiated in theory and in practice, marital therapy will become more separated from family therapy.

Vincent (1977), however, questions the possibility that "Marital Health" will develop as a separate discipline from family therapy, by citing four obstacles: (1) the failure to distinguish between concepts of "healthy marriages" and "Marital Health" as a health field; (2) erroneous assumptions that Marital Health already exists as a health field; (3) the preindustrial myth of naturalism, which assumes that marriage is a natural occurrence and therefore should not be altered; and (4) the inability to develop a health model based on neutral, value-free concepts and terminology. It must be noted, however, that in spite of these inherent obstacles, interest in "Marital Health" as a unit of study and intervention has increased noticeably in the past decade, primarily because of vast societal changes and demands. Broad segments of our society are concerned with the question of what constitutes a healthy marriage, and there is a growing awareness that there is no singular definition of "health." The idea that marriage is a stable unit of two individuals is no longer accepted. Instead, there is a growing acceptance of the idea that marriage is a changeable unit of individuals that requires numerous accommodations and adaptations throughout its life cycle.

Marital problems present a significant proportion of all mental and emotional disorders. In fact, Gurin, Veroff, and Feld (1960) reported on the basis of a nationwide survey that marital difficulties were the most frequently cited reason for consulting a mental health professional. Of those respondents who had sought professional help, 42 percent had done so because of problems with the "spouse" or "marriage." This figure is over twice that for the next leading cause for seeking help: "nonjob adjustment problems in the self (general adjustment, specific symptoms, etc.)," which was the reason cited in 18 percent of the cases. The great importance of marital problems in psychiatric disorders was further confirmed in a more recent survey by Sager et al. (1968). They found that fully one-half of those individuals seeking psychotherapy were largely motivated to do so because of marital problems. It was found that another one-fourth of the patients in psychotherapy had marriage-related difficulties. Marital problems were the single major precipitating stress in approximately one-half of all first admissions to state mental hospitals.

It seems clear that the number of referrals to mental health professionals represents a gross underestimate of the number of individuals experiencing marital disharmony. The percentage of couples who are unhappy in their marriages is generally placed at 25 percent. This situation does not appear to be improving spontaneously, as evidenced by a rising divorce rate.

Marital problems appear to have deleterious effects that extend beyond the unhappiness experienced in the married state. Cahalan, Cisin, and Crossley (1969) determined that alcoholism is greater among those individuals who are separated, while others (Monahan, 1957; Siegman, 1966; Silver & Derr, 1966) determined that delinquency is more prevalent among children who come from broken homes.

In addition to the obvious need for therapeutic interventions for marital problems as such, a good case can be made for the position that many forms of individual psychopathology would be better treated within the context of the family or the marriage. This argument follows from Haley's (1963) observation that when one spouse becomes more functional as a result of individual counseling, there is a tendency for the behavior of the other spouse to deteriorate. Haley (1963) attributes this phenomenon to an implicit agreement between the two spouses to relate in a dysfunctional manner. This pattern of expected behaviors has been labeled by Lidz and Fleck (1965) "homeostasis of the dyadic relationship." Satir (1967) also argues that therapy should be conducted within a family context. She believes that a person cannot present an accurate image of himself or herself in individual therapy. A closer approximation to an accurate perception may, however, be obtained by involving members of the client's family in the counseling process. The great importance of accurate role perceptions in marital counseling is suggested by the research of Lucky (1964).

A somewhat discrepant conclusion emerges from the Sager, et al (1968) study. Of the treated patients they reviewed, 60 percent showed "moderate or marked improvement." They also found a strong positive correlation between a patient's improvement in psychoanalysis and improvement in the mental status of the spouse; however, 51 percent of the spouses had themselves been in psychoanalysis! "Of those spouses who were not in any treatment, about 6 percent were said to be greatly improved as a result of therapy of the primary person, 65 percent were reported to be relatively unaffected, and about 8 percent were rated as worse" (p. 217). A positive relationship was found between individual progress in therapy and improvement in the state of the patient's marriage. The Sager, et al (1968) study appears to open up the possibility that marital functioning may be improved through individual treatment. The study suffers from the serious defect that all data derive from the global ratings of therapists, however.

There is a growing acknowledgment that the institution of marriage must alter itself in order to accommodate to rapid cultural changes. Cultural change is seen in the current divorce rate of one of every three marriages and in current mental health statistics, which indicate that marital difficulties are among the three most common reasons that individuals seek the help of mental health professionals (Prochaska & Prochaska, 1978). Furthermore, the current Women's Movement has challenged the traditional authoritarian marriage by emphasizing the equality of women. This increased emphasis on women's equality has undoubtedly altered both the lay and the professional communities' conceptions of what is expected of the marital relationship. As a result of altered expectations, new marital forms such as companionship marriages and serial monogamy are becoming increasingly prevalent, with accompanying disruption and uncertainty among individuals concerning the structure and status of their marriages.

Concurrent with changing expectations, economic changes have altered the traditional structure of marriage. The traditional nuclear family, consisting of one wage earner, constitutes the minority of families, for the dual-wage couple continues to be a necessity rather than a choice for most couples.

In the past, the growth of marital therapy and interventions has emerged not only from demand but in many instances from the academic and professional luxury of interest. Those professionals who were interested in marriage as an entity of study ultimately developed interventions and other therapies.

The field of marital interventions and therapies can no longer be considered a luxury for those with expressed interest, however, but is instead a professional necessity. Societal changes have forced an awakening to numerous unresolved issues concerning the nature, quality, and future of the marital relationship.

Changes in society's views of marriage are now reflected in the commonalities across all marital treatment approaches. These commonalities are the goals of increased role flexibility/adaptability, a more equitable balance of power, open and clear communication, and increased self-esteem (Gurman, 1978). Treatment approaches differ, however, in terms of emphasis on the etiology and locus of pathology and the types of methods that can most effectively achieve therapeutic goals.

In attempting to assess current methods of marital intervention, we must stress the need for more controlled inquiries concerning the effectiveness of interventions, regardless of their theoretical orientation. No single approach has been found to be inherently more effective than another. Instead, various approaches have differing strengths and weaknesses.

Gurman (1978), in his comparative analysis of the three major contemporary models of treatment (psychoanalytic, behavioral, and systems), examined four specific dimensions by which the marital treatment and intervention process can be examined: (1) the role of the past and the unconscious, (2) the nature and meaning of the presenting problems and the role of assessment, (3) the relative importance of mediating versus ultimate treatment goals, and (4) the nature of the therapists' roles and functions. In his analysis of these four dimensions, Gurman predicted that in the field of marital therapy, the basic theoretical orientations may remain, but that ultimately the blending of these orientations will produce different combinations and permutations from their original "parent" ideas. He also predicted that further increases in empirical evidence will show that no single theoretical approach can be effective for all marital problems and that competition among proponents of various approaches will give way to more collaboration, as well as to more temperate and moderate allegiances and claims.

To Gurman's analyses of methods of marital intervention, this book adds two perspectives that have been overlooked in the past. The first is the presence and impact on marriage and marital therapy of the humanistic movement. Thus we have attempted to review the various humanistic approaches that are available in methods of marital intervention. The second perspective is one of viewing current methods of marital intervention along a continuum, ranging in degree of structure from remedial preventive skill-training programs to unstructured remedial therapies. The commonalities presented by the variety of preventive skill-training programs include a focus that integrates the primary aspects of human behavior. These aspects are *emotionality*, which represents the viewpoint of subjective experience presented by humanists; *rationality*, which represents the rational viewpoint presented by psychoanalysis, reality-oriented therapy, and Bowenian therapy; *activity*, which represents the behavioral viewpoint presented by behaviorists; *awareness and feedback*, which represents the gestalt-experience viewpoint presented by humanistic and Eastern philosophies; and, finally, *context*, which represents the systemic view of relationships

Table 1-1
Classification of Intervention Methods According to the E-R-A-Aw-C Model

A. Emotionality & Awareness	B. Rationality	C. Activity	D. Context (Systemic, Structured, Strategic)
Methods focus on experiential exercises that differentiate feeling states of solitude and solidarity. 1. Developing intrapersonal awareness through individual exercises of mediation fantasy trips, imaginary dialogues, here-and-now awareness.	*Methods focus on the development of conscious understanding that supports reality-based control.* 1. Teaching new facts, concepts, and theories through lectures, readings, and discussions.	*Methods focus on the application of scientific principles to shape and control behavior.* 1. Solving behavioral problem through experimental analysis—quantifying behavior, determining controls, implementing interventions, and evaluating.	*Methods focus on adjusting dimensions of cohesion and adaptability that maintain family functioning.* 1. Establishing appropriate boundaries for cohesion and autonomy through a. Directives given in session (e.g., spatial rearrangements, reenactments of events demanding specific interactions, blocking other members of the social network) b. Behavior assignments for daily context (e.g., rituals, paradoxical exercises, age-appropriate tasks, activities to support coalitions to limit enmeshment).
2. Developing awareness of interpersonal relationships through interactional tasks of role play, sculpting, etc.	2. Relating past influence to present functioning through cognitive recreation of past events (e.g., psychoanalytic dialogues, genograms, rational reevaluations).	2. Teaching and increasing desired behavior and extinguishing inappropriate behavior through techniques of a. Respondent conditioning (e.g., stimulus pairing, desensitization) b. Operant conditioning (e.g., positive reinforcement, punishment).	2. Restructuring operations in response to situational stress and/or developmental change through a. Assigning linear task to directly change operations (e.g., rescheduling, assigning family duties) b. Assigning paradoxical tasks that emphasize

operational problems (e.g., role reversals, behavioral extremes).

3. Developing bodily awareness through physical exercises of creative movement and interpersonal body contacts.

3. Developing insight to differentiate feelings from actions through analysis of one's present and past relationships (e.g., working through transference, understanding defense operations and ego controls).

3. Teaching desired behavior through social learning (e.g., modeling, films).

4. Teaching skills of interpersonal sensitivity and communication through lectures, readings, demonstrations, and practice exercises.

4. Teaching skills of rational thinking and ego control through lectures, discussions, and practice in rational problem-solving and decision-making.

4. Increasing and maintaining behavior through evaluative feedback.

5. Practicing application of learned behavior through role play and simulated exercises.
6. Implementing desired behavior or its approximation through behavioral tasks performed in daily context.
7. Teaching behavioral principles through lectures, models, and practice exercises, with feedback or by programmed instruction.

From Ulrici D, L'Abate L, & Wagner V. The E-R-A- model: A heuristic framework for classification of skill training programs for couples and families. *Family Relations*, 1981, *30*, 307-315.

presented by Systems Family Therapists (the Palo Alto and Milan Groups), Structural Family Therapists (Minuchin), and Strategic Family Therapists (Haley and Modanes).

By noting these components of preventive skill-training programs, one can clarify the various theoretical orientations and interventions presented throughout this book according to their emphasis on various aspects of information processing. Emotionality represents input reception functions; rationality represents processing or through-put functions; activity represents the observable output and outcome of a process; awareness represents a feedback and self-regulation function; and context includes the transactional (spatial and temporal) and interpersonal components of any interaction.

In this model, the relationships between and among these five components is not linear; therefore one cannot predict how change in one component will affect change (if any) in the other components. Thus we cannot expect that changes in awareness, for instance, will affect how one couple thinks or acts about their marriage. By the same token, changes in feelings (emotionality) will not necessarily produce changes in activity. The fallacy in some of the methods presented in this book lies in their assumption that change is a linear phenomenon.

This information processing model of classification also allows us to clarify the various underlying theoretical orientations (Table 1-1). For example, humanistic approaches, such as the Minnesota Couples Communication Program and Effectiveness (see Chapter 3), should emphasize the subjective experience and awareness.

On the basis of this classification system, one trend in virtually all methods of marital intervention becomes apparent: a psychoana-

lytic influence is present in only a small degree (i.e., in logical understanding, rationality-oriented programs). If this trend is consistent, a further lessening of the psychoanalytic influence on the field of marital therapy may be predicted.

Thus, in considering any of the methods of marital intervention presented in this book, we should be able to trace the origins of each model on the basis of the E-R-A-Aw-C classification, finding that, except for a few extreme cases, most models are eclectic and include an emphasis on varying components represented by this classification system.

Although most methods are eclectic, there are basic apparent differences among models of intervention. There is a distinct emphasis on either a remedial therapeutic approach or a preventive, education-oriented, social-skills-training approach. Currently, most therapists display little interest in prevention, while most social-skills trainers show little interest in remedial approaches. This schism in emphasis between practitioners will be apparent to the reader throughout this book: while methods of marital intervention have become more clearly defined in the past decade, major differences in treatment focus have appeared.

In conclusion, the field of marital interventions and therapies has grown into a full-fledged profession worthy of its own identity and its own distinction from other therapeutic specialties. It possesses its own body of theories, methods, and techniques that overlap minimally with those used in individual, group, and family therapies. Therefore it deserves to be considered separately and independently from all the other therapies. Thus this book attempts to consider the current state of the art of the field of marital intervention.

REFERENCES

Bardwick J. *In transition*. New York: Holt, Rinehart & Winston, 1979

Broderick CB, & Schrader SS. The history of professional marriage and family therapy. In AS Gurman & DP Kniskern (Eds.), *Handbook of family therapy*. New York: Brunner/Mazel, 1981

Burgess EW, & Cottrell LS, Jr. The prediction of adjustment in marriage. *American Sociological Review*, 1936, *1*, 737–751

Cahalan D, Cisin IH, & Crossley HM. *American drinking practices. Rutgers Center of Alcohol*

Studies Monograph No. 6 New Brunswick, N.J., Rutgers Center of Alcohol Studies, 1969

Fleck S, Freedman D, Cornelson A, Lidz T, & Terry D. The family environment of schizophrenic deficits. V. Understanding of symptomatology through the study of family interaction. In T Lidz, S Fleck & A Cornelson (Eds.), *Schizophrenia and the family*. New York, International Universities Press, 1965

Gurin G, Veroff J, & Feld S. *Americans view their mental health: Joint Commission on Mental*

Health. Monograph Series No. 4. New York: Basic Books, 1960

Gurman AS. Contemporary marital therapies: A critique and comparative analysis of psychoanalytic, behavioral and systems theory approaches. In TJ Paolino & BS McCrady (Eds.), *Marriage and marital therapy: Psychoanalytic, behavioral and systems theory perspectives.* New York: Brunner/Mazel, 1978

Gurman AS. Dimensions of marital therapy: A comparative analysis. *Journal of Marital & Family Therapy*, 1979, *5*, 5–16

Haley J. *Strategies of psychotherapy.* New York: Grune & Stratton, 1963

Hansen JC, & L'Abate L. *Approaches to family therapy.* New York: Macmillan, 1982

L'Abate L. Skill training programs for couples and families. In AS Gurman & DP Kniskern (Eds.), *Handbook of family therapy.* New York: Brunner/Mazel, 1981a

L'Abate L. Toward a systematic classification of counseling and therapy theorists, methods, processes and goals: The E-R-A model. *The Personnel and Guidance Journal*, 1981, *59*, 263–265b

L'Abate L, & Frey J, III. The E-R-A model: The role of feelings in family therapy reconsidered; implications for a classification of theories of family therapy. *Journal of Marriage and Family Therapy*, 1981, *7*, 143–150

L'Abate L, Frey J III, & Wagner V. Toward a classification of family theories: Further elaboration and implications of the E-R-A-Aw-C model. *Family Therapy*, 1982 (In press)

L'Abate L, & Thaxton ML. The differentiation of resources in mental health delivery: Implications for training. *Professional Psychology*, 1982, *12*, 761–768

Landis JT. Social correlates of divorce or nondivorce among the unhappy married. *Marriage and Family Living*, 1963, *25*, 178–180

Lederer WJ, & Jackson DD. *The mirages of marriage.* New York: Norton, 1968

Lidz T, Fleck S. Family studies and a theory of schizophrenia. In T Lidz, S Fleck & A Cornelison (Eds.), *Schizophrenia and the family.* New York: International Universities Press, 1965

Lucky EB. Marital satisfaction and its concomitant perception of self and spouse. *Journal of Counseling Psychology*, 1964, *11*, 136–145

Monahan TP. Family status and the delinquent child: A reappraisal and some new findings. *Social Forces*, 1957, *35*, 250–258

Mudd E. *The practice of marriage counseling.* New York: Association Press, 1951

Olson D. Marriage and family therapy: A critical overview. In A Gurman & D Rice (Eds.), *Couples in conflict.* New York: Jason Aronson, 1975

Patterson GR, Weiss RL, & Hops H. Training in marital skills: Some problems and concepts. In H Leitenberg (Ed.), *Handbook of behavior modification and behavior therapy.* Englewood Cliffs, NJ: Prentice-Hall, 1976

Plateris AA. Increases in divorces in U.S.—1967. *Vital and Health Statistics*, 1970, HEW Series 21, No. 20, pp 1–18

Prochaska J, & Prochaska J. Twentieth-century trends in marriage and marital therapy. In TJ Paolino & BS McCrady (Eds.), *Marriage and marital therapy: Psychoanalytic, behavioral and systems theory perspectives.* New York: Brunner/Mazel, 1978

Renne KS. Correlates of dissatisfaction in marriage. *Journal of marriage and the Family*, 1970, *32*, 54–67

Rosenzweig S. A transvaluation of psychotherapy: A reply to Hans Eysenck. *Journal of Abnormal and Social Psychology*, 1954, *49*, 298–304

Sager CJ, Gundlach R, Kremer M, Levy R, & Royce JR. The married in treatment. *Archives of General Psychiatry*, 1968, *19*, 205–217

Satir V. *Conjoint family therapy* (2nd rev. ed.). Palo Alto, CA, Science and Behavior Books, 1967

Satir V. *Peoplemaking.* Palo Alto, CA, Science and Behavior Books, 1972

Schultz DA, & Rogers SF. *Marriage, the family, and personal fulfillment.* Englewood Cliffs, NJ: Prentice-Hall, 1975

Siegman AW. Father absence during early childhood and anti-social behavior. *Journal of Abnormal Psychology*, 1966, *71*, 71–74

Silver AW, & Derr J. A comparison of selected variables between parents of delinquent and nondelinquent adolescents. *Journal of Clinical Psychology*, 1966, *22*, 49–50

Ulrici D, L'Abate L, & Wagner V. The E-R-A model: A heuristic framework for classification of skill training programs for couples and families. *Family Relations*, 1981, *30*, 307–315

Vincent CE. Barriers to the development of marital health as a health field. *Journal of Marriage and Family Counseling*, 1977, *3*, 3–11

Weiss RL, Hops H, & Patterson GR. A framework for conceptualizing marital conflict, a technology for altering it, some data for evaluating it. In LA Hamerlynck, LC Handy, & EJ Marsh (Eds.), *Change: Methodology, concepts, and practice.* Champaign, IL: Research Press, 1973

SECTION I

Educational and Preventive Social Skills Training Methods

2

Assertiveness Training

In the past decade, assertiveness training has enjoyed a growing popularity and an increase in its use as a clinical method. This training is now employed as either the sole treatment for a specific problem or as an adjunct to ongoing psychotherapy or other forms of intervention. Although assertiveness training was initially employed with individuals and addressed difficulties in interpersonal relationships in a general way, this method is now used to address specific problems in clearly defined interpersonal settings. Among those issues specific to marital relationships that are now treated by assertiveness training are sexuality (Carlson & Johnson, 1975; Liss-Levinson, et al, 1975), sexual dysfunction, increased assertiveness by both spouses (Eisler, et al, 1974), increased assertiveness by one spouse (Baer, 1976), closeness (Fensterheim & Baer, 1975), and communication (Simon, 1975).

Assertiveness Training (AT) can be defined as a behavioral technique to help individuals substitute withdrawn or inhibited behavior with socially appropriate, expressive, outgoing behavior. Assertiveness is defined as the antithesis of inhibition, whereby individual expression is positive and productive, appropriate eye contact with others is maintained, grievances are stated to others, and one can say no when one wants to respond with no (Rathus, 1973).

BACKGROUND AND DEVELOPMENT

Aggressiveness has been a focus of clinical interest since Freud's (1920) first writings on the subject. Whether clinicians are interested in the phenomenon from a theoretical or an empirical vantage point, they are forced to address the issue of aggressiveness for pragmatic reasons. It is an innate characteristic of the individual and couples' relationships. In extreme forms (violence or abuse), the clinicians' responsibility for assessing aggressiveness may become highly critical, for a decision must be made as to when it is safe for a couple to stay together.

On a continuum with aggressiveness, since the beginning of the 1970s, there has been a burgeoning interest in assertiveness (as opposed to aggressiveness), which Lange and Jakubowski (1976) have defined as "a capacity to stand up for personal rights and express thoughts, feelings, and beliefs in direct, honest, and appropriate ways which do not violate another person's rights" (p. 7).

Assertiveness has become a popular target for intervention efforts with psychiatric patients as well as with individuals without diagnosable symptoms. On the basis of some empirical evidence (Bates & Zimmerman, 1971; Gay, Hollandsworth & Galassi, 1975; Percell,

Berwick & Beigel, 1974) and widespread assumptions that assertiveness is associated with good psychological adjustment, attempts have been made on a large scale to increase assertiveness in psychiatric patients. The rationale for assertiveness training frequently includes arguments for the utility of assertive behavior as an alternative to aggressive behaviors in situations of interpersonal stress. Thus assertiveness training has been reported as having been used successfully in the treatment of antisocial aggressive behavior (Rimm & Masters, 1974).

Originally developed by Wolpe (1958) for treatment of the anxious, inhibited individual, assertiveness training has also been used successfully in treating a variety of clinical problems, including depression (Piaget & Lazarus, 1969), alcoholism (Martorano, 1974), hallucinations and delusions (Nydegger, 1972), and homosexual pedophilia (Edwards, 1972). Thus, acting on an assumption promoted by Wolpe (1969) that nonassertiveness is a frequent component of many broader clinical problems, treatment specialists have chosen to view increased assertiveness in patients as an important goal of the helping process in both outpatient and inpatient settings. Although a few agree with Fensterheim and Baer's (1975) rather extreme view that increased assertiveness is "the goal of all therapies" (p. 11), numerous clinicians of a variety of theoretical orientations do believe that increasing assertiveness is one valid treatment goal for a variety of patients.

Thus many clinicians are currently involved in attempts to assess and alter levels of "aggressiveness" and "assertiveness" in a variety of populations. These attempts are accompanied by little empirical data distinguishing between the terms "aggressiveness" and "assertive," however. Theoreticians have not reached consensus on the definition of assertion or aggressiveness (Macdonald, 1975; Rich & Schroeder, 1976; Selg, 1975) or on the theoretical relationship between these two constructs.

The development of different definitions and conceptualizations of assertiveness and aggressiveness has been accompanied by the development of numerous self-report measures for degrees of assertiveness (Galassi & Galassi, 1977) and/or aggressiveness (Rathus, 1973a, b,

and c; *see* Appendix A). Nevertheless, the "nomological networks" of self-reported assertiveness and aggressiveness are not well elaborated. Furthermore, little empirical information exists about the personality correlates of these constructs as measured through self-report inventories. The shortage of information on psychiatric patients is particularly acute. Existing published studies of personality correlates of assertiveness (Bates & Zimmerman, 1971; Galassi, et al, 1974; Gay, Hollandsworth & Galassi, 1975) have involved normal, not psychiatric, samples. Remarkably, considering current societal concern about aggression, no published studies exist of the personality correlates of self-reported aggressiveness in any type of subject sample.

Assertiveness and Aggressiveness

The terms "assertion" and "aggression," and "assertiveness" and "aggressiveness" were not invented by social scientists. Rather, these terms, as well as the confusion about them, existed in popular language long before clinicians and researchers began attempting to define them as theoretical constructs. Although evidence of the lack of a clear semantic distinction between these terms is abundant in everyday language, the synonymous use of the words "assertion" and "aggression" is by no means peculiar to the layman: a similar conceptual confusion can be found in books purported to teach assertion to the layman (Bach & Goldberg, 1974; Fensterheim & Baer, 1975), as well as in the psychological literature (Marlatt & Perry, 1975). Goldberg (1977) has posited a theoretical continuum of "aggressive behavior" ranging from "submissive" to "assertive" (p. 19). Marlatt and Perry (1975) state that nonassertive individuals "can be taught to be more outgoing and aggressive through the use of modeling techniques" (p. 133). Even Wolpe (1958), credited with the founding of assertion training, drew no distinction between the terms in his earliest definition of assertive behavior: "The word *assertive* has a rather wide meaning here. It refers not only to more or less aggressive (anger-expressing) behavior, but also to the outward expression of friendly, affectionate, and other nonanxious feeling" (p. 72).

The problems inherent in the frequent confusion of assertive and aggressive behavior in assertion literature and training efforts are highlighted by Lazarus (1973), who made the observation that much of the literature on "assertiveness training" emphasizes "the ability to contradict and verbally attack other people." Lazarus argued that "there is little to be gained (and perhaps much to be lost) from the acquisition of abrasive and obnoxious interpersonal behaviors in the guise of 'assertiveness training' " (p. 698).

Lazarus is not alone in his view that a distinction between assertiveness and aggressiveness should be maintained in assertion training. A trend toward emphasizing that distinction can also be noted among authors of recent books on assertion training (Alberti & Emmons, 1974; Bower & Bower, 1976; Cotler & Guerra, 1976; Dawley & Wenrich, 1976; Lange & Jakubowski, 1976; Liberman, et al, 1975). These authors argue that people can learn to be assertive (to express personal rights and feelings) without learning to be aggressive (to abuse others physically or emotionally). In fact, among these authors, training people to avoid being aggressive in interactions with others is a goal as important in assertiveness training as teaching trainees to overcome interpersonal timidity.

Background and Development

The origins of behavioral assertiveness training can be traced to Salter's (1949) work, *Conditioned Reflex Therapy.* Using Pavlov's discovery of the learning of conditioned reflexes, Salter developed a program for treating people with nervous disorders. He suggested that the etiology of nervous disorders is an improper balance of inhibitory and excitatory brain processes with insufficient excitation. Therefore his treatment required that the patient act in an excitatory manner in order to alter inhibition. To bolster an individual's excitatory brain processes, he taught clients to make statements beginning with "I" ("I" statements), to behave spontaneously, and to communicate feelings nonverbally. Salter stated that behavioral changes lead to physiological changes, and that increasing the individual's excitatory processes helps teach the person to be more direct, make decisions, and enjoy responsibility.

Wolpe's (1958) therapy by reciprocal inhibition added to Salter's (1949) concepts by stating that "when a response is inhibited by an incompatible response and if a major drive reduction follows, a significant amount of conditioned inhibition of the response will be developed" (p. 30). The treatment, reciprocal inhibition, consisted of eliminating or weakening old anxiety-producing responses by acquiring new responses that are incompatible with the old ones and that counteract the anxiety. Wolpe (1958) stated that, "If a response inhibitory of anxiety can be made to occur in the presence of anxiety-invoking stimuli, it will weaken the bond between the stimuli and the anxiety" (p. 67). Wolpe's treatment procedures consisted of teaching clients to behave so as to inhibit anxiety during an interpersonal encounter in which they usually experience anxiety. In treatment, Wolpe used counterconditioning (assertive responses and relaxation responses were encouraged to occur simultaneously), positive reconditioning (the desired response was rewarded and the undesired responses were consistently not rewarded or were punished), and experimental extinction (continued nonreinforcement of the habit occurred).

Wolpe implemented his treatment techniques for assertive training, stating, "Assertive training, generally speaking, is required for patients who in interpersonal contexts have unadaptive anxiety responses that prevent them from saying or doing what is reasonable or right" (Wolpe, 1969, pp. 59-60). Wolpe also found that simple instruction using examples from other cases was sometimes sufficient to cause assertive behavior, as was behavior rehearsal. In addition, he employed assertiveness training for a variety of presenting problems, including impotence, frigidity, and phobias.

Lazarus (1973) added to concepts of assertive training by stressing that one should stand up for one's rights as well as respect the rights of others. He stated that being assertive allows an individual to be free emotionally and that an assertive person knows and expresses his or her feelings. His resulting treatment procedure of rehearsal desensitization is a five-step procedure:

1. Nonthreatening role-playing situations are employed until the patient enjoys the procedure.
2. Very mildly threatening encounters arranged in a hierarchy are enacted.

3. The therapist models the way in which he or she thinks the patient should respond to an item.
4. The patient attempts to enact the role only when the therapist's modeling leads the patient to feel that he or she can do so adequately.
5. New items are attempted only when the patient and therapist are satisfied with each performance and when the new, expressive behavior is followed by positive consequences of various kinds (Wolpe & Lazarus, 1966).

Since 1966, the number of articles on assertion training and assertion-related procedures has increased dramatically. As assertiveness training developed, so did ideas about what constitutes assertiveness. Definitions have evolved from general ones (e.g., "all socially acceptable expressions of rights and feelings," Wolpe & Lazarus, 1966; "the ability for self-expression," Liberman, 1970) to more specific behavioral definitions (e.g., "behavior which enables a person to act in his own best interests, to stand up for himself without undue anxiety and to express his rights without destroying the rights of others," Alberti & Emmons, 1974). Alberti and Emmons categorized interpersonal behaviors as either nonassertive, assertive, or aggressive. The types of behavior, feelings, and consequences associated with each category are shown in Table 2-1.

Other definitions have attempted to define response classes. Rich and Schroeder (1976, p. 1081) defined four specific response patterns of assertive behavior: (1) the ability to say no; (2) the ability to ask for favors or to make requests; (3) the ability to express positive and negative feelings; and (4) the ability to initiate, continue, and terminate general conversation. Other response classes in definitions of assertive training include the following:

1. *assertive talk* (Wolpe, 1969)—statements that attempt to correct or amend an injustice that the client experiences;
2. *commendatory statements* (Wolpe, 1969)—statements that provide others with pleasure;
3. *expression of feelings* (Rathus & Ruppert, 1973; Salter, 1949)—the open and frank expression of feelings in order to avoid suppressing emotions, likes, and dislikes;
4. *disagreement* (Salter, 1949)—openly disagreeing;
5. *asking why* (Rathus, 1973)—asking for clarification of what others ask one to do;
6. *talking about oneself* (Salter, 1949)—the use of "I" statements;
7. *rewarding others for compliments* (Salter, 1949)—expressing agreement when one is praised;
8. *refusal to justify opinions to disputatious persons* (Rathus, 1973)—not arguing with

Table 2-1
The Continuum of Behavior

Nonassertive Behavior	Assertive Behavior	Aggressive Behavior
As Actor	*As Actor*	*As Actor*
Self-denying	Self-enhancing	Self-enhancing at expense of another
Inhibited, hurt, anxious	Expressive, feels good about self	Expressive, deprecates others
Allows others to choose for him	Chooses for self	Chooses for others
Does not achieve desired goal	May achieve desired goal	Achieves desired goal by by hurting others
As Acted Upon	*As Acted Upon*	*As Acted Upon*
Guilty or angry	Self-enhancing	Self-denying
Deprecated actor	Expressive	Hurt, defensive, humiliated
Achieves desired goal at actor's expense	May achieve desired goal	Does not achieve desired goal

From Alberti RE, Emmons ML: *Your Perfect Right: A Guide to Assertive Living* (4th ed). Reproduced by permission of Impact Publishers, Inc., P.O. Box 1094, San Luis Obispo, CA 93406. Further reproduction prohibited.

individuals who argue for the sake of arguing;

9. *maintaining eye contact with others;*
10. *engaging in antiphobic responses*—responding in ways that one has habitually feared.

Since Salter's (1949) and Wolpe and Lazarus's (1966) work with developing assertiveness training, its use as a treatment technique has grown in popularity and use. Flowers, et al (1975) have proposed several factors that have promoted the interest in assertiveness training. First, there has been an increasing amount of attention to assertiveness training in both professional and popular publications. Second, there has been a growing concern for the rights and personal power of the individual in society. Third, there is a concern with nonaggressive means of reducing and resolving conflicts. Fourth, human liberation movements have identified assertive behavior as a growth-enhancing strategy for dealing with social oppression. Fifth, there is a professional move toward short, educative, preventive workshops that address specific topics (i.e., the Social Skill Training movement). These workshops stress educational rather than therapeutic models of intervention.

Major Philosophy and Current Concepts

Assertive training currently fits the preventive, educational, social skills model of intervention. It is a systematic, structured, learning program that employs the traditional behavioral techniques of behavioral rehearsal, modeling, successive approximation, response shaping, and positive reinforcement. It also involves cognitive restructuring of the individual's belief systems.

As a treatment technique, assertive training may be employed on a one-to-one basis, but it is usually used in a group setting, primarily because of the presumed modeling effects of group treatment. It has been shown that modeling effects may increase learning over a shorter period of time, as well as help to reduce an individual's fear of social interactions (Bandura, Blanchard & Ritter 1969).

As has been discussed in this section, the philosophy of assertive training is primarily related to a broad theoretical agreement concerning the sources of noninhibited, nonassertive behavior (i.e., that nonassertive behavior is related to anxiety and inhibitions in the presence of others). Included in the philosophy of assertive training is a growing valuation of individual self-assertion as both a cause and an outcome of increased self-esteem.

THE TREATMENT PROCESS

Although assertiveness training procedures may vary from situation to situation, depending on the leaders, the general formats are similar, and most assertiveness training programs are conducted in group settings.

Assertion groups usually meet weekly for 1.5 to 3 hours per session. The group format is time-limited (6 to 12 weeks) or can be open-ended (with new members entering as old members leave). Group size generally ranges from 8 to 12 members, with 1 or 2 therapists or leaders present. In some groups, members are either referred or screened prior to the beginning of the group; in others, group membership is open.

The first meeting consists of the leaders' presenting a general philosophy of self-dignity and its relationship to assertive behaviors. Case examples may be given of nonassertive, aggressive, and assertive behaviors, in addition to ways to address various problem situations. The behavioral goals of the group are discussed, as are the procedures that will be used (i.e., homework assignments, role-playing, coaching).

Participants may be asked to describe and keep a record of their assertive, nonassertive, or aggressive behaviors outside the group, in addition to noting situations in which they would like to improve their assertive skills. These situations constitute many of the situations that are role-played, coached, and discussed during the group, along with common and "canned" situations presented by the group leader. An assortment of other teaching procedures are also used, including behavior rehearsal, shaping, modeling, coaching, and homework assignments. Relaxation training and systematic desensitization may also be used (Geisinger, 1969; Lazarus, 1968; Lesser, 1967). When individuals reach their goals, they are praised by the group leader(s).

In working with the nonverbal aspect of

communication (Booraem & Flowers, 1972; Guerra & Horskey, 1973), attention is given to maintaining eye contact, to voice characteristics, and to body and facial movements. Some group formats also provide video and/or audio feedback as a learning device (Cotler & Guerra, 1976; McFall & Marston, 1970).

Assertive training generally consists of five stages. First, the individual becomes aware of the extent of his or her nonassertive or aggressive behaviors and the negative repercussions of the behavior. Second, the individual gains an appreciation for the potential of assertive behaviors. Third, the individual attempts to act in an assertive manner. Fourth, the individual begins to use acquired assertive skills in increasingly appropriate ways (i.e., expressing feelings and standing up for rights more consistently while discriminating the circumstances under which assertive responses may be inappropriate or maladaptive). Finally, the individual becomes aware of a growing mastery of various interpersonal situations, supposedly with a resulting improvement in self-concept and greater self-respect.

ASSERTION TRAINING WITH COUPLES

Alberti and Emmons (1974) proposed the use of assertiveness training in marital therapy based on the assumption that marital conflict often results from selecting an inappropriate style for expression of strong feeling. A relationship between assertive near-equals is measurably more satisfying to each partner than one in which one partner is dominant and the other a compliant, nonassertive servant. Inadequate communication and nonassertive behavior are viewed as often having been established during "courtship and honeymoon" days when partners were still trying to "impress" each other. Thus hurtful aggressiveness or self-denying nonassertiveness becomes destructive of communication in the intimate dyadic relationship.

The authors distinguish between aggressiveness, which is self-enhancing at the expense of another while attempting to achieve desired goals by hurting others; nonassertiveness, which is self-denying and allowing others to choose for themselves; and assertiveness, which

is self-enhancing, choosing for self, and expressive. The ultimate goal of assertion is for both marital partners to become more self-expressive in a positive, nonhostile style, bringing them closer together as a cohesive unit rather than driving them apart. They propose the following systematic method to facilitate assertiveness in couples:

Paying attention to the components of behavior. In defining and facilitating assertive behavior, the therapist systematically pays attention to:

1. Eye contact between the couple
2. Body posture
3. Gestures
4. Facial expression
5. Timing of communication
6. Fluency of speech
7. Content of speech

Facilitating assertion.

1. *Assessment.* Role-playing by the couple is recommended as a method of visual assessment.
2. *Situation definition.* Individual situations that are sources of difficulty in the clients' relationship are defined. Clients are asked to explain in detail what happens in conflict situations.
3. *Covert rehearsal.* Clients are asked to close their eyes and imagine how they typically respond to the conflict situation.
4. *Modeling.* The therapist role-plays the scene, taking the respondent's part, and demonstrates one effectively assertive response.
5. *Feedback.* Clients are instructed to review the modeled response with an emphasis on discriminating the nonassertive, assertive, and aggressive qualities in each behavioral component.
6. *Covert rehearsal.* Clients are asked to repeat step 3 but to visualize a successful assertion and positive response.
7. *Client role-play.* Clients role-play new responses and interchanges.
8. *Feedback.* The therapist provides specific, directed feedback to the client on each of the components of his or her behavior. Videotape is used if available.

9. *Coaching.* Steps 6, 7, and 8 are repeated to give clients practice in achieving self-expression.
10. *In vivo rehearsal.* Clients are encouraged to practice at home.
11. *Follow-up.* The therapist maintains contact with the clients while they practice at home in a variety of situations.

Lehman-Olson (1976) has discussed the theoretical and clinical implications for assertiveness training with couples:

Consider some topical patterns: husband and wife argue incessantly with little resolution (aggressive–aggressive), husband and wife share little of their thoughts, feelings, and desires with each other (passive–passive), or one spouse is typically angry and demanding while the other is compliant and withdrawn (aggressive–passive).

If both spouses were trained to be more assertive, their relationship world become closer to what is implied as a "healthy relationship" (p. 93).

According to her, assertiveness training is compatible with the goals of Rogers' client-centered theory, Freud's psychoanalytic theory, and Ellis' cognitive, rational-emotive therapy. Assertiveness training addresses Rogerian goals by aiding a person to feel more self-confident, more self-directing, and more open to feelings, resulting in expression of thoughts, feelings, and desires without undue anxiety. Psychoanalytic goals are included when the ego is strengthened by the acquisition of new behaviors, and rational-emotive therapy goals are achieved when an individual rids himself or herself of irrational beliefs and establishes realistic goals. She proposes that assertiveness is the behavioral analogue of the concepts of unconditioned positive regard (Rogers), ego strength (Freud), and self-worth (Ellis).

Lehman-Olson (1976) views assertiveness training as compatible with family therapy in the following ways:

1. Assertive behavior provides a means of measuring concepts such as "differentiation of the family ego mass," differentiation, separation of family members, legitimate self-regard, and the "good family."
2. Assertiveness training provides a set of procedures for training family members to negotiate conflict issues and to eliminate unchangeable rules in relationships.

3. Assertive behavior can provide a referent to understanding diverse theoretical conceptualizations.
4. Assertive behavior can provide a means of assessing dysfunctional communication patterns, nondifferentiation of family members, and pathological forms of seeking self-regard (p. 100).

She also suggests that assertive behavior might serve, at least in part, as an operational definition of differentiation, which can ultimately be measured behaviorally, both as a diagnostic tool and as an outcome measure. She added that, "once the problems of assertiveness have diagnosed within a marriage, the therapy context provides a unique opportunity for training, rehearsal, coaching, and modeling *in situ* as opposed to in vivo" (p. 112). The therapist can assess which behaviors among partners (interpersonal) increase the likelihood that beliefs and myths (intrapersonal) related to worthlessness, anger, and blame will be maintained.

Fensterheim and Baer (1975) add the following four key steps concerning the use of assertive training with couples.

1. A careful behavioral formulation is crucial. There are many causes of marital discord, and treatment must vary according to cause. This formulation cannot be kept in general terms but must be specifically applied to the major source of dissension between the partners.
2. The behavioral formulation must be communicated to the couple in both general and concrete terms. Discussion of specific incidents and the ancillary use of role-playing help achieve this latter result. Such procedures help structure the problem for the couple, set goals, and help them to understand the impact of the assertive problems upon even their most trivial interactions. They also serve to focus attention on "What can I do differently?" rather than on "He should be different!"
3. The specific treatment modalities must flow from the behavioral formulations and be designed to meet the specific problems presented by the couple. Some assertive techniques may be used for many different couples, but for some couples it is necessary to devise fairly ingenious methods to

cope with special problems. Other techniques, such as systematic desensitization, may also be called into play. Whatever techniques are used, the couple should be encouraged to work at home on the problem as much as possible.

4. The couple should be taught skills enabling them to cope with future problems. This may be done by teaching them to analyze their problems in assertive and communication terms and by teaching them to use "feeling talk" in the life situation (pp. 17–18).

Fensterheim and Baer have also discussed a five-step procedure designed to help couples become closer. Their procedure requires the active participation of both the therapist and the clients.

First, the therapist helps each spouse identify the specific behaviors that he or she wants changed in the marriage. Second, the spouses are taught the ways to change these behaviors. Third, they are taught how each spouse's behavior helps maintain the other spouse's behavior in terms of reinforcement theory.

It is important that the couple understand that they are probably maintaining the disruptive behaviors to which they object by continuing reinforcement. By providing or withholding reinforcements for specific behaviors, each partner exercises control over the other. Assertiveness training teaches that instead of saying, "My spouse should be different," you must learn to ask yourself, "What am I doing to reinforce the very behavior I want to stop?" (Fensterheim & Baer, 1975, p. 125)

Fourth, each spouse is taught how to communicate more clearly, both verbally and nonverbally. This makes "mind reading," a behavior that often leads to misunderstandings and problems in marriage, unnecessary. Fifth, the therapist helps the couple set short-term goals. It is presumed that when couples set attainable goals they are rewarded by their success and will continue to work on improving their relationship.

Couples actively participate in their training, which leads to a major change in their style of behavior. Spouses practice many of the same methods that are used with individuals, such as feeling talk and behavior rehearsal, as well as exercises designed specifically for married couples. For instance, there is one exercise that

is designed to help spouses choose specific target behaviors that they wish to change. Each spouse is asked to list specific behaviors that he or she would like the other spouse to do more often. The spouses exchange their lists and clearly explain what they mean by each item. Partners then agree as to whether or not they can behave in the desired way for each of the items. When the lists are agreed upon, spouses begin to keep a count to determine the number of times the partner behaves in the desired manner. At a preset time, such as just before bed or dinner, they share the count and tell each other how they felt when the spouse behaved in the new way. This sharing serves to reinforce the new behavior. A very similar exercise is used by Baer (1976).

A communication exercise, designed to bring the couple closer, is also used. Each spouse writes a message that he or she would like to tell the other. The spouse then tape-records the message, listens to it, and makes any changes necessary. The couple then agree upon a time to talk about the messages with each other, and do so. If one spouse is afraid to bring up a certain issue, two alternatives are offered. One possibility is to make a list of the potential ways in which the other spouse might respond. This list is recorded. The spouse who is afraid then practices responding to these imagined comments from the other spouse until satisfied with his or her response. The couple then agrees on a time to talk about the issue. If, however, the afraid spouse still cannot bring himself or herself to talk about the issue after practicing responding to imagined reactions, the spouse is advised to tell the partner that there is something that he or she wants to say but cannot. The other spouse is asked to listen to the taped message; after the spouse has done so, the couple can discuss the issue.

Fensterheim and Baer (1975) conclude with danger signals that couples should be alert to: (1) analyzing the wherefores of the spouse's behavior, (2) neglecting to see one's own part in the marital difficulties, (3) using "we" constantly and never using "I," and (4) not allowing themselves or each other independence. Baer (1976) further addressed the marital relationship in a book written for women. Exercises are designed for the wife, but can be done by both spouses.

The process begins with a request for the

woman to determine her problem areas. Baer described 11 roles played by women that often lead to marital difficulties: (1) the unfulfilled woman, (2) the manipulator, (3) the dwarf, (4) the child-wife, (5) the emotional blackmailer, (6) the get-even girl, (7) the nag, (8) the egotist, (9) the servant, (10) the disciple, and (11) the woman with health problems. The recognition of role-playing allows the realization that one is actively determining one's own behavior. The next step requires the couple to set marital goals. Baer believes that closeness should be the major goal of an intimate relationship.

In the assertiveness training approach to closeness, the word "closeness" means an ever-increasing ability to share more and more of your personal feelings, fantasies, thoughts, ideas, and concomitantly, a similar, ever-growing ability to act in such a way that your partner is able to share more and more of his personal feelings, fantasies, thoughts, and ideas . . . and at the same time, both of you feel free to be a "self" and express your own individuality (Baer, 1976, p. 182).

Couples rate their marital happiness, and specific goals are decided upon.

Baer then described a "behavioral change program for marital happiness." To improve communication, she tells couples to (1) determine how their conversations can be improved, (2) discuss trivial matters, and (3) speak up always, being sure to find the appropriate way and time. Baer breaks down this last proposition into four parts:

1. Spouses too often rationalize that speaking up will hurt the partner. This must be stopped.
2. It is important to be sure that you are sending the message you want to send.
3. Use conversation to express your feelings, not as a chance to put down your partner.
4. Always express your feelings honestly, in a straightforward manner, and with concern for your spouse.

Baer's program also includes a variety of other exercises. One requires clients to tape a significant emotional experience, listen to it, change it to reveal more feeling, and then tell the story to the partner. Another set of exercises addresses decision-making. The Moon Game requires the couple to rank the importance of certain equipment for survival. They

must, after discussing their ideas, come up with a consensus decision. She also suggested writing a marital decision contract covering all areas of importance to the couple: childrearing, sexual exclusivity, financial matters, etc.

Baer also described traps that will decrease the couple's opportunity for a satisfying marriage. First, she asserted the importance of not feeling guilty when changing. Also, couples should not adopt adversary positions, trying to produce evidence that the other spouse is responsible for all individual and couple difficulties. This blaming accomplishes nothing. Finally, the couple must realize that being assertive does not mean that each person will always be satisfied with the outcome of an interaction: "Don't think that it's always assertive to speak up in the close relationship. Sometimes real assertiveness is saying nothing" (Baer, 1976, p. 212).

Baer (1976) and Fensterheim and Baer (1975) also address asserting oneself in a sexual relationship. Couples are instructed to specify their sexual pleasures and dissatisfactions and to discuss only the behaviors they wish their partners to increase. Dissatisfactions are changed into requests for more satisfying behaviors. Exercises are also outlined that ask the couple to share their sexual fantasies, feelings, and sensations before, after, and during lovemaking. Finally, these authors also advise couples to make behavioral contracts and to learn "fair fighting."

As part of a couples enrichment series, Simon (1975) devised a program to help couples who are unable to be equally assertive. The goal of his program is to equalize the level of assertiveness so that neither partner is more dominant or submissive than the other. Building on the foundation of Wolpe's reciprocal inhibition therapy, Simon developed an assertiveness training program of cognitive and affective components. It begins with cognitive exercises designed to increase the couple's understanding of their difficulties. The affective exercises assist the couple to experience themselves emotionally and perceptually as they proceed along the various points or levels on the submissiveness–assertiveness continuum. Role-playing exercises are the major training tool, with the program divided into six lessons. Pretests, posttests, and follow-up sessions are also conducted.

Session 1 is called "Give and Take."

Spouses are asked to discuss what is meant by a "give and take" relationship, assertiveness, dominance, and reciprocity. These concepts are then clarified by the enricher/ instructor. The two following exercises require the couple to discuss, first, whether or not they are able to make themselves clearly understood when speaking to the spouse and, second, to decide whether or not they would like to increase the reciprocity in their marriage. They are told that by practicing more assertive behavior through role-playing, they will be able to increase the amount of reciprocity in their marriage. A homework assignment asks each spouse to list specific instances of assertiveness or submissiveness with the partner.

Session 2, titled "Responsibility," begins by reviewing the homework lists and asking spouses to describe how they felt (what were their specific emotions) during each of the incidents listed. The next exercise tries to elicit a response from the couple to indicate that they are aware that they are responsible for making sure that the message they wish to send is the one sent. When the partners agree that the individual is responsible for communicating the message that he or she wishes to send, the actual training begins.

The trainer explains to the couple that certain skills need to be developed in order to behave assertively and that these skills can be developed by practicing assertive behavior. The trainer, looking toward the dominant partner, also notes the importance of listening to others and compromising. The couple is then asked to role-play a nonmarital situation. Simon suggested that the dominant partner go first since he or she "is probably more skillful in these types of assertive responses . . . and can serve as a model" (p. 122). The dominant partner may behave aggressively rather than assertively, however, thus being as much in need of learning the skills of assertive behavior as the passive or submissive partner. A mirror is used and spouses rate each other on (1) eye contact and facial expression, (2) speech fluency and voice loudness, (3) duration of the assertive statement, and (4) distance from the image in the mirror. Each spouse is also given an opportunity to describe feelings during the role-play. Couples are asked to practice asserting themselves at home in front of the mirror using made-up situations. Spouses are asked to

rate each other's performance according to the dimensions discussed and to give the other spouse feedback. Spouses are also encouraged to compliment each other when they have performed well.

Over the next four sessions, couples are asked to role-play numerous situations, beginning with everyday, nonmarital issues. After the spouses become comfortable with these role-plays, they are asked to role-play situations that are relevant to their marriage. This role-play procedure is based on Lazarus' "rehearsal desensitization" (1971). Spouses are asked to give each other feedback throughout this process. They are taught that when one spouse speaks, the other should listen carefully, commend the spouse on clear expression, and then either agree or disagree, clearly stating his or her own opinion. Spouses are also taught to rephrase angry statements into positive language and still get their messages across. During the final lesson, the couple learns how to be diplomatic and how to compromise. All concepts taught during the program are practiced at home to reinforce the new behaviors. At the conclusion of the program, the couple is asked if there are any exercises that they would like to practice again. If there are none, the trainer compliments the couple for their willingness to work together to improve their relationship. The program is then concluded.

Alberti and Emmons (1974) present another program of assertiveness training for marital counseling in which they emphasize that it is crucial to differentiate between assertive, aggressive, and nonassertive styles of interpersonal interaction. "Assertion is not 'constructive aggression' nor 'successful intimidation' " (Alberti & Emmons, 1974, p. 49). In this way, they differ with Simon, who failed to differentiate clearly between assertive and aggressive behavior. Since "assertive" and "aggressive" apply to concepts that are often confused, Alberti and Emmons strongly suggest that marital counselors stress the difference to their clients. They further propose that, insofar as couples rarely have a clear picture of precisely what assertive behavior is, the counselor should model assertive behavior for them.

The therapist next analyzes the communication/behavioral patterns of the relationship and determines the problem areas. The couple is helped to learn new and more effective behaviors. The important consideration is to change behaviors that are causing the difficulties. The therapist rates the number of times the client (1) maintains eye contact; (2) leans toward spouse; (3) does not use gestures that threaten (clenched fists), or show capitulation (open palms facing upward) or resignation (hands thrust into pockets); (4) uses facial expressions congruent with verbalizations; (5) uses appropriate timing (does not let bad feelings fester and then burst out angrily); (6) speaks without hesitation in voice or pauses (fluency); and (7) makes statements in which the words are appropriate to the content.

The therapist and couple then determine the situations specific to the couple's relationship in which they are unable to behave assertively. A typical conflict situation is decided upon and one spouse covertly rehearses a typical response. (The client is asked to close his or her eyes and imagine the scene and how he or she would normally respond.) The therapist then role-plays the scene, playing the part of the client and demonstrating an assertive response. The therapist tells the client that this is only one possible assertive response and that there are many other ways to respond assertively. The client is then told to watch how the therapist responds, not necessarily what the therapist says (modeling). Partners are then asked to offer feedback on the therapist's performance. The client once again covertly rehearses the behavior, adding a visualization of himself or herself making an assertive response and receiving a positive reply. When the client can imagine this scene, he or she role-plays responding assertively. The client is then offered specific feedback about each of the behaviors that compose an assertive response. (Videotape may be used at this point.) The last three steps are repeated until the client can successfully respond in an assertive manner. (Coaching is used.) Alberti and Emmons (1974) believe that it will be easier for the client to practice if the spouse is not present. They recommend that the spouse, rather than being present, be kept informed of the progress of treatment.

The client practices the new behavior in his or her "natural" environment (in vivo rehearsal). The client is alerted to reinforcers in his or her natural environment such as the way the spouse responds. This awareness of re-inforcers is considered crucial if the new behavioral style is to take hold, since the therapist will not be present to support the client in the new behavior. Finally, after treatment ends, Alberti and Emmons (1974) follow up clients to ensure maintenance of these new behaviors.

EVALUATION

Numerous studies, conducted since the early 1970s on the outcome of assertiveness training for individuals, show post-test behavior change (Russell, 1981). Long-term behavior change has not been measured, however, and there is some evidence that lasting gains in response to acquisition interventions are obtained only by using cognitive self-statement approaches (Glass, et al, 1976).

An early case study of assertiveness training documented successful treatment of a marital problem by teaching a couple how to utilize assertive skills (Fensterheim, 1972). Eisler and his co-workers (Eisler et al, 1973; Eisler, et al, 1974) were the first to report an empirical investigation on the effects of assertiveness training on marital interaction. Prior to training husbands to be more assertive, Eisler, et al (1973) studied the effects of videotape and instructional feedback on nonverbal marital interaction. This study was undertaken to investigate the separate and combined effects of videotape feedback and focused instructions before embarking on a full-scale study to determine the effects of assertiveness training on marital interaction.

The subjects of this investigation were 12 married couples. (In each case the husband was a patient at a local VA Hospital.) Target behaviors were looking and smiling. Using an interval recording procedure, trained observers rated videotapes of the couples interacting to determine the number of smiles and looks during the session.

Three couples were sequentially assigned to one of the following experimental conditions:

1. *Videotape feedback alone.* In this condition, the couple were asked to talk with each other on a topic selected prior to the taping. They were taped for 6 minutes (baseline). After the taping, the last 2 minutes of the videotape were replayed for

them and they were asked to interact for another 2 minutes. This playback continued until the couple had received 6 minutes of feedback. Baseline and feedback phases were then repeated.

2. *Irrelevant feedback.* This condition was identical to the first, with one exception: instead of feedback, the couple's interactions were interrupted by 2 minutes of local television programs.

3. *Videotape feedback and focused instructions.* This condition was also identical to the first. In this case, however, focused instructions such as, "We would like you to pay attention to how much you are looking at each other" (Eisler et al, 1973), were offered after each 2-minute videotape feedback.

4. *Focused instructions alone.* This condition was, again, identical to the others, with the one exception that no videotape feedback was given—just focused instructions every 2 minutes.

Videotape feedback in the absence of instructions effected a slight increase in nonverbal interactions of the married couples. Focused instructions led to marked changes in the target behavior of looking. A combination of videotape feedback and focused instructions was not significantly more potent than instructions alone. However, the combined design led to an increase in the related behavior of smiling (Eisler, et al, 1973, p. 551).

Eisler, et al (1974) investigated the "effects of assertiveness training on marital interaction." Specifically, they examined how marital interactions were affected when husbands were trained to be more assertive. Tree dysfunctional couples were studied. Prior to treatment each couple was videotaped discussing their marital difficulties. From these videotapes, trained observers recorded (1) duration of looking at spouse; (2) duration of speech, (3) number of positive statements categorized by the frequency of verbal expressions of affection, approval, or agreement; (4) number of negative statements categorized by the frequency of verbal expressions of criticism, disapproval, or disagreement; (5) number of questions asked; and (6) number of smiles exhibited by the couple. Couples 2 and 3 were also videotaped. Similar measures were chosen based on the specific difficulties experienced by these couples. These behaviors were shown by Eisler, et al

(1973) to be related to overall assertiveness. These recordings provided a pretreatment measure. Inter-rater reliability for each of these measures was above 90 percent.

Sessions for husband 1 were led by one of the authors with the assistance of a female research assistant who role-played the man's wife based on observations of the initial videotape. The husband was required to perform successively more difficult assertive behaviors that stressed the six features mentioned earlier. Following treatment, the couple was again videotaped. Both the husband and wife were recorded as behaving more assertively on the aforementioned criteria. Additionally, they both reported greater satisfaction in their posttreatment interaction.

Husband 2 was trained using role-playing situations that were based on everyday nonmarital situations. Findings indicated that generalization to marital interaction was only partially successful, and there was no change in the wife's behavior.

Husband 3 was trained on marital situations that were typical of interactions between him and his wife. The female research assistant was again cast as a surrogate wife. In this case, as was true of couple 1, learning in the practice situation generalized to the actual marital interaction.

Eisler, et al (1973) found that assertive behaviors learned during role-playing situations generalized to real-life marital interaction. Additionally, they determined that if the role-playing situations simulated relevant marital problems, the wives would also become more assertive, even though they were not directly involved in the training. Unfortunately, the study's conclusions are limited because of the use of a small number of subjects.

Shoemaker and Paulson (1976) and Blau (1978) investigated the effect of marital interaction when the wife alone received assertiveness training. Shoemaker and Paulson (1976) worked with 16 "wife-mothers" who reported difficulty raising their children. Pre- and posttest measures of both spouses were taken, using the Inventory of Marital Conflicts (Olson & Ryder, 1970), which is a simulated conflict situation. In addition, both parents rated their child's unsatisfactory behavior on the Devereux Child Behavior Rating Scale (Spivac & Spotts, 1966). Each woman received 5 weeks of assertiveness training in an assertiveness training group. Post-tests revealed a significant increase in assertive behavior for both spouses. This study supports Eisler, et al's (1973) findings that assertiveness training with one spouse can positively affect the marital relationship.

Blau (1978) studied the effect on marital interaction of assertiveness training with wives. Participants were 40 married couples; 30 of the women were volunteers who had responded to a newspaper advertisement. They were randomly placed in either a general assertiveness training group, a martial situations assertiveness training group, a marital situations assertiveness training group, or a waiting list, no-treatment, control group. Also used as controls were 10 other women who were friends or neighbors of the researcher.

Female graduate students who had been trained by the researcher conducted 2-hour sessions. They met once a week for a period of 5 weeks, using methods of role-playing, modeling, behavior rehearsals, and homework assignments. Pre- and post-tests, and follow-up measures were taken using the Adult Self-Expression Scale, the Assertion Inventory, and a 5-minute joint-problem task. Trained observers recorded four dimensions of assertive behavior while watching the couple perform the task: (1) the number of explicit agreements, (2) the number of explicit disagreements, (3) the number of "I" statements, and (4) the response latency.

Findings indicated, in contrast to Eisler, et al's (1973), that there was no significant difference in the increased level of assertiveness between the two types of assertiveness groups. Husbands of the women in these two groups also significantly increased their assertive behavior. Women in the control groups showed no increase in assertiveness, nor did the spouses. These findings support the conclusions of Eisler, et al (1973) and Shoemaker and Paulson (1976) that training one spouse to behave more assertively can increase the assertive behavior of the other spouse. Blau (1978) also found that there was a positive relationship between levels of assertiveness and marital happiness. This supports May's (1969) proposal that assertive behavior between spouses is necessary for a vital relationship.

The appendix describes some of the instruments and methods used specifically to study assertiveness and outcome. Muchowski and Valle (1977) measured the effects of a four-week assertive training program for wives. Using the methods of Alberti and Emmons (1974), the 22 voluntary subjects were assessed pre- and post-treatment by the Wolpe-Lazarus Assertive Inventory (Wolpe & Lazarus, 1966), the Interpersonal Relationship Rating Scale (Hipple, 1977), and a content inventory designed by the authors.

A series of 2 x 2 analyses of variance tests were conducted to assess what effect assertive training had on trainees and their husbands. None of the analyses were significant, and some spouses reported their wives higher after assertive training, while some spouses rated their wives lower after assertive training. The authors concluded that inclusion of significant others in a client's training program is advantageous.

Epstein, Degiovanni, and Lazarus (1978) trained conjointly 20 couples in assertiveness and compared them with 10 couples who had received only "minimal," or nominal, training. As outcome, they found that there was a significant increase in verbal assertion and a significant decrease in verbal aggression for the experimental couples. Other positive results related to self-reported clarity by self and spouse and a positive interaction between the spouses.

Russell (1981) reviewed and synthesized nine studies in which one or both marital partners received assertiveness training to enhance the marital relationship. Russell concluded that the limited number and quality of these studies made conclusions about the efficacy of assertiveness training tentative. Results about the relationship between assertiveness and marital satisfaction have been mixed, but positive correlations between these two factors were reported more frequently. Russell recommended that more and better controlled studies are needed, especially concerning couples treated as units rather than separately:

One implication is that assertiveness training is not for everyone, that while it might improve the marital satisfaction of one or both partners, it might also have the opposite effect with others. The improved communication of thoughts and feelings and standing up for one's rights cannot ensure that greater marital satisfaction will result. Thus, the purpose of the use of assertiveness training primarily or adjunctively should be clarified since positive correlations between assertiveness and marital satisfaction have not been consistently found (Russell, 1981, p. 17).

DISCUSSION

Assertiveness training has become a widely used educational skills training program that addresses both interpersonal and intrapersonal dynamics. Within couples' interaction, spouses learn to express clearly their feelings, opinions, and wishes, based on the assumption that they will be more able to satisfy their needs. Therefore, assertiveness training may be classified as a communication training program as well as a training program in self-assertion and negotiation skills. Because it can be a concrete behavioral program, it can be taught to trainers/educators in a relatively simple format, and outcome can be reliably measured according to acquisition of defined assertive behaviors. If one accepts Lehman-Olson's (1976) postulate that assertive behavior can demonstrate differentiation, unconditional positive regard, self-worth, and ego strength, or Blau's (1978) postulate that marital happiness and assertiveness are positively correlated, assertiveness training offers the potential for a powerful educative or re-educative intervention.

Assertiveness training provides a behavioral intervention with the underlying assumption that a change in behavior will cause a change in feelings, self, and other perceptions. Therefore, as with other skills training programs reviewed in this book, it offers a structured intervention that addresses the couple's interactional system on an observable, problem-behavior level. Thus a concrete intervention is offered to the clients. One must caution, however, that there are no long-term outcome evaluations of couples' assertiveness training programs to indicate that changing behavior changes underlying feelings and perceptions about marital satisfaction.

The role of the therapist in assertiveness training is primarily an educational one. This educational role provides several ramifications for the training and availability of the therapist/educator. Conceivably, assertiveness training leaders could be paraprofessionals who have been trained by professionals. Thus there is a capacity to provide more available group leaders who have been trained in a relatively short time. The use of paraprofessionals also makes lower cost services available to clients. As with all educational skills training programs, however, the extent of therapeutic skills re-

quired to conduct the program successfully is as yet unclear.

As a treatment, assertiveness training provides a time-limited, short-term approach that can reach a wide range of clients. How wide this range can be is yet unknown. Nevertheless, its feasibility as a therapeutic intervention that can be implemented in a variety of settings is without question. Assertiveness training can be used as a sole treatment of choice, as an adjunct to ongoing psychotherapy, and as an individual, couple, or group treatment. One must, however, wonder if some clients will not benefit from assertion training, and which clients will benefit most. Unfortunately, as with most other methods of marital treatment, only relatively functional, well-educated, verbal, middle-class clients have been treated with assertiveness training. Other client populations have not been addressed.

Although current research is favorable on the outcome of assertiveness training, the problems that plague the state of the art of outcome research also plague assertiveness training studies. Sample-size effects are rarely addressed, and long-term follow-up is usually less than six months after treatment. Controls are rarely used, and different studies are rarely comparable. Outcome research primarily needs to address long-term follow-up with adequate behavioral measures.

The role of values in the growth of assertiveness training cannot be ignored. Currently, there is a cultural emphasis on the positive value of self-assertion and standing up for one's rights. Assertion training would certainly not be a widely used intervention if its participants did not value its assumptions. Little has been written about any disadvantage that might occur from assertive behavior, however. The possibility of any negative ramifications of assertiveness training must certainly be considered.

THE FUTURE

The interest in assertiveness training continues to grow. Whether or not assertiveness training will continue to be a popular intervention remains to be seen, however. In the meantime, as with all marital treatment, further research is needed concerning the long-term effects of assertiveness training on both the individual and the couple.

REFERENCES

Alberti RE, & Emmons ML. *Your perfect right: A guide to assertive behavior.* San Luis Obispo, CA: Impact Publishers, rev. ed. 1974

Bach, G, & Goldberg H. *Creative aggression: The art of assertive living.* Garden City, NY: Doubleday, 1974

Baer J. *How to be an assertive, not aggressive, woman, in life, in love, and on the job.* New York: Signet, 1976

Bandura A, Blanchard EB, & Ritter B. Relative efficacy of desensitization and modeling approaches for inducing behavioral, affective, and attitudinal changes. *Journal of Personality and Social Psychology,* 1969, *13,* 173–199

Bates H, & Zimmerman S. Toward the development of a screening scale for assertive training. *Psychological Reports,* 1971, *38,* 99–107

Blau J. Changes in assertiveness and marital satisfaction after participation in assertiveness training group. Temple University, Order No. 7812186, 1978

Booraem CD, & Flowers JV. Reduction of anxiety and personal space as a function of assertion training with severely disturbed neuropsychiatric inpatients. *Psychological Reports,* 1972, *30,* 923–929

Bower S, & Bower S. *Asserting yourself: A practical guide for positive change.* Reading, MA: Addison-Wesley, 1976

Carlson N, & Johnson D. Sexuality assertiveness training: A workshop for women. *The Counseling Psychologist,* 1975, *5*(4), 53–59

Cotler S, & Guerra J. *Assertion training.* Champaign, IL: Research Press, 1976

Dawley H, & Wenrich W. *Achieving assertive behavior: A guide to assertive training.* Monterey, CA: Brooks/Cole, 1976

Edwards NB. Case conference—Assertive training in a case of homosexual pedophilia. *Journal of Behavior Therapy and Experimental Psychiatry,* 1972, *3,* 55–63

Eisler RM, Miller PM, Hersen M, & Alford H. Effects of assertiveness training on marital interaction. *Archives of General Psychiatry,* 1974, *30,* 643–649

Epstein N, DeGiovanni IS, & Lazarus CJ. Assertion training for couples. *Behavioral Therapy and Psychiatry,* 1978, *9,* 149–155

Fensterheim H. Behavior therapy: Assertive training in groups. In CJ Sager & HS Kaplan, (Eds.), *Progress in group and family therapy.* New York: Brunner Mazel, 1972

Fensterheim H, & Baer J. *Don't say yes when you want to say no: How assertiveness training can change your life.* New York: David McKay, 1975

Flowers J, Cooper C, & Whiteley J. Approaches to assertion training. *The Counseling Psychologist,* 1975, *5*(4), 308

Freud S. *A general introduction to psychoanalysis.* New York: Boni and Liverwright, 1920

Galassi J, DeLo J, Galassi M, & Bastien S. The College Self-Expression Scale: A measure of assertiveness. *Behavior Therapy,* 1974, *5,* 165–171

Galassi J, & Galassi M. Assessment procedures for assertive behavior. In RE Alberti (ed.), *Assertiveness: Innovations, applications, issues.* San Luis Obispo, CA: Impact Publishers, 1977

Gay M, Hollandsworth J, & Galassi J. An assertiveness inventory for adults. *Journal of Counseling Psychology,* 1975, *22,* 340–344

Geisinger DL. Controlling sexual and interpersonal anxieties. In J Krumboltz & C Thoresen (Eds.), *Behavioral counseling: Cases and techniques.* New York: Holt, Rinehart & Winston, Inc., 1969

Glass CR, Gottman JM, & Schmurak SH. Response-acquisition and cognitive self-statement modification to dating-skills training. *Journal of Consulting Psychiatry,* 1976, *23,* 520–526

Goldenberg H. *Abnormal psychology: A social/community approach.* Monterey, CA, Brooks/Cole, 1977

Guerra J, & Horskey D. *The use of graduated clients as role models in an assertion training group at a free clinic.* Paper presented at the Western Psychological Association Convention, Anaheim, California, April, 1973

Hipple J. The interpersonal relationship rating scale. In W Pfeiffer & J Jones (Eds.), *The 1977 handbook for group facilitators.* Iowa City: University Associates, 1977

Lange A, & Jakubowski P. *Responsible assertive behavior: Cognitive/behavioral procedures for trainers.* Champaign, IL: Research Press, 1976

Lazarus AA. Behavior therapy in groups. In G. M. Gazda (Ed.), *Basic approaches to group psychotherapy and group counseling.* Springfield, IL: Charles C Thomas, 1968

Lazarus AA. On assertive behavior. A brief note. *Behavior Therapy,* 1973, *4,* 697–699

Lazarus AA. Behavior therapy and beyond. New York: McGraw-Hill, 1971

Lehman-Olson D. Assertiveness Training: Theoretical and clinical implications. In DHL Olson (Ed.), *Treating Relationships.* Lake Mills, IA: Graphic Publishing, 1976, pp 93–116

Lesser E. Behavior therapy with a narcotics user: A case report. *Behavior Research and Therapy,* 1967, *5,* 251–252

Liberman R, King L, De Risi W, & McCann M. *Personal effectiveness: Guiding people to assert themselves and improve their social skills.* Champaign, IL: Research Press, 1975

Liberman RP. Behavioral approaches to family and couple therapy. *American Journal of Orthopsychiatry,* 1970, *60,* 106–118

Liss-Levinson N, Coleman E, & Brown L. A program of sexual assertiveness training for women. *The Counseling Psychologist*, 1975, *5*(4), 74–78

MacDonald M. Teaching assertion: A paradigm for therapeutic intervention. *Psychotherapy: Theory, Research, and Practice*, 1975, *12*, 60–66

Marlatt G, & Perry M. Modeling methods. In F Kanfer & A Goldstein (Eds.), *Helping people change.* New York: Pergamon Press, 1975

Martorano R. Mood and social perception in alcoholics: Effects of drinking on assertion training. *Quarterly Journal of Studies on Alcohol*, 1974, *35*, 445–457

McFall RM, & Marston AR. An experimental investigation of behavior rehearsal in assertive training. *Journal of Abnormal Psychology*, 1970, *2*, 295–303

Muchowski PM, & Valle SK. Effects of assertive training on trainees and their spouses. *Journal of Marriage and Family Counseling*, 1977, *3*, 57–62

Nydegger RV. The elimination of hallucinatory and delusional behavior by verbal conditioning and assertive training: A case study. *Journal of Behavior Therapy and Experimental Psychiatry*, 1972, *3*, 225–227

Olson DH, & Ryder RG. Inventory of marital conflict (IMC): An experimental interaction procedure. *Journal of Marriage and the Family*, 1970, *32*, 443–448

Percell L, Berwick P, & Beigel A. The effects of assertion training on self-concept and anxiety. *Archives of General Psychiatry*, 1974, *31*, 502–504

Piaget G, & Lazarus A. The use of rehearsal-desensitization. *Psychotherapy: Theory, Research, and Practice*, 1969, *6*, 264

Rathus S. Principles and practices of assertiveness training: An eclectic overview. *Counseling Psychologist*, 1973a, *5*, 9–20

Rathus SA. A 30-item schedule for assessing assertive behavior. *Behavior Therapy*, 1973b, *4*, 398–406

Rathus SA, & Ruppert C. Assertion training in the secondary school and the college. *Adolescence*, 1973c, *8*, 251–264

Rich AR, & Schroeder HE. Research issues in assertiveness training. *Psychological Bulletin*, 1976, *83*, 1081–1096

Rimm C, & Masters J. *Behavior therapy: Techniques and empirical findings.* New York: Academic Press, 1974

Russell, RA. Assertiveness training and its effects upon the marital relationship. *Family Therapy*, 1981, *8*, 9–20

Salter A. *Conditioned reflex therapy.* New York: Capricorn, 1949

Selg H. What is aggression? In H Selg (Ed.), *The making of human aggression.* London: Anchor Press, 1975

Shoemaker ME, & Paulson TC. Group assertion training for mothers: A family intervention strategy. In EG Marsh, LC Handy, & LA Hamerlymch (Eds.), *Behavior modification approaches to parenting.* New York: Brunner/Mazel, 1976

Simon S. In L L'Abate (Ed.), *Manual: Enrichment programs for the family life cycle.* Atlanta: Social Research Laboratories, 1975

Spivack G, & Spotts J. Devereux child behavior rating scale manual. Devon, PA, Devereux Foundation, 1966

Wolpe J. *Psychotherapy by reciprocal inhibition.* Stanford: Stanford University Press, 1958

Wolpe . *The practice of behavior therapy.* New York: Pergamon Press, 1969

Wolpe J, & Lazarus AA. *Behavior therapy techniques: A guide to the treatment of neurosis.* New York: Pergamon Press, 1966

3

Communication Training Programs

The communications approach to marital difficulties has become the most widely adopted theoretical and practical orientation in the field of marital therapy. Contemporary marital therapists urge couples to negotiate their differences successfully, generate new ideas, and change patterns of interaction in the face of new or modified information. They also attempt to help couples listen attentively to each other, to value their own and others' input, to speak for themselves, and to share their feelings.

The communications approach is a relatively new one, having been developed only since the mid-1960s. Its basic premise is that problems involve ongoing behavior and interaction between persons in some system of social relationships. Thus the following questions are relevant of treatment: (1) What is going on? (2) How does it continue when people want things to be different? (3) How can the functioning of the system be altered for the better even though no solution will be final or perfect? (Watzalawick et al, 1974). As a logical outcome of these three questions, the focus of both study and treatment becomes the communication patterns, both verbal and nonverbal, of the couple, and the significance of these patterns for the shaping of actual behavior. In an early formulation of this focus, Bardill (1966) noted:

Couples with marital problems tend to communicate progressively less as their conflict deepens. When

communication does take place, it is often ambiguous or contradictory. Even simple tasks often result in arguments because of the nature of the ambiguous communications and on other occasions, there are contradictions between the different levels of communications (p. 71).

More currently, the communications approach to treatment involves two clearer central ideas: (1) that specific behavior of all kinds is primarily an outcome or function of communicative interaction within a social system, and (2) that "problems" consist of persisting undesired behavior (Weakland, 1976, p. 121). Thus the logical focus of treatment becomes one of changing communication patterns that help to maintain the problem behavior.

In addition to the widespread adoption of the communications approach by marital therapists, there has also been a recent development of structured communication training programs for couples. These programs not only address specific problems within the marital dyad, but also provide educational training experiences that may be classified as preventive in nature; i.e., they teach couples communication skills that can then be employed by the couple as problems arise within the marital relationship. Therefore the communications approach currently provides a model of intervention that can be classified as both a preventive and a treatment-oriented intervention.

BACKGROUND AND DEVELOPMENT

The development of communications theory in marital and family therapy can be traced to the now-classic research project on communication conducted by Gregory Bateson and his colleagues (1956) at the Palo Alto VA Hospital. The project evolved from concern with studying communication in general to the examination of the communication of schizophrenics, and led to the formulation of the concept of the double-bind, which described schizophrenic speech and other symptomatic behavior as a response to incongruent messages of different levels within an important relationship and as instances in which escape from the field and comment on the incongruity were both blocked. The necessary components of a double-bind situation were described as:

1. Two or more persons
2. Repeated experience
3. A primary negative injunction
4. A secondary injunction conflicting with the first at a more abstract level and, like the first, enforced by punishment or signals that threaten survival
5. A tertiary negative injunction prohibiting the victim from escaping the field
6. The complete study of injunction is no longer necessary when the victim has learned to perceive his universe in double-bind patterns (Hausen and L'Abate, 1982)

Bateson emphasized the pathological nature of the double bind and concluded that a history of exposure to double binds can be schizophrenogenic.

Other theorists and practitioners also addressed the interactional nature of communication and its impact on the formation and maintenance of behavior. Grinker (1967) stated:

Each has an effect on the other that is specific to the situation in which they exist. One acts on the other, whose response in turn feeds back on the first. The process is cyclical. The setting of the system in which the transacting persons or foci exist determines and is determined by the processes going on (p. 200).

Satir (1964) elaborated further by stating that any behavior occurring between two people is the product of both of them so that behavior can be understood once the premises from which the behavior is derived are made explicit and clear. All communication carries meaning and is either modificatory, informative, reality testing, and/or satisfying needs for self-expression.

Watzlawick, et al (1967) added that one cannot *not* communicate. Communication not only conveys information but imposes behavior. The verbal content of the message conveys content and information. The command aspect, however, refers to how the message is interpreted as well as how it comments on the relationship. The relationship comments can be interpreted as either confirming, rejecting, or disconfirming, depending on the interaction.

Haley (1970) added the concept of rules whereby couples establish implicit and explicit rules to govern their relationships. These rules also govern communication patterns and may reinforce the continuation of interpersonal problems, particularly when the couple struggles with who is to make the rules. Spouses also communicate at more than one level, so that a message may define one type of relationship at one level and an incompatible type of relationship at another level. Symptoms result when there are incompatible definitions of the relationship.

Berne (1964) conceptualized the breakdown of communication as the result of crossed transactions rather than a misunderstanding of the level at which a message is being communicated. Individuals can communicate only when their ego states (Parent, Adult, Child) are complementary (Parent to Parent, Adult to Adult, or Child to Child).

As a result of theory, the treatment focus in the communication approach becomes one of correcting communication, which will lead to self-correction in the interactional system. Symptoms are viewed as a resulting from the interaction within the marital system so that both members are involved in and are influencing the production of the dilemma. Furthermore, the resolution of the problem becomes a here-and-now-oriented approach because it primarily requires a change in the problem-maintaining behavior (communication) in order to interrupt what has usually become a vicious positive feedback circle—the attempted solution to the problem often maintains the problem. (Watzlawick, Weakland & Fisch, 1974).

MAJOR PHILOSOPHY AND CURRENT CONCEPTS

Ultimately, the communications approach views both the problem and the cause of the problem as inadequate or destructive patterns of communication. Therefore, treatment aims at altering communication patterns in the context of the interrelationship of the couple. This approach is a systems approach, for essentially, the actions and reactions of one influence the actions and reactions of the other so that all behavior is a product of the ongoing interrelationship.

Within this framework, treatment stresses (1) the specification of problem(s), (2) clarification of attempting solutions, (3) redefinition of problems, (4) recognition of mutual contributions to problem(s), (5) clarification/specification of individual desires and needs in the relationship, (6) increased reciprocity, (7) decreased coercion and blame, and (8) recognition and modification of communication patterns and rules. Presenting problems are seen as communicational messages about the marital relationship or as the result of faulty problem definition or faulty previous change efforts. Therefore the focus of treatment is on the communication patterns within the relationship.

Although it is difficult to describe the implementation of the communications approach by marital therapists, this approach has been altered only slightly in its translation into structured training programs. All current communication training programs for couples stress the essential theoretical and treatment components that have been addressed by communications theorists.

Couple Communication Training Programs

Minnesota Couples Communication Program

The most widely known and thoroughly researched couples communications program is the Minnesota Couples Communication Program (abbreviated variously as MCCP, CCP, and CC). This program (abbreviated here as CC) was developed in 1968 at the University of Minnesota Family Study Center by Miller, Nunnally, and Wackman (1975b).

Development of the program included synthesizing the additions of the concept of "process" to the traditional cognitive model of learning, the concepts of growth and development as aspects of adjustment, a systemic approach to the conceptualization of families and couples in addition to the individual perspective, recognition of strengths and methods for utilizing them, and a humanistic psychological orientation that stressed learning by experimenting with different ways of communicating.

The rationale underlying the development of the program consisted of two major premises. The first was the importance, emphasized by Foote and Cottrell (1955), of developing interpersonal competence to accommodate and create change in order to keep the marital relationship viable over time. The second was a concern with equipping couples with interpersonal competence for creating their own marital scripts rather than teaching "correct" marital role behavior.

Two primary theories provided the theoretical framework for the program: systems theory and communications theory. From the systems theory perspective, families are characterized as "rule-governed systems": the rules define and limit how the system interacts and how these rules affect the system's functional effectiveness. From the communication theory perspective, communication becomes the index for understanding the system and the vehicle for changing it.

Several major concepts related to intrasystem processes were presented by Miller, et al (1975a) within the two theoretical systems. The first concept is *awareness*, defined as the internal experience of the person. Much of what occurs in communication depends on the internal state of the person communicating. Therefore, the assumption is made that each person must be an authority on his or her own awareness and have responsibility for what he or she does with it.

The second concept is *rules*. How one addresses one's awareness depends to a large extent on social rules and expectations. Every interrelationship has boundaries, or constraints, that either encourage or discourage certain types of awareness and various types of behavior. Rules are generally outside direct awareness; they operate to create and maintain meaning and order in relationships. They are conceptualized in terms of who can do what, when, how, for what length of time, and can be applied to any issue in a relationship. Rules become apparent by the consequences that occur when they are broken. Families and couples have rules about how they address issues, and formal rules within families often prohibit and discourage the negotiation of important issues. The third concept, *metacommunication*, or talk about communication, enables couples to establish procedures for self-monitoring, regulating, and directing the rules of their relationships and, thus, the relationship itself.

The fourth concept is that of *disclosure and receptivity*. The individual has a choice, once aware of a thought, feeling, or desire, of whether to disclose verbally its content. How something is disclosed is as important as what is disclosed. Hill (1968) explored the relationship between different content dimensions and levels of disclosure (awareness foci and communication styles) and concluded that various styles could be categorized under one of two basic models of communication: "nonwork" and "work" modes, the former characterized by behaviors that reflect no intent to explore and change personal and relationship issues, the latter by behaviors that facilitate negotiation within the relationship. Jourard (1964) also identified the "dyadic effect": within significant relationships, disclosure tends to encourage disclosure.

The fifth concept is that of *skills*, defined as behaviors that facilitate effective communication. They include speaking for self and owning one's own statements, giving specific examples and making feeling statements. Focusing on skills enables one to describe concretely those aspects of one's awareness that in the past may have been implicit and, often, vague.

The sixth concept is *esteem building*. It became apparent that heightening one's awareness and learning skills to express that awareness could not only improve communication, but could also equip a person to become a more sophisticated and destructive communicator. Therefore, the intent or spirit of communication is important. Sorells and Ford (1969) suggested an esteem component: by the way people communicate with each other, they demonstrate their intent to maintain and build

or to destroy their own and the other person's esteem. When a person's intentions do not match actions, he or she behaves incongruently. Satir's (1964) four stress patterns (blamer, placater, computer, distracter) are employed when self-esteem is threatened. Congruent communication is honest communication whether or not it is "open." Esteem building is reflected in the types of messages couples send to each other, and each person takes responsibility for his or her own messages and response to the messages received.

Finally, Miller, et al (1975b) conceptualized a symmetrical system as an ideal structure for a dyadic relationship: "Positive symmetry in husband–wife input regarding significant interaction characteristics contributes to marital satisfaction and to the vigor and growth of the marital system" (p. 63). A key feature of symmetry is that it is a function of the system and therefore cannot be individually incorporated by the members of the system, although each member can unilaterally terminate the systemic balance. They also cited findings from empirical research that support the importance of symmetry for marital satisfaction and growth:

1. Couples in which both husband and wife used communication styles involving high disclosure reported higher levels of marital satisfaction than couples in which one or both partners used low disclosure styles.
2. Couples in which both husband and wife were high in accurately understanding the partner's view on a number of issues were more satisfied with their marriages than couples in which one or both partners were low on accuracy (Miller, Corrales, & Wackman, 1975).
3. In a series of studies, couples with equalitarian power structures were higher in marital satisfaction than were couples with other kinds of power structures (Blood & Wolfe, 1960; Lu, 1952).

Positive symmetry is further advanced as an important characteristic of the marital relationship by Boszormenyi–Nagy and Spark (1973), who built a theory of family therapy on the notion of maintaining a balanced ledger of indebtedness within and between generations, promoting healthy individual growth:

The fact that the total end result of the ledger may be imbalanced at any given time is not the crucial determinant of health versus pathogenicity of a relationship. In that it requires a new effort at rebalancing, transitory imbalance contributes to the growth of relationships. Only fixed, unchangeable imbalance with its consequent loss of trust and hope should be considered pathogenic (p. 101).

Miller and his colleagues concluded that the symmetry observed in the various identified components of marital communication may indeed contribute to the balance or imbalance of the marital ledger.

As a result of this conceptual framework, two sets of skills were seen as necessary to improve communication: (1) *awareness* skills, which enable couples to understand their rules and interaction patterns; and (2) *communication* skills, which enable them to change the rules and interaction patterns. In addition, metacommunication can be taught, enabling couples to discuss the rules of their relationship.

Two goals were identified in designing CC: (1) to increase each couple's ability to reflect on and accurately predict their own dyadic processes by refining each member's private self-awareness, heightening each partner's awareness of his or her own contribution to the interaction and helping couples explore their own rules of relationship, particularly their rules for conflict resolution and their patterns of maintaining self and other's esteem; (2) to increase each couple's capacity for clear, direct, open metacommunication, especially about their relationship. The focus of these goals was on helping couples establish common perspectives and skills for monitoring and altering their own interaction patterns related to developmental issues, on their own time and by their own choice, rather than trying to solve pathogenic relationship problems.

Six dimensions underlie the model:

1. An educational developmental orientation, with a focus on equipping rather than repairing.
2. A focus on the system. Both partners are included and the emphasis is on their interaction, with the assumption that how a message is sent is as important as why it is sent. Four styles of communication, based on Hill's Interaction Matrix, are presented with the idea that a complete repertoire of skills enables flexibility and adaptability.
3. A skill orientation. The presentation of skills for heightening self, other, situation, and system awareness distinguishes CC from the sensitivity and encounter experiences of the mid-1960s when the model was developed.
4. Presentation of conceptual frameworks. Four conceptual frameworks are presented in order to eliminate some of the mystery surrounding relationships by helping couples systematically understand predictable properties of relationships, to serve as advanced organizers for learning specific skills and making sense of the program, and to provide common bases from which couples can amplify their awareness.
5. Volunteerism and participant choice. The assumption is that the learning process is most effective when voluntary; therefore, there is an initial interview prior to the program in which each partner agrees on a contract to ensure conjoint participation.
6. Group context as a learning environment. The group serves as sources for feedback and multiple models to emulate or avoid, but the pressure to conform is thought to come largely from within the dyad itself.

Structure of the program. Groups that are limited to five to seven couples meet with one or two certified instructors for three-hour sessions, one night a week for four consecutive weeks. The texts are the CC Workbook and *Alive and Aware* (Miller Nunnally, & Wackman, 1975a).

Session 1: Definition of Awareness Wheel. The Awareness Wheel, a visual model that has five sections, is presented by the instructors. These sections are acting, sensing, thinking, wanting, feeling. The presentation of the framework creates an overview for understanding complete and congruent, as well as incomplete and incongruent, self-awareness. Couples are also taught six skills for verbally expressing their awareness: (1) speaking for self, (2) making sense statements, (3) making interpretive statements, (4) making feeling statements, (5) making intention statements, and (6) making action statements.

Session 2. The focus shifts to learning how to accurately exchange important information with one's partner. Four additional skills are taught as part of the "Shared Meaning Framework": (1) checking out what is heard, (2) stating intentions and asking for acknowledgment, (3) acknowledging the sender's message, (4) confirming/clarifying the sender's message.

Session 3. The "Communication Styles Framework" is presented. Four styles with different impact are identified, each associated with different intentions and behaviors (Hill Interaction Matrix). With Style I, information meeting social expectations is exchanged; little is disclosed about the self. In Style II, the intention is to force change in another person or in a situation: this style usually involves interpretations (judgments) and actions (should/ought) and can be useful in signaling that there are areas of tension in the relationship. Style II limits the possibility of dealing effectively with the situation, however. Style III's intention is to reflect and explore, to examine an issue or event; it is a tentative and speculative style. It can be helpful in identifying and clarifying issues, in examining background information relevant to the issue, and in generating alternatives. In Style IV, the intentions and behaviors signal a commitment to deal completely and congruently with the issue; the person is in contact with his or her self-awareness and shares this awareness. The 10 skills taught in Sessions 1 and 2 are used in Style IV.

Session 4. In the final session, attention centers on heightening each partner's awareness of one's intentions to build, maintain, or diminish one's own and another's esteem. The fourth framework presented integrates all material presented and facilitates the creation of verbal work patterns. The model for self–other esteem may be compared with the four stances of Transactional Analysis (Berne, 1964): "I count, you count," "I count, you don't count," etc. A work pattern is defined as follows: (1) identify the issue; (2) use a mini-contract to work; (3) deal with the issue by using Styles III and IV, or IV alone.

Miller and his colleagues see several limitations in the CC program: it is designed as an educational rather than therapeutic experience; it is designed for nonclinical couples—clinical couples' relationships are not seen as flexible enough; the limited size of the groups increases the cost of the program; and it attracts rela-

tively highly educated people. Several potential strengths are identified by the authors: by January 1976, more than 1500 CC groups had been conducted. They were found to be beneficial to couples at any point in their marital careers since the program is not limited to any stage of the family life cycle; the groups can be conducted in a number of different settings such as churches, university continuing education divisions, social agencies; and the program offers a meaningful supplement or alternative to more traditional methods of preparation for marriage.

Research evaluating CC programs. As indicated previously, CC is the most widely known and thoroughly researched of the structured communication programs. In the instructors' manual (Miller, Nunnally, & Wackman, 1975b), eight studies had been completed, evaluating the program's impact (Brown, 1976; Campbell, 1974; Dillon, 1976; Miller, 1971; Nunnally, 1971; Schwager & Conrad, 1974; Thielen, et al, 1976; Zimmerman & Bailey, 1977).

Of the eight studies, seven used an experimental design, six of the seven used pre- and post-test measures, and all seven took immediate postgroup measures. One study took a second postgroup measure after 10 weeks. Comparison of the experimental subjects with no-activity control groups was made in seven studies. All studies used random assignment of couples to experimental and control groups. One study included a survey of couples who had participated in CC 6 months to 5 years earlier.

All of the studies used small samples, the largest using 30 couples in both experimental and control groups. Typically, 15 to 20 couples were assigned to each condition. The sample subjects were generally better educated than the general population, although one study used "rural disadvantaged adults." Early studies used engaged couples; later studies included persons ranging from their late 20s through their early 40s. One study used German couples. The populations used in these samples can be considered representative of the population of couples who would volunteer for marital enrichment programs. The studies covered a broad geographical range within the United States (as well as one outside the United States).

Usually, the studies used self-report measures: three used observational techniques, and five used measures of various aspects of interpersonal communication behavior. Other outcomes, such as acceptance of self and partner, self-esteem, marital satisfaction, and sexual stereotyping, were measured in four studies.

Self-disclosure communication was assessed in three of the studies. In all but one comparison, experimental subjects increased self-disclosure more than the controls. In one study, experimental subjects increased accuracy in recalling interaction patterns more than the control subjects.

The one survey study assessed impact on communication behavior between self and partner, and communication styles used in conflict situations. A large majority reported improvement in their own communication; more than 75 percent reported increased use of positive styles, integration, and compromise.

Three studies measured couple interaction using observational techniques and found that the experimental subjects increased in disclosures of feelings and work pattern communication. There was no change in the control subjects. Both self-reports and behavioral measures, then, indicated an increase in the use of communication skills following participation in CC.

The measurements of noncommunication outcomes yielded positive results with few exceptions: a greater acceptance of self and partner, increased self-esteem, and lower sex-role stereotyping when compared with the controls. Measurement in these studies of change in marital satisfaction yielded no differences between experimental and control groups immediately after CC, but one study that ran a second post-test after 10 weeks found that the experimental couples increased marital satisfaction "somewhat," while the controls did not change. There was a high correlation in this study between changes in communication behavior and changes in marital satisfaction.

The survey study assessed aspects of satisfaction with CC: 97 percent were highly or moderately satisfied; 19 percent felt CC was worth the time and money; 75 percent recommended the program to their friends; 75 percent recalled most elements of the program; and 90 percent who recalled a framework or skills indicated that it was helpful.

All eight studies indicated positive results in terms of increased communication skills. The studies do *not* indicate that all couples learn all skills taught in CC, but most learn some skills. The impact was clearly seen to be due to the program, not to the individual instructors.

More recently, Wampler (1982) reviewed all of the outcome studies on CC, evaluating results on the basis of self-report and behavioral measures. On the Marital Communication Inventory of Bienvenu (1971), three studies showed no effects, two showed positive effects maintained at follow-up, and one study was questionable. On the Primary Communication Inventory of Locke (1951), three studies showed positive effects. On the Self-Disclosure Questionnaire revised by Bienvenu (1971), two studies showed no effects. On the Self-Disclosure Questionnaire by Miller et al (1975a), two studies showed no effects. On a Recall and Predictive Accuracy measure developed by Nunnally (1971), no effects were found, and two studies found "positive effects on recall only." On the spouse's ability to predict the spouse's responses to the same measure, two studies found no effects and one found positive effects on recall maintained at follow-up.

On the Marital Adjustment Test of Locke and Wallace (1959), no effects were found in four studies and positive effects in two. On the Interpersonal (Adjective Checklist) by La Forge, Saczek, and Leary (Leary, 1957), two studies found no effects, one found positive effects, and one found a questionable effect. On the Relationship Inventory of Barnett-Lennard (1962), positive effects were found in one study and questionable effects were found in another. On the Semantic Differential of "my marriage," "myself," and "my spouse," one study found that changes at post-test were not maintained at follow-up. On the Interpersonal Relationship Scale by Schlein, Guerney, and Toller (Guerney, 1977), one study found positive effects. On the Relationship Change of Scale of Schlein and Guerney (Guerney, 1977), one study found questionable results. On Shostrom's (1966) Caring Relationship Inventory, one study found no effects. Nor were any effects found on the FIRO-B Reciprocal Compatibility. On the Tennessee Self-Concept Scale by Fitts (1970), one study found no effects, one found positive effects that were not maintained at follow-up, and one study found improved scores for males but not for females.

On the Self-Actualization Scale of the Personal Orientation Inventory by Shostrom (1966), one study found positive effects. On Gough's Adjective Checklist (Gough and Heilburu, 1965), one study found positive effects on degree of sex-role stereotyping self's spouse.

On behavioral measures, four studies found positive effects on increased percentage of work statements and on increased percentage of time spent in productive communication styles. Of the three CC skills, Speaking for Self, Making Feeling Statements, and Making Intervention Statements, one study found positive results for the first two, while two studies found no effects for the first and third skills.

On other behavioral measures, positive effects were found on the Communication Rapid Assessment Scale by Joanning (in press) for frequency of interruptions, defensive communication, supportive communication, and no response. No effects were found on amount of silence and amount of talking time. No negative or deterioration effects were reported in these studies.

Wampler (1982) concluded,

CCP appears to produce immediate positive changes in communication behavior and relationship satisfaction with improvement in these areas maintained after the immediate impact of the program has passed. The quality of research on CCP has been improving, but partly because of the relative unavailability of research reports, CCP research frequently has not built on previous research (p. 352).

Joanning, in an unpublished paper, assessed the immediate and long-term impact of CC with 33 couples assigned to either training (17) or control (16) groups. Change was measured by self-reports of marital adjustment, trust and intimacy, and communication quality, with behavioral ratings of couple verbal interaction. Trained couples increased significantly on all measurements at immediate post-test. At five months follow-up, marital adjustment scores returned to pretest levels. Trust, intimacy, couple-perceived communication quality, and rater-judged communication quality, however, kept their post-test levels. Joanning recommended an increase in the length of the program, especially as far as specific skills were concerned, and a continued use of behavioral and self-report measures of changes due to training.

An investigation by Rosella (1981) attempted to establish a connection between communication-systems theory and psychosomatic disorders. There is no evidence that previous studies have been conducted linking a couples communication program with the incidence of psychosomatic complaints. Rosella thus hypothesized that a Couples Communication Workshop would effect a change in the incidence of somatic complaints of a medically selected group of married couples.

Subjects for the study were selected by physicians from the populations of four suburban Philadelphia, Pennsylvania, medical centers. In addition, the Wahler Physical Symptoms Inventory (WPSI) and Taylor-Johnson Temperament Analysis (T-JTA) were employed to select subjects. A "matched pair" experimental group and control group were chosen based on physician recommendation, WPSI, and J-JTA raw scores. In addition, subject availability to participate in the study and testing program were considerations, as were factors such as age, number of years married, and education of the participants.

Statistical analysis of the preceding factors, utilizing the F test for equality of variance and the t test for independent sample means, showed that no significant differences existed between the two groups at the 0.05 level. Furthermore, no significant differences were found between the experimental group and control group on the WPSI, T-JTA Anxiety Pattern Self and Spouse Perception, Nervous Scale, and Depressive Scale at the 0.05 level. In addition, no statistically significant differences were found at the 0.05 level between Self and Spouse Perception on the Nervous and Depressive Scales employing the t test for dependent means. It was therefore concluded that the experimental and control groups were equally matched.

After the subjects were selected, 10 couples (20 subjects) attended 4 (3-hour) sessions at which communications techniques were taught. Participants were post-tested 4 to 8 weeks later. Results of these tests showed that the experimental group had a significant decrease in physical symptoms as measured by the WPSI self-reported scores at the 0.01 level. The Mann-Whitney U Test and the t test for independent sample means were employed to analyze data. In addition, the T-JTA Nervous and Depressive Scales Self-Perception scores each showed a significant decrease at the 0.01 level. The *t* test for dependent means was used to analyse these data. Spouse perception scores also indicated a decrease on the Nervous Scale score at the 0.05 level of significance. Decreases on scores on the Anxiety Pattern Self and Spouse perception and the Depressive Scale Spouse perception revealed no significant decrease at the 0.05 level.

Data for the control group were treated similarly. No significant decreases in raw scores were found for the control group scores on the WPSI self-report score, the T-TJA Anxiety Pattern, self and spouse perception scores, and the Nervous and Depressive Scales.

Experimental group subjects reported in a postworkshop questionnaire that they believed that the Couples Communication Workshop had benefited them by improving their emotional well-being, communications skills, interpersonal relationships, and, to some extent, their physical health.

The Couples Communication Workshop assisted in reducing self-perceived somatic complaints as measured by the WPSI scores for the experimental group. There was also a decrease in self-perceived nervousness and depression as measured by the T-JTA Nervous and Depressive Scales. Furthermore, spouses perceived a decrease in nervousness in each other but did not report noticing a decrease in symptoms of spouse-perceived depression. Finally, there was no decrease in anxiety as measured by the T-TJA Anxiety Pattern scores on either self or spouse perception.

The control group showed no statistically significant decreases in the WPSI score, T-JTA Anxiety Pattern scores, Nervous Scale scores, or Depressive Scale scores in either self or spouse perception. Control group subjects did perceive themselves as somewhat less depressed, but the decrease was not statistically significant.

Limitations of the study included difficulties with the T-TJA test instrument, in that the Anxiety Pattern Subjective and Hostile Scales may not have measured what the experimenters expected concerning their effects upon their relationships with psychosomatic complaints. Second, obtaining subject cooperation and biasing variables that could not be controlled were also problems.

Brock and Joanning (1980) compared 26 couples trained in Guerney's (1977) Relationship Enhancement versus 20 couples trained with the Minnesota Couples Communications Program (CC). A control group of eight couples was used. Both experimental groups were rather heterogeneous in age, years of marriage, and other demographic variables. However, they were similar on scores achieved on Spanier's Dyadic Adjustment Scale (1976). All couples were evaluated on this scale in pre-, post-, and follow-up testing. A rapid assessment measure of actual communications between spouses was also used. On follow-up, RE showed statistically significant changes in scores of pertaining to "general relationship satisfaction, general communication patterns, and expression of affection, whereas CC did not. In addition, this comparison found RE to be more effective in increasing spouses' general agreement and actual communications skills. Neither program was effective in increasing marital cohesion-couples' 'frequency of joint activities' " (Brock & Joanning, 1980, p. 7). The authors explained the results in terms of differences in program format, focus, functions, and facilitations. For instance, RE is more applicable than CC to low-satisfaction couples, while CC was designed to improve already functional relationships.

Witkin (1977) compared a behaviorally oriented communication skills workshop (CSW) based on social learning theory with CC. He recruited couples through newspaper and radio advertising, letters, agency referrals, and a feature story in the local newspaper. All couples were evaluated pre- and post with the Marital Adjustment Questionnaire, Areas-of-Change Questionnaire, and Marital Communication and Marital Interaction Coding System. Of the couples, five attended CC and eight attended CSW. Evaluation was conducted at one week and seven weeks following training. The results indicated that CC training produced significant increases in nonverbal positive messages relative to CSW and no training. CC training also resulted in significant decreases in nonverbal negative messages as compared with CSW, even though both training conditions significantly reduced negative verbal messages. Self-report measures revealed no significant differences at follow-up testing. Witkin concluded that CC appears to be a viable alternative to behavioral programs like CSW. These and other findings would also support the need for addressing emotional affects in addition to the cognitive and the nonverbal.

In a comparison of CC and behavioral exchange, with 32 couples randomly assigned to treatment and control conditions, Russell, et al (1980) had difficulty finding significant differences in either approach.

Communication Training

Gottman, et al (1976a) have developed a program that has, as its philosophical base, an empirical rather than a behavioral orientation. The program is also designed for individual couples rather than groups.

Gottman traces the history of his program from the cybernetics research during World War II, which was generalized by Norbert Weiner to the behavioral sciences, and the double-bind theory of schizophrenia, the study that has stimulated interest in the social interaction of distressed families. Gottman and his colleagues saw a need for further descriptive information about interacting systems, especially in nondistressed families.

Although the concept of quid pro quo, or positive reciprocity, has been assumed to characterize successful marriages, Gottman believes there is no evidence to support this theory:

We believe in positive reciprocity primarily because first Lederer and Jackson (1968), then Richard Stuart (1969), and then Nathan Azrin (Azrin, Naster and Jones, 1973) and now the whole brass ensemble is out playing the "Quid Pro Quo March" (Gottman, et al, 1976a, pp. x-xi).

Gottman and his associates set out "to describe systematically what it is that nondistressed couples do differently than distressed couples to resolve marital conflict and how they themselves perceive the messages they exchange" (Gottman, et al, 1976a, p. xi).

Gottman et al challenged the idea that positive reciprocity discriminates between distressed and nondistressed couples. He and his group ran two studies of nondistressed and distressed couples and found no evidence to support the positive reciprocity model; in fact, they concluded that the data support a "bank account" model rather than a reciprocity model:

Positive codes or "deposits" must exceed negative codes or "withdrawals." Perhaps it is precisely this lack of contingency on positive interaction that characterizes satisfying and stable nondistressed marriages. Nondistressed couples in the second study, who had been married longer than nondistressed couples in the first study, showed less reciprocity than nondistressed couples in the first study. In fact, in the interactions in this book we stress the concept that behavior change be "unlatched" or *not* contingent (p. xviii).

The rationale for their program, therefore, is a bank account rather than a reciprocity model.

In addressing Behavior Exchange Theory, Gottman, et al (1976b) discussed the interpretations of the proposal that a dyad engaged in a mutually satisfying relationship will exchange behaviors that have low cost and high reward to both members (Thibault & Kelley, 1959). One interpretation of the reward–cost idea is that *producing* a specific behavior has a specific reward and a specific cost to the person producing the behavior (Gergen, 1969). A second interpretation is that in a satisfying dyadic relationship, a person will receive behaviors that have high reward for himself or herself, the implication being that a person will perceive the relationship as satisfying to the extent that he or she codes the behaviors *received* as positive. According to the widely accepted communication deficit explanations of marital distress, distressed couples are presumed to intend their messages to be received as far more positive than they are in fact received. Gottman suggested that distressed couples perhaps *intend* their messages to be more negative, or less positive, than do nondistressed couples. His studies did not confirm this idea, however.

One of the innovations created by Gottman and his colleagues is the use of a "talk table," which was used in their studies to record the "intended impact" and "actual impact" of messages sent and received. They wanted subjects, rather than outside observers who might misjudge established dyadic communication behaviors, to code their own behaviors. After speaking, the first partner coded the intended impact of his or her message. Before responding, the listener coded the actual impact of the message. The talk table is described as a double, sloping table on the side of which is a toggle switch, operated by the couple, that lights a button on the side of the spouse who has the floor to speak. It has two rows of five buttons: those on the left are used by the speaker to code the intended impact of the message sent; those on the right are used by the listener to code the actual impact of the message received. The buttons are labeled "super negative," "negative," "neutral," "positive," and "super positive." Although the partners can see one another across the table, a metal shield blocks the buttons from the view of the other person so that neither can see the codes assigned by the partner.

The results of their two studies supported a deficit model of marital distress. For distressed couples, behavior was coded as far less positive than was the intention. In both studies, although distressed and nondistressed couples did not significantly differ in the way they intended their messages to be received by their spouses, they did differ significantly on how the messages were actually received. Gottman, et al concluded that reciprocity variables do not discriminate between distressed and nondistressed couples, again supporting his noncontingent "bank account" model.

Gottman and colleagues' resulting communication program was presented in *A Couple's Guide to Communication* (1976a). Unlike CC and Carkhuff's (1973) programs, this guide is intended for couples to use on their own, outside a group experience, although it also lends itself to incorporation into a group program. The central theme is that therapy interventions are "unlatched," or noncontingent, on the behavior of the other spouse (i.e., "I won't change until my spouse changes"), for contingency produces resistance to change.

Effective communication consists of five skills: listening and validation, leveling, editing, negotiating agreements, and hidden agendas.

Skill 1: Listening and Validation. This skill reduces the proportion of summarizing self-statements (SS), ending what is called the "SS Syndrome"—circular repetition of each person's point of view without acknowledging the other's point of view. The skill taught is checking out and paraphrasing, which has five steps: (1) Call Stop Action, (2) Feedback, (3) Listen to Feedback, (4) Summarize and Validate, and (5) Check Impact.

The cognitive organizer for this section is the Intent/Impact model from the talk table studies, i.e., intent does not always equal impact. Validation is defined as related to "accepting" behaviors: when a spouse expresses feelings, the other spouse does not have to agree but responds with "I can see how you think and feel that way even if I don't see it the way you do."

The objective is to enable couples to get feedback on Intent/Impact discrepancies, call a "Stop Action" when there is a discrepancy, use the "Interim Trouble-Shooting Guide" (a manual identifying problems and suggesting solutions), and find an intervention to improve communication. The section also begins to build a language of "marital games," which can be used as tags of specific behavior patterns so that the couple can monitor and intervene to change these patterns. The couple is also introduced to the concept of mindreading as a way of attributing blame; the expectation is not to eliminate mindreading but to affect its nonverbal delivery.

Skill 2: Leveling. This skill deals further with mindreading, defined as attributing feelings, thoughts, motives and behaviors, and blaming. The behavioral objective is to transform the general attack to a specific statement: "When you do X in situation Y, I feel Z," so that the statement can become an agenda item for negotiation.

The concepts of constructive and destructive leveling are presented. Four destructive modes are presented with constructive alternatives:

1. *Character assassination.* For example, the charge, "You're insensitive," can be presented in terms of action with specific example: "You didn't ask my opinion about where to go for dinner tonight."
2. *Insults.* The charge, "You're a slob," can be presented by describing specifically what the spouse does in which specific situations and how it makes the partner feel: "When you don't wear a shirt at the dinner table, I feel that you don't think I'm special."
3. *Kitchen sinking.* "I'm fed up with the house, with not going anywhere, with our

sex life, with our whole lifestyle." The constructive alternative is to choose one important gripe and state, "When you do X in situation Y, I feel Z."

4. *Cross-complaining, airing resentments without listening to each other (SS Syndrome).* The constructive alternative is to stick at one issue at a time.

The techniques used in this section include a feeling chart, which labels positive and negative feelings, assertion instructions, a discussion of catastrophic expectations, and the idea of suggestion boxes (one for each partner, with specific times scheduled to open the suggestion boxes and discuss their contents). Couples who have difficulty leveling and talking honestly are the conflict avoiders who feel lonely and cut off, or who intellectualize feelings and issues. Leveling can help this type of couple learn to deal with conflict avoidance.

Skill 3: Editing. Contrasted with couples who typically avoid conflict are those who continually bicker and escalate quarrels. The skills in this section are designed for couples who engage endlessly in arguments. The behavioral objectives are to proofread one's own behavior to self-control escalating quarrels, to learn to "edit" the scripts of other couples, and to learn nine rules of politeness (specific etiquette rules) with one another.

The theory behind this section is that it is well known that even highly distressed couples are capable of being nice to strangers. Editing works as a renewal process so that couples can back off, act like strangers, get in touch, and level within a climate of positive or considerate behavior.

Examples of the rules of etiquette include (1) don't say what you can't do, or what you don't want to do; say what you can do and what you want to do; (2) don't complain or nag, give sincere and positive appreciation—if you have an issue to resolve, schedule a leveling session; (3) don't be selfish, be courteous and considerate.

Skill 4: Negotiating Agreements. The behavioral objective is to identify three parts of a "family meeting": gripe time, agenda-building time, and problem-solving time; to learn to change negative, nebulous complaints into specific negative complaints (leveling) and then into positive suggestions; to use closure with an "up deck," a deck of cards containing specific behaviors the couple decides to increase in frequency. The cards include such behaviors as getting a household repair done, balancing the checkbook, doing the dishes. Finally, a behavioral contract is used to close the deal made by the partners in their meeting.

Skill 5: Hidden Agendas. This skill addresses "wheel spinning." Gottman, et al found that many couples learned Skills 1 through 4 and resolved the surface issues in their relationships but still felt bored with their relationship. He believes that hidden agenda dimensions, when addressed, get at the underlying issues of the marriage.

A Couple's Guide to Communication includes four additional chapters, "Solving Your Sexual Problems, "Making a Good Thing Better," "Getting Through a Crisis," and "Getting Out of a Bad Marriage." These chapters are not based on the group's research, but the authors added the material to address other components of the marital relationship.

Gottman and colleagues' program is couple-individuated, designed for couples to use on their own at their own pace. As such, the material would appeal to those highly motivated, relatively highly educated couples who want to improve their relationships.

Marital Communication and Decision-Making

Thomas (1977) developed a behaviorally based program for couples that defined verbal behavior as an operant under control of its consequences and as a stimulus for future interactions with dual functions: message sending and behavioral guidance. Thomas suggested eight basic steps to answer the four main questions of assessment:

1. Is there a problem of marital communication that warrants intervention?
2. If so, what are the specific verbal behaviors that define that problem operationally?
3. What are the probable sources of the communication difficulty?
4. What should be the behavioral objectives of intervention?

The eight steps of assessment are (1) filling out an inventory of problem areas, (2) selection of and contracting for target behavior, (3) commitment to cooperate, (4 and 5) response specification and identification of probable sources of difficulty, (6) assessment of behavioral and environmental resources, (7) specification of behavioral objectives, and (8) respecification of contract for target behavior.

His plan of modification consists of four steps: (1) formulations, (2) implementation, (3) monitoring of outcomes, and (4) maintenance of change. In addition, Thomas suggested principles for partners to keep in mind when working with each other:

1. Tailor plans for modification procedures to each partner and to the couple.
2. Formulate the modification plan for a few key target responses.
3. Include both partners as targets of modification even if one contributes much more than the other to the interactional difficulties.
4. Choose a setting for modification (e.g., office, house, or both) that is consonant with the modification objectives and distinctive capabilities of the interventional methods.
5. Direct intervention toward altering the sources of communication difficulty when these are known.
6. Give priority to alteration of sources of communication difficulty derived from external sources before focusing on partner interaction itself.
7. When possible, combine modification to accelerate desirable verbal responding with intervention intended to decelerate responding for unacceptable behavior.
8. When focusing on partner interaction, modify complementary target behaviors of both partners when possible.

Corrective feedback and instruction for both partners are based on a set of 23 rules designed to set events favorable for marital communication, to separate marital decision-making from noncontroversial verbal exchange, to structure couple communication, and to settle noncontroversial discussions. There are also nine procedural steps to implement the use of these rules.

An exchange system between partners is then developed on the basis of the following steps: (1) the appropriate form of exchange is selected, (2) the desirable and undesirable behaviors to be included in the system are specified exactly and fully, (3) the target behaviors are determined to be within the response capability of the partner, (4) all privileges are specified exactly and fully, and (5) values are allocated for potential earnings for behaviors and costs for privileges, using a token or point system, with full details of exchange for continuous contracts.

In addition to the preceding eight principles for marital communication, Thomas added five more principles for marital decision-making.

9. Difficulties involving nonrecurring decision issues should generally be addressed before any decision-making difficulties for recurring issues.
10. Operational targets of intervention for difficulties in handling recurring decision issues should generally be the sources of such difficulties, if these sources have been identified.
11. Before endeavoring to modify sources of decision-making difficulty rooted in partner interaction, attention should be given to alteration of other sources of decision-making difficulty.
12. Operational targets of intervention for difficulties in handling nonrecurring decision issues should generally be particular responses relating directly to these issues.
13. A problem-solving approach to marital decision-making should be emphasized, rather than a bargaining approach.

In suggesting critical activities in decision-making, Thomas followed the usually steps given by other negotiation programs: (1) recognition that a problem situation requiring joint decision exists, (2) agreement to try to work together toward a solution, (3) isolation of a specific and workable contract, (4) generation of solution alternatives without evaluation or judgment ("brainstorming"), (5) selection of solution(s) for implementation, (6) deciding on which action to follow and who will do what, when, and how, (7) taking action, and (8) reviewing action. Here again, Thomas listed a set of 16 rules for marital decision-making to address, establishment of facilitative conditions, decision-making procedures, and increasing partner interaction. He follows up implementation procedures through an approach based on "coaching."

There is no question that his method is complete, for Thomas leaves little room for variations and/or deviations. He also illustrates through case studies how his procedures are applied with couples. There is currently no outcome data for this program, however. The major question about this method relates to the number of steps and rules that couples follow. Will so many rules confuse couples? Will they be able to follow and implement so many rules? Can a marriage survive on rules? Are so many rules necessary?

Couples Communication and Negotiating Skills

This program, developed by Garland (1978, 1981), is a couples communication workshop designed for use with groups.

In 1974, the Family Service Association appointed a National Task Force on Family Life Education, Development and Enrichment. Their recommendations included "to recognize family life education, development and enrichment as one of the three major services of the family service agency: family counseling, family life education and family advocacy (Garland, 1978, p. iii). This recommendation became basic policy for the Association. Accordingly, a series of workshop manuals were developed for Family Life Education, "to promote the exploration of new alternatives and the utilization of new options in day-to-day living through programs in family education" (Garland, 1978, p. iii).

The workshop for couples communication focuses on teaching skills that will enable young couples to develop changing, open, growing communication systems. The concern of the program is with one aspect of marital interaction: verbal interaction as it occurs in communication and negotiating conflicts.

The theoretical framework of the program comes from the findings of Lewis, et al (1976), whose study of healthy families identified eight characteristics. Garland focuses on three of the eight characteristics, which form the basis for the development of the skills taught in her program: (1) respect for one's own world and the subjective world of others; (2) openness in communication versus distancing, obscuring, and confusing mechanisms; and (3) spontaneity versus rigid, stereotyped interactions.

The program teaches two sets of skills, communication and negotiation. The communication skills include listening (attending, observing, and paraphrasing) and reaching for information. The negotiation skills include pinpointing the question, staying with the question, deferring the question, labeling behavior, determining whether the question is one of fact or opinion, and negotiating questions of opinion.

There are two overall educational goals: (1) to give information on how to communicate more effectively in marriage, and (2) for participants to understand and analyze their own communication patterns and gain skill in communicating and negotiating more effectively. The goals are presented within the theoretical framework cited earlier.

The program is designed for use by two leaders, male and female, for role-modeling purposes, but can be adapted for use by one leader. It is also designed for 10 couples per group, but as long as the number of couples is even, the number of participants can be flexible. In addition, couples participating in the program should be committed to a long-term relationship. The program is designed for four sessions of two to two-and-a-half hours each. The program is also evaluated by means of pre- and post-tests, as well as by ratings during role-plays provided with the manual.

Session 1. The objectives are to teach the knowledge that communication may occur in a number of channels, that a person cannot *not* communicate, and that perceptions of the same experience may be quite different. It is presumed that this knowledge base will help participants begin to develop their own guidelines for effective marital communication.

Role-plays and exercises include demonstrating that a person cannot *not* communicate (an exercise involving sitting with backs to one another to demonstrate the importance of nonverbal communication) and the development of guidelines for communication, with leaders role-playing, including instances of attempts not to communicate, incongruent messages, and different perceptions of the same stimulus.

Participants then discuss and brainstorm guidelines.

Session 2. The objective is to teach listening skills of attending, observing, paraphrasing, and reaching for information. Role-plays and exercises include paraphrasing; observing and attending skills, with leaders simulating arguments, using interpretations, and misconstruing messages; and reaching for information when role-playing of simulated dialogue includes use of open- and close-ended questions.

Session 3. The objective is to teach the negotiation skills of pinpointing the question, staying with the pinpointed issue, deferring the question, labeling behavior, and determining whether the question is one of fact or opinion. Sidetracking issues are mindreading, refusal to discuss, bringing up past issues, and name-calling.

Session 4. The objectives are to explore the difficulties in agreeing on matters of fact and in negotiating matters of opinion in marital discussions, and to help participants generalize and apply this understanding to their own marital disagreements. Two sets of concepts are presented: (1) facts and (2) opinions.

(1) Fact: Each partner must understand the question; there is a need to define how each partner can help solve the problem. Each partner needs to be aware of the potential helpfulness of the other in solving the problem rather than seeing the other as a mind to be changed; each partner needs to be aware of the other's viewpoint.

(2) Opinions. An acceptance of individual differences allows for individual and marital growth; issues that are opinions are not matters of right or wrong, but matters on which persons can agree. These are the questions addressed: Why do we have to agree? On what must we agree? How strongly do we feel about our positions? Who is most affected? Can we make a swap of some kind?

In summary, Garland's program is designed primarily for young couples in a structured setting. It is not designed for distressed couples. The skills and concepts are similar to those presented in other communication programs; however, the material is more cognitively presented than in other programs. There are also some creative exercises presented for experiential learning. The program is also not as highly organized as the others presented.

Systematic Helping Skills Program

Pierce (1973) described the use of Carkhuff's (1969) systematic helping skills program for partners in distressed marriages. Working independently of the Minnesota group, Carkhuff believed that the communication problem had been attacked in three ways up to that point: through traditional insight counseling, through behavioral change, and through programmed, cognitive approaches. Carkhuff's method of training in interpersonal skills sought to integrate the cognitive and behavioral approaches in order to combine the exploration and understanding of self and others with the action goals and systematic methodology of the behaviorists. His program also attempted to integrate experiential and didactic sources of learning.

In this program, two sets of skills are taught: the responsive skills of empathic understanding, positive regard, and concreteness of specificity of expression, which are dimensions responding to another's frame of reference; and initiative or action-oriented skills, including facilitative gentleness, confrontation, and interpretations of immediacy.

The program uses as its text *The Art of Helping* (Carkhuff, 1973). The material is first presented didactically, including a structured behavioral means of communicating the dimensions taught. The trainees practice, in systematic steps, communicating the responsive and initiative dimensions to each other, and they receive concrete and immediate feedback from the trainer and other group members.

Pierce's (1973) study was the first use of the training model with deteriorated marriages. He advanced several hypotheses: training will significantly raise the level of constructive communication between spouses in problem marriages; the level of interpersonal functioning of the trained partners will be higher than the functioning of those partners treated by traditional insight methods; the trained groups will have significantly better communication than those partners left in a time control.

Pierce used four groups: a time control group consisting of eight couples; two treatment control groups of eight couples each, both from an earlier project and a fourth, experimental group of five couples seeking marital counseling who acknowledged poor communication as a major problem in their marriages.

The procedure involved 2-hour sessions once a week for several months for a total of 25 hours. Trainees were taught the responsive dimensions—empathy, regard, and concreteness of expression—as well as the initiative dimensions—genuineness, confrontation, and interpretations of immediacy—but the primary focus was on the development of empathy. In the first stage, "pre-helping" skills of attending, observing, and listening are presented and practiced in role-playing situations; in the second stage, responding to feelings is role-played; in the third stage, responding to feeling and meaning (reason for feeling) is practiced; and in the fourth stage, the helper learns to go beyond what the helpee has expressed to understand what the helpee is really saying about himself or herself. Appropriate behavior is modeled by the trainer, and immediate feedback is given by the trainer and the other members of the group. Both aspects of training shape the behavior of the trainee.

The two treatment control groups also meet for a total of 25 hours, receiving traditional insight therapy. Interviews of 15 minutes were conducted pre- and post-training, in which one spouse was designated helper and the other helpee; roles were then reversed. Rating scales of 1 through 5 (1 = low, 5 = high) were used on the responsive and initiative dimensions. The ratings were done by three trained raters with rate-rerate and interrater reliabilities in the 0.80s and 0.90s in earlier studies.

The results showed that trained couples increased significantly on the critical response and initiative dimensions of communication, which confirmed the first hypothesis. Depth of self-exploration also increased significantly as a result of the increase in interpersonal skills, which confirmed the hypothesis that increased communication skills would lead to increased self-exploration in the marital partner. A comparison of the training group with the treatment and time control groups, using Duncan's

multiple range test, indicated a significant difference from the mean level of communication, confirming the third hypothesis that training is more efficient than insight therapy in increasing interpersonal skills. Schauble and Hill (1976) followed up on Pierce's (1973) work by describing in greater detail their method of teaching spouses specific communication skills that can be used in lieu of, or in conjunction with, more traditional marital counseling. They believe that this approach would be most effective with couples who do not have a long history of communication problems.

Marital Effectiveness[1]

Although Gordon (1976) believes himself "far from having a marital effectiveness training program," his organization, Effectiveness Training Associates, markets three programs, *Effectiveness Training for Women, Youth Effectiveness Training*, and *Marital Effectiveness Training*.

Gordon rejects the medical model and, instead, reiterates the need to present an educational, skill-oriented, low-cost model to be broadly available to a vast range of families, settings, and socioeconomic levels. Effectiveness Training is an example of how a method originally constructed to address the parent–child relationship was transformed to address the marital interaction, similar to Relationship Enhancement (see Chapter 6), whose theoretical roots it shares. Its theoretical background can be found in Rogers' (1959) nondirective psychotherapy in terms of unconditional positive regard, active listening, warmth, and empathy.

Gordon's basic tenets are essentially included in "A Credo," which condenses the basic assumption of this program.

A Credo for My Relationships with Others

You and I are in a relationship which I value and want to keep. Yet each of us is a separate person with unique needs and the right to meet those needs.

When you are having problems meeting your needs I will try to listen with genuine acceptance in order to facilitate your finding your own solutions instead of depending on mine. I also will respect your

[1]We are grateful to Greg Samples for his critical help with this section.

right to choose your own beliefs and develop your own values, different though they may be from mine.

However when your behavior interferes with what I must do to get my own needs met, I will tell you openly and honestly how your behavior affects me, trusting that you respect my needs and feelings enough to try to change the behavior that is unacceptable to me. Also whenever some behavior of mine is unacceptable to you, I hope you will tell me openly and honestly so I can try to change my behavior.

At those times when we find that either of us cannot change to meet the other's needs, let us acknowledge that we have a conflict and commit ourselves to resolve each such conflict without either of us resorting to the use of power or authority to win at the expense of the other's losing. I respect your needs, but I also must respect my own. So let us always strive to search for a solution that will be acceptable to both of us. Your needs will be met, and so will mine—neither will lose, both will win.

In this way, you can continue to develop as a person through satisfying your needs and so can I. Thus, ours can be a healthy relationship in which both of us can strive to become what we are capable of being. And we can continue to relate to each other with mutual respect, love and peace. (Used by permission of Thomas Gordon, 531 Stevens Avenue, Solana Beach, CA 92075.)[2]

Gordon labels his program "no-lose," in contrast to the win–lose aspect of other methods. Both husband and wife have to win, rather than one winning at the expense of the other. Winning is based on clarifying what one individual can and cannot accept in himself or herself and in the behavior of the mate. Acceptance is equated with feeling "good" about oneself, while nonacceptance is equated with feeling "bad" about oneself. False acceptance is a gray area between acceptance and nonacceptance, in which one mate may act outwardly in an accepting manner, but inwardly may be unaccepting. Thus two of the major obstacles to creative marital relationships are inconsistency, and vacillating and contradicting one's words with deeds and incongruity, i.e., feeling one thing and saying another. Gordon acknowledged that as humans we cannot nor do we need to be perfect; no matter what, we will be inconsistent and incongruous. Feelings are transitory. Relationships endure.

---

[2]Copyright 1972, 1978, Effectiveness Training, Inc.

Gordon distinguished between ineffective solutions to conflict and value collisions. Skills for dealing with value collisions are modeling, consulting, changing self, and prayer. Effectiveness training addresses conflicts. Another basic premise of this method is a clear separation between personality and performance. Mates may love each other but need not accept certain behaviors in themselves or in their mates, i.e., "I love you, but that does not mean I accept your behavior, regardless." Unconditional acceptance is directed toward the individual. Conditional nonacceptance is directed toward the specific behavior that is problematic to the pair.

Nonacceptance is demonstrated through verbal and nonverbal means, such as nonintervention or avoidance of confrontation, passive listening, or methods that fail to "draw a line" where a line needs to be drawn. Win–lose methods of negotiation and drawing lines are: (1) ordering, directing, commanding; (2) warning, admonishing, threatening; (3) exhorting, moralizing, preaching; (4) advising, or giving solutions or suggestions; (5) lecturing, teaching, giving logical arguments; (6) judging, criticizing, disagreeing, blaming; (7) praising, agreeing; (8) name-calling, ridiculing, shaming; (9) interpreting, analyzing, diagnosing; (10) reasoning, sympathizing, consoling, supporting; (11) probing, questioning, interrogating; and (12) withdrawing, distracting, humoring, diverting. These are the typical 12 win–lose methods that fail to resolve an issue but guarantee that the same issue, perhaps in some other form, will reappear. Since there is no resolution, the issue is not finished. They are strategies used when partners subscribe to either Method I (authoritarian and power-oriented) or Method II (passiveness and permissiveness).

The most constructive aspects of effectiveness are: active listening, "I" messages, and Method III, the no-lose method of negotiation. One constructive no-lose gambit is to "open the door" and allow the mate to say more. Depending on who owns the problem, such a goal is achieved through the use of "door-openers" that are directed toward the goal of greater self-disclosure on the part of each mate ("Tell me more"). Once the door is opened, it must be kept open for further and more detailed discussion and negotiation. The door is kept open through active listening, the basic principle on which most marital and interpersonal effectiveness is based.

The two major ingredients of active listening are (1) paying attention and (2) letting the mate know that one has heard what the other has said. Thus active listening means checking back and rephrasing what on has heard to communicate to the mate that he or she has been heard and to give the other the chance of affirming or clarifying what he or she meant to say originally. To use active listening, each spouse must want to hear what the other spouse has to say and want to be helpful to the spouse by accepting his or her feelings, whatever the feelings may be. Wanting to help is based on trusting the partner and realizing that most feelings are transitory and change, and that one feeling is different and separate from another feeling. One does not have the same or similar feelings as one's mate. Trust is related to ownership of the problem—whose feelings are whose and who owns the problem? Acceptance is directed toward clarification of ownership of specific feelings related to specific problematic behaviors. No solution is needed or forthcoming. At this point, feelings are clarified first. Common errors in active listening at this juncture are (1) manipulating the mate through "guidance," (2) opening the door and then slamming it shut (typical 12), (3) parroting what the mate has said instead of rephrasing it to clarify it, and (4) listening without empathy and feelings for the mate or failing to feed back the feelings. Another significant issue relevant to problem ownership is helping each individual to be responsible for his or her own problems and responsive to the spouse's ownership of his or her problems. Indirectly, Gordon acknowledged the presence of triangulization, the family ego mass, and the need for successful individuation so that each partner achieves an appropriate balance of closeness and distance.

Confrontation of issues between mates is most often ineffective because of giving quick solutions that bypass feelings or putting the mate down, directly or indirectly, by withdrawing or criticizing. Effective confrontation takes place when "you-messages" give place to "I-messages" that deal with how on feels about the issue at hand. After the couple has slowly fallen into the "you-trap" or entrenched projective identification, the use of I-messages is a difficult one to adopt. Thus the clear switch from ineffective to effective marital communication finds its basic solution in the substitution of I-messages for you-messages. This switch is at the very core of marital effectiveness or ineffectiveness.

Once I-messages are exchanged about how each mate feels about a particular issue, and after these feelings have been received and a basic sharing and exchange has taken place at the feeling level, mates can start looking for possible solutions and changes in their interaction and in their environment. They can find solutions by simplifying, limiting, expanding, or substituting less satisfactory activities for more satisfactory ones for both mates.

Negotiation of conflict needs to be done in terms of the relationship so that solutions are determined in terms of how can WE solve it? The inevitable power struggle that takes place between partners is dealt with after recognizing that neither authoritarianism (Model I) nor permissiveness (Model II) is effective in problem-solving and decision-making. The costs of ineffective negotiation are resentment, anger, and losing relationships. Model III, the effective no-lose method, requires negotiating a solution with which both mates can "feel good." Model III includes recognizing the ineffectiveness of all the methods already outlined and confronting each issue from the viewpoint that both partners must be satisfied with the outcome. The creative no-lose solution does not mean compromise, it means finding a completely new solution that unites rather than separates the couple. Negotiation takes place along the same steps involved in the problem-solving process (see also Chapter 9) as previously discussed by Thomas (1977):

1. Identify and define the conflictual issue.
2. Generate possible alternative solutions.
3. Evaluate alternative solutions in terms of payoffs and costs.
4. Decide on the best solution that is *equally* acceptable to both mates.
5. Work out a plan that will allow implementation of the solution.
6. Implement the solution.
7. Follow-up to evaluate the solution and make whatever adjustments are necessary to make it better.

What if one partner fails or is unwilling to subscribe to this method? This is probably the most crucial question in marital effectiveness. According to Gordon, one partner alone can use this method: if he or she uses it consistently, it may eventually influence the other partner to negotiate according to a no-lose process.

There are numerous claims of success as measured by thousands of testimonials ("It works!") and the popularity of the movement. However, this program has not been critically evaluated against either contrasting theoretical positions or evidence gathered outside the Parent Effectiveness Training movement by investigators who are neutral toward the outcome measures.

Marital effectiveness training stresses premises and procedures that can improve communication, problem-solving, and decision-making between spouses. Its major assumption, like other communication training programs, that marital partners can and should behave as adults in confronting and negotiating issues, indicates that its major focus is a preventive one, i.e., useful with functional and mildly dysfunctional couples. Coupled with other structured treatment methods, it may increase the effectiveness of other forms of marital intervention.

Unilateral Marital Intervention Program

Most marital communication skills training programs are designed for participation of both the husband and the wife. Little attention has been given to the development of skills training methods for couples in which one partner is either unable to unwilling to participate. Recent research on this population has shown, however, that there are three subgroups of couples who may respond to unilateral marital skills programs (Brock, 1978a, 1978b, 1979). One subgroup is composed of high relationship-satisfaction couples whose lifestyles are so hectic that managing the attendance of both spouses at conjoint training sessions is difficult. A second subgroup comprises low-satisfaction couples in which both spouses are interested in changing their relationship but one partner is reluctant to use professional resources in doing so. The third subgroup consists of low-satisfaction couples in which one spouse is not

willing to work with the other in changing the relationship. Professionals often assume that all couples in which one spouse is either unable or unwilling to participate in relationship-change efforts belong in this third subgroup. As a result, the unwarranted assumption may be made that no individuals are interested in training programs designed for the participation of only one spouse. Tentative evidence indicates, however, that up to one-third of the individuals who seek psychological treatment fall into the third subgroup (Goldstein & Francis, 1969). Similarly, one follow-up study of the outcome of marriage counseling showed that one-quarter of the population receiving services was made up of spouses without partners in treatment (Cookerly, 1973). Presumably, then, there may be a large and diverse population of potential users of unilateral intervention programs in which only one spouse is required to interact with professional helping resources.

The only intervention method that has been available for use with one member of a marital relationship is individual counseling in which the focus of intervention is on the intrapersonal functioning of one spouse, not on the relationship comprising both the husband and the wife. Evidence of the effectiveness of individual counseling for marital problems has shown it to be less effective than conjoint intervention methods and more likely to incur relationship deterioration (Cookerly, 1973). As a result, individual counseling is not recommended as a treatment for marital problems (Gurman & Kniskern, 1978). Apparently, effective intervention methods for marital couples must involve both husband and wife, and the focus must be on some aspect of the marital relationship (e.g., communication, problem-solving).

The primary goal of the Unilateral Marital Intervention Program is to improve the communication functioning of both marital partners while maintaining professional contact with only one member of the relationship system. This goal is accomplished by first training one spouse in communication skills and then training that same spouse to change the partner's skills. The program is implemented in two parts over a 10-week period. During the first five weeks of the program, groups of up to 20 participating spouses are trained in empathy and self-disclosure skills, following the procedures outlined by Danish and Hauer (1973). Weeks 1 and 2 are devoted to empathy skills, while weeks 3, 4, and 5 focus on self-disclosure and feedback skills. At the beginning of each session, the rationale for learning a skill is presented and discussed, and then the skill is modeled by the group leader. After the modeling, participants practice the skill both in and out of class. Since one objective of the program is to help participants develop a high skill level before the skills are introduced to their partners, participants are cautioned not to practice the skills with their spouses prior to the second phase of the program.

In the second phase of the program, the participants learn methods of changing their partners' communication behavior. Those participants with partners who are willing to work on the relationship spend two hours each week for five weeks simply putting their partners through the same training that they received in the first five weeks of the program. Each week participants meet with the group leader and practice the training steps for that week. Also, a discussion is held each week so that participants may talk about their successes and frustrations in working with their partners. For participants with unwilling partners, the first two weeks of the second phase consist of instruction in behavior change methods, such as removal of reinforcement, planned positive reinforcement, spontaneous reinforcement, and substitution of alternative behaviors. These behavior change methods have been found successful when used by wives in changing their husbands' behaviors (Goldstein, 1971; Goldstein & Francis, 1969). The primary method of behavior change for this group, however, is modeling (Bandura, 1969). Participants are trained to use and demonstrate their new communication skills with the spouses whenever possible. Weeks 3 through 5 are spent practicing methods of implementing the behavior change strategies and designing specific communication behavior change programs for each relationship.

The effectiveness of the Unilateral Program has been assessed with high relationship-satisfaction couples in which one spouse was unable to attend training sessions (Brock, 1978b). The participants who trained their partners, as compared to those in a relationship discussion group, were successful in increasing their partners' self-disclosure and empathy skills. In a second study (Brock, 1979), 10 low-satisfaction participants were trained to instruct their partners in communication skills. Preliminary analyses indicated that a group of trained spouses were more successful in training their partners in these skills than were a contact control group.

It is apparent that although the field of marital social skills training has focused on conjoint methods, there is ample room for the development of unilateral training strategies. It is probable that unilateral methods can be developed that have an impact on both members of the marital relationship system and that spouses can be trained as relationship change agents. Future research will need to examine the effectiveness of the unilateral intervention approach in teaching other skills (e.g., behavior exchange, problem-solving) to this population.

DISCUSSION

Of the six programs presented, CC (the Minnesota Couples Communication Program) is the oldest, most widely known, and most extensively researched, and Gottman's and Carkhuff's programs are the only ones that have been used with distressed or clinical couples. Each program has in common an underlying humanistic treatment philosophy and communications theory: The problem is caused and maintained by faulty and ineffective communication skills. Therefore the solution to interpersonal problems is to alter ineffective patterns of communication, which will in turn alter the problematic interpersonal relationship.

Because of this common underlying theoretical assumption, each of the six programs varies somewhat in structure, but relatively little in content. Self-awareness, other-awareness, self-responsibility, checking out communication, altering feedback, and negotiation skills are integral components of the alteration of the couple's communication process.

These programs have as advantages their structured formats, which make training leaders a short-term endeavor; group formats, which increase availability to clients; group formats, which can reduce the cost of services to clients; and a prevention focus, which may constitute early and short-term intervention for some couples' problems. Furthermore, each program equally values each individual within the marital relationship and stresses that change is ultimately the responsibility of each individual within the dyad. The marriage is viewed, ideally, as a relationship consisting of equals, a distinct outcome of the underlying humanistic philosophy.

These programs have, however, several disadvantages that raise questions about their efficacy. From a theoretical perspective, it is assumed that increasing empathy, understanding, and effective communication skills will alleviate marital distress and dissatisfaction. Therefore, marital distress is primarily caused by faulty communication skills. Although it is a systems theory, communications theory may ultimately be a unilateral one and too simplistic. It is conceivable that a dissatisfied couple may experience relatively few difficulties in communication, with the source of dissatisfaction stemming from other factors (e.g., intrapersonal issues, external variables in the environment, interpersonal value conflicts, one partner's desiring a different kind of partner based on maturation over time).

From a treatment perspective, research on the effectiveness of communication training programs has generally focused on short-term assessment of skill maintenance and relationship satisfaction. Middle- and upper-middle-class populations in and around college communities have been the primary recipients of this training. Evaluation of these programs has led to several conclusions about communication training in marriage: (1) social skills training programs for marriage can be effectively developed and evaluated through an educational model approach; (2) marital partners are capable of learning a wide variety of social skills that they can successfully employ in relationships with significant others; and (3) demonstrated acquisition of these skills has led to increased relationship satisfaction and adjustment for those couples involved.

Nevertheless, many studies are based on self-report data alone; appropriate control groups are not always used, and measurements lack validity and reliability. Furthermore, there are no long-term follow-up studies of skill maintenance and/or relationship satisfaction or measures of the extent to which participants employ the skills they have learned. In addition, most studies have used middle-and upper-middle-class participants, so that any conclusions apply only to educated, white, middle-to upper-middle-class, motivated clients.

Furthermore, although the formats of these programs appear to be relatively concrete, it is not known what leader qualities or attributes influence the successful teaching of skills. No data are provided on couples who drop out of these programs or on couples who are inappropriate for these programs. As a result, these programs have face validity with little to no evidence of construct or criterion validity.

THE FUTURE

Communication Skills Training programs for couples appear to be potentially effective. Further empirical data are needed, however, in order not only to assess the current state and impact of these programs, but to assess needed future directions. Currently, communication training programs for couples remain primarily a philosophy and a movement because of the lack of empirical data. Thus whether or not communication training remains a movement will be dictated by further integration of theory, practice, and research.

REFERENCES

Azrin NH, Naster BJ, & Jones R. Reciprocity counseling: A rapid learning-based procedure for marital counseling. *Behavioral Research and Therapy*, 1973, *11*, 365–382

Bandura A. *Principles of behavior modification*. New York: Holt, Rinehart & Winston, 1969

Bardill DR. Relationships-focused approach to marital problems. *Social Work*, 1966, *11*, 70–77

Barrett-Lennard GT. Dimensions of therapist response as causal factors in the therapeutic change. *Psychological Monographs*, 1962, *76* (43, Whole No. 562)

Berne E. *Games people play*. New York: Grove Press, 1964

Bateson G, Jackson DD, Haley J, & Weakland J. Toward a theory of schizophrenia. *Behavioral Science*, 1956, *1*, 251–264

Bienvenu MJ. An interpersonal communication inventory. *The Journal of Communication*, 1971, *21*, 381–388

Blood R, & Wolfe DN *Husbands and wives*. Glencoe, IL: Free Press, 1960

Boszormenyi-Nagy I, & Spark G. *Invisible loyalties*. New York: Harper & Row, 1973

Brock GW. *Unilateral marital intervention: Training spouses to train their partners in communication skills*. Unpublished doctoral dissertation. Pennsylvania State University, 1978a

Brock GW. *Training spouses to train their partners in communication skills*. Paper presented at the Annual Meeting of the National Council on Family Relations, Philadelphia, October 1978b

Brock GW. *Training spouses as relationship change agents*. Paper presented at the National Symposium on Building Family Strengths, University of Nebraska, Lincoln, May,1979

Brock GW, & Joanning H. *Structured communication training for married couples: A comparison of the relationship enhancement program and the Minnesota couples communication program*. Paper presented at the Annual Meeting of the National Council on Family Relations, Portland, Oregon, 1980

Brown R. *The effects of couple communication training on traditional sex role stereotypes of husbands and wives*. Unpublished master's thesis, Appalachian State University, 1976

Campbell EE. The effects of couple communication training on married couples in the child-rearing years: A field experiment. *Dissertation Abstracts International*, 1974, *35*, 1942–1943A

Carkhuff RR. *Helping and human relations: Volume I: Selection and training; Volume II, Practice and research*. New York: Holt, Rinehart & Winston, 1969

Carkhuff RR. *The art of helping*. Amherst, MA: Human Resource Development Press, 1973

Cookerly JR. The outcome of the six major forms of marriage counseling compared: A pilot study. *Journal of Marriage and the Family*, 1973, *35*, 608–611

Danish SJ, & Hauer AL. *Helping skills: A basic training program workbook*. New York: Behavioral Publications, 1973

Dillon JD. Marital communication and its relation to self-esteem. *Dissertation Abstracts International*, 1976, *37*, 5862B

Fitts W. *Tennessee self-concept scale manual*. Nashville, Counselor Recordings and Tests, 1970

Foote N, & Cottrell LS Jr. *Identity and interpersonal competence*. Chicago: University of Chicago Press, 1955

Garland DR. *Couples communication and negotiation skills*. New York: Family Service Association of America, 1978

Garland DR. Training married couples in listening skills: Effects on behavior, perceptual accuracy and marital adjustment. *Family Relations*, 1981, *30*, 297–306

Gergen K. *The psychology of behavior exchange*. Reading, MA: Addison-Wesley Publishing Co, 1969

Goldstein MK. Behavior rate change in marriages: Training wives to modify husbands' behavior (Doctoral dissertation, Cornell University, 1971). *Dissertation Abstracts International*, 1971, *32*. 5593

Goldstein MK, & Francis B. *Behavior modification of husbands by wives*. Paper presented at the National Council on Family Relations Annual Meeting, Washington, DC, 1969

Gordon T. *Parent effectiveness training*. New York: Peter H. Wyden, 1970

Gordon T. *PET in action: Inside PET families, new problems, insights, and solutions*. New York: Wyden Books, 1976

Gottman J, Notarius C, Gonso J, & Markman H. *A couple's guide to communication*. Champaign, IL: Research Press, 1976a

Gottman JM, Notarius C, Markman H, Bank G, Yoppi B, & Rubin ME. Behavior exchange theory and marital decision making. *Journal of Personality and Social Psychology*, 1976, *34*, 14–23b

Gough HG, & Heilbrun AB. *The adjective check list manual*. Palo Alto, CA: Consulting Psychologists Press, 1965

Grinker RR, Sr (Ed.). *Toward a unified theory of human behavior*. New York: Basic Books, 1967

Guerney BG, Jr. *Relationship enhancement*. San Francisco: Jossey-Bass, 1977

Gurman AS, & Kniskern DP. Research on marital and family therapy: Progress, perspective, and prospect. In S Garfield & AE Bergin (Eds.), *Handbook of psychotherapy and behavior change*. New York: Wiley, 1978

Haley J. Family therapy. *International Journal of Psychiatry*, 1970, *9*, 223–242

Hansen JC, & L'Abate L. *Approaches to family therapy*. New York: Macmillan, 1982

Hill WF. *Hill interaction matrix: A method of studying interaction in psychotherapy groups*. Los Angeles: Youth Studies Center, University of Southern California, 1968

Joanning H. The long-term effect of the couple communication program. *Journal of Marital and Family Therapy* (in press)

Jourard SM. *The transparent self: Self-disclosure and well-being*. Princeton: D. Van Nostrand Co, 1964

L'Abate L. The goals of family therapy: Toward a negotiated life-style. In L L'Abate, JC Hansen, & G Ganahe (Eds.), *Key Concepts and Methods in Family Therapy*. Englewood Cliffs, N.J., Prentice-Hall (in press)

L'Abate L, & Milan M (Eds.). Handbook of social skills training and research. New York, Wiley & Sons (in press)

Leary T. *Interpersonal diagnosis of personality*. New York: Ronald Press, 1957

Lederer WJ, & Jackson DD. *The mirages of marriage*. New York: W. W. Norton, 1968

Lewis JM, Beavers WR, Gossett JT, & Phillips VA. *No single thread*. New York: Brunner/Mazel, 1976

Locke HJ. Predicting adjustment in marriage. New York: Henry Holt & Co., 1951

Locke HJ, & Wallace KM. Short-term marital adjustment and prediction tests: Their reliability and validity. *Journal of Marriage and Family Living*, 1959, *21*, 251–255

Lu Y. Marital roles and marital adjustment. *Sociology and Social Research*, 1952, *36*, 364–368

Middleman RR, & Goldberg G. *Social service delivery: A structural approach to social work practice*. New York: Behavior Books, Inc, 1972

Miller S. *The effects of communication training in small groups upon self-disclosure and openness in engaged couples' systems of interaction: A field experiment*. Unpublished doctoral dissertation, University of Minnesota, 1971

Miller S, Corrales R, & Wackman DB. Recent progress in understanding and facilitating marital communication. *The Family Coordinator*, 1975, *24*, 143–152

Miller S, Nunnally EW, & Wackman DB. *Alive and aware: Improving communication in relationships*. Minneapolis, MN: Interpersonal Communications Program, 1975

Miller S, Nunnally EW, & Wackman DB. *Minnesota couples communication program: Instructor's manual*. Minneapolis, MN: Interpersonal Communications Program, 1975b

Miller S, Nunnally EW, & Wackman DB. A communication training program for couples. *Social Casework*, 1976, *57*, 9–18

Nunnally EW. *Effects of communication training upon interaction awareness and empathic accuracy of engaged couples: A field experiment*. Unpublished doctoral dissertation, University of Minnesota, 1971

Pierce RM. Training in interpersonal communication skills with partners of deteriorated marriages. *The Family Coordinator*, 1973, *22*, 223–227

Rogers CR. A theory of therapy, personality, and interpersonal relationships as developed in the client-centered framework. In S Koch (Ed.), *Psychology: A study of a science* (Vol. 3): *Formulations of the person and social context*. New York: McGraw-Hill, 1959

Rosella JD. *The effects of a couples communication workshop upon the incidence of somatic complaints of a medically selected group of married couples*. Doctoral dissertation, Walden University, 1981

Russell CS, Bagarozzi DA, Atilano RB, & Morris, JE. *A comparison of two approaches to couple communication training: MCCP and behavioral-exchange*. Paper presented at the annual meeting of the National Council of Family Relations, Portland, Oregon, October, 1980

Satir V. *Conjoint family therapy*. Palo Alto, CA: Science and Behavior Books, 1964

Schauble PG, & Hill CG. A laboratory approach to treatment in marriage counseling: Training in communication skills. *The Family Coordinator*, 1976, *25*, 277–286

Schwager HA, & Conrad RW. *Impact of group counseling on self and other acceptance and persistence with rural disadvantaged student families*. (Counseling Services Report No. 15). Washington, DC: National Institute of Education, 1974

Shostrom EL. *Caring relationship inventory*. San Diego: Educational and Industrial Testing Service, 1966

Sorrells J, & Ford F. Toward an integrated theory of families and family therapy. *Psychotherapy: Theory, Research and Practice*, 1969, *6*, 150–160

Spanier GB. Measuring dyadic adjustment: New scales for assessing quality of marriage and similar dyads. *Journal of Marriage and the Family*, 1976, *38*, 15–28

Stuart RB. Operant interpersonal treatment for marital discord. *Journal of Consulting and Clinical Psychology*, 1969, *33*, 675–682

Thibault M, & Kelley HH. *The social psychology of groups*. New York: Wiley & Sons, 1959

Thielen A, Hubner HO, & Schmook C. *Studies of the effectiveness of the Minnesota couple communication program on relationships between partners*. Unpublished manuscript, Institute of Psychology, University of Heidelberg, 1976

Thomas EJ. *Marital communication and decision making: Analysis, assessment, and change*. New York: Free Press, 1977

Wampler KS. The effectiveness of the Minnesota couple communication program: A review of research. *Journal of Marital and Family Therapy*, 1982, *9*, 345–355

Wampler KS, & Sprenkle DH. The Minnesota couples communication program: A follow-up study. *The Family Coordinator*, 1980, *42*, 577–584

Watzlawick P, Beavin JH, & Jackson DD. *Pragmatics of human communication: A study of interaction patterns, pathologies and paradoxes*. New York: W. W. Norton and Co, 1967

Watzlawick P, Weakland J, & Fisch R. *Change: Principles of problem formation and problem resolution.* New York: W. W. Norton & Co, 1974

Witkin SL. The development and evaluation of a group training program in communication skills for couples. *Dissertation Abstracts International,* 1977, *37*(8-A) 5362

Zimmerman A, & Bailey J. *The Minnesota couple communication program: An evaluation of the training and post-training communication behavior of its participants.* Unpublished manuscript, University of Minnesota, 1977

4

Covenant Contracting

'*Covenant contracting*' describes a specific method of treatment developed by Sager (1976), in which the couple, with the aid of the therapist, works toward the goal of fulfilling a negotiated behavioral contract. Sager's method is somewhat different from contingency contracting, a method employed as a component of Behavioral Marital Therapy (BMT), for it focuses on the emotional as well as the behavioral components of the couple's relationship.

BACKGROUND AND DEVELOPMENT

The use of verbal and written contracts between spouses has been an inherent component of marriage. In the early Middle Ages in Western Europe, written contracts were based on economic and legal agreements concerning property exchange and financial protection for the bride if her husband died or if he deserted or divorced her. By the 16th century, oral promises made before witnesses (the spousals, or contract) were considered a legally binding agreement, and by the 18th century, the church wedding was considered a legally binding contract promising specific roles for each spouse (Stone, 1977).

Within the institution of Western marriage in this century, the concept of contracts is still not only a legal and economic one, but is ac-

knowledged as a psychological one as well. Individuals agree to specific, acknowledged as well as unacknowledged contracts related to both concrete and abstract behaviors in the marital relationships.

In the field of marital therapy, the concept of contracts has been used to make explicit those behaviors that are desired and/or not desired in the marriage, as well as to diagnose interactions that spouses report as unsatisfactory. Behavioral marital therapists have focused on overt written contracts related to specific, concrete behaviors desired by each spouse, while therapists of other theoretical orientations have focused on the unwritten, unspoken, or unconscious contracts that guide spouses' interactions with each other (Berman & Lief, 1975; Dicks, 1967; Lederer & Jackson, 1968). Thus, from an interactional viewpoint, the concept of spouse contracts or agreements (both conscious and unconscious) is a crucial component of diagnosis and change.

Behaviorists were quick to address the concept of contracts as well as to make the negotiation of contracts an overt process and a component of therapeutic change (Patterson, et al, 1973; Stuart, 1969).

The use of contracts in marital therapy from a nonbehavioral orientation is more recent, however, and was not systematically addressed until the early work of Sager and his colleagues (1971) and Sager's (1976, 1981a, 1981b) further elaboration of this work into a specific treatment strategy.

PHILOSOPHY AND MAJOR CONCEPTS

Sager's basic assumption is that couples develop operational, interactional contracts for their marriages. The interactional contract consists of the conscious and unconscious ways in which two people work together or against each other to try to fulfill the terms of their respective individual contracts while preserving the marital system.

According to Sager, individual contracts are on tri-leveled and comprise three categories. These levels are conscious and verbalized, conscious but unspoken, and beyond awareness. Categories of expectations are based on (1) expectations of a relationship, (2) needs arising from the individual's psychological and biological make-up, and (3) external foci of problems that are usually rooted in the first two categories. The interactional contract is operational in the marriage, ideally derived from negotiating the requirements of each individual's contract. It is a dynamic contract in that it changes at many points in the marriage. Sager maintains that congruence at the conscious and verbalized level usually leads couples to go ahead and marry; disparity on the second level (conscious but unspoken) leads to marital discord early in the marriage; and disparity at the unconscious level leads to trouble later in the marriage's development. Sager further believes that the spouse is often an even better authority on the partner's unconscious expectations than is the partner himself (or herself). Therefore each partner brings to a marriage, as a result of social, familial, individual values as well as social and biological needs, an implicit (often unconscious) contract that is modified in interaction with the implicit contract of the spouse.

This basic philosphical premise is one of reciprocity; however, different from the behavioral theory of reciprocity, more levels of exchange are included than just concrete, overt behavior. Sager's concept of contracts is also similar to Lederer & Jackson' *quid pro quo* metaphor (1968), but includes needs, motives, attributions, and feelings. Each partner's contract is thus a set of conscious (and unconscious) agreements, negotiated overtly and covertly, by which each partner hopes to get his or her needs met by fulfilling the needs of the other.

Contradictions between each individual's expectations and between the individual contracts and the operational reality of marital interactions lead to the midunderstanding and chronic frustration of both partners. These contradictions and the resulting inability to get one's needs met in the relationship create dysfunction and also exist between different levels of each individual's contract. These contradictions are evidenced in a large variety of no-win interactions, with behavior predicated on ambivalence.

DIAGNOSIS

In Sager's treatment approach, diagnosis is considered a dialectic process with treatment. Both treatment and diagnosis are considered dynamic and changing as the therapy progresses; therefore both must be continually adapted to the couple as the couple's dynamic relationship evidences additional dimensions and change.

Initial diagnosis and assessment consist of elucidating each spouse's separate contracts in order to pinpoint sources of malfunction within the marital system and to begin working out a schematic model of the couple's probable interactional contract. Diagnosis becomes the beginning of treatment as couples learn the concept of contracts, supply data about their contracts, and initially write their contracts with each other. Sager (1976) noted, however, that requesting couples to write their contracts

is contraindicated if (1) the partners see their problem as confined to one specific area and will not consider further exploration; (2) one mate has a secret of major proportions, whose maintenance would negate the entire process; or (3) one mate is so paranoid and/or destructive that the technique would be counterproductive (p. 49).

The contract reveals the dynamics at work both within individuals and within the interactional system. Behavioral profiles and the consequent partner combinations are considered useful in the diagnosis of the marital system because they provide a topographical map of the system. Marital profiles developed from initial diagnosis are equal, romantic, parental, childlike, rational, companionate, and parallel, and each essentially describes the predominant way in which individuals tend to connect intimately with others. Combinations of profiles are examined with the assumption that in most good relationships, there tends to be complementarity and compatibility of style and purpose without ambivalence and with a relative lack of hostility.

Couple covenants can be based on individual convenants that are congruent, complementary, or conflictual. Ideally, one should be able to convert conflict into congruence or complementarity. It is not necessary that individual contracts be identical. What is required is that the partners be aware of their differences. Sager places a great deal of importance on the couple's being conscious of their expectations and differences, because their awareness puts them in the position of being able to negotiate their differences rather than unconsciously sabotaging each other. His diagnosis, then, as well as his therapy, is predicated at least in part on making conscious the unconscious desires and motives in the marriage.

In approaching diagnosis and therapy, the therapist looks beyond the level of external foci of complaints to the other two levels of relational expectations and individual needs. Initial assessment/therapy involves explication of the interactional contract, communication, goal-setting, and tasks that are used to reflect the goals of therapy.

Sex is often viewed as a diagnostic microcosm of the relationship. Sager notes, however, that the couple's sexual relationship does not always parallel other marital dynamics. When sex is dissociated from other dynamics, it is viewed as diagnostic of a marriage that is, on the whole, unhealthy. The more sex is integrated into the marital context, the better the prognosis and the less difficult the therapy. Sager identified three types of sexual adaptations in troubled marriages: (1) a sexual dysfunction leading to marital discord; (2) marital discord in some areas, impairing sexual satisfaction, and (3) severe marital discord impairing sexual satisfaction. In diagnosing/treating the sexual relationship, the important interaction terms of the sexual contract are attraction, initiation, roles, frequency, relative importance of sex in living, pleasure issues, who or what is included in the sexual relationship, and the point in the marital cycle at which the couple find themselves.

Ultimately, diagnosis is viewed as an integral part of treatment. The therapist makes explicit the implicit individual and relationship contracts, not only to diagnose the state of the marital relationship but to begin to identify those areas of the relationship that need to be altered or renegotiated. Both the therapist and the couple initially identify one of the three types of couple contracts as a means of diagnosis, treatment focus, and goal setting:

1. Congruent interactional contracts on a quid pro quo basis, emphasizing the idea that "trading off" is a basic, "more mature" interpersonal skill.
2. Complementary interactional contracts, which are more common than congruent ones and are based on both the neurotic and realistic needs of the partners fitting together well: one uses the traits of the other to fulfill oneself rather than negotiating something for something. This is a workable approach to marriage, but is considered less mature than a quid pro quo agreement.
3. Conflictual interactional contracts in which conflict emerges from a basic and primitive level of intrapsychic functioning and precludes the couple's resolution or acceptance of it. In this type of contract, the biological and psychological levels of each individual's needs are considered the prime determinants of the primacy and/or irreversibility of the conflict between the two spouses.

THE TREATMENT PROCESS

The treatment process consists primarily of the explication of the interactional contract. Therapy is a further extension of the diagnostic assessment, which includes communication, goal-setting, and tasks that are used to reflect the goals of therapy. Tasks are used to work through or bypass relationship issues as well as to change the couple's relationship system.

The therapeutic process evolves from the basic premise that dissatisfaction occurs in a marital relationship when implicit contracts are violated without the individuals' awareness of what is being violated, with a resulting generation of intense, often negative, feelings. Diagnosis provides a topographical map of the relationship from an organic, system-transactional, psychodynamic, learning theory perspective and, as a result, dictates the focus of the treatment. Therefore, treatment is the process of contracting (renegotiating) between the two spouses who are in treatment and between the spouses and the therapist, as well.

Each partner writes what he or she wants and expects. In this process, the therapist not only sees the levels of awareness of the couple (realistic and unrealistic expectations, feasible and unfeasible demands), but negotiates with the couple the goals of the therapy. The more explicit the contract, the clearer are the expectations and roles of everyone involved in the therapeutic process. The focus on contracting also clearly addresses four separate sets of issues pertaining to the marriage: (1) issues pertaining to the self, (2) issues pertaining to the spouse, (3) issues pertaining to the marriage, and (4) issues pertaining to the children.

Treatment involves fulfilling a negotiated contract with an emphasis on the flexibility of the concept and the incorporation of it into the therapist's own theoretical framework and personal style.

In therapeutic application, the contract organizes materials, pinpoints the areas of marital discord, and helps the partners examine the relationship. Flexibility involves changing the contract over the course of therapy based on individual sessions, dream analysis, the spouses' assessment of the marriage, and spouses' and therapists' observations and hypotheses formulated throughout therapy.

Treatment is thus a process by which the therapist helps the couple discover and put into writing their individual contracts, examine their interactional contracts, and then, together, write a single contract that encompasses the others, which begins to resolve (or at least recognize) conflicts. The negotiated, working contract is then addressed in therapy from a number of perspectives. These perspectives include couple therapy as a continuing exploration of the implicit contracts each partner brings to marriage (their expectations of marriage and of the spouse); exploration of marital dynamics, stabilizing the system by assertive as well as defensive maneuvers, exploration of double binds, of the double parental

transference (each spouse views the other as his or her parent), of similar anxieties and varied defenses against them, and of uneven development of various parts of the marital system.

Ultimately, a single contract of agreement is negotiated by the two spouses, and therapy is completed. Each spouse, after exploration of the self and the relationship, is able to interact within a quid pro quo congruent relationship. Thus the couple has negotiated a viable interactional contract.

Sager's approach stresses the intrapsychic determinants of behavior. Therefore the contracting process is not a static, concrete approach to behavioral profile types, but an interplay between the process of the marriage (the interactional contract) and the individual; between diagnosis/history-taking and observation of and intervention in the current, ongoing process; and between interpretation and insight as therapy and behavior change as therapy. Transference and countertransference issues are also acknowledged and addressed. As a result the final contract between the partners is not negotiated by homogenizing the two individual sets of expectations, but by uncovering and exploring the incongruities and contradictions in the original contracts. The couple is guided through a process of negotiating agreements concerning ways in which both partners can attain the major goals they have for the marriage. Since many goals and expectations can be contradictory, trade-offs become a basic part of the negotiation process. The contracting process thus highlights and utilizes the reciprocal nature of individual and marital contracts in improving committed relationships.

THE ROLE OF THE THERAPIST

In covenant contracting, the therapist must provide guidance based primarily on an eclectic theoretical approach for treating the marital relationship. The therapist must be cognizant of psychodynamic theories of interactional behaviors, and must also be cognizant of cultural ramifactions of the institution of marriage on individuals' expectations of marriage. Therefore the use of covenant contracting in therapy requires a therapist who is highly trained and able to use a complex repertoire of behaviors. He or she must be able to observe and analyze the marital relationship, including a number of simultaneous concerns and unconscious processes, and must also have the skills to address therapeutically a number of simultaneous levels of behavior (in each partner's self as well as in the couple's relationship), including conscious and unconscious dynamics.

THE INITIAL CONTRACT IN TREATMENT

The written explication of the individuals contracts include self, marriage, mate, and children (when applicable). The following is an example of an initial contract written by a couple who had been separated and were thinking of living together again.

Wife

1. Self
   a. I want to feel more adequate, secure, and self-confident.
   b. I want to feel more joyful about life.
   c. I want to regain my strengths and realize my hopes.
   d. I want to WRITE.
   e. I want to practice psychotherapy.
   f. I want to exercise my creativity.
   g. I want to be involved in positive, working relationships with others and have the special one-to-one relationship on a permanent basis as reality allows.
2. Marriage
   a. I want a vital marital relationship. I want to care about someone's needs and know that he cares enough about mine to be generous, flexible, and specific in meeting them. When feelings are strong, most obstacles can be overcome with feelings of relative ease, and frustrations are minimal. I have been willing to undergo many hardships—my strength has been and is constantly being sapped. I cannot give and do as I have in the past, now.
   b. I want to enjoy a variety of experiences—play tennis, go skiing, go to the mountains, go swimming, have picnics, go to concerts and plays and dancing, auctions, etc.

     c. I want a maid once or twice a week. I am not a talented housecleaner.
   d. I want a warm, fun, full sex life.
   e. I want a trustworthy *commitment* and sharing of responsibilities.
3. Mate
   a. I want someone who is proud of himself and glad to share his person and possessions.
   b. I want someone who cares about his family as individual personalities and people with strengths and weaknesses.
   c. I want someone who likes me and cares and believes in me.
4. Children
   a. I want children to enjoy learning, life, challenge, and responsibility.
   b. I want children to know life involves ups and downs.
   c. I want children to value commitment.
   d. I want standard bedtimes in general.
   e. I want care of self-bathing and dressing.
   f. I want children to manage money.
   g. I want children to have "good" feelings about self in all respects.

Husband

1. Self
   a. I want to support the family to the best of my ability.
   b. I want to be with my family whenever possible but not to put family ahead of everything else.
   c. I expect time for myself to relax and to do some things that I would like to do.
   d. I want to see that the yard is kept intact.
   e. I want to be a father to my children in a way that I see fit—not as others would like me to be.
   f. I want to be the strength in times of need.
   g. I want to pay all the bills.
   h. I want to share with my wife certain activities (such as spectator sports, bowling, bridge, social functions, etc.)
   i. I want to give of myself sexually.
   j. I want to express devotion and affection.

2. Mate
   a. I want her to take the responsibility of keeping the house clean and neat.
   b. I want her to see to it that repairs are taken care of.
   c. I want her to take care of shopping for the house, the children, and herself during the week while I'm not at home so that the weekends will be left open for family activities.
   d. I want her to take care of phone calls during daytime hours so that we could have the evenings to ourselves.
   e. I want her to drop all social work activities.
   f. I want her to be sure to be home at dinner time before I am and to take care of seeing to it that the table is set, etc.
   g. I need to feel welcome and for it to be understood that when I come home I am tired and need just a little bit to get my second wind.
   h. I want her to look nice when I do come home and not like something the cat dropped in.
   i. I want her to be natural about her person and get rid of all that garbage coloring of her hair.
   j. I want her to allow the leisure of talking to the kids until their bedtime before starting to tell me all her problems.
   k. I want her to express herself sexually.
   l. I want her to be strong enough to deal with things and to take a positive outlook on life without leaning on me for every little thing.
   m. I want her to be available for trips at any time—especially for weekends without the children.
   n. I want her to arrange for babysitters so that we can get away in the evenings or for weekends.
   o. I want her to have some fun out of life.
   p. I want her to help promote my business where possible.
3. Marriage
   a. I want for each to take their own responsibilities.
   b. I want to share time together.

   c. I want to make the other feel wanted and noticed.
   d. I want to put each ahead of others.
   e. I want to express love and affection and to enjoy sexual togetherness. Compatibility is important in sex.
4. Children: Children are like ships that pass in the night. When they are grown and start their own lives, then you only have each other—so:
   a. Children have to be taught that the world doesn't center around them.
   b. Family activities should include children, but children should not dictate family activities.
   c. Children should be exposed to the world and should also learn from experience.
   d. They should assume family responsibilities as they reach certain ages.
   e. Parents' spats should not be held in front of the children.
   f. Children should help make decisions concerning family problems.

Thus one can see different levels of needs, wants, and expectations that the couple must successfully negotiate in an interactional context.

EMPIRICAL ASSESSMENT AND EVALUATION

There is currently no empirical assessment of this treatment approach other than Sager's use of follow-up sessions with couples after termination.

DISCUSSION

Contract negotiation as a therapeutic treatment focus is described by Sager as a process based on confrontation of issues, negotiation, give and take, and an integration into a compromise representing the best of alternatives for the couple. Contracting provides both the diagnostic and treatment foci and, ideally, is a focus that is flexible enough to be altered when needed.

There are at least four apparent advantages in the contracting process as advocated by Sager. First, written contracts provide a method for the delineation and confrontation of issues. They also force the couple in treatment to address their issues actively outside the therapist's office. Second, written contracts provide a means of clarification of issues, whether they are feelings, goals, expectations, or concrete behaviors. Third, written contracts provide a means by which the couple can change past or self-defeating ways of transacting and strctures the couple to communicate more clearly with each other. Finally, written contracts provide a tool for the teaching and learning of give-and-take negotiations.

There are also many differences between covenant contracting and behavioral contingency contracting methods. Sager's contracts operate on many levels of the marital relationship. Covenant contracting not only addresses overt behavior and the elimination of conflict in the relationship, but also teaches the couple negotiation skills. In addition, the couple, instead of the therapist, determines the contract and then actively negotiates its implementation. Sager's emphasis on agreements, conflict, and complementarity between the two partners' contracts goes beyond the contingency contracting model of addressing overt behavior problems by also addressing issues of value differences as well as the spouses' attitudinal and personal differences that underlie the behavior problems. Covenant contracting focuses on satisfactions and positives, as well as on difficulties and problems, in the relationship. Covenent contracting provides a model that is less oriented toward teaching the couple reinforcement techniques to apply to each other and more concerned with separating the spouses' contributions to the relationship so that they can modify the relationship for themselves. Although quid pro quo exchanges of behavior are valued, one-for-one behavior exchanges are not necessarily the primary determinants of a healthy marital relationship. Sager's covenant contracting is, however, similar to behavioral contingency contracting in the sense that Sager addresses the marital quid pro quo, or equal reciprocity of need systems and behavioral exchanges, at the relationship level. He emphasizes that marital partners must consider what they are willing to exchange with each other in order to receive what they want from the marriage.

O'Leary and Turkewitz (1978), therapists of a cognitive behavioral approach, stated,

The present authors would argue that much of what occurs in good marital therapy of *any* variety involves discussions of the assumptions that each spouse has: (1) about what was expected of the marriage, and (2) about what the marriage is providing relevant to those expectations. In this sense, the writings of Sager (1978) regarding the development of informal contracts appear to have critical yet unrecognized import for behavioral marital therapists (1978 stat). (p. 247)

Nadelson and Paolino (1978), psychoanalytic marital therapists, describe their extensive questionnaire developed to evaluate couples' process: "The model used in the procedure is not very different in its conceptualization from the marriage contract (Sager, 1976)" (p. 130). Sager's marriage contracts have much in common with the systems theorists' formulations of interactional processes (Gurman, 1978; Haley, 1963).

Theoretical formulations of marriage and marital therapy similar to Sager's are found in Martin (1976) and Strong (1975). These other approaches also emphasize the underlying value differences between the spouses, which become symptoms or problems at the relationship level. Their approach is to seek mutual adjustment and better alternative solutions rather than simply to eliminate conflict. Bancroft (1975) has emphasized the importance of changing attitudes because they can obstruct behavior change. In addition, Ziegler and Mazen (1975) have developed a structural model of relationship counseling to address the often unspoken expectations of marriage and to provide a model for negotiation of issues. Thus, not only is there a recent interest in contracting as hypothesized and implemented by Sager, but other theoreticians are beginning to address the importance of the couple's expectations in the underlying dynamics of the overt marital relationship.

Although Sager addresses issues and techniques recognized by other marital therapists, his approach adds to existing methods by more intensively addressing the unconscious psychodynamics of the individual and the relationship. He transforms the concept of contracts from outlining concrete behaviors to including the interactional or transactional rules of the couple, as well as including the effects of biological, social, and unconscious motivations. His approach also has the advantage of emphasizing to the couple the importance of their expectations—of marriage as an institution, of themselves, and of their partners.

Seaburg (1976), in an earlier work, reviewed most of the literature on the use of contracts in social work practice. His criticisms, even though applied to the use of contracts *in general* may be useful in considering the use of covenant contracts, for some of his comments are relevant to contracts between spouses, regardless of the negotiation approach used. First, Seaburg stressed that contracts cannot only be incomplete but can also focus only on selected aspects of a relationship, which may in some cases be irrelevant to the continuance of that relationship. Second, he noted that contracts need to be used judiciously (at the right time and in the right place) and that not all marital therapists may be able to integrate the use of contracts appropriately. Third, contracts cannot be used with every couple. There are many couples who are too distressed or disturbed even to be able to focus initially on an insight-oriented approach to treatment. Further, there are some couples who may not be motivated to make the effort necessary to successfully complete the contracting process.

Wells (1976) was even more critical than Seaburg of marriage contracts. These criticisms focused on several aspects of contracting: (1) their questionable legality, (2) their inability to anticipate problems in the marriage, (3) the lack of evidence of attitude changes in long-term follow-up, (4) the lack of flexibility in directing change, and (5) a pessimistic outlook reflected in the contracts. To add to these concerns about contracting, Ziegler and Mazen (1975) developed a treatment program that expanded negotiation to include non-negotiable issues in the marriage. They pointed out that some issues in marital relationships are issues of acceptance rather than negotiation. Other problems with contracting include (1) that contracting may limit a couple's creativity in finding their own solutions to their problems because the area of change and the mechanisms of change are outlined by the therapist; (2) contracting may foster a mechanistic exchange model of human beahvior that does not encourage or value other forms of interpersonal dynamics (i.e., a quid pro quo model of behavior is valued to the exclusion of any other "appropriate" dynamics); (3) covenant contracting is a method requiring skills that all marital therapists may not possess; and (4) there is no empirical evidence available of its claimed efficacy in treating couple relationships.

THE FUTURE

Covenant contracting may provide a valuable and important addition to marital therapy, for it extensively addresses underlying as well as overt issues in the marital relationship. The use of covenant contracting is, however, limited to clients who are motivated for, available to, and capable of insight therapy. Therefore, future development needs to delineate those couples who are appropriate for contracting techniques. In addition, empirical evidence is needed to demonstrate efficacy for those couples who are considered appropriate treatment candidates.

REFERENCES

Bancroft J. The behavioral approach to marital problems. *British Journal of Medical Psychology*, 975, *48*, 147–152

Berman EM, & Lief HI. Marital therapy from a psychiatric perspective: An overview. *American Journal of Psychiatry*, 1975, *132*, 583–592

Dicks HV. *Marital tensions*. New York: Basic Books, 1967

Gurman AS. Contemporary marital therapies: A critique and comparative analysis of psychoanalytic, behavioral, and systems theory approach. In TJ Paolino, Jr & BS McCrady (Eds.), *Marriage and marital therapy*. New York: Brunner/Mazel, 1978

Haley J. *Strategies of psychotherapy*. New York: Grune & Sratton, 1963

Lederer W, & Jackson D. *The mirages of marriage.* New York: W. W. Norton & Co., Inc., 1968

Martin P. *Marital therapy manual.* New York: Brunner/Mazel, 1976

Nadelson CC, & Paolino TJ Jr. Marital therapy from a psychoanalytic perspective. In T. J. Paolino, Jr. & B. S. McCrady (Eds.), *Marriage and marital therapy.* New York: Brunner/Mazel, 1978

O'Leary KD, & Turkewitz H. Marital therapy from a behavioral perspective. In TJ Paolino, Jr & BS McCrady (Eds.), *Marriage and marital therapy.* New York: Brunner/Mazel, 1978

Patterson GR, Hops H, & Weiss RL. A social learning approach to reducing rates of marital conflict. In R Stuart, R Liberman, & S Wilder (Eds), *Advances in behavior therapy.* New York: Academic Press, 1973

Sager CJ. *Marriage contracts and couple therapy.* New York: Brunner/Mazel, 1976

Sager CJ. Couples therapy and marriage contracts. In AS Gurman & DP Kniskern (Eds.), *Handbook of family therapy.* New York: Brunner/Mazel, 1981a

Sager CJ. Marital contracts. In GP Sholevar (Ed.), *The handbook of marriage and marital therapy.* New York: SP Medical & Scientific Books, 1981b

Sager CJ, Kaplan H, Gundlach R, Kremer M, Lenz R, & Royce J. The marriage contract. *Family Process*, 1971, *10*, 311–326

Seaburg BA. The contract: Uses, abuses, and limitations. *Social Work*, 1976, *34*, 16–21

Stone L. *The family, sex, and marriage in England, 1550–1800.* New York: Harper & Row, 1977

Strong J. A marital conflict resolution model: Redefining conflict to achieve intimacy. *Journal of Marriage and Family Counseling*, 1975, *1*, 269–276

Stuart RB. Operant-interpersonal treatment for marital discord. *Journal of Consulting and Clinical Psychology*, 1969, *33*, 675–682

Wells J. A critical look at personal marriage contracts. *The Family Coordinator*, 1976, *25*, 33–37

Ziegler D, & Mazen D. Contractual marriage counseling: A new look at intimate relationships. *Journal of Family Counseling*, 1975, *3*, 29–35

5

Encounter

Marriage Encounter is a two-day marriage enrichment program sponsored by several religious organizations. Of all the marriage enrichment programs that have been developed during the past decade, Marriage Encounter is perhaps the only one that has become a movement. As of 1976, approximately half a million couples had participated in the program (Koch & Koch, 1976), and by 1977 weekends had been sponsored in every state in this country (DeYoung, 1979).

The objectives of Marriage Encounter are twofold: first, to allow married couples to experience genuine communication with their spouses, and second, for those believing in transcendence, to experience the presence of God in moments of shared intimacy (Regula, 1975). According to the National Marriage Encounter Board, the program is:

not a sensitivity session, Cursillo, couples retreat, counseling session, T-group, group therapy, or prayer meeting. The Marriage Encounter is not oriented towards problem solving. . . . It is an opportunity to discover again the meaning of married love *(Chicago Supplement to the National Marriage Encounter Manual, 1976, p. 5).*

BACKGROUND AND DEVELOPMENT

Marriage Encounter is a weekend marriage enrichment program open to all married couples, particularly through a set of church-

related organizations. Although its specific beginnings as a program originated within the Catholic Church in Spain, Marriage Encounter can be traced to earlier ideas in the United States. Shortly after World War II, a young couple, Pat and Patty Crowley, thought that something could and should be done to foster the enrichment of family life in America. Thus they began a small discussion group based on the principles of observation, judgment, and action as espoused by the Belgian priest, Canon Cardijn, with social action in the community as the ultimate goal of the group. The Crowleys' initial idea spread within their church, and by 1950 the Christian Family Movement (CFM) had become an international movement connected with the Catholic Church.

In 1962, Fr. Gabriel Calvo in Spain started the first Encounter program, Encuentro Conyugal, with his goal being to "help couples serve God and their fellow men through their marriages" (Calvo, 1975, p. 2). He believed that the couple needed to understand the marriage relationship in its deepest sense and to use this understanding as a foundation for achieving the qualities that St. John Chrysostrom had described when he called Christian families "miniature churches" (Bosco, 1973). The Spanish word *encuentro* means "surprise discovery," and to Calvo this concept seemed to describe what was taking place in the encounter program.

Calvo worked to recruit couples and to build his program; as a result, during the 1960s the marriage Encounter movement grew rapidly into an international movement within the Catholic Church. The program was presented at the International Confederation of Christian Family Movements in Venezuela in 1966, and in 1967 the first English-language weekend program was conducted in the United States (Buettner, 1976). Encounters were held in Montreal, Detroit, Chicago, and New Jersey, and by 1969 the movement was large enough to create its own national board of directors. After creating its own board, Marriage Encounter became separate from the Christian Family Movement, although it maintained close ties (Genovese, 1975a, 1975b).

In 1970 a schism developed within the movement, splitting Marriage Encounter proponents into two antagonistic groups. The principal issues in the dispute were the admission or nonadmission of non-Catholics into leadership positions and the adherence or nonadherence to a specific, written, dialogue technique (Doherty, et al, 1978). Other issues included a dispute concerning which group represented the "true" experience and a dispute concerning whether or not to continue a fundamentalist approach.

As a result of this schism, Marriage Encounter is currently represented nationally by two separate groups. National Marriage Encounter is a loose-knit ecumenical organization with local affiliated groups who advocate adherence to Calvo's original manual. Worldwide Marriage Encounter is a more structured organization and maintains a stronger Catholic identity, although it does have Protestant and Jewish affiliates. Both the National and Worldwide Marriage Encounter groups actively recruit couples of any or no religious faith.

THE PHILOSOPHY OF MARRIAGE ENCOUNTER

There is a general consensus concerning the fundamental goal of Marriage Encounter across the various divisions within the movement. The goal of Marriage Encounter is to promote unity in marriage. This unity is considered God's plan for married couples. The concept of unity, however, is not clearly defined. Gallagher, the leader of Worldwide Marriage Encounter, states that the aim of marriage is "full integration, true oneness, complete involvement." He adds, "We are not seeking partnership but coupleness" (Gallagher, 1975, p. 143). Kligfield, a leader of Jewish Marriage Encounter, claims that "the goal of marriage in this light is not happiness. The goal is unity. Unity is not just togetherness; it consists of totally and absolutely feeling the beloved" (Kligfield, 1976, p. 140).

The basic rationale underlying the Encounter experience is that a community set in a framework of honesty, openness, and responsibility is enlivening and healing. Thus a purpose of Marriage Encounter is to live more fully and experience more deeply (Burton, 1970). The rationale and purpose have been borrowed from the encounter group movement, as has the main idea of what consititutes a healing experience. Different from Encounter groups, however, the encounter in Marriage Encounter is primarily dyadic, focusing on the couple rather than the group. The entire weekend experience focuses on the relationship between the husband and the wife; interaction with other couples is minimal.

Attending to one's feelings and becoming more aware of what one feels are stressed as crucial components of growth. It is emphasized that couples may have been so busy that they have not given much thought to themselves or that they may believe that it is wrong to concentrate on or to think too much about the self. Therefore couples have to be encouraged to stop, turn inward, and take a hard look at themselves, their strengths, and their weaknesses in order to appreciate themselves more. This integration of attention and awareness, a primary goal of Gestalt therapy (Enright, 1970), is borrowed by the Marriage Encounter Movement and becomes the first step in creating what is supposedly the most fulfilling love relationship possible between the spouses.

Jourard's (1959) theory of self-disclosure underlies much of what is addressed during the encounter. Letting another person know what one thinks, feels, or wants is considered the most direct means (though not the only means) by which an individual can make himself or herself known to another person. Thus the ability and willingness to self-disclose is considered a necessary part of personality health as well as a prerequisite for satisfying interpersonal relationships. Jourard's theory stresses that, in marriage, couples oftentimes know the spouse as a "role" but never as a "person." A husband's or a wife's subjective side (i.e., what he or she thinks, feels, believes, wants, fears, worries about) remains largely unknown. The subjective side is not revealed because it is a threatening experience to expose those deeper portions of the self to possible rejection by a "significant other" (Jourard, 1959). In Marriage Encounter, couples are encouraged and supported in revealing themselves to each other, first through their written reflections and then through their dyadic dialogue. Consistent with Rogerian philosophy, an atmosphere of genuineness, caring, and nonjudgmental understanding is considered a prerequisite for the depth of sharing of one's self that is expected to take place in the encounter.

The rationale for the use of written reflections in Marriage Encounter is that the act of writing one's thoughts and feelings oftentimes helps to clarify and organize information for the writer. Writing is also a way to avoid distractions that often occur when communication is only oral, as well as a way to make it impossible to forget, ignore, repress, confuse, or sidetrack feelings (L'Abate, 1977).

Caldwell (1977) has suggested that Marriage Encounter, although expressly not therapy, encompasses several of Yalom's (1970) curative factors: the imparting of information, the instilling of hope, universality, imitative behavior, and interpersonal learning. Marriage Encounter per se does not, however, provide as clear a theory or theories for its program as do others who have commented on its organization. For example, Calvo (1975) has stated:

·The Golden Rule is that all that promotes real marital and family unity (people, circumstances, things) is in accordance with the plan of God and anything that endangers or corrupts marital and family unity (people, circumstances, things) is not in accordance with the plan of God. This rule is for the solution of all problems and marriage cases in the light of the Word of God (p. 22).

The philosophy underlying the program's dialogue technique for couples is not one of understanding or problem-solving but is instead one of experiencing "oneness" and an emotional high:

The thrust and focus are to feel that person, to get inside his or her skin, and to be a part of who he or she is. The result is a new closeness and an overwhelming exultation that both experience (Gallagher, 1975, pp. 95–96).

. . . to revel in one another's personhood the way they did in their days of early marriage (Gallagher, 1975, p. 42)

One may summarize the overall goal of Marriage Encounter as one of encouraging a rebirth to closeness, transformation, and a life-changing experience that will foster a couple's unity (Kligfield, 1976). In the words of the *National Marriage Encounter Manual*, "Aloneness or loneliness, i.e., independence or individualism, is harmful" (Calvo, 1975, p. 20). As a result of clearly stated doctrines, it is probably more accurate to describe the philosophy of Marriage Encounter as a religious ideology rather than a theoretical or philosophical orientation.

THE TREATMENT PROCESS

The basic rationale for Marriage Encounter is simple: open dialogue promotes unity. As a result, the Marriage Encounter Weekend is a structured format, encouraging open dialogue between spouses. Couples are told that they are free to accept or ignore the religious aspects of the weekend; therefore any married couple, regardless of religious orientation, is eligible to participate in Marriage Encounter. Severely distressed couples are urged not to use Marriage Encounter as a substitute for marital therapy (Genovese, 1975a, 1975b). There are, however, no procedures by which to screen severely disturbed couples from participation.

Role of the Leader

Present at the Marriage Encounter are one or more Team Couples who have participated previously in a Marriage Encounter Weekend and who have volunteered to share their experiences with the group. They are there primarily to tell their "before" and "after" stories and to provide role models with whom the participating couples can identify

(Regula, 1975). They reveal themselves as "ordinary folks" who have problems and concerns but who have found a "better way" of dealing with those concerns. They supposedly serve as models of behavior as they share their experiences, express feelings, and take risks in relating to their spouses. In many ways, the Team Couples serve as co-leaders or co-facilitators of the group. Also present is a priest or minister of the church sponsoring the weekend. He or she has been trained to participate in and lead the session. It is the task of the priest or minister, along with the Team Couples, to present a program of structured exercises to the couple participants.

Calvo's (1975) *Marriage Encounter Manual* lists the desired characteristics of a Team Couple:

1. They are living their Encounter and are growing in their own conjugal dialogue.
2. Their life is a manifestation of couple dialogue.
3. Both wish to be a team couple.
4. As a couple they must express love, stability, and unity.

Their mission is described as follows:

1. To establish an atmosphere and to create a good climate.
2. To motivate couples by sharing from their own life experiences.
3. To inspire each couple to give their best efforts to their encounter, so that they truly encounter or rediscover each other.
5. To be loyal to the objective of each step of the weekend.

There is no specific training provided for the Team Couples. During the planning sessions for an Encounter Weekend, each couple chooses the talk they would like to give to participants. These talks are fairly well structured by the *Marriage Encounter* manual, and the couple "fills in the blanks" with their personal experiences. During the planning sessions, the talks are rehearsed and critiqued by other Team Couples. In some cases, the preparation sessions may include outside speakers for further enrichment or instruction. Generally, however, there is no real training involved. Enthusiasm is the main ingredient of the team preparation.

The Marriage Encounter Program

Most Marriage Encounter weekends are structured in the same way. From Friday night through Sunday afternoon, 10 to 25 couples meet at some suitable retreat house. One to three previously "encountered" couples and a priest, or clergyperson, are present as a team to instruct and encourage the participants in their efforts to explore the meaning of their lives and their marriages.

Four general themes are addressed during the weekend: I, We, We-God, and We-God-World. The "I" theme involves the relationship with the marriage partner. The "We-God" theme involves revelation of God in the marriage relationship, and the "We-God-World" theme involves the demonstration of the Spirit to the world through service.

The "presenting team" (the Team Couples) give short talks throughout the weekend on the four major themes. After each talk the speakers give each participating couple a list of questions on which to reflect. Time is then allowed for the husband and the wife to write separately their individual responses in a notebook, with the instructions emphasizing getting in touch with feelings. After writing, the couple comes together to exchange notebooks, read what the other has written, and then talk about what the other has written. The stated objective of these exercises is to establish a real understanding of the partner's feelings, hopes, dreams, wishes, etc.

On Friday evening, all couples attending the Marriage Encounter are introduced to the Team Couples, who have previously participated in Marriage Encounter, and the clergy, who will lead the weekend. After introductions, the first ground rules are stated. Couples are instructed to remove or alter watches and clocks, not to watch television in their rooms, and not to communicate with the world outside their motel rooms or the room in which the presentations are made. Secrecy is emphasized: couples are instructed not to ask questions about the proceedings.

During the first session on Friday night, the questions for reflection and dialogue concern the couple's reasons for coming and the positive aspects of their relationship. For example, "What are my feelings about coming here? What do I hope to gain?" Husbands and wives are also asked to introduce each other and state each other's most endearing quality. Following this exercise, the first presentation is made, in which one of the presenting couples describes the natural reaction many couples feel at having to stand up before 40 or so strangers and say something meaningful.

During the first presentation, participating couples are given notebooks and pens and asked to record important information from each presentation. They are also told that they will be writing love letters to their spouses on the topics addressed by the presenting couples. Alternately, all the men and then all the women return to their rooms so that each member of the couple can write in solitude a response to the initial questions of why they have come and what they hope to gain. After a limited time period, participants return to the meeting room to hear a presentation concerning the four themes for the weekend. An emphasis on recognition and expression of feelings is added to the presentation, and a qualitative discussion of the best characteristics of oneself, one's spouse, and both individuals as a couple takes place. Participants engage in letter-writing related to these characteristics and return to their rooms to have a dialogue or share the letters they have written.

The first Saturday session is a time for personal reflection. There is a presentation on opening oneself to critical examination. Individuals reflect, in writing, on the questions "What do I like about myself? What do I dislike? What masks do I use?"

The focus on the "we" phase begins with a presentation on the cycle of romance, disillusionment, and joy, which "married singles" go through as the pressures of the outside world force each spouse to react as individuals. The technique of the daily writing of love letters and dialogues is discussed as a way to remove isolation between two partners in a couple.

After a love-letter-writing session, the couples engage in exchange and dialogue on the topic of sadness and/or emptiness. This letter-writing session is followed by a presentation on accepting the feelings of the other, both as a way of seeing into the other's feelings and to further encourage the trust of the other per-

son in revealing those feelings. Nonverbal communication is also discussed.

The last dialogue question of the "we" phase is to reveal to one's spouse the innermost feelings that one has difficulty accepting. Following the writing of love letters in which the members of the couple describe the feelings they have difficulty accepting, the exchange of letters, and the dialogue, participants return to the presentation room for the beginning of the "we-God" phase.

In the "we-God" phase, "coupleness" is explained as resulting from God's love and plan. The married couple is seen as a basic unit in God's community, and it is only through God's love that coupleness is possible. The first dialogue in this phase concerns naming three specific instances when each member of a couple felt close to the other member and how these times of closeness made each spouse feel. In the second "we-God" presentation, participants are told that the ultimate meaning of marriage and closeness is God's love. The dialogue question for couples in this presentation is "What feelings do I have that I find most difficult to share with you?"

On Sunday morning, marriage is discussed as a sacrament, and the Team Couples serve as witnesses and give examples. The participating couples are then introduced to the Marriage Evaluation Questionnaire, which they answer in writing. This questionnaire is a 50-question instrument designed to force a deep look within one's self at one's attitudes about life and its meaning, about God, children, relatives, neighbors, and responsibility to others.

The final session of the weekend involves couples' agreeing on a joint plan for the future concerning their commitment to each other, to the family, and to the world, the "I-we-God" theme. This session may or may not include a renewal of marriage vows in a group ceremony.

At the end of the Marriage Encounter Weekend, couples are urged to join various follow-up programs that are available to give support to the newly "encountered" couples. In particular, couples are encouraged to commit themselves to the daily practice of 10 minutes of writing and 10 minutes of couple dialogue.

After the Marriage Encounter Weekend is completed, volunteers are recruited for training as lead couples from those couples who report having experienced positive effects, and, in some instances, considerable pressure is brought to bear on couples to continue to take part in the movement. For example, to reluctant couples, it might be suggested that they have never made a *real* encounter. As an example of continued involvement, Bosco (1973) noted that in the New York area, the movement among former participants is highly organized, even to the distribution of Marriage Encounter pins, sweatshirts, and bumper stickers.

Depending upon the organization sponsoring the weekend, activities and specific exercises may vary somewhat. The entire weekend, however, consists of the structure of providing *Inspiration and Information*, wherein former participants share experiences and a lecture is given; *Personal Reflection*, wherein one writes his or her thoughts and feelings on the topic presented by the leaders; and *Couple Dialogue*, wherein members of a couple share verbally with each other what they have written.

Types of Marriage Encounter

Various religious denominations, especially the larger Protestant ones, now have some type of Marriage Encounter. Among the most prominent non-Protestant ones are the Roman Catholic Marriage Encounter and the Jewish Marriage Encounter.

Marriage Encounter

Offered by the Roman Catholic Church, this program is highly structured and is based on an ongoing dialogue between the husband and wife to symbolize a rebirth of communication. Writing, along with structured discussion, is utilized as an expression of self. Leadership is provided by a priest and a couple who have previously experienced Marriage Encounter (Bosco, 1973).

Jewish Marriage Encounter

In this program, the focus is on an educational experience, addressing the meaning of marriage and attempting to strengthen Jewish family life by strengthening the marriage. Home is considered a sanctuary; the spiritual aspects of Marriage Encounter are considered essential, and the encounter is primarily a dialogue between the husband and the wife (Kligfield, 1976). Usually, Jewish Marriage Encounter occurs in a weekend-retreat setting involving 30 couples, a rabbinic couple, and facilitating couples. The weekend experience stresses an active, process-centered group, oriented toward addressing a couple's "decision to love" (Genovese, 1975a, 1975b).

RESEARCH AND EVALUATION

Little research has been conducted on the outcome of Marriage Encounter weekends. A dissertation study by Neuhaus (1977) found that after an encounter weekend, couples showed significantly increased scores on a modified form of the Barrett-Lennard Relationship Inventory. This inventory measures openness, sensitivity, constancy, understanding and regard for spouse, closeness, unconditional regard, collaboration, appreciation by spouse, self-awareness, and empathy. Pre- and posttesting was conducted on experimental and control groups of similar backgrounds. On all 10 dimensions, the means for the experimental group increased significantly after exposure to the encounter weekend. On most dimensions, the means did not decrease significantly a month later.

Huber (1977) examined the effects of the dialogue technique, using the dimensions of Loving and Caring on Shostrom's Caring Relationship Inventory. The experimental group consisted of 77 married couples participating in one of three Marriage Encounter weekends. The control group was made of up 31 couples on a waiting list for the weekend. The pretest was completed on the Friday night before the regular activities started, and the post-test on the Sunday evening after completion of the weekend. Follow-up tests were given six weeks later. Huber found significant changes for the experimental group between pre-, post-, and follow-up tests on the scales Affection, Eros, and Empathy. No changes were found in the control group. In the experimental group there were no general changes between post-test and follow-up, indicating that positive changes lasted at least 6 weeks. Husbands showed a greater pre–post test increase in scores than did wives.

Research not specific to Marriage Encounter but on encounter groups in general includes a study by Burns (1972), using the Taylor-Johnson Temperament Analysis—one pre-test, two post-tests—that showed greater congruence in perceptions of spouse and in perception of self after encounter-group training. The experimental group became more open and less defensive as measured by the attitude scale of the Temperament Analysis.

Increasing the effectiveness of encounter group experiences is addressed by Bolan (1973). A combination of verbal encounter and designed nonverbal activity was found to be more effective than verbal activity alone. This combination was correlated with greater gain scores for encounter group participants on Time Competence, Inner-Direction, and the Self-Acceptance scales of the Personal Orientation Inventory.

Loomis (1972), in an interesting study of the effects of time distribution on encounter-group learning (marathons versus spaced groups) found that there were more significant positive changes for the twice-weekly groups than for the marathon groups on three measures: Personal Orientation Inventory, Rotter's Locus of Control, and Shapiro's Adjective Check List.

DISCUSSION

The growing popularity of Marriage Encounter points to the concern of many individuals in this country with experiencing greater intimacy and meaning within significant relationships. One must certainly take note of any program that is increasingly reaching thousands of couples. This almost overwhelming response by couples to the topic of intimacy may point to limitations with other forms of marital intervention and may be Marriage Encounter's most valuable contribution to the field of marital and family therapy to date. There are thousands of couples responding to a program that purports to increase closeness and unity within the couple relationship. Therefore one must assume that the need to further address issues of intimacy within couple relationships not only exists but is openly acknowledged by the consumer of mental health services (Stedman, 1982).

It is difficult to assess Marriage Encounter as a form of psychological treatment per se, however, because of the numerous inherent religious tenets as well as the adamant ideology espoused by its proponents. Although Marriage Encounter is primarily a structured educational format that focuses on teaching self-awareness and communication skills, it is also a quasimystical movement claiming to help couples do "God's will." Although one can assess the value or end result of teaching communication skills, one cannot assess "God's definition" of a happy marriage without engaging in subjective discussions of religious ideology. It is important to note the underlying ideology of Marriage Encounter, however. Underlying this religious philosophical movement is the belief that "autonomy is bad," that differences are bad, and that was is "good" is to recapture some sort of enlightened oneness with another individual. Closeness or oneness is the answer for any marital difficulty. Although achieving a oneness may indeed lead to some form of "ecstasy," it may also lead to fusion and symbiosis, and loss of individual ego boundaries. More importantly, the goal of union, or fusion, may simply not be attainable except by sacrificing the individual in the relationship.

One certainly might point to the couple leaders as examples to others of the attainment of some sort of union and oneness. The team leaders, by definition, however, are couples who are constantly working on achieving and maintaining the goal of union and oneness. Therefore it is difficult to point to any evidence that a union and oneness occurs, for team leaders are, in a sense, constantly in treatment. It is more difficult still to point to lasting outcome effects for participants, for there are no long-term follow-up studies of the effects of Marriage Encounter.

Although the treatment may seem straightforward and clear-cut, several issues concerning the format need to be addressed. DeYoung (1979) has described his experience in Marriage Encounter as like an initiation ceremony whereby one learns important and mystical facts that enable one to be an adult. In his experience leaders were often authoritarian and coercive with those couples who failed to experience an "encounter," telling them that they were in danger of losing their relationships if they did not succeed, continually stressing that having an "encounter" is a wonderful high. Although some participants do report achieving a "high," there is no data concerning those who do not achieve the "high." One might draw a parallel between Marriage Encounter and EST. It is not known how many participants in EST fail to get "it." It is not known how many participants in Marriage Encounter fail to have an "encounter." This lack of knowledge of failures is in part due to the lack of adequate outcome studies, but may also be due to the tremendous pressure to get "it." It would simply be difficult for individuals to report their failures to have an encounter.

DeYoung (1979) criticized Marriage Encounter on the basis of his experience as a participant-observer. He questioned the recruitment approach to lure couples into the process and the "halo" effect of religious and, in some cases, charismatic and mystic emphasis. He was also critical of the claims made by the proponents of this approach, summarizing his experience thusly;

If the majority of such Marriage Encounter sessions approximate the one described, more serious investigations of theory and practice involved should be a major project supported by the therapeutic professions (DeYoung, 1979, p. 34).

It would certainly be unfair to ignore the fact that numerous participants report feeling better, feeling closer to their spouses, and believing that they have had an "encounter." The long-term effects are, however, still questioned.

Regarding clients served, not only are there no data for long-term follow-up of treatment effects, but Marriage Encounter also offers no data concerning those participating couples who are considered inappropriate for Marriage Encounter. It is difficult to ascertain the interventions that would occur with those couples who indicate, once in the program, that they are clearly inappropriate for the experience. It is thus difficult to ascertain whether all couples are considered appropriate or whether no interventions are made for inappropriate couples.

Praise, as well as criticism, for Marriage Encounter is in many ways premature, for there is virtually no outcome research available. The few studies available suffer as much from difficulty in quantifying outcomes as they do from lack of numbers. Assessment of such abstract concepts as "happiness," "satisfaction," or "adjustment" requires much more sophisticated, as well as objective, measures than are now available (Stedman, 1982).

Finally, one must look closely at the value system espoused in Marriage Encounter. One goal (unity) is presented for marriage, and this goal is presented as being divinely sanctioned. Thus, with this divine sanction, only Marriage Encounter *knows* the way in which couples should be married. To assume that there is only one way to be married is at best limiting and at worst ignorant of the large bodies of biological, sociological, and psychological literature concerning the existence of individual differences in human behavior.

Doherty, et al (1978) have likened Marriage Encounter's combination of great promises and terrible threats to a fundamentalist revivalism, while DeYoung (1979) has stated that the teachings are primarily male-centered, with females encouraged to be followers while males take the lead. These two criticisms raise the question of whether or not we are witnessing a quasireligious-political movement rather than a mental health movement, for Marriage Encounter undoubtedly offers a traditional, conservative view of marriage. One could hypothesize that Marriage Encounter offers a reaction to the numerous self-growth therapies, stressing individuation and individualism, and that it may be indicative of other societal trends towards renewed conservatism.

More recently, Doherty and Walker (1982) reported on 13 case reports obtained by seven marriage therapists that showed deterioration after a Marriage Encounter weekend. This deterioration may take the form of: (1) increased marital conflict; (2) avoidance of constructive problem solving; or (3) marital enmeshment at the expense of the children. These authors believed "that the most harmful effect of the Marriage Encounter experience is its induction of intense couple-centered communication, leading to emotional overload in some couples" (p. 15). To lower risks connected with participation in this experience, the authors recommended that (1) more systematic effort should be made to screen out distressed couples; (2) couples who need to seek professional help should be encouraged by team leaders to do so; (3) one of the team leaders should have training and experience in crisis intervention; (4) couples should be alerted to the possibilities of a post-weekend upset; and (5) proper referral channels for distressed couples should be available.

Stedman (1982) has attempted to refute some of the foregoing criticisms, pointing out that the good of the majority may be paramount and that casualties are a small cost to pay for all the good received.

THE FUTURE

The outcomes of Marriage Encounter are not known and certainly need to be further explored, for Marriage Encounter is a growing movement, making numerous claims concerning efficacy in helping marriages become more intimate. Marriage Encounter currently not only addresses thousands of individuals each year but also offers a definition of the marital relationship that differs from other marital theories and therapies. Therefore its impact, whether positive or negative, cannot be overlooked or ignored.

REFERENCES

Bolan SL. A study exploring two different approaches to encounter groups: The combination of verbal encounter and designed nonverbal activity versus emphasis upon verbal activity only. *Dissertation Abstracts International*, June 1973, *33*, 6070B

Bosco A. *Marriage encounter: The rediscovery of love.* St. Meinrad, IN, Abbey Press, 1973

Buettner J. A history of marriage encounter in the United States. *Agape*, February 1976, 4, 12–15

Burns CW. Effectiveness of the basic encounter group in marriage counseling. *Dissertation Abstracts International*, September 1972, *33*, 1281B

Burton A (Ed). *Encounter: The theory and practice of encounter groups.* San Francisco, Jossey-Bass, Inc., 1970

Caldwell AT. *The therapeutic implications of marriage encounter.* Paper presented at meeting of Southeastern Psychological Association, Hollywood, Florida, May 1977

Calvo Fr. G. *Marriage encounter.* St. Paul, MN: Marriage Encounter, Inc. 1975

Chicago Supplement to the National Marriage Encounter Manual. Published by National Marriage Encounter, 1976

DeYoung AJ. Marriage encounter. A critical examination. *Journal of Marital and Family Therapy*, 1979, *5*, 27–34

Doherty WJ, McCabe P, & Ryder RG. Marriage encounter: A critical appraisal. *Journal of Marriage and Family Counseling*, 1978, *4*, 99–108

Doherty WJ, & Walker BJ. Marriage encounter casualties: A preliminary investigation. *American Journal of Family Therapy*, 1982, *10*, 15–25

Enright JB. An introduction to gestalt techniques. In J Fagan & IL Shepherd (Eds.), *Gestalt therapy now.* New York: Harper & Row, 1970

Gallagher C. *The marriage encounter: As I have loved you.* Garden City, NY: Doubleday, 1975

Genovese RJ. Marriage encounter. In S Miller (Ed.), *Marriage and families: Enrichment through communication.* Beverly Hills: Sage Publications, 1975a

Genovese RJ. Marriage encounter. *Small Group Behavior*, 1975b, *6*, 45–56

Huber W. *Marriage encounter evaluated by CRI.* San Diego; Edits Research and Developments, 1977

Jourard SM. Healthy personality and self-disclosure. *Mental Hygiene*, 1959, *43*, 499–507

Kligfield B. The Jewish marriage encounter. In HA Otto (Ed.) *Marriage and family enrichment: New perspectives and programs.* Nashville, TN: Abingdon Press, 1976

Koch J, & Koch L. The urgent drive to make good marriages better. *Psychology Today*, 1976, *10*, 33–35

L'Abate L. *Enrichment: Structured interventions with couples, families, and groups.* Washington, DC: University Press of America, 1977

Loomis TP, Skin conductance and the effects of time distribution on encounter group learning: Marathon vs. spaced groups. *Dissertation Abstracts International*, 1972, *33*, 5275A

Neuhaus RH. A study of the effects of a marriage encounter experience on the interpersonal interaction of married couples. *Dissertation Abstracts International*, 1977, *37*, 6793A

Regula M. Marriage encounter: What makes it work? *The Family Coordinator*, 1975, *24*, 153–160

Stedman JM. Marriage encounter: An "insider's" consideration of recent techniques. *Family Relations*, 1982, *31*, 123–129

Yalom ID. *The theory of practice of group therapy.* New York: Basic Books, 1970

6

Relationship Enhancement

Relationship Enhancement (RE) is another program that attempts to assist couples in improving communication skills, broadening and deepening emotional lives, and reinforcing and fostering existing marital strengths (Guerney, 1977a). This program is a structured couples group format that addresses the communication deficits within the relationship. Although RE has been expanded to include several different training formats, couples usually meet 2 hours weekly for 10 weeks and learn skills by practicing systematically according to principles of social reinforcement, learning theory, and behavior modification. Initially, spouses learn skills while discussing neutral and positive relationship issues, and they gradually move toward applying these skills to difficult interpersonal issues over the 10-week meeting period. Like other educational programs designed to promote growth, its main orientation is one of skills-training. According to its originator, Bernard G. Gureney Jr. (1977a, p. 19), Relationship Enhancement aims to alter ways in which each individual views the deepest emotions and most interpersonal behaviors of him/herself and of other significant people in the interpersonal environment'' (p. 19).

BACKGROUND AND DEVELOPMENT

One can view RE as yet another response to several cultural changes within American society. There has been an increasing focus on the quality of marital relationships within the field of marital therapy as opposed to an initial problem-alleviation orientation (see Chapter 9). Concurrent with this focus, there has been, since the mid-1960s, an increasing societal emphasis on individual growth and personal enhancement. Whether cultural concerns about the quality of emotional life reflect trends within marital therapy or whether trends within marital therapy reflect cultural concerns is at times unclear. It is hypothesized, however, that what can be called the results of the individual personal growth movement have finally begun to raise a concern for the dangers of a focus on only individual growth when that individual is part of a dyadic or family system. Growth within an intimate relationship is now seen as a necessary joint effort, for the relationship may fail as one partner, focusing on personal enhancement, moves away from the other. Furthermore, partly due to growing concerns about the cost of mental health services, there has been an increasing concern with prevention. To provide an educative, preventive approach to mental health issues is viewed as less costly in the long run than to provide only a treatment approach aimed at the alleviation of an existing problem. Finally, from a theoretical viewpoint, the field of marital therapy has been significantly influenced by communication theorists who have focused on the importance of communication skills in a functional marital relationship (Haley, 1959a, 1963, 1971; Jackson,

1965; Lederer & Jackson, 1968; Ruesch & Bateson, 1951).

In a recent study of practicing marital and family therapists who were also clinical members of the American Association for Marriage and Family Therapy (AAMFT), Sprenkle and Fisher (1980) found that 8 of the top-10-ranked goals of family therapists were "effective communication skills." Concurrent with this focus, RE can be viewed as an intervention focusing primarily on the goal of teaching and/or improving effective communication skills.

Geurney (1977a), the creator of RE, reports that as he researched various methods of improving a couple's understanding of one another, he decided to reject both the spiritual and the medical approaches to "helping." He denounced the pre-20th-century spiritual model, which viewed problems as evolving from a spiritual deficit, supposedly making it impossible for anyone except witch doctors and exorcists to make people feel better. Similarly, he rejected the medical model as placing the control of problems (i.e., sickness and neurosis) in the hands of a healer, in this case, a physician (psychiatrist), who has curing powers. Guerney (1977b) criticized both the medically and the spiritually oriented healers and stated that, "instead of the urge to instruct and engineer, many professional helpers seem to provide the direction, the nurturance, the succorance, and the solution to the problem" (p. 79).

In addition to his criticism of traditional therapeutic orientations, Guerney's RE model evolved from his concept of education, which incorporates many psychotherapeutic methods that address the learner's conflicting motivations, self-concept, and ambivalent feelings. In Guerney's model, however, the learner engages in feeling (recognizing and accepting emotions), thinking (rationally integrating feelings and making logical decisions), and doing (acquiring skills that improve interpersonal communications) in order to learn to resolve his or her difficulties.

Guerney (1964) first combined his educational model with client-centered behavioristic and social learning theories to address the issues in families of emotionally disturbed children. He designed a program of "filial therapy" in an attempt to provide professional assistance to more children and families than had been provided for by traditional methods.

The rationale behind filial therapy is that a child's primary source of maladjustment could be traced to his or her interpersonal relationships within the family. Therefore the resources for the child's improvement lie within the family constellation.

The filial therapy process involved training three or four pairs of parents in a group setting to conduct private play therapy sessions with their emotionally disturbed youngsters. At first, parents would practice this client-centered play therapy while being supervised and encouraged by the group leader. Parents were taught to communicate acceptance and appreciation of their child's play activities. The child was encouraged by the parents to choose his or her own games and activities. If the child chose to engage in any potentially dangerous activity, the parents were to ask the child to choose another activity. If the child continued in dangerous play, the parent was to end the session abruptly. Thus filial therapy aimed at developing an empathic understanding between parents and child, in addition to teaching the child limits by showing him or her the consequence of misbehavior.

After mastering basic empathic skills, the parents were asked to practice the play sessions at home. Typically, as parents became less inhibited in their communication, children would exhibit more self-directed appropriate play with more self-confidence.

An additional result of filial therapy was that parents reported being better able to communicate with each other. Thus Guerney (1964) made his first attempt at conjugal marital relationship enhancement in which spouses with troubled relationships were successfully taught to use therapeutic communication skills with each other. Out of filial therapy emerged relationship enhancement between couples, between mothers and adolescent daughters, within nonclinical families, and between premarital couples. Guerney (1969) also began to train paraprofessionals to conduct his treatment program.

PHILOSOPHY AND MAJOR CONCEPTS

Guerney (1977a) believes that the disillusionment experienced by many married individuals is caused by a lack of training and role models in effective communication. He also believes that, through improving one's intimate interpersonal relationships, an individual may gain personal satisfaction and allow both self and partner more growth. Thus, conceptually, three clients are treated: the husband, the wife, and the marital relationship. The treatment consists of increasing the clients' understanding of themselves and their spouses along the dimensions of communication that are directly pertinent to the relationship. The understanding centers on the needs, desires, aspirations, values, and motivations of self and partner.

Guerney reframes problems and abnormality as conflicts and dissatisfactions. The diagnosis may be renamed prioritization and may be done by the individual with the aid of a therapist or teacher. Together, they design an instructional program (versus prescription) that aims at greater personal satisfaction (versus cure). Thus Guerney conceptualizes the therapeutic process as a psychosocial educational process.

Within the educational model, the concepts of prevention and treatment merge. Remedial instruction (treatment) is skill instruction (prevention), and both processes involve competency training. Remedial instruction in communication skills is necessitated by some deficiency in earlier experiences; for example, children whose mothers never listen, whose fathers are demanding, who are not encouraged to express their feelings, whose parents don't discuss and/or argue in front of them may in adulthood be unaware of how to communicate with their spouses. Guerney (1977a) emphasizes the importance of skill training in the therapeutic process:

Unless and until someone can describe the skill a person needs to avoid developing a specific problem—including a problem such as schizophrenia—and these specific skills are incorporated into a program, it makes very little sense to expect to either overcome or prevent the problem (p. 4).

Essential to Guerney's view of education is his belief in encouraging participants to learn new skills that may allow them to communicate with each other on both cognitive and affective levels.

The theoretical rationale for Relationship Enhancement reflects the importance of integrating emotions, cognitions, and behaviors. Skinner's theory of operant conditioning is employed and integrated with Rogerian client-centered principles. Roger's client-centered approach is employed early in the process by both leader and participants. Both are trained to be unconditionally accepting and respectful of the feelings and thoughts of others. Early in the RE process, each spouse grapples with the paradox of listening to one with whom many intimate investments and connections have been formed without allowing his or her own reactions, opinions, and values to interfere with hearing. Operant methods are applied to further the teaching of client goals through the co-leaders, who are generous and spontaneous in giving praise and who utilize a wide range of social reinforcement phrases, ranging from simple acceptance to enthusiastic praise. In the initial sessions, reinforcement may be given immediately following any appropriate remark made by a group member. In subsequent sessions the co-leaders reinforce "successive approximations" to more complete expressive and empathic statements by the participants.

Other principles involved in Relationship Enhancement skill-training are derived from Bandura's social learning theory. All skills are modeled by the co-leaders before being practiced by the participants. Also, vicarious learning may occur when couples acquire skills that were modeled (and reinforced) by other group members.

THE TREATMENT PROCESS

The treatment process occurs in a couples group format with at least three couples per group. Two-co-leaders aid the spouses in replacing vicious communication cycles with more direct and open cycles of communication. The process involves first separating the communication process into distinct components or "modes." Participants are systematically taught each mode of expressing feelings and thoughts clearly, emphasizing and accepting the expressions of another, facilitating and critiquing their own communication skills from moment to moment, and maintaining a dialogue on the constructive resolution of conflicts. When in the mode of *expressing* a feeling, opinion, experience, or reaction, a spouse learns to state his or her views subjectively by communicating how the issue is personally meaningful. The expresser is also asked to attach a feeling to the statement, to tie the general statement to specific behaviors or actions, to include basic positive feelings that may underlie a concern or problem, and to connect a statement of hope and desire with any statement of criticism. In teaching a mode, the leader concentrates on teaching one aspect of the expression (or any mode) at a time, with the purpose of enlarging the participants' repertoire of expressive techniques.

The responsive mode involves receiving and reacting to an expresser's statement in an open-minded manner. The responder learns to place himself or herself in the expresser's place in order to ascertain what the expresser is communicating. The responder may then demonstrate understanding of that statement by repeating its main contents. Ultimately, the empathic responder should be able to convey acceptance of his or her partner's views, utilizing tone, facial expression, posture, etc., while restating not only the other's thoughts, but also the major conflicts, feelings, and desires that are implicit or explicit in the expresser's statement. While the responder attempts to be as accurate as possible in his or her responses, the major objective is to encourage the expresser to complete a congruent, clear statement. Therefore there are usually several interchanges between expresser and responder before the expresser feels satisfied that his or her message has been understood.

Once the expresser feels satisfied that he or she has expressed himself or herself, or exhausted his or her attempts to communicate that message, or is anxious to receive feedback or suggestions from the spouse, the expresser may request a *mode switch* (i.e., let the spouse be the expresser while assuming the responder mode). At times, after delivering an empathic response, the responder may feel an urgent need to introject some views of his or her own and may also request a mode switch. In either case, both partners must agree to exchange modes. Through becoming more sensitive to needs to switch modes, the partners learn to complete their messages, to engage in productive dialogue, and to collaborate in the resolution of conflicts.

These skills may at first appear simple to master, thereby creating some frustration for participants in the initial sessions when they are confronted with the complexity and hard work of mastering the skills. Here, the co-leaders become *facilitators* by monitoring and encouraging the communicators. In order to build and refine communication skills, participants must be made aware of exactly what they are doing to encourage or impede the process. During the early sessions, the group leaders serve as the only facilitators. In effect, they are modeling and teaching facilitation skills to the group members. Sometime after the 10th hour, however, participants practice facilitating each other's discussions. During the final sessions, facilitation responsibility is evenly dispersed throughout the group, with all participants offering praise, constructive criticism, and alternative empathic responses to the "focus couple." In this way, group members gain additional skill practice and provide modeling and support for each other. Facilitation exchanges also promote group cohesiveness throughout the RE process.

Intake Interview/Assessment

There is no initial assessment or diagnosis in RE. The first interview is structured, however, so that it serves the purpose of an intake interview. The intake interview provides useful information about the couple that the structured program format might mask. The intake provides both participants and leader with an opportunity to become known to each other. Rather than assessment per se, however, the leader's main objectives are to establish rapport and trust with the couple, to introduce and explain the major components (modes) of effective communication patterns, and to stress the value of learning and practicing these skills. At the conclusion of the intake, the leader discusses any doubts and concerns the participants may have about the program.

The Role of the Group Leader

An RE leader is ultimately concerned with "giving the client the capacity to win empathy and respect from other people by his own behaviors" (Guerney, 1977a, p. 319). The leaders do not encourage or utilize the client's transference, though the leaders do attempt to foster a strong, trusting relationship with the clients. During the initial session, the leaders present an appearance and an attitude of warmth and friendliness toward the participants. Guerney suggests that leaders should be attired comfortably but neatly, and should relate to participants on a first-name basis. The group meets in a large, comfortable space, and members are permitted to come and go as they please during the sessions.

Guerney trains his leaders to refrain from the powerful "healer" image. Instead of concentrating on the participants' abnormalities, the leader from the start expresses appreciation for the difficulty in acquiring interpersonal skills and then continually offers support and praise for participants' approximations of effective communication skills. Guerney likens the leader's teaching role to an advanced stage of parenthood: while supervising and supporting, the leader/parent is consciously teaching the learner/child skills that will foster independence and self-reliance.

Meanwhile, the leader is discouraged from self-disclosing and sharing personal feelings with participants. The only reactions that are supposed to be shared are those that may serve to illustrate specific skills to the couples. Guerney (1977a) believes that the leader's introjected opinions and experiences would serve to remove the participants further from their own subjective experiences: "A therapist or educator whose professional behaviors are determined mainly by personal momentary impulses is about as useful as a drunken brain surgeon" (p. 117). This is a particularly provocative statement, since many marriage therapists at times utilize quite effectively their personal reactions and opinions to guide the therapeutic process.

RE co-leaders must also address clients who are forgetful, balky, resistant, distressed, etc. With the difficult or uncooperative client, after a wide variety of teaching methods and reinforcement techniques have proved ineffective, the RE leader may employ the "trouble-shooting" procedure. In this structured problem-solving procedure, the leader assumes an expressive mode; the uncooperative client or couple is placed in the responsive mode, and the other group members participate as facilitators. In this way, the leader may vent his or her anger, disappointment, etc. in a productive problem-solving framework. While trouble-shooting, the leader discusses X

behavior that makes him or her feel Y with person Z, and then allows Z to respond. Both leader and participant repeatedly switch modes until some resolution is achieved.

Guerney believes that teaching methods need to be flexible yet specific enough to be described clearly in behavioral terms. Therefore specificity and quantification of leadership functions facilitate the teaching of leadership roles to trainees and the replication of the methodology for research. In order to define more clearly the leadership process, Guerney has developed a classification system for leadership responses. Leaders' statements may be coded by an observer, supervisor, trainee, or the leader (if audio or video tape is employed) into broad categories of appropriate (A) and inappropriate (I) responses. Inappropriate responses may be defined as statements that do not fit into the structure of Relationship Enhancement. Inappropriate responses are often made in reaction to the leader's personal needs, or they are made because the leader would use them in other forms of marital intervention (see Table 6-2). In addition, the recipient of the remark may be coded Group (G), Co-leader (C), Expresser (E), Responder (R), Facilitator (F).

There are 19 basic subdivisions of appropriate responses for group leaders (see Table 6-1). Many leader statements may be encoded into two or more categories.

During the first 16 hours of RE training, the co-leaders take an active role in facilitating group discussion. Eventually, as participants learn to give social reinforcement and model the modes for one another, the group may be more self-propelling. Still, the leader continues to offer praise and encouragement to each group member. The leader is also responsible for monitoring the time spent on each couple so that, over several sessions, each couple receives ample time to practice their skills in the presence of the group.

The leader's role is largely defined in terms of the empathic and behavioral skills that he or she employs rather than in terms of personal characteristics and complex interaction that he or she should have with the participants. Guerney does recognize qualities that contribute to making an effective group leader (e.g., empathy, self-confidence, warmth, verbal expressiveness); however, he also believes that a variety of people may be trained to develop and demonstrate these leadership qualities.

Table 6-1
Appropriate Responses

Administrative response	Statements that are necessary for the smooth running of the group; Procedural reminders, etc.
Social reinforcement response	Frequently used phrases of encouragement and praise for appropriate comments by participants.
Social reinforcement (nonverbal)	Body communications that express acceptance or praise; head nods, forward postures, smiles, etc.
Structuring response	Responses made when participants err, which remind them of guidelines and rationale for roles.
Modeling on empathic response	Providing the responder with a good example of a statement that demonstrates understanding.
Modeling on expressive response	Providing the expresser with an example of a statement that clearly expresses feelings and ideas.
Encouraging a mode switch	Suggesting to the couple that they exchange modes when it seems appropriate.
Encouraging problem-solving	Defining the nature, parts of, and feelings behind a problem in the hope that the couple may begin to generate alternative solutions.
Direct acceptance in trouble-shooting	Dealing with issues that seriously impede group functioning; working through the conflict using the RE model.

Guerney also believes that a male/female pair of co-leaders would provide maximum sensitivity to both sexes among group members. In addition, a male and female team would provide more face validity when modeling relationship communication skills for groups of male and female couples.

THE ENHANCEMENT PROCESS

If a couple elects to return to the second RE meeting after the intake interview, they are greeted by a group comprising two co-leaders and three to four married couples. The activities that take place throughout the program

Table 6-2
Inappropriate Responses

Directive lead	Steering statement usually made out of a leader's desire to move the conversation toward more productive content.
Interpretation	Insight regarding contradictions in a participant's statement; generalization from statement about a personality trait of a participant.
Suggestion, advice	Descriptive statement about how participant should be or act.
Approval, reassurance	Comforting response made to participant in reaction to the *content* of the statement.
Personal criticism	Belittling, critical comments usually arising out of leader's personal reaction to a participant.
Diversion	Extraneous thoughts, judgments, and anecdotes that are shared with the group.
Inappropriately directed responses	Making an empathic response that is directed at the expresser, or reformulating an expressive statement for the responder.
Failure to correct	Allowing a significant mistake to pass uncorrected.

are divided into four levels. Beginning at level one, the co-leaders once again explain and model expressive and responsive skills for the group. Participants are then asked to begin practicing expressive and responsive skills; to converse with group members other than their partners about issues that are unrelated to the marriage. Therefore, in level one, participants attempt to assume the expresser and responder roles under less intense, less emotional circumstances than those of their own marital relationship. This cross-couple communication may help couples feel more connected with the other group members so that in subsequent sessions, when there are few cross-couple direct interchanges, group members may still feel comfortable self-disclosing in front of one another.

At the conclusion of the first group meeting, the leader distributes several copies of the Relationship Questionnaire, an assessment tool that directs each spouse to identify in writing several pleasing aspects of the relationship and other aspects that could be developed, enhanced, or changed (including conflicts and problems). The Relationship Questionnaire is continually revised by the participants throughout Relationship Enhancement and serves as a springboard for discussions in the group sessions.

When participants return for their second group session, spouses are asked to practice both expressive and responsive modes together. Once again, they are allowed to discuss only those issues that do not relate directly to their relationship, thereby encouraging them to concentrate on skills and processes and avoid difficulties of getting bogged down in the emotionality of the content. At the conclusion of session two, couples are asked to select from their Relationship Questionnaire a positive aspect of their relationship for discussion at the third session.

When the co-leaders are confident that the participants have practiced all aspects of basic skills, they permit the couples to discuss the aspects of their relationship that either or both spouses would like to alter, including problems and conflicts. These level-four dialogues constitute the remainder of the sessions.

After the first week, participants are asked to practice their communication skills at home. Each assignment provides an opportunity to revise and refine the principles taught in the preceding session; thus homework assignments are ordered so as to complement the increasing levels of session difficulty. At the beginning of each session, the homework is reviewed, and participants are reminded of the importance of trying out these skills in a variety of real-life situations.

Guerney (1977a) offers the following outline/check list for sessions:

I. Review Homework
   A. Collect any written work and reinforce.
   B. Discuss any difficulties and questions.
II. Discuss Generalization
   A. Discuss the importance of using skills in everyday situations.
   B. Ask participants for specific examples of when they could have or did use skills since the last session.
   C. Encourage use of skills between now and next session.
III. Skill Practice
   A. Participants practice with their partners only.
   B. Subject area of discussions progresses in the order listed below (Points 1 and 2 are required topics only in the early hours of training):
     1. At about the third hour of training, partners talk with each other about an area outside their relationship.
     2. At about the fifth hour of training, partners discuss an area of their relationship that engenders positive feelings (Relationship Questionnaire category 1).
     3. At about the seventh hour of training, partners talk about either a previously discussed high-priority item or other areas from the Relationship Questionnaire (categories I, II, or III)
IV. Homework
   A. Give assignments and have each dyad agree on the time they will do them before the next session.
   B. Ask participants to review Relationship Questionnaire and make changes if desired; periodically distribute extra, blank Relationship Quesionnaires.
   C. Come to the next session prepared to discuss issues from the Relationship Questionnaire (pp. 187–188).

TRAINING GROUP LEADERS

Guerney has developed a leadership training program for graduate students and paraprofessionals based on the assumption that in addition to providing the public with more economical help (with several paraprofessional group leaders reporting to one professional supervisor), these leader trainees will receive valuable supervision and experience in group dynamics and communication facilitation. According to Guerney, graduate students may be trained in as few as 80 hours by professional Relationship Enhancement leaders.

Much of this training has been conducted at Pennsylvania State University where Guerney developed the Enhancement program. Professionals may be trained in an intensive 3- to 5-day workshop. A professional marriage therapist has the additional task of learning to ignore and repress some of his or her personal therapeutic techniques when learning to lead Relationship Enhancement groups. If the professional intends to use pure Relationship Enhancement, he or she may want to spend more than a few days studying and practicing the process. In addition, on-site training and/or supervision is available anywhere in the country from a recently formed nonprofit organization, the Institute for the Development of Emotional and Life Skills. This institute also disseminates information and aid to mental health programs that are based on an educational model.

RESEARCH AND EVALUATION

Despite the relative ease with which RE research could be conducted, few studies have addressed outcome research. There are, however, several studies that attempt to define more clearly the results of improving communication between spouses.

Although Guerney has utilized a variety of assessment tools in his research, including the Primary Communication Inventory, the Marital Adjustment Test, the Family Life Questionnaire, the Interpersonal Relationship Scale, and the Satisfaction Change Scale, none of these mesasures have reliability or validity data.

Nevertheless, the majority of Relationship Enhancement research has incorporated relatively large numbers of subjects and randomly assigned, "no treatment" control groups. Assessment of behavioral and self-report measures on a variety of dependent variables, including communication patterns, trust, satisfaction, and problem-solving abilities, has also been included in the studies.

The first comprehensive research in Conjugal Relationship Enhancement was conducted by Collins (1971) under the supervision of Guerney. Collins supported the goals of Relationship Enhancement by citing studies in client-centered therapy that suggested that genuineness, nonpossessive warmth, and accurate empathy are characteristics shared by effective relationship-oriented therapists (Carkhuff & Berenson, 1967). He also reported evidence that nonprofessional trainees can improve their empathic abilities and that nonprofessionals who demonstrate high levels of warmth, genuineness, and empathy may not be differentiated from professional therapists on measures of client progress (Carkhuff & Truax, 1965b). Next, Collins reviewed literature that repeatedly showed that therapists emphasize improving spouses' communication during marital therapy. Finally, Collins connected these findings:

It is not unreasonable to expect husbands and wives as nonprofessionals to learn to provide higher levels of warmth, genuineness, and empathy to each other and to become effective psychotherapeutic agents for their own marital relationship (Guerney, 1977a, p. 193).

Collins (1971), after acknowledging that marital therapists are often concerned with improving communication in marriage, attempted to determine to what extent general marital adjustment would be benefited by improving communication techniques. Given only six months of communication training, would husbands and wives see improvements in their relationships? Collins hypothesized that through a six-month Relationship Enhancement program, couples would improve their communication as measured by the Primary Communication Inventory (PCI) and the Marital Communication Inventory (MCI). He also hypothesized an improvement in overall marital adjustment as measured by the Marital Adjustment Test and the Conjugal Life Questionnaire.

Collins recruited a wide variety of subjects through contacting Pennsylvania State's married students and faculty, local newspapers, lawyers, and clergy. The typical spouses who participated in the program were 30 years old and had 2 children. Their pretest scores indicated that most couples were not as happy together as the average married couple, yet not as distressed as the typical clinical couple. Collins randomly assigned 21 "no treatment" control couples and 24 experimental couples to two groups. The experimental group was further subdivided into four Relationship Enhancement groups, each containing 3 couples and 2 co-leaders (graduate students with 10 to 20 weeks of training). These subject groups attended RE sessions for one-and-a-half hours per week over a six-month period. All couples were pretested and post-tested on the measures previously mentioned. They also completed 30-minute homework assignments each week, compiled from a manual, *Improving Communication in Marriage*, developed by the Human Development Institute (1970).

Collins' results indicated a high correlation between communication and marital adjustment variables. The Marital Communication Inventory evidenced a significant improvement and difference between experimental and control groups. Similarly, a significant improvement in marital adjustment was indicated on the Marital Adjustment Test. Both of the other measures (PCI and CLQ) detected insignificant differences in the hypothesized direction.

Rappaport (1976) designed a two-month, intensive, conjugal-relationship-modification program. His 21 couples indicated on self-report measures that a significant improvement in their marriages had taken place during the Enhancement process. Improvement, in this case, may be defined as enhanced adjustment, communication, trust, intimacy, and problem-solving ability. Behavioral scales indicated that significant improvements in group members' speaking and listening abilities had also taken place.

DISCUSSION

In comparison with other forms of marital intervention, RE is relatively structured, with is own set of theories and techniques.

Similarities may, however, be drawn between RE and unstructured marital therapies. In both forms of treatment, the therapist or co-leader offers support and constructive tactics. Therapists and leaders also allow the couple to choose the context of the sessions, while being more professionally concerned with the process of the relationship; both, to some extent, model and teach empathic and expressive skills. One of Guerney's major beliefs is that there are numerous ties between "therapeutic" and "educational" processes; he asserts that no major psychotherapeutic goal is abandoned when moving from a medical to an educational model. RE may also be compared to other structured interventions, such as Enrichment (see Chapter 7) and the Minnesota Couples Communication program (see Chapter 3). In these programs, short-term, programmed interventions, often employed by trained paraprofessionals, aim to improve relatively functional marriages. Process rather than content is the focus, and a linear process is employed to teach simple-to-complex communication skills systematically.

The strengths of RE can be seen in its relative simplicity. Theoretically and practically, communication skills are the main focus of treatment. The leader can be trained relatively quickly. In addition to the short leader-training period, the use of paraprofessionals provides an economical form of intervention. Group treatment versus individual couple treatment further provides an economical intervention.

RE also provides a program by which the main concepts of communication training can be incorporated into a variety of therapeutic modalities. Often, the presenting problems that couples bring to therapy have been perpetuated because couples are unable to communicate effectively about the issues; initial or adjunct communication skills training could further more quickly the process of problem resolution in therapy. In addition to aiding couples in communication skills, the leadership training would also aid professional and paraprofessional helpers to review or improve their own communication skills.

Unfortunately, as in most other forms of therapy, many of the strengths of Relationship Enhancement are also its limitations. Theoretically, Relationship Enhancement is clear, somewhat concrete, and related directly to practice. One question concerning the underlying theoretical rationale, however, is whether or not its major assumptions are simplistic. Presumably, poor communication skills are causal factors in couples' inabilities to resolve their difficulties. The reverse of this assumption may also be true, however. It is possible that underlying issues are causal factors in communication skills deficits. Furthermore, communication skills deficits may be present in a "satisfactory" marriage, and "good" communication skills may be present in a dysfunctional marriage. The assumption of a linear cause–effect relationship between "poor" communication and marital issues may miss other important factors related to the perpetuation of dysfunctional patterns within a marriage.

The role of the co-leader, although apparently easy to learn, may at second glance be more difficult than presumed. Although the structured group format allows few deviations from that which is taught, the co-leader must in reality draw upon a wide repertoire of psychologically sophisticated skills. For example, the co-leader must understand when to intervene in a dialogue and when not to intervene. The co-leader does not focus directly on content, and therefore must attend to a wide variety of verbal and nonverbal cues. It is possible that couples can easily digress to a discussion of trivia that may be totally unrelated to the core of the identified conflict if the co-leader is not highly sensitive to the underlying meaning of the communication.

Concerning the treatment employed, empathy, understanding, and support are stressed. There is a noticeable lack of emphasis on the negotiation and resolution of conflicts of specific behavioral change, however. It is certainly conceivable that two members in a dyad can understand each other and still not agree on the joint resolution of an issue.

Concerning the clients served, this highly specific, detailed communication system limits itself to serving two spouses who are willing to participate actively in the therapeutic process. Regardless of any modeling, prompting, and positive reinforcements that the participants may receive from the group co-leaders, a group member may not want to invest himself or herself in the Relationship Enhancement

process. Guerney contends that those whose values conflict with the values of Relationship Enhancement (i.e., open communication, honesty, equalitarianism) would probably not benefit from the process. Thus many couples who prefer to operate under unilateral decision-making and minimal expression of emotions would not be appropriate participants. Guerney also concedes that the highly verbal, interactive, logical basis of Relationship Enhancement would exclude those who have a mental age below 10 years, those who have psychosis or psychotic tendencies, those who are severely depressed and/or insecure, and those with metabolic disorders (including alcoholism and other drug dependencies). The sum of all of these inappropriate clientele clearly indicates that Guerney's approach, despite its low cost and relative inefficiency, may, like most other therapies, benefit only the verbal, intelligent, highly motivated, and already highly functional individuals and couples.

Concerning the research related to RE, there are still too little empirical data to ascertain its presumed effectiveness. The short-term, structured format does lend itself to short-term research and follow-up, however. RE lends itself to further, one hopes, well designed, long-term follow-up studies, primarily because it is definable in terms of methodology and theory.

Finally, the underlying values of RE raise several questions about its impact on clients. The major premise is that a couple's difficulties can be solved by an open, empathic dialogue. The abuses of "openness" have been well documented by the failure of the Encounter Group movement (Lieberman, et al, 1973; Rogers, 1970). Conceivably, openness can be used for a variety of interpersonal abuses. Another underlying assumption concerns the value of education and the learning of skills. Not all individuals under all circumstances are educable, nor can all individuals learn a specific skill. Finally, there is an underlying assumption that all issues can be resolved. This somewhat utopian view of the impact of communication-skills training may present a value and standard that few can meet, and may have some negative impact on those couples who find that they cannot learn "simple" communication skills.

THE FUTURE

There is no doubt that the future will see more structured, educationally oriented programs for couples and couples' issues. In the beginning rush to provide education and prevention, however, it is important that several major concerns that have yet to be addressed in the field of marital therapy be borne in mind. Theoretically, the field is still unable to delineate those factors defining a dysfunc-tional marriage versus a functional one. It is still not clear what leaders/teachers are teaching, and the effective components of treatment have not been defined. Clients are still limited to middle-class, functional couples, and no long-term outcome effects are noted. Lastly, a new unachievable norm for marital satisfaction may simply replace old unachievable norms, thereby fostering dissatisfaction for a number of couples.

REFERENCES

Carkhuff RR, & Berenson BG. *Beyond counseling and therapy*. New York: Holt, Rinehart and Winston, 1967

Carkhuff RR, & Truax CB. Training in counseling and psychotherapy: An evaluation of an integrated didactic and experiential approach. *Journal of Consulting Psychology*, 1965a, *29*, 333–336

Carkhuff RR, & Truax CB. Lay mental health counseling: The effects of lay group counseling. *Journal of Consulting Psychology*, 1965b, *29*, 426–431

Collins JD. *The effects of the conjugal relationship modification method on marital communication and adjustment*. Unpublished doctoral dissertation, Pennsylvania State University, 1971

Guerney BG, Jr. Filial therapy: Description and rationale. *Journal of Consulting Psychology*, 1964, *28*, 304–310

Guerney BG, Jr (Ed.). *Psychotherapeutic agents: New roles for non-professionals, parents and teachers*. New York: Holt, Rinehart & Winston, 1969

Guerney BG, Jr. *Relationship enhancement: Skill training programs for therapy, problem prevention and enrichment*. San Francisco: Jossey-Bass, 1977a

Guerney, BG, Jr. *The great potential of an educational skill-training model in problem prevention*. Unpublished manuscript, The Pennsylvania State University, 1977b

Guerney LF. Filial therapy. In DHL Olson (Ed.), *Treating relationships*. Lake Mills, IA: Graphic, 1976

Guerney LF. *Parenting: A skills training manual*. State College, PA: Institute for the Development of Emotional and Life Skills, 1978

Haley JA. An interactional description of schizophrenia. *Psychiatry*, 1959a, *22*, 321–332

Haley, JA. The family of the schizophrenic: A model system. *Journal of Nervous and Mental Disease*, 1959b, *129*, 357–374

Haley JA. Marriage therapy. *Archives of General Psychiatry*, 1963, *8*, 213–234

Haley JA. Review of the family therapy field. In *Changing families: A family therapy reader*. New York: Grune & Stratton, 1971

Human Development Institute. *Improving communication in marriage*. Atlanta, GA: 1970

Jackson D. The study of the family. *Family Process*, 1965, *4*, 1–20

Lederer W, & Jackson D. *Mirages of marriage*. New York: Norton, 1968

Lieberman MA, Yalom ID, & Miles MB. *Encounter groups: First facts*. New York: Basic Books, 1973

Rappaport AF. Conjugal relationship enhancement programs. In DHL Olson (Ed.), *Treating relationships*. Lake Mills, IA: Graphic, 1976

Rogers C. *On encounter groups*. New York: Harper & Row, 1970

Ruesch J, & Bateson G. *Communication: The social matrix of psychiatry*. New York: Norton, 1951

Sprenkle D, & Fisher B. An empirical assessment of the books of family therapy. *Journal of Marital and Family Therapy.*, 1980, *6*, 131–139

7

Enrichment

Since the early 1970s there has been an increase in both the development and utilization of programs designed to "enrich" marital and family relationships. The term "marital enrichment" refers to those experiences designed to induce psychological "growth" in couples whose interactions are considered basically sound but who are seeking ways to make their relationships more psychologically satisfying.

Enrichment programs are structured, time-limited, educational experiences, usually conducted with groups of participants. The program structures usually consist of alternating didactic and experiential exercises. The focus of almost all such marital programs is the enhancement of communication skills, the broadening and deepening of emotional and/or sexual lives, and the reinforcing and fostering of existing marital strengths (Gurman & Kniskern, 1977). Enrichment per se is therefore primarily a movement toward preventive rather than remedial work with couples.

Marital enrichment may also be considered a component of the general area of Social Skills Training (SST) programs. Among these training programs are assertiveness training, communication training, relationship enhancement, structured learning therapy, and problem-solving techniques. All of the SST programs, including enrichment, share a structural nature (i.e., a pre-arranged, preprogrammed, time-limited sequence of lessons) and a focus on interpersonal skills (i.e., the skills taught are designed to improve the quality of

relationships with others, whether at home or at work). In addition, time-limited working contracts are negotiated with couples who do not necessarily see themselves as "sick" or dysfunctional but who want specific, circumscribed learning in a given area (L'Abate, 1980).

The term "enrichment" includes a variety of programs, such as "encounter," communication, and relationship enhancement (Hof & Miller, 1981; L'Abate, 1981; Sell, et al., 1980). In an early survey regarding the use of enrichment programs in the United States, Otto (1975) found that 23 professionals were conducting marital enrichment programs and reported having enriched a total of approximately 60,000 couples. More recently, Hof and Miller (1981) have listed at least 50 different existing enrichment programs, which have attracted from a handful to thousands of couple participants.

In order to condense and discuss the basic components of enrichment programs, this chapter reviews and summarizes three major program areas: (1) the enrichment model of David and Vera Mace, (2) the structured enrichment model of L'Abate and associates, and (3) miscellaneous programs that address the enrichment of couples.

BACKGROUND AND DEVELOPMENT

The historical antecedents of marital enrichment may be traced to several sources, including one of the first social skills training programs—Parent Effectiveness Training (Gordon, 1970). Gordon developed a time-limited, structured, educational group format designed to teach Rogerian communication skills to parents of small children. His program, like others that followed, was a direct outgrowth of the human potential movement in psychology. Resulting treatment emphases included direct confrontation skills, role-playing and psychodrama techniques, increased awareness, and attention to nonverbal behavior. In addition, sensitivity training and marathon group approaches, as opposed to individual treatment approaches, were used. These group approaches increasingly de-emphasized accepted traditional mental health treatment models, with a growing tendency to criticize and move away from the traditional "medical model" of "illness." Rather than viewing psychological difficulties as the result of an illness that needed to be treated, the human potential movement emphasized enhancing assets and strengths.

Parallel to the growth of the human potential movement in the late 1960s and early 1970s was an increase in the growth of self-help groups (e.g., Gamblers Anonymous, Neurotics Anonymous, Parents Without Partners). Self-help groups, like the human potential movement, rejected the medical model of illness and instead stressed personal growth and the learning of more effective ways to live with oneself and the world. In addition, self-help groups also rejected the presumed need for the extensive training of credentialed professionals in psychology, stressing not only the use of, but the growth of paraprofessionals in the field of mental health.

Other important historical antecedents of and continuing influences on the growth of marital enrichment and other social-skills training programs have been changes in consumer trends and increasing demands for brief, affordable treatment programs. This emphasis on affordability has stemmed in part from major mental health funding sources that began to demand cost-effectiveness and accountability of services. The creation of short-term, affordable treatment programs has also been increasingly influenced by consumers who have demanded not only more effective, but relatively quicker solutions to difficulties.

An additional antecedent of and influence on marital enrichment programs has been the growth of behavior therapy and behavioral technologies that emphasize, among other things, self-control strategies and gradual, linear, step-by-step problem-solving approaches. As a precursor of marital enrichment programs, behavioral approaches have developed programmed, interpersonal relations techniques that can be conducted in educational group formats.

Finally, there has been a re-emerging emphasis on family-life education since the latter half of the 1970s. Family-life education programs have increasingly stressed psychological health and the learning of skills that will enhance the existing mental health of the family.

The first marital enrichment programs in the United States were developed by David Mace, who began to conduct weekend retreats for the Quakers in 1961 (Mace, 1975a, 1975b); Herbert Otto, who began the Family Resource Development Program (Otto, 1975); Antoinette and Leon Smith, who in 1966 began to train leader couples in the United Methodist Church (L'Abate, 1977); and the Catholic Marriage Encounter movement, which was brought to the United States from Spain in 1967 (Doherty, et al., 1978). Thus the first sources of enrichment were primarily nonprofessional and religious in nature. Since the early 1970s, however, the majority of enrichment programs have not been religious in nature, but, instead, have been developed within the field of professional psychology—e.g., Association of Couples for Marital Enrichment (Mace & Mace, 1976a, 1976b), Minnesota Couples Communication Program (see Chapter 3), Conjugal Relationship Modification—CRM (Chapter 6), Pairing Enrichment Program (Travis & Travis, 1975a, 1975b), Marriage Diagnostic Laboratory (Stein, 1975), and Enrichment (L'Abate, 1977).

MAJOR PHILOSOPHIES AND CURRENT CONCEPTS

Enrichment defines a particular approach that is unique from other types of marital intervention. L'Abate (1977) defined enrichment as "a process of intervention based on prearranged, programmed lessons and exercises dealing with interpersonal relations between and among members" (p. 5). This process emphasizes the systematic arrangement of exercises and lessons in a gradual hierarchical sequence that is assumed to be helpful to the family or to family members. It is neither primarily educational nor primarily therapeutic, but combines a preventive educational/therapeutic model, presumably administered to nonclinical couples. Its practitioners can also be individuals with less extensive training than marriage therapists.

Otto (1976, p. 13) defined marriage enrichment as "programs for couples who have what they perceive to be fairly well functioning marriages, and who wish to make their marriages even more mutually satisfying." VanderHaar and VanderHarr (1976, p. 195) claimed that the purpose of enrichment is "to enable couples to discover deep love, intimacy, and joy in marriage by: developing better communication patterns, learning to accept one another's strengths and weaknesses, and establishing mutually acceptable goals."

Hopkins and Hopkins (1976, p. 230) wrote, concerning their labs, that "the lab is education, not therapy," while Smith and Smith (1976, p. 240) claimed that "the purpose of a Marriage Communication Lab is to make good marriages better—to assist couples who have fully satisfying marriages to improve their relationships." Thus marital enrichment programs may be viewed as existing on a continuum somewhere between therapy and family-life education. Unlike many other educational programs, however, marital enrichment includes structured, experiential activities integrated within the didactic components of the program.

In general, enrichment may be conceptualized as an affirmative educational process (Otto, 1975; Satir, 1975) that attempts to teach couples skills by which they can develop the full potential of their relationships (Mace & Mace, 1976a, 1976b). Change presumably occurs through experiential learning; therefore the process of marital enrichment programs is considered their most important component.

Enrichment is a growth model that stresses the basic philosophy of the human potential movement. Therefore enrichment programs usually contain an underlying belief that most of what is present psychologically in humans can be accepted and enhanced to produce a higher level of health and functioning; that is, one can more fully develop what is already

healthy rather than attempt to remedy interpersonal and intrapersonal deficits.

Finally, the enrichment movement seeks to reconceptualize marriage, not as a static institution, but as a dynamic dyadic relationship in which increased intimacy enhances the individual's freedom within the relationship (Mace & Mace, 1975a, 1975b). Thus, psychological growth is the major emphasis and philosophy underlying enrichment.

THE INTERVENTION PROCESS

As has been stated, the major rationale of enrichment programs is the enhancement of the growth of the dyadic relationship. Since this enhancement or growth focuses on an already satisfactory, or functional, relationship, assessment and/or screening techniques for potential participants are rare. Clients, who are usually volunteers, are assumed to be normal, and the group leader or enricher is viewed as a teacher/leader. Concerning the role of the teacher/leader, many enrichment programs emphasize the use of male–female co-leadership in order to provide satisfactory relationship models.

The following are the major techniques used in enrichment programs:

1. *Role-playing.* Participants may create roles, change roles with others, or act out assigned roles in order to become aware of specific attitudes and behaviors.
2. *Teaching communication skills.* These skills usually involve "checking out" what is heard; restating what is heard to achieve a shared meaning; making prescribed statements about feelings, wants, thoughts, actions, sensations; speaking for oneself by using "I" statements; and negotiating agreements to communicate with others on specified topics.
3. *Action imagination.* Participants are asked to fantasize situations, then imagine and/or rehearse their responses to them.
4. *Movement.* Movement may be free movement or prescribed movement exercises (e.g., trust walks).

Most enrichment programs involve either a weekend retreat or six to eight weekly sessions for 8 to 10 couples. Couples who are clearly dysfunctional are usually excluded from enrichment programs, although criteria for exclusion are rarely clarified in most programs. The format is usually highly structured, although some programs are fairly unstructured. The degree of involvement by participants varies, as do the specific techniques used.

Some programs offer an advanced enrichment or follow-up experience, whereas others encourage informal, ongoing support groups of enriched couples and families. Religion-sponsored programs are usually eclectic, while secular programs usually stress one major theoretical orientation and/or theme (e.g., humanistic, experiential, communications). The majority of Enrichment programs, however, focus on the development of communication skills.

Religious Enrichment Programs

Christian Marriage Enrichment Retreat. This program is Baptist-sponsored and focuses on an effort to integrate Christian values into the couple's marriage. The program includes couples' discussions of priorities, a focus on verbal and nonverbal communication skills, and instruction and discussion about the meaning of love, intimacy, and individuality (Cowley & Adams, 1976). Satirian family sculpture techniques and written exercises are employed as diagnostic tools (Green, 1976). Usually, 10 couples participate in a weekend retreat away from home.

Marriage Enrichment Program. This program is sponsored by the Reformed Church in America. Its rationale of "relational theology" states that Christ's sacrifice of Himself for the church is an appropriate model for marriage; a couple's relationship should be "as intimate as Christ's love for the church" (VanderHaar & VanderHaar, 1976). Experiential aspects of the relationship are stressed, as is unstructured experience, with little cognitive input. Sessions include the use of body awareness techniques, nonverbal exercises, films, discussions of the Bible, and exercises with building blocks to symbolically address various issues (Otto, 1976). Maximum emphasis is placed on spouse interaction, with a minimal emphasis on group interaction.

Marriage Enrichment Lab. This program is the second phase of the Reformed Church's Marriage Enrichment Program. Phase II is based on Frankl's logotherapy, which stressed that man is free to choose his own attitudes and create his own meaning. In the course of the group sessions, spouses interact apart from and with the group (Van Eck & Van Eck, 1976). Marriage is viewed as a system wherein partners negotiate and express their wants in an effort to attain intimacy. Intimacy is conceptualized as the "key value" of marriage within this formulation (Clinebell, 1976).

The Marriage Communication Lab. This program is sponsored by the Church of the Disciples of Christ (Hopkins & Hopkins, 1976) and is modeled on the Reformed Church of America's (VanderHaar & VanderHaar, 1976) program. The religious dimension of the Marriage Communication Lab is, however, less explicit than that of the Reformed Church. The Lab follows a health and process-centered model by which couples help other couples. This format permits an almost leaderless enrichment process (Mace & Mace, 1975a, 1975b); couples participate in an experiential, educational group process in which they draw their own conclusions about their marital interactions after a period of reflection. A number of cognitive components are emphasized such as the use of poetry and books as educational tools, a discussion of conflict (Satir, 1972), and a discussion of values (Simon, et al., 1972). A section on sexuality, which utilizes Otto's (1976) *Love Life Development Test*, is also included.

Secular Enrichment Approaches

More Joy in Your Marriage Program. This program (Otto & Otto, 1976) is based on the assumption that all relationships need to be rejuvenated after a certain length of time. Otto theorized that his program is applicable to all motivated couples who are willing to make a commitment to change. Structured as a weekend retreat, "More Joy" includes writing exercises that enable couples to specify issues within their relationships. Among the topics addressed in various sessions are constructive and destructive patterns of conflict, primal sensory experiences, and marital strengths and weaknesses. Otto also described an "action" program that couples may follow at home to bridge the gap between the enrichment experience and home life.

Marriage Renewal Retreat. This program (Schmitt & Schmitt, 1976) is based on the Rankian idea that experience itself heals. Thus "emotional insight" is more important than cognitive insight in any human relationship. As part of their framework, Schmitt and Schmitt forsee the possibility of changing the name of their enrichment program to Marital Rebirth Retreats. According to them, during the process of rebirth, the individual goes from a state of union, to separation, and back to union. Union is abandoned because of a will to grow and to avoid annihilation of the self. The union that follows the rebirth of self is then viewed as a "peak experience." Theoretically, after affirmation of the self, the individual returns to union with a capacity for deeper encounter. The goal of marriage, according to this model, is growth toward fulfillment. Within this context, marital happiness results from learning to come to terms with the paradox of union and separation in a "mature" way. Therefore renewal weekends are spent identifying and analyzing four distinct stages of marriage: ecstasy, conflict, ecstasy, and freedom.

Positive Partners. This program (Hayward, 1976) is a marital communication course involving three to six couples who actively participate in four to six sessions, each two hours long. Every marriage is considered unique; therefore no prescriptions for "good" marriages are offered. Group encounter is balanced with couple interaction in an effort to break the "intermarital taboo" that prevents couples from openly discussing their marriages with other couples.

Gestalt Marriage Enrichment. This program (Zinker & Leon, 1976), like Gestalt therapy, is process-centered (i.e., the process of communication takes precedence over the content). Thus awareness exercises are used to help couples focus on how people communicate. Criticism, support, and confrontation are used to provide adequate feedback for future change. Couples engage in "Creative Conflict," in which they release their conflict by beating pillows and shouting and by imitating and reversing roles. As described by Zinker and Leon, Gestalt

Marriage Enrichment is relatively unstructured, focuses on affects, and is both preventive and therapeutic.

Preventive Maintenance. This program (Sherwood & Scherer, 1975) is a cyclical model, describing how relationships are established and maintained over time. Couples learn to apply new theoretical concepts to their marriages, based on the authors' assumption that individuals *need* concepts to guide their behaviors. These concepts include sharing, negotiation, role clarity, stability, and the meaning of disruptions. Affective and cognitive concepts are considered, although the main emphasis of this program is a cognitive one. Role clarity is linked to commitment (i.e., as roles become clearer, commitment is possible, and as commitment occurs, there is predictability in the relationship, greater stability, and more commitment). The authors state that, inevitably, an individual in a relationship will feel "pinched." A "pinch" is defined as a point at which there is an awareness of discomfort in the relationship. If a couple does not address the "pinches," more problems will arise, leading to an increase in conflict and greater disruption. Disruption may be dealt with in three ways: (1) by renegotiating the expectations of the relationship, (2) by reconciling prematurely, or (3) by terminating the relationship. Sherwood and Scherer consider fighting and "pinches" the sources of new information. If the new information is not utilized for change through renegotiation, disruption becomes more and more intense. Ignoring a "pinch" or disruption can lead to psychological divorce, or what is called a "comfortable disaster."

The ACME Movement. Mace and Mace are the married founders of a Marriage Enrichment Movement called ACME—Association of Couples for Marriage Enrichment (Mace & Mace, 1976a, 1976b). ACME is a national organization composed of married couples whose primary goal is to develop and maintain effective support systems for Marriage Enrichment. The organization has stated its purposes as follows:

1. To encourage and help member couples to seek growth and enrichment in their own marriages.

2. To organize activities through which member couples can help each other in their quest for marital growth and enrichment.
3. To promote and support effective community services designed to foster successful marriages.
4. To seek to improve the public image of marriage as a relationship capable of fostering both personal growth and mutual fulfillment (Hopkins, et al., 1978, p. 1-7).

The Maces' approach to the problem of marital disharmony emphasizes prevention. Mace (1975a, p. 172) states that "what we wish to stress is the improvement of the relationship by the development of its unappropriated inner resources." Thus this movement is part of a growing concern for "redirecting the focus of psychology from a problem-oriented, negativistic emphasis on psychopathology which posits 'adjustment' as the ultimate goal of therapeutic intervention to a new awareness of man's strong positive potential for growth and self-actualization" (Nadeau, 1971, p. 1). Therefore, couples meet primarily to try to help each other improve, rather than adjust to, their marriages:

What we are now seeking to do, late in the day when the scene is already strewn with marital wrecks, is to equip married couples with the insight and training that will keep their marriages in such good order that the danger of going on the rocks will be as far as possible avoided (Mace, 1975b, p. 33).

Mace and Mace have cited two obstacles in American society that block the attempts of couples to achieve happier and more fulfilling marriages. The first obstacle is the myth of naturalism, which has asserted that success in marriage should come almost effortlessly to the normal adult and that anyone who has difficulties in this area is thereby identified as an inadequate person (Mace & Mace, 1976a). The second obstacle is the intermarital taboo that states that marriage is very private and very personal, and therefore, one must never talk to anyone else about what occurs in one's marriage. Because of these two cultural restraints, the married couple is often prevented from seeking or receiving help until they are in a state of desperation.

In its preventive efforts, ACME offers weekend retreats as one of its programs. In the retreat, one couple serves as participating facilitators rather than as leaders. There is no structured agenda; instead, topics initiated by the participants are addressed. These retreats, however, are seen as one-time experiences that are only the beginning of improvement in a couple's relationship. After the initial weekend retreat, additional marriage enrichment supports are provided by local chapters of ACME, which offer various programs and services.

ACME's main philosophy is that in each marital dyad, there exists inherent capacity for mutual fulfillment and development. Thus the programs offered by ACME are designed for couples who have fairly functional marriages and who desire additional growth.

Anecdotal reports suggest that involvement in ACME is a meaningful experience for couples, but no data on the effectiveness of ACME are available. Mace (1975a) himself, however, has issued an eloquent call for the collection of such data.

The Pairing Enrichment Program. This program (Travis & Travis, 1975a, 1975b) is based on the principles of self-actualization and interpersonal growth. The program is offered as a group experience for couples and consists of five sessions:

1. Being Aware, which focuses on awareness and acceptance of feelings.
2. Being Authentic, which attempts to teach the couple how to share genuinely in the relationship.
3. Being Free, which attempts to create an openness for experiencing each other.
4. Being Secure, which focuses on helping the couple support and appreciate each other's individuality.
5. The Beginning, which attempts to encourage ways in which the couple can keep their partnership moving in the direction they want it to grow.

Sessions are conducted in either a weekend format or a three-week format. The weekend format consists of five three-hour sessions that begin on Friday evening and terminate on Sunday evening. The sessions are separated by a three-hour session in which the couple privately practice suggested exercises. The three-week format consists of three weekly sessions that are held for three hours each. Suggested exercises are practiced at home rather than within the time period of the weekend format.

The Pairing Enrichment program is an action-oriented experience in communication, involving a blend of couple and limited group discussions, fantasy experiences, educational films, exploration of feelings and attitudes, sensory awareness exercises, communication exercises, intimate encounter exercises, leader-modeling, role-playing, and discussions of exercises (Travis & Travis, 1975a, 1975b).

Structured Marriage Enrichment Program. This program (L'Abate, 1977; L'Abate & Rupp, 1981) is a didactic, structured approach, using a number of distinct programs. Each program is designed with the goal of utilizing effective, humane, and inexpensive techniques for couples so that they may achieve greater self-differentiation and a higher quality of family life. In this approach, the marriage enrichment programs are constructed for specific purposes and/or situations, and they attempt to combine both the affective and cognitive aspects of living.

The programs are arranged for both clinical and nonclinical couples in preplanned and structured sequences. Each program is composed of three to six lessons, with each lesson containing five to six exercises.

The program is administered to a participating couple by the leader or the leader couple through a general procedure that involves several steps. In the first step, the participating couple is interviewed so that rapport may be established, an explanation and description of the enrichment program may be given, and the suitability for enrichment may be determined. A clear working contract is then negotiated. The second step involves an evaluation of the couple, using rating sheets and various tests. Evaluation includes the use of a Family Information Sheet, a Marital Questionnaire, a Semantic Differential Sheet, the Azrin Marital Happiness Scale, as well as several other scales (L'Abate & Rupp, 1981). In the third step, the couple is informed of the type of enrichment program that, based on the evaluation, best suits their needs. They are then given a series of six weekly enrichment lessons, focusing on a specific topic or issue. Re-evaluation or post-test of the couple is the fourth step, using the same instruments used in the initial

evaluation. The last step is a feedback session in which the couple's reactions to enrichment are elicited and recorded; the leader's feedback to the couple is given in a positive fashion, and various possibilities for any future work are considered.

The following are examples of the types and range of programs offered for couples:

1. Confronting Change. This program is designed to help the couple realize their need for change by addressing why the relationship should change, helping each individual to accept personal responsibility for his or her own change, and helping the couple establish short- and long-range individual, marital, and familial goals.

2. Sexual Clarification. This program is designed to help couples learn more about each other's sexual attitudes. It involves the couple's learning to talk more openly about sex. After addressing communication, the program focuses on the meaning of sex and sexuality in marriage, learning to laugh about sex, and learning to give pleasure to each other.

3. Sexual Fulfillment for Couples. This program is designed to teach communication skills concerning anxiety-provoking sexual issues.

4. Cohabitation. This program is designed for couples who cannot make up their minds whether to separate, continue cohabiting, or marry. It involves helping couples clarify both their values and their issues.

5. Reciprocity. This program helps the couple to explore and understand why they married, to increase old marital satisfactions, to elicit new marital satisfactions, and to teach compromise. This program is based on the behavioral concepts developed by Azrin and his co-workers (see Chapter 11).

6. Marital Negotiation. This program helps the couple realize false assumptions that exist in their marital relationship, helps them increase awareness of how each partner communicates with the other, and instructs them in bargaining with each other about conflicts.

7. Assertiveness. This program teaches couples to communicate effectively their points of view, rights, and desires.

8. Working Through. This program is designed to help couples focus on and resolve their problems.
9. Conflict Resolution. This program is designed to teach couples step-by-step skills in order to negotiate conflict issues.

EVALUATION AND RESEARCH

In their review of marital enrichment programs, Gurman and Kniskern (1977) noted that although a number of studies have concluded that such programs are effective, there have also been numerous methodologic problems in assessing the outcome of marital enrichment. Gurman and Kniskern located 29 marital and premarital enrichment studies, of which 23 used untreated control groups. Of these studies, 86 percent were conducted in non-church-related programs, with close to 75 percent of the subjects recruited from university communities. Of the programs, 93 percent were conducted in a group setting, most with weekly meetings over an average span of 7 weeks.

The outcome criteria in most studies were self-reports of overall marital satisfaction and adjustment, measures of communication skills, and various individual and personality variables (e.g., introversion–extroversion, stability–instability, self-actualization, self-esteem, and perception of spouse or partner). Positive change was consistently demonstrated on 60 percent of the criterion tests. However, 84 percent of the criterion measures used were participants' self-reports, with 58 percent of the studies using participants' reports as the sole criterion for change and another 26 percent relying partially on self-report data. Furthermore, follow-up of participants to assess any enduring changes was conducted in only four of the studies reviewed (Burns, 1972; Nadeau, 1971; Swicegood, 1974; Wieman, 1973). In all of these studies, only a moderate maintenance of gains was found. Overall, however, the results of controlled studies are positive; 67 percent found that program effects exceeded those of no-treatment control groups. Nevertheless, of the 29 studies reviewed, 11 showed no significant differences.

Hof and Miller (1981) reviewed most of the relevant literature on marital enrichment. They compared outcome studies of marriage enrichment experiences with the Minnesota Couples Communication Program (reviewed in Chapter 3), the Conjugal Relationship Enhancement Program (reviewed in Chapter 6), and other miscellaneous communication and behavior exchange training programs (reviewed in various parts of this book). They found results similar to those in Gurman and Kniskern's earlier review.

Ganahl (1981) investigated the efficacy of the Structured Enrichment Programs (SEP) of L'Abate and associates in producing changes in couples' marital adjustment, satisfaction, and communication. The effects of the enrichment program type, sex, number of facilitators used, and clients' initial level of adjustment were also assessed. Subjects were 127 married couples who were either clients at the Family Study Center of Georgia State University or university students who volunteered for research credit as part of an introductory psychology course. Subjects were in their late 20s, well-educated, of diverse occupational backgrounds, and had been married for 2 to 7 years, with 0 to 1 children. The population was composed predominantly of Caucasian couples, with either Protestant or no religious preference.

Enrichment group results were compared with a no-treatment control group, a group receiving written homework instructions in communication, an enrichment group with homework assignments, and a clinical enrichment group composed of couples who presented with marital difficulties. The clinical enrichment group was contrasted with a clinical sample receiving marital therapy.

Results were analyzed using one-factor analyses of variance, with analysis of covariance applied to positive results of groups that were significantly different from one another on pretest scores. Improvement was assessed by the Locke-Wallace Short Marital Adjustment Test (MAT), the Primary Communication Inventory (PCI), the Marital Happiness Scale (MHS) of Azrin, and a composite test battery composed of questions concerning marital satisfaction with a variety of areas of functioning. Tests were administered on a pre–post basis, with 6 to 7 weeks intervening between pre- and post-testing.

Results indicated that SEP was effective

in producing improved marital satisfaction and adjustment. Results were mixed for improved communication. The enrichment group showed positive changes on the MAT, the composite test battery, and the communication item of the MHS. The enrichment and homework group produced positive results on the battery and the PCI. The homework group produced positive results on the battery scores alone. No significant differences were noted between the raw gain scores of these groups on any measure.

Clinical groups were not evaluated on the MAT or PCI. The clinical enrichment group achieved significant improvement on the MHS only, while the clinical therapy group showed significant improvement on the battery, the MHS, total score and the communication item of the MHS. Differences between the clinical and nonclinical groups, following analysis of covariance, were nonsignificant. The clinical enrichment group was found to be inferior to the therapy group on the battery and communication item of the MHS.

No sex differences were found in response to treatments, program types, or therapist sex and number. Minimal differences were found between programs, and nonsignificant trends were found favoring male therapists, but these latter trends are highly speculative.

Results were discussed in terms of their implications for the extension of enrichment programs to clinical populations and to nonclinical settings using paraprofessionals as facilitators/educators.

It was recommended that future research include a biased assignment procedure for subjects in order to address the pretest differences of clinical and nonclinical groups and that nonparticipant and behavioral measures be included. Replication studies on diverse populations were also recommended in order to test the generalizability of results. More attention to isolating the active components of successful treatments was also recommended.

Some studies yielding data on the effectiveness of other forms of marital enrichment have been conducted. Nadeau (1971) treated 13 couples in a "Marital Enrichment Group" (MEG). This group was designed to "help them focus on the positive qualities of their relationship, to increase their awareness of feelings and sensitivity to their marriage, and to improve the communication patterns between them" (p. 5). The Marital Communication Scale, the Marital Roles Scale, the Personality Trait List, Interaction Testing, and the Group Experience Evaluation were administered to these couples and to 13 couples in a no-treatment control group on a pre–post test basis: "Results from this study suggest that participation in the MEG increases non-verbal communication skills, causes one's view of self, spouse, and marriage to be more positive, and increases the effectiveness of interaction patterns between spouses" (p. 84).

Bruder (1972) found that couples who participated in a marital enrichment program focusing on communication skills showed improvements on the Conjugal Life Questionnaire and the Relationship Change Scale when compared with couples who had not participated in the program.

Wittrup (1973) had four couples participate in a semi-structured, eight-session, marital enrichment program that involved work in the areas of goal-contracting, communication skills, role and value clarification, spouse role expectations, sexuality, resolution of differences over in-laws, and "marital contracting." No significant pre- to postintervention changes on the Interpersonal Check List were noted. Positive changes in attitudes toward the marriage on a specially designed instrument, the Wittrup Marriage Inventory, were found for three of the four couples. All but one of the couples reported the resolution of significant relationship problems that had existed prior to their participation in the marriage enrichment program, and all four couples described their marriage relationships as improved at the time of the postintervention interview. Wittrup (1973) concluded from his study that,

the Marriage Enrichment Program was effective in changing the marriage relationship; that the Marriage Enrichment Program may be an alternate form of marriage counseling; and that the amount of marriage relationship change is related to the degree of resistance exhibited by the individuals in the sample group (p. 77).

The results of Nadeau (1971), Bruder (1972), and Wittrup (1973) are encouraging, but they failed to document rigorously the overall improvements in the marriages on a comprehensive or objective multi-level basis.

Sauber (1974) addressed the outcome of

preventive enrichment programs by evaluating the Methodist Enrichment approach developed by Carl Clarke (1970). He evaluated the outcome of this approach, using 35 couples drawn from a university community who had participated in the program. On the basis of the couples' responses to open-ended questions, he developed a list of 34 outcomes related to the respondents, their spouses, and their marital relationships. Percentages were given for each item in terms of marginal influence, negative effect, considerable influence, or positive effect. Most of the responses were highly positive. This kind of subjective assessment makes it difficult to reach any conclusion or assessment of change, however, since no baseline evaluation or objective measures were used. Nevertheless, Sauber advocated marital enrichment as a model of primary prevention.

Another study (Wagner, et al., 1980) addressed the hypothesis that paradoxical and linear written messages (Selvini-Palazzoli, et al., 1978) as supplements to marital enrichment programs increase the programs' effectiveness:

Four groups of couples were investigated before and after a six-week session of marriage enrichment. Group I received no enrichment and Group II received only the enrichment program. Group III received the enrichment program and paradoxically worded messages. Group IV received enrichment plus linear letters. Pre- and post-assessment were done on a happiness scale, communication sale, and a marital progress scale. Although the enrichment group utilizing paradoxical letters did demonstrate positive pre–post changes, they changed less than the couples who only had the enrichment or the enrichment plus linear messages. The lack of support for the paradoxical messages was partially attributed to the fact that the outcome measures were linear and possibly missed the complexity assessed by paradoxical intervention (Wagner, Weeks & L'Abate 1980, p. 44).

DISCUSSION

The fact that the number and use of marital enrichment programs are growing cannot be overlooked. Currently, marital enrichment programs constitute a distinct and separate entity within the field of marital therapy, with their use as a form of intervention gaining both popularity and acceptance with consumers of psychological services.

The major potential and focus of enrichment programs is preventive; that is, specific attempts are made to prevent current and future deterioration in a functioning marriage. In addition, many, if not most, of the marriage enrichment programs address specific issues and concerns that may be viewed as potential problem areas in any dyadic relationship. Marriage enrichment programs also offer a humanistic promise of growth rather than remedial intervention; that is, the potential of relationships is addressed, rather than the treatment of a problem in order to return a couple to a normative mode of functioning. From a theoretical viewpoint, marital enrichment programs offer the antithesis of the medical model, for the components stress growth through education, experience, and, in many cases, self-help.

The role of the therapist/facilitator in marital enrichment programs is consistent with an antimedical model orientation, for many of the programs use trained paraprofessional leaders to treat couples in group formats. The use of leaders without traditional forms of mental health training can not only provide a large number of leaders/facilitators, but can also be viewed as a separate and distinct force in the mental health field. As an outgrowth of self-help movements, both the philosophy and type of leader in marital enrichment programs is revolutionary: there is an increasing, visible rejection of the traditional view that dysfunctional couples need to be treated by experts.

The short-term, structured group formats offer the potential not only for addressing large numbers of consumers, but also for providing a cost-effective intervention for couples. If, as a few seminal studies indicate, marriage enrichment programs can produce long-term, positive changes within couple relationships, they can then provide a relatively inexpensive format affordable to a vast majority of couples, rather than to primarily middle to upper class couples. In addition, structured group formats are easy to implement and do not require the leader to initiate a broad range of skills. Therefore, cost-effectiveness can also be viewed from the standpoint of the cost of training leaders.

Marital enrichment programs have been designed primarily for use with the functioning couple. There is the possibility, however, that some programs have applicability to more dysfunctional couples. In addition, all of the programs described in this chapter have the potential for use as an adjunct form of treatment for the dysfunctional couple who is being treated with traditional forms of marital therapy. Paraprofessionals might provide another dimension to the therapeutic process by offering enrichment services concurrent with marital therapy.

Some marital enrichment programs have been widely researched, whereas the outcome of others has not been addressed. Data exist to indicate the potential of marital enrichment programs, however, at least in the area of communication skills. If marital enrichment programs should prove only to facilitate couples communications skills, however, a primary aspect of couples' relationship problems will have been addressed in a format that is, at the least, more efficient and cost-effective than traditional couples therapy.

The values espoused by marital enrichment programs offer a positive view of marriage: it is not seen simply as an institution, but as a dynamic relationship with the potential for increased personal and interpersonal satisfactions. The values of marital enrichment programs are consistent with their underlying theoretical assumptions, for the values are humanistic and growth-oriented, rather than remedial-oriented.

Although one can view a number of positive potentials for the marriage enrichment movement, one must also consider the potential negative impact of this movement. Concerning the underlying theoretical orientation of marital enrichment programs, it has been stated that most programs are educational, with an underlying rationale of developing the full potential of a relationship through experience (Mace & Mace, 1976a, 1976b). This development of potential is assumed to build on an already existing level of health, in the belief that enhancement will occur primarily by improving communication and negotiation skills.

These underlying assumptions raise several questions that have not been empirically validated. First, what exactly is the full potential of a human relationship? Second, does one always learn by experience, and what does one learn by which experience? Third, is there an existing specifiable mode of health in most marriages? And, fourth, do improved communi-

nication skills improve what is presently a nebulously defined quality of a relationship?

Although the use of paraprofessionals suggests numerous possibilities, one must question the training of leaders. At present, there is little data on how leaders are selected, how they are trained, and in some cases, exactly what they are trained to do. The leader in most programs is assumed to be a model, and if a high degree of learning does indeed occur through modeling, one would then assume that the leader's qualities would be crucial to the program's success. No current marital enrichment programs, however, address the issues of selection and training of leaders.

The majority of marital enrichment programs teach specific skills that presumably promote growth. In some programs, however, primarily the religiously oriented ones, it is not clear what underlies concepts such as the true nature of marriage or God's purpose for marriage. Other programs provide a number of experiential exercises without stating or defining clearly what is to be learned.

Concerning the clients served, it is clear that marital enrichment programs are affordable to a large number of couples. As with almost all forms of intervention in the field of mental health, however, clients must be verbal, able to understand a variety of concepts, and, until it is proved different, fairly well educated. How disadvantaged groups can enhance their relationships is not addressed, nor is the issue of relationships among various ethnic groups and subcultures. It is difficult to imagine financially impoverished, uneducated, racially or ethnically varied couples benefiting from enrichment in the same way as middle-class, educated, white couples.

The outcomes of enrichment have yet to be rigidly measured, and available information on outcome, although seemingly positive, should be cautiously studied. Five important issues related to outcome have yet to be addressed. They are the durability of enrichment-induced change, the effects on the marriage of enrichment-induced change, the range of potential participants, demonstration of change through nonparticipant rating sources, and the specification of change-inducing components.

Marital enrichment programs tend to be associated with highly enthusiastic testimonials by participants and program leaders. In reviewing the outcome data from these programs, however, growing controversy becomes evident regarding long-term effectiveness. Critics suggest that benefits may be illusory and may produce negativism and discouragement when the emotional "high" is replaced by the stark reality of an unchanged relationship.

Hof, Epstein & Miller (1980) have questioned the quality of outcome studies that over-rely on participant self-reports, inadequate control groups, failure to differentiate varieties of enrichment programs that have different goals, and a lack of consensus in defining what is a valid, clinically relevant effect.

Another issue related to all enrichment programs is the effective screening of participants. Although some programs make references to screening procedures, there is a lack of basic or obvious criteria to exclude or refer elsewhere those couples who are (1) uncooperative, extremely hostile, or angry, and indicate the existence of projective identification and excessive use of blaming ("you") and generalizations ("never," "always"); (2) chaotic, disorganized, and in crisis, and indicate that they are considering or have considered separation or even divorce, and in the screening interview show confusion of goals in their own lives or marriages, or think that the structured experience will have magical results or be a substitute for therapy; (3) experiencing a recent loss (death of close relative, moving away of children) and are attempting to reinstate this loss through the experience of enrichment; and (4) exhibiting entrenched psychosomatic or delusional systems that make them externalize most of their tensions outside themselves or their marriage.

In addition to a more specific taxonomy in screening procedures, a more detailed taxonomy for screening excessive, defensive narrowness needs to be ascertained before admission to a structured program, i.e., (1) defensive statements, such as strong denial of any tension and/or conflict, suggesting either a digital (either–or) or vague view of life and the self; (2) superficial goals and views about the nature of life; (3) mixed or confused priorities about self, marriage, children, work, and family (L'Abate, 1976); (4) inappropriate or incongruent affect, with a minimum of congruent "I" statements; (5) excessive polarization in the marriage, as shown by overexpressivity in the woman and underexpressivity in the man (sometimes this pattern is reversed).

Furthermore, no matter how carefully participants may be screened, with assumptions of functionality, it is inevitable in any program that occasionally a dysfunctional couple will become participants in an experience that requires minimum levels of marital health and functionality. If and when the dysfunctional couple become participants in an enrichment program, the leader must be able to intervene to defuse the impact of the dysfunctional couple on the group participants, neutralize the dysfunctional couple's behavior, or terminate their participation in the enrichment program. Currently, however, not only are there no existing guidelines for the problem of the inappropriate participant in most marital enrichment programs, but there are no assumptions that leaders/trainers must have a minimal level of clinical therapeutic expertise in order to address difficulties with couples who would be labeled clinical, rather than functional or healthy.

Concerning the underlying and overt assumptions of enrichment, numerous value questions are raised. There are inherent assumptions that a marriage will be "happier" if certain role clarities are achieved. What exactly are these role clarities? Do they conform to traditional views of the husband–wife relationship or do they espouse other ways of relating? There are also assumptions that intimacy is an ultimate, almost peak-experience, goal. Is intense intimacy attainable by most couples and, if achieved, can it be sustained? There are also assumptions that there is one way (although rarely clear) to relate. What is *the* way to relate? Does this one way ignore other potentials in human relationships? Finally, there is an inherent approval of only a legal marriage as a viable dyadic relationship. Couples who live together are ignored, as are same-sex couples, couples who are involved but do not live together, and varied group forms of relationships.

THE FUTURE

Smith, Shoffner, and Scott (1979), in a review of the Marriage and Family Enrichment movement, expressed several major concerns about marriage enrichment as a new professional area. They stated that it offers a new cure-all for everyone, with questionable training of leaders, higher expectations, beliefs that couples and families will be either "totally enriched" or "closed," and a major assumption that enrichment may become one of life's peak experiences. Finally, they state that no hard evidence is as yet available to claim any preventive benefits.

Even beyond Smith, et al.'s (1979) concerns, the underlying assumptions of enrichment need to be further questioned. The training of leaders, as well as the content of what they are teaching, needs to be evaluated. Clients other than middle-class whites must be considered, and both process and outcome research is needed. Finally, one must question whether the theories of marital enrichment simply support a set of values related to traditional, idealistic views of the marital relationship, which in turn support traditional views of sex roles and functions in our society. For marital enrichment to become a viable and professional treatment modality, it must still be adequately defined, implemented, and evaluated.

REFERENCES

Bruder RC. *Effects of a marriage enrichment program upon marital communication and adjustment.* Unpublished doctoral dissertation, Purdue University, 1972

Burns CW. Effectiveness of the basic encounter group in marriage counseling. *Dissertation Abstracts International,* 1972, *33,* 3–B, p. 1281

Clarke, C. Group procedures for increasing positive feedback between married partners. *The Family Coordinator,* 1970, *19,* 324–328

Clinebell HJ. Cassette programs for training and enrichment. In HA Otto (Ed.), *Marriage and family enrichment: New perspectives and programs.* Nashville, TN: Abingdon, 1976

Cowley ADS, & Adams RS. The family home evening: A national ongoing family enrichment program. In HA Otto (Ed.), *Marriage and family enrichment: New perspectives and programs.* Nashville, TN: Abingdon 1976

Doherty WJ, McCabe P, & Ryder RG. Marriage encounter: A critical appraisal. *Journal of Marriage and Family Counseling,* 1978, *4,* 99–107

Ganahl GF. *Effects of client, treatment and therapist variables on the outcome of structured marital enrichment.* Unpublished doctoral dissertation, Georgia State University, 1981

Gordon T. *Parent effectiveness training.* New York: Peter H. Wyden, 1970

Green H, Jr. A Christian marriage enrichment retreat. In HA Otto (Ed.), *Marriage and family enrichment: New perspectives and programs.* Nashville, TN: Abingdon 1976

Gurman AS, & Kniskern DP. Enriching research on marital enrichment programs. *Journal of Marriage and Family Counseling,* 1977, *3,* 3–10

Hayward D. Positive partners: A marriage enrichment communication course. In HA Otto (Ed.), *Marriage and family enrichment: New perspectives and programs.* Nashville, TN: Abingdon 1976

Hof L, & Miller WR. *Marriage enrichment, philosophy, process, and program.* Bowie, MD: Robert J. Brady Co., 1981

Hof L, Epstein N, & Miller WR. Integrating attitudinal and behavioral change in marital enrichment. *Family Relations,* 1980, *29,* 241–248

Hopkins L, Hopkins R, Mace C, & Mace V. *Toward better marriages: The handbook of the Association of Couples for Marriage Enrichment (ACME).* Winston-Salem, NC: ACME, 1978

Hopkins P, & Hopkins L. The marriage communication labs. In HA Otto (Ed.), *Marriage and family enrichment: New perspectives and programs.* Nashville, TN: Abingdon, 1976

L'Abate L. *Understanding and helping the individual in the family.* New York: Grune & Stratton, 1976

L'Abate L. *Enrichment:. Structured interventions with couples, families, and groups.* Washington, DC: University press of America, 1977

L'Abate L. Screening couples for marital enrichment programs. *American Journal of Family Therapy,* 1980, *8,* 74–77

L'Abate L. Skill training programs for couples for families. In AS Gurman & DP Kniskern (Eds.), *Handbook of family therapy.* New York: Brunner/Mazel, 1981

L'Abate L, & Rupp G. *Enrichment: Skills training for family life.* Washington, DC: University Press of America, 1981

Mace DR. Marriage enrichment concepts for research. *The Family Coordinator,* 1975a, *24,* 171–173

Mace DR. We call it ACME. *Small Group Behavior,* 1975b, *6,* 31–44

Mace DR, & Mace V. Marriage enrichment: A preventive group approach for couples. In DHL Olson (Ed.), *Treating relationships.* Lake Mills, IA: Graphic, 1976a

Mace DR, & Mace V. The selection, training and certification of facilitators for marriage enrichment programs. *The Family Coordinator*, 1976b, *25*, 117–125

Nadeau KG. *An examination of some effects of the marital enrichment group*. Unpublished doctoral dissertation, University of Florida, 1971

Otto HA. Marriage and family enrichment programs in North America: Report and analysis. *The Family Coordinator*, 1975, *24*, 137–142

Otto HA (Ed.). *Marriage and family enrichment: New perspectives and programs*. Nashville, TN: Abingdon, 1976

Otto HA, & Otto R. The more joy in your marriage program. In HA Otto (Ed.), *Marriage and family enrichment: New perspectives and programs*. Nashville, TN: Abingdon, 1976

Satir V. *Peoplemaking*. Palo Alto, CA: Science & Behavior Books, 1972

Satir V. Family life education—A perspective on the educator. In S Miller (Ed.), *Marriages and families: Enrichment through communication*. Beverly Hills, CA: Sage Publications, 1975

Sauber SR. Primary prevention and the marital enrichment group. *Journal of Family Counseling*, 1974, *2*, 38–44

Schmitt A, & Schmitt D. Marriage renewal retreats. In HA Otto (Ed.), *Marriage and family enrichment: New perspectives and programs*. Nashville, TN: Abingdon, 1976

Sell HD, Shoffner SM, Farris MC, & Hill EW. *Enriching relationships: A guide to marriage and family enrichment literature*. Greensboro, NC: Department of Child Development and Family Relations, University of North Carolina, 1980

Selvini-Palazzoli M, Boscolo L, Cecchin G, & Prata G. *Paradox and counterparadox*. New York: Jason Aronson, 1978

Sherwood JJ, & Scherer JJ. A model for couples: How two can grow together. *Small Group Behavior*, 1975, *6*, 11–29

Simon S, Howe L, & Kirshenbaum H. *Values clarification*. New York: Hart Publishing, 1972

Smith I, & Smith A. Developing a national marriage communication lab training program. In HA Otto (Ed.), *Marriage and family enrichment: New perspectives and programs*. Nashville, TN: Abingdon, 1976

Smith RM, Shoffner SM, & Scott JP. Marriage and family enrichment: A new professional area. *The Family Coordinator*, 1979, *28*, 87–93

Stein EV. MARDILAB: An experiment in marriage enrichment. *The Family Coordinator*, 1975, *24*, 167–170

Swicegood MS. *An evaluative study of one approach to marital enrichment*. Unpublished doctoral dissertation, University of North Carolina (Greensboro), 1974

Travis P, & Travis R. Marital health and marriage enrichment. *Alabama Journal of Medical Sciences*, 1975a, *12*, 172–176

Travis P, & Travis R. The pairing enrichment program: Actualizing the marriage. *The Family Coordinator*, 1975b, *24*, 161–165

Van Eck B, and Van Eck B. The Phase II marriage enrichment lab. In HA Otto (Ed.), *Marriage and family enrichment: New perspectives and programs*. Nashville, TN: Abingdon, 1976

VanderHaar D, & VanderHaar T. The marriage enrichment program—phase I. In HA Otto (Ed.), *Marriage and family enrichment: New perspectives and programs*. Nashville, TN: Abingdon Press, 1976

Wagner V, Weeks G, & L'Abate L. Enrichment and written message with couples. *American Journal of Family Therapy*, 1980, *8*, 36–45

Wieman RJ. *Conjugal relationships. Modification and reciprocal reinforcement: A comparison of treatments for marital discord*. Unpublished doctoral dissertation, Pennsylvania State University, 1973

Wittrup RG. *Marriage enrichment: A preventive counseling program designed to attain marriage potential*. Unpublished doctoral dissertation, Western Michigan University, 1973

Zinker JC, & Leon P. Gestalt perspective: A marriage enrichment program. In HA Otto (Ed.), *Marriage and family enrichment: New perspectives and programs*. Nashville, TN: Abingdon, 1976

8

Conflict Resolution

Anger as a primary factor underlying marital dysfunction has been noted and discussed in numerous theoretical and applied works (Bach & Wyden, 1969; Bahr & Boyd, 1971; Blood, 1960; Blood & Blood, 1978; Mace, 1976; Schwartz & Schwartz, 1980). It is also an accepted clinical belief that anger and conflict are inevitable in a marital relationship. As a result of this belief, marital therapeutic interventions inherently and overtly address conflict and conflict resolution.

In the past decade, structured intervention methods have been developed that focus on the expression of anger and constructive fighting. To date, several specific approaches for couples' nonaggressive reduction and resolution of conflict have been developed. These approaches are primarily educational in nature and, for the most part, do not presuppose therapy per se.

BACKGROUND AND DEVELOPMENT

As structured interventions, conflict resolution programs can be considered variations of assertiveness training programs (see Chapter 2), the genesis of which can be traced to the publication of Salter's (1949) *Conditioned Reflex Therapy*. As a specific intervention, assertiveness training is designed to address specific, nonassertive, dysfunctional, interpersonal behaviors in which transactions with other persons are the focus of behavior (Flowers, et al., 1975).

The growth in the popularity of assertiveness training for individuals and the emphasis on interpersonal skills for couples can be traced to several recent trends. First, there is a growing concern with the rights and needs of the individual. Then, there is an increasing awareness of a need for nonaggressive means of reducing and resolving conflicts, and there is also the growing trend in counseling and psychotherapy to provide short-term, preventive treatment programs designed to resolve specific issues. The impact of the Women's Movement, the Gay Liberation Movement, and other human liberation movements have increased awareness of and concern with cognitive and behavioral changes that give individuals equal rights and status in relationship to others. Finally, there has been a growing professional and public concern with the nature and ramifications of aggression in American society (Flowers, et al., 1975).

Within interpersonal conflict resolution, a major inherent component has been the delineation of aggression and aggressive behaviors versus assertion and assertive behaviors. The resulting clinical work with assertive behavior has derived from several theoretical influences. In addition to Salter's (1949) work with inhibited individuals, Dollard and Miller (1950) added a learning theory explanation to the individual's inability to get his or her needs met within a relationship. Kelly's (1955) fixed role therapy, Ellis's (1962) rational emotive therapy, and behavior therapy (Wolpe, 1969;

Wolpe & Lazarus, 1966) all subsequently provided specific approaches aimed at altering the individual's cognition of the conflict situation and the resulting behavior.

Assertive behavior can be viewed as the primary influence on and component of conflict resolution programs. Although assertiveness training is not overtly acknowledged as a major influence, its emphasis on the expression of oneself in a positive, productive manner (Rathus, 1975) is the primary focus of conflict resolution with couples. The acquisition of assertive behavior involves an incorporation of Rogerian communication skills, problem-solving techniques, and negotiation skills into what is then considered a rational communication process.

THE MAJOR PHILOSOPHY OF CONFLICT RESOLUTION PROGRAMS

The major philosophy of conflict resolution programs for couples is that anger and fighting within a marital dyad are inevitable. It is believed that the couple can creatively utilize their inevitable aggressive impulses (Dayringer, 1976) rather than ignoring them or attempting to dissolve them through therapy. A couple is taught to use anger creatively, with the underlying assumption that they can learn new communication techniques that will help them address the underlying issues of the conflict situation. Thus, conflict resolution programs are based in learning theory and are educational in nature. They are also considered preventive in the sense that they teach couples skills that can be utilized in future conflict situations.

TECHNIQUES

Fair Fight Training (FFT)

One of the major methods of conflict resolution is fair fight training (FFT). The term "Fair Fight Training" evolved from Bach's (Bach & Goldberg, 1974) approach and denotes an educational, structured format that teaches couples a step-by-step methodology for constructively resolving and dissipating areas of

marital conflict marked by the anger of one or both marital partners (Bach & Bernhard, 1971; Bach & Deutsch, 1970; Bach & Goldberg, 1974; Bach & Wyden, 1969).

The underlying theory of this approach is that fighting between mature, intimate partners is inevitable, but that the expression by couples of angry feelings is a pathway for achieving true intimacy in marriage. Bach (Bach & Goldberg, 1974) believes that many of the problems in marriages emerge from the inability of couples to address positively their aggressive feelings because societal training has defined anger as bad and evil. Bach (Bach & Bernhard 1971) stressed couples' need for permission to fight, as well as training in fighting productively.

Bach's (Bach & Goldberg 1974) theory of aggression differs from the classic Frustration–Aggression hypothesis posed by Dollard and Miller (1950), which states that aggression is motivated by a desire to remove the frustration caused by the blockage of a goal-directed behavior. In Dollard and Miller's (1950) theory, the infliction of injury terminates the aggressive sequence. Bach's Impact–Aggression Theory proposed instead that in the real-life context of fights, aggression arises in most individuals not only from their desire to remove frustration, but also from their desire to influence each other, promote the maintenance of contact and fun, and for individual catharsis.

Seven issues that inevitably arise in marriages are considered central to personality development in marriages (Bach & Goldberg, 1974, pp. 281–294). These issues concern identity and relationship formation:

1. *Optimal distance.* The question of how close, how intimate, and how different a couple will be.
2. *Centricity struggles.* Struggles designed to discover the extent of the partner's commitment to the relationship and the partner's priorities.
3. *Power struggles.* The issue of who will dominate the relationship or life style.
4. *Trust formation.* The question of how sure a person can be of the partner. Trust formation develops slowly and with clashes in three areas: the revelation of critical areas of emotional vulnerability, called "beltlines"; behavior manifested during a

crisis (e.g., how a partner reacted when the other spouse lost his or her job); imbalances in physical strength, intellectual ability, or social facility.

5. *Preservation of self.* The question of autonomy. Bach believes that a totally nonintrusive life style, "You do your thing and I'll do mine," is psychologically impossible.

6. *Social boundaries.* The question of friends, social activities, and relatives. For example, must all friends be mutual to both partners?

7. *Romantic illusions.* The important question, "Are you the person I married?" Disillusionments about the other person are inevitable consequences of the phony courtship rituals in which most people engage. Bach, however, believes that vital relationships grow from the conflict-laden dimensions discussed in each of the issues that arise in marriage. Conflicts are the way to intimacy.

Although the release of aggressive feelings serves several purposes for each partner, aggression's primary function is considered the information and change that it produces for the intimate relationship. Fighting furnishes information to the couple about where they stand with one another in their relationship, where they have been, and where they are going. It enables both partners to locate their optimal distance from one another: the range at which each is close enough not to feel left out, yet free enough to engage in his or her own thoughts. The change or impact produced by the information is the terminal point of the fight.

Aggression is defined as a wide range of feelings, thoughts, actions, and interactions that naturally occur when partners frustrate or quarrel with each other as they demand or resist change (Bach & Wyden, 1969). It can be broken down into two categories: hurtful aggression and impact aggression. Hurtful aggression is the hostile, violent, and irrational part of aggression, as opposed to impact aggression, which is the part of aggression that desires change and influence. Although both types have potential for destruction, they may be channeled into constructive expressions—hurtful aggression may be released cathartically or deflected ritually, and impact aggression may be routed by maximizing explicitly the information that is being communicated.

Bach & Goldberg (1974) hypothesized four ways of expressing aggression constructively in order to achieve intimate relationships: fair fighting, fighting over trivia, ritual fighting, and fighting against nice crazymakers and hidden aggressors. Fair fighting, also known as fighting for change, has received the most emphasis in Bach's constructive aggression program. Its focus is on using impact aggression constructively so that the relevant information and the impact-for-change portion of aggression is greater than the hostile portion.

FFT is a communicative technique–process designed to focus on a single issue concerning a specific behavior pattern, with a demand for change by one of the partners. The following 15 steps, which may be done with or without a third partner, are used as a guideline (Bach & Wyden, 1969):

1. *Engagement.* The initiator makes a request to his or her partner to engage in a fight.

2. *Meditation.* The initiator meditates upon the exact thought and working of his or her issue.

3. *Huddle.* The initiator holds dialogue with a third party or within himself or herself so that he or she may become more aware of the gripe.

4. *Beef.* The initiator presents the gripe to the partner.

5. *Feedback and reward.* The partner repeats the initiator's gripe and is rewarded with a thank-you.

6. *Meditation.* The initiator meditates again on the behavior that he or she wishes the partner to change.

7. *Huddle.* The initiator enumerates with a third party or within himself or herself possible options for change that he or she may present to the partner.

8. *Demand.* The initiator states specifically the change that he or she wants the partner to make.

9. *Feedback and reward.* The partner repeats the initiator's demand and is rewarded with a thank-you.

10. *Evocation.* The initiator asks the partner if he or she will make the change.

11. *Meditation.* The partner mediates on the initiator's demand.
12. *Huddle.* The partner holds a dialogue concerning the initiator's demand with a third party or within himself or herself.
13. *Unconditional or conditional acceptance.* The partner communicates his or her decision.
14. *Planning next engagement.* If either of the partners has another issue to consider, a time is set for the next engagement.
15. *Closure.* Goodwill is expressed by both partners.

In Bach's training program, a scoring system and/or a trained observer evaluates for partners the fairness or unfairness of the fight. The scoring system consists of nine dimensions, which are rated with a positive (good style of aggression), negative (poor style of aggression), or zero (neutral style of aggression), score:

1. *Reality.* Measures the authenticity of the fight.
2. *Injury.* Measures fairness, unfairness, or meanness of the fight.
3. *Involvement.* Evaluates the activeness or passiveness of the fighters.
4. *Responsibility.* Rates the extent to which the fight participation is claimed by the fighters.
5. *Humor.* Measures the purpose of humor in terms of relief or ridicule.
6. *Expression.* Evaluates the openness of the fighter's aggression.
7. *Directness.* Measures the degree to which aggression is focused on the present.
8. *Communication.* Measures clarity of verbal and physical communication.
9. *Specificity.* Measures specific issues and behaviors addressed or generalizations made.

The degree of change that has taken place as a result of the fight is registered by the Fight Effects Profile. It breaks down the impact of the fight into 12 categories, using the same scoring process used to evaluate the fairness or unfairness of a fight.

1. *Hurt.* Measures the hurt experienced by the fighter.
2. *Information.* Measures the knowledge that a fighter gained about where he or she stands.

3. *Positional movement.* Measures the extent to which a fighter believes the fight issue has been resolved.
4. *Control.* Evaluates how much influence the fighter can exert over the opponent's behavior as a result of the current conflict.
5. *Fear.* Measures how a fighter's fear of the fight situation has been affected by the fight.
6. *Trust.* Measures the fighter's trust in the opponent.
7. *Revenge.* Rates the amount of retaliatory or grudge feelings.
8. *Reparation.* Rates any move designed to undo or repair injuries.
9. *Centricity.* Rates changes that have taken place in the fighter's central value within the opponent's heart and private world.
10. *Self-count (autonomy).* Evaluates any changes in the fighter's feelings of self-worth.
11. *Catharsis.* Rates to what extent the fighter came out of the fight with a cleansed feeling.
12. *Cohesion affection.* Records what the fight did to the fighter's feeling of optimal distance from the opponent.

A second component of Bach's constructive aggression program is "fighting over trivia," also known as "fighting for fun"—a kind of expression that channels hostile, irrational aggression into a constructive outlet. It is a fight without real issues, serving sensible functions such as preventing boredom and entertaining audiences. Bach assumes that spouses who do not fight over "nothing" actually miss out on a great deal, especially the revived courtship pattern in which attraction and repulsion alternate in cycle (i.e., attraction–repulsion, counterattack–chasing, refusing–forgiving, etc.). This type of fight is urged as long as neither partner attempts to hurt the other and the topics are kept current. Fighting over trivia may have underlying causes, however. In this case, the fight should be decoded and discussed by the fair-fighting method.

Ritual fighting, the third component of Bach's constructive aggression program, is another method of expressing irrational, hostile anger in constructive ways. It is an adult game in which the basic rules are designed to promote dramatic display and communication of irrationally hostile feelings and thoughts so vicious and foul that they usually are kept secret (Bach & Bernhard, 1971). In ritual fighting, all fair-fighting rules are suspended, since no fighting is done seriously.

Ritual fighting is encouraged as a part of everyday life for couples. Two notable rituals designed by Back for couples are the Virginia Woolf and the Batacca-style fight. The Virginia Woolf fight is an all-out fight, involving the exchange of deep blows and insults by the couple. A Batacca-style fight allows the expression of hostile feelings through the mock beating of one partner by the other. Other names of ritual fights include Haircut, Vesuvius, Slave Market, Attraction-Reservation, Self-reproach, Persistence–Resistance, Hurt Museums, Beltline Sharing, and Insult Clubs. These rituals should be a starting point from which couples may develop their own structure for expressing aggressive feelings.

The fourth component is fighting against "nice crazymakers" and "hidden aggressors," wherein one recognizes and combats dirty fighters. There are two types of dirty fighting—crazymaking and hidden aggression.

Crazymaking may be identified by its passive-indirect style of aggression, which is particularly destructive to interpersonal intimacy. The "crazymaker" displays a conning influence in communicating in order to camouflage the ulterior motives in his or her manipulative maneuvers. Consequently, the victim ends up feeling confused about where he or she stands with the crazymaker. One cannot drive another crazy without that other's full cooperation, however, even if the cooperation is largely unconscious. A crazymaking relationship contains four basic and necessary ingredients: emotional dependency and vulnerability on the part of one of those involved, an unequal power balance, an intense core of rage and resentment indirectly expressed by the crazymaker, and a socially traditional relationship. Nine types of interactions by crazymakers are identified:

1. The *double bind* communicates a message from the crazymaker of "damned if you do, damned if you don't."
2. The *mind rape* tells the other spouse what he or she really thinks or feels (mindread-

ing) because it serves the convenience and need of the crazymaker.
3. The *guilt maker* represents a form of manipulation of the partner's fear of aggression by the crazymaker's use of words, silence, hurt looks, or intentional bungling.
4. *Nonengaging* by the crazymaker makes the victim feel like a troublemaker, thereby generating insecurity and self-doubt.
5. *Thinging* characterizes the victim only as an object or in a segmented way.
6. The *mystifier* communicates to the spouse a message of "If I weren't around to fulfill your needs, you couldn't survive."
7. The *crisismaker* aborts communications and instills frustration, fear, and confusion by strategically dropping threats of abandonment, suicide, divorce, illness, or emotional breakdown whenever the spouse attempts to come to grips with a threatening issue.
8. In *closure blocking or derailing*, the Crazymaker shifts the context in the middle of an aggressive confrontation to prevent the resolution of the conflict.
9. The *occasional reinforcer* keeps the victim tied to a destructive relationship with occasional crumbs of love, affection, flattery, or material reward.

"Hidden aggression" may be identified as an unconscious and automatic style of masking hostility. The hidden aggressor, unaware of the real intentions of his or her own behavior, disguises hostility behind the noblest and most loving intentions. Eight types of hidden aggression interactions are recognized:

1. In *collusion*, both partners work hard to convince themselves of a false perception of reality in the hope that this will decrease the fear of losing love.
2. The *passive aggressor* expresses anger to the partner in inert ways, such as forgetting, misunderstanding, procrastinating, arriving late, and no carry-over of learning.
3. The *moral one-upmanship persecutor* exhibits a "holier-than-thou" attitude toward the spouse, with the purpose of creating feelings of doubt, guilt, and unworthiness.
4. The *intellectualizer* relates through mechanical words and ideas to keep the partner at an emotional distance and to avoid the experience of feelings.

5. The *nonrewarder* expresses hostility by never giving positive, rewarding feedback.
6. The *doubter* arouses anxiety and insecurity in the spouse in the name of concern at critical moments when the spouse is most vulnerable.
7. The *helpless aggressor* utilizes weakness, fears, vulnerability, hurt, and fragility as a way of generating guilt, thereby avoiding responsibility and, at the same time, controlling and engulfing the partner.
8. The *sickness tyrant* uses illness to assert himself or herself and to gain control and power over the spouse.
9. The *Red Cross nurse aggressor* seeks out and nourishes himself or herself on the weakness and vulnerability of the partner.

Several guidelines are suggested for partners who have to deal with crazymakers or hidden aggressors. These include diagnosing the interaction of the relationship, recognizing the items each person is gaining or losing in the relationship, and directing, confronting, and demanding change.

Bach's approach has addressed anger in several ways. First, it has given people permission to have and to express feelings of anger. As Bach has noted, the taboo against anger in American society has led many people to repress their feelings in order to appear "nice." This taboo, however, can prove detrimental to one's personality and growth. Second, Bach has also shown people how to fight by establishing guidelines. These guidelines may provide an important step for those who have never expressed anger or who are afraid that their anger will get out of control in destructive ways. Third, Bach has recognized that anger may be motivated by a desire to improve the relationship rather than a desire for injury that may contribute to the termination of the relationship.

Nevertheless, FFT has several major flaws in its content. Bach has presented a structured program that demands that individuals be rational with their feelings of anger. Individuals, however, are not always rational, nor is anger the only "negative" emotion that couples must address with each other. Bach has also demanded a high level of sophistication in the differentiation of modes of anger. It would take an intelligent, educated, and articulate couple

to separate the aspects of various modes and forms of fighting. Finally, Bach may overly emphasize anger, neglecting other important relationship issues. Thus he may encourage a couple to focus on issues related to anger, thereby perpetuating rather than resolving some of the issues underlying the anger.

Fair-Fight-For-Change

Another program similar to Bach's (Bach & Goldberg 1974) FFT is Dayringer's (1976) fair-fight-for-change (FFFC). Dayringer states that one of the most difficult problems in marriage counseling is the anger that spouses have toward one another. His method, which is essentially one of negotiation, attempts to utilize creatively and helpfully the aggressive impulses involved in most marital issues.

Dayringer (1976) defines anger as an emotional and physiological feeling of reactive displeasure to interference with the attainment of goals. He defines aggressiveness as constructive self-assertion or self-protection, signifying action carried out in a forceful but not necessarily destructive way. Anger is the emotion or feeling, and aggressiveness is how emotion is acted out.

In the FFFC program, the counselor or therapist ritualizes marital arguing, thus presumably decreasing its intensity so that reasoning can be introduced into what is initially pure emotion. FFFC provides a step-by-step procedure whereby partners can constructively express criticism of one another and assertively demand and negotiate changes. Dayringer adds that it is the counselor's task to see that the fight is fair, exciting, and, if possible, joyful, rather than the usual "dirty" fighting with many "fouls" and unnecessary hurting (Dayringer, 1976).

The FFFC technique is primarily a communication technique, designed to establish a process for negotiating any one particular issue. The technique focuses on one "gripe" or "beef" about a specific behavior pattern, with a demand for change. The step-by-step, structured fighting procedure is outlined:

1. *Engagement to fight.* Either of the two spouses or the therapist can initiate the fight by inviting the other spouse to fight. The invited spouse may accept, postpone,

or reject engaging in a fight. Engagement may also mean setting an appointment for a fight at another time or place. If both spouses are willing to fight, the spouses place themselves physically at their optimal distance from one another and proceed.

2. *Selection of beef.* A "beef" is a gripe or complaint that one spouse has toward the other about a single issue. It is stated and contains a behavior or action and a feeling of hurt or anger. Both the therapist and the couple select the beef.

3. *Huddle for rehearsal.* A huddle is a strategy conference between the counselor and one spouse to clarify the beef. Huddles are open so that the other spouse listens attentively but does not say anything. The therapist sits close and blocks the view of the spouses to enable them to get their cues from within rather than nonverbally from each other.

4. *Statement of beef.* The beef is stated by the spouse.

5. *Feedback and reward.* Feedback is as nearly as possible a verbatim replay of what was said in order to clarify what was heard. The spouse then thanks the other for listening. The purpose of feedback is to teach spouses to listen to one another. It also slows the fight.

6. *Huddle to determine request for change.* The therapist helps the "beefer" clarify what behavior change is really needed, not simply wanted. The change requested should be large enough to help the beefer and small enough to be seriously considered by the "beefee."

7. *Request for change.* The request for change is made.

8. *Feedback and reward.* The spouse gives feedback and reward to the request and to the way it was requested.

9. *Evocation.* "Will you change?" The beefer asks directly for change after having the request understood.

10. *Huddle to consider change.* The therapist helps the beefee decide whether or not he or she wants to make the change and if he or she can do it and maintain integrity. Bargaining is discouraged. The therapist also explains alternative responses that the beefee may use.

11. *Unconditional or conditional acceptance.* If the request is not unconditionally accepted, the therapist helps the couple negotiate alternative choices or amended agreements.

12. *Planning next engagement.* Another engagement is planned if needed.

13. *Closure.* The agreement becomes a commitment and is sealed with verbal and physical expressions of good will.

Dayringer's approach is similar to Bach's FFT program in the sense that it demands that couples approach their anger and related issues rationally. Like Bach's FFT program, however, the FFFC program can only be used by those couples who have the ability to address their emotional issues in a rational way. In addition, couples must be willing to negotiate mutual solutions to their issues.

The Rational Emotive Approach

Ellis (1976) has employed an approach to anger that is the complete antithesis of Bach's and Dayringer's methods. It diverges from the "hydraulic theory of anger," which proposes that unless individuals can in some way express their hostile feelings, these feelings will grow to enormous proportions and damage the intimate relationship. According to Ellis, a great deal of psychological research has not only revealed the limitations of the hydraulic theory of anger, but has also shown that the more people directly or indirectly express their feelings of anger, the more irate they feel and the more punishing their actions become toward others.

Ellis believes that marriage counselors should show couples how to eliminate their feelings of anger toward each other. His approach is derived from his popularly known A–B–C–D–E theory of rational emotive therapy.

The A–B–C–D–E theory of rational emotive therapy is based on the hypothesis that individuals cause their own emotional disturbance by the ways in which they interpret events. It is not the activating event (A), but the underlying belief system (B) of the individual that directly causes one's emotional consequences (C). The emotional consequences (C) lead to a decision (D) that will have some effect (E) on behavior. A partner does not feel anger because of the way the spouse acts, but because of what he or she tells himself or herself about the spouse's act. Those thoughts or beliefs usually contain "shoulds," "oughts," or "musts"; e.g., "My mate should not treat me that way. Anyone who treats a mate that way acts not only badly, but horribly."

The goal of rational emotive therapy is to replace irrational beliefs containing "shoulds," "oughts," or "musts" with rational beliefs consisting of "wishes" or "prefers." The result will range from feelings of mild disappointment to feelings of strong displeasure and annoyance but will not include violent, hostile, or angry feelings toward the other spouse.

Ellis recommends two major methods of dissipating anger. Both derive from the concept of the angry partner's relieving himself or herself of disturbing beliefs and thoughts. The first technique employs diversion methods for the angry partner. These methods include counting to 10 or 100 before trying to reply to the "unfair" spouse, going for a walk or drive, putting off discussion of the mate's unfairness until another time or day, interrupting anger by doing a pleasant or diverting activity, or performing various kinds of relaxing exercises. Ellis's hypothesis is that once a partner stops devoutly believing the irrational belief, even for a few minutes, he or she automatically cools off and starts thinking differently. This cooling-off technique will not, however, help the angry partner arrive at the source of the anger. Rather, it is a stopgap to thwart angry encounters.

The second technique is considered the more basic and permanent solution to the dissolution of anger. It consists of eight steps that the partner uses when angry:

1. *Acknowledge the anger to yourself.* This allows the irate partner to get in touch with the anger.
2. *Assume full responsibility for the anger.* The partner should admit that he or she feels annoyed and irritated about the spouse's behavior.
3. *Accept yourself with the anger.* The partner should accept himself or herself no matter how he or she feels or acts.
4. *Stop making yourself anxious, depressed, and self-downing.* The partner should not feel bad because of his or her own actions or feelings.

5. *Look for the philosophical source of the anger.* The partner should look for the statement that contains the "should," "ought," or "must." Two irrational beliefs, in particular, lead to anger: "You must treat me kindly, considerately, lovingly, and approvingly" and "The conditions under which I love must turn out nicely and be nonfrustrating so that I get practically everything I want without too much effort."
6. *Discriminate wishes from demands and commands.* The partner should separate very clearly the wishes he or she has regarding the mate and marriage from his or her other *must*urbatory commands.
7. *Dispute and debate the absolutistic musts.* The partner should actively question and challenge his or her beliefs and demands or he or she will never give them up. Beliefs and demands should not be suppressed or swept under the rug.
8. *Employ behavioral and emotive means of undermining the feelings of anger.* The partner should use a variety of active-directive approaches to eliminate anger. For instance, emotively, he or she could deliberately act lovingly rather than angrily toward the mate. He or she could also use behavior rehearsal methods.

Ellis's method, although based on premises different from Bach's and Dayringer's, is similar to them in its emphasis on rationality. Like FFT and FFFC, rational emotive therapy emphasizes the importance of adding a rational component to anger. The same limitations are noted, in that couples must be able to address their emotional issues in a rational way. In addition, one can also question the assumption that one can rid oneself of the human emotional response of anger. However, Ellis, unlike Bach and Dayringer, has noted the limitations of his method, stating that it is not applicable to more severely disturbed individuals.

Sharing Hurt Feelings Approach

L'Abate (1977) views anger in a context different from those of Bach, Dayringer, and Ellis. He asserts that in most cases anger is the result of hurt feelings and the fear of being hurt. Underneath the emotion of anger is unresolved and unexpressed pain, and the fear of further hurt. The resolution of anger and increased intimacy occur when these painful feelings and fears are shared by the couple.

L'Abate believes that the hurt feelings and fears that underlie anger arise from unresolved grief issues, past frustrations and failures, feelings of inadequacy, present loneliness, or poor self-esteem (L'Abate, 1977). These underlying emotions, rather than anger, must be addressed, for to address only the anger is to treat the symptom rather than the cause. Analogous to the situation of smoke indicating a fire, if the fire (underlying emotions) is addressed, the smoke (anger) then disappears. Thus an awareness of both the verbal and nonverbal aspects of the self gives rise to a congruence in the couple relationship.

Once the couple is aware of underlying feelings, they must then address their emotional issues positively. Five steps are suggested for the individual as guidelines for examining and resolving anger and hurt:

1. When there is anger, recognize that there is also hurt.
2. Address these hurt feelings and express them to the spouse in terms of "I feel . . ." or "It hurts me when you . . ."
3. Avoid projecting these feelings onto the other spouse, and assume responsibility for your own hurt.
4. Forgive yourself for trying to be perfect and invulnerable by trying to deny awareness of hurt feelings.
5. Redefine the self, in terms of errors and weaknesses, as human, not "crazy." Do not demand invulnerability ("perfect supermen and superwomen") of yourself (L'Abate, 1977; L'Abate & L'Abate, 1979).

L'Abate offers an approach to anger that is similar to Bach's and Dayringer's methods in that it stresses both the emotional and the rational components of anger. Unlike FFT and FFFC, however, the sharing-hurt-feelings approach requires the couple to address objectively their emotions related to intrapsychic hurt rather than to anger. Therefore couples must have the ability to be aware of their inner subjective emotional states before they can address their anger with each other constructively.

The Conflict Resolution Model

Strong's (1975) conflict-resolution model (CRM) proposes another skill development model that redefines conflict as arising from alternative choices. Behind the formation of the CRM are six assumptions about conflict. The author assumes, first, that conflict is a natural phenomenon and that it arises in part from the different perceptions of each individual. The different ways in which individuals perceive the world allow for alternative choices (conflicts); if there were no choices, there would be no conflict. Second, it is assumed that conflict involves personal values, the need to love and be loved, and the need to feel worthwhile in relation to oneself and to others. One's values and previous experiences help determine the direction of attempts to gain need fulfillment. Third, conflict manifests itself at an issue (symptom) level. A particular conflict issue may be regarded as a symptom of an unfulfilled psychosocial need. Resolution of conflict at the symptom level is less effective than resolution at the level of psychosocial needs. Fourth, conflict is generally not addressed openly between individuals because of the lack of knowledge of effective ways of dealing with (processing) it. Minor conflicts are sometimes ignored in order to maintain the status quo in relationships, a habit that sets up a pattern of avoiding the resolution of more serious conflicts. Attempts to deal with major conflicts (i.e., those with a high degree of emotional involvement) are accompanied by feelings of hurt, resentment, and vindictiveness that reinforce the pattern of not openly addressing the conflict. The fifth assumption is that conflict provides opportunity for growth in a relationship. Effective resolution of conflicts leads to both personal and relationship growth. The final assumption is that unresolved conflict interferes with satisfying interaction because it leads to individuals' establishing a defensive distance in order to avoid being hurt. This distance then diminishes the depth and intensity of their potential positive interactions with others.

The CRM model is also based on the assumption that the presentation of the conceptual framework to couples will help them identify their issues within the model. As a result, they can then understand its ability to help them resolve their issues. The author also believes that an educational, rather than a treatment, approach allows couples to view conflicts as both natural and healthy. This educational approach also provides a learning process that enhances relationship viability over time rather than producing a treatment program for crisis or momentary difficulties. This educational approach uses skill orientation as the basis of intervention, with the added assumptions that voluntary participation of couples is important and that group participation and interaction facilitate the learning of the model because of the opportunity it provides to gain insight from others.

The purpose of CRM is to make changes in the relationship in order to help each partner fulfill his or her needs as well as the needs of the relationship. Mutual adjustment, rather than compromise, is the goal. Thus alternatives are sought that better fulfill each partner's basic needs versus obtaining a compromise of the wishes, wants, and desires of the two individuals.

Strong (1975) also bases his model on his stated principles of human interaction and relationships:

1. Individuals seek meaning that arises from their relationship to others. To be able to communicate thoughts, feelings, and ideas and to work through alternative choices with one's partner provides meaning and verification of the worth and dignity of each individual.
2. Taking responsibility for one's own actions and responses is essential for growth and change. As individuals focus on their own actions and their responses to others, they are in a position to make changes that will be essential to further development and growth of the relationship.
3. Unless individuals feel understood by others, they are not open to suggestions from them. Through an understanding of oneself and the other, the couple gains support for mutually choosing the best alternative to conflict.
4. Within limits, the lack of willingness to forgive the other person is a greater deterrent to relationship development than

are the offenses of the other person. Estranged or restrained individuals limit relationship interaction.
5. When an individual has been offended, he or she should go to the offender, who may not even be aware of the offense.
6. Being an example, rather than a judge, is a key to the human influence process. As one person uses a particular skill in the interaction, he or she gives the other person an invitation to follow in like manner, thus increasing the desire and courage to attempt a mutual understanding.
7. An individual can work out in his or her own mind the dynamics of the interaction with another individual and make it a model for the actual experience.
8. To rebuilt a relationship, one must be released from the other person's prison. Often, in conflict situations, the person offended takes the position of the plaintiff, the prosecutor, and the judge, as well as the jury and the jailer, placing the offender in a prison and keeping him or her there until restitution, as judged by the offended one, has been made.
9. Talking with the other person about feelings concerning the importance of the relationship should precede confronting the person with negative feelings about a conflict issue. Less hurt comes to the total relationship by working through the feelings about the conflict than by ignoring such feelings.
10. The offender should be involved in the problem, not in one's suggested solution to the problem. If one person imposes a solution on the other, the relationship and each individual suffer.

The skills involved in CRM are skills that lead to an understanding of oneself and one's partner in the interaction of conflict situations. Presumably, the understanding of one another then allows choices that will help each individual grow and develop as an individual, while helping the relationship grow and develop positively. There are five basic skills involved in CRM:

1. *Listening.* Listening is divided into two parts: positive attitudes and actions, and negative attitudes and actions. The posi-

tive attitudes and actions are those that facilitate an understanding as well as an encouragement of the other person to interact at a deeper level. Rapport is developed through positive listening attitudes and actions, giving greater meaning to the relationship and appreciation for one another. These attitudes and actions are empathy, acceptance, verification feedback response, and silence. The negative aspects of listening decrease appreciation in the relationship and include defending one's position, giving advice, seeking entrance into the conversation, not having time, taking a dogmatic position, and assuming an understanding that has not been clarified. Listening means gaining understanding, and it can be learned.

2. *Speaking.* Speaking is a skill analogous to listening and has both positive and negative aspects. Speaking enables the individual to convey intent concerning feelings, needs, meaning, and ideas so that the listener may gain an accurate understanding. Speaking conveys a congruent message in which the individual expresses as clearly as possible what is in his or her awareness. The positive aspects of speaking include the prefacing of threatening remarks, taking responsibility for one's statements, inviting participation of a listener, and granting the right to be understood. The negative aspects of speaking include attitudes of being better than or not equal to the listener; attitudes of being unqualified to speak; speaking too slowly, rapidly, or loudly; talking to fill a void; and placing on the other person the responsibility for what one says.

3. *Deciphering basic needs.* This skill involves the ability to discover the relationship between one's basic needs and the conflict issues. Each person can develop the skill of finding the relationship between a specific issue and the way it relates to the need for loving, being loved, and feeling worthwhile.

4. *Unlocking alternative choices.* The alternatives to the symptom (conflict) are processed in terms of other considerations. When a choice is made, it is important to have a period of evaluation so that both partners can see that the choice adequately

fits the needs of both the individuals and the relationship.

5. *Introspecting about the process.* Individuals in the relationship need to be able to step back and ask themselves what is happening in terms of their listening abilities and their speaking skills with one another.

In this model, the procedures for resolving all conflict situations are the same. The steps, which are to be memorized by the participants, are as follows:

1. *Recognize conflict issues.* When conflict arises, it should be accepted as an opportunity to gain self-understanding and understanding of the other person. A specific issue should be selected for work, and issues should be defined so that there is agreement regarding what is being considered. Initially, the immediate alternatives and the choice of each partner is listed.

2. *Select the most appropriate time.* The couple selects a time (if the present is not appropriate) that will allow the greatest understanding and cognitive effort. The time selected should not be too far in the future. It is important for the couple to be certain that the issue under consideration is defined in enough detail so that they can come back to it in the future; the issue also needs to be written. A future setting gives each person time to reflect on feelings and basic needs before trying to resolve it (Ard, 1971). To force an issue to completion results in wasted time and wounded dignity.

3. *Find the defined issue–basic-needs relationship.* Each individual looks for the relationship between the defined issue and his or her basic psychological needs. It is recommended that individuals put their feelings in writing in order to help produce a clearer understanding of how the issue relates to one's basic needs and values.

4. *Provide feedback to the other person.* Through verification procedures, each individual conveys his or her feelings to the other person about the relationship of the issue (conflict) to the basic needs. In early experiences of processing conflict situations, the verification feedback material should be written in order to assure greater understanding.

5. *Seek appropriate, need-oriented alternatives.* The couple looks for alternatives that meet basic, need-oriented interactions. Within limits, the more alternatives that can be found and considered before one is chosen, the greater the opportunity for experiencing mutual care and concern for the other person.

6. *Select the best alternative and use it.* The partners choose an alternative(s) for mutual good and specify how to carry it out.

7. *Specify an evaluation time and seek better alternatives.* A particular period of time is selected for evaluation of the new interaction. Additional alternatives are sought that may better fit the needs of growing individuals in a deepening relationship.

Strong's CRM provides a detailed problem-solving model that is similar to and includes most of the steps in traditional problem-solving systems. Like other approaches to the resolution of anger, CRM demands that the individual possess insight, objectivity, and good communication skills. Thus its limitations are similar to the limitations previously discussed concerning other conflict resolution models, in that participants must be psychologically highly functioning. Low-level-functioning individuals or more disturbed individuals would not be appropriate for this approach to conflict resolution.

BEHAVIORAL APPROACHES TO CONFLICT RESOLUTION

Although considered an integral part of behavioral marital therapy rather than a specific method addressing anger and conflict (Chapter 11), behavioral approaches to conflict resolution are similar to the existing, structured models presented in this chapter. Behavioral techniques focus on interrupting coercive relationships and reciprocal exchanges of negative behavior, and on fostering reciprocal exchanges of positive behavior (Wills, et al., 1974). Therapists teach couples to improve their communication and problem-solving skills and to negotiate behavioral contingencies (Patterson & Hops, 1972; Weiss, 1975; Weiss, et al., 1973).

The behavioral approach is structured and educational in nature and addresses problem-solving by focusing on communication skills, contracting, and homework.

Problem-solving. Behavioral marital therapy alters the couple's aversive problem-solving style by teaching the couple a specific problem-solving format consisting of three steps. The first step is selecting and stating a problem in specific, descriptive, behavioral terms (Jacobson, 1977, 1978). Initially, small, nonthreatening problems may be addressed so that the couple can focus on the learning of skills rather than the content of the problem. It is believed that couples are unlikely to be able to resolve emotionally laden issues until they learn prerequisite skills (Lester, Beckham & Baucom, 1980). The second step is to list possible alternative solutions, which are stated in specific behavioral terms. The couple, depending on their preferences, may offer an alternative, evaluate it, and discard it if it is unacceptable; or they may "brainstorm" a list of alternatives and then review them. The final step in the problem-solving process is for the couple to choose their best alternative and agree to implement it.

Communication skills. The therapist monitors the couple's communication skills during problem-solving, stops them when there are destructive interactions, and instructs them in ways to improve their verbal communications. When the therapist intervenes during destructive or aversive communication, the undesirable behavior is labeled, and a rationale for change is given (Lester, Beckham & Baucom, 1980).

Contracting. Once a couple has learned to use problem-solving skills and has begun to demonstrate improved or good communication skills, they are taught to use their skills in writing behavioral contracts. The contracts, which are behavior change agreements, take the form of either a "good faith" contract (Weiss, Hops & Patterson, 1973), in which the partner making a behavioral change agrees to change noncontingent on a reinforcer from the other partner, or a "quid pro quo" contract (Lederer & Jackson, 1968), in which the behavioral exchange stops if one member of the couple does not perform the agreed-upon, contracted behavior.

Homework. Homework is assigned because an argumentative, inefficient, problem-solving style may be an ingrained habit, and most couples need practice to become effective problem-solvers. Homework consists of regularly scheduled times during which the partners practice skills. The therapist monitors the homework, thereby monitoring the couple's progress and encouraging them to address problem areas (Lester, Beckham & Baucom, 1980).

The behavioral approach to problem-solving is similar to Strong's CRM. Unlike the other models presented in this chapter, however, the behavioral approach stresses the specification of behavior in detailed and concrete ways, necessitating intervention by a therapist or other facilitator. Because of its detailed and somewhat objective behavioral approach, it may demand more rationality from couple participants than any of the other currently available conflict resolution models.

EVALUATION

Little evaluation has been conducted on the six models presented in this chapter. There are a few studies related to the efficacy of structured models for conflict resolution, however. Frey, Holley, and L'Abate (1979) investigated and compared Ellis's (1976) rational–emotive approach, Bach's (Bach & Goldberg, 1974) fair-fighting approach, and L'Abate's sharing-hurt-feelings approach (L'Abate, 1977). In comparing the three approaches, they hypothesized that females would react more favorably to the sharing-hurt-feelings approach and consider it more conducive to intimacy, whereas males would react more favorably to the rational approaches of Ellis (1976) or Bach (Bach & Wyden, 1969). Two studies were conducted to test this hypothesis; the first used videotaped scenarios and the second used an enrichment approach (Wright & L'Abate, 1977; see also Chapter 7).

In the first study, 18 males and 18 females enrolled in an introductory psychology class at Georgia State University were employed as subjects. The subjects saw videotaped scenes of a couple resolving the same conflict, using the three different approaches. Ratings and preferences for each method were obtained through the completion of two questionnaires. The data collected did not support the hypothesis concerning sex differences in the preference of conflict resolution models. However, a significant number of the subjects did consider the sharing-hurt-feelings approach the most intimate while preferring to learn the rational–emotive approach in a training program.

The second study used 22 married couples, of whom one spouse of each couple was enrolled in an introductory psychology course. Of the couples, 12 were randomly assigned to an experimental group and the other 10 were assigned to a control group. Each experimental couple attended four training sessions, with the first three addressing conflict resolution according to Bach's, Ellis's and L'Abate's models, presented in random order; the last session consisted of a follow-up and debriefing. The results showed that subjects considered L'Abate's approach the most intimate, Ellis's approach the most suited to their styles of interpersonal behavior, and Bach's approach the best liked, as well as the one they preferred to learn.

Several limitations of both studies were noted. The use of college sophomores limited generalization of findings to other populations and settings. Additionally, subjects' reactions to the different methods of conflict resolution was the topic studied. Although these methods supposedly increased intimacy, the subject of intimacy was not studied.

The researchers, in their assessment of the data, believed the results were understandable if examined from the functional significance of each approach. Although the subjects considered the sharing-hurt-feelings approach more intimate, they were less willing to learn and use it. This result was considered due to the great amount of risk and vulnerability involved in the use of a more intimate approach. Although the subjects considered the fair-fighting and rational–emotive discussions more effective for resolving conflicts, the researchers pointed out that these methods may also avoid the deeper issues involved in many marital conflicts.

In two studies related to behavioral marital techniques, Jacobson (1977) first found that couples receiving behavioral marital therapy improved significantly more than a waiting-list control group, and that gains were maintained at a one-year follow-up. Later, Jacobson

(1978) compared the effects of two different types of behavioral contracting in a treatment approach that also included training in communication and problem-solving skills. The two types of contracting were (1) quid pro quo, in which the behavior change of the husband was the reward for the wife's changing her behavior and vice versa, and (2) good faith, in which changes in one partner were not contingent upon changes in the other. Jacobson (1978) found no differences in effectiveness between the two contracting groups, but both behavioral treatment groups showed greater improvement than a nonspecific treatment group and a waiting-list control group.

DISCUSSION

Seven structured models that directly address the resolution of anger and conflict, using an educational communication paradigm, have been presented. All of the models, except for Ellis's (1976) RET approach, assume that anger and conflict are inevitable and that the resolution of conflict leads to greater intimacy and marital satisfaction. Each method is somewhat different in that the theoretical conceptualizations of intimacy vary. Bach views intimacy as "two people openly expressing their unique needs" (Bach & Wyden, 1969, p. 283). Therefore, to achieve intimacy, couples must openly conflict and appropriately display their anger toward each other.

Dayringer's (1976) definition of intimacy is similar to Bach's, whereas Ellis (1976) believes that anger destroys intimacy. L'Abate (1977) believes that communicating hurt increases intimacy; Behavioral marital therapy (see Chapter 11) and Strong's (1975) CRM view intimacy as being achieved through the resolution of conflict and the negotiation of reciprocal altered behaviors.

These methods are important theoretically in that they add to the classic frustration–aggression hypothesis (Dollard & Miller, 1950) by conceptualizing the purpose of anger in addition to the causality of anger. Anger is not viewed solely as a reaction to not having one's needs met. Rather, it can also serve the purpose of maintaining contact and attempting to communicate a desire for change within a relationship.

Additionally, the therapist provides an educational role, whereby he or she directly addresses learning deficits that, for most couples, may be defined as cultural deficits (i.e., inability to express anger and difficulties in communicating clearly). Treatment consists primarily of a corrective educational experience through which couples are not only taught skills for a present crisis but are taught a method of conflict resolution that one hopes is applicable to other situations and issues. Furthermore, couples can be treated on a short-term basis and are taught that difficulties in a relationship are inevitable and to be expected.

Nevertheless, these conflict–resolution models raise several issues that merit further consideration. Although it is important that anger be acknowledged as a normal and inevitable response to a number of life situations, it has not been sufficiently demonstrated that increased intimacy is a byproduct of conflict resolution. Each method presented in this chapter either states or assumes that closeness, intimacy, and growth result from conflict negotiation. It is not only possible that some conflict–resolution situations lead to further distance between partners, but that increased intimacy may be an ideal rather than an achievable goal in many relationships. The cause-and-effect connection between conflict resolution and increased intimacy has yet to be demonstrated.

Theoretically opposing conceptualizations of anger are also presented by these models. Bach (Bach & Bernhard, 1971) encourages expressing aggression "creatively," stating that aggression can be fun, whereas Ellis (1976) stresses that one needs to ignore and not express anger or it will become destructive to the relationship. In viewing Bach's model, not only is it difficult to understand what is meant by "creative" aggression, but it is hard to conceive of an encounter such as ritual fighting as fun. In viewing Ellis's model, it is also debatable whether an individual can ignore his or her feelings. L'Abate's (1977) stress on the importance of viewing anger as symptomatic of underlying hurt and as a complex reaction within a couple's relationship raises further considerations about treatment. Expressing hurt feelings may not alleviate the conflict or the anger.

The therapist, as well as the treatment, function as educators in all of the models presented in this chapter. Therefore, treatment is, to some extent, technical in that it demands that participants be objective and rational about their own feelings, motivations, and behaviors. The question is raised; however, as to whether a couple can objectively rate how fair or unfair they are with each other or objectively clarify the hurtful behaviors they exhibit when fighting. From a clinical standpoint, it is the rare and almost nonexistent couple who can, in any way, be objective about their conflicts.

Unfortunately, new techniques are presented that, like other methods discussed in previous chapters, presuppose insightful, verbal, educated clients. One can hypothesize that those couples engaging in educative communication approaches will be those couples who already possess an adequate degree of the skills being taught. Again, as in other marital approaches, educated, middle-class, fairly well-integrated individuals will benefit the most. It is difficult to imagine the use of any of these methods with severely disturbed couples.

From a research perspective, one must point out that none of these approaches have been validated. The few studies that do exist define "better" in subjective terms (e.g., self-reports of marital satisfaction or behavioral inventories). Even if behavior "improves," feelings within a relationship may not change.

Finally, these conflict–resolution models present programs that value the expression of anger as a means of growth and state that they are applicable to any conflict situation. Thus the expression of anger is valued, the ultimate goal of intimacy is valued, and the successful negotiation of any conflict is valued.

As has been mentioned in this discussion, it is not yet clear whether or not increased intimacy is always a realistic outcome of conflict resolution. Many couples may resolve behavioral issues without resolving underlying emotional issues. All conflict issues within a relationship may not be satisfactorily negotiable to both partners, and individual needs may not always be fulfilled in a relationship context.

Finally, one can question the potential fallacy of not only promising too much with simplistic rational approaches, but presenting a new norm for "successful" marriages which, by and large, may be unattainable. The value

of teaching conflict resolution skills cannot be underestimated, for the unsuccessful resolution of conflicts leads to the dissolution of marital relationships. Nevertheless, the proposal of treatment models that imply an intimate couple relationship (i.e., all needs are successfully negotiated and met) may reinforce cultural myths of marriage as an always-satisfying relationship.

THE FUTURE

With the growing popularity of short-term, educative, preventive approaches to mental health, there is no doubt that structured conflict–resolution models will continue to exist. More integrated theories concerning the causes, purposes, and dissolution of anger in relationships need to be developed, however. The only two theoretical views of anger in a marital relationship are either that anger must always be expressed or never expressed. The role of the therapist and therapist qualifications also need to be clarified, for it is the therapist who defines "effective" communication as well as "effective" behavior. These judgments of effectiveness are still primarily subjective.

The outcome of treatment as well as the appropriate applicability of treatment must also be investigated. It is not clear, as in most therapies, what treatment is appropriate for which clients under what circumstances. One must certainly question the assumption that conflict resolution models are applicable to all conflicts with all couples.

Finally, the inherent values in conflict–resolution models for couples' relationships need to be addressed as an integral part of the treatment. One must remember that the field of psychology has a history of positing, for mental health, norms that have often proved unfeasible. For example, one can point to the failure of the encounter-group movement (see Chapter 5) in its encouragement of self-revelation to others as a norm for mental health, as well as the ultimate limitations of any treatment that has promised applicability to every client, regardless of client characteristics.

The reduction of anger is a necessary component of any conflict resolution approach. It is not, however, a sufficient treatment for all conflict issues. In addition to the reduction of anger and the constructive expression of feelings, couples need to master a variety of intrapersonal and interpersonal relationship skills in order to negotiate successfully the variety of issues that confront them over the course of the marital relationship. These varied skills are still either ignored or simplified as easily mastered by most couples. Thus conflict resolution models need not only further exploration but additional explication as well.

REFERENCES

Ard B. Communication in marriage. *Rational Living*, 1971, *5*, 20–22

Bach G, & Bernhard Y. *Aggression lab: The fair fight training manual*. Los Angeles: Kendall/Hunt Publishing Co., 1971

Bach G, & Deutsch RM. *Pairing*. New York: Peter H. Wyden, Inc., 1970

Bach G, & Goldberg H. *Creative aggression*. Garden City, NY: Doubleday & Co., 1974

Bach G, & Wyden P. *The intimate enemy: How to fight fair in love and marriage*. New York: William Morrow & Company, 1969

Bahr SJ, & Boyd CR. Crisis and conjugal power. *Journal of Marriage and the Family*, 1971, *33*, 360–367

Dayringer R. Fair-fight for change: A therapeutic use of aggressiveness in couple counseling. *Journal of Marriage and Family Counseling*, 1976, *2*, 115–130

Dollard J, & Miller N. *Personality and psychotherapy*. New York: McGraw-Hill, 1950

Ellis A. *Reason and emotion in psychotherapy*. New York: Lyle Stuart, 1962

Ellis A. Techniques of handling anger in marriage. *Journal of Marriage and Family Counseling*, 1976, *2*, 305–315

Flowers J, Cooper C, & Whiteley J. Approaches to ascertain training. *The Counseling Psychologist*, 1975, *5*(4), 3–9

Frey J, Holley J, & L'Abate L. Intimacy is sharing hurt feelings: A comparison of three conflict resolution models. *Journal of Marital and Family Therapy*, 1979, *5*, 35–41

Jacobson NS. Problem solving and contingency contracting in the treatment of marital discord. *Journal of Consulting & Clinical Psychology*, 1977, *45*, 92–100

Jacobson NS. Specific and nonspecific factors in the effectiveness of a behavioral approach to the treatment of marital discord. *Journal of Consulting & Clinical Psychology*, 1978, *46*, 442–452

Kelly GA. *A theory of personality* (vol. 2). New York: Norton, 1955

L'Abate L. Intimacy is sharing hurt feelings: A reply to David Mace. *Journal of Marriage and Family Counseling*, 1977, *3*, 13–16

L'Abate L, & L'Abate BS. The paradoxes of intimacy. *Family Therapy*, 1979, *6*, 175–186

Lederer WJ, & Jackson DD. *The mirages of marriage*. New York: W. W. Norton and Co., 1968

Lester G, Beckham E, & Baucom D. Implementation of behavioral marital therapy. *Journal of Marital and Family Therapy*, 1980, *6*, 189–199

Patterson GR, & Hops H. Coercion, a game for two: Intervention techniques for marital conflict. In RE Ulrich & P Mountjoy (Eds.), *The experimental analysis of social behavior*. New York: Appleton-Century-Crofts, 1972

Rathus S. Principles and practices of assertive training: An eclectic overview. *The Counseling Psychologist*, 1975, *5*, 9–20

Salter A. *Conditioned reflex therapy*. New York: Creative Age Press, 1949

Schwartz R, & Schwartz L. *Becoming a couple*. Englewood Cliffs, NJ: Prentice-Hall, Inc., 1980

Strong J. A marital conflict resolution model: Redefining conflict to achieve intimacy. *Journal of Marriage and Family Counseling*, 1975, *1*, 269–276

Weiss RL. Contracts, cognition, and change: A behavioral approach to marriage therapy. *The Counseling Psychologist*, 1975, *5*, 15–26

Weiss RL, Hops H, & Patterson GR. A framework for conceptualizing marital conflict, a technology for altering it, some data for evaluating it. In LA Hamerlynck, LC Handy & EJ March (Eds.), *Behavior change: Methodology, concepts, and practice*. Champaign, IL: Research Press, 1973

Wills TA, Weiss RL, & Patterson GR. A behavioral analysis of the determinants of marital satisfaction. *Journal of Consulting and Clinical Psychology*, 1974, *42*, 802–811

Wolpe J. *The practice of behavior therapy*. New York: Pergamon Press, 1969

Wolpe J, & Lazarus AA. *Behavior therapy techniques*. New York: Pergamon Press, 1966

Wright L, & L'Abate L. Four approaches to family facilitation: Some issues and implications. *The Family Coordinator*, 1977, *26*, 176–181

9

Problem-Solving

In the field of psychology, problem-solving has been and continues to be the main focus of research and therapeutic endeavor. A problem is defined as any perplexing question or situation, especially one difficult or uncertain of solution. A problem can also be defined as any puzzling or difficult circumstance or person. Solving the problem entails arriving at or working out an explanation or solution so that the difficult circumstance is resolved.

In the past decade, interest in problem-solving as a specific method of intervention has led to the development of a variety of structured programs and treatment strategies aimed specifically at developing cognitive problem-solving skills in couples as well as individuals. As a rule, problem-solving programs can be defined as any structured cognitive procedures having as their goal the active resolution of an immediate and identifiable problem.

BACKGROUND AND DEVELOPMENT

The growth of cognitive literature related to the nature of problem-solving can be dated to the earlier research of Wertheimer and Köhler (Kohler, 1947) in the 1920s and 1930s. Their research in Gestalt psychology was conducted in part as a reaction to the atomistic beliefs of behaviorism and concluded succinctly with the maxim that the whole is greater than the sum of its parts. Wertheimer maintained that sensory elements do not form a bundle and

associations do not serve as a means of binding together (Wertheimer, 1959). This view of a lack of innate logical organization then led to an attempt to describe the mediating or organizing processes of human thought.

Wertheimer (1959) stated that one of the most important elements of productive thinking is appreciation of the overall problematic situation, or the Gestalt, while Kohler (1947) added, from his studies with primates, both the importance of "hypothesis testing," or the subsequent search for solutions, and the concept of developing "insight." Wertheimer also noted the limitations of habitual interpretation or productive problem-solving. Habitual interpretation, which is similar to the later notion of "functional fixedness" (Adamson & Taylor, 1954; Dunker, 1945), referred to the fact that habitual judgment of the utility of objects can restrict their novel application to problem solution. For example, in one problem-solving study, a bottle cork could be used as a lever to provide the solution to the problem at hand. This solution was easily reached by subjects if the cork was presented independently but seldom reached if the cork was presented in its usual position, with the cap in the bottle. This principle of "functional fixedness" was subsequently applied by Osborn (1963) in his development of the "brainstorming" procedure in industrial psychology. One of the assumptions of "brainstorming" is that the deferment of judgment will allow for more novel ideas in the problem-solving process.

Although most of the literature on problem-solving consistent with the early work of Wertheimer and Kohler, has addressed impersonal problem-solving situations in laboratory settings, there are some fundamental conclusions from the literature that delineate a problem-solving process:

1. Covert problem-solving procedures involving symbolic stimulus transformations and cognitive rehearsals are more effective than overt problem-solving procedures involving rudimentary trial-and-error procedures. Covert procedures, however, involve the input of more relevant information and the acquisition of the sophisticated skills of innovative response generation and integration.
2. Problem-solving strategies include a bifocal tendency toward flexibility or fixation that is greatly influenced by immediate circumstances.
3. Problem-solving is a step-wise process, consisting of (a) general orientation (set and attitudinal factors), (b) problem definition and formulation, (c) generation of alternatives, (d) decision-making (evaluation of alternatives), and (e) evaluation (retrospective evaluation of performance).

Of the stages delineated, problem definition and formulation have commanded the most attention in the literature and have been considered the most important in the successful solution of laboratory problems (D'Zurilla & Goldfried, 1971). The emphasis on problem definition and formulation has, however, been based primarily on impersonal problem-solving tasks in laboratory settings, and the laboratory situation has been acknowledged as simplistic and stilted by many cognitive theorists (Mahoney, 1974; Thoresen & Coates, 1978). More recently, the application of problem-solving principles to interpersonal situations has led to some changes in formulating the problem-solving process.

Problem-solving as a method of interpersonal intervention has been used primarily in the areas of industry, education, and clinical psychology. In industry, four influential models have been proposed. Simon and Newell (1971) conducted numerous studies on the decision-making process within economic organizations. Simon also pioneered concepts

of artificial intelligence and has done much to integrate the use of computers with the study of human problem-solving. One of his earliest assumptions was that the "human organism's simplifications of the real world for the purpose of choice introduce discrepancies between the simplified model and the reality; these discrepancies, in turn, serve to explain many of the phenomena of organizational behaviors" (Simon and Newell 1971). Their model of human problem-solving, which includes the stages of: (1) settling payoff functions, (2) information gathering, (3) ordering of payoff values, and (4) obtaining a unique solution, has influenced researchers/practitioners such as Patterson and Hops (1972), D'Zurilla and Goldfried (1971), and Spivack, et al (1976) in stressing the reward aspects of conjoint marital problem-solving.

Osborn's (1963) "brainstorming" method was developed in 1938 as a method of idea generation within groups in business organizations. This "brainstorming" procedure has been used as a clinical concept (D'Zurilla & Goldfried, 1971), using the principles of "deferred judgment" and "quantity breeds quality." In "brainstorming" procedures, the goal is the generation of creative alternative solutions. Criticism is ruled out; freewheeling, or the-wilder-the-ideas-the-better is welcomed; quantity is wanted; and a combination and improvement of ideas is sought.

A method related to "brainstorming" is the Synetics program developed by Gordon (1961). Three modes of analogical thinking are considered to enhance creative thinking: direct analogies are made in which the problem at hand is compared to a parallel or similar problem; personal analogies are made in which the problem at hand is imagined to be an aspect of oneself; and fantastic analogies are made in which active, even bizarre, fantasizing is encouraged.

The fourth major problem-solving method from industry is the Bionics program (Papanek, 1969). In this model, biological prototypes are used in the design planning of man-made systems.

In the area of educational problem-solving, there has been a focus on the development of problem-solving skills in children. Early efforts focused on "inquiry training" (Suchman, 1960, 1969) and skill training in "hypothesis testing" (Olton & Crutchfield, 1969), with early studies concluding that problem-solving training in children contributes positively to later, increased problem-solving abilities.

An important outcome of early studies in education has been the differentiation of problem-solving skills from overall intelligence (Shantz, 1975). Social competence (i.e., interpersonal and intrapersonal sensitivity, perspective-taking, and problem-solving skills) has been described as an area related to but distinct from intelligence (Spivack, et al., 1976). An important underlying assumption is that problem-solving is, to an extent, a learned skill and, therefore, remedial training is possible.

By the early 1950s, the earlier problem-solving paradigms had undergone numerous modifications in an effort to incorporate a multiplicity of variables in interpersonal situations. Clinical psychologists did not find it sufficient to focus only on the area of problem definition and formulation. The problem-solving process was considered much more complex because circumstantial variables were numerous and intrapsychic emotional factors influenced problem-solving in ways that could not be explained by the somewhat concrete quality of impersonal problem-solving paradigms.

Jahoda (1953) observed that simply noting the existence of a personal problem is difficult for some people under stressful circumstances. Due to anxiety or fear of failure, the individual may avoid confronting an issue. If the anxiety is great enough, it may shortcircuit the individual's normal problem-solving abilities, leading in most cases to impulsive and inefficient action. The usual mediation of rational thought between emotion and action is then lost. Jahoda was the first clinician to relate problem-solving skills to social adjustment, as well as stressing that problem-solving includes the stage of "admitting the problem" (Spivack, et al., 1976).

Weinstein (1969) postulated a group of factors that combine to provide degrees of interpersonal competence: empathy, acquisition of a repertoire of interpersonal tactics, and personality factors that inhibit or augment these factors (i.e., rigidity, internal locus of control, and self-esteem). Like Jahoda, Weinstein implied that problem-solving is an independent skill and that it is affected by other, more emotional aspects of adjustment.

Aldous, et al. (1971), from a sociological

perspective, attempted to "isolate and define the central issues pertaining to research on the family as a problem-solving group" (p. vi). They attempted to delineate the areas of felt intuitive problems versus consensually validated problems, goal-less versus goal-oriented dissatisfaction, and external versus internal sources of problems. Weick (1971) added that ambiguity of role structure, problem definition, or negotiation procedures will lead to a shorter attention span on the part of the family members and a general regression to more primitive modes of problem-solving. That is, family problem-solving may be more characterized by digital thinking (Haley, 1976), or lack of differentiation between emotionality and rationality (Bowen, 1976), and a degeneration from constructive to destructive conflict resolution. This destructive conflict resolution has been defined as a shift in focus from issues to individuals (Duetsch, 1973).

Behavioral theorists were slow to address the issue of problem-solving, probably because of the need to address mediational cognitive aspects of behavior. The operational methodology of behavioral assessment, however, proved to be analogous to the skills required for efficient problem solving by individuals. In their earlier, extensive review of the cognitive problem-solving and behavior modification literature, D'Zurilla and Goldfried (1971) noted that previous behavioral studies on self-control training are similar to the issues of import in problem-solving. Unlike the early, traditional behavioral interests in discrete response training, the evolution of self-control training involves a mediating skill. Furthermore, self-control training utilizes known controllable behaviors to shape less integrated problem behaviors in much the same way that other problem-solving paradigms have used known information and skills to arrive at previously unknown solutions.

D'Zurilla and Goldfried (1971) proposed the following definitions related to problem solving:

Problem. Specific situations or related situations to which a person must respond in order to function effectively in his environment

Problematic. Descriptive of a situation in which no effective response alternative is immediately available

Problem-solving. A method that makes available a variety of effective response alternatives and increases the probability of selecting the most efficient of these alternatives

They further viewed difficulties with problem-solving as primarily a skill deficit that is the outcome of an inadequate learning history. Ineffective problem-solving was also considered to cause sufficient consequences to precipitate emotional or behavioral disorder. They further postulated that the most effective intervention for psychological problems is general training to increase problem-solving ability and to allow clients to resolve independently problematic situations.

In D'Zurilla and Goldfried's (1971) proposed treatment process, an individual is led through the stages of problem-solving by the therapist in a dyadic/didactic approach within the context of a specific problematic situation faced by the client in real life. There are five stages and their primary components:

1. *General orientation.* Acceptance of the fact that problems are a normal part of life is considered fundamental to confronting any problematic situation. Recognition of problematic situations as they occur is also viewed as a function of prior exposure to a standard repertoire of such situations. In treatment, inhibition of the tendency to respond with the first impulse is stressed. The methods used to convey these major points and fill deficits as needed include description of some problematic areas (e.g., family, home) and factors that can precipitate problematic situations (e.g., role changes, new environments), and teaching clients to use emotional responses as cues to the existence of a problem.
2. *Problem definition and formulation.* All relevant aspects of the problematic situation are defined in clear, operational terms. These elements are then classified in a consistent fashion. The authors consider the case of a housewife who entered therapy with the following complaint: "I became upset and depressed last night because my husband was out late working and I was home alone." After training, this "rough" description was refined into the following statement:

My husband and I have been married for 3 years and have a 2-year-old son. During the past 6 months, my husband has had to work late in the evenings, usually until about 10 p.m. . . . I have been feeling increasingly lonely, anxious, and depressed in the evenings after our child goes to bed and I am waiting for my husband to come home. I have been trying to amuse myself by watching t.v., but . . . etc. (p. 110).

3. *Generation of alternatives.* D'Zurilla and Goldfried apply Osborn's "brainstorming" virtually verbatim in this stage. Their aim is simply to generate the alternatives that will be evaluated in the next stage. Thus clients are trained in the rules of "brainstorming" and supervised in its practice. A distinction is also made between the generation of strategies and the generation of specific behaviors, both of which are necessary to the problem-solving process.
4. *Decision-making.* The client is trained in making subjective estimations of the probability that each alternative will achieve its expected outcome and of the value of that outcome. The evaluation of the value of outcome involves the consideration of consequences of the various alternatives over the short and long terms, in the eyes of the client and the rest of society.
5. *Verification.* The client is trained to make structured observations of his or her behavior during the first four stages. Criteria for acceptable problem resolution are practiced. Unlike impersonal problem-solving, there is rarely a categorically correct solution to personal problematic situations. Thus criteria for "exiting" from the problem-solving process must be determined.

Goldfried and Goldfried (1975) extended this structured treatment program by suggesting the use of adjunct behavioral procedures (i.e., relaxation training) when necessary. They added a consideration of the influence of emotional factors and also stated that problem-specific skill-training procedures may be most useful in crisis intervention when normal skills may suffer a deficit.

Spivack, et al. (1976) took a more wholistic stance toward problem-solving and were the first to distinguish interpersonal problem-solving skills from impersonal problem-solving skills. It was their contention that the skills required in interpersonal problem-solving are different from the skills required in impersonal problem-solving and that these skills develop at different times in an individual's development, as a function of experience and degree of differentiation. The traditional, impersonal stages of problem-solving were modified to include five skills:

1. Awareness of the variety of possible interpersonal problem situations, acceptance of the inevitability of conflicting desires between individuals, and the ability to view such differences objectively.
2. Ability to generate a variety of alternate solutions and consider them all as options.
3. Ability to spell out step-by-step means to solution (means–ends generation), including foresight, familiarity with possible obstacles, and the ability to delay gratification.
4. Consequential thinking and awareness of social impact of actions.
5. Causal thinking, awareness of social/interpersonal etiology of problems and establishing a continuity of events.

Not all of the steps outlined by Spivack, et al. (1976) were new: delayed gratification is reminiscent of the "inhibition of immediate response" of D'Zurilla and Goldfried (1971), and consequential thinking has also been included in past paradigms. Means–ends generation is similar to the "generation of strategies and specific behaviors" put forth by D'Zurilla and Goldfried (1971). Spivack, et al. (1976), however, added a different focus from past problem-solving paradigms. Most notably, they deemphasized the importance of problem definition and formulation, which had been a holdover from early laboratory and cognitive studies. Instead, they focused on the skill of means–ends generation. In addition, they placed a great emphasis on other variables, which were less operational but widely utilized by various therapeutic approaches; for example, the ability to view differences objectively is reminiscent of the "toleration of differences" noted by Satir (1967) as an indication of level of self-esteem and dysfunction within family communication patterns.

Using a procedure called means–ends problem-solving (MEPS), the authors demonstrated that the ability to generate means–ends differentiated significantly between "normal" controls and various subjects ranging from chronic psychiatric patients to disturbed adolescents. The authors concluded that means–ends generation was sufficiently related to social adjustment to be useful in training programs in problem-solving. In their study, generation of alternative solutions was found to be closely related to IQ. Furthermore, abnormals (psychiatric patients) were able to select as well as normals the most efficient means–end alternatives on a recognition basis. Thus it was the actual *generation* of alternative courses of action toward solution, not the ability to select the best solution nor the ability to recognize from several choices the most expedient means to solution, that was clearly related to degree of social adjustment.

MAJOR PHILOSOPHY AND CURRENT CONCEPTS

Currently, problem-solving theories and treatment programs view problem-solving as a skill that can be learned. Deficits in problem-solving skills are viewed as deficits in learning that can be remedied or as deficits in one's cognitive behavioral repertoire that may result from the impact of a stressful emotional situation or crisis. The problem-solving process is considered a step-wise procedure, with acknowledgment that external and intrapersonal factors will influence the individual's effective or ineffective problem-solving abilities.

One can view the theoretical development of problem-solving as primarily a cognitive behavioral endeavor. Although other theoretical orientations might explain problem-solving differently, little work in the area of specific problem-solving skills has been generated by other major theoretical orientations.

PROBLEM-SOLVING TECHNIQUES THAT CAN BE IMPLEMENTED WITH COUPLES

The so-called Oregon Group (Patterson & Hops, 1972; Weiss, Hops & Patterson, 1973) has developed a comprehensive behavioral treatment program for couples in which one of the program's three areas of concentration is the teaching of problem-solving skills. Marital conflict is hypothesized as arising from the couple's attempts to effect behavior change in one another when coercion is used to the exclusion of productive problem-solving and affectional exchange. Coercion is defined as the use of aversive behavior and negative reinforcement to effect behavior change in the spouse. Treatment focuses on the partners' exchange of affectional behavior and positive reinforcement, and on the use of problem-solving behavior over a wide range of specific issues.

In treatment, the marital dyad is trained jointly to reduce their rate of aversive behavior when attempting to negotiate behavior change. Videotapes of their interaction, therapist modeling of nonaversive negotiation, and supervised practice trials are used to produce initial change. The couple is also taught to "pinpoint," or operationalize, the specific behavior changes sought (much like D'Zurilla and Goldfried's operationalization of problem definition and formulation). "Please" behaviors, which are the desired substitution for the "displease" behaviors originally cited by the complaining spouse, are exchanged through a "quid pro quo" or "good faith" negotiation process. The negotiated exchange is formalized in a contract with contingencies for noncompliance, and daily records of "pleases" and "displeases" are kept by both spouses. Typically, the couple will also maintain daily telephone contact with their therapist.

In the Oregon model, problem-solving is a joint, verbal negotiation process by the couple. In this joint negotiation process, spouses exchange, or barter, desired behaviors with each other.

Blechman and others (Blechman, 1974; Blechman & Olson, 1976) have developed the Family Contract Game, which incorporates the program developed by the Oregon Group. It is a board game designed for eventual independent use by clients. Although targeted for use with multigenerational families, it can also be applied to couples.

The game format is an operationalization of the steps toward successful problem resolution proposed initially by Aldous (1971). Thus Aldous's stages of (1) identification and definition; (2) collection of information; (3) innovation of action alternatives; (4) choice of course of action; and (5) evaluation of consequences

are specified as: (1) pinpointing problems in observable, quantifiable terms; (2) tracking problem baseline frequency; (3) selecting "pleasing" replacement behavior; (4) selecting reward; and (5) tracking frequency of "pleasing" and "displeasing" behaviors.

The procedure of the game is as follows:

1. The complainant writes a problem in operationalized terms on a game card. The card cannot include any speculations about the motives of the offender or feeling statements of the complainant.
2. Through a series of board moves, the complainant and the offender attempt to reach a quid pro quo exchange of "pleases" for "displeases." Rewards and fines in game money and household tasks are allocated on the basis of efficacy in reaching a contract.
3. The contract is taken home by the family and enforced as homework. Frequency counts of the specified "pleases" and "displeases" are kept, and problems for "play" in the next session are noted.
4. Each new session is opened with a review of the success of the previous week's contract. The previous offender can then become the complainant if the contract has been successfully observed.
5. After the fourth session, the family may be able to use the game independently.

An adapted version of the Marital Interaction Coding Scale (MICS), developed by the Oregon Group (Weiss, et al., 1973), is used as an observational measure of outcome. Frequency counts of agreements reached, number of "pleases" versus "displeases," and a self-report scale on marital happiness are used. The authors specify that this procedure is most beneficial with families having short attention spans, a concrete approach to problems, low levels of self-disclosure, and meager social skills in general. They suggest that the Family Contract Game can be used as an evaluative instrument, a gentle introduction to family therapy, as a substitute for therapy during the therapist's absence, or as a brief therapy procedure with continued use by the family at home.

Some of the less obvious advantages of the Family Contract Game include its relatively nonthreatening nature (i.e., no self-disclosure is asked for), that it is not therapist-bound, and that it places the family in an active, responsible role, allowing them to take credit for the successes they achieve. The structure of the game also discourages hostile or aversive behavior by focusing on task-oriented behavior, removing preinsulting cues, and reducing the opportunities for conflict. The game is a somewhat more accessible method for therapists and interveners than the procedures of the Oregon Group, for it is more highly structured and, thus, more easily learned. It also has a more specified course of treatment (six to eight weeks).

Another simulated game developed by Olson and Straus (1972) is the Simulated Family Activity Measurement. SIMFAM is a game-like task that is played with a pusher and balls on a 9 by 12-foot court that has two large targets at one end. The instructions to the couple or family are to learn the rules of the game and make more points than the average family who plays the game. Stop (red) and go (green) lights are controlled by an observer.

The couple or family play the game for eight three-minute trials, separated by one-and-a-half-minute rest periods. After each trial, a total family score is posted in comparison to the "average" scores of other families who have played the game. The same scores are always posted, regardless of the family's performance or behavior.

In the first four trials, couples are led to believe that they are improving, with green lights signaling that they are accurately discovering the rules of the game. In the last four trials, red lights indicate that the family is no longer accurately discovering the rules of the game, thereby inducing an "experimental crisis." As family members attempt to resolve the crisis, hidden observers code their behavior, using the dimensions of power, support, creativity, and problem-solving ability.

Although the SIMFAM technique has been used primarily as a diagnostic task, it does present a couple with a problem-solving situation and could be used as an educational or treatment component related to addressing couple problem-solving abilities. SIMFAM has received little attention in subsequent literature, however; perhaps because it is a lengthy, complicated, and costly procedure.

Other problem-solving models, although not currently applied to couples, do possess the potential for adaptation to interpersonal problem-solving skills. In addition to the D'Zurilla and Goldfried (1971) model already discussed in this chapter, Spivack and Levine (1963) have developed a problem-solving procedure for adolescents.

The means-end problem solving (MEPS) involves presenting to a subject the beginning and end of several "stories," with instructions to connect the beginning that is supplied with the end that supplied, or, in other words, to make up the middle of the story. The following is an example of such a story:

Mr. C. had just moved in that day and didn't know anyone. Mr. C. wanted to have friends in the neighborhood. The story ends with Mr. C. having many good friends and feeling at home in the neighborhood. You begin the story with Mr. C. in his room immediately after arriving in the neighborhood (Spivack, et al., 1976, p. 85–86).

The subject's responses are then scored in terms of predetermined categories of "relevant" and "irrelevant" means ($\bar{x}$ interrater reliability of .84). Clearly, the subject matter of the stories can be altered to fit varied populations. Although this procedure is not used in Platt and Baker's treatment program with adults, similar procedures with TAT cards are used. Thus the authors offer a projective technique by which to identify problem-solving abilities.

Spivack, et al. (1976) have developed a training program for adults and young adults that involves problem-solving training without the context of specific presenting problems by the clients. Instead, group members engage in a series of exercises designed to enhance problem-solving skills. Only late in the program are actual personal problems introduced, and then only on an optional basis. The program format consists of 19 structured units that were originally presented on a once-weekly basis. The exercises within these units are presented in order of increasing difficulty, and some of the early exercises can be dropped for groups exhibiting a higher level of social competence.

The fundamental assumption of this program is that the skills practiced in the group will be acquired by its members and that they will use them in their various life situations. The exercises address the following key skills:

1. Recognizing problematic situations by emotional cues.
2. Discriminating facts from opinions: a consensus procedure using TAT cards provides the content material for group members to discriminate facts from opinions in themselves and other group members.
3. Using facts one can see: TAT cards are flashed with the instruction to remember as many facts as possible from each card; attending to facts.
4. Using facts one cannot see: induction is used to fill in the gaps; fill-in-the-blank sentence exercises, practice of direct questions, and homework assignments using direct questions are also used.
5. Using facts as others see them: comparison is made of values lists, and there is use of consensus TAT procedure to compare interpretations.
6. Recognizing feelings in self and others: there is a focus on communication and recognition of pleasure and displeasure on verbal and nonverbal levels, and application of these skills to real problem situations of members.
7. Using memory aids.
8. Thinking before acting: attempts are made to decrease impulsive action; there is use of Kagan's (1965) "matching familiar figures task," in which careful discrimination between similar cards is necessary to complete the task successfully; thinking aloud is used to ensure mediation of thought between feeling and action; and there is listing of means–end options to cartoons (i.e., means–ends generation).
9. Consequential thinking: there is evaluation of alternatives in a forced-choice cartoon situation.
10. Analyzing an argument between a husband and wife to evaluate each one's viewpoint.
11. Focusing: individuals attend to the problem at hand; there is transcription of a problem tape and real situational problems into skits.

Although the use of this procedure with couples has not been established, the program has potential for couple programs. The program is noteworthy because it is more experientially oriented than other problem-solving training programs and acknowledges the disrupting effect that feelings can have on problem-solving abilities. The authors note, however, that the program is not designed to resolve intrapsychic conflict but could be incorporated into insight-oriented therapeutic treatment approaches. Their assumption is related to their belief that deficient problem-solving skills can be secondary to either deficient cognitive skill-training and stimulus exposure or to situation-specific emotional responses that disrupt normal social sensitivity and/or cognitive functioning.

As a part of his series on human resource development, Carkhuff (1973) developed a structured problem-solving procedure. His procedure is designed primarily to help paraprofessionals and professionals learn to apply the system to clients. The procedure is highly structured and situation-specific and is used with individuals who are functioning at less than optimal levels. The time needed to learn the procedure is not specified and probably varies greatly from individual to individual. The system is designed for eventual independent use in any situations that require organized decision-making.

Carkhuff outlined four steps for problem solving: (1) developing the problem, (2) breaking down the problem, (3) considering courses of action, and (4) implementing courses of action:

1. *Developing the problem.* Initially, the client must take responsibility for changing the problematic situation. The situation is then explored in terms of its physical, emotional, and intellectual aspects, and the resultant limitations on functioning are outlined.
2. *Breaking down the problem.* The problematic situation is formulated in specific, measurable terms. A problem can generally be stated as a deficit, and a mathematical equation is formulated to express this deficit (i.e., responsibility unit > time units). The goal then becomes to reverse the equa-

tion (i.e., responsibility units < time units), illustrating the belief that the clear problem definition leads to goal specification.

3. *Considering courses of action.* Means–ends are generated in a nonjudgmental "brainstorming" fashion. Then, a value hierarchy is developed for the specific problem situation. Values are described in terms of degree of significance (rank ordering) and weight of influence (assignment of a value from 1 to 10). A table is then constructed with the alternative courses of action as the abscissa and the value hierarchy as the ordinate.

4. *Developing courses of action.* Plus or minus values are assigned to each combination of alternative courses of action and values on the table (more than one plus or minus may be assigned to each combination). Each combination value (i.e., two plusses) is then multiplied by the weighted numerical value of the corresponding personal value. These products are summed over each course of action. The course(s) of action with the highest sum(s) is then considered the most efficient. A similar systematic process is used to determine the most efficient means of implementation.

SPECIFIC PROBLEM-SOLVING TECHNIQUES WITH COUPLES

Rausch, et al. (1974) present a six-stage problem-solving process designed for couples' treatment. Although primarily presented from a theoretical stance, the process bears much resemblance to that of D'Zurilla and Goldfried (1971). The six stages of the problem-solving process are outlined by the authors as follows: (1) identifying the problem, (2) exploring alternative solutions, (3) selecting the best alternative, (4) implementing the decision, (5) rebuilding the relationship, and (6) reviewing the decision-making process.

The theoretical basis of this outline is that problem identification in long-term relationships can be more difficult than in other situations and that symptoms of complaint can mask underlying problems. For example, nagging is a problem that may be symptomatic of another issue in the relationship. The emotional charge behind side-taking on given issues is consid-

ered a major obstacle to effective decision-making, and taking a rigid stance on an issue is considered threatening to the other spouse's emotional investment in the issue, often leading to greater conflict.

The authors state that "rebuilding the relationship" is a new category unique to long-term relationships and especially important to conflict resolution in marriage. Several possible outcomes to disagreement in marriage are seen. The most favorable of these is consensus, whereby the same resolution to the problem is satisfactory to both spouses. Most issues are too complex for couples always to arrive at a consensus, however. Other possible outcomes include accommodation, whereby the alternative solutions held by either spouse are each put into effect, compromise, or concession, when one spouse gives in to the wishes of the other.

The use of "brainstorming" is suggested, as a digital right/wrong attitude is discouraged in the negotiation of conflict. As a means of helping partners see the other side, the use of role-reversal is suggested, and it is emphasized that, in the decision-making process, the couple can learn new things about each other, thus optimizing the growth potential in conflict.

Another procedure for use with couples, *The Marriage Game*, developed by Greenblatt, et al. (1974), was designed primarily as a teaching aid for use with high-school and college-age students, with the goal of providing them with a realistic expectation of marriage. The program was an innovative curriculum addition at the time of its development, and it received much press coverage. The authors note, however, that the game can also be used by married couples as practice in solving the problems common to most marriages at different stages of the marital relationship.

The game covers the course of marriage; players must make decisions on whether to marry, whether to stay married, how to utilize finances, whether or not to have children, etc. Each time around the board represents one year of marriage. There are seven kinds of points a player can win as a result of the decisions that he or she makes in the game: security points, respect and esteem points, freedom points, enjoyment points, sex gratification points, marital and parental status points, and ego-support points. The points earned are also contingent on other points (e.g., deciding to have an income of $16,500 instead of $10,000 results in a forfeit of 100 sex gratification points). The game can be played by a group divided into dyads (its original design) or by one dyad alone (i.e., a married couple).

The theoretical orientation of *The Marriage Game* is game theory. Game theory assumes that rapid feedback of information in simulated situations provides a learning experience in which participants do not have to experience real-life consequences. The game's ultimate focus is the enhanced awareness of possible problem areas in marriage.

Kieren, et al. (1975) present a more limited approach to problem-solving in marriages. They define problem-solving as "the process of working through commonly agreed upon goals of the marriage system" (p. 22), and they propose a traditional seven-step problem-solving process. The seven steps are recognition, involvement, generation of alternatives, assessment of alternatives, selection, action, and evaluation. The authors also delineate several problem areas common to most marriages such as finances, sex, in-law problems, parenting, and morale, and describe some of the adjunct variables in problem-solving in marital dyads.

Low self-esteem in either or both of the partners is considered to decrease the number of alternatives generated to problem situations because of the correlation of low self-esteem with a high level of conformity and a low level of risk-taking. Self-awareness is considered important for two reasons: first, it can help decrease or control the interference of emotional conflicts and, second, it expands or makes more realistic the personal resources that are considered in solution-finding. The authors suggest that self-disclosure is one of the best ways to increase self-awareness within the marriage. Therefore the importance of communication is stressed in problem-solving. Unclear communication can obstruct the problem-solving process, and dysfunctional communication can completely disrupt any movement toward the solution of the originally addressed problem.

This program consists of three sessions that are delivered by two trained co-enrichers who may also be trained paraprofessionals. The outline of the major skills covered is as follows:

I. The Problem-Solving Process Explained
   A. Recognition
   B. Involvement
   C. Generation of alternatives
   D. Assessment of alternatives
   E. Taking action
   F. Evaluation
II. Developing Communication as a Resource
   A. Opening up to each other
      1. ability to ask for help
      2. sending clear messages when emotionally worked up
      3. counting to 10 before responding
   B. Rational thinking and emotion in communication
      1. balancing the two
      2. achieving different balances for different situations
   C. Verbal and nonverbal communication
      1. cues
      2. "checking out"
      3. incongruence
   D. Becoming sensitive
      1. "checking out"
      2. learning each other's signals
III. Developing Conflict as Resource
   A. Understanding your own goals
   B. Conflict techniques
      1. listening to the other's side
      2. signals of conflict
      3. counting to 10
      4. maintaining rational judgment
      5. using positive reinforcement, avoiding aversive behavior
      6. admitting errors
      7. patience
      8. sticking to designated issues

This enrichment program combines several of the previously developed techniques in communication skills. The program incorporates the rational step-wise elements of the behavioral programs with some of the less cognitive, more experiential elements of communication-oriented programs, such as Spivack's (Spivack, et al., 1976).

Harrell and Guerney (1976) have developed a similarly eclectic program, which they call Behavioral-Exchange Negotiation. The nine stages of this program parallel the stages of traditional problem-solving paradigms: (1) listening carefully, (2) locating a relationship issue, (3) identifying one's own contribution to the issue, (4) identifying alternative solutions, (5) evaluating alternative solutions, (6) making an exchange, (7) determining conditions of exchange, (8) implementing the behavioral-exchange contract, and (9) renegotiating the behavioral-exchange contract.

Techniques ranging from the use of listening skills to phrasing problems in "we" statements and negotiating an adapted quid pro quo contract are incorporated. Unlike the programs from which these techniques were drawn, participants meet in groups of three couples with one trained professional therapist/trainer. The sessions are primarily didactic, with one stage covered per week and two contracts negotiated throughout the program.

A new contribution to problem-solving techniques with couples has been made by Kessler (1978). This program is designed for couples in conflict, and attempts to structure such conflict along the constructive lines defined by Deutsch (1973): i.e., cooperative conflict and a focus on issues rather than individuals. This program is eclectic, but its overall structure follows a traditional problem-solving-stage outline. These stages and some of their component exercises are listed:

A. Setting the Stage
    1. Establishing rules
    2. Setting tone
    3. Obtaining commitment
    4. Foreshadowing
B. Defining the Issues
    1. Checking out assumptions
    2. Fact-finding
    3. Determing the real issues
C. Processing the Issues
    1. Managing the emotional climate
        a. timing
        b. questions
        c. nonverbal communications
        d. covert competition
        e. impasses
    2. Encouraging empathy
        a. over styles
        b. over needs
        c. over issues
    3. Maintaining equality

D. Resolving the Issues
    1. Encouraging creative alternatives
        a. means–ends shift: shifting from the desired end to the possible means of getting there
        b. expanded boundaries: looking outside normal area of evaluation for solutions

Kessler (1978) also reviews areas of conflict (i.e., excess dependence on drugs, friends, spouse, division of labor, labor of communication, etc.) and notes that the program is applicable to individual couples or groups of couples.

Another more recent treatment program designed specifically for couples provides a systematic, problem-solving approach to the issue of jealousy (Teismann, 1979). The approach is based on the works of Haley (1976) and Weakland et al., (1974); couple awareness of intrapsychic and interpersonal dynamics is considered unnecessary.

Treatment follows a symptom-oriented, goal-directed, task-focused, and short-term procedure whereby specific behavioral sequences are viewed as the key to the maintenance of the problem. Repeated ineffective attempts at problem resolution are viewed as factors that perpetuate the problem itself. These attempts include explanations that may help the couple continue rationalization of the problem.

The problem is viewed as a developmental rather than a pathological one, as residing in the system's interaction rather than in individual psyches, and as the responsibility of both therapist and clients rather than the sole responsibility of the clients. Therapy, thus, is a directive, demanding, continual use of strategies by the therapist in order to realize goals. These strategies include the use of both logical and illogical remedies, including paradoxical methods.

The therapist labels the problem as a jealous system rather than a jealous individual. The therapist then maps the problem by asking how the problem developed, what previous attempts have been used to solve the problem, what triggers begin the problem sequence, and what rules and sequences are working to prevent appropriate management. In beginning the work, the therapist attempts to discover who is pivotal in the change process, beginning change with the person who is most interested in change. The therapist, however, must also have the ability to neutralize his or her position as a rival to the jealous partner(s).

Techniques employed include phoning the extramarital rival in front of the couple and asking him or her to attend sessions. When the rival refuses to come, as is usually the case, the therapist tells the rival to continue the extramarital contact so that the therapist will know how to treat the couple. This intervention ritualizes the therapist's control and excludes the rival through the rival's refusal. Reframing and relabeling the problem (i.e., romantic, loyal, devoted, rather than dependent, possessive, and insecure) are used to alter perspective, promote action, and provide the hope necessary for system change. Since the norms and beliefs of a system are reflected in and controlled by the language of that system, altering the language alters norms and beliefs. System transfer is also employed, whereby the therapist ascribes to the nonjealous person emotions and reactions similar to those experienced by the jealous person. The purpose of system transfer is to redirect the jealous person from his or her intense self-focusing toward the struggles of the partner. The jealous person is assigned the role of Helper rather than the Helped. For example, a wife, jealous of her husband's recently terminated extramarital affair, was assigned the role of helping her husband recover from his guilt and depression.

In this treatment modality, the therapist has the role of a social engineer, realigning structures, hierarchies, values, norms, roles, and sequences. The therapist has the tasks of providing brief, specific problem-solving therapy; tracking the problem sequences; providing task assignments, paradoxical directives with client resistance, and reframing of the negative connotations of behavior; and breaking-up coalitions.

Unlike the other problem-solving programs discussed in this chapter, Teismann's approach incorporates numerous therapeutic, rather than educational, techniques. Traditional marital therapy focusing on marital happiness or satisfaction is restructured to provide specific problem focus and problem resolution. Although a problem-solving treatment paradigm, it is not highly structured, nor does it proceed in a step-wise fashion.

EVALUATION

Although a growing body of literature and structured problem-solving treatment programs now exist, little evaluation of results is available.

Of the earlier programs in industry—Gordon's (1961) Synetics program, Papanek's (1969) Bionics program, and Osborn's (1963) "brainstorming" model—only Osborn's (1963) model has been rigorously studied. His method has been demonstrated as more effective in terms of generation of quantity and quality of solutions than critical or selective idea generation (Parnes, 1959).

In the area of education, training students in problem-solving skills has been demonstrated to have four major effects. First, it enhances alternative consequential and cause-and-effect thinking. Second, it decreases superfluous and irrelevant thinking. Third, it enhances problem-solving ability in those who need it most, and, fourth, it shifts the priority away from aggressive solutions and trains children to see nonforceful possibilities. Other follow-up studies have also suggested the generalization of training to play and domestic settings (Spivack, et al., 1976).

D'Zurilla and Goldfried's (1971) structured problem-solving training has no formal assessment of its efficacy, nor does it address emotional factors that can disrupt the problem-solving process. The authors do, however, cite the need for outcome research and the need to assess the relative contribution of each of the five postulated problem-solving stages to the overall process, and state their intentions to develop a programmed, self-instructing procedure that will not be didactic and therapist-bound.

The Oregon Group has included in their treatment program several measures of outcome evaluation, using both self-report and observational measures, including the Marital Interaction Coding Scale (MICS, Weiss et al., 1973). In studying the outcome of treatment with two groups of five couples, their measures indicated a general increase in problem-solving behavior, a decrease in non-problem-solving behavior, a decrease in negative verbal and nonverbal behavior, and an increase in positive verbal and nonverbal behaviors.

There is no available research concerning

the relative efficacy of the Family Contract Game (Blechman, 1974; Blechman, et al., 1976) with parental dyads, although evaluative research is reported as being currently conducted (O'Callaghan, 1979). The protocols also tend to address the concrete areas of disagreement common to homes with children, and complicated behaviors are not addressed.

Although substantial evaluative research has been conducted with some of Carkhuff's other systems, his problem-solving program (Carkhuff, 1973) has not been formally evaluated (Warsaw, 1975). The advantages, however, include its possible implementation by paraprofessionals and its emphasis on personal values in the problem-solving process. It would thus seem to be most applicable to individuals unclear about their specific goals (e.g., whether or not to return to work, whether or not to move, etc.). It would also seem most applicable to concrete issues as opposed to more abstract problems such as poor communication.

The senior author's enrichment programs used various self-report measures, including an adapted version of the Azrin Marital Happiness Scale. These self-report measures have indicated improvement in subject couples' satisfaction with various aspects of their relationships *(see* Chapter 7).

Harrell and Guerney (1976) have evaluated their Behavioral-Exchange Negotiation program with a battery of self-report and observational measures, one of which, the Marital Conflict Negotiation Task (MCNT), was developed by the authors. Their evaluation of the program revealed mixed results. Generally, significant improvement was found in the measures of marital conflict-management skills, although no significant improvement was found on the measures of marital happiness. In explaining the latter, unexpected result, the authors suggested that the skills taught might not have generalized to everyday life but were more likely reserved for crisis situations, that there might have been insufficient time for the couples to apply the skills to everyday life, that the nonromantic philosophy inherent in behavioral-exchange negotiation might not have been appealing enough to encourage couples to practice skills, and that overt reciprocity (as taught in the program) is not as conducive to enhancing marital satisfaction as a perceived altruistic form of reciprocity.

There is no follow-up data available on the other programs discussed in this chapter; therefore one can only conjecture as to what valid outcomes might be. One would assume that some of the skills that are taught will have relevancy to real-life problem situations. Achieving valid skill training in problem-solving skills with couples, however, remains to be confirmed.

DISCUSSION

It can be concluded that problem-solving is a cognitive, intrapsychic function, highly influenced by social and interpersonal factors, that it is a rational procedure highly contingent upon emotional response to the content that is being evaluated and to other individuals involved, and that problem-solving is both intra- and interpersonal, both rational and affective.

Unfortunately, the definition of problem-solving is as broad and general as most existing programs designed to enhance or teach problem-solving skills. From a theoretical perspective, researchers and practitioners involved in problem-solving stress a skill that is primarily linear in nature. A therapist/teacher either focuses on skill-deficit training or, as in some later programs, focuses on a structured balancing of emotional and rational factors in highly emotionally charged problematic situations.

Although is is conceivable that high-level functioning clients could benefit from a rational educational approach to problem-solving, current approaches may oversimplify the process of problem-solving. Problem-solving is more than mere social competence or judgment; productive problem-solving entails an element of creativity that defies definition within the terms available. There is also a difference between problem-solving/decision-making in laboratory or research settings and real-life settings, for external stimuli that may enhance or detract from the problem-solving process increase outside the laboratory setting.

Unfortunately, little is known about the nature of intuitive problem-solving versus structured problem-solving: its processes are covert, its methods apparently hit-or-miss on the overt level, and the nature of intrapsychic synthesis is unknown. What is known is that some individuals are better at intuitive approaches to problems than at systematic approaches and that some problems are more amenable to intuitive "Aha"-type solutions than others.

Current problem-solving paradigms may be too simplistic to incorporate the myriad complex issues in a couple relationship; to view problem-solving as a skill deficit ignores the interactional nature of the couple relationship. To view problem-solving as a balance between rational and emotional factors may oversimplify human behavior: it may be impossible for any individual ever to achieve balance between rationality and emotionality.

In addition to exploring the nature of problem-solving and acknowledging its complexities, the values inherent in some programs must be noted. Harrell and Guerney (1976) have already raised the question of viewing couple problem-solving as a behavioral exchange rather than involving any altruistic components. Bartering for desired outcomes focuses

on individual gains and may ignore other components of the relationship. In a similar vein, board games in which one collects sex-gratification points, freedom points, and ego-support points may present an inherently individualistic rather than a relationship emphasis.

CONSIDERATIONS FOR THE FUTURE

Whether or not current problem-solving programs are too simplistic to be of any value remains to be seen, for sufficient evaluation is lacking. It is important in the further development of problem-solving paradigms to assess the carryover of teaching problem-solving skills to problematic real-life situations. Finally, one must assess the value of a primarily cognitive approach to human problem-solving when it involves complex interpersonal and intrapersonal emotional factors.

REFERENCES

Adamson RE & Taylor DW. Functional fixedness as related to elapsed time and to set. *Journal of Experimental Psychology*, 1954, *47*, 122–126

Aldous J, Condon T, Hill R, Straus M & Tallman I. *Family problem solving: A symposium on theoretical, methodological, and substantive concerns.* Hinsdale, IL: Dryden Press, 1971

Blechman EA. The family contract game. *The Family Coordinator*, 1974, *23*, 269–281

Blechman EA, & Olson DHL. The family contract game: Description and effectiveness. In DHL Olson (Ed.), *Treating relationships*. Lake Mills, IA: Graphic Publishing, 1976

Blechman EA, Olson DHL, Schornagel CY, Halsdorf M & Turner AJ. The family contract game: Technique and case study. *Journal of Consulting and Clinical Psychology*, 1976, *44*, 449–455

Bowen M. Principles and techniques of multiple family therapy. In PJ Guerin (Ed.), *Family therapy: Theory and practice.* New York: Gardner Press, 1976

Carkhuff R. *The art of problem solving.* Amherst, MA: Human Resource Development Press, 1973

Deutsch M. *The resolution of conflict.* New Haven: Yale University Press, 1973

Dunker K. On problem solving. *Psychological Monographs*, 1945, p. 58

D'Zurilla TJ, & Goldfried MR. Problem solving and behavior modification. *Journal of Abnormal Psychology*, 1971, *78*, 107–126

Goldfried MR, & Goldfried AP. Cognitive change

methods. In FH Kanfer & AP Goldstein (Eds.), *Helping people change: A textbook of methods.* New York: Pergamon Press, 1975

Gordon WJJ. *Synetics.* New York: Harper & Row, 1961

Greenblatt CS, Stein P, & Washburne N. *The marriage game: Understanding marital decision making.* New York: Random House, 1974

Haley J. *Problem-solving therapy.* San Francisco: Jossey-Bass, 1976

Harrell J, & Guerney B. Training married couples in conflict negotiation skills. In DHL Olson (Ed.), *Treating relationships.* Lake Mills, IA: Graphic Publishing, 1976

Jahoda M. The meaning of psychological health. *Social Casework*, 1953, *34*, 349–354

Kagan J. Impulsive and reflective children: Significance of conceptual tempo. In JD Krumboltz (Ed.), *Learning and the educational process.* Chicago: Rand McNally, 1965

Kessler S. *Creative conflict resolution mediation: Leader's guide.* Atlanta: National Institute for Professional Training, 1978

Kieren D, Henton J, & Marotz R. *Hers and his: A problem-solving approach to marriage.* Hinsdale, IL: Dryden Press, 1975

Kohler W. *Gestalt psychology.* New York: Liveright Publishing, 1947

Mahoney MJ. *Cognitive and behavior modification.* Cambridge, MA: Ballinger Publishing, 1974

O'Callaghan JB. *The relative effectiveness of mari-*

tal and parent–child treatments in the amelioration of referred child behavior problems. Doctoral dissertation, Georgia State University, 1979

Osborn AF. *Applied imagination: Principles and procedures of creative problem solving* (3rd ed.). New York: Scribner's, 1963

Olson DH, & Straus MA. A diagnostic tool for marital and family therapy: The SIMFAM technique. *The Family Coordinator*, 1972, *21*, 251–258

Olton RM, & Crutchfield RS. Developing the skills of productive thinking. In P Mussen, J Langer, & MV Covington (Eds.), *Trends and issues in development psychology*. New York: Holt Rinehart & Winston, 1969

Papanek VJ. Tree of life: Bionics. *Journal of Creative Behavior*, 1969, *3*, 5–15

Parnes M. Evaluation of training in creative problem solving. *Journal of Applied Psychology*, 1959, *43*, 189–194

Patterson GR, & Hops H. Coercion, a game for two: Intervention techniques for marital conflict. In RE Ulrich & P Mountjoy (Eds.), *The experimental analysis of social behavior*. New York: Appleton-Century-Crofts, 1972

Rausch H, Barry WA, Hertel RK, & Swain MA. *Communication, conflict, and marriage*. San Francisco: Jossey-Bass, 1974

Satir V. *Conjoint family therapy*. Palo Alto: Science and Behavior Press, 1967

Shantz CU. The development of social cognition. In EM Hetherington (Ed.), *Review of child development research* (Vol. 5). Chicago: University of Chicago Press, 1975

Simon HA, & Hewell A. Human problem solving: The state of the theory in 1970. *American Psychologist*, 1971, *26*, 145–159

Spivack G. Problem-solving thinking and mental health. *The Forum*, 1973, *2*, 58–73

Spivack G, & Levine M. *Self-regulation in acting-out and normal adolescents* (Report M-4531). Washington, DC: NIMH, 1963

Spivack G, Platt J, & Shure M. *The problem-solving approach to adjustment*. San Francisco: Jossey-Bass, 1976

Suchman JR. Inquiry training in the elementary school. *Science Teacher*, 1960, *27*, 42–47

Suchman JR. *Evaluating inquiry in the physical sciences*. Chicago: Science Research Associates, 1969

Teismann M. Jealousy: Systematic, problem-solving therapy with couples. *Family Process*, 1979, *18*, 151–160

Thoresen C, & Coates T. What does it mean to be a behavior therapist? *The Counseling Psychology*, 1978, *7*, 3–21

Warsaw G. *Effects of problem-solving training upon ability to generate alternative solutions*. Unpublished doctoral dissertation, Georgia State University, 1975

Watson RI. *The great psychologists*. Philadelphia: J. B. Lippincott, 1971

Weakland J, Fisch R, Watzlawick P, & Bodin A. Brief therapy: Focused problem resolution. *Family Process*, 1974, *13*, 141–168

Weick K. Group processes, family processes, and problem solving. In J Aldous, T Condon, R Hill, M Straus & I Tallman (Eds.), *Family problem solving*. Hinsdale, IL: The Dryden Press, 1971

Weinstein EA. The development of interpersonal competence. In DA Goslin (Ed.), *Handbook of socialization theory and research*. Chicago: McNally, 1969

Weiss RL, Hops H, & Patterson GR. A framework for conceptualization of marital conflict, a technology for altering it, some data for evaluating it. In LA Hamerlynck, LC Handy, & EJ Marsh (Eds.), *Behavior change: Methodology, concepts, and practice*. Champaign, IL: Research Press, 1973

Wertheimer M. *Productive thinking*. New York: Harper and Brothers, 1959

10

The Treatment of Sexual Dysfunction

Since the early 1970s and the publication of Masters and Johnson's (1970) monumental work, there has been not only an increase in consumer requests for treatment of sexual problems, but also a seemingly overnight growth of sex therapy centers and the establishment of at least two consortia of medical school sex therapy programs. As the interest in and openness to addressing sexual dysfunction continue, new sexual treatments are being employed by a rapidly increasing number of clinicians from diverse professional backgrounds.

Sex therapy may be defined in its purest sense as treatment that is limited to relief of the client's sexual dysfunction. It can be distinguished from other forms of therapy primarily by its use of educational, sexual, and communicative tasks as an integral part of the treatment. Kaplan (1974) defined sex therapy as, "the integrated use of systematically structured sexual experiences with conjoint therapeutic sessions which are the main innovation and distinctive feature of sex therapy" (p. xii).

Lowry and Lowry (1975) defined sex therapy as having the goal of reversing such problems as premature ejaculation, impotence, and ejaculatory incompetence in males; vaginismus, anorgasmia, and dyspareunia in females; sexual aversion in either sex; differing levels of sexual interest in a couple; and other concerns that, if present, patients may identify as undesirable (p. 229). Thus sex therapy specifically addresses the alleviation of a definable sexual dysfunction or concern, and in comparison with the objectives of the two traditional forms of treament for sexual dysfunction (i.e., psychotherapy and marital therapy), the goals of sex therapy are much more limited. Within the context of psychotherapy or marital therapy, sexual symptoms are usually seen as reflections of underlying conflicts and problems, and the relief of the symptoms is seen as a product of the resolution of basic intra- and interpersonal issues. Most sex therapies, however, view sexual dysfunction as caused by faulty previous learning experiences or early traumatic events. Consequently, treatment goals are usually aimed at ameliorating the presenting complaint of the individual or couple.

Most sex therapy approaches are composed of cognitive, behavioral, and emotional components. The cognitive aspect usually consists of an educational component based on the rationale that many sexual difficulties can be corrected or prevented through correcting misconceptions, information-giving, and instruction in proper technique (Hogan, 1978; McCary, 1977).

The behavioral component of treatment is usually homework assignments to be carried out between therapeutic sessions, and the emotional component is addressed according to the philosophy and style of various therapists. Depending on the particular therapist, emotional reactions are considered on a continuum ranging from being peripheral to treatment to being absolutely crucial to successful treatment.

BACKGROUND AND DEVELOPMENT

Historically, sexual dysfunctions were regarded as manifestations of serious psychopathology, with a poor thearapeutic prognosis (Leiblum & Pervin, 1980; Sederer & Sederer, 1979). In addition, the clinician attempting to treat sexual disorders did not possess accurate knowledge about human sexuality on which to base interventions. Sexual behavior had never been directly and systematically studied in the laboratory; consequently, basic data were virtually nonexistent.

This lack of data resulted in the adherence to incomplete and inaccurate therapeutic concepts derived from theoretical speculations and unsubstantiated hypotheses. One poignant example of the confusing influence of inaccurate concepts can be seen in Freud's (1935) assertion that vaginal orgasms express normal and healthy female functioning, while a preference for clitoral stimulation reflects a deep-rooted neurosis. This misconception was not corrected until Masters and Johnson's (1966) demonstration of a single type of orgasm. One consequence of this misconception was the effect on women of prolonged psychanalysis that failed to eliminate the "neurotic" clitorial orgasms.

Several events eventually led to the rapid development of sex therapy as a separate therapeutic entity. Although the development of any psychotherapeutic activity may be outlined arbitrarily, it appears that sex therapy was influenced by a few specific events, beginning with Alfred Kinsey's studies (1948, 1953) of sexual behavior in males and females. He and his colleagues interviewed some 18,000 individuals in an attempt to describe the types of sexual behaviors in which people engage. His work revealed some startling discoveries. These discoveries included the fact that women were not frigid, that approximately one-third of all males had had at least one homosexual experience, and that one-half of all males and one-fourth of all females had engaged in an extramarital affair. Kinsey's report not only removed long-held ideas about male and female sexuality but, for the first time, considered sex from a scientific, descriptive viewpoint, rather than a moralistic one.

Kinsey's work created the *Zeitgeist* for the eventual, extensive, physiological research conducted by Masters and Johnson (1970). Their work was embraced, not only by professionals, but eventually by lay individuals and the general public. Beginning in the 1970s, Masters and Johnson provided remarkable advances in knowledge of human sexuality and tentative evidence that sexual problems are not invariably manifestations of profound emotional disturbance or emotional illness. They posited that sexual problems also commonly occur in persons who function well in other areas of their lives and have no other presenting psychological symptoms. Masters and Johnson (1970) showed that, in many cases, sexual dysfunctions have their etiology in more immediate and simpler problems, such as the anticipation of failure to function, real or imagined demands for performance, and fear of rejection by one's partner. Their data were derived from the study of sexual behavior of men and women under laboratory conditions for two decades, a period during which they observed and recorded approximately 14,000 sexual acts. Their observations included a spectrum of sexual behavior under a variety of conditions. They studied coitus between strangers, between happily married couples, and between couples who had sexual and interpersonal difficulties. Different techniques of erotic stimulation were explored under a variety of conditions.

Kinsey's and Masters and Johnson's studies provided a fairly accurate picture of the basic psychophysiology of human sexuality and reproductive functioning. Their studies subsequently led to the development of a number of treatment approaches for sexual disorders. Although Masters and Johnson's later treatment techniques and outcome reports have come under some criticism (Szasz, 1980; Zilbergeld & Evans, 1980), their physiological data on sexual functioning remain a landmark source from which both medical and nonmedical practitioners have developed their sexual treatment programs.

In addition to the publication of these two major descriptive studies, other professionals, beginning in the 1950s, began to condone a much greater variation of personal preference in sexual behaviors (Ellis, 1971; McConnell, 1977). Furthermore, cultural changes, particularly during the 1960s, led to a greater openness as well as individual concern about sexuality and sexual functioning. As American society became more permissive, sexuality became a more accepted rather than a secretive, hidden aspect of human functioning.

MAJOR PHILOSOPHY AND CURRENT CONCEPTS

The sexual dysfunctions most commonly seen in the context of a couple relationship can be divided into male dysfunctions, female dysfunctions, and dysfunctions that may occur in either sex. One of the basic redefinitions by Masters and Johnson (1970), however, was to consider all sexual dysfunction as part of a dyadic process, both in conception and treatment. Although dysfunctions are described in terms of one partner, they are also considered a problem of the sexual relationship. Any sexual dysfunction can have elements of more general difficulties between partners and/or, depending on the philosophy of the therapists, intrapsychic difficulties of one of the partners.

The major male dysfunctions are defined as follows:

1. *Premature ejaculation.* The male ejaculates so rapidly after vaginal penetration that the female has little or no opportunity to achieve orgasmic return, assuming the capability of orgasm. The man is basically unable to exert voluntary control over his ejaculatory reflex, with the result that once he is sexually aroused, he reaches orgasm very quickly.
2. *Secondary impotence.* The male has been successful in achieving and keeping an erection adequate for penetration of his partner but currently fails to do this at least 25 percent of the time. The most common cause of secondary impotence is aging, in which case it is not a dysfunction, but a natural process. Secondary impotence can also be a common development in response to premature ejaculation. Whether because of his own anxieties or because of communication between the partners, the man realizes that he is not performing adequately for his partner. He begins to worry and try too hard, and the result is impotence. The many organic and medical difficulties that can lead to impotence will not be considered here, except to underscore the importance of medical examination prior to sex therapy.
3. *Primary impotence.* In an interpersonal setting, the man has never had an erection sufficient to allow penetration of his partner. Primary impotence is considered a more serious problem than secondary impotence and may require a longer term of treatment.
4. *Ejaculatory incompetence (retarded ejaculation).* This problem may be considered primary or secondary but is less frequently seen than premature ejaculation or impotence. Although the partner may not be disturbed by the "problem," the couple may seek help when conception is desired. The man responds to sexual stimuli with erotic feelings and erection. Ejaculation, however, is retarded, ranging from occasionally involuntary inhibition of ejaculation to a broad inhibition such that the man has never experienced orgasm in his life.

These are the major female dysfunctions:

1. *General sexual dysfunction.* There is an inhibition of the general arousal aspect of the sexual response. Along with a lack of erotic feelings, there is an impairment of vasocongestion, and there is usually no orgasm.
2. *Primary orgastic dysfunction.* The female has never had (or at least never identified) any orgasmic response. This female is commonly found to have been strictly socialized, with prohibitions about sexuality, pleasure, and touching.
3. *Situational orgastic dysfunction.* The woman has had some orgasmic experience by some methods or a single method, but only in certain situations. She may feel that she lacks important ways of attaining orgasm, such as through intercourse. The inhibition may be random or in specific situations. When the problem is specific to intercourse, it raises the question of whether the woman has unrealistic expectations. Until further research is performed, Kaplan (1974) believes that coital orgastic inhibition may be a normal variation of the female sexual response.
4. *Vaginismus.* There are involuntary contractions of the pelvic musculature that prevent penetration or render penetration

uncomfortable or painful. Vaginismus may accompany primary impotence of the male and may, therefore, have existed for some time without being recognized. In some cases, marriage will not have been consummated.

The following dysfunctions may apply to either sex:

1. *Sexual aversion.* The aversion may be directed to the partner or to certain sexual activities. Curing the aversion may often be a simple matter, requiring either permission or basic information from the therapist or physician.
2. *Dyspareunia.* There is painful intercourse, which can occur for either partner. The cause may often have a medical basis unique to the individual. Therefore the partner who is experiencing the pain is usually examined for medical difficulties, with other possible treatment considered. At the same time, psychological bases for the painful experience are examined, and an individualized treatment is designed.
3. *Low sexual desire.* The dysfunctions of low sexual desire has been posited by Kaplan (1979) as occurring in the first phase of her triphasic conception of sexual reponse. She considers three phases: desire, excitement, and orgasm; thus the dysfunction is a desire problem. Kaplan hypothesized that the etiologic basis of low sexual desire has both physiological and psychological roots. Kaplan suggested that the most frequent physiological correlates of low sexual desire include depression, high stress, and low testosterone level, and the use of certain drugs, such as alcohol, sedatives, or antihypertensive agents. These causes, however, tend to be secondary in frequency to psychological factors. The most immediate psychological antecedent of low sexual desire is the patient's unconscious suppression of the sexual desire. This suppression may occur through those physiological inhibitory centers that act to reduce sexual desire. This "turn-off" mechanism may be activated by the client by a selective focus on some unattractive feature of the partner, such as overweight, or the client's self-defeating cognitions, e.g., "I am too ugly."

ASSESSMENT

Among sex therapists, the initial model for assessing sexual dysfunction was presented by Masters and Johnson (1970). Masters and Johnson examined human sexual response on a physiological level and identified the four states of excitement, plateau, orgasm, and resolution. Another model, similar to that of Masters and Johnson, was suggested by Kaplan (1974). Her model included a biphasic response pattern based on the components of genital vasocongestion and those muscular contractions that produce orgasm in both sexes. Vasocongestion refers to the genital swelling in males and vaginal lubrication in females. Further refinements in assessment occurred when a consideration of the client's subjective experience of sex entered the definition of the dysfunction. The importance of the client's subjective experience developed from clinical experiences suggesting that the question of desire for sex was an issue that needed to be addressed separately from the physiologic response. Unfortunately, the wholehearted acceptance by the therapeutic community of a physiological paradigm overshadowed for some time the importance of subjective factors. Early rationale for treatment was that increasing physical arousal would increase subjective interest. All assessments now attempt to separate emotional from physiological causes, however. Several assessment models incorporate both physiological and pyschological elements. A component model (Zilbergeld & Evans, 1980) assesses the elements of interest, arousal, physiological readiness, orgasm, and satisfaction. Kaplan (1979) suggested her triphasic model, which contains the elements of desire, excitement, and orgasm. She stated:

The three phases are physiologically related but discrete. They are interconnected but governed by separate neurophysiological systems. Metaphorically, orgasm, excitement, and desire may be thought of as having a "common generator," but each has its own "circuitry." And the existence of a separate system of neural circuits creates the possibility for separate and discrete inhibitions of the three phases. Certain kinds of trauma, if sufficiently intense, disturb the entire system, but often only a component is disrupted (p. 3–4).

Kaplan's model was the first to address the question of desire, a phenomenon that perhaps has contributed to many therapeutic failures previously ascribed to client resistance (LoPiccolo, 1980).

Another conceptualization (Walen, 1980) of sexual arousal focuses on the importance of perceptual accuracy and the ability to utilize rational processes in the conduct of sexual functioning. Walen proposed an eight-link arousal cycle that includes (1) perception of a sexual stimulus, (2) evaluation of the sexual stimulus, (3) physiologic arousal, (4) the perception of the arousal, (5) evaluation of the arousal, and (6) the overt response of sexual behavior, followed by (7) the perception and (8) evaluation of that behavior.

Each of these models adds to the clinician's initial assessment of the dysfunction by helping him or her clearly pinpoint specific areas for intervention. Although no one model has been universally accepted by sex practitioners, as a general rule all practitioners examine both the physiological and the psychological etiology in varying degrees and by various classification systems. Since all forms of sexual therapy have as their goal the relief of the sexual symptoms presented by the individual or couple, an initial, thorough assessment of sexual functioning is considered essential prior to treatment.

Lobitz and Lobitz (1978) developed an assessment format that is representative of how most initial assessments are conducted. Their assessment consists of three steps: (1) evaluation of the client's suitability for therapy, (2) development of the client's sexual history and problem list, and (3) ongoing evaluation of the client's progress during treatment.

In their treatment program, the initial session is structured around a discussion of each individual's perception of the sexual difficulty. Lobitz and Lobitz state that they anticipate the couple's inhibitions about discussing sex but do not dwell on desensitizing the inhibition. The session is structured and consists of the following topics: (1) demographic data, such as occupation, current length of relationship, previous marriages; (2) the couple's description of the nature of the sexual problem, including the personal hypotheses of etiology and attempts to resolve it; (3) a description of the couple's current sex life, including questions about frequency of intercourse, female's potential for orgasm, and man's latency to ejacu-

lation; (4) psychosexual history of each partner, including past and present psychological difficulties, traumatic events, and any psychotherapy related to the difficulties; (5) each person's physical health and medical history; and (6) their method of birth control.

Lobitz and Lobitz use the preceding information to evaluate several individual and relationship factors that contribute to a decision as to the couple's appropriateness for sex therapy. These factors include (1) the presence of organic pathology that may influence an individual's ability to perform, (2) the degree of psychopathology in either partner, and (3) each person's motivation for treatment, including commitment to the relationship and willingness to participate. The relationship factors about which Lobitz and Lobitz inquire and that they observe include the relative degree of hostility and intimacy of each partner. The assessment of these areas is conducted to determine whether the couple can be treated via the techniques of sex therapy or if marital therapy would be more appropriate. This initial stage of assessment concludes with either telling the couple that sex therapy would be appropriate or explaining the reasons that they are not suitable candidates for sex therapy. The purpose of this first phase is to identify any problems that would prohibit the couple from treatment with the techniques of sex therapy.

The second phase is conducted to identify the specific psychosexual problems that contribute, either directly or indirectly, to the couple's sexual dysfunction. The interview attempts to specify these problems, with treatment focused on their improvement. This phase is typically conducted with each therapist individually interviewing the same-sex client for one to two hours. The therapists then process this information between themselves before proceeding to interview the opposite-sex client.

The interviews may be considered active–directive, with the general purpose of determining those conditions and situations that have contributed to the development of the sexual problem, as well as those factors that may be maintaining it. Lobitz and Lobitz inquire into the following areas in order to better decide what has predisposed an individual to develop a problem: (1) sexual attitudes and behaviors of parents and other authority figures; (2) sources of early sexual information; (3) nature of early sex play, e.g., same or opposite sex; (4) self-discovery of one's sexuality, e.g., erection, orgasm; (5) masturbation; (6) types of sexual fantasies during masturbation; (7) the development of social-sexual values; (8) first intercourse; (9) first and subsequent social-sexual involvement with current partners; (10) onset and course of specific sexual dysfunctions; (11) attempts that have been made to change the dysfunction.

Lobitz and Lobitz employ Lazarus's (1974) multimodal approach to identify the factors that maintain the sexual problem. The therapists attempt to identify deficits in behavior, cognitions, affect, sensation, imagery, interpersonal relations, biology, and personality. In addition to identifying weaknesses, the therapists also identify strengths that can be used as resources in the course of treatment.

After these interviews are completed, a list of problems, derived from the various areas of inquiry, is formulated. The interaction among problems is considered, as are hypotheses about their development. For Lobitz and Lobitz, hypotheses are formulated as behavioral responses that have been learned in order to give clients hope that they may be unlearned.

The second phase concludes with feedback sessions in which clients are given impressions that the therapists have developed through the first two phases. An attempt is made to increase the clients' commitment and cooperation by eliciting their reactions to the therapists' impressions. The end result of this discussion is that therapists and clients arrive at mutually agreeable goals for treatment.

THE TREATMENT PROCESS

Before Masters and Johnson's work, treatment approaches varied and were based on analytic or other therapeutic intervention styles, as well as on marital counseling (Heiman, et al, 1981). The therapist looked at the deeper issues for the individual or couple, with the assumption that sex was only a symptom; it was not to be focused on and certainly not to be treated directly. In recent years, an analytic emphasis now represents one end-point of a continuum, and exclusive, symptom-focused in-

terventions represent the other end-point. Clinical case reports by a variety of sex therapists (Sotile & Kilman, 1977) suggest that a consensus now exists on initial sex-therapy interventions. Most therapists begin by prescribing low-intensity sex exercises for the couple. The point of therapeutic divergence occurs when these tasks are met with noncompliance. For some therapists (Kaplan, 1974, 1979), this resistance allows entree to an examination of the individual dynamics or dyadic difficulties maintaining the problem, while, for others, treatment may be terminated as unsuccessful.

A body of techniques compose the overall treatment repertoire of most sex therapists. The first technique concerns giving couples information about the sexual response. Treatment includes information about sexual functioning, physiology, and the range of sexual behavior that is common and uncommon. This information is given to correct the couple's possible misinformation about their sexuality and sexual functioning.

The second area of techniques is contributed by behavioral therapy. The techniques include desensitization based on reciprocal inhibition, deep relaxation exercises, operant training, successive approximation of new behaviors, and assertiveness training, as well as the identification and training of specific social skills. Behavioral techniques in general lend themselves to short-term treatment, allow an individualized treatment to be designed, and give specifiable and teachable techniques that can be evaluated. The behavioral rationale is that sexual dysfunction is a problem of prior learning (LoPiccolo & Lobitz, 1973) and can thus be corrected by new learning.

Systematic desensitization (Wolpe, 1973) in particular is one of the basic techniques of many sex therapies. It is used both to address directly a specific dysfunction and to densensitize the individual to the anxiety that may accompany certain social or sexual activities. Much of Masters and Johnson's exercises, as well as most sex therapy treatment procedures, focus on creating a relaxed sexual atmosphere to counteract learned, negative behaviors. The basic relaxation principle is that of reciprocal inhibition, which states that if a response that is inhibiting anxiety (such as relaxation) can be connected with stimuli that usually arouse anxiety, the response that is inhibiting anxiety will weaken the later arousal of anxiety by those stimuli.

Medicine and medical clinics have contributed a group of specific techniques. These include the Kegel (1952) exercises, Semans' (1956) stop–start technique, the "squeeze" technique (Masters & Johnson, 1970), the Valsalva technique (Marcotte & Weiss, 1977) for premature ejaculation, the Haslam method of vaginismus (Haslam, 1965), nondemand pleasuring (Masters & Johnson, 1970), the quiet vagina exercise (Hartman & Fithina, 1974), sensate focus (Masters & Johnson, 1970), masturbation training, and the use of fantasy.

The Kegel exercises are based on the finding that in women the development of the pubococcygeus muscle increases sensation and response of the vagina during intercourse, tends to eliminate pain during intercourse, and often produces a greater capacity for experiencing orgasms. The exercises consist of identifying and learning to develop this muscle.

The Semans technique, the "squeeze," the pause, and the Valsalva technique (Marcotte & Weiss, 1977) are all basic techniques used in the couple context to help the man control his ejaculation. The Semans technique and the pause technique are simply to stop and start stimulation; the Masters and Johnson idea is to add a squeeze just below the head of the penis to reduce erection. The Valsalva technique teaches the male to relax his pubococcygeus muscle and use this relaxation to delay orgasm (Marcotte & Weiss, 1977).

Kaplan (1974) reported treating 32 couples, using the pause technique, with a 100 percent cure rate. Semans (1956) reported a 100 percent success rate in eight cases with the pause technique. LoPiccolo and Lobitz (1973) treated six cases with a 100 percent success rate, using the squeeze technique. Masters and Johnson (1970) reported treating 186 cases, using the squeeze technique, with only four failures. Only Cooper (1968, 1969) reported discouraging results with both techniques. In one study, only one client of nine improved, while in a second study of 60 clients, only 43 percent improved, and 7 percent became worse.

The Haslam method for vaginismus consists of a series of graduated dilators used to inhibit the involuntary spasm, eventually allowing penetration and intercourse.

Nondemand-pleasuring, the quiet vaginia,

and sensate focus are all variations on the idea of increasing sexual stimulation in a relaxed atmosphere without any pressures to perform.

The use of masturbation-training and fantasy has many purposes. They are used to condition the sexual response to different situations as well as to distract a person from viewing his or her own performance in an anxious or judgmental way. They are also used to help an individual increase his or her arousal.

Masturbation has been widely employed in many sex therapy programs for the treatment of erectile failure (Annon, 1971, 1974), premature ejaculation (Annon, 1974), general sexual dysfunction (Annon, 1975), primary orgasmic dysfunction (Annon, 1974, 1975; Hastings, 1963, 1966), and secondary orgasmic dysfunction (Annon, 1975). Hogan (1978) cites the following reasons for the utility of masturbation in therapy:

1. It is less anxiety-provoking than heterosexual behavior for some clients.
2. The client is able to discover his or her own arousal response and then teach the partner.
3. Women are more likely to reach orgasm through masturbation than through any other technique.
4. Masturbation leads to more intense orgasms than intercourse or manual stimulation by the partner.
5. It may be used by clients who do not have partners.
6. Males can practice the squeeze or pause technique without a partner's performance demands.
7. It may be used to increase the frequency of orgasm, leading to a longer ejaculation latency in men who suffer from premature ejaculation.

The use of cognitive and attention-focusing techniques are also widely used in the treatment of sexual dysfunction (Ellis, 1971; Kaplan, 1974; Lazarus, 1968; Masters & Johnson, 1970). These techniques include fantasy and pornography to increase sexual arousal (Kaplan, 1974), thought-stopping to reduce obsessions about performance (Garfield, McBrearty & Dichter, 1969), and a logico-empirical approach to stop irrational thoughts about performance (Ellis, 1971). The most widely used cognitive approach is the simple instruction that the client direct attention to his or her own physical sensations, as opposed to worrying about performance or trying to control orgasms. Hogan (1978) reported several successful case studies using these techniques.

Other techniques include group therapy, communication training, assertiveness training, and the use of co-therapists.

Gestalt theory has also contributed the use of body and imagery and the idea of building self-esteem through positive self-imagery. Self-imagery is best illustrated in the work of Hartman and Fithian (1974), who use nude self-examination with mirrors to change individuals' body images and therapist-directed sensitivity exercises in order to help the couple become more aware of their sensations.

MAJOR MODES OF TREATMENT

It is difficult to divide the treatment of sexual dysfunction into structured and nonstructured approaches. Since the pioneering work of Masters and Johnson, there has not only been a proliferation of sexual treatment theories and approaches, but most approaches have shared structured formats that rely on established techniques. Disregarding the work of unqualified sex therapists and less reputable approaches, there remains a continuum of structured treatment approaches. For this reason, only the major treatment approaches will be considered, beginning with the less structured and proceeding to the most structured. Each treatment approach will be identified by author.

Kaplan

Kaplan's (1974) approach uses a therapist of either sex who is a trained psychotherapist. Therapy is individualized, dynamic, and is conducted during a two-week, intensive, and, to the client, expensive format. The assigned sexual tasks are expected to evoke personal and dyadic conflicts that can then be addressed by the therapist. One of the primary tasks of the therapist is considered the management of resistance.

One of Kaplan's major points is that the therapist needs to be flexible and to tailor the treatment procedures to the needs of the couple.

Sensate focus and other exercises are used if and when indicated. Exercises and experiences are arranged to meet specific psychotherapeutic objectives. The sexual tasks are seen as directly changing a problematic sexual system, such as helping to resolve sexual conflicts and bringing into focus personal and interactional problems that can be handled by the therapist. Sensate focus is used to help the couple relax in an intimate setting and to reduce worry about performance and emphasis on orgasm. Great emphasis is placed on helping the individual or couple to achieve adequate sexual functioning one time. This success encourages the couple and provides the therapist with an opportunity to show the couple that progress is possible and that changes need to be made for continued success.

Kaplan considers the couples' sexual assignments part of the assessment of the problem. By the couple's resistance to carrying out the tasks and by their reactions to the results, the therapist is able to identify the sexual inhibitions operating within the individuals and the dyad.

The therapist uses the information from assigned tasks to plan the therapeutic sessions. The therapist clarifies the couple's sexual transactions for them and attempts to change problematic behaviors by fostering insight into underlying, unconscious dynamics. The use of this psychodynamic therapy focuses only on the specific sexual problem and is meant to address only the obstacles that interfere with the improvement of the sexual difficulties.

Hartman and Fithian

Hartman and Fithian's (1974) approach uses dual-sex therapists and also takes place in a two-week, intensive format. The initial assessment includes a detailed sexual history, as well as psychological testing.

Hartman and Fithian believe that the dual-sex team is essential, considering the strong differences in how men and women are reared. It is thought that the dual-sex team minimizes the problem of sexual involvement and the handling of sexual interest that can occur between therapist and client. It allows easier touching between client and therapist and encourages the clients to touch each other more easily.

After extensive psychological testing, these

authors conduct a thorough sex history. The history is used as an educational as well as an information-gathering opportunity. Testing is followed by physical and sexological examinations. The sexological examination is unique to Hartman and Fithian's approach.

The female's sexual organs are physically examined, with the examiner carefully checking the sexual response. This response is discussed with the female as it takes place, giving valuable information and correcting any misinformation she may have. At the same time, she is being given permission to have sexual feelings. The husband is brought in for the last part of this sexological examination of the woman, and the exploration and information-giving continues. A male sexological examination is also conducted, and the wife is included, to teach her male physiology, as well as the squeeze technique if this technique is to be used later in treatment.

Body-imagery work is used and stems from research the authors have conducted on nudism. Their basic goal is to encourage the acceptance of one's nude body, with the addition of self-touching and exploration. The work is done with each individual standing in front of a tailor's mirror. The therapist tries to be objective as well as reassuring in helping to point out and emphasize the positive aspects of the individual's appearance. Common worries such as the size of sexual organs and concerns about the shape or appeal of parts of the body can then be discussed with each person. A series of fantasy exercises concerning the images each person has about his or her own body are also used, as are sensitivity exercises between the partners.

Hartman and Fithian begin with the couple's pleasuring exercises with nonthreatening touching, such as foot and face caresses. The couple then moves to body caressing, breathing together, and, finally, sexual caressing. The homework assignments are carried out in the motel where the couple stays during treatment. Assignments include nondemand-caressing and the quiet-vagina exercise, a Hartman and Fithian idea. In this latter assignment, the woman inserts the penis into her vagina when she is ready, after which the people lie quietly together for a half-hour. They are told to move just enough to maintain erection. This exercise serves as a bridge between the nondemand, noncoital exercises and coital functioning. It is meant to provide a non-pressure situation in which the couple is in close intimate contact, without worry about performance.

Various audio-visual aids are used, in which actors model the behaviors of the various exercises and homework assignments. The couple can view videotapes or films and listen to audio tapes of persons who have gone through treatment for particular dysfunctions and who describe how they have come to function well sexually.

Lobitz and LoPiccolo

According to Lobitz and LoPiccolo (1972), sexual dysfunction is a learned phenomenon, maintained by a parnter's anxiety as well as those difficulties with the spouse that fail to reinforce healthy responses. The program as originally designed was conducted by graduate doctoral students. After an initial screening of up to 50 percent of applicants because of severe personal and dyadic difficulties, the selected clients pay, in advance, their fees and refundable penalty deposits. The penalty deposit is refunded if the client follows all the treatment rules and procedures. For each session missed or rule violated, a certain portion of the penalty deposit is forfeited.

A dual-sex therapy team is used, and treament begins with a sexual physical examination designed to be disinhibiting and educational. For all couples, intercourse is at first prohibited, while the therapist team works to rebuild the couple's repertoire of sexual behaviors. In addition to standard techniques that have been discussed in this chapter, this program also uses some innovative techniques.

The first is the penalty deposit. Second is a daily record form, used to collect data on sexual activity as well as numerical ratings of arousal and sexual pleasure. This daily record form provides for the therapists data that can be used to readjust the treatment program, when needed. The third is a group of masturbation-training techniques. These techniques may be used with fantasy to help each partner become more aroused by the other or to produce orgasm for anorgasmic women. In increasing arousal, the client is instructed to masturbate, using already arousing stimuli or visual materials, and to switch before orgasm to a fantasy of the partner.

For women who have never achieved orgasm, a nine-step masturbation program is used. The program begins by having the woman examine her body, including her genitals, with mirrors, and having her begin the Kegel exercises. She next explores her genitals, first without paying attention to sensation, then with the idea of locating sensitive areas. She is then told how to concentrate on stimulating the sensitive areas and how to use a lubricant. She is told to increase the intensity and length of time of self-stimulation; if orgasm does not result, she is to begin to use a vibrator to stimulate herself. After orgasm is attained, the husband is involved, first by having him observe her stimulating herself, then having him stimulate her in the way he has observed. Finally, intercourse is included, with the husband additionally stimulating the wife manually or with the vibrator.

In order to teach deficit social skills, Lobitz and LoPiccolo also use modeling and role-playing. They teach clients to share feelings as well as to assert themselves in important situations. They also use role-playing of orgasm to disinhibit many types of control the woman may be using against her sexual behavior. A final innovation is to have the clients help in planning the final session so that they will be better able to handle problems that may arise after treatment is terminated.

The Plissit Model

The Plissit Model (Annon, 1976) is a conceptual scheme used by a number of different treatment approaches. Annon noted that although the treatment in many clinics starts with a comprehensive assessment, the resulting treatment formats remain fairly standard for all clients. He made the point that the initial assessment should dictate the treatment that follows. In addition, Annon stated that considering the broad range of techniques available for bevahioral treatment of sexual dysfunction, a plan is required for ordering and selecting the techniques for any particular case. A plan is essentially what the Plissit model provides. After analyzing the client's sexual problem, the therapist is encouraged to look at the relevant behavioral repertoires in order

to make a behavioral diagnosis. A treatment approach can then be planned that will include priorities for different interventions, as well as a way of ordering and timing the different interventions. The basic scheme consists of four levels: permission, limited information, specific suggestions, and intensive therapy.

In the first level of permission-giving, the client is seen as needing reassurance from a professional that he or she is normal or that the type of sex that he or she is interested in is acceptable. The giving of permission is considered both a prevention for future problems and a treatment technique. The areas requiring permission might include thoughts, fantasies, dreams, and feelings, as well as behaviors.

Annon makes the point that there are limitations to the giving of permission. First, the therapist should be encouraging the client to make an informed choice. For example, although the therapist could give the client permission to enjoy any fantasy while masturbating, there is evidence that a systematic association of sex with any kind of fantasy will tend to condition arousal to that kind of stimuli. This could, of course, work to the benefit or the detriment of the client. The values of the therapist may make it difficult to give permission for some things; in those cases, he or she would need to express the difficulty clearly and refer the client to someone else.

The second level is the giving of information. In this level, the giving of specific information is related to the concerns of the client. Annon cites evidence that the giving of a limited amount of information of direct concern to the patient will be more helpful than a more comprehensive, longer presentation of general sex information. The information given can help to overcome common cultural misconceptions. These misconceptions include myths about genital size, differences in sexual interest between the sexes, the harms of masturbation, oral sex, and frequency of sexual performance. The manner of presenting the information must, of course, be suited to the client.

The third level is the giving of specific suggestions. To understand the sexual difficulty well enough to proceed to this level, the therapist needs more information, which is acquired by taking a sexual-problem history. This problem history is basically an attempt to look at the behavioral system that is maintaining the problem. It resembles other brief-therapy information-gathering in that it looks at the current problem, when and how it developed, what the individual sees as the cause, what keeps the problem going, what other treatment has been attempted, and what the goals and expectations of treatment are. By carefully collecting this information, the clinician is able to discern the cause of the problem, what keeps it going, and what the client hopes to get from treatment.

The suggestions given depend on the problem and on the therapist's preferred techniques. They can include all the standard techniques used in sex therapy and can be suggestions given to a male or a female alone, or to a couple. For the individual who has no partner available, some form of masturbation-training would probably be most helpful. These first three levels form the brief therapy component of the Plissit model.

The fourt level is intensive therapy. Therapy consists of more involved, longer-term treatment of dysfunctions that, for various reasons, are more difficult to treat. Here the individual skill of the therapist becomes much more important.

Masters and Johnson

Masters and Johnson's (1970) treatment takes place in a two-week, intensive format, with the couple staying at a motel near the clinic. Treatment is conducted by a dual-sex team, one of whom is always a physician. Initially, each individual is separately interviewed by one therapist and there is a complete medical examination for each partner. The therapists and the couple then meet to discuss the problem and the treatment goals. After the initial examination, the couple is seen every day, usually conjointly by both therapists, with occasional individual sessions when required.

The basic format is designed for couples. In the past, Masters and Johnson have provided a surrogate partner for the individual who has no current partner or whose partner is not available for treatment. In addition to criticism of the use of surrogates (Appelbaum, 1977), however, there have been legal problems, and

Masters and Johnson have discontinued the use of surrogates.

The basic treatment philosophy is that sexual dysfunction is a problem of the couple; both partners are involved in treatment, and treatment focuses on education and re-education. The same routine and series of tasks are used for all couples. Treatment always begins with a prohibition of intercourse and with the sensate focus exercises. After the couple reports an increase in pleasure, they carry out specific exercises designed for their particular dysfunction.

Because the Masters and Johnson approach is so basic to many sex therapies, their treatment will be described in some detail. Therapy for the couple is aimed at developing a functional interaction between the partners that will support both individuals. Healthy interaction and communication are encouraged, focusing on sexual functioning. Since sex is only one way in which the partners communicate and express their sexuality, attention is paid to the total way in which the couple interacts. The dual-sex, co-therapist approach in treatment is based on the idea that the female therapist supports the female client and the male therapist supports the male client. A basic principle of sexual communication stressed by Masters and Johnson is that each partner must express himself or herself and risk letting the partner know his or her needs.

Both partners are considered equal in that they must take responsibility for their desires, needs, and sexual satisfaction. On the other hand, the basic values of the clients must be respected. Since sexual communication and social communication are related, as the therapy focuses on sexual communication, it will also naturally extend to social communication. Males are understood to be often socialized to be nonfeeling and performance-oriented; females are understood to be more often socialized to look for security in relationships and to downplay sex. Physiologically, the female is seen as the more versatile in terms of sexual capability.

The treatment begins with the sensate-focus exercises. In these exercises, one partner receives pleasuring as the other gives it. The receiving partner is told to be completely selfish, concentrate on his or her sensations, and communicate to the partner what feels best and how to provide pleasure. Different positions are used in sensate focus, beginning with nongenital caressing and, later, including genital pleasuring.

The treatment for premature ejaculation is as follows: The female uses the squeeze technique on the penis during sexual activity. This technique is used three to five times before vaginal intromission for three months, for one-half of sexual activities for the following three months, and after that, whenever three to five days have passed since sexual activity. The female may be unable to achieve orgasm with intercourse, and she may have much resentment about the time she has "put up with" her husband's problem. Therapy then focuses on communication about issues that trouble the couple.

The treatment for secondary impotence first involves education about the effects of aging on sexuality. The documented decrease in frequency of need to ejaculate, rapidity of erection, volume of ejaculation, and force of ejaculation, with increasing age, may be the cause of the "problem." A single failure in an aging male may cause a fear of sex and lead to a pattern of repeated failures or avoidances. Use of alcohol or certain drugs are also considered possible causes.

Therapy for secondary impotence involves unlearning and reorienting for the couple. Information is given and the communication system of the couple is worked with to enhance total communication. The basic treatment tasks include nondemand pleasuring, dispelling the fear of failure, and building up to intercourse once erectile confidence has been established.

The treatment of primary impotence is based on the idea that this dysfunction stems from an individual's own fears, not necessarily aroused or aggravated by the partner. Treatment is generally more difficult and has a less favorable prognosis. The therapeutic tasks are more dependent on the male's sexual inhibitions, his interaction patterns, and physical examination.

Therapy for ejaculatory incompetence starts with an educational component, in which this relatively infrequent dysfunction is explained in terms of its usual various causes. After this, the male (or his partner) stimulates himself to the point of ejaculatory inevitability. At this point, intercourse may be attempted, with the female thrusting at the male's command. If intercourse is unsuccessful, manual

stimulation is repeated. Although it may take some time to accomplish the first ejaculation in the vagina, progress is rapid after one success. The process described may, when necessary, proceed by graduated steps.

The basic treatment for orgasmic dysfunction in women, whether primary or secondary, is as follows: First, the therapists look for things the husband does or does not do that interfere with his wife's sexual pleasure. The wife's attitudes and history relative to sex are also examined. The sensate focus exercises are prescribed, with daily discussion to allow examination of the interference with the orgasmic reflex. The woman is helped to understand that orgasm comes from allowing herself to be overcome by erotic stimulation instead of "trying" to do something. The woman is at the same time given permission to have sexual feelings. After the sensate-focus exercises, genital caressing is prescribed. The woman reclines against the seated male and directs his hand to provide a maximum of stimulation for her. The husband has access to his wife's entire body in this position, and the woman can feel protected and less self-conscious. The male is told not to approach the clitoris directly, as it may be too sensitive. Rather, he is to caress the general mons area, the shaft of the clitoris, the upper thighs, and outer lips. The husband should spread vaginal lubrication to the clitoral area. Stimulation should be teasing, should center on various parts of the body, and should always try to maximize pleasure, according to the wife's desires.

Coitus is next attempted in the female-superior position. The husband lies still while his wife moves so as to explore possibilities for increasing her excitation. Later, the husband may thrust at a pace dictated by his wife. This coitus should stop periodically to allow embracing in each other's arms. If the husband ejaculates, he can reassure his wife that there will be another opportunity to resume the experience. If this position successfully provides pleasure to the wife, a lateral position is next used for intercourse. In this position, both partners have the most freedom to move their bodies. Through this procedure, it is hoped that the woman can develop a pattern of orgasms.

Treatment for vaginismus begins with a physical demonstration for the husband of the vaginal muscle spasm. After this, graduated dilators are used by the husband under the wife's direction. The dilators, in graduated sizes, will be inserted for several hours each night. The use of the dilators builds to the size at which penile insertion is possible. Therapy is directed toward the interaction between the couple, since the husband will often be afraid of hurting his wife.

Miscellaneous Programs

Adaptations of the Masters and Johnson format have been used in different settings. One such adaptation is a short-term workshop format. In this approach, a multidisciplinary team operated a weekend workshop based on Masters and Johnson ideas. Reported success figures for treatment were reasonably close to the original Masters and Johnson figures (Blakeney, et al, 1976).

Another adpatation is a sexual enrichment program of a more preventive nature (L'Abate, 1975a). Entitled the Program for Sexual Fulfillment of Couples, it consists of six programmed lessons based on the ideas of Masters and Johnson. It is designed to promote an awareness of each partner's sexuality and to allow experiences that will enhance the couple's enjoyment of thseir sexual experience. It can be carried out in a once-a-week time structure, more easily usable to the average practitioner. The homework assignments begin with the sensate focus exercises and proceed through intercourse.

There are two other enrichment programs for sexuality available from L'Abate (1975a). These include a sex-attitudes clarification program and an adolescent sexual-awareness enrichment program. The second program is designed for teachers, parents, or adolescents, and is based on the idea that well clarified, healthy attitudes in parents aid the development of healthy attitudes in their children. The conveying of biological information about sex is considered only part of the process; the other part must address values and attitudes about sex and sexuality. Entitled the Sexual Attitudes Clarification Workshop (L'Abate, 1975a), it consists of six lessons. These lessons cover talking about sex, laughing about sex and sexuality, the meaning of sex and sexuality, pleasuring, sexuality and responsibility, and ethnic, cultural, and occupational role differences in sexuality.

The third enrichment program is entitled the Adolescent Sex Awareness Enrichment Program. This program is meant to encourage open discussion of sexuality among adolescents. It provides accurate information, dispels myths, and challenges double standards and existing contradictions. This program is basically preventive, as are the other enrichment programs, and also helps to prevent illegitimacy, venereal disease, inappropriate mate selection, and conflicts between sexuality and romantic love (L'Abate, 1975a).

The enrichment program for adolescents is one of a large number of programs for sex education. Sex education can be a component of sex therapy, in that it is ideally preventive by providing information about sex and sexuality. McCary (1977) has advocated that most sexual difficulties could be prevented by timely education, and that most clients seeking sex therapy expect a heavy emphasis on discussion of specific content (Rose, et al, 1974). Currently, there are a substantial number of documented sexual education programs in the literature.

Another sexual enrichment/educational program is presented by Kaufman and Krupka (1975). This program is designed as a way for couples to enhance their sexual relationships. Through a series of seven weekly sessions led by dual-sex enrichers, the couples learn to build good communication, to resolve conflict, and to pleasure each other in nondemanding ways. Improving communication is emphasized in this program.

Rosenberg and Rosenberg (1976) report on a two-day experiential educational program for adolescents and their families. They used a multimedia presentation, including small group sessions with parents and teenagers discussing their reactions to the materials. In a self-report follow-up, participants found the program helpful, informative, and facilitative of communication.

Diamond (1976) reported the use of commercial television as a medium to transmit sexual information, and in his study, he found it effective in transmitting information in an entertaining way. He also found the community reaction to the programming to be positive.

Duehn and Mayadas (1977) made the point that sex educators need to use media and structured learning formats to create effective group sex-education programs. They have found it possible to teach adolescents interpersonal skills that are usable in sexuality. Snegroff (1976) also found that parents and their adolescent children could be successfully involved together in sexual education, and that one result was an increase in communication. Monge, Dusek, and Lawless (1977) examined the information gained by adolescents through a sex education class. They found, first, that sex education courses can provide information not gained by other adolescents who were not in such a course. Second, they found that peers were not as important a source of information when sex education was made available to adolescents.

Mayadas and Duehn (1977) reported the effects of a short-term sex education program for nearly married couples. They found that the sexual knowledge-base of the couples increased, that couples became more involved during sexual interaction, and that the couples experienced a broadening of sexual behaviors, with positive results.

Self-Help Program

A number of structured self-help programs are advocated as both prevention- and treatment-oriented. The proliferation of self-help books has been phenomenal since the mid 1970s, and although this chapter will not review self-help bibliotherapy, we note that an increasing number of books about sexuality have been published by both professionals and nonprofessionals. Although some reiterate the important components of sex therapy, others advocate increased sexuality and sexual performance as more of a value system than a solution to dysfunction.

EVALUATION

Kuriansky and Sharpe (1976) proposed guidelines for evaluating therapeutic procedures. Although these guidelines are reasonable, it is difficult to find any single study that meets all the requirements for a thorough evaluation. This may be due in part to the newness of the field, but it probably also reflects the difficulties, as well as lack of emphasis on evaluation, in the therapy field in general. The guidelines proposed were (1) the use of standard interviews both before and after treatment; (2) a careful specification of treatments used, and how they are standardized; (3) an assessment of psychosocial as well as

sexual functioning; (4) criteria for diagnosis and outcome; (5) the use of control of other comparison groups; (6) methodical in-person follow-up.

The most impressive outcome study (for visible results) is probably that of Masters and Johnson (1970). Over a 10-year period, they evaluated the therapy of hundreds of couples and reported an 80 percent overall cure rate, with some specific dysfunctions responding more favorably to treatment. A careful 5-year follow-up showed a relapse rate of only 5 percent. There were no controls, however, and clients who did not complete treatment were not counted. In addition, couples were carefully screened for entry.

In general, many therapies using variations of the Masters and Johnson techniques report good results (Lobitz & LoPiccolo, 1972; Marshall, 1973; Kaplan, 1974; Wish, 1975). Lobitz and LoPiccolo (1972) rigorously studied changes in behavior during sex therapy, using a Sexual Interaction Inventory, and report success rates comparable to those of Masters and Johnson. Hartman and Fithian (1974) did not report any figures but said that their results were comparable to those of Masters and Johnson.

Wabrek and Wabrek (1975) reported on the use of systematic desensitization with graduated dilators for the treatment of vaginismus. Their findings are in line with success rates reported by Masters and Johnson.

Barbach (1974) reported a group treatment for preorgasmic women. (The label of preorgasmic is noted as a helpful way of relabeling a problem to increase the hope for change.) Women in this group treatment explored their own physical response at home through masturbation. The group shared experiences about their homework assignments and their difficulties or fears about the homework, as well as other issues. The format was a weekly session for five weeks. A high percentage of women were orgasmic at the end of treatment, and many of them also showed transfer of response to an interpersonal context. In addition, other aspects of sex and their relationships showed significant results after follow-up. It should be noted that this study presents workable alternatives to the couple-in-therapy format or the use of surrogates.

Nims (1975) reported on the success of shaping of masturbatory fantasies, which can then be incorporated into intercourse, to increase excitatory and orgiastic capabilities. Zilbergeld (1975) presented a successful program for treatment of sexual dysfunction in men without partners. He used masturbation training, self-disclosure, assertiveness, relaxation, and information to explode myths. He found that, in more cases, men prefer the use of a female co-therapist. Schmidt, et al (1976) presented a model for treating a male without a partner, using short-term behavioral sex therapy. Rosen (1976) used a biofeedback technique in sexual therapy. Male and female subjects received feedback on their rate and amplitude of tumescence (arousal for man or woman), and seemed to acquire greater voluntary control of the response.

Segraves (1976a) examined the outcomes of all the principal treatments of sexual dysfunction for the purpose of identifying the basic treatment components of successful programs. He found that masturbation training, the Masters and Johnson techniques, and systematic desensitization combined with other therapeutic procedures all showed fairly successful outcomes. All three approaches use some kind of graduated exposure to erotic stimulation; therefore erotic stimulation may be an essential treatment element. In addition, all successful approaches appeared to involve some directive kind of psychotherapy. This psychotherapy ranged from training of social skills such as assertiveness, expressing affection, and asserting one's wishes and desires, to a more general, Satir-type, communications training program. The basic elements might be considered teaching someone to differentiate himself or herself from others, discarding sexual myths and other distractions, and encouraging the growth of self-expression. There was no evidence that any of the sexological exams, dual-sex therapy teams, or the use of the Kegel exercises made any difference in treatment outcome.

Segraves also noted that there are mixed findings on whether successful outcome is enhanced by treating individuals or couples. The marital issues that may arise in couple therapy may be therapeutically difficult, thus interfering with successful outcomes for the treatment of the sexual dysfunction. Yet, Lobitz and LoPiccolo (1972) showed higher success treating couples than did the Barbach (1974) programs, which treat individuals in groups.

There is currently too little evidence to enable the clinician to decide which situations would be suitable for couple treatments. Nevertheless, much clinical observation supports the fact that symptoms exist in a marriage or relationship context and that this context needs to be considered for effective treatment.

Godow (1977) proposed that there are essential elements in all effective treatments for female sexual dysfunction. These include legitimizing sexuality, reducing anxiety, providing basic education, promoting effective sexual communication, and encouraging acceptance of responsibility by the client. Godow provided a slightly different perspective from that of Segraves.

An interesting qualification of the results of sex therapy was proposed by Levay and Kagle (1977). They reported on 19 couples who returned for treatment some time after completing a Masters and Johnson-style sex therapy. Of these couples, eight required only additional short-term sex therapy, while the other 11 couples were treated for an extended length of time with either individual dynamic therapy or conjoint therapy. These authors believe that an overload of the intensity of the original treatment, the severity of the original symptoms, and the presence of psychopathology relating to pleasure, intimacy, and cooperation all interefered with continued or maintained progress. They argue, as does Kaplan, that some cases require a more open-ended treatment, paced according to the abilities of the couple and in conjunction with pscychotherapy as necessary.

In a departure from the nearly total acceptance of the methods of Masters and Johnson by sex therapists, Zilbergeld and Evans (1980) provide a substantive criticism of their work. Although this criticism is unique to the literature, the authors have assembled a compelling critique of the Masters and Johnson research. Since many research studies report outcome results similar to those of Masters and Johnson, (Wright, et al, 1977), it is important to examine this criticism.

One general criticism reported by Zilbergeld and Evans concerns the difficulty of replicating Masters and Johnson's work. Replication is difficult because of the critical omission of relevant methodological data as well as nonspecified reporting of outcome data. Masters and Johnson's definition of treatment failure, that "Failure as defined as indication that the two-week rapid treatment phase has failed to initiate reversal of the basic symptomatology of sexual dysfunction" (1970, p. 38), will illustrate the issue of the specification of the outcome criterion to be reached. Using anorgasmic women as an example, failure to initiate reversal may have any of several meanings, none of which are specifically stated by Masters and Johnson. Several questions are left unanswered: failure may mean that the females failed to enjoy sex more, or became less performance-oriented, or failed to become less guilty. It may also mean that the client failed to experience orgasm with intercourse but may have become orgasmic with masturbation. No criteria are reported, so it is impossible to know exactly how Masters and Johnson assessed outcome. Additionally, no rate of improvement is reported (i.e., what percentage of failure can occur and still be considered a success?).

This same criterion problem exists for the reporting of male secondary impotence, which Masters and Johnson define as occurring when an individual male's rate of failure at successful coital connection approaches 25 percent of his opportunities. An ambiguity exists about the meaning of success since it is not known whether this term refers to firmness of the erection, duration of erection, or satisfaction of the male or his partner. Concerning premature ejaculation, Masters and Johnson are quoted as defining this dysfunction as one in which "a man cannot control his ejaculatory processes long enough during intercourse to satisfy his partner at least 50 percent of the time" (1970, p. 92). Zilbergeld and Evans raise a question about the subjective experience of satisfaction by asking how one is to evaluate therapy if it did not help the male to delay his ejaculation and his partner did not have orgasm during intercourse, yet the partner was no longer dissatisfied.

Another area of criticism levied against the work of Masters and Johnson concerns the treatment sample. Again, several questions are left unanswered, such as what procedures are used to screen candidates for acceptance to treatment. Masters and Johnson give no descriptive features of those persons rejected. It is not possible to determine how dropouts are tabulated in the outcome presentation, nor is it possible to know who made the decisions about the provision or rejection of treatment.

Zilbergeld and Evans are critical of the follow-up data of Masters and Johnson because the entire sample of participants is not evaluated; this fact is not made explicit by Masters and Johnson. Zilbergeld and Evans also expressed surprise at Masters and Johnson's reported 7 percent relapse rate as they compare this figure with 54 percent reported by Masters and Johnson-trained psychiatrists.

Zilbergeld and Evans speculate on possible explanations for the low relapse rate, suggesting that since no specifics are given about how people are prepared for termination, perhaps telephone calls constitute one part of the follow-up. Criticism is made of the lack of rigor in defining relapse since Masters and Johnson reported that 23 men treated for premature ejaculation relapsed but were not counted as relapses. Zilbergeld and Evans are concerned that it was not known whether differences in relapse rate were a result of the quality of treatments or different criteria for relapse.

Questions related to the duration and nature of therapy are also left unanswered. One criticism exists with respect to the differential treatment given to St. Louis residents versus those patients coming from out of town. Approximately 10 percent of the persons treated are St. Louis residents and are treated for three weeks, presumably because the impact of the treatment experience is somewhat diluted by returning home each evening. Length of treatment is not equal for all participants, however.

Zilbergeld and Evans conclude their comments on Masters and Johnson's work by suggesting a few reasons that criticism of Masters and Johnson has not occurred previously. They state that the very cumbersome writing style and the self-critical attitudes of Masters and Johnson tend to reduce the initiation of critical inquiry by others. They also report that the very exacting and superior physiological data collected by Masters and Johnson (1970) cast a halo upon all subsequent publications. Finally, they conclude that unequivocal acceptance of a new treatment entity is normal in the psychotherapeutic field. Only after some time do people begin to evaluate more critically a new treatment paradigm.

The importance of Zilbergeld and Evans' criticism must not be underestimated, since the omissions noted in Masters and Johnson's research affects most sex therapy. The implication of their criticism is that sex therapists must become more concerned with the efficacy of minimally evaluated technology. Much of the strength of clinical effectiveness of the brief sex-therapy format lies in the tenets of Masters and Johnson's work, as evidenced by the descriptions of similar format and outcome data as "comparable to Masters and Johnson." Certainly, the Zilbergeld and Evans' criticism forces sex therapists to join the ranks of other clinical researchers in refining all phases of their research. This is not to deny the tremendous contributions of Masters and Johnson, including the viability of many of their techniques. Instead, it may be construed as a challenge to the rank-and-file clinicians and researchers to continue the struggles inherent in developing a clinical specialty.

Although numerous techniques are employed in the conduct of sex therapy, what evidence do we have for their effectiveness? Fortunately, the maturity taking place in this specialty is reflected by an increase in critical self-examination of methodology and outcome. Kilmann (1978) provided a methodologic review of the literature for the treatment of primary and secondary orgasmic dysfunction. The methodological shortcomings that he noted include (1) ambiguous descriptions of subject characteristics; (2) the heavy reliance on a woman's self-report of outcome in the absence of her partner's evaluation; (3) neglecting to ferret out the effects of the woman's partner on her orgasmic responsivity; (4) the use of different criteria for treatment success, making generalization from results difficult. Kilmann states that these problems make it impossible to specify a treatment format that is most successful for a specific treatment population of women who experience a specific form of primary or secondary orgasmic dysfunction. Kilmann's review highlights a few findings that need to be evaluated in the controlled research of the treatment of primary and secondary orgasmic dysfunction. These findings suggest that (1) secondary nonorgasmic women would show greater gains than primary nonorgasmic women in treatments emphasizing sexual and nonsexual communication techniques, (2) primary nonorgasmic women would show greater gains than secondary nonorgasmic women in

desensitization and sexual-technique training procedures, and (3) desensitization may be the proper treatment for women whose sexual anxiety contributes to secondary orgasmic dysfunction.

Other methodological criticisms reported by Kilmann concern the small number of women used as subjects, the procedures used to screen subjects, and how dropouts are included in outcome reports. No studies reviewed by him reported an attention-placebo group to control for expectancy factors.

Several comments concern the lack of information about therapist characteristics in outcome studies; for example, often, neither the therapist's sex nor the number of therapists is mentioned. In addition, no studies that employed two or more therapists separated therapist from treatment effects. Further, most studies provided little information about the education and training of therapists. Bias was also presumably present in those studies in which the therapists were also the experimenters, thus presumably aware of the criterion variables under investigation.

Hogan (1978) considered the evidence for clinical effectiveness of several popular techniques used in the treatment of sexual dysfunction. One caveat, previously noted by Kilmann, is that nearly all of the studies were of the case-study method and, hence, lacked controls. Sex therapists have generally been practicing clinicians with only marginal interest in psychotherapy outcome research and thus have not conducted a great deal of rigorous experimental research.

Hogan characterizes the use of structured sexual experiences (e.g., actual physical involvement with a partner) as either graduated or nongraduated. The tentative conclusion that he draws as to which kind of experience is more useful was stated as follows:

Although there is little evidence on which to decide the issue, theoretical reasons and some empirical evidence indicate that graduated sexual experiences are preferable to nongraduated experiences (p. 235).

A related dimension is that of the level of involvement in the sexual experience. Participation may occur directly, in imagination, or vicariously via films or tapes. No conclusions as to the preferred mode of involvement are possible, as the only experimental studies

(Husted, 1972, and Wincze & Caird, 1976, both cited in Hogan, 1978) yielded ambiguous results. One may speculate that the mode of sexual experience interacts with such client variables as degree of sexual anxiety, sexual knowledge, and skill level.

Although much has been published on the successful outcome of sex therapy, scrutiny of existing evaluative research yields the same difficulties found in outcome research of all therapies. Studies are rarely replicable, control groups are lacking, and methodologies are not specified. Client selection varies, as do measurements and outcome criteria. One can only conclude that there exist numerous self-reports of satisfaction with sex therapy but little data exists about dropouts and/or failures.

ETHICAL ISSUES

Due to the nature of sex therapy as it is most commonly practiced, a number of ethical issues are raised for the sex therapist. Lowry and Lowry (1975) noted that interviews and inquiries concerning sexuality and sexual dysfunction must be void of personal curiosity or voyeurism, while stating that skillful, goal-directed, psychosexual history-taking is usually not provided in training programs or texts. They added that sex therapy provides a context for the abuse of psychological intimacy. Lowry and Lowry also raised the ethical issues of physical intimacy with clients and overt sexual activity with clients. Witkin (1977) added the problem of the imposition of the therapist's sexual values on the client, while Lassen (1976) suggested that much more importance be given to ethical issues than has been heretofore.

In addition to these author's' concerns, sex therapy as a field may promise too much to too many while advocating a new and often unrealistic norm for sexual behavior. Thus the ethical issue is raised of promising an effect that cannot be provided, as well as advocating changes in sexual attitudes rather than providing objective treatment.

DISCUSSION

In the last two decades, numerous advances in the treatment of sexual dysfunction have occurred. In the current proliferation of sex therapists and sex-therapy programs throughout the country, the majority are primarily educational in nature. This educational aspect of sex therapy may constitute, to date, sex therapy's greatest contribution, since sexual dysfunction is no longer considered a sign of a deep emotional disturbance but rather an indiciation of a learning deficit or a reaction to intra- and/or interpersonal stress. Thus symptoms can be corrected without intensive, long-term therapy. In addition, the legitimacy of sex therapy as a therapeutic focus per se has encouraged individuals to be more communicative about their sexual difficulties and more likely to seek help for sexual dysfunction.

To sexual functioning theory, the field of sex therapy has contributed revolutionary information about human sexuality, most notably through the work of Masters and Johnson (1966, 1970). Information on the vast range of "normal" sexual functioning can be viewed as a move from the dark ages of psychological understanding of sexuality. Women are no longer viewed primarily as the identified patients in couples' sexual difficulties, and men are no longer viewed as expressing their sexuality solely through orgasm.

Nevertheless, current theory in sex therapy may in essence be replacing one unrealistic hypothetical understanding of sexual function with another. Much of the current theory focuses on educational deficits and may offer a simplistic view of human sexual functioning. One trend in this mechanistic vein is illustrated by the popularity of sexual self-help manuals (Comfort, 1972; McCarthy, 1977), which essentially claim that if one merely follows instructions, one will experience a heightened awareness and enjoyment of sex. From a theroetical standpoint, sex therapy may advocate goals consistent with current cultural values (i.e., sexuality and sex are no longer hidden, taboo aspects of one's life; in order to be "healthy," one must experience maximum enjoyment in life, not only in sexual performance).

Cleveland (1976) maintains that both traditional and "new" norms concerning sexual behavior during and beyond middle age are unrealistic in terms of the physiological, behavioral, and emotional realities of aging. Instead of a "performance" orientation, which may be more frequent before middle age, he stresses that sexual activity can be oriented not just toward orgasm but toward greater intimacy, joy, and personal fulfillment through a broad spectrum of sexual interactions.

Sexual dysfunction is still frequently a symptom of other underlying conflicts and cannot be corrected or changed without some resolution of more basic underlying issues. As with other areas of human functioning, sexual activity includes numerous aspects of an individual's personality, in addition to sexual pleasure. A sexual relationship also involves issues of self-identify, self-esteem, power, and aggression, depending on the context. Sexual activity is not always a vehicle for expressing pleasure and/or love. Unfortunately, most sex therapy programs stress only the pleasure and love aspects, possibly ignoring underlying dynamic issues.

Sederer and Sederer (1979) have argued that focusing on sexual dysfunction is often used by both the couple and the therapist to ignore more fundamental issues of relating, which contribute to sexual difficulties. This viewpoint is in contrast to the more simplistic behavioral view that the symptom is the problem.

Although current treatment may be viewed positively as revolutionary and potentially helpful, one must note that treatment emphasizes pleasure and improved performance. Whether or not this goal is realistic remains to be seen, for evaluation and long-term follow-up of results are still virtually nonexistent.

The values of the sex therapist must also be addressed as part of current theory. Pleasure may be viewed as the ultimate value in treatment. In addition to providing a potentially unrealistic view of sexual relationships, sex therapists may also be encouraging the value of constant pleasure, with an overemphasis on sexual pleasure (Hartman & Fithian, 1974; Kaplan, 1974; Lobitz & Lobitz, 1978; Heiman, et al, 1981; Masters, et al, 1977). This value of seemingly always achieving sexual pleasure may simply replace an historical Victorian view of sex with a new value system that has the potential for equally detrimental results. In the early part of this century, an individual was considered to have problems if he or she enjoyed sex "too much." In the latter part of this century, sex therapists may be promoting a new value system that indicates that an individual has problems if he or she does not enjoy sex "enough."

Concerning treatment, when one reads the texts by Masters and Johnson (1966, 1970), Kaplan (1974), and most writers in the field, one is struck by their technical proficiency. Too often, however, this technical proficiency gives these writings a professional detachment and a coldness that is somehow incompatible with the goals of sexual expression as an intimate, natural function.

As sexual functioning may involve deficits other than educational ones, the role of the sex therapist may not always primarily involve an educational function. The sex therapist, at a minimum, needs general therapeutic skills and probably requires therapeutic competencies of the highest order. Without a high level of therapeutic skill, the sex therapist can at best provide education for those sexual dysfunctions that are the result of ignorance about sexuality. Although lack of education about one's sexuality is certainly a result of past morés in this culture, other identity issues and relationship issues must also be addressed.

Furthermore, there is not consensus about standard training for sex therapists. Various training programs offer various forms of education to the sex therapist, while practical application of theory to treatment is often ignored. Training is offered as if providing information to the potential sex therapist will make him or her an effective sex therapist.

Kaplan (1974) stressed the importance of general therapeutic skills for the sex therapist. These are important in the recognition of when to use or not to use sex therapy, what some of the marital and personal issues are for the couple, and how to handle the common but importance transferance reactions in sex therapy.

In all of the major approaches to sex therapy, there appear to be common elements that require specific therapist skills that are not stressed either by practitioners or by training manuals. These include a basic foundation of information about sexual functioning, training in communication skills, and general directive therapeutic skills. The competent sex therapist would thus require rigorous training in psychotherapy, as well as specific information and techniques in sex therapy.

Any practitioner of sex therapy will also find his or her own values and stereotypes challenged by the therapy and contact with a variety of people and experiences. Although many standard sex therapy formats are designed for the heterosexual couple, the sex therapist must also competently treat the homosexual, as well as other triadic or group relationships. Treating the homosexual for sexual dysfunction requires special knowledge and sensitivity; homosexuality, as well as heterosexuality, includes a large number of diverse experiences. These experiences include dimensions such as the extent to which an individual is homosexual, the amount of the individual's sexual interest and activity, the nature of the individual's sexual behavioral repertoire, the extent of any sexual dysfunction, and the individual's attitude toward his or her homosexuality. Only the clinician who is able to help the homosexual evaluate himself or herself along these dimensions is able to help the individual decide what is dysfunctional and how change is to occur. For many therapists, particularly heterosexual therapists, additional training related to homosexuality is required.

Maddock (1975) raised some questions about time and its importance in sex therapy. Timing and initiation of sex is frequently a problem area for males and females. There is a somewhat paradoxical structuring of time in brief sex therapy, however. According to Maddock, the couple who enters sex therapy basically turns over to the therapist the responsibility for their sex lives. The therapist accepts this responsibility and then immediately begins to give it back to the couple through homework assignments. One way of structuring sessions is the two-week, intensive, away-from-home format used by Masters and Johnson, Kaplan, and others; another is using daily or weekly homework assignments. Maddock suggested a third possibility, that of using variable appointment scheduling at the pace of the couple rather than at a pace defined by the therapist.

The paradoxical element in sex therapy noted by Maddock is worth considering further. Most approaches emphasize the spontaneity of sex, yet, paradoxically, totally direct the clients in their sexual activity. The paradoxical command, "Be spontaneous," is therefore consistent in sex therapies. In addition, some of the nondemand exercises have a paradoxical nature. The male may be instructed to lose his erection with his wife several times, freeing him to defy the therapist eventually and keep the erection. The couple is often prohibited from having intercourse at the beginning of treatment, which allows them to experience sexual desires without having to perform. They are free to feel controlled by the therapist; thus their failure to successfully complete sexual activity is no longer a symptom, but a command of the therapist assumed to be leading to improved sexual functioning.

The question is raised of which clients, if any, do not respond to the paradoxical nature of sex therapy. Without outcome and evaluation data specifically related to failures and dropouts, this question cannot be answered. Other questions about treatment that cannot be answered without further research are: How many clients have psychogenic sexual dysfunctions that will not respond to short-term structured treatments? What are long-term results in success cases? How effective is treatment for homosexual, bisexual, and/or asexual individuals? What effects does treatment have on the sexual values of the client?

Most sex therapy literature and treatment are directed toward married couples. Although most of this material is also applicable to nonmarried couples, the problems of "singles" and homosexuals are frequently not addressed. What are the parameters of the "commitment bond" in a casual sexual encounter? How does a therapist treat a single person who has no regular partner, yet wishes enriched sexual functioning? Legalling, a therapist cannot provide a sex partner nor, in most states, even advise a single person to engage in sexual intercourse (Cohn, 1974). Although these sex laws are under attack in most areas and are rarely enforced, clients and therapists are faced with numerous issues of judgment in what is a nonjugemental therapy. Refusing to treat an unmarried couple or individual might also be construed as discrimination or a violation of civil rights. An adult's natural functions do not change with the issuance of a marriage license; hence the need for sexual expression in individuals who are not legally married should be addressed.

Masters and Johnson (1974) have responded to criticisms that sex therapy is mechanistic and simplistic by adding an emphasis on the twofold nature of sexual responsibility, stating that individuals are ultimately responsible for themselves, for full communication of their wants, and for physical expression of their sexual drives. Awareness and increased awareness of one's own and one's partner's needs is stressed as a primary emphasis. Sager (1975) added that sex therapy goes beyond sexual functioning and involves and influences crucial aspects of the relationship, particularly the partners' feelings of love, concern, and commitment. Nevertheless, in the currently popular, brief sex therapies (Hartman & Fithian, 1972; Kaplan, 1974; Masters and Johnson, 1970), the focus is almost entirely on the sexual dysfunction. How many sex therapists stress affects and interpersonal expressions of love and affection is unknown.

Concerning the clients served, many of the well-known sex therapy programs are prohibitively expensive for participants. Thus there is a notable lack of participation in sex therapy by clients of lower socioeconomic status. Devaneson, et al (1976) have stressed that treatments for lower socioeconomic groups, in order to be successful, must include the use of informal therapeutic settings, flexible hours, immediate contact with a therapist, equal time for education and communication skills, and directive/permissive techniques to bridge communication gaps. Few if any sex therapy programs, however, address the lower socioeconomic groups or even those couples who have poor or nonfunctional communication skills.

THE FUTURE

The numerous publications and treatments available from the specialty of sex therapy have, no doubt, contributed to radical changes in attitudes, beliefs, and morés about sexuality. Data based on objective observation have dispelled numerous myths about "normal" sexual functioning, particularly as it relates to women. The field of sex therapy must, however, confront a number of issues about both its theory and its practice. These issues are (1) the extent to which it may advocate new norms of sexuality for society and the potential impact of these new norms (e.g., increased functioning and pleasure), (2) the actual success rate of sex therapies, (3) a further delineation of those clients who are inappropriate for sex therapy, (4) a further definition and delineation of adequate training for sex therapists, (5) further development of sex therapy for clients who are not married and/or heterosexual, (6) further development of available sex therapy for those clients who are other than middle or upper-middle class, verbal, and able to understand and act on the concepts presented to them, and (7) further theoretical delineation of those interpersonal factors that contribute to sexual dysfunction.

Like any new field, sex therapy currently claims to treat everyone successfully. It is beginning to become more differentiated, however, as some practitioners begin to address specific issues and populations, i.e., sexual deviants (Barlow & Wincze, 1980), coronary and heart disease victims (Stein, 1980), diabetics (Ellenberg, 1978; Renshaw, 1978), the elderly (Sviland, 1978), and spinal and injury victims (Higgins, 1978). In order to develop further as a specialty, sex therapy as a field must address itself to a number of specific questions about its actual efficacy and impact.

REFERENCES

Annon JS. *The extension of learning principles to the analysis and treatment of sexual problems.* Unpublished doctoral dissertation, University of Hawaii, 1971 (Abstract)

Annon JS. *The behavioral treatment of sexual problems.* Honolulu: Mercantile Publishing, 1974

Annon JS. *The behavioral treatment of sexual problems. Vol. 1: Brief therapy.* Honolulu: Enabling Systems, Inc, 1975

Annon JS. The PLISSIT model: A proposed conceptual scheme for the behavioral treatment of sexual problems. *Journal of Sex Education and Therapy*, 1976, 2, 1–16

Appelbaum B. The myth of the surrogate. *Journal of Sex Research*, 1977, *13*, 238–249

Barbach LG. Group treatment of preorgasmic women. *Journal of Sex and Marital Therapy*, 1974, *1*, 139–145

Barlow D & Wincze J. *Treatment of sexual deviations: Principles and practice of sex therapy.* New York: Guildford, 1980

Blakeney P, Kinder BN, Creson D, Powell LC, & Sutton C. A short-term, intensive workshop approach for the treatment of human sexual inadequacy. *Journal of Sex and Marital Therapy*, 1976, 2, 124–129

Cleveland M. Sex in marriage: At 40 and beyond. *The Family Coordinator*, 1976, *24*, 233–240

Cohn F. *Understanding human sexuality.* Englewood Cliffs, NJ: Prentice-Hall, 1974

Comfort A. *The joy of sex.* New York: Simon & Schuster, 1972

Cooper A. "Neurosis" and disorders of sexual potency in the male. *Journal of Psychosomatic Research*, 1968, *12*, 141–144

Cooper A. Clinical and therapeutic studies in premature ejaculation. *Comprehensive Psychiatry*, 1969, 30, 285–295

Devaneson M, Tiku J, Massler D, Calderwood MD, Samuels RM, & Kaminetzky HA. Changing attendance patterns to sex therapy programs as a function of location and personnel. *Journal of Sex and Marital Therapy*, 1976, *2*, 309–314

Diamond M. Human sexuality: Mass sex education, student and community reaction. *Journal of Sex Education and Therapy*, 1976, *2*, 1–11

Duehn WD, & Mayadas NS. Integrating communications skills with knowledge: A conjoint adolescent/parent format in sex education. *Journal of Sex Education and Therapy*, 1977, *3*, 15–19

Ellenberg M. Impotence in diabetics: The neurological factor. In J LoPiccolo & L LoPiccolo (Eds.), *Handbook of sex therapy.* New York: Plenum Press, 1978

Ellis A. Rational-emotive treatment of impotence, frigidity, and other sexual problems. *Professional Psychology*, 1971, *2*, 346–349

Freud S. *Letters of Sigmund Freud* (EL Freud, Ed.). New York: Basic Books, 1960 (Originally published, 1935)

Garfield Z, McBrearty J. & Dichter M. A case of impotence successfully treated with desensitization combined with in vivo operant training and thought substitution. In RD Rubin & CM Franks (Eds.), *Advances in behavior therapy.* New York: Academic Press, 1969

Godow AG. Female sexual dysfunction: Contributory factors and treatment considerations. *Journal of Sex Education and Therapy*, 1977, *3*, 8–10

Hartman WE, & Fithian M. *The treatment of the sexual dysfunctions.* Long Beach, CA: Center for Marital and Sexual Studies, 1972

Hartman WE, & Fithian MA. *Treatment of sexual dysfunction.* New York: Jason Aronson, 1974

Haslam M. The treatment of psychological dyspareunia by reciprocal inhibition. *British Journal of Psychiatry*, 1965, *111*, 280–282

Hastings DW. *Impotence and frigidity.* Boston: Little, Brown & Co, 1963

Hastings DW. Can specific training procedures overcome sexual inadequacy? In R Brecher & E Brecher (Eds.), *An analysis of human sexual response.* New York: The New American Library, 1966, pp. 221–237

Heiman JR, LoPiccolo L, & LoPiccolo J. The treatment of sexual dysfunctions. In AS Gurman & DP Kniskern (Eds.), *Handbook of family therapy.* New York: Brunner/Mazel, 1981

Higgins G. Aspects of sexual response in adults with spinal cord injury: A review of the literature. In J LoPiccolo & L LoPiccolo (Eds.), *Handbook of sex therapy.* New York: Plenum Press, 1978

Hogan DR. The effectiveness of sex therapy: A review of the literature. In J LoPiccolo & L LoPiccolo (Eds.), *Handbook of sex therapy.* New York: Plenum Press, 1978

Husted JR. Effect of method of systematic desensitization and presence of sexual communication in the treatment of sexual anxiety by counterconditioning. *Proceedings of the 80th Annual Convention of the American Psychological Association*, Honolulu, Hawaii, 1972, *7*, 325–326

Kaplan HS. *The new sex therapy.* New York: Brunner/Mazel/1974

Kaplan HS. *Disorders of sexual desire.* Simon & Schuster, 1979

Kaufman G, & Krupka J. A sexual enrichment program for couples. *Psychotherapy: Theory, Research, and Practice*, 1975, *12*, 317–319

Kegel AH. Sexual function of the pubococcygeus muscle. *Western Journal of Surgery*, 1952, *60*, 521–524

Kilmann P. The treatment of primary and secondary orgasmic dysfunction: A methodological review of the literature since 1970. *Journal of Sex and Marital Therapy*, 1978, *4*, 155–175

Kinsey AC, Pomeroy WB, & Martin CE. *Sexual behavior in the human male.* Philadelphia: W. B. Saunders, 1948

Kinsey AC, Pomeroy WB, Martin CE, & Gebbard PH. *Sexual behavior in the human female.* Philadelphia: W. B. Saunders, 1953

Kuriansky JB, & Sharpe L. Guidelines for evaluating sex therapy. *Journal of Sex and Marital Therapy*, 1976, *2*, 40–42

L'Abate L. *Manual: Enrichment programs for the life cycle.* Atlanta: Social Research Laboratories, 1975a

L'Abate L. A positive approach to marital family intervention. In RL Wolberg & ML Aronson (Eds.), *Group therapy 1975—An overview.* New York: Stratton Intercontinental Medical Books Corporation, 1975b

Lassen CL. Issues and dilemmas in sexual treatment. *Journal of Sex and Marital Therapy*, 1976, *2*, 32–39

Lazarus A. Multimodal behavior therapy: Treating the "basic id." In CM Franks & GT Wilson (Eds.), *Annual review of behavior therapy: Theory and practice.* New York: Brunner/Mazel, 1974

Lazarus AA. Behavior therapy and marriage counseling. *Journal of the American Society of Psychosomatic Dentistry and Medicine*, 1968, *15*, 149–56

Leiblum S, & Pervin L. Introduction: The development of sex therapy from a sociocultural perspective. In S Leiblum & L Pervin (Eds.), *Principles and practice of sex therapy*. New York: Guilford, 1980

Levay AN, & Kagle A. A study of treatment needs following sex therapy. *American Journal of Psychiatry*, 1977, *134*, 970–973

Lobitz W, & Lobitz G. Clinical assessment in the treatment of sexual dysfunctions. In J LoPiccolo & L LoPiccolo (Eds.), *Handbook of sex therapy*. New York: Plenum Press, 1978

Lobitz WC, & LoPiccolo J. New methods in the behavioral treatment of sexual dysfunction. *Journal of Behavior Therapy and Experimental Psychiatry*, 1972, *3*, 265-271

LoPiccolo L. Treatment of sexual desire disorders. In S Leiblum & L Pervin (Eds.), *Principles and practice of sex therapy*. New York: Guilford, 1980

LoPiccolo J, & Lobitz W. Behavior therapy of sexual dysfunction. In LA Hammerlynck, LC Handy & EJ Marsh (Eds.), *Behavior change: Methodology, concepts, and practice*. Champaign, IL: Research Press, 1973

Lowry TS, & Lowry TP. Ethical considerations in sex therapy. *Journal of Marriage and Family Counseling*, 1975, *1*, 229–236

Maddock JW. Initiation problems and time structuring in brief sex therapy. *Journal of Sex and Marital Therapy*, 1975, *1*, 190–197

Marcotte DB, & Weiss DS. An alternative to the squeeze: A new rapid treatment for premature ejaculation in the male. *Journal of Sex Education and Therapy*, 1977, *2*, 26–27

Masters WH, & Johnson VE. *Human sexual response*. Boston: Little, Brown & Co, 1966

Masters WH, & Johnson VE. *Human sexual inadequacy*, Boston: Little, Brown & Co, 1970

Masters WH, & Johnson VE. *The pleasure bond*. Boston: Little, Brown & Co, 1974

Masters WH, Johnson VE, & Kolodny RC (Eds.). *Ethical issues in sex therapy and research*. Boston: Little, Brown & Co, 1977

Mayadas NS, & Duehn WD. Measuring effects in behavioral sexual counseling with newly married couples. *Journal of Sex Education and Therapy*, 1977, *3*, 33–37

McCarthy B. *What you still don't know about male sexuality*. New York: Crowell, 1977

McCary JL. Sexual concerns of counseling clients. *Journal of Sex Education and Therapy*, 1977, *3*, 40–42

McConnell LG. The sexual value system. *Journal of Marriage and Family Counseling*, 1977, *3*, 55–67

Monge RM, Dusek JB, & Lawless J. An evaluation of the acquisition of sexual information through a sex education class. *Journal of Sex Research*, 1977, *3*, 170–184

Nims JP. Imagery, shaping, and orgasm. *Journal of Sex and Marital Therapy*, 1975, *1*, 198–203

Renshaw D. Impotence in diabetics. In J LoPiccolo & L LoPiccolo (Eds.), *Handbook of sex therapy*. New York: Plenum Press, 1978

Rosen A, Duehn WD, & Connaway RS. Content classification system for sexual counseling: Method and application. *Journal of Sex and Marital Therapy*, 1974, *1*, 53–62

Rosen RC. Genital blood flow measurement: Feedback applications in sexual therapy. *Journal of Sex and Marital Therapy*, 1976, *2*, 35–42

Rosenberg PP, & Rosenberg LM. Sex education for adolescents and their families. *Journal of Sex and Marital Therapy*, 1976, *2*, 53–67

Sager CJ. A false dichotomy. *Journal of Sex and Marital Therapy*, 1975, *1*, 187–189

Schmidt G, Nederlander C, & Drake L. Non-surrogate single sex therapy in the treatment of primary impotence. *Journal of Sex Education and Therapy*, 1976, *2*, 16–21

Sedere LI, & Sedere N. A family sex therapy gone awry. *Family Process*, 1979, *18*, 315–321

Segraves RT. Conditioning of masturbatory fantasies in sex therapy. *Journal of Sex Education and Therapy*, 1976a, *2*, 53–54

Segraves RT. Primary orgasmic dysfunctions: Essential treatment components. *Journal of Sex and Marital Therapy*, 1976b, *2*, 115–123

Semans J. Premature ejaculation: A new approach. *Southern Medical Journal*, 1956, *49*, 353–357

Snegroff S. Understanding puberty: A community school program designed to improve knowledge and communication between parents and their children. *Journal of Sex Education and Therapy*, 1976, *2*, 41–44

Sotile WM, & Kilman PR. Treatments of psychogenic female sexual dysfunctions. *Psychological Bulletin*, 1977, *84*, 619–633

Stein R. Sex therapy with special populations. In S Leiblum & L Pervin (Eds.), *Principles and practice of sex therapy*. New York: Guilford, 1980

Sviland M. Helping elderly couples become sexually liberated. In J LoPiccolo & L LoPiccolo (Eds.), *Handbook of sex therapy*. New York: Plenum Press, 1978

Szasz T. *Sex by prescription*. Garden City, NY: Anchor Press, 1980

Wabrek AJ, & Wabrek CJ. Vaginismus. *Journal of Sex and Marital Therapy*, 1975, *1*, 21–25

Walen SR. Cognitive factors in sexual behavior. *Journal of Sex and Marital Therapy*, 1980, *6*, 87–101

Wincze JP, & Carid WK. The effects of systematic desensitization and video desensitization in the treatment of essential sexual dysfunction in women. *Behavior Therapy*, 1976, *7*, 335–342

Wish PA. The use of imagery-based techniques in the treatment of sexual dysfunction. *The Counseling Psychologist*, 1975, *15*, 52–60

Witkin M. Ethical issues and sex therapy. *Journal of Sex Education and Therapy*, 1977, *3*, 8–12

Wright J, Perrequit R, & Mathieu M. The treatment of sexual dysfunction: A review. *Archives of General Psychiatry*, 1977, *34*, 881–890

Zilbergeld B. Group treatment of sexual dysfunction in men without partners. *Journal of Sex and Marital Therapy*, 1975, *1*, 204–214

Zilbergeld B, & Evans M. The inadequacy of Masters and Johnson. *Psychology Today*, August 1980, pp. 29–43

SECTION II

Remedial Techniques:
Therapeutic Interventions

11

Behavioral Marital Therapy

Since the early 1970s, behavioral therapy and accompanying treatment techniques have been increasingly utilized in marital therapy. This still-growing utilization can, in part, be traced to five factors. The first and most obvious factor is the growth in popularity of behavioral techniques among clinicians in general. The second factor is a continued disillusionment with various intrapsychic approaches to treatment. The third factor is an increasing empirical emphasis on a more rigorous application of the scientific method in clinical practice, and the fourth factor is a growing emphasis on the relevance of the outcome of treatment to the client's presenting problem. Finally, there are increasing demands by those clients presenting marital problems for behavioral changes within the marital relationship.

Behavioral treatment approaches to marital problems now represent distinct approaches that differ in clear and separate ways from other major marital treatment interventions. Although theoretical formulations and resulting treatment approaches vary somewhat, all current behavioral marital theorists conclude, consistent with social learning theories, that marital distress is caused by the failure of a couple's interaction to provide mutual, positive social reinforcement at an equitable rate. Therefore all treatment approaches have as their basic goal the increase of positive acts and the decrease of negative acts within the dyadic relationship. As a result, behavioral marital therapy (BMT) can be defined as therapy that attempts to increase mutual positive rein-

forcement, with an accompanying decrease of mutual negative reinforcement within the marital dyad. Reinforcement is defined as verbal and nonverbal means of giving attention and recognition: a positive reinforcer is a stimulus, the presentation of which increases the strength of a response; a negative reinforcer is a stimulus, the removal of which increases the strength of a response (Travers, 1972). All reinforcers are events subsequent to behavior that change the probability that the behavior will recur.

Unlike other major theories and approaches that address the understanding of dyadic interaction, BMT is a logical extension and application of interpersonal interaction concepts initially formulated to explain the acquisition and maintenance of behavior. Behavioral therapy began as a response to personality theories that saw symptoms as a result of the individual's unconscious inner forces and as an attempt to bring precision to the study of personality and behavior change through a more rigorous application of the scientific method. The primary theoretical tenet of all behavioral concepts is that all behavior is learned and that learning is an associative process. Thorndike's initial law of effect can still be quoted verbatim as the explanation of the learning process:

Any act which in a given situation produces satisfaction becomes associated with that satisfaction so that when the situation recurs, the act is more likely than before to recur also. Conversely, any act which in a given situation produces discomfort becomes dissociated from that situation so that when the situation recurs the act is less likely than before to recur (Thorndike, 1905, p. 203).

Although Thorndike's early formulations, which are central to instrumental learning, and Pavlov's discovery of classical conditioning phenomena and its subsequent application in Watson's early experiments (Watson, 1914; Watson & Raynor, 1920) aroused academic interest in the United States, it was not until the work of Skinner (1953) that behavioral theory received wide attention. In the 1960s, behavioral therapy began to be widely applied and further refined by clinicians with the treatment of individuals, and in the late 1960s, therapists began to apply BMT to the treatment of marital distress. Further development of BMT in the 1970s has consistently focused on the basic tenet that all behavior can be explained and altered by principles of learning.

HISTORICAL BACKGROUND AND DEVELOPMENT

Pavlov's systematic and intensive early studies led him to formulate the paradigm that classical conditioning involves the presence of an unconditioned stimulus that automatically evokes an unconditioned response. In his now classic experiments, the presentation of meat powder (the unconditioned stimulus) evoked salivation in dogs (the unconditioned response). A conditioned stimulus that is similar to or part of the unconditioned response can evoke a conditioned response. In his experiments, the presentation of a light (the conditioned stimulus) with the meat powder ultimately evoked salivation (the conditioned response) in dogs when the light was presented alone. Learning thus takes place when the conditioned stimulus is paired with the unconditioned stimulus so that the conditioned stimulus becomes associated with the unconditioned response and in the future will elicit that response when presented alone. Therefore Pavlov demonstrated that learning occurred through generalization. The learned behavior could also be eliminated, however. Pavlov demonstrated the principle of extinction, which is the gradual diminution of a conditioned response by the repeated absence of the unconditioned stimulus (i.e., in his

experiments, presenting the light to dogs with no further presentation of the meat powder led to a cessation of the dogs' salivation).

Unlike classical conditioning in which behavior is said to be elicited by some identifiable stimulus, Thorndike's early investigations on the consequences of behavior were later elaborated by Skinner (1953), who posited that the acquisition of learning of behavior is accomplished by instrumental learning and operant conditioning. The instrumental learning model refers to the organism's being actively instrumental in obtaining consequences in the environment and the organism's voluntarily or spontaneously emitting behavior. Operant conditioning refers to the organism's actively initiating behavior and operating on the environment rather than simply reacting to it.

In operant conditioning, which is the cornerstone of behavioral marital therapy and treatment, voluntarily or spontaneously emitted (operant) behavior is strengthened or discouraged by positive reinforcement (reward) or by negative reinforcement. Learning takes place because positive reinforcement increases the behavior it follows, negative reinforcement supposedly decreases the behavior it follows, and lack of reinforcement or punishment decreases the behavior it follows. Variable schedules of reinforcement also have variable effects on the acquisition or extinction of behavior. Rather than a passive association learning model, the operant conditioning paradigm presents the organism as actively seeking in the environment and acting on it.

Miller and Dollard's (1941) landmark treatise added to the importance of the role of observational learning in the acquisition of behavior. They identified two types of observational learning. In the first type, copying, individuals learn from others by endeavoring simply to reproduce their behavior. For copying to be successful, the copiers must know or be told whether their responses are acceptable reproductions. In the second type, matched-dependent behavior, a leader or model is able to read in the environment certain critical cues that the follower cannot detect. The follower is therefore dependent on the leader's behavior as a cue to guide his or her actions. It is assumed that the follower begins to imitate the behavior of the leader in order to gain the rewards that the leader has obtained.

In addition to their theories of observational learning, Miller and Dollard (1950) elaborated learning theory by applying it to the acquisition of neurosis. They defined the unconscious as unlabeled drives. They also stressed that symptoms are learned as habits by the phenomena of reinforcement principles, generalization from stimuli, and anticipatory responses. Therapy, then, was essentially conceived of as a situation in which neurotic responses are extinguished, and better, more normal responses are learned. Their work not only expanded behavioral principles to explain the unconscious but also made behavioral principles of learning more acceptable as a rationale for therapeutic interventions.

Bandura (1973), in a series of studies, further elaborated principles of observational learning and stressed the importance of modeling and vicarious processes of learning. In essence, observational learning can occur without specific instruction. In the therapeutic situation, the acquisition of new behaviors can also occur when the client, or patient, models the therapist's behavior, often without awareness that he or she is doing so.

Lindsley (1956) began to experiment in lab settings with operant conditioning in treating neurotic and psychotic conditions. Wolpe (1958), influenced by the work of Pavlov and the drive theories of Hull (1943), formulated psychotherapy in terms of reciprocal inhibition. To Wolpe, the inhibition, elimination, or weakening of old responses occurs simultaneously with an incompatible response. If a major drive reduction follows the incompatible response, a significant amount of conditioned inhibition of the response will occur.

In his experiments with induced neurotic anxiety in cats, Wolpe concluded that neurotic anxiety had been conditioned to intrinsically nonharmful stimuli. It is a form of unadaptive behavior that can be weakened and eliminated by principles of classical conditioning, whereby a more favorable competing response is developed through reciprocal inhibition (i.e., "If a response inhibitory of anxiety can be made to occur in the presence of anxiety-evoking stimuli, it will weaken the bond between those stimuli and the anxiety" (1958, p. 15). Thus counterconditioning and operant conditioning occur simultaneously. In addition to reiterating the principle that all behavior is learned,

Wolpe added to Miller and Dollard's (1950) formulations that emotional disturbance or neurosis is learned through conditioning and is characterized by unadaptive behavior accompanied by anxiety.

Rotter (1954) added an expectancy–reinforcement theory that considers the value of any reinforcement a function of the reinforcements with which it has been previously paired. The potential for the occurrence of a particular behavior in a particular situation is a function of the expectancy of the occurrence of the reinforcement following the behavior in the situation and the value of the reinforcement. Rotter also formulated psychotherapy as a learning process in which the individual changes expectancies and reinforcements, resulting in changes in unrealistic and maladaptive behavior.

During the growth and evolution of behavior theory, a number of investigators began to apply its principles to treatment for a variety of problems (Bandura, 1969; Eysenck, 1960; Lazarus, 1958; Yates, 1975), with a growing emphasis on specific performance-stated behavioral objectives as the goals of counseling and therapy (Krumboltz, 1966; Krumboltz & Thoresen, 1969; Michael & Myerson, 1962).

In the past decade, as the body of work by cognitive behavioral therapists has grown, there has also been an increasing emphasis on self-management techniques and cognitive change, with an added focus on the learning of cognitions; i.e., much more than simple sequences of behavior are learned. Individuals also learn which categories to use in structuring their thoughts about the physical world, what processes to use in retrieving information from memory, how to relate one thought to another, as well as ways to enact complex sequences of action. Therefore cognitive behavioral therapists focus not only on maladaptive learned behavior but on maladaptive learned cognitions that are the stimuli for maladaptive behavior (Vincent, 1980).

With the growth of behavioral therapy as a more comprehensive theory has come a variety of behavioral treatment techniques. In a review of behavioral therapies, Thoresen and Coates (1978) noted that in 1969 the major techniques of behavior therapy were aversive conditioning, contracts, guided practice, instruction, modeling, programmed materials, punishment, reinforcement, role-playing, simulation, systematic desensitization, and token systems. Since 1969, behavior therapy has added the techniques of aversive counterconditioning, cognitive restructuring, covert reinforcement, covert sensitization, differential feedback, extinction, flooding (implosion), focused imagery, guided practice (behavioral rehearsal), homework assignments, information-giving, intermittent reinforcement, paradoxical intention, reinforcement of incompatible alternatives, relaxation, satiation, self-instruction, self-monitoring, self-punishment, self-reinforcement, shaping, thought-stopping, and time-out procedures.

Although there are divergences in theoretical formulations and a variety of treatment techniques, behavioral therapy has continued to emphasize that the nature of reinforcements in a social context can be understood and treated by learning principles.

The stimulus-organism response (S-O-R) model that underlies all behavioral theories stresses the interaction between the individual and his or her environment. Although the occurrence of unobservable mental processes is acknowledged, the focus of understanding and treatment is on the input (stimulus) and output (reponse) elements of human behavior, which can be directly observed, quantified, and measured and which are current problematic behaviors for the individual. Epstein and Williams (1981), Jacobson (1978), Weiss (1978), Bagarozzi and Wodaski (1978), and Jacobson and Margolin (1979) are some among the many reviewers of BMT.

PHILOSOPHY AND MAJOR ASSUMPTIONS

The first advocacy of BMT based on a social learning model appeared in 1968 (Lazarus, 1968), and work by subsequent researchers and clinicians began to integrate several theoretical models (Liberman, 1970; Rappaport & Harrell, 1972; Stuart, 1969a, 1969b). Most influential among these models were the operant learning approach and social exchange theories (Thibault & Kelley, 1959), with later minor contributions from general systems the-

ory (Vincent, 1980) and attribution theory (Margolin & Weiss, 1978b).

Social exchange theory (Thibaut & Kelley, 1959) states that a relationship is satisfying if the benefits obtained outweight the costs inherent in being in the relationship. Hence a partner's degree of marital satisfaction is determined by a minimum reward/cost ratio that Thibaut and Kelley (1959) labeled the comparison level. The rate of reinforcers obtained from one's spouse determines not only the level of marital satisfaction but also the rate of reinforcers given to the partner in return. This premise, that reinforcers received in a relationship are correlated, is labeled reciprocity (Gottman, et al, 1976). Furthermore, the persistence of a relationship is greatly determined by the rewards and costs available from the environment external to the marriage (i.e., is it more rewarding and/or less costly to be married or single?). Lovinger (1965) proposed that the stability of a marriage is "a direct function of the attraction within and barriers around the marriage, and an inverse function of such attractions and barriers from other relationships." Hence exchange theory provides a way to predict what choices a person will make in social situations by determining the standard by which an individual assesses the alternatives (comparison level) and the superiority of one alternative over another (comparison level for alternatives). Cognition plays a crucial role because partners must assess their alternatives (estimate their value based upon their expectations) to determine a comparison level of alternative relationships. In this model, therefore, social behavior is maintained by the ability of each partner to give the other low personal cost, highly rewarding behavior. The relationship will continue as long as each partner's perceived cost/reward ratio is more favorable than alternative courses of action. For example, the wife of an abusive alcoholic husband, whose marriage clearly provides her with no visible positive rewards, may remain in the marriage because of her perception that leaving the marriage would provide her with fewer positive rewards and more distress (i.e., difficult economic conditions, loneliness, depression, and difficulties in reorganizing her life as a single person).

Thibaut and Kelley's formulation asserted

that as the relationship progresses over time, the interaction of a particular dyad is facilitated by a set of norms that reflect a balance between rewards and costs. In the event that one partner's behavior upset the equilibrium, the other partner will try to re-establish a balance. An equilibrium is again achieved at the point at which rewards and costs are again balanced. For example, if one partner begins to withhold sex in the relationship, the other partner might initiate such behaviors as displaying anger, nagging, or coercion in an attempt to re-establish the former level and frequency of sexual relations. If the first partner responds by displaying the former level of behavior, the second partner's responses will end, and a balance will be regained.

Another exchange theory formulated by Homans (1961) and similar to the theory of Blau (1964) summarizes the relevant aspects of the exchange model (Homans, 1961, pp. 51–82). Its underlying rationale is that:

1. *Responses are conditioned.* If, in the past, the occurrence of a particular stimulus situation has been the occasion on which an individual's activity has been rewarded, the more similar the present stimulus situation is to the past one, the more likely the individual is to emit the activity or some similar activity in the present.
2. *The individual is pleasure-seeking.* The more often, within a given period, an individual's activity rewards the activity of another, the more often will the other emit the activity.
3. *The individual values positive reinforcement.* The more valuable a unit of activity given by another is to an individual, the more often will the individual emit activity rewarded by the activity of the other.
4. *The individual thrives on novelty.* The more often an individual has, in the recent past, received a rewarding activity from another, the less valuable any further unit of that activity becomes.
5. *Interpersonal relationships are internally mediated.* The individual has a perception of what is fair, and anger is a consequence when attempts to negotiate "fairness" have failed.

Stuart (1969a, 1969b) added the concept of *reciprocity*, or *quid pro quo* (something for something). Successful marriages are characterized by reciprocity when there is an equitable exchange of reinforcement between spouses. Conversely, unsuccessful marital relationships are described as those relationships that employ either or both of the two dysfunctional patterns of behavior control: coercion and withdrawal. The use of coercion is described as "one member seeking to gain positive reinforcement from the other in exchange for negative reinforcement" (Patterson & Reid, 1967, cited in Stuard, 1969a, p. 676). Withdrawal is defined as withdrawal from the spouse, thereby decreasing the opportunity for the exchange of positively reinforcing events. Although the dynamics of coercion and withdrawal are different, the end result is a low rate of positively reinforcing interactions.

The effect of this low rate of positive reinforcers exchanged by spouses is a decrease in the level of attraction each spouse has for the other, with a consequent deterioration in the marital relationship.

Since 1970, the major theorists and researchers in exchange theory have been Patterson, Weiss, and their colleagues at the University of Oregon, collectively known as the Oregon Group. Patterson and Reid (1970) elaborated the behavioral exchange model by categorizing marriages as two basic types of marital interaction: *reciprocity*, wherein partners tend to give each other equal amounts of reinforcement and punishment, and *coercion*, wherein one partner is punished until he or she complies with the other's demands. Simply increasing positive behaviors within a marriage does not increase global feelings of marital happiness. Distressed marriages are characterized by coercive interaction sustained by mutual reinforcement through which partners dispense aversive stimuli to control the behavior of their mates. Wills, Weiss, and Patterson (1974) also added the basic premise that communication influences the level of satisfaction experienced in a relationship.

Based upon social exchange models, distressed couples are noted to exhibit fewer rewarding exchanges and more aversive exchanges than nondistressed couples. Such discrepancies are detected both in their verbal behavior (Birchler, et al, 1975; Gottman, et al, 1977) and in their nonverbal behaviors (Robinson & Price, 1980). Another distinction between distressed and nondistressed couples is that distressed partners reciprocate the spouse's use of punishment more readily and frequently than nondistressed couples (Jacobson, 1979). Many spouses of distressed couples are sensitive and reactive to immediate aversive stimuli (Jacobson & Margolin, 1979; Weiss, 1978). Gottman, et al (1976) proposed that nondistressed couples interact according to a "bank account" exchange model, in which consequences (both reward and punishment) are put into a "relationship account," thereby circumventing quid pro quo exchanges. In other words, distressed couples react to aversive or negative stimuli immediately; whereas nondistressed or satisfied partners tend to react more to the total amount of accumulated rewards than to the immediate stimulus. Interestingly, this difference in reactivity applies only to aversive stimuli, since research has demonstrated that distressed couples are no more likely to respond to immediately positive stimuli than are nondistressed couples, and they may even be less likely to exhibit such reactivity (Gottman et al., 1977; Jacobson, 1979). Jacobson (1980) suggests that perhaps other variables may counteract the tendency for distressed couples to be reactive to immediate positive stimuli. Robinson and Price (1980) suggest that distressed couples selectively attend to negative behavior.

Another distinction between distressed and nondistressed couples is that the distressed group does not view positive communication to be as reinforcing as does the nondistressed group. Distressed couples also do not view negative communication to be as nonreinforcing as do nondistressed couples (Jacobson, 1980). Control is exercised in distressed couples by withholding positive exchanges and exhibiting primarily negative behaviors. Additionally, sharing activities is perceived as reinforcing by nondistressed couples but not so by distressed couples. In general, research thus far supports the tenet of behavior exchange that dissatisfied spouses apply aversive contingencies to induce behavioral changes in their partners.

Thus social learning theory of marital interaction emphasizes the variables that are maintaining positive and negative behaviors, regardless of whether these variables refer to the spouse's behavior, the social environment, or individual factors. The assessment of marital conflict thus attempts to detect and analyze these variables.

In the operant model, emphasis is placed on the probability that a certain behavior will occur and is ultimately influenced by positive and negative reinforcers as well as by punishment and extinction. The basic paradigm for the operant learning approach, then, is antecedent – behavior – consequence. Based upon this paradigm, marital interactions are viewed as patterns of discriminative stimuli (antecedents), conditioned responses (behaviors), and reciprocal reinforcement and punishment (consequences). Each spouse's behavior is determined by both the cueing and reinforcement given by the partner and by the individual's own history of reinforcement. It is assumed that individuals enter marital relationships because of the positive reinforcers obtained from the relationship. Therefore each partner has important control of the other partner's behavior via the reinforcements dispensed.

Marital distress, interpreted from an operant learning perspective, can emerge when deficits occur in any of the three components of the antecedent–behavior–consequence paradigm. Antecedent deficits occur when marital behavior is not under appropriate stimulus control. For example, the misreading of cues (which frequently results in misunderstanding and frustration), such as readiness for sexual activity, may result in conflict between the spouses. The importance of stimulus control necessitates the need for rules to govern the relationship. Without such rules, the marital relationship is generally chaotic (Jacobson & Margolin, 1979; Weiss, 1978).

Behavioral deficits limit the couple's ability to exhibit adaptive relationship skills. For example, a deficit in appropriate problem-solving skills to negotiate conflicts of disagreements will result in marital discord. Contingency deficits refer to the lack of appropriate reinforcement. Initially, individuals marry for expected and obtained benefits; however, such rewards may lose their strength because of satiation effects. As Jacobson and

Margolin (1979) state, if this "reinforcement erosion" is perceived as falling out of love and/or if the spouses do not expand or alter their repertoire of reinforcers, marital dissatisfaction is likely. In addition, couples may experience the loss of reinforcement from an aversive exchange (Patterson & Reid, 1970). Patterson and his associates termed the development of this aversive exchange the "coercion process," whereby a spouse uses an aversive stimulus to initiate a change in the partner. Instead of asking for or negotiating a change, partners apply aversive strategies such as demanding, threatening, and inducing guilt to obtain a change in the spouse. The coerced partner then makes the behavioral change in order to terminate the aversive stimulus, which reinforces the coercive behavior exhibited by the manipulative spouse. Thus one partner is positively reinforced for applying coercive strategies, and the other is negatively reinforced for acquiescing to the request, resulting in the maintenance of this dysfunctional interaction.

General systems theory (Alexander & Barton, 1976) and attribution theory (Margolin & Weiss, 1978) have made minor contributions to learning theory. According to Vincent (1980), general systems theory has influenced social learning theory by supplementing "microbehavioral analyses of family interactions with somewhat more abstract theoretical constructs" (p. 3). In other words, therapists are encouraged not to focus primarily on small details but to attend to the function of the behavior (e.g., an alcoholic husband is gratifying his wife's need to be nurturant). Attribution theory has influenced social learning theory by noting that the spouse's interpretation of the partner's behavior determines the reinforcing or punishing effect of that behavior (Gottman, et al, 1976).

THE TREATMENT PROCESS

Behavioral Assessment of Marital Conflict

The behavioral assessment of marital discord involves using various procedures designed to measure both the strengths and the weaknesses of marital interactions via assessing the rewards and punishments exchanged, and the spouse's subjective assessment of marital satisfaction (Jacobson, 1981).

According to Jacobson and Margolin (1979), the main function of assessment for the behavioral therapist is to obtain the necessary information to (1) identify and define problems in the marriage; (2) determine the controlling variables related to the conflictive behaviors; (3) determine appropriate treatment strategies; and (4) identify whether and when the treatment is successful by assessing behavior on a continuous basis, thereby providing feedback to the therapist, which allows for modification of treatment procedures when necessary. These authors also stress that a complete assessment is crucial to the selection and application of effective therapeutic interventions and should not be considered important only as research information.

The emphasis in behavior assessment has been on the utility of various instruments for selecting therapeutic approaches. Although instruments and assessment techniques vary, the behavioral approach involves a direct measurement of a person's response to various dyadic situations. For example, the couple who approaches the behavioral therapist for help because of frequent fighting will most likely receive, as part of the initial assessment, instructions in recording various discrete components of the fighting behavior.

Reid (1978) stresses the following factors in the behavioral approach to assessment:

1. *Assessment of antecedent stimuli that may evoke or elicit the problem behavior.* A focus is placed on one spouse's specific behaviors (antecedent stimuli) that appear to encourage the responding behavior of the other spouse. Assessment is usually conducted with various spouse self-report procedures that force each partner to examine the relevant aspects of his or her behavioral contribution to the problematic situation.

2. *Assessment of the magnitude of the maladaptive behavior.* An attempt is made to analyze a problem with respect to its degree and frequency.

3. *Assessment of both antecedent and consequential behaviors that might involve the reinforcement of the problem behavior and*

the extinction or punishment of adaptive behavior. Antecedent and consequential behaviors are identified in concrete, measurable terms.

4. *Assessment of interactional patterns that continue the problem behavior.* An attempt is made, usually by spouse verbal report, to identify sequences of behavior that continue the problem behavior. For example, a sexually relatively inexperienced spouse may attempt to initiate sex, be ridiculed (punished) for being inept, and thus continue to have difficulties initiating sex.

5. *Assessment of client variables that might affect the function of naturally occurring events.* Other intervening variables, such as physical health or social relationships, are assessed for interference with the couple's interaction. For example, one spouse's ongoing extramarital affair may provide reinforcement that decreases the commitment to improve the marital relationship.

6. *Assessment of each spouse's behavioral assets and deficits.* An ongoing attempt is made to assess whether the desired behavior is lacking because of a behavioral deficit. For example, one spouse may state a desire for increased affection from the other spouse. An assessment must be made as to whether or not the specified spouse has the ability to display the desired affection.

Some of the self-report measures that have been used include the Locke-Wallace Marital Adjustment Scale (MAS) and the Dyadic Adjustment Scale (DAS) (Spanier, 1976). Both tests provide a validated measure of subjective marital satisfaction. Their value is limited, since the information provided is subjective; however, both tests correlate highly and are useful in determining specific conflictive behaviors.

Perhaps the most extensive development of and research on assessment have taken place at the Oregon Research Institute and the University of Oregon (Olson & Sprenkle, 1976; Patterson & Hops, 1972; Weiss et al., 1973). The so-called Oregon Group has developed a set of assessment procedures using both self-report and observational data.

Among their assessment procedures are *The Willingness to Change Scale,* which is an instrument designed to assess conflict by asking each partner to mark on a seven-point scale whether the other partner should engage less, the same, or more in particular activities; and *the Marital Activities Inventory,* which assesses patterns and sources of social reinforcement by surveying 85 common recreational activities. Each spouse is asked to estimate frequency of participation in these activities for the preceding month and whether he or she was alone, with spouse, or with others at the time.

The Oregon Group (Weiss, Patterson, and their associates) also devised an instrument, the Spouse Observation Checklist (SOC) (Christensen & Nies, 1980; Patterson, 1976a, 1976b; Weiss, 1978; Weiss & Margolin, 1977) to assess spouse relationships by examining daily exchanges of rewarding and punishing behaviors. This checklist contains about 400 spouse behaviors that have been classified as pleasing and displeasing events. SOC behaviors are also categorized into 12 areas of marital interaction: companionship, affection, sex, consideration, communication, process, coupling activities, child care, household management, financial decision-making, employment, personal habits, and self–spouse independence. Couples are instructed to check all items or behaviors that have occurred during the previous 24-hour period. SOC data is collected throughout the assessment and intervention phases of therapy. Normative data on the SOC demonstrate that mean ÷ displease ratios are about 4:1 for distressed couples and 12:1 to 30:1 for nondistressed couples (Margolin, 1979). In addition to obtaining frequency data on specific behaviors, the SOC provides information on overall marital satisfaction by requiring partners to rate their marital satisfaction daily on a scale of 1 to 7, 7 being totally satisfied and 1 being totally dissatisfied.

Stuart (1980) developed the Stuart Marital Precounseling Inventory, which provides data on specific behaviors exhibited. Stuart also devised a Marital Happiness Scale (MHS), in which couples are required to rate their level of happiness in 12 categories related to married life. This rating scale is a subscale of Stuart's Marital Precounseling Inventory. Azrin, et al (1973) devised a marital happiness scale consisting of nine categories related to marital life. O'Leary and Turkewitz (1978) developed an 18-item questionnaire designed to evaluate the emotional quality of the marriage. This questionnaire, "Feelings Toward Spouse," asks spouses how they feel about their partners' variable behaviors. Overall, these self-report measures provide not only information pertinent in determining a treatment plan but also a means of assessing treatment effects via a pre-and postcomparison. The reliability and validity of pre- and postmeasures may, however, be affected by difficulties in recall, along with social desirability variables (Murstein & Beck, 1972).

Another procedure for monitoring spouses' behavior was devised by Stuart (1969a, 1969b). He had each partner list three behaviors that he or she wished the spouse to exhibit. These lists were posted in the home and the recipient marked instances of receiving the desired behavior.

The pleasurable–displeasurable count (P's and D's), developed by the Oregon Group, provides a comprehensive list of specific pleasant or unpleasant behaviors in several marital areas by having each spouse make frequency recordings of various behaviors. More recently, supposedly behavioral instruments are: (1) the Spouse Observation Checklist (Christensen & Nies, 1980); (2) the Area-of-Change Questionnaire (A–C), developed by Weiss and Perry (1979), in which couples note which of 34 positive behaviors they would like changed, along with the amount of change and the direction of change desired; (3) the Marital Status Inventory, created by Weiss and Cerreto (1980), a true–false questionnaire concerning what steps have been taken toward separation and divorce.

Although interview and self-report methodology in the assessment of marital conflict have been widely used, a recent emphasis has included in vivo observational measures. Observational assessment techniques used by the Oregon Group include the following:

1. A structured conflict interview in which the interviewer makes a continuous record of positive and negative behaviors and awards a final global rating on a seven-point scale of marital distress.
2. Samples of ongoing, problem-solving interactions, using the Marital Interaction Coding System (MICS). The MICS was de-

veloped as a laboratory tool for the assessment of marital interaction along two dimensions: rewardingness and problem-solving. Rewardingness is the extent to which spouses emit reinforcing as opposed to aversive interactions with one another. Problem-solving is the efficiency of marital communication in solving problems in the relationship. Husband-and-wife interaction concerning a problem is videotaped in 10-minute segments and played back for scoring in 30-second units, with a minimum interrater reliability of 70 percent. The 30 verbal and nonverbal behavior categories used include Agree, Approval, Laugh, and Positive Physical Contact.

Other observational procedures in assessment have ranged from structured problem-solving discussion in the laboratory (Gottman, et al, 1976) to home observations (Patterson, et al, 1976). Recently, laboratory assessment has attempted to analyze spouses' patterns of solving conflicts about real-life relationship problems. These discussions are videotaped and then coded by trained observers using elaborate coding systems that analyze the ongoing verbal interactional patterns. Gottman and his associates (Gottman, et al, 1976) devised an even more complex coding system whereby both verbal and nonverbal behavior is recorded.

Another method used to obtain observational data is to observe the spouses' behavior in the home. The validity of such data is questionable, however, since observers may affect the occurrence of target behaviors. To counteract this reactivity to live observers, tape recorders that automatically activate at specific time intervals or certain decibel levels have been placed in the home (Christensen, 1979).

An innovative electromechanical assessment device has been used by Thomas and his associates (Carter & Thomas, 1973; Thomas, 1977). The Signal System for the Assessment and Modification of Behavior (SAM) is an electronic system consisting of five units: client button boxes to receive light signals, client button boxes to transmit light signals, a therapist control box to regulate circuits of the signal system and to intervene by signals in interaction of the couple, a relay box, and an event recorder. A partition is used to prevent clients' visual interaction. SAM is used to measure verbal behavior of the interacting partners, the signals they emit during interaction, and the particular inter-relationship of the signal and verbal behavior.

Aside from the number of behavioral assessment procedures available, the majority of practicing therapists exclusively use verbal reports and self-report checklists in the initial assessment of the couple's problem.

Generally, the initial assessment occurs over two or three conjoint interview sessions, which serve several purposes. One purpose is to engender positive expectancies, to create a structure that discourages complaining and blaming, and to dispel the idea that each spouse's unilateral goals will be supported (Jacobson & Margolin, 1979; Weiss & Birchler, 1978). Another purpose is to examine the marriage partners' thoughts and behaviors that are relevant to their marital happiness. A third and crucial purpose is to obtain information during the sessions about how the marital partners interact with each other, how they present themselves to another person, how they describe and understand their conflict, and how they make requests of each other. In addition to gathering this information verbally, additional data on marital satisfaction and interactions are obtained via one or more objective tests and/or observational procedures.

Behavioral Treatment of Marital Conflicts

The structure of BMT usually entails a specified number of conjoint therapy sessions, with the context of meeting being highly structured. Regardless of the couples' presenting complaints, the two goals of therapy are to improve the quality and quantity of positive experiences in the marriage.

The initial phase of BMT involves inducing positive expectancies and developing a collaborative set. "Successful marital therapy is predicated on the spouses' willingness to work collaboratively to improve their relationship" (Jacobson, 1981, p. 567). Generally, behaviorists contend that producing an expectation that therapy can help the relationship can be of therapeutic value by alleviating anxiety and hopelessness. Also, positive expectancies may facilitate therapeutic success by increasing the couple's willingness to participate and follow

instructions. The therapist attempts to engender positive expectancies by encouraging the couple to identify strengths as well as weaknesses in the relationship. For example, Jacobson and Margolin (1979), in their initial interview, focus upon the early history of the relationship (i.e., how they met, what attracted each to the partner, etc.) rather than attending to the problems in the relationship.

The therapist initially tries to develop a collaboration set at the conclusion of the pretreatment assessment phase by stressing reciprocal causality and mutual responsibility for the present conflicts. Also, a strategy applied to facilitate collaborative behavior in the spouses is obtaining the couple's commitment to follow therapeutic instructions by having the couple sign a written therapy contract. Finally, BMT attempts to make easy the initial tasks or requirements in therapy so that the spouses can avoid failure and be reinforced for their successes, thereby encouraging their cooperation in future, more demanding tasks.

Techniques in BMT

Empirically, five marital intervention procedures have been examined: (1) communication training, (2) problem-solving training, (3) behavioral exchange procedure, (4) miscellaneous behavioral techniques, and (5) contingency contracting.

Behavioral communication training (BCT) developed from the nondirective therapy movement (Carkhuff, 1969, 1973; Guerney, 1977; Rogers, 1951). The more nondirective communication approaches emphasize the expression and reception of feelings, however, whereas behavioral therapists instruct couples in communication primarily to facilitate conflict negotiation and resolution. The speaker is taught to be direct, clear, and specific, and to express both thoughts and feelings. Being direct means to speak for oneself or to own one's feelings and behaviors instead of blaming another, invoking support from others, or speaking in abstract terms. Also, each spouse is encouraged to use "I" statements ("I want," "I feel") rather than "we should" or "others do." Expressing feelings refers to describing one's emotions, as opposed to name-calling and denigrating one's partner. For example, instead of a spouse saying, "You're mean," the spouse is directed to say, "I feel angry." Being specific is saying how one feels in reference to specific events. For example, a spouse would say, "It upsets me when you don't call and say you'll be home late," rather than "I feel hurt because you're not considerate of me." Besides learning speaking skills, the couple is taught how to be a "good listener." This role entails demonstrating to the speaker that he or she has been heard by the listener's repeating, paraphrasing, or summarizing what has been said. This technique enables the speaker to clarify or correct any misunderstanding of what he or she said.

In teaching couples these specific communication skills, behavioral therapists may differ somewhat in their approaches and in their emphasis on different skills. Despite the content of the program, however, all behaviorists base their method of training communication skills on the concept of reinforced practice, which includes instructions, feedback, and behavioral rehearsal.

Another treatment procedure that is sometimes a second component in BMT is termed problem-solving (Jacobson & Margolin, 1979; Weiss, 1978) or conflict-resolution skills (Birchler, 1979). Training in the use of communication can facilitate understanding of problems, but it does not ensure the generation of appropriate solutions. Hence BMT may be a necessary but insufficient step in the solving of marital conflict.

Problem-solving involves the couple's learning to define their problems, to "brainstorm" for possible solutions to their distress, to assess or evaluate those solutions, and, lastly, to negotiate agreements to observe these solutions. Couples are encouraged specifically and descriptively to define clearly their problems and to agree upon a solution.

Several guidelines are followed by behavioral therapists who use problem solving procedures (Jacobson, 1981), including the following:

1. Discuss one problem at a time.
2. Paraphrase by having each spouse begin his or her response to the partner's statement by summarizing what the other has said.
3. Avoid attempting to attribute feelings, attitudes, or motivation to one's spouse.

4. Avoid aversive verbal exchanges (i.e., blaming, humiliating, etc.).
5. When defining a problem, first say something positive.
6. When defining a problem, be specific and precise.
7. Feelings should be appropriately expressed.
8. There should be recognition by both partners of their responsibility in perpetuating the problem.
9. Definitions of problems should be brief.
10. After a problem has been defined, the discussion should be focused on generating solutions.
11. Behavior change must be based upon compromise and mutuality.
12. The agreed-upon solution should be specific and put in writing.

A third intervention approach is the behavioral exchange procedure, which refers to any technique used in therapy that enables spouses to acquire an increased frequency of desired behaviors (Jacobson & Margolin, 1979). Although the term "behavioral exchange" may refer to negotiation procedures used in problem-solving, most often the term is used to describe procedures directed at increasing behaviors that are no conflictual issues for the couple. Thus the couple is encouraged to exchange pleasing behaviors that are desirable and then to attempt to increase the occurrence of those behaviors. Stuart's (1969a, 1969b) approach involved four steps. First, he explained the approach logically to the couple. Next, each spouse listed three behaviors that he or she wished the spouse to exhibit more frequently. Each spouse had to agree to exhibit either those behaviors selected by the other spouse or an alternative behavior. Third, these selected behaviors were posted at home and the recipient recorded on a chart the instances when he or she received the agreed-upon behavior. The final step involved negotiating contracts to describe how each partner would "compensate" the other for the delivered behavior. Stuart also proposed incorporating the use of a token economy in this intervention approach, which appeared to be effective even with couples with a several conflict or those who were potential candidates for divorce.

Another behavioral exchange procedure is referred to as "love days" (Weiss, et al, 1973) or "caring days" (Stuart, 1980). Caring days is a technique whereby couples are told to demonstrate caring behaviors in an effort to facilitate caring feelings toward one another. Each spouse is asked how he or she would like the partner to demonstrate caring for the other. Responses must be specific, positive, small (can be emitted at least once daily), and must not be the subject of a severe conflict. Positive requests focus upon increasing constructive behaviors, and not decreasing unwanted responses (e.g., "Please ask me what I'd like to do tonight" instead of "Don't neglect me"). The caring list should initially include at least 18 items (Stuart, 1980), and the couple should be encouraged to add to the list weekly. After the list is completed, each request is discussed and each spouse should agree to exhibit at least five of the behaviors daily. Stuart stresses that this minimum number will ensure frequent demonstrations of the couple's willingness to please each other. Also, each partner is requested to emit these "caring" behaviors whether or not the other partner has made similar gestures.

The spouses record on the sheet the date on which each has received a positive gesture from the other. Thus this written record not only serves to remind the couple to demonstrate such behaviors but also serves as data by which the therapist can assess progress. Stuart (1980) suggests using this procedure early in treatment to facilitate positive feelings between the spouses. Applying behavioral exchange procedures and increasing positive behaviors in this manner may be a powerful therapeutic tool, since distressed couples frequently withhold positive behaviors as a means of minimizing the costs of a conflictual relationship.

Additional Techniques

Homework assignments

Homework is another procedure that is often utilized by BMT (Lester, Beckham & Baucom, 1980), but it has not received extensive research attention. Homework is typically assigned by the therapist to ensure the practice of skills learned in therapy and also to facilitate generalization of such skills to the home environment. Typically, homework involves a daily 15-minute period when the couple practices one or a combination of communication, problem-solving, and/or contracting skills. If contracting is being practiced, the couple writes the problem, generates solutions, agrees upon a solution, and determines the contingencies. Also, functional and dysfunctional communications are often written (e.g., improved eye contact; wife interrupted husband three times).

The therapist reviews these written notes from the previous week, usually at the start of each therapy session. This review enables the therapist to monitor the couple's progress, detect recurrent problems, and make suggestions for improvement. Also, if the couple is not completing homework tasks, the therapist frequently aids the couple in problem-solving whatever difficulty is preventing homework completion.

Extinction

This procedure involves the consistent withdrawal of a reinforcer in order to decrease the frequency of a behavior. For example, the marriage in which one spouse is demanding and the other spouse reluctantly gives in to demands may be altered by one spouse's consistent ignoring of the other's demanding behavior. Extinction is often combined with positive reinforcement procedures to reinforce alternative desirable responses to the behavior being extinguished. To continue the example, one spouse may verbally reinforce the other for being less demanding.

Modeling

Modeling is used to demonstrate and teach some behavior, skill, attitude or feeling (Friedman, 1972; Liberman, 1970). The principles of modeling as formulated by Bandura (1969) within the context of social learning theory simply state that modeling is a method of instruction in which an individual demonstrates the behavior to be acquired by the observer, who learns by imitation. For example, a therapist may model communication skills.

Videotape feedback

A recent augmentation to the use of modeling has been the use with a couple of videotape feedback of their learning of new behaviors. Modeling has been combined with videotape feedback, practice procedures, and peer feedback to further facilitate learning (Alger & Hogan, 1969; Canter, 1969; Eisler & Hersen, 1973). The procedure is not widely used, however, primarily because of its cost.

Cognitive restructuring (reframing or reattribution)

The use of this procedure is not the sole domain of behavioral therapists and has been used by others in a variety of ways (Bowen, 1971; Friedman, 1972; Haley, 1963; Lazarus, 1971; Minuchin & Montalvo, 1971). Cognitive restructuring helps spouses to reconceptualize the definition of a chronic problematic event by relabeling the problem. This relabeling is designed to overcome the couple's resistance to giving up the problematic behavior. For example, when a couple engages in the reciprocally negatively reinforcing relationship of an alcoholic marriage (one spouse is an alcoholic), the alcoholic spouse may blame the other for causing the drinking or not helping the alcoholic to stop drinking. The blamed spouse feels guilty and helpless, initiating no different interaction, and the alcoholic spouse continues to drink and blame the other for the behavior. Cognitive restructuring or a positive relabeling might be accomplished by the therapist's defining the behavior of the blamed spouse as concerned and protective rather than causal.

Therapists also reframe the problem as dysfunctioning in the relationship rather than in the individual. Margolin and Weiss (1978) found that BMT that emphasized attributing success and failure to mutual rather than individual functioning was more effective than BMT alone, as measured by self-report and observational measures.

Paradoxical injunctions

Another intervention strategy not derived strictly from a behavioral approach is paradoxical injunction (see Chapter 12). Paradoxical injunctions entail instructing spouses "to engage in the very behavior that has been identified as a target for elimination in therapy" (Jacobson & Margolin, 1979, p. 150). Jacobson and Margolin warn that paradoxical injunctions should not be used by the inexperienced clinician and that when they are applied, four guidelines should be followed. First, the injunction should be given in the context of concern for the couple. Second, the therapist must exhibit both a sense of humor and an acknowledgment of the severity of the couple's problems. Third, the therapist must give a believable rationale for the paradoxical injunction, and, fourth, later in therapy, the therapist must not debrief the couple. Hence these authors suggest that paradox be used with caution and then only rarely.

Thought-stopping

This covert procedure, made popular by Wolpe (1969) and Lazarus (1971), is directed toward the treatment of obsessional thoughts by interfering with the obsessional thought. Rosen and Schnapp (1974) reported a case in which the husband's constant rumination of the details of his wife's recent extramarital affair was treated. During treatment the wife and husband were instructed to role-play a typical obsessional sequence in which the husband would think aloud about some of the details of his wife's affair. Gradually, he would bring his wife into the picture by crossexamining her on certain details of her affair. Control over obsessional thinking, as well as the crossexamination, was obtained by instructing the husband to covertly verbalize "Stop!" when he became aware of obsessional thoughts. Additionally, when questioning became painful, the wife was instructed to shout to her husband, "Stop!" It was reported that three sessions of rehearsal between spouses resulted in a cessation of the husband's obsessional thinking.

Coaching

This procedure is related to modeling and involves the therapist's overall guiding and instructing function. It is a cognitive and behavioral procedure in which the therapist explains concepts or theories, gives examples, draws diagrams, asks questions, and suggests a range of choices for the problem under consideration.

Role-playing

Although role-playing has been used in traditional approaches for years (King, et al, 1960), the major function of role-playing in BMT is usually to re-create problem situations as they have occurred between spouses to help the therapist determine which contingencies contribute to the problem situations. In performing a behavioral assessment, the therapist may ask the couple to role-play a hypothetical situation (e.g., discussion of an in-law's upcoming visit) with one for, and one against. Thus the therapist is able to gain information about interactional patterns as a prelude to formal treatment. Role-playing assumes that spousal patterns of interaction do not change greatly with the setting.

Behavioral rehearsal

Related to the concept of role-playing is behavioral rehearsal (Rimm & Masters, 1974). The emphasis in behavioral rehearsal, as applied to the marital dyad, is to introduce new verbal and nonverbal behaviors into the participants' repertoire. In this technique, the therapist first models an appropriate interactional reponse with one spouse, then instructs the observing person to interact in a similar way. The procedure is repeated until the therapist is satisfied that the behavior has been learned.

Contingency contracting

Contingency contracting is currently the most widely used technique in the repertoire of the behavioral marital therapist (Jacobson & Margolin, 1979; Knox, 1971; Lederer & Jackson, 1968; Rappaport & Harrell, 1972; Stuart, 1969b; Weiss, et al, 1974). Its use is justified as a means of reversing a distressed couple's reliance on aversive communication patterns, and its goal is to foster an increase in reciprocally reinforcing behaviors through adherence to the tenets of the contract. Weiss,, et al (1974) started the objectives of contracting:

1. to identify for the spouses those behaviors which are positively or negatively reinforcing to the partners;
2. to establish the public market value of targeted annoying behaviors which occur at either high or low rates;
3. to provide a procedure for contracting behavioral contingencies such that predetermined (agreed upon) rewards and penalties reliably follow compliance and noncompliance with the terms of the contract (p. 323).

In the contracting procedure, couples begin by identifying ways in which each partner could change to make the relationship more satisfying. To accomplish this goal, the therapist helps each partner to pinpoint specific behaviors that the other could exhibit to improve their relationship. The couple then negotiates an agreement in which positive consequences for positive behaviors are established. Weiss, et al (1974) suggest that since most distressed marriages are characterized by high rates of aversive control, the focus should be on increasing the frequency of desirable behaviors rather than on decreasing undesirable behavior.

Contingency contracts, first used by Stuart (1969a, 1969b), refer to the negotiation of written behavior change agreements between the spouses. Spouses agree to quid pro quo contractual exchanges of reinforcing or pleasing behavior to replace behavior displeasing to the spouse (Rappaport & Harrell, 1972).

Another type of contingency contracting promoted by Weiss, Hops, and Patterson (1973) is the "good faith" contract whereby each spouse agrees to reinforce positive behavior in the other spouse, independent of any quid pro quo exchange of behaviors.

Margolin (1980) called *parallel* contracts the type in which "reward that each spouse receives for contractual compliance is totally independent from the other partner's targeted behavior change" (p. 72). She also noted that her study has isolated contingency contracting from other behavior exchange and/or problem-solving procedures and studied its relative effectiveness. Among the hazards she mentioned were: (1) the difficulty in identifying reinforcers for adults; (2) that the specification of the reward actually reduces its reinforcing power; (3) emphasis on issues that are irrelevant to or are a "smoke screen" for underlying difficulties the couple may be avoiding; and (4) lack of adequate problem-solving skills in the couple. By the same token, training a couple is a relatively cost-efficient process that may pay dividends in the long run (L'Abate & L'Abate, 1977). Jacobson (1978a, 1978b) has arugued that since there is no direct evidence on the efficacy of contingency contracting, it is unnecessary and, indeed, counterindicated on logical and empirical grounds.

Contract revisions

Revisions of established contracts are a part of the contracting process and are accomplished whenever they are needed. Occasionally, the contract is revised because it is ineffective, and revisions involve simplifying the contract by reducing the level of responsibilities and privileges or redesigning the responsibilities or privileges to make them less demanding, more easily monitored, or more salient (Weiss, et al, 1974).

Generally, contracts are revised to permit a fading of the intensity of treatment or to increase the amount or quality of work required for privileges (Weiss, et al, 1974). A fading in reliance on the contract occurs as individuals develop skills in reciprocity (Weiss, et al, 1974). Treatment goals in contracting include the skill to initiate and formulate contracts without therapeutic guidance (Patterson, et al, 1976); the flexibility to revise and renegotiate contracts in an ongoing process provides a foundation for this skill.

Behavioral marital therapists usually employ some combination of problem-solving skills, behavioral exchange tactics, communication training, and contingency contracting, with the goal that couples begin to solve their marital conflicts and thereby increase their marital satisfaction. An essential part of behavioral marital intervention is the manner in which the therapist teaches couples these skills and thereby induces change. Procedures or tactics for teaching skills that are used in communication training, problem-solving, and to a lesser extent in behavioral exchange and contingency contracting, include all of the techniques previously reviewed.

Initially, the therapist presents the content of the program or treatment plan. This presentation may use prepared materials (written descriptions or tape-recorded presentations), verbal instructions, and/or modeling. Following the instructions, the couple engages in behavioral rehearsal or role-play, thereby practicing the skills presented. The therapist then instructs the couple to practice at home and assists the couple in structuring these practice sessions to avoid annoyances or interruptions (Jacobson & Margolin, 1979). The last component of the skill-training is feedback, including the therapist's describing the couple's behavior (pointing out specific behaviors and emphasizing their impact), as well as the couple's providing feedback to one another on the success of their efforts. Typically, feedback is given verbally; however, the couple may listen to an audiotape or view an audiovisual recording exemplifying their interactions (Gottman, et al, 1976; Margolin & Weiss, 1978b).

There is a paucity of empirical data analyzing the specific effects of instructions, practice, and feedback in BMT. Mead (1981) reviewed the scant literature on feedback in BMT (Alkire & Brunse, 1974; Jacobson, 1979) and concluded that although feedback can be effective in inducing change, is may also be "destructive" when used with some couples. Thus Mead suggests that feedback must be used cautiously; however, feedback, instructions, and practice have all received indirect empirical support from BMT outcome studies.

SPECIFIC TREATMENT PROGRAMS

This section provides a review of four representative BMT programs; most include, as major components, training in basic communication skills and negotiation strategies. Although each of these programs overlap in procedures used, each program incorporates enough unique features to warrant individual consideration.

Token Rewards

This intervention consists of one or both spouses' receiving tokens as reinforcement for performing specified behaviors. The tokens function as interpersonal currency and may be exchanged for goods, services, or privileges as agreed upon by both partners. Stuart's (1969a, 1969b) use of this procedure trained wives to dispense tokens to husband as rewards for conversing together. Husbands could then redeem these tokens for sexual contact.

Stuart (1969) indicated that the following features of tokens make them appealing as an intervention when trust is lacking in the marital relationship: (1) they are given immediately, (2) they can be redeemed for the specific consequences that the recipient deems desirable at that time, (3) they are concrete and unambiguous, and (4) the giving and receiving of tokens is customarily associated with positive social interchanges.

Stuart's (1969) program is cited as the first data-based study providing evidence of the use of behavior modification within the marital dyad (Greer & D'Zurilla, 1975). Stuart's treatment program is based on the concept of reciprocity and coercion, and his "operant-interpersonal" approach is founded on the following assumptions: (1) that the exact pattern of interaction between spouses is, at any time, representative of the most rewarding of all available alternatives; (2) that a positive quid pro quo arrangement characterizes successful marriages; and (3) that training is required in distressed marriages in order to allow spouses to mediate rewards for one another.

Stuart's program is conducted in four steps:

1. The couple is trained in the logic of the approach. During this stage, Stuart's goals are twofold: to convince each spouse that the problem does not reside within the other, and to persuade each spouse to take initiative for changing his or her own behavior. The benefits of the first step are to free each spouse from his inaccurate and negative biasing prejudices and to allow spouses to participate fully through understanding of the program rationale.
2. Each spouse lists the three behaviors that he or she would most like to see the other spouse improve. Emphases during this step include a focus on positive behaviors, stating desires in specific behavioral terms, the need for open communication of wishes, and re-education of each spouse's participation in various difficult behavior sequences.
3. Each spouse is asked to record on a behavior checklist the frequency with which the spouse has performed the desired act elicited in step 2. The behavior checklist is posted in a visible place in the house.
4. A quid pro quo series of exchanges are monitored, using the behavior monitoring form.

As noted earlier, Stuart states that severely distressed marriages, characterized by lack of trust, require immediate reinforcement in the form of tokens. In his study, each couple recorded daily conversation and physical activity prior to, during, and for 24 to 48 weeks following the end of treatment. Results indicate that, in all four cases, rates of conversation and sexual activity increased substantially.

**The Oregon Marital
Studies Program**

The second program for consideration is the modular treatment program developed as part of the Oregon Marital Studies Program.

The Oregon Group offers a 10-session assessment treatment program that begins with the couple's receiving through the mail a set of precounseling marital inventories. This battery (Margolin, et al, 1975) is designed to assess global marital satisfaction, marital problem areas, and steps toward divorce.

The first two weeks are spent making baselines recordings (i.e., spouse observation and self-recording of pleasing and displeasing events as they occur at home). During this time, couples also provide 40 minutes of videotaped samples of their marital communication and problem-solving skills, which are analyzed with the MICS.

Following assessment, the couple is given a summary of strengths and weaknesses in their relationship, conceptualized from a behavioral perspective, and a treatment contract is formally negotiated. At this time, the first 3 of 6 treatment modules are simultaneously implemented: continued tracking of pleases (Ps) and displeases (Ds) at home, pinpointing contingencies and discrimination training, and communication skills training.

In the first module, couples are instructed to continue tracking Ps and Ds at home on a daily basis, reporting every few days by phone. The second module is designed to help couples reconceptualize their complaints from vague awareness (e.g., "My wife's always yelling" (into specific behaviors that can be increased (e.g., "I would like my wife to speak with me in a conversational tone when discussing finances"). The third module consists of communication skills training and skills related to conflict resolution. This procedure is conducted at both a process and a content level and is facilitated by the use of videotape feedback, modeling, behavioral rehearsal, and homework assignments.

The fourth intervention module, developing behavioral utility matrices, is presented when skills in the first three modules have been successfully demonstrated. This module consists of the couple's developing a menu of potential rewards and penalties to be used contingently in the negotiation and contracting phases that follow. These menus include both positive and negative consequences, which are later paired with specific behavior changes.

The fifth treatment module is negotiation and contracting. During this phase of treatment, couples are taught how to restate undesirable, negative behaviors into observable behaviors that are to be accelerated. These rather formal agreements, initially mediated by the therapist, involve explicit statements of the behavior that each partner wants increased. At the outset, the desire for more conversational time with the spouse may take the somewhat artificial form of "John will spend 20 uninterrupted minutes talking to me about our relationship within one hour after he returns from work." Contracts used by the Oregon Group are typically of the good faith variety.

The final step in the Oregon program is that of termination, maintenance, and evaluation. Termination is accomplished through the gradual fading of therapist support, concurrent with an increase in couple responsibility for their relationship. The fading process is mediated over the contracting procedure (i.e., the therapist becomes decreasingly influential in the couple's negotiation process and allows them to rely on their own skills). Final assessment is conducted by the readministration of the initial assessment procedures.

Negotiation Training

The behavioral marital program presented by Liberman, et al (1976a, 1976b) is different from the Oregon Group's in that treatment consists of 8 to 10 two-hour sessions in which participants meet conjointly in groups of 3 to 5 couples.

Intake and assessment procedures, lasting from one to three sessions, are conducted individually, and many of the instruments used in assessment overlap with those of the Oregon Group. Initially, clients are individually allowed to ventilate their dissatisfactions with their marriages.

Liberman, et al (1976a, 1976b) describe the major elements of treatment as "(1) specifying and acknowledging how each spouse could please the other in reciprocal ways; (2) engaging in behavioral rehearsals to learn more constructive verbal and non-verbal communication strategies; (3) negotiating an agreement on a contingency contract" (p. 468).

As in the Oregon approach, contingency contracting represents the culminating activity of the program. Prior to this contracting module, couples participate in four modules conducted in a group setting: programming of social and recreational activities; pinpointing and discriminating pleasing events; com-

munication training; and development of core symbols.

Pinpointing and discriminating "pleases" is conducted by use of a large checklist, "Catch Your Spouse Doing Something Nice and Let Him/Her Know About It," as well as a diary for daily narrative recordings of spouse.

The development of "core symbols" has been advocated as a discrimination stimulus for mutual dyadic pleasing. Couples are encouraged to recall or develop activities, places, or objects that signify special positive meanings to the relationship.

The development of shared mutually rewarding activities has been stressed in response to Birchler, et al's (1975) findings that distressed couples tend to engage in few shared activities with only the spouse. In this spirit, the module helps couples view the importance of prioritizing mutually reinforcing activities.

The most important treatment element, according to Liberman, et al (1976a, 1976b), is that of communication training. This component is characterized by the practice of positive and negative statements, as well as discussion of the roles of sex and affection in the marriage. Structured exercises, along with coaching, modeling, behavioral rehearsal, and homework assignments are used to facilitate training.

The specific nature of these lessons may be illustrated by examples provided by Liberman, et al (1976b, pp. 470–471), in which each spouse is instructed to complete a response (e.g., "I like it when you do . . ."; "It would make me feel good if you would do . . ."; or "When you do . . . it makes me feel good"). Examples of homework assignments include participation in "Executive Sessions," defined as periods of conversing without distraction at a designated time and place.

Contingency contracting features written contracts of the good faith type and are framed to the couple as temporary aids to help structure the development of positive exchanges. Evaluation of this package involves use of the Locke-Wallace Marital Adjustment Scale as well as monitoring of contract performance.

The use of this approach in a group evaluation, comparing it with a more traditional approach, is cited for its methodological soundness. Four couples received training as outlined earlier, while five couples were placed in an "interactional-insight" comparison group that focused on group support, problem discussion, and emotional expressiveness. Treatment was conducted for 16 hours.

A number of pre- and post-treatment measures were obtained, including spouse observations (counting Ps received and given); self-report (hours spent together, shared recreational activities, Marital Activities Inventory, Areas of Change Questionnaire, Marital Adjustment Test); and observational techniques (MICS, frequencies of looking, smiling, and touching). Results did not conclusively demonstrate superiority of one treatment method over another, but did suggest that the combined use of communication skills training and contracting produced objective behavioral changes.

Reciprocity Counseling

Azrin, et al (1973) departed significantly from a simplistic response–reinforcement notion by expanding the behavioral approach to a concept of "reciprocity" that would take into account factors that have been overlooked or denied (oftentimes vehemently) by many radical behaviorists. These factors, according to Azrin, et al, would be "personality, attitudes, expectations, role factors, communication, sex or social customs in determining marital happiness" (p. 366). On the basis of a "reciprocity" notion of marital interaction that would place them within the social-exchange rather than social-learning school, Azrin, et al coined the termed "reciprocity counseling" for a fairly structured sequence of step-wise interventions.[1]

Since their original article, a variety of studies have replicated some of the procedures and some of the outcomes (Mead, 1981). Dixon and Sciara (1977) applied the concept to a group format, while Glisson (1977) compared it with communication training according to the Minnesota Couples Communication Program (see Chapter 3). Despite several methodological weaknesses in this study, Glisson found that the best outcome was a combination of *both* communication training and reciprocity counseling.

More recently, Azrin, et al (1980), in a larger test (55 couples) of the usefulness of this approach, compared 28 couples administered reciprocity counseling for approximately 7 sessions with 27 couples who received discussion-type therapy. They found that the group receiving reciprocity counseling had significantly more improvement than the discussion-type group on three different self-report marital adjustment measures. This improvement was maintained during a 24-month follow-up period. As far as scores are concerned, however, the final differences in scores for the three groups were very similar. It is difficult, on the basis of these scores, to agree with the authors that reciprocity counseling was superior to the discussion-type approach.

RESEARCH AND EVALUATION

In addition to the adherence to principles of learning that can be validated in the laboratory and in controlled studies with human subjects, a distinguishing characteristic of the behavioral approach to marital therapy has been its emphasis on objectification, measurement, and quantification of its subject matter. Measurement has consisted largely of single-case, repeated-measures methodology with a continuing and growing emphasis on therapeutic outcome.

Direct testing of the basic propositions of social exchange theory has yielded significant findings concerning its support. In a 1974 study, Wills, Weiss, and Patterson had seven nondistressed married couples count the frequency of their spouses' pleasing and displeasing responses toward them over a 14-day period. The hypothesis of reciprocity within a marriage was supported when computed separately for each couple over the 14-day period for affectional behaviors, showing a stronger tendency to reciprocate displeasurable behaviors than to reciprocate pleasurable behaviors. This tendency was in contrast to results for average levels of pleasing and displeasing behavior, which suggested that greater reciprocity exists for pleasing than displeasing responses. A tentative conclusion from this data is that some inequity in aversive control may be more characteristic of distressed marriages than inequities in levels of positive affection.

Using both observational and self-report

---

[1]This program has been reduced to an enrichment format by Wildman and O'Callaghan, 1975 (see Chapter 7).

assessment methods, Birchler, Weiss, and Vincent (1975) compared distressed and non-distressed couples on mean rates of rewarding and punishing behaviors. They found that distressed couples had lower rates of rewarding behaviors and higher rates of punishing behaviors. In addition, couples were able to make rewarding responses more frequently with opposite-sex strangers than with their spouses.

A study by Gottman, et al (1976) found relatively little support for the social exchange theoretical formulation that views distressed marriages as characterized by less positive, or more negative, reciprocity than nondistressed marriages. Gottman, et al's research suggested that nondistressed marriages were characterized by a "bank account" conceptualization of reinforcing behaviors (i.e., spouses could give and "draw" reinforcers in a noncontingent manner). The results of Gottman, et al (1976) are in agreement with a review by Jacobs (1975) that reported difficulty in obtaining consistent differences across studies between distressed and nondistressed families.

Jacobson and Martin (1976), in their review of research in BMT, have specified five criteria by which to assess behavioral outcome studies: (1) the suitability of outcome measures, including specificity, multidimensionality, and freedom from sources of bias; (2) sufficient control to demonstrate the effectiveness of the technique; (3) identification of the components of treatment that effect change; (4) demonstration of the persistence of change after treatment over time via follow-up measures; (5) identification of the conditions that maximize or maintain the treatment effects. Selected studies representative of both the content and methodology of BMT outcome studies are examined here, incorporating Jacobson and Martin's criteria for evaluation.

Most of the evaluations of BMT have involved contingency contracting, communication training, problem-solving, and reciprocal reinforcement, either alone or in combination. The effectiveness of these strategies with couples in therapy has not yet been experimentally established, however. Studies, for the most part, are still based on uncontrolled clinical data or on highly controlled but questionably relevant laboratory analogue material (Gurman & Kniskern, 1978; Jacobson, 1978a; Jacobson & Martin, 1976).

Stuart (1969a, 1969b), in his first study, which is cited frequently in the course of this chapter, used contingency contracting with four sexually distressed couples, reporting positive results. He used a quid pro quo procedure in which the target behavior of one person was contingent on the appearance of the behavior desired in the other spouse. Tokens were given to husbands for engaging in conversation with their wives. These tokens could, in turn, be exchanged for various forms of sexual contact with their wives. Stuart used a single-subject design with daily measures of the frequency of contracted target behaviors; daily measures were obtained prior to, during the 10-week program, and at 24 and 48 weeks after the end of treatment. He also administered a marital satisfaction inventory prior to treatment, at the termination of treatment, and between 24 and 48 weeks after treatment. Stuart thus used an A–B–A single-case design, with a more global measure repeated after each phase of the study.

His study was limited, however, in that he lacked a nontreatment control group and used client self-report measures exclusively. Additionally, there was wide variability in the data recorded by spouses, which raises questions concerning the extent to which the behaviors were influenced by uncontrolled factors extraneous to the treatment program.

Azrin, et al (1973) made some methodological improvements on Stuart's study. Based on the theory that marital problems result from insufficient reciprocal reinforcement in the relationship, Azrin, et al attempted to train couples to behave in ways that were more reinforcing to each other. Through structured tasks and homework assignments, couples were taught to identify those behaviors desired by the spouse as well as those behaviors aversive to the spouse, and how to change these behaviors in exchange for reciprocal desirable changes by the spouse. Reciprocity counseling included instruction in reciprocity notions, contracting, interpersonal feedback, and sexual communication.

The treatment program consisted of a basic A–B design, beginning with a three-week, nondirective, catharsis counseling phase that would control for placebo effects, client expectancy effects, and demand characteristics, and would offer a contrasting, unstructured experience to the more structured reciprocity counseling. In this control condition, the therapist "attempted a 'talking out' of the marital problems, by encouraging and prompting communication of the client's feelings about any area of the marriage to each other and to the therapist" (p. 371). This was followed by four weeks of reciprocity counseling.

Couples were required to complete the Marital Happiness Scale (MHS) as the sole dependent outcome measure each evening from day of intake until termination and at follow-up intervals of one month. The MHS is a rating scale on which each spouse rates the degree of happiness on a 10-point scale for each of 9 aspects of marriage and estimates the general marital happiness for that day. An advantage of the structured format of this program over that of Stuart's is that it addresses subgroups of problems on the MHS sequentially, allowing assessment of differential effects of the procedures in target areas. Unfortunately, and curiously, the investigators only presented in their data the daily MHS ratings for the last week of each phase of the procedure, not for the duration of the phase as a whole.

Ratings on MHS items changed a maximum of three points versus a one-point change during the baseline phase. Azrin, et al (1973) collapsed the total 10-point range of the scale to indicate only the range of variability of the actual data. Thus the impression at first glance is that the effects were greater in magnitude than they in fact were. Their data raise issues concerning clinical versus statistical interpretation; given the possible range of 10 points, the reported positive change of 2 to 3 points is of doubtful clinical significance.

Overall, of 12 couples participating in the study, all but one individual reported statistically more marital happiness during the last week od reciprocity counseling than at the end of the catharsis procedure. At one-month follow-up, 96 percent of the clients increased in self-reports of marital happiness over pretreatment levels, and 88 percent of the spouses indicated more happiness than was reported on the last day of the treatment phase. Azrin, et al (1973) concluded that this study provided experimental evidence of the effectiveness of the procedures.

These conclusions seem to have been premature, for a variety of reasons. The three-week placebo baseline phase may not have been as innocuous as Azrin, et al assumed. As Jacobson and Martin (1976) have noted, the effects manifested during the reciprocity counseling phase may have been attributable in part to this vaguely described catharsis phase in the form of carry-over effects. Some evidence for this is the one-point mean overall increase in ratings, based on the last six factors of the MHS during the initial counseling phase. Another confounding factor is that exchange of ratings between partners was initiated during the reciprocity counseling phase, which could account for the change in ratings attributed by the authors to the structured program. The exclusive reliance on client self-reported measures has been discussed and is a serious limitation in this study. Also, the behavioral referents of overall marital happiness, as well as individual items, are not specified, making questionable the reliability and validity of the measurement between spouses. Lastly, the authors apparently did not monitor other factors pertinent to the study. Since most of the husbands involved were graduate students, it is quite possible that high MHS ratings reflect desirable changes in scale items due to increased free time at the end of a quarter or semester. In spite of these limitations, however, the Azrin study represents a methodological advance in the form of a delayed treatment, placebo baseline phase, which enabled within-client comparisons.

Aspects of reciprocity counseling were replicated in a group setting by Dixon and Sciara (1977), using seven nondistressed couples. The format consisted of eight weekly sessions of two hours each. The workshop provided sequenced instruction in assessment of marital resources, development of open communication, and exchange of reciprocally satisfying behaviors. Assessment of resources consisted of the Marital Pre-Counseling Inventory (Stuart & Stuart, 1973) and the Reciprocity Awareness Procedure (Azrin, et al, 1973). This latter measure required each spouse to list 10 behaviors currently done by the other spouse that were satisfying to him or her and 10 behaviors currently done by the other spouse that were dissatisfying to him or her. The communication phase attempted to "encourage nonjudgmental, behaviorally descriptive communication" (Azrin, et al, 1973), p. 78) and was assessed via negotiation procedures targeting, in sequence, subgroups of items on the MHS.

This study combined a group statistical comparison approach with a multiple baseline, single-case design. The Marital Pre-Counseling Inventory was administered during the first week of the workshop and during the last session. Pre- and post-treatment differences on a summary subscore reflecting commitment to and optimisim about the marriage were analyzed via a *t* test. Average ratings for each item on the MHS for the weeks preceding session 3 and session 8 were compared via *t* tests. A multiple baseline analysis was performed on the weekly ratings of three couples to document the hypothesized causal relationship between MHS ratings and initiation of reciprocity counseling procedures.

Results indicated that three areas on the MHS significantly increased from week 3 to week 8, while six factors showed a nonsignificant increase in the desired direction. The multiple baseline analysis demonstrated the contingency relationship between the introduction of specific reciprocity exchange procedure and increased ratings of happiness on MHS items when they were targeted by the reciprocity procedures.

This study demonstrates the usefulness of single-case designs in addressing more directly the issue of which outcome effects are attributable to which treatment techniques. The group statistical comparison approach demonstrates a statistical difference between pre- and post-treatment scores. Causal inferences, however, can only be made to the extent that the treatment program is unidimensional and/or that the extraneous variables are highly controlled. In applied clinical settings, neither condition is likely to exist. The Dixon and Sciara study was also limited by an exclusive reliance on client self-report data. A second limitation is the lack of any follow-up assessment.

An important advance in the behavioral assessment of marital dysfunction has been made by Weiss, et al (1973) and their associates (the Oregon Group). These researchers have provided outcome studies on their treatment package, which includes communication skills-training, problem-solving, reciprocity, and contingency contracting, as well as a marital assessment battery that includes both client self-report rating scales and observational instruments.

The Oregon Group's treatment package includes both a baseline phase and a follow-up assessment. Patterson (1976) treated 10 couples with their structured program and found improvement among husbands and wives on only three problem-solving behaviors of 29 categories on the Marital Interaction Coding System (Weiss, et al, 1973). On the Spouse Observation Checklist, which provides a daily rating by each spouse of the mate's behaviors that are pleasing and displeasing to him or her, husbands and wives both increased in number of Pleases from pre- to post-test, and husbands showed a significant decrease in Displeases.

A second outcome study by Weiss, et al (1973) found that five treated couples improved over baseline levels on the MICS items of compromise and behaviors antagonistic to successful negotiation. Wives' critical behavior was reduced to a post-treatment level similar to that of their husbands' critical behavior. There was also a significant pre- to post-treatment increase in rate of Pleases.

Weiss, et al (1973) conducted a third study that assessed for effectiveness of the Oregon modular approach on five couples treated for 56 to 91 days, plus a follow-up at six months post-treatment. All couples improved on four of the five measuring instruments; four couples improved on the Lock-Wallace Marital Adjustment Scale (Locke & Wallace, 1959), which provides a global estimate of marital distress. Frequency of Pleases and Displeases changed nonsignificantly in the desired directions.

Although the data from the Oregon Group are by no means conclusive, they demonstrate the importance and feasibility of multiple measurement, including both self-report and observational measures. Efforts to replicate and validate studies also exemplify the self-corrective nature of the scientific enterprise. Whether or not the assessment instruments devised by this group withstand the stringent requirements of reliability and validity, this group has given the impetus to both behavioral and nonbehavioral clinical researchers in the marital field to objectify their therapeutic procedures and outcome assessment.

Jacobson (1977a, 1977b) attempted to evaluate a behavioral treatment program for couples involving problem-solving and contingency contracting, using a waiting-list control group.

Participants were 10 married couples who had responded to a newspaper advertisement offering a new program for troubled marriages. Couples were assessed in terms of self-report and observational measurement via the MAS and MICS. In addition, each spouse recorded daily the rate of occurrence of the mate's target behaviors. The rate recordings were assessed via a single-case design. All target behaviors to be changed were identified at intake, and the frequency of two target behaviors of each spouse was recorded for a two-week baseline period prior to treatment.

The treatment format was essentially a replication of the approach of the Oregon Group, consisting of eight weekly sessions, including problem-solving and contingency contracting, plus related homework assignments. The control group completed the MAS and participated in problem-solving sessions nine weeks after pretest. The treatment group, 12 months after termination, completed the MAS and returned it by mail.

Results indicated that the treatment group changed in the desired direction on positive and negative behaviors on the MICS compared to the control group, whose positive behaviors decreased slightly and whose negative behaviors increased slightly. Similarly, mean total marital satisfaction scores from the MAS increased significantly for the treated group but not for the control group. These change levels were maintained at follow-up. There were no differences in the treatment group between husbands and wives on marital satisfaction.

Additionally, multiple baselines on target behaviors were kept for four out of five treatment couples. These data indicated a change in the desired direction on each target behavior in a sequence contingent on the implementation of a contract to modify that behavior. Thus Jacobson demonstrated that the single-case design and group-comparison approaches could be usefully combined in an outcome study in such a way that each design provided information not addressed by the other. The single-case, multiple baseline design permitted the assessment of the effectiveness of the treatment on the idiosyncratic problems of each couple, as well as the corroboration of the data for the group as a whole.

Limitations of Jacobson's study (pointed out by him) include the fact that participating couples were not necessarily comparable to distressed couples in other studies or to distressed couples in mental health agencies. Also, couples' problem-solving interaction and monitoring of each other's behavior were not done in vivo. Therefore the fabrication of rating scores or collusion of spouses on these ratings cannot be ruled out. The small sample size limits confidence in the group data, since one couple could have exerted an inordinate influence on the group averages. The investigator also served as the principal therapist in the study, suggesting experimenter bias. Finally, the study assesses a treatment package rather than the relative efficacy of each treatment intervention alone.

Jacobson (1978b) has followed up this study with another study investigating the relative effectiveness of the quid pro quo versus the good faith method of contingency contracting. This study represents the increasing methodological sophistication of current research in BMT. It constitutes one of the few examples of systematic replication across settings and subjects. Subjects were either solicited by an announcement in the media or referred from mental health agencies or clinicians in private practice. Participating in the study were 30 couples who were initially interviewed and administered the Marital Pre-Counseling Inventory (Stuart & Stuart, 1973); three therapists participated, including the investigator. Measures were the MICS, MAS, and MHS, plus ratings by undergraduates of descriptions of the behavioral treatments and nonspecific treatments as a measure of credibility. In addition to two treatment groups, each of which received one form of contracting, two control groups were utilized. A nonspecific control group received elements of treatment packages assumed to be partly responsible for previously demonstrated effectiveness of nonbehavioral methods. The good faith group was a replication of a prior study by Jacobson (1977b). The quid pro quo group replicated the good faith group in all ways except that it received training in quid pro quo contracting. The nonspecific control group duplicated the treatment groups in all respects except procedures related to contracting. The waiting-list control group was offered treatment after pre- and post-testing were completed.

Results indicated that both contracting groups, compared to the nonspecific and waiting-list control couples, decreased the number of negative behaviors and increased the number of positive behaviors from pre- to post-test. Neither behavioral group differed from the other on these measures. On the marital satisfaction scale, the two behavioral groups improved considerably from pre- to post-test, with no differences for the nonspecific group and a deterioration effect for the waiting-list group. Neither behavioral group differed from the other on this measure. These differences were also maintained at follow-up. On the MHS, both behavioral groups and the nonspecific group, in contrast to the waiting-list group, increased from pre- to post-test and did not differ from each other.

Jacobson noted that a nonspecific treatment group, perceived as credible, showed effects comparable to two forms of contracting on the one self-report measure (MHS) that seemed to be the most susceptible to demand characteristics. He concluded that improvement following contracting procedures is not due to nonspecific factors. Also, this study suggested that neither form of contracting is preferable to the other, at least with nonseverely distressed couples. There were no therapist–treatment interaction effects, even though one therapist was the investigator. A limitation of this study, however, is that MICS ratings were based on a hypothesized rather than an actual conflict situation pertinent to the couple (Gurman & Kniskern, 1978a, 1978b).

A persistent criticism of many of the applications of BMT to date has been that the techniques have been developed on young, fairly well functioning, nondistressed couples, representative of highly educated, middle-class university communities (Liberman, et al, 1976a, 1976b; Weiss, 1980). As Gurman and Kniskern (1978a, 1978b) have noted, the techniques and procedures of BMT have yet to be demonstrated with severely distressed couples. Jacobson's (1977a, 1977b), 1978a) success with couples who were not directly associated with a university community has somewhat muted this criticism. Two other recent studies (Liberman, et al, 1976a; O'Leary & Turkewitz, 1978) have applied these procedures to more severely distressed, non-university-affiliated couples.

The study of Liberman, et al (1976a) illustrates the art and science of systematic replication. This group applied the Oregon treatment model and assessment battery to distressed couples in a group setting. They also made some innovative changes in the treatment format and in the assessment procedures. The study also illustrates the fruitfulness of combining the group statistical comparison approach with the single-case, repeated-measures design.

The study examined the effectiveness of a behavioral treatment package comprising reciprocity training, communication training, and training in contingency contracting, including relevant homework assignments. A comparison group (interactional group) was geared toward increasing expression of feelings, modeling of empathy and warmth, clarity of communication, providing advice on reciprocal behavioral exchange, and fostering insight into and awareness of interpersonal behavior. Both groups were led by the same three therapists, a psychiatrist, a psychiatric social worker, and a mental health nurse, all of whom were experienced in group work.

Subjects were referred from a local mental health center or from area practitioners. To be included in this study, subjects had to be nonpsychotic, non-drug-addicted, living together and considering separation or divorce but willing to postpone any action on separation until after the treatment program. Participating couples reported unhappiness at pretest, measured by the Marital Pre-Counseling Inventory, in the areas of social, affectionate, and sexual interactions, child management, financial management, lack of free time, and sharing of household reponsibilities.

The program consisted of pretest, a two-week baseline period, eight weekly group sessions of two hours' duration, and a follow-up session one month after termination. Results indicated that both groups improved significantly on all the self-report measures from pre- to post-treatment. Marked differences were noted on the observational measures, however. After treatment, the behavioral group members, compared to members of the interactional group, showed significantly more understanding and congruence in their estimates of what changes in their behavior were desired by their spouses. Also, the behavioral group members looked and smiled at their spouses significantly more often than did members of the interactional group. On the MICS in pre- and post-treatment comparisons, the behavioral group members, compared to members of the interactional group, showed significant decreases in negative verbal and nonverbal behaviors, and significant increases in positive nonverbal behaviors. Frequency of Pleases declined for the behavioral group but remained the same for the interactional group over the nine weeks of treatment. There was also low interspouse reliability (.40) for this measure, thus invalidating the test of the reciprocity hypothesis. This decrease in Pleases for the treatment group is at odds with Weiss, et al (1973) and, according to the investigators, may have reflected social desirability, demand characteristics, and/or fatigue effects of daily recording. Liberman, et al view this study as providing substantial support for the applicability of BMT techniques to distressed couples and as demonstrating the importance of using both client self-report and observational measures of outcome. They view the similarity of the two groups on self-report measures as evidence against the influence of placebo factors on the outcome of the behavioral group. The authors also conclude that their study demonstrates that a comprehensive behavioral assessment and treatment of couples in distress is both logistically and financially feasible in a community mental health setting, thus refuting some criticisms of the work of the Oregon Group. A limitation of the study from the viewpoint of a group statistical comparison approach was the small number of couples in each group.

A more recent study, using BMT procedures with distressed couples, has been reported by O'Leary and Turkewitz (1978). They attempted to test their observations and those of Liberman, et al that contingency contracting is worthless if the couple has insufficient communication skills. They used 30 couples, two-thirds of whom had been referred by local mental health clinics or by clinicians in private practice, and one-third of whom had responded to announcements in local newspapers. Couples were matched into three groups, based on their scores on the Locke-Wallace Marital Adjustment Scale and on number of years of marriage, and were assigned to one of two treatment groups or to a waiting-list control group. The first treatment group received communication training; the second group was taught communication skills plus behavioral contracting skills, which were drawn up in writing and implemented at home.

Criteria for inclusion in the study were that the couple must have been married for at least five years, must currently live together, and must score in the distressed range on the MAS. Couples were excluded if there was evidence of chronic alcoholism, psychotic disorders, or sexual dysfunction. Based on these criteria, four couples were excluded. Couples averaged 12.4 years of marriage, 35.4 years of age, and had two children, a $12,000 annual income, and a high-school education.

Assessment consisted of the following;

1. *Primary Communication Inventory* (Navran, 1967), a 25-item questionnaire on which a respondent rates the frequency of various communication behaviors on a 5-point scale. This inventory served as both a diagnostic and as an outcome measure.
2. *Feelings Toward Spouse Questionnaire* (O'Leary & Turkewitz, 1978), which assesses feelings not necessarily communicated verbally or nonverbally. Frequency of these feelings are rated on a 5-point scale.
3. *Target problems*, either pertaining to the marriage or identified with either self or spouse, as elicited from a questionnaire.
4. *Marital Adjustment Scale*, as described earlier.

These measures were obtained at intake, termination, and at four-month follow-up. At intake, couples were assigned a problem-solving exercise similar to Jacobson's (1978a) and told to try to resolve it. This discussion was tape-recorded and coded by trained raters. The waiting-list control group couples completed pre- and post-treatment questionnaires, with a 10-week interval, and subsequently received therapy. The study utilized five therapists, each of whom worked alone, with two couples in each group. Therapists consisted of the two authors, a clinical psychologist, a social worker, and a doctoral-level student in clinical psychology, all of whom were trained for this study. Treatment consisted of 10 weekly sessions plus follow-up and related homework assignments.

Results indicated that both treatment

groups, compared with the control group, showed positive prepost treatment changes on the communication questionnaire, the self-reported marital problems, and on behavior change desired by the spouse. Wives in the two therapy groups, compared with wives in the control group, reported more positive changes on nonmarital personal problems. Husbands showed no such changes. There were no differences between groups on the problem-solving exercise. Follow-up data indicated that couples in both treatment groups improved on the communication questionnaire and on the MAS. There were no differences between treatment groups on these measures. Therapist behaviors with couples in each group, rated by both therapist self-report and by observers, indicated that each group was receiving the designated intervention by the therapists, thus assuring the integrity of the design.

The data supported the inference addressed elsewhere (Jacobson, 1978b) that written agreements were a superfluous component of contingency contracting; however, consistent with the possibility that group averages obscure important treatment effects (Bergin & Strupp, 1972; Hersen & Barlow, 1976). O'Leary and Turkewitz (1981) re-analyzed the data from the MAS and the communication questionnaire according to age of the couples. Younger couples across the two treatment groups averaged 29 years of age and seven years of marriage. The older group averaged 41 years of age and 18 years of marriage. This analysis revealed that the communication plus written agreements was very effective for all younger couples but less so for most of the older couples. The younger couples also improved more than the waiting-list couples. The older couples, in contrast with the waiting-list couples, showed more positive response to the communication intervention. the same pattern held for the follow-up MAS ratings. The investigators speculated that these data suggest that older distressed couples may have more entrenched pathological communication patterns, requiring more intensive therapeutic focus. In any case, in light of these results, O'Leary and Turkewitz reiterated Jacobson and Martin's (1976) exhortation that BMT procedures should not become so prepackaged and standardized that they cease to be tailored to the individual client. Such rigidity and regimentation

would violate the tradition and the unique contribution of the behavioral approach.

Some laboratory analogue research is worthy of mention for its relevance to clinical settings. Thomas and his associates (already reviewed in Chapter 3) have extensively researched the area of modifying problematic verbal communication through brief, direct instructional feedback and specific suggestions. They developed a procedure to assess communication via in vivo ratings of conversation in 49 categories of problem communication (Thomas, et al, 1974). They developed the instrument called Signal System for the Assessment and Modification of Behavior, or SAM (Thomas, 1977). SAM is an electronic apparatus which, through lights as signals, allows for both client-controlled and therapist-controlled signaling during ongoing couple interaction. The therapist and client-couple can receive signals from each other, allowing for both assessment and modification of their verbal behavior (Thomas, 1977). This group has attempted to simplify complex verbal communication between clients into small response units, and they have reported successful application of the SAM procedure in improving a distressed couple's specificity of communication about sexual problems.

A recent study by Mayadas and Duehn (1977) utilized 19 desirable and undesirable behaviors identified by Thomas (1977) to develop a stimulus-modeling videotape on which a couple role-played these behaviors. This tape was used in a subsequent study to assess the differential effects of stimulus modeling, videotape feedback plus modeling, and traditional verbal-counseling procedures. Participants were 30 couples who were being treated in a private marriage and family counseling center for communication problems. There were 10 couples in each group. Each couple was treated by one of three social workers for eight one-hour sessions. Stimulus-modeling plus videotape feedback consisted of viewing the SM tape, followed by videotaped role-playing of the desired behavior by the couple, and replaying of the client couple's role-playing segment, along with therapist critique.

Each couple was asked to indicate problematic behaviors, based on the list of 19 behaviors that were modeled on the SM tape and had been identified by Carter and Thomas as salient behaviors for distressed couples. The five most frequently checked behaviors served as the dependent variables. When pre–post treatment scores were examined, it was found that all couples improved on all five behaviors across the three therapists. Couples exposed to the SM tape only improved on three of five communication behaviors. In the SM tape-videotape feedback group, couples improved on all five behaviors. Couples receiving verbal counseling only improved on one of five target communication behaviors. The investigators viewed these results as a partial validation in a clinical setting of the analogue work of Thomas and his associates.

The work of Gottman, et al (1976) provides a second illustration of the relevance of laboratory analogue research to clinical applications of BMT. As reviewed further in Chapter 16, Gottman, et al developed a device called the "talk table," which was used to operationalize aspects of behavior exchange and reciprocity theories. In essence, this instrument is a panel board for each spouse, containing two rows of buttons. One row pertains to intended impact of a message given by the spouse; the other row pertains to the felt impact of messages received from the other spouse. Each row of five buttons represents a continuum with extremes of "super positive" and "super negative." Each verbal message given and received is rated by each spouse on this continuum.

Gottman, et al reported two studies utlizing this device to test the reciprocity hypothesis of Birchler, et al (1975) that nondistressed couples are characterized by a high degree of reciprocally reinforced behavior, whereas distressed couples show a deficit of reciprocally reinforced behavior. Gottman, et al noted that the key variable in distinguishing these couples might be their base rates of reinforcing behaviors rather than whether these behaviors are reciprocally based or mutually contingent. Gottman emphasized in these studies the importance of client self-report data as much as observational data.

By enabling the couples themselves to judge messages as positive or negative via the talk table, Gottman both utilized the phenomenological experience of each spouse and refined theoretical notions of communication deficit. Thus he was able to test whether distressed couples intend their messages to be more negative or less positive or whether they are just received as such. Communicational deficit was thus operationalized as the correspondence between the intent of the message sender and the impact on the recipient.

Gottman, et al conducted two studies, using distressed and nondistressed couples as identified by a self-report questionnaire. In the first study, he assessed their communications via the talk table under three levels of stress associated with three different conflict situations. Results from 10 distressed couples and 6 nondistressed couples referred from local mental health clinics, university counseling centers, and a newspaper advertisement indicated that distressed couples emit more negative and fewer positive messages than nondistressed couples. It was also found that distressed couples had less correspondence between intent and impact of communications, whereas nondistressed couples had almost identical levels of intent and impact. The ratio of agreements to disagreements, based on observers' ratings of videotapes of four randomly selected couples (two distressed, two nondistressed), was higher in the problem-solving tasks for nondistressed couples. Analysis of probability of positive impacts for each spouse, based on impacts on the other spouse, provided support for the reciprocity theory of distressed marriages.

The second study was an extension of the first, using 30 older couples (mean age 32.5, mean years of marriage 9.4) and a high- and low-conflict task. Results replicated the first study in degree of greater correspondence on intent and impact of message in nondistressed marriages. The difference in correspondence for distressed couples seemed to be attributable to differences between spouses concerning how messages are received rather than how they are intended. The ratio of agreements to disagreements for two couples in each group in the conflict situation was higher for nondistressed couples only on the high-conflict task. Gottman, et al concluded that the conflict level of the task influences how messages are coded and that high-conflict tasks discriminate more reliably the distressed from nondistressed couples.

In the second study, the reciprocity theory was not substantiated. Data were interpreted in terms of the base-rate model of reinforcement. The authors formulated a "bank account" model of reinforcement for nondistressed marriages in which reinforcing behavior has a high frequency relative to aversive behaviors and is noncontingent on reinforcing behavior by the spouse. Gottman, et al note that observers' ratings of a couple's communications may be insensitive to the ideosyncratic or contextual determinants of how these behaviors are experienced by the couple. Consequently, couple self-reports may be the more reliable and valid measurement. Although these studies were vulnerable to couple and experimenter expectancy effects, as the investigators noted, they illustrate the advantages of controlled analogue research.

In attempting to evaluate behavioral marital research, Jacobson and Martin (1976) have offered several recommendations for future research:

1. More controlled studies with either group-comparison designs or single-subject designs must be done to identify which components of treatment packages are the most effective.
2. There is a need to evaluate alternative ways of implementing different techniques (e.g., quid pro quo or good faith models of contracting).
3. There is a need for increased use of direct observation methods in addition to client self-report inventories.
4. Consistent with the behavioral approach of examining each case differently, any standardized treatment package or procedure should be sufficiently flexible to adapt to each case.
5. The development of standardized assessment techniques will facilitate comparisons across studies.

Gurman and Kniskern (1978a) have updated Jacobson and Martin's (1976) and Greer and D'Zurilla's (1975) reviews of BMT in the context of reviewing outcome research on marital therapy in general. Gurman and Kniskern note the lack of any controlled comparison study of BMT with severely disturbed couples. They cite Jacobson's (1977, 1978b) as most closely approximating a controlled study with disturbed couples, but criticized Jacobson (1978b) for assessing couples' problem-solving behavior on hypothetical rather than actual marital problems. They criticize the methodological limitations (lack of control groups, lack of adequate follow-up), over-reliance on small samples of nondistressed couples, absence of replication, and lack of evidence of differential effectiveness of each component of the treatment packages, which characterize most of the BMT studies to date. They also question the use of outcome measures that function as both an assessment instrument and an intervention strategy. The resulting reactive effect may produce inflated and meaningless outcome data. They also note and examine in more detail elsewhere (Gurman & Kniskern, 1978b) strands of evidence from these same instruments, indicating deterioration effects. Gurman and Kniskern conclude that the empirical literature to date does not demonstrate the superiority of BMT over other approaches.

According to Patterson, et al (1976), research in the area of marital intervention is "limited in both quality and quantity." Then, only six published controlled outcome studies examining the effect of BMT existed. Only four of these studies applied BMT to distressed couples, while the other two were analogue studies.

The results of one of the four controlled outcome studies involving distressed couples (Tsoi-Hoshmand, 1976) will not be considered, since Jacobson (1981) reported that this study "failed to meet minimal methodological prerequisites for establishing internal validity" (p. 586). The other three controlled outcome studies (Jacobson, 1977a, 1978b; O'Leary & Turkewitz, 1981) examined the effects of a BMT treatment package that included communication training and some type of behavioral exchange components (i.e., negotiation, problem-solving, contracting).

Jacobson's methodologically sound studies (1977a, 1978b) demonstrated the effectiveness of BMT as compared with waiting-list control groups and, in the second study, with a placebo control group. In these studies, BMT consisted of teaching couples problem-solving skills and contracting procedures. In Jacobson's initial study (1977a), however, good faith contracts were taught; whereas, in his later study (1978b) he compared a behavioral treatment group learning quid pro quo contracting with a behavioral treatment group learning good faith contracting. He found no differences between these two behavioral treatments, both proving equally effective. The effectiveness of BMT in these studies was demonstrated both by self-report measures of marital satisfaction and by observational measures of the spouses' problem-solving skills. Both of these studies are also noteworthy in that the effects of treatment maintained, as measured by one-year and six-month follow-ups, respectively.

O'Leary and Turkewitz (1981) compared the effectiveness of behavioral contracting plus communication training with communication training alone. The communication training group worked more intensely on expressing feelings than did the group who worked on a combined contracting and communication training. A waiting-list control group was also used to determine the effectiveness of the treatment groups. The results indicated that both treatment groups improved significantly on self-report measures but not on behavioral measures. No overall differences between treatment groups were found. Couples in treatment groups reported increases in marital satisfaction and communication from pretreatment to a four-month follow-up. An interesting finding in this study was that young couples exhibited more positive change in the behavioral contracting and communication group; whereas older couples responded far better to communication training. Although this study lends support to the effectiveness of BMT, the differences between the findings of behavioral and self-report measures render the results inconclusive.

Liberman, et al (1976a) have reported that BMT applied in a group setting was significantly superior to an insight-oriented couples group as assessed by objective measures of marital communication. Couples in both groups however, improved significantly on ratings of marital satisfaction. A one-year follow-up revealed that these results were maintained. O'Leary and Turkewitz (1981), however, stated that the results of Liberman, et al (1976a) should be viewed skeptically, since their study was plagued by methodological flaws (i.e., lack of a control group, nonrandom assignments to groups).

Margolin and Weiss (1978b), in an analogue outcome study, compared three groups: (1) a behavioral communication training group that included a cognitive restructuring component, (2) a behavioral-communication-only group, and (3) a nondirective treatment group. The findings indicated that the behavioral treatment with the cognitive restructuring compo-

nent was more effective than the behavioral treatment alone, and both of these groups were more effective than the nondirective treatment group as measured by both observer-coded and spouse-coded measures of positive behavior. All three treatment groups were effective in decreasing the occurrence of negative behavior.

Jacobson (1979) examined the effectiveness of problem-solving training upon severely distressed couples in an uncontrolled series of single-subject design. This is the only BMT study to date using "severely" distressed couples. The results demonstrated the effectiveness of the problem-solving training as measured by spouse records of positive and negative behaviors exhibited in the home. These results were maintained at six-month and one-year follow-up in four of the six couples studied.

In conclusion, based upon a review of the existing literature (Gurman & Kniskern, 1978b; Jacobson, 1978b; Jacobson & Margolin, 1979; Weiss, 1978) including both analogue and naturalistic studies, BMT appears to be no more effective than nonbehavioral approaches to marital therapy, with both approaches demonstrating approximately 66 percent effectiveness (Vincent, 1980). Also, Gurman and Kniskern (1978b) warn that the results presented in the BMT literature should be viewed cautiously for the following reasons: (1) an insufficient number of group design studies presently exist, (2) many studies use nonclinical analogue demonstrations with minimally distressed couples, (3) there is lack of replication of studies, and (4) there is infrequent collection of follow-up data. In addition to these criticisms of the empirical literature about BMT, issues concerning BMT's conceptual model and its application have also been subject to scrutiny.

In concluding this section, a word of caution offered by Margolin and Christensen (1981) seems necessary. These authors stress that behavioral therapists should be careful not to rely heavily or become overly dependent on specific therapy procedures and thereby neglect the specific needs of each couple. Although research on BMT interventions indicates that BMT is applicable to all couples, its applicability has not been demonstrated. Hence therapists should continually assess couples' progress during therapy and be ready to alter strategies as needed.

DISCUSSION

Although the use of applied behavioral principles in marital therapy is certainly in its infancy, in the last 10 years there have been an increasing number of somewhat successful applications of behavioral principles to the treatment of difficulties within the marital relationship (Greer & D'Zurilla, 1975; Jacobson & Martin, 1976). Although there is some divergence in thinking concerning treatment applications, ranging from classical and operant conditioning approaches to cognitive behavioral approaches, the common element in all the behavioral marital approaches remains the theoretical base of social learning theories that is directly translated into a behavioral change approach. In BMT, the interactive, quantifiable aspects of observable human behavior are emphasized. Treatment focuses on current problematic behaviors while acknowledging the importance of behavior that takes place outside the treatment setting, and there is a concern with the exact specifications of problematic behaviors and the measurement of those interventions that produce behavioral change.

Behavioral marital therapy appears primarily to emphasize learning and the contigencies by which learning takes place. The behavioral approach, however, as has been true in the development of individual therapies, is beginning to converge with other theoretical viewpoints. Communication theories have been incorporated into theory and treatment as has an interest in how stimulus events are mediated by cognitive processes. This expanding theoretical approach continues to be implemented with an increasing variety of presenting problems.

Perhaps the greatest contribution to date of the behavioral approach is its critical examination of the specificity of treatment goals and treatment designs, with a primary concern for the outcome of therapy. The devotion to scientific method has led to the primary goal of change in maladaptive behavior and an increasing emphasis on the measurement and assessment of problems, expanding research strategies and statistical procedures. This change is accomplished by the clients' taking action, rather than the client's actions and new behaviors resulting from insight and/or understanding of the problem.

While the behaviorists point to the question of specified change, other marital therapists are questioning their own effectiveness in the treatment of dysfunctional relationships. With the continued prodding of behavioral research, one must acknowledge the issue of specificity and continue to ask Kiesler's (1966) original question: What treatment under what conditions in which settings is the most effective for which clients? Concerning this question, behavioral marital therapists have offered the most systematic rationale and accompanying intervention strategies for the implementation of change. They have also offered a theoretical approach that differs in major ways from those of other schools.

The behavioral approach differs from other schools of thought in that it does not specifically focus on intrapsychic processes. Although internal cognitive processes that mediate behavior are acknowledged and increasingly considered important, insight with an emphasis on past development is not considered of primary importance. Diagnosis is not used; instead, a behavioral diagnosis focuses on personal and interpersonal sources of strength. The foundation of change is strengths rather than weaknesses or labeled personality defects. The detailed assessment of treatment goals, using the clients' presenting problem, not only acknowledges and responds to the clients' stated goals but provides a mechanism for isolating causes of improvement. Problems are broken down into manageable components, and treatment strategies can be altered in an orderly and logical fashion during the course of treatment.

Human behavior is viewed as determined by an individual's history of social reinforcement and consequent learning, as well as by the current environmental antecedents and consequences that impinge on the behavior in question. Ultimately, that which is learned can be unlearned, and new learning can take place by altering environmental conditions. Rather than change that addresses an individual's hypothesized internal processes, the components of change in behavior can be concretely identified in one's external world and therefore altered.

In attempting to assess the contributions of BMT, one must also note its liabilities. Although specificity is stressed, there is no universally accepted definition or consensus as to what constitutes BMT. Behavioral treatment approaches are still general ones, emphasizing communication, negotiation, and homework. They also overlap with a variety of other approaches.

This overlap can primarily be seen in the reliance on the therapeutic relationship, suggestion and manipulation of client expectancies, and focus on underlying themes to which behavior might be traced. Behavioral treatment approaches are increasingly addressing the individual's private events (unconscious), which is no different from all major therapies. The general approaches used in behavioral treatment then lead to the very old question related to the specificity of change: Is it the treatment technique or the relationship with the therapist that has the most impact on inducing change?

Knudson, et al (1980) have presented several assumptions seemingly characteristic of BMT that address inherent practical and conceptual limitations of this approach. A major criticism of BMT stated by these authors is that the approach assumes that both partners agree that the problem is relational and, therefore, the situation in which one person is presented as the problem is neglected. According to Knudson, et al (1980), it is the exception for a couple to present themselves as a dyad for therapy. More frequently, one spouse presents as the "identified patient" and, therefore, marital conflict is often disguised as one spouse's vague complaints, such as anxiety, depression, etc. Thus, if couples fail to perceive their situation as a relational dysfunction, resistance to a behavioral intervention that focuses on the dyad is practically guaranteed. Also, resistance is not restricted to couples who obviously present with one spouse ill, but resistance is probably inherent in all attempts to make important changes in any relationship. The concept of resistance has received minimal attention in the BMT literature to date, with several behaviorists denying its importance. For example, Jacobson and Weiss (1978, p. 152) state that "as an a priori assumption, we have found it more useful to assume that when a couple seeks therapeutic assistance . . . they do, in fact, want to change their relationship." Also, Jacobson and Margolin (1979, p. 5) stated that, "rather than adhering to the homeostatic conception of a family striving for maintenance of maladaptive behavior patterns and resist-

ing change, behavior therapists assume that couples who ask for help generally wish to be helped," and that anticipating resistance may promulgate its emergence. Although Knudson, et al (1980) agree with these behaviorists that expecting resistance may act as a self-fulfilling prophecy, they sugest that one's model be cognizant of resistance when it does emerge and also be able to prescribe a therapeutic response when such resistance is encountered. Hence, as Bancroft (1975) noted, the behavioral approach expects both spouses to act like rational adults, open to logical instruction, and the success of BMT will depend greatly on the therapist's ability to persuade the couple to maintain such an adult role, often when behaving in an emotional, childlike manner has been a well-established pattern of marital interaction.

Another criticism of BMT offered by Knudson, et al (1980) is that BMT's avoidance of cognitions and mediating processes results in the neglect of emotions and intentions. Jacobson and Margolin (1979, p. 12) state that,

a behavioral exchange model does not accept the assumption that most target behaviors presented by the couple can best be understood as metaphors serving a communication and relationship defining function. Rather, behavior is seen as primarily a function of its environmental consequences, for the individual engaging in that behavior, and the topography of particular responses is viewed literally rather than symbolically.

Weiss (1978), however, states that behavioral models are attempting to include the role of cognitions in behavior change, but that the main focus continues to be upon the effects of behavior. Hence, in focusing upon behaviors, the behaviorist may miss an important underlying message. For example, a husband bought his wife a fur coat, not to please her but to defer and/or alleviate the guilt of his having an affair. The wife reports that such behavior makes her suspicious, not grateful. Therefore the behaviorist's persistent focus upon content and reliance on first-order changes (a linear perspective) such as increasing positive behavior to ameliorate marital distress, may not lead to a change in the system or how one spouse feels about the other.

Another criticism, offered by Knudson, et al (1980) is that behaviorists' insistence upon increasing positive behaviors and decreasing negative ones may be useless and/or counter-productive. For example, Luthman (1974, p. 57) stresses that "anger is very much attached to aliveness, sexuality, and creativity. To repress it is to deaden oneself in these areas." Knudson, et al (1980) contend that expression of negative feelings is often an important component of changing. Also, these authors stress a primary emphasis on overt behavior that may inhibit rather than enhance clinical understanding. For example, a wife may tell her husband that when it comes to dancing, he is a klutz, and a behaviorist may note this response as negative although, in fact, the relationship message may be, "I have confidence in you and our relationship and I know that this statement doesn't really bother you."

Weiss (1978) has criticized BMT on the grounds that behavior modification is based upon a technology that, derived from learning principles, neglects to address the issue of a theory of adult intimacy in relationships. Weiss also criticizes BMT for its interpretation of marital conflict as representing skill deficiencies. Weiss maintains that not all problem exemplify skill deficits and that if each partner had every social skill teachable, this would probably not ensure marital happiness.

A third criticism offered by Weiss is that spouses in BMT may perceive "rewards" as given because of obligation rather than as a favorable evaluation of the spouse's worth. Thus the paradox, "The strength of BMT, which lies in reinforcing—contingency control of behavior—flies in the face of cognitions about desirability in an intimate relationship" (Weiss, 1978, p. 173).

Other criticisms presented in the literature (Gurman, et al, 1978; Gurman and Kniskern, 1978,a, 1978b) include (1) lack of application of BMT to severe marital disorders (i.e., psychotic, alcoholic, or schizophrenic spouse); (2) adherence to emphasizing only quantifiable data, possibly resulting in the ignoring of therapeutic concerns (i.e., feelings, cognitions); (3) the assumption that altering behaviors will definitely result in increased marital satisfaction; and (4) lack of emphasis on therapist–client relationships.

In conclusion, Jacobson and Weiss (1978) assert that the model for BMT is still an infant, and therefore, one hopes it will continue to develop and expand, perhaps addressing some of its current limitations. Also, such inherent limi-tations may be alleviated through an integration of BMT with other approaches to therapy, specifically the systems theory approach (Gurman, 1980; Weiss, 1980).

Concerning specificity and the role of theory in BMT, one can point to the assets of preciseness and clarity, for theories are understandable, internally consistent, and free from ambiguities. There is a minimum of complexity and few assumptions, so that behavioral theories are comprehensive as well as operational. The difficulty with the emphasis on specificity, however, is that theory becomes simplistic, viewing human behavior as caused by a narrow set of determinants. This reductionistic stance has already led to a growing realization of limitations, for the current treatment concern with the feeling state known as "mutual satisfaction" is not always correlated with specific and identifiable reinforcing behaviors. For example, contracting procedures designed to provide increased social reinforcement have been shown ineffective when one or both spouses do not have an ideology of equality of power or role function (Gottman, 1979). The spouses' perceptions, cognitions, and attributions (about their own feelings) may be crucial in defining the impact of contracted behaviors (Gottman, et al, 1976). Gottman's findings are crucially important if one remembers that most marriages are not based on the underlying assumption of equality of power and role.

Although the importance of the individual's attributions has been acknowledged and there is an increasing emphasis on cognitive aspects of behavior, most studies have continued to address reinforcement principles, with little study of the role of cognitions. Cognitions are acknowledged to be important but are not addressed in identifying relevant components of behavior and change. Although there is a growing consensus that behavioral change is short-term unless there is some cognitive change (Thoresen & Coates, 1978), BMT has so far added little, other than reinforcement principles, to the knowledge of the etiology of maladaptive behaviors.

Concerning the role of the BMT therapist, he or she is an expert in assessment, treatment planning, treatment initiation, and follow-up. Although often viewed as technicians, behaviorists have contributed to the field of marital therapy by stressing the educative functions of the therapist. Therapy is not necessarily a treatment for a deficit; rather, it is an educative process, using couples' strengths. Two crucial issues in the role of the behavioral marital therapist involve function and training, however.

The therapist must define maladaptive behaviors. It is easy to define maladaptive behavior when fighting and violence is a presenting problem. It is difficult to define maladaptive behavior when the presenting problem is a general state of dissatisfaction, however. Therefore, although one might think that the therapist is merely a technician or teacher, the therapist, instead, must address a complex set of interactions and construct effective interventions. By virtue of his or her role, the therapist must be highly trained and skilled. Not all clients present a specific behavior problem; translating "feeling better" or "feeling more satisfied" into behavior components is a complicated task at best. Unfortunately, training issues are rarely, if ever, addressed in current behavioral literature.

Since not all clients present an overt behavioral problem to the therapist, the question must still be asked, which behaviors and which clients benefit from BMT? Unfortunately, most outcome studies are conducted with white, educated, middle-class couples who present specific problems (e.g., sexual dysfunction, poor communication). Results of applicability to specific clients so far indicate only that BMT is effective with fairly high-level functioning, educated couples who present specific behavioral difficulties. One must also add that this middle-class bias is further complicated by the fact that currently proposed detailed assessment and client follow-up procedures are costly, as well as limited to those clients who are capable of assessing themselves and giving the therapist self-report data. At this time, it is difficult to imagine the use of behavioral treatment approaches in treating a psychotic or educationally deprived individual or couple.

Although the behavioral marital therapists are to be commended for stressing the importance of outcome studies, there are many inherent difficulties in assessing the outcome of treatment. The difficulty of identifying the role of the individual therapist has already been mentioned. In addition, the almost exclusive reliance on the use of single-case studies further raises the question of generalizability. Re-

sults can only be generalized to specific, small populations with specific and somewhat concrete difficulties. Furthermore, when multiple interventions are used, it is difficult to identify significant treatment components and their interactions in producing or impeding change. In addition, most behavioral outcome studies still rely on self-report data that can be both positively and negatively biased by a number of factors (e.g., clients' desire to please the therapist, social desirability, and the clients' justification for involving themselves in treatment). Concerning therapist bias, most outcome studies have a confirmatory bias that shows behavioral treatment to be effective when pitted against no treatment or a placebo.

Finally, one must address the role of values in BMT. No therapy approach is free from inherent theoretical and individual values; rather than attempt a value-free formulation, one must acknowledge ideological and value-laden issues as they relate to psychological intervention in clients' lives. BMT is based theoretically and philosophically on a bargaining-and-exchanging-goods model, as well as acknowledgment that change of another's behavior can be initiated without his or her express consent. One spouse is sometimes treated with the goal of helping to teach effective operant conditioning principles by which the other spouse will conform to the desired behavioral outcome. Not only does the issue of manipulation become important as related to defining exactly what it is one manipulates, but the issue of treatment without consent is raised.

There is also a general emphasis on stopping aversive emotions and statements, with a unidimensional focus on the content level of behaviors. Restricting one's behavior to positive content may constrict the range of emotions and behaviors allowable within a viable relationship, thus robbing it of spontaneity as well as vitality.

An example of the importance of values can be seen in Stuart's (1969a) treatment of married couples. Husbands were rewarded by their wives for engaging in behaviors desired by the wives (i.e., more communication). They could, in turn, exchange their tokens for sex. One can raise numerous value-laden issues about this study. One can see the relationship as viable only when there is a concrete reward. Sexual relationships, then, are not valued as spontaneous, nor is a voluntary giving and cooperation in the marital relationship. One can easily deduce that the wife is a sexual object from whom the husband "buys" sexual favors. Carried further, Stuart's study inadvertently confirms the centuries-old disparaging belief that women are sexual objects to be bought and owned.

One might conclude that behavioral therapy and therapy merely extend to the therapy setting the economic values inherent in American society. Individuals are not valued as giving or sharing voluntarily. Instead, receiving and exchanging goods is the ultimate goal of the marital relationship. The therapist and the therapy can be criticized as a technician's implementation of a technology that defines maladaptive behaviors as behaviors that do not allow an individual to collect a vast number of "goods."

In summary, BMT has contributed to the field of couples therapy by providing a systematic and, in some reported cases, effective treatment for changing some behaviors in couples' relationships. Its shortcomings, however, are many. It is still a general approach that overlaps with many other therapy techniques, and the specific components of treatment that effect change cannot be defined. The importance of an individual's attributions and motivations are often ignored, and interventions have been used primarily with white, educated, middle-class clients. Its theory is limited and ignores unseen events in an individual's life. There is no emphasis on therapist training, no generalizable outcome studies showing any long-term change, and there is a question concerning the nature of its inherent values.

THE FUTURE

Clearly, BMT is still in its infancy, and its needs related to its future growth are many. Although trends continue to emphasize education, using reinforcement principles, the rationale lacks comprehensiveness and generalized applicability. Future treatment and research must address a number of key issues: (1) a clearer understanding of the etiology of maladaptive and distressed behaviors and states; (2) the applicability to the more severely disturbed, the economically disadvantaged, and the racially and culturally different client; (3) the issue of providing treatment that produces a long-term and/or lasting change; (4) an understanding of the role of affects and intimacy in the marital relationship; (5) the nature of its role in shaping and/or maintaining values in the marital relationship.

It is hoped that, with its focus on the scientific method, future BMT-derived or BMT-oriented research and treatment will address these issues. Until these issues are addressed, BMT may remain a limited technique, for its applicability to more general abstract issues (e.g., dissatisfaction) has not been demonstrated. Rather, BMT has demonstrated a rational treatment program for specific concrete issues.

REFERENCES

Alexander JR, & Barton C. Behavioral systems therapy with families, in DH Olson (ed), *Treating relationships*. Lake Mills, IA: Graphic Press, 1976

Alger I, & Hogan P. Enduring effects of videotape playback experience on family and marital relationships. *American Journal of Orthopsychiatry*, 1969, *39*, 86–94

Alkire AA, & Brunse AJ. Impact and possible causality from videotape feedback in marital therapy. *Journal of Consulting and Clinical Psychology*, 1974, *42*, 203–210

Azrin NH, Basalee VA, Bechtel R, Michalicek A, Mancera M, Carroll D, Shuford D, & Cox J. Comparison of reciprocity and discussion-type counseling for marital problems. *The American Journal of Family Therapy*, 1980, *6*, 27–28

Azrin NH, Naster BH, & Jones R. Reciprocity counseling: A rapid learning-based procedure for marital counseling. *Behavior Research and Therapy*, 1973, *11*, 365–382

Bagarozzi DA, & Wodaski JS. Behavioral treatment of marital discord. *Clinical Social Work Journal*, 1978, *6*, 135–154

Bancroft J. The behavioral approach to marital problems. *British Journal of Medical Psychology*, 1975, *48*, 147–152

Bandura A. *Principles of behavior modification*. New York: Holt, Rinehart & Winston, 1969

Bandura A. *Aggression: A social learning analysis*. Englewood Cliffs, NJ: Prentice-Hall, 1973

Bergin AE, & Strupp HH. *Changing frontiers in the science of psychotherapy*. New York: Aldine-Atherton, 1972

Birchler GR. Communication skills in married

couples, in AS Bellach & M Hersen (eds), *Research and practice in social skills training.* New York: Plenum, 1979

Birchler GR, Weiss RL, & Vincent JP. A multidimensional analysis of social reinforcement exchange between maritally distressed and nondistressed spouse and stranger dyads. *Journal of Personality and Social Psychology*, 1975, *31*, 349–360

Blau PM. *Exchange and power in social life.* New York: Wiley, 1964

Bowen M. Family and family group therapy, in HT Kaplan & BJ Sadock (Eds), *Comprehensive group psychotherapy.* Baltimore: Williams & Williams, 1971

Canter A. Discussion of enduring effects of videotape playback experience on family and marital relationships. *American Journal of Orthopsychiatry*, 1969, *39*, 96–98

Carkhuff RR. *Helping and human relations.* New York: Holt, Rinehart & Winston, 1969

Carkhuff RR. *The art of problem solving.* Amherst, MA: Human Resource Development Press, 1973

Carter RD, & Thomas EJ. Modification of problematic marital communication using corrective feedback and instruction. *Behavior Therapy*, 1973, *4*, 100–109

Christensen A. Naturalistic observation of families: A system for random audio recordings in the home. *Behavior Therapy.* 1979, *10*, 410–422

Christensen A, & Nies DC. The spouse observation checklist: Empirical analysis and critique. *The Journal of Family Therapy*, 1980, *8*(2), 69–79

Cookerly J. The outcome of the six major forms of marriage counseling compared: A pilot study. *Journal of Marriage and the Family*, 1973, *36*, 608–611

Dixon DN, & Sciara AD. Effectiveness of group reciprocity counseling with married couples. *Journal of Marriage and Family Counseling*, 1977, *3*, 77–83

Eisler R, & Hersen M. Behavioral techniques in family-oriented crisis intervention. *Archives of General Psychiatry*, 1973, *28*, 111–116

Epstein M, & Williams AM. Behavioral approaches to treatment of marital discord, in GP Sholevar (ed), *The handbook of marriage and marital therapy.* New York: SP Medical and Scientific Books, 1981

Eysenck HJ (ed). *Behavior therapy and the neuroses.* New York: Pergamon, 1960

Friedman P. Personalistic family and marital therapy, in A Lazarus (ed), *Clinical behavior therapy.* New York: Brunner/Mazel, 1972

Glisson DH. A comparison of reciprocity counseling and communication training in the treatment of marital discord. *Dissertation Abstracts International*, 1977, *37*, No. 12

Gottman JM. *Marital interaction: Experimental investigation.* New York: Academic Press, 1979

Gottman J, Markman H, & Notarius C. The topography of marital conflict: A sequential analysis of verbal and nonverbal behavior. *Journal of Marriage and the Family*, 1977, *39*, 461–477

Gottman J, Notarius C, Markman H, Bank S, Yoppi B, & Rubin M. Behavior exchange theory and marital decision making. *Journal of Personality and Social Psychology*, 1976, *34*, 14–23

Greer S, & D'Zurilla T, Behavioral approaches to marital discord and conflict. *Journal of Marriage and Family Counseling*, 1975, *1*, 299–315

Gureney BG, Jr. *Relationship enhancement.* San Francisco: Jossey-Bass, 1977

Gurman AS. Behavioral marriage therapy in the 1980's: The challenge of integration. *American Journal of Family Therapy*, 1980, *8*, 86–96

Gurman AS, & Kniskern DP. Behavioral marriage therapy: II. Empirical perspective. *Family Process*, 1978a, *17*, 139–148

Gurman AS, & Kniskern DP. Research on marital and family therapy: Progress, perspective and prospect, in S Garfield & AE Bergin (eds), *Handbook of psychotherapy and behavior change* (2nd ed). New York: Wiley, 1978b

Gurman AS, Knudson RM, & Kniskern DP. Behavioral marriage therapy: IV. Take two aspirin and call us in the morning. *Family Process*, 978, *17*, 165–180

Haley J. Marriage therapy. *Archives of General Psychiatry.* 1963, *8*, 213–224

Hersen M, & Barlow D. *Single-case experimental design.* New York: Pergamon Press, 1976

Homans GC. *Social behavior: Its elementary forms.* New York: Harcourt, Brace, & World, 1961

Hull CL. *Principles of behavior.* New York: Appleton-Century-Crofts, 1943

Jackson D. Family rules: The marital quid pro quo. *Archives of General Psychiatry*, 1965, *12*, 589–594

Jacobs LJ. Family problems of childless adopting couples concerned with their role as parents. *Dissertation Abstracts International*, 1975, *35*(8-B)

Jacobson NS. Problem solving and contingency contracting in the treatment of marital discord. *Journal of Consulting and Clinical Psychology*, 1977a, *45*, 192–100

Jacobson NS. Training couples to solve their marital problems: Part II: Intervention strategies. *International Journal of Family Counseling*, 1977b, *5*, 120–28

Jacobson NS. A review of the research on the effectiveness of marital therapy, in T Paolino & B McCrady (eds), *Marriage and marital therapy.* New York: Brunner/Mazel, 1978a

Jacobson NS. Specific and nonspecific factors in the

effectiveness of a behavioral approach to the treatment of marital discord. *Journal of Consulting and Clinical Psychology*, 1978b, *46*, 442–452

Jacobson NS. Increasing positive behavior in severely distressed marital relationships: The effects of problem-solving training. *Behavior Therapy*, 1979, *10*, 311–326

Jacobson NS. Behavioral marital therapy: Current trends in research, assessment and practice. *The American Journal of Family Therapy*, 1980 (Whole No. 8)

Jacobson NS. Behavioral marital therapy, in AS Gurman and DP Kniskern (eds), *Handbook of family therapy*. New York: Brunner/Mazel, 1981

Jacobson NS, & Margolin G. *Marital therapy: Strategies based on social learning and behavior exchange principles*. New York: Brunner/Mazel, 1979

Jacobson NS & Martin WB. Behavioral marriage therapy: Current status. *Psychological Bulletin*, 1976, *83*, 540–556

Jacobson NS & Weiss RL. Behavioral marriage therapy. III. Critique: The contents of Gurman et al. may be hazardous to our health. *Family Process*, 1978, *17*, 149–163

Kiesler DJ. Basic methodological issues implicit in psychotherapy process research. *American Journal of Psychotherapy*, 1966, *20*, 135–155

King GF, Armitage SG, & Telton JR. A therapeutic approach to schizophrenics of extreme pathology. *Journal of Abnormal and Social Psychology*, 1960, *61*, 276–286

Knox D. *Marriage happiness: A behavioral approach to counseling*. Champaign, IL: Research Press, 1971

Knudson RM, Gurman AS, & Kniskern DP. Behavioral marriage theory: A treatment in transition, in CM Franks & GT Wilson (eds), *Annual Review of Behavioral Therapy:* Vol. 7, New York: Brunner/Mazel, 1980

Krumboltz JD. Behavioral goals for counseling. *Journal of Counseling Psychology*, 1966, *13*, 153–159

Krumboltz JD, & Thoresen CE (eds). *Behavioral counseling: Cases and techniques*. New York: Holt, Rinehart & Winston, 1969

L'Abate L, & L'Abate B. *How to avoid divorce: Help for troubled marriages*. Atlanta: John Knox Press, 1977

Lazarus AA. New methods in psychotherapy: A case study. *South African Medical Journal*, 1958, *33*, 660–664

Lazarus AA. Aversion therapy and sensory modalities. *Clinical Impression—Perceptual and Motor Skills*, 1968, *27*, 178

Lazarus AA. *Behavior therapy and beyond*. New York: McGraw-Hill, 1971

Lederer W, & Jackson D. *The mirages of marriage*. New York: W. W. Norton Co., 1968

Lester GW, Beckham E, & Baucom DH. Implementation of behavioral marital therapy. *Journal of Marital and Family Therapy*, 1980, *2*, 189–199

Levinger G. Marital cohesiveness and dissolution: An integrative review. *Journal of Marriage and the Family*, 1965, *27*, 19–28

Liberman RP. Behavioral approaches to family and couple therapy. *American Journal of Orthopsychiatry*, 1970, *40*, 106–118

Liberman RP, Levine J, Wheeler E, Sanders N, & Wallace C. Experimental evaluation of marital group therapy: Behavioral vs. interaction-insight formats. *Acta Psychiatrica Scandinavica*, 1976a (Supplement)

Liberman RP. Wheeler E, & Sanders N. Behavioral therapy for marital disharmony: An educational approach. *Journal of Marriage and Family Counseling*, 1976b, *12*, 383–395

Lindsley O. Operant conditioning methods applied to research in chronic schizophrenia. *Psychiatric Research Reports*, 1956, *5*, 118–153

Locke HJ, & Wallace KM. Short-term marital adjustment and prediction tests: Their reliability and validity. *Journal of Marriage and Family Living*, 1959, *21*, 251–255

Luthman SG. *The dynamic family*. Palo Alto, CA: Science and Behavior Books, 1974

Margolin G, Christensen A & Weiss RL. Contracts, cognition, and change: A behavioral approach to marriage therapy. *The Counseling Psychologist*, 1975, *5*, 15–26

Margolin GA. Conjoint marital-therapy to enhance anger management and reduce spouse abuse. *American Journal of Family Therapy*, 1979, *7*, 13–23

Margolin GA. Contingency contracting in behavioral marriage therapy. *The American Journal of Family Therapy*, 1980, *6*, 171–74

Margolin GA, & Christensen A. The treatment of marital problems, in RT Daityman (ed), *Clinical behavior therapy and behavior modification* (Vol. 2). New York: Garland Publishing, Inc., 1981

Margolin GA, & Weiss RL. Communication training and assessment: A case of behavioral marital enrichment. *Behavior Therapy*, 1978a, *9*, 508–520

Margolin GA, & Weiss RL. Comparative evaluation of therapeutic components associated with marital treatments. *Journal of Consulting and Clinical Psychology*, 1978b, *46*, 476–486

Mayadas N, & Duehn W. Stimulus-modeling videotape for marital counseling. *Journal of Marriage and Family Counseling*, 1977, *3*, 35–42

Mead DE. Reciprocity counseling: Practice and research. *Journal of Marital and Family Therapy*, 1981, *2*, 189–200

Miller N, & Dollard J. *Social learning and imitation.* New Haven: Yale University Press, 1941 (1953)

Miller N, & Dollard J. *Personality and psychotherapy.* New York: McGraw-Hill, 1950

Minuchin S, & Montalvo B. Techniques for working with disorganized low socioeconomic families, in J Haley (ed), *Changing families.* New York: Grune & Stratton, 1971

Murstein BI, & Beck GD. Person perception, marriage adjustment, and social desirability. *Journal of Consulting and Clinical Psychology,* 1972, *39,* 396–403

Navran L. Communication and adjustment in marriage. *Family Process,* 1967, *7,* 173–184

O'Leary KD, & Turkewitz H. The treatment of marital problems from a behavioral perspective, in T Paolino & B McCrady (eds), *Marriage and marital therapy.* New York: Brunner/Mazel, 1978

O'Leary KD, & Turkewitz H. A comparative outcome study of behavioral marital therapy and communication therapy. *Journal of Marital and Family Therapy,* 1981, *9,* 159–169

Olson D, & Sprenkle D. Emerging trends in treating relationships. *Journal of Marriage and Family Counseling,* 1976, *2,* 317–329

Patterson GR. Some procedures for assessing changes in marital interaction patterns. *Oregon Research Institute Bulletin,* 1976, No. 16

Patterson GR, & Hopes H. Coercion: A game for two: Intervention techniques for marital conflict, in R Ulrich & P Mountjoy (eds), *The experimental analyses of social behavior.* New York: Appleton-Century-Crofts, 1972

Patterson GR, & Reid JB. Reciprocity and coercion: Two facets of social systems. In C Neuringer and L Michael (eds), *Behavior modification in clinical psychology.* New York: Appleton-Century-Crofts, 1970

Patterson GR, Weiss RL, & Hops H. Training in marital skills: Some problems and concepts. In H Leitenberg (ed), *Handbook of behavior modification.* New York: Appleton-Century-Crofts, 1976

Rappaport A, & Harrell J. A behavioral-exchange model for marital counseling. *The Family Coordinator,* 1972, *21,* 203–212

Reid JB. *A social learning approach to family interventions.* Eugene, OR: Castalia, 1978

Rimm DC, & Masters JC. *Behavior therapy: Techniques and empirical findings.* New York: Academic Press, 1974

Robinson EA, & Price MG. Pleasurable behavior in marital interaction: An observational study. *Journal of Consulting and Clinical Psychology,* 1980, *48,* 117–118

Rogers CR. *Client-centered therapy.* Boston: Houghton-Mifflin, 1951

Rosen RC, & Schnapp BJ. The use of a specific behavioral technique (thought stopping) in the context of conjoint couples therapy: A case report. *Behavior Therapy,* 1974, *5,* 261–264

Rotter JB. *Social learning and clinical psychology.* Englewood Cliffs, NJ: Prentice-Hall, 1954

Skinner BF. Operant behavior. *American Psychologist,* 1963, *18,* 503–515

Skinner BF. *Science and human behavior.* New York: Free Press, 1953

Spanier GB. Measuring dyadic adjustment: New scales for assessing the quality of marriage and similar dyads. *Journal of Marriage and the Family,* 1976, *38,* 15–28

Stuart RB. Operant-interpersonal treatment for marital discord. *Journal of Consulting and Clinical Psychology,* 1969a, *33,* 675–682

Stuart RB. Token reinforcement in marital treatment, in R Rubin & C Franks (eds), *Advances in behavior therapy.* New York: Academic Press, 1969b

Stuart RB. *Helping couples change.* New York: The Guilford Press, 1980

Stuart RB, & Stuart F. *Marital pre-counseling inventory.* Champaign, IL: Research Press, 1973

Thibaut JW, & Kelley HH. *The social psychology of groups.* New York: Wiley, 1959

Thomas EJ. *Marital communication and decision making: Analysis, assessment and change.* New York: The Free Press, 1977

Thomas EJ, Walter CL, & O'Flaherty K. A verbal problem checklist for use in assessing family verbal behavior. *Behavior Therapy,* 1974, *5,* 235–236

Thoresen CE, & Coates TJ. What does it mean to be a behavior therapist? *The Counseling Psychologist,* 1978, *7(3),* 3–21

Thorndike EL. *The elements of psychology.* New York: Seiler, 1905

Travers R. *Essentials of learning:* New York: Macmillan, 1972

Tsoi-Hoshmand L. Marital therapy: An integrative behavioral-learning model. *Journal of Marriage and Family Conseling,* 1976, *2,* 179–191

Vincent JP. The empirical-clinical study of families: Social learning theory as a point of departure, in JP Vincent (ed), *Advances in family intervention, assessment, and theory* (Vol. 1). Greenwish CT: Jai Press, Inc., 1980

Watson JB. *Behavior: An introduction to comparative psychology.* New York: Holt, 1914

Watson JB, & Raynor R. Conditioned emotional reactions. *Journal of Experimental Psychology,* 1920, *3,* 1–14

Weiss RL. The conceptualization of marriage from a behavioral perspective, in T Paolino & B McCrady (eds), *Marriage and marital therapy from three perspectives: Psychoanalytic, behav-*

ioral, and systems theory. New York: Brunner/ Mazel, 1978

Weiss RL. Strategic behavioral marital therapy: Toward a model for assessment and interaction. In JP Vincent (ed), *Advances in family intervention, assessment, and theory: A research annual.* Greenwich, CT: JAI Press, 1980

Weiss RL, & Birchler GR. Adults with marital dysfunction, in M Hersen & AS Bellack (eds), *Behavior therapy in the psychiatric setting.* Baltimore: Williams & Wilkins Co., 1978

Weiss RL, Birchler G, & Vincent P. Contractual modes for negotiation training in marital dyads. *Journal of Marriage and the Family,* 1974, *36,* 321–330

Weiss RL, & Cerreto MC. The marital status inventory: Development of a measure of dissolution potential. *American Journal of Family Therapy,* 1980, *8,* 80–85

Weiss RL, Hops H, & Patterson GR. A framework for conceptualizing marital conflict, technology for altering it, some data for evaluating it, in LA Hamerlynck, LC Handy & EJ Marsh (eds), *Behavior change: Methodology, concepts, and practice.* Champaign, IL: Research Press, 1973

Weiss RL, & Margolin G. Marital conflict and accord, in AR Ciminero, KS Calhoun & HE Adams (eds), *Handbook for behavioral assessment.* New York: Wiley, 1977

Weiss RL, & Perry BA. *Assessment and treatment of marital dysfunction.* Eugene: Oregon Marital Studies Program, 1979

Wildman RW, II, & O'Callahan JB. Reciprocity enrichment program. In L L'Abate and collaborators, *Manual: Enrichment program for the family life cycle.* Atlanta, GA: Social Research Laboratories, 1975

Wills T, Weiss R, & Patterson G. A behavioral analysis of the determinants of marital satisfaction. *Journal of Consulting and Clinical Psychology,* 1974, *42,* 802–811

Wolpe J. *The practice of behavior therapy.* New York: Pergamon, 1969

Wolpe J. *Psychotherapy by reciprocal inhibition building.* Stanford, CA: Stanford University Press, 1958

Yates AJ. *Theory and practice of behavior therapy.* New York: Wiley, 1975

12

Counseling and Psychotherapy

Marital therapy continues to be increasingly accepted as a needed and valid treatment modality (Gurman & Rice, 1978). The number of professional and popular books and articles concerning marriage problems and their solutions has grown tremendously in the past two decades, as has public awareness of and willingness to acknowledge difficulties and issues within marital relationships (Allred, 1976; Gurman, 1979; Hunt & Rydman, 1976; Lasswell & Lobsenz, 1976). Currently, marital therapy is used for a wide variety of clinical problems that were formerly treated by individual psychotherapy (e.g., affective disorders, alcoholism, and sexual dysfunction), and there appears to be no foreseeable end to marital therapy's application to the treatment of interpersonal as well as intrapersonal difficulties.

As with any growing profession, terms are often vague, theories are not often well developed, and treatment cannot always be related to theory. There is, however, beginning to be some consensus regarding the definition of marital therapy as well as regarding the definitions of various divergent treatment approaches within the field. Ultimately, there is no accurate unitary description of the field of marital therapy, partly because of divergent theoretical orientations and resulting practices, and partly because of the lack of empirical research on marital therapy and specific treatment outcomes. One can, however, define marital therapy by the growing consensus on its purpose and function.

The terms "marriage counseling" and "marital therapy" have appeared interchangeably in the literature since the 1960s. Silverman (1972) stated that the difference between marriage counseling and marital therapy is that marriage counseling focuses on less severely disturbed individuals and more conscious processes, while marital therapy focuses on more severely disturbed individuals and unconscious problems. Olson (1970) stated that marriage counseling, as opposed to marital therapy, does not convey a wide range of services; whereas other authors (Bowen, 1978; Gurman, 1973b; Leslie, 1964) used the terms interchangeably.

It appears that, in the past, attempts to distinguish martial therapy from marriage counseling have been related to the debate over whether counseling and psychotherapy are the same or different. Patterson (1974) noted the inability of practitioners to diffentiate between what is called counseling and what is called psychotherapy, and found no essential differences in practice between the two in severity of psychological disturbance, presenting problems, goals, methods, or techniques.

The American Association of Marriage and Family Counselors, in discussing its name change to the American Association of Marriage and Family Therapists, made no distinction between the terms "marriage counselor" and "marital therapist," but indicated that the name should be changed from counselor to therapist to qualify for various third-party payments and other mental health benefits and to indicate to the public that marriage and family therapists are not advice-givers (AAMFC Newsletter, 1978, pp.l, 7). The distinction between therapy as applicable to more severely disturbed individuals and counseling as applicable to less severely disturbed individuals is noted only in the context of how others will view the profession (AAMFC Newsletter, 1978, pp. 1, 7). Therefore, there appear to be no essential distinguishing differences between the terms marriage counseling and marital therapy other than connotative ones related to professional identity issues.

Martial therapy has been defined as a treatment that focuses on the marriage relationship when the couple is interviewed conjointly by the therapist (Haley, 1963a), a treatment whereby the therapist is interested in the dynamic interaction between two married persons (Mace, 1967), a specialized form of psychotherapy (Hudson, 1972), and the "application of any planned therapeutic techniques to modify the maladaptive relationships of married couples" (Gurman, 1973b, p. 146). Others have defined marital therapy as a therapy that treats the marriage (Bell, 1975), a therapy that is not only a treatment but a new way of conceptualizing the cause and cure of psychiatric problems (Stierlin, 1977, p. 13), and a treatment for the marriage in which both spouses attend sessions together (Bowen, 1978). The American Association of Marriage and Family Therapists' current definition of the functions of a marriage and family therapist states that a marriage and family therapist is "one who is required to possess/exhibit a unique understanding and conceptualization of relationships; interpersonal interactions and systems theory" (AAMFC Newsletter, 1978, pp. 1, 7).

The goal of marital therapy can be generally defined as improving the marital relationship in some way. Statements of goals have included changing the rules of the system (Haley, 1963a, 1963b; Satir, 1965), "living effectively and wholesomely within the framework of responsibilities, relations and expectancies that constitute the state of marriage" (Silverman, 1972, p. 23), improving the marriage (Olson, 1970), improving marital relationships (Bell, 1975), bringing happiness into the marriage and restoring the lost equilibrium or

balance (Knox, 1971), and creating intimacy (Strong, 1975).

Therefore marital therapy can be defined as some type of intervention that treats the marital relationship independent of the method of treatment employed; its goal is some type of improvement in the marital relationship. It must be noted that this definition is global in nature and based on numerous definitions from current literature, and that specific theorists and practitioners may define and describe marital therapy in other ways, some of which may differ from the global definition.

BACKGROUND AND DEVELOPMENT OF THE FIELD

Although numerous theories are currently offered to explain the widespread recognition of marital incompatibility in the United States (Melville, 1977), neither widespread marital incompatibility nor various forms of therapy are new phenomena. Aries (1962) and Stone (1977) have both documented the fact that until the present century, the historical position of the institution of marriage in Western Europe was primarily one of an arranged, economic, often distant relationship. Lantz (1976), in a study of 18th-century American documents and publications, found that marital incompatibility in the American colonies was widespread and differed little from current statistics and estimates.

Throughout history, men and women have traditionally sought help for marital difficulties from shamans, priests, friends, and relatives. In this century, however, marital therapy has appeared as a formally recognized profession, perhaps mostly due to demand by consumers.

Although many explanations have been offered for the growing verbalized public and professional concerns about marital difficulties and the institution of marriage, the fact remains that many individuals experience difficulties in living within a marriage and that increasing numbers of individuals and couples are seeking marital therapy. In 1960 in a nationwide sample, Gurin and others found that only one person in seven had ever sought outside help for emotional problems (Gurin, et al, 1960).

Of the number who had sought outside help, almost half listed the presenting problem as a marriage problem. In later studies, Sager, et al, (1968) estimated that one-half of all individuals seeking psychotherapy were motivated by marital problems and that another one-fourth in psychotherapy had marital-related problems. In addition, marital problems were the largest precipitating factors in admissions to state hospitals, and Renne (1976) concluded that the percentage of couples who are unhappy in their marriages is between 20 percent and 25 percent.

In conjunction with the growing awareness of marital difficulties and requests for therapy, the major national organization exclusively for marriage and family counselors, the American Association of Marriage and Family Therapists, has recently been approved by the Department of Health, Education and Welfare as the national accrediting organization in the field of marriage and family counseling and is actively lobbying for the licensing of marriage and family counselors throughout the nation (AAMFC Newsletter, 1978). In addition, this organization has hired a public relations firm to advertise and promote its services as a profession (AAMFC Newsletter, 1978).

One must, therefore, recognize that not only is awareness of and seeking treatment for marital difficulties a still-growing phenomenon, but that the treatment of marital difficulties is part of a rapidly growing and increasingly recognized profession.

In the United States, marital therapy dates from the late 1920s and early 1930s, when the first clinics opened to treat couples with marital problems. The three major centers and founders of the practice of marital therapy were the Marriage Consultation Center in New York, started by Abraham and Hannah Stone in 1929, the American Institute of Family Relations started by Paul Popenoe in 1929, and the Marriage Council of Philadelphia started by Emily Mudd in 1932 (Olson, 1970). The beginnings of these centers were influenced theoretically by writings in the social sciences concerning the individual personality as an interacting member of a group (Burgess, 1926), and practically by need as requests for services for marital problems increased after World War I (Erickson & Hogan, 1972; Foley, 1974; Kaslow, 1975). During the 1920s, marital therapy was usually conducted with only one spouse and

was considered a specialty in the field of Family Counseling (Silverman, 1972); its goal was to help an individual adjust to the roles required of him or her by the institution of marriage.

With the advent of the relative popularity of psychoanalysis and the child-guidance movement in the 1930s, the relationship of the couple was largely ignored because of the increased focus on the psychoanalytic view of the individual and the Adlerian-influenced view of the mother–child relationship as it pertained to childhood disturbances. In the 1930s, marital therapy was still usually conducted with only one spouse and was still a specialty of family counseling, espousing an adjustment model of treatment.

The focus on and the treatment of marital difficulties was largely ignored professionally until the late 1940s, when the relative failure of the child-guidance movement created a focus on the mother–father relationship, with a resulting interest in the nature of the marital interaction (Bell, 1967; Bowlby, 1949). The rapid growth of family therapy, beginning in the 1950s with the Bateson project to study schizophrenia (Bateson, et al, 1968, pp. 31–55; Ruesch & Bateson, 1951), gave further impetus not only to the practice of marital therapy but to increasing theoretical considerations of the individual in a marital relationship.

In 1942, the American Association of Marriage Counselors (AAMC) was organized by a small group of practitioners to facilitate the development of the new profession (Peterson, 1968). In 1970, the AAMC officially changed its name to the American Association of Marriage and Family Counselors (AAMFC) to include family therapists who had previously had no nationally affiliated group (Olson, 1978).

Since the 1960s, marital therapy and the treatment of marital dysfunction has not only grown rapidly but has grown separately from the field of family therapy. Although the two fields are moving in similar directions, their development continues to be somewhat unrelated to each other. Marital therapy is and has been considered since the early 1960s as a field separate from family therapy (Silverman, 1972).

Currently, the major difference between marital therapy and family counseling/therapy, by consensual definition (Nichols, 1974), is that marital therapists treat primarily the marital relationship, whereas family therapists treat primarily the family system. Olson (1970) summarized the major descriptive differences between marital therapy and family therapy by stating that marital therapy grew out of a social need for practitioners to treat marital problems, whereas family therapy grew out of a realization of inadequate treatment methods. Marital therapists traditionally came from interdisciplinary programs or have been social workers or ministers, whereas family therapists originally came from the field of psychiatry. In Olson's (1970) review, he could find no functional differences between marital therapy and family therapy, and concluded that the functions of both appeared to be ill-defined. In attempting to distinguish the practice of family therapy from the practice of marital therapy, it is still difficult to separate the two in current literature. The family therapist often works only with the couple; the marital therapist sometimes works with the family.

In a later review, Olson (1978) states that the two fields appear to be moving in similar directions with parallel but generally unrelated developments. Marital therapists generally use the theoretical framework of family sociology or clinical psychology; family therapists use either psychodynamic formulations or ideas espoused by eminent family therapists. In spite of similarities in approaches, marital therapy and family therapy function rather autonomously and do not influence each other to a great extent in either theory or practice, even though this lack of interdisciplinary influence may be changing. Marital therapy could be considered a phase of treatment in dealing with the whole family.

The theoretical growth and practice of marital therapy have been influenced by a number of ideas, including family systems theory. Systems theory, as initially defined by Bateson (Bateson, et al, 1968, pp. 31–55), states that in a relationship there is a dynamic interaction among the parts rather than a sum of their absolute characteristics. This departure from a linear, individually oriented, cause-and-effect theory is currently widely acknowledged in theories of marital therapy. Other theoretical concepts incorporated into marital therapy are (1) Bateson's (Bateson, et al, 1968) double-bind theory of communication and its subsequent emphasis on the nature of communication in marital and family relationships, (2) Wynne's (Wynne, et al, 1958) concepts of pseudomu-

tuality and pseudohostility as they relate to the emotional nature of the marital relationship. (3) Jackson's (1965) concept of the marital quid pro quo and its resulting emphasis on role expectations, and (4) Lidz's (1968) concepts of marital schism and skew as they relate to the results of failure of role complimentarity in marital relationships.

The communication theorists and their emphasis on clarifying communication to affect the individual and the relationship have led to a growing emphasis on therapies that focus on improving communication and communication skills (Haley, 1959; Lederer & Jackson, 1968; Satir, 1967). Gestalt (Kempler, 1973) and nondirective theories (Rogers, 1972) have also contributed to the theory and practice of marital therapy by emphasizing the feeling state of the marital relationship, and an abundance of behavioral approaches (Knox, 1971; Patterson & Hops, 1972; Stuart, 1969a, 1969b; Weiss, et al, 1974) have contributed to theory and practice by focusing on the reciprocal behavioral nature of the relationship.

Other theorists have focused on isolation and loneliness in modern American society, resulting in increased expectations of the marital relationship (Ackerman, 1958), role and role confusions and conflicts (Ellis, 1973; Haley, 1963a, 1963b; Saxton, 1968; Silverman, 1972), and transference issues as they relate to unreal expectations (Goldberg, 1974; Boszormenyi-Nagy, 1965; Stierlin, 1977; Schwartz & Leder, 1972).

Marital therapy has been characterized as both a unique and effective form of treatment (Leslie, 1964) and an ill-defined (Nichols, 1974) field with no integrated theory or validated hypotheses (Ackerman, 1972). It is unique, in that marital therapy is the only form of treatment that specifically and primarily addresses the marital relationship. It is ill-defined, however, in that theoretical orientations are diverse and represent numerous nonintegrated approaches.

MAJOR PHILOSOPHIES AND CURRENT CONCEPTS

Green (1965) proposed a classification system to describe the various current approaches to marital therapy:

1. Supportive Therapy and Counseling

2. Intensive Therapy
   a. Classical individual psychoanalysis
      b. Collaborative therapy between two therapists treating two spouses individually
      c. Concurrent therapy whereby both spouses are treated individually by the same therapist
      d. Conjoint couple therapy whereby spouses are seen together
      e. Combined and mixed approaches

Crowe (1973) classified approaches to treatment as behavioral, interpretive, or supportive. A more recent approach has consisted of marital group therapy in which couples are treated in a group of other couples (Leichter, 1973; Markowitz, 1968).

These classification systems may currently be subsumed under four major nonbehavioral theoretical orientations to marital therapy: (1) systems theory that considers the marital relationship as an interacting system (Haley, 1963a, 1963b; Kantor & Lehr, 1975; Olson & Sprenkler, 1976, (2) psychoanalytic theory that considers primarily the intrapersonal nature of the individual in the marital relationship (Bockus, 1975; Bowen, 1978; Dicks, 1967; Eckland, 1972; Skynner, 1976; Stierlin, 1977), (3) communications theory that considers the nature of verbal communication in maintaining dysfunctional marriages (Bolte, 1970; Gurman, 1975; Haley, 1973; Mace, 1972; Strong, 1975), and (4) humanistic theory that considers primarily the phenomenological; existential, and experiential aspects of the relationship. In addition, there are other, eclectic theories and treatments that incorporate aspects of the four major theoretical positions. There is also a large body of sociological theory related to dysfunctional marriage; however, these thoeries are, for the most part, ignored in current marital therapy literature (Bayer, 1971; Blood & Wolfe, 1960; Rainwater, 1965).

Systems theory is concerned with the spouses as they interact. Essentially, the actions and reactions of one member of the dyad are viewed as influencing the actions and reactions of the other member. The spouses' problems are viewed as having structural, not intrapsychic, causes; i.e., their problems arise from their interaction as members of a social system that they have formed and within which

they perform the roles appropriate to the system to achieve goals associated with their values (Hurvitz, 1975). Influenced by family theory, primarily the early work of Bateson and his colleagues (Bateson et al.; 1968), systems theorists do acknowledge that the roles and values, as well as the rules of the system within which a couple operates, may be primarily unconscious. A dysfunctional marriage then has some disturbance or disequilibrium within the system.

Psychoanalytic theory is concerned primarily with unconscious drives and needs within the individuals in the dyad, specifically as they relate to paternal introjects (Eckland, 1972). It is assumed that a partner brings into a marriage paternal introjects that he or she projects onto the other spouse. This unconscious projection, depending on the original parental relationship, can lead to a functional relationship or a dysfunctional one (Russell & Russell, 1977; Willi, 1982).

Communication theory is perhaps the most widely used theory in marital therapy. It states that marital problems are the result of ineffective patterns of communication (Gurman, 1975). The vehicle for studying the relationship is the verbal and nonverbal communication within the dyad; in a dysfunctional marriage, communication is conflictual, in that there are disagreements about the rules for living together (Bolte, 1970). The communications view of marriage, like systems theory, grew out of the Bateson project (Bateson, et al, 1968) and views all behavior within the marital dyad as an outcome or function of communicative interaction within the social system. All behavior is viewed as maintained by current communicative interaction (Guerin & Guerin, 1976).

It must be noted that most practitioners describe themselves as eclectic, with an emphasis on communication theory (Sprenkle & Fisher, 1980); few practioners can be described as adhering to any one pure theory. Current views of marriage and marital dysfunction incorporate Jackson's (1965) marital quid pro quo (something for something) theory and note the importance of a reciprocal relationship, joint definition of the relationship, and the negotiation of rules for living together (Haley, 1963a, 1963b). There is also an increasing interest in the nature of intimacy within the marital dyad and couples' strategies for maintaining distance and closeness (Kantor & Lehr, 1975; Schwartz & Schwartz, 1980). Finally, there is an overall emphasis on growth and health within the marital dyad (Ard, 1967; Crosby, 1976; Luthman, 1977; Satir, 1971; Sprendle & Olson, 1978; Whitaker, et al, 1979).

Theories are relatively diverse; however, ranging from psychoanalytic to behavioral approaches, with little to no integration of the various theoretical approaches. For the most part, marital theory is borrowed from individual and family conceptualizations, with minimal empirical observation of couples.

SPECIFIC THEORETICAL APPROACHES TO MARITAL THERAPY

Humanistic Approaches

Humanistic psychology represents a theoretical orientation of relatively recent origin, which can be traced primarily to the work of Rogers (1951) and Maslow (1962). As a movement, it represents a reaction to dissatisfaction with psychoanalysis and behaviorism. The humanistic orientation also represents what many authors have termed the "third force" in psychology (Misiak & Sexton, 1973) because of its emphasis on the innate strengths of the individual. The therapeutic focus of humanistic psychology is the facilitation of self-actualization with an emphasis on subjective phenomena rather than an objective and scientific reality (Misiak & Sexton, 1973; Welch, et al, 1978). Humanistic approaches include several different schools of thought, including the phenomenological, the existential, and the experiential (L'Abate & Frey, 1981). The experiential–phenomenological approaches have as their underlying philosophical premise that reality consists of internal and external dimensions. The external world is perceived only through internal experience. Therefore the only thing human beings can ever know for certain is that they are experiencing streams of thoughts and feelings.

With the adoption of a humanistic position, the task of the therapist changes from one of interpretations of intrapsychic functioning as observable behavior to one of illuminating the subjective, experiential world of the client.

Rogers' (1951) method of therapy, called nondirective, client-centered therapy, emphasized the view that people are basically co-operative, constructive, and trustworthy, and when free of defenses, their reactions are innately positive and forward-moving. Therefore, therapy consists of an experience in which the therapist relates to the client as one person deeply involved in the feelings of another. Treatment avoids suggestion or direction and, instead, fosters self-actualization by providing an atmosphere of acceptance, warmth, empathy, and nonjudgment whereby the therapist encourages emotional ventilation (with a decrease in defenses) and insight. For the Rogerian therapist, behavior change is best achieved by, first, effecting alterations in the concept of the self so that the client can become more congruent, more open to experience, less defensive, more realistic, and more effective in problem-solving. Threat is reduced as the client perceives the ideal self in a more realistic and achievable manner (Ewing, 1977).

With the adoption of a phenomenological position, the task of the therapist becomes one of unbiased exploraton of consciousness and experience. Phenomena are intuited, analyzed, and described as they appear, without any preconceptions (Misiask & Sexton, 1973).

Phenomenological psychology originates from phenomenological philosophy, the use of Husserl's phenomenology as a method of direct inquiry (i.e., direct intuition as a way of knowing), and the intuitive study of essences, Misiak & Sexton, 1973), as well as from the Gestalt school of Koffka (1922), Kohler (1947), and Wertheimer (1944). A European phenomenon before the Second World War, this psychology permeated the U.S. intellectual community after the Nazi occupation of Germany and the departure of many German scholars. Since the early 1950s, it has been absorbed primarily by existential and experiential approaches (Mahrer, 1978), which emphasizes the importance of the therapist's focusing on the inner experience of the client and developing awareness of feelings "as one penetrates the other's world" (Havens, 1973, p. 157). According to proponents of the existential school, it is through the engagement of subjective feelings and experiences of the client and therapist that therapeutic change is possible.

Although the initial focus of client-centered, phenomenological, existential, and experiential therapies was an individual one, these therapies have been increasingly influenced by the realization that the structure of therapy (the format in which it should be conducted and who should be included) should approximate as closely as possible the social, interpersonal nature of the lives of the clients (Haley, 1963a). Shifts away from solely individual treatment have occurred; shifts that take into account the interpersonal aspects of clients' lives and how these aspects may directly influence both functional and dysfunctional psychological processes. As a result, marriages and families have commanded growing attention as this shift from an individual to a more complex frame of reference has occurred (Haley, 1971a, 1971b).

An interpersonal frame of reference is included in the existential idea of "being-in-the-world" (Havens, 1973; Laing, 1967), which refers not only to a person's ability to live and be with himself or herself but also involves an interpersonal dimension, the suggestion that a functional aspect of being involves a person's ability to live in nondomineering relation to the physical and interpersonal environment (L'Abate, et al, 1980).

The existential mix of the intra- and interpersonal aspects of living has been ardently described by Laing (1967). He proposed that behavior cannot be considered apart from the experience of those who are behaving. Similarly, he noted that a failure to view the experience and behavior of one person in relation to others fosters both theoretical and therapeutic confusion. Effective therapy can only be transexperiential in nature, in the sense that an effort is made to reintegrate the behavior and experience of those in therapy (Laing, 1967; Mahrer, 1978). These ideas have served as a conceptual springboard for Laing's investigation of pathological processes in families (Laing & Esterson, 1973).

Currently, the humanistic position is widely espoused within the field of martial therapy (Bandler & Grinder, 1976; Hale, 1978; Laing, 1967; Napier & Whitaker, 1978; Satir, 1972), with the primary focus of treatment continuing to be the inner experiences of each individual in the couple relationship. There is no clear specification of the theoretical and therapeutic aspects of the humanistic position as

it pertains to marital therapy, however, because various theorists incorporate various aspects of humanistic psychology into their treatment orientations.

The reason for the lack of specification is a logical outgrowth of theory. The therapist meets each couple idiographically, in terms of their patterns and needs, and is, therefore, flexible in approach, depending on the presenting problem (Bockus, 1980). The commonality in all humanistic approaches to treatment, however, is a respect for each individual's inner, subjective experience of the world and a focus on altering the individual's phenomenological world in order to ultimately alter feelings and behavior intrapersonally and within the marital relationship.

Olson and Sprenkle (1976) have noted the increasing influence of client-centered approaches to couples therapy based on the Rogerian model of expressing feelings and empathic listening. In addition, most approaches to improving a couple's communication skills incorporate the principles of client-centered therapy (Guerney, 1976; Rappaport, 1976).

Levant (1978) summarized the orientation of the Rogerian marital family therapy: the person exists in a phenomenological world of which he or she is the center and which includes internal and external realms of experience. The internal realm includes his or her experience of his or her intrapsychic dynamics; the external realm includes each individual's experience of family systems in response to his or her perceived experience in both realms. This view assumes that individuals are motivated for maintenance and enhancement of growth (self-actualization) rather than motivated to oppose change and growth.

As a result of this theoretical orientation, the client-centered approach to marital therapy begins with a trust in the ability of family members to assume the responsibility for their own change and growth, and a respect for their ability to make the decisions that will be best for them in all aspects of the therapy. Related to trust and respect, the therapist experiences a sense of nonpossessive caring and warmth for the family. The therapist attempts to gain an appreciation of the internal frames of reference of the family members and to communicate empathic understanding of family experiences. The therapist tries to stay in contact with and follow the moment-to-moment changes in the family's experiential flow. He or she interacts with the family members on a genuine basis, being transparent about his or her own feelings and congruent with personal experience.

In this therapy, the therapist is not an expert but a co-participant in and facilitator of the process of therapy. The role does not involve history-taking diagnosis, treatment-planning, or the use of therapeutic techniques to induce change. Rather, it facilitates the release and development of self-regenerative and self-enchancing powers within the dyadic unit. It also involves direct person-to-person encounter, based to a large extent on the person of the therapist.

The Experiential Approach

From the experiential perspective, theoretical formulations have largely been directed not toward conceptualizing the process of marriage but toward the elaboration of dysfunctional marital arrangements and how these arrangements can be changed (Bandler, et al, 1976; Napier & Whitaker, 1978). The process of change for the experiential therapist is closely aligned with the humanistic concepts of growth and self-actualization. Therapy is commonly seen as aiding the growth process that, under optimal conditions, should have occurred naturally in the lives of those who enter therapy. A common underlying assumption is that human nature is such that there is a universal need to expand and integrate experience (Napier & Whitaker, 1978). Martial therapy is thus necessitated when there has been a blockage of this naturally occurring process, with the therapy serving as an agent that will unblock the resources inherent in the couple. The experiential school places considerable emphasis on the clients to work in therapy in order to experience the therapy as something that can help release innate potentials (Napier & Whitaker, 1978).

Bandler, et al (1976), one group of practitioners within the experiential school, discuss what could be described as the task of the experiential therapist, as well as the goal of the therapy itself. They suggest that a major task is to change the *system* (italics theirs) of how messages are given and received from one spouse to another. Here, change is assessed at a process rather than a content level. Therefore,

the therapist elicits from each person in therapy his or her hopes and wants (e.g., love, affection, trust, privacy, etc.). The therapist then surveys each individual to determine which input and output channels (visual, auditory, kinesthetic) are essential in order for the individual to know when he or she is getting what is wanted from the partner. Bandler, et al (1976) suggest that comparing what people want with what they currently have provides the therapist with valuable information. This information can be used as an initial focus of change, in that the therapist can pick a set of hopes mentioned by the couple a new experience that is congruent with the hopes described by each. The extent to which this initial goal is reached depends on the skill of the therapist in creating for the couple in therapy experiences that necessitate a change in the way information is given to and received from one another. Ultimately, the major focus of intervention is the need of a couple to actively experience positive changes, which are initially orchestrated within the context of therapy.

Napier and Whitaker (1978) address the factors that are often operational in causing difficulties that prompt a couple to engage in marital therapy. When a couple begins therapy, there is often an emotional separateness between the spouses (commonly termed an emotional divorce). This separateness often results from the couple's realization of the extent of their dependency on each other. This realization occurs as a result of a complex process. Many spouses marry the "American Marital Dream" rather than a marital partner. The marriage is initially viewed as an oasis from which spouses will be able to get all of the love, attention, affection, etc. that may not have been present in their families of origin. The marriage then tends to operate relatively smoothly until one spouse panics at the thought of losing individual identity as a result of the forced dependency in the relationship (a process that may mirror earlier experiences in the family of origin).

The loss of individual identity is often realized as a result of an escalating set of demands made by one spouse of the other. The spouse who is asked for more and more assistance may suddenly experience concern that he or she will not be able to meet the seemingly new demands. Typically, this concern in unspoken, something that the concerned spouse keeps to himself or herself. Feelings of panic and of being trapped result, and the process of emotional distancing begins as a defense against dependency.

Each spouse is often alarmed at the emotional retreat that is experienced, and each may try nonverbally to teach the other a lesson by finding a substitute interest (e.g., a job, hobby, an affair, etc.) to fulfill dependency needs. In actuality, these substitutes are often sought as a cushion against the experience of loneliness and feelings of abandonment. By finding other interests, spouses are often attempting to prove to themselves that what was once obtained from the spouse can be obtained elsewhere. In actuality, emotional involvement with the spouse is still wanted, but each is too proud to state his or her need. As a result, bitterness tends to build as the emotional distance between the spouses increases.

Napier and Whitaker (1978) note that partners often enter marriage with the assumption that the contract promises sexual satisfaction, companionship, romantic love, and security. There is often an unspoken assumption, as well, that the marriage will serve as a kind of psychotherapy for each partner, a context in which the wounds from the family of origin of each spouse can be healed. After a period of emotional distancing, however (and a downplaying of problems), many spouses realize that all of the expected components of the marital contract cannot be upheld. Many spouses then assume that the problem lies not within their expectations of marriage but with the inability of the spouse to meet the expectations. For these people, divorce and remarriage, or a continuing search for the martial dream, is common (Napier & Whitaker, 1978).

From a therapeutic stance, Napier and Whitaker (1978) see the issue of dependency as a central one in marital difficulties. They suggest that many people who are near divorce actually have a poor sense of self and a lack of individuation. The marriage is characterized by overdependency, leading to the reaction of emotional distance.

Marital interventions are thus often directly focused on the feelings expressed by the marital pair concerning dependency. The therapeutic task, by focusing on such perceived experiences, is to create a sense of individua-

tion in the members present, hopefully leading the couple to a position of functional interdependence.

The ideas of Napier and Whitaker (1978) are also paralleled by those of Jourard (1978). Like Napier and Whitaker, Jourard speaks of the fallacies of the ideal marriage: the myth that there is an ideal partner and the myth that there is a way to behave that will guarantee happiness and marital success. Neither myth is true; by adopting these myths, spouses accept the idea that change is bad. As a result, rather than viewing change as an inevitable part of the relational process, some spouses react in horror if a change occurs in the relationship. Jourard sees many divorces as attempts by such spouses to search for an unchanging partner, one who will allow him or her to continue the search for the marital dream (and also avoid the prospect of changing himself or herself).

Jourard (1978) notes that marriage is at its best when the likelihood of change in each spouse is accepted and when changes are generated by the way spouses relate to one another—what he described as the dialogue between them. From the humanistic perspective, within this dialogue, there is the potential for growth, identity, and rootedness in the relationship, largely because such dialogue requires commitment, courage, and honesty from the spouses, as well an acceptance of change as a way of experiencing relational growth.

Jourard (1978) places relatively little value on marriage counseling as a way of contributing to a couple's or a family's quality of life, since he does not believe that there is a general plan to point out to couples the way they should live (something he apparently sees as necessary if such therapies are to be effective). For Jourard, change in the marriage occurs from the context of dialogue within the relationship and the experiences of the couple around issues of commitment, honesty, and change.

When viewed in the context of the writings of Napier and Whitaker (1978) and Bandler, et al (1976), experiential therapy, whether it addresses the establishment of a functional interdependence between spouses (through the facilitation of individuation) or the alteration of the way in which information is given or received, is a means of freeing the couple from existing interactional patterns so that the dialogue between them can begin again. Therapeutic change is thus a process that helps a couple toward growth, actualization, and dialogue.

Other experiential approaches also view therapy as redecision (Goulding & Goulding, 1979). The presenting problem, similar to psychodynamic formulations, is hypothesized as resulting from repetitive interaction sequences, which are based on early childhood conflicts within the family of origin and projected onto the partner in the dyad.

Assessment is not formalized but focuses on understanding the past and unconscious material in the couple's lives in order to understand the recurring childhood themes that are enacted in the present. Attention to slips of speech, key words, subject–object assignments, symbolic interactions, and parallels between past and present patterns helps the therapist separate key past issues from the symbolic presenting problem (Bockus, 1980). Exploration of the past and the unconscious is significant in that it helps create an experiential simulation that replicates as much as possible the client's present life situation.

The treatment goal consists of aiding the couple to understand present interactions separately from unconscious re-creations of past experiences in the belief that conscious understanding will create a change in emotion and behavior.

The role of the therapist, then, is to provide an environment in which an individual's frame of reference can be revealed and carefully traced. Interaction sequences, themes, and outcomes are monitored; concealed, denied, and distorted experiences are evoked in the present to bear immediately on the client's reenactment of the past. Clients are confronted with their life patterns with present immediacy. The experiential therapist may also use a mixture of methods, such as Gestalt exercises, sculpting, psychodrama, communication, and directives, in order to make visible the basic feelings, attitudes, and behaviors in the client's life.

The Existential Approach

The existential approach has evolved from two primary movements: phenomenology and existentialism. While phenomenology emphasizes the importance of subjective experience, existentialism, influenced by philosophers such as Jaspers (1955), Heidegger (1949), and Sartre (1953), emphasizes the understanding of human beings in their total existential reality, especially the subjective relationship of a person to the self, the world, and others in it. The data of interest include consciousness, feelings, moods, and experiences, stressing that each individual has a unique inner life. The works of Laing (1967) and Frankl (1967) fall within this tradition, and others such as Gordon Allport, Abraham Maslow, Carl Rogers, and Rollo May are also aligned with this school of psychology (Misiak & Sexton, 1973).

The traditional existential view grew out of a disdain for and a reaction to mechanistic conceptualizations of human beings as espoused around the time of the Second World War. An alternative conceptualization, one based on the existence of human beings and their being-in-the-world and on the importance of meaning as opposed to existence, became a hallmark of the traditional existentialists (Misiak & Sexton, 1973). This emphasis on the importance of individual meaning has been addressed by Laing (1967), particularly in his discussion of the relationship of family processes to psychopathology, and by Boerop (1975), who focused on the meaning of the relational process of marriage. The concern for meaning rather than existence also appears in works of Frankl (1967).

Frankl (1967), the originator of logotherapy, noted that therapy involves more than an analysis of existence, or being. The central concern of logotherapy is that the individual discover meaning, a concept that serves as the basis for an explicit philosophy of life. This philosophy is based on three primary, interrelated assumptions: (1) that there is a freedom of will, (2) that there is a will to meaning, and (3) that there is a meaning of life.

According to Frankl (1967), the first of these, freedom of will, belongs to the immediate data of experience, that which is tapped via the phenomenological method. Human beings are free, within limits, yet restricted by biological, social, and psychological conditions. Even with these restrictions, however, people can choose the stand they take and their attitude toward these restrictions.

With the second assumption, the will to

meaning, Frankl makes more specific statements about the role of meaning. Human beings cannot struggle for identity in a direct fashion but must be committed to a cause that is greater than themselves. In logotherapy, clients are not spared the inevitable discomfort that arises from confronting issues of meaning and finding meaning. Meaning is described not as coinciding with being but as being ahead of it. Existence carries meaning only when it is lived in terms of a willingness to transcend itself. When a meaning orientation turns into a meaning confrontation, the possibility of maturation and development of the client is reached. At this point, freedom becomes responsibility, and the client is responsible for the fulfillment of the particular meaning of his or her life (Frankl, 1967).

Frankl (1967) also addresses the types of meaning that can come to human beings if they take responsibility. He proposes that life can be meaningful according to (1) what we give to it (creative output), (2) what we take from it (the experiential), and (3) the stand we take against things we cannot change (e.g., the inevitability of pain, death, and guilt).

Since meaning is the key factor in health, alternatively, the loss of meaning of life can result in psychological dysfunction. Frankl (1967) therefore views methods of intervention based on theories of drive, homeostasis, or self-actualization as limited. An appropriate view of human beings can only result when there is a consideration for what we will do and what we will be in the objective world of meaning and values, i.e., a consideraton of the importance of meaning in life (Frankl, 1967).

Boerop (1975) has added to Frankl's work by noting that the existential view of human beings suggests that we are not simply passive beings, but that we are active, free agents who have been thrown into a world in which no rules exist. There are no instructions for the tasks of life. Given the introspective nature of human beings, we not only respond to reality, but also to our own images of reality. Reality does not exist in and of itself but is created by us.

According to Boerop (1975), it is meaning that differentiates being from existing. To be, humans must superimpose their subjective reality onto reality, thus creating meaning. From Boerop's existential view, marriage by itself has no meaning. It is simply an institution.

The meaning of a marriage must come from those who are married, i.e., it must be created and superimposed onto the marriage.

Boerop (1975) provided a series of pragmatic descriptions of the marriages of some of his clients. He noted that bad marriages are typically defined with reference to three possible levels: (1) at the cognitive level, the marital couple may see the marriage as simply a legal contract, something they got into and which they now (often) see as a trap; (2) at an affective level, the marital couple may define the marriage through their descriptions of boredom, hostility, frustration, or depression; and (3) at a behavioral level, the reaction of the couple to the marriage may be suggested by the limited social life they have, the existence of affairs of one or both partners, etc.

In describing the process of marital therapy, Boerop (1975) noted that an initial task is for the therapist to share his or her philosophical bias with the couple, noting to them that options other than marriage are available to them and that these options should be carefully evaluated.

Once other options have been assessed and a decision has been made to work on the marriage in therapy, work begins at the cognitive level to try to change the couple's perception of their marriage from something molded and unchangeable to something that can be positively altered. Questions such as "What does the marriage mean to you?" and "What do you want it to mean?" are described as useful (Boerop, 1975). Boerop noted that if there is a change in the cognitive impression of the couple about their marriage, a change is likely at the affective level, as well. Here, the depression of the couple may quickly lift, or they may feel less restricted and more outgoing.

For Boerop (1975), an existential intervention at the behavioral level begins with the couple's shared feelings with each other. This sharing, interactive process is viewed as an essential component if new meaning is to be superimposed onto the marital relationship. Ultimately, the couple creates together a new, shared meaning of the marital relationship.

The Gestalt Approach

The Gestalt approach to marital therapy represents yet another experientially-oriented subset of the humanistic school. Although the focus of the therapy is relational in nature, the methods and techniques used are often identical to those that have traditionally been used in individual Gestalt therapy.

Kaplan and Kaplan (1978) have noted an increase in the use of Gestalt, experiential approaches as a means of disrupting and breaking entrenched family patterns. Gestalt techniques are also viewed as being of value as tools to help a family member reintegrate relationships with other family members once the relationships with these others have been altered.

The goal of Gestalt marital therapies is to help clients achieve self-awareness, a heightened clarity of experience, and increased self-direction. In helping the couple achieve these goals, the therapist serves as a facilitator rather than a strategist. The therapeutic task, then, is to help the couple become aware of entrenched, growth-limiting patterns of behavior within the dyad (Kaplan & Kaplan, 1978).

As in individual Gestalt treatment, the initial step of therapy is to help clients attend to what they are currently experiencing, i.e., bodily experiences, muscular actions, emotional experiences, etc. The therapist then aids the couple to focus on here-and-now experiences. The purpose is to allow the members of the dyad to explore the areas in which awareness may be blocked and to facilitate the discovery and expression of new experiences as well as experimentation with individuation within the couple context. Clients are encouraged to move freely out of the roles that they have typically played in the relational system in order to create new experiences and to break established patterns of functioning (Kaplan & Kaplan, 1978).

Hale (1978) made specific reference to efforts to break stereotyped, entrenched patterns of behavior between the marital pair, patterns in which there is no spontaneity. He proposed that experientially-oriented techniques are often more useful than verbal procedures simply because the couple's discussion about the entrenchment they are experiencing is likely to proceed according to the very role-bound patterns that are the focus of therapy. These techniques (e.g., awareness continuum, push-when-pulled, pull-when-pushed, empty chair, etc.), get the couple to focus on the here-and-now and to behave and experience their behavior in a way that is totally separate from that characteristic of their entrenched pattern of living. The focus is on creating new experiences and more spontaneity between the marital pair (Hale, 1978).

Psychoanalytic Approaches

Psychoanalytic approaches are subsumed under traditional psychoanalytic marital therapy, the more recent object-relations theory and therapy, and Bowenian theory and treatment.

These approaches stress the development of the individual personality, the nature of marriage, mate selection, sustaining the attachment, and the nature of the marital difficulties. These approaches also stress the importance of understanding intrapsychic as well as interpersonal processes and, more than any other marital therapy approach, emphasize the importance of individual psychodynamics.

Traditional Psychoanalytic Marital Therapy

Psychoanalytic marital therapy is, in some ways, indistinguishable from individual psychoanalysis, for each spouse addressed primarily his or her individual dynamics in the marital relationship (Giovacchini, 1965). Presenting problems are viewed as symptoms of unconscious individual as well as dyadic conflicts, with the underlying theoretical assumption that current issues and difficulties represent a projection of parental introjects and a reenactment of earlier struggles and conflicts within the spouse's family of origin (Dicks, 1967; Stierlin, 1977).

Assessment is important, although there is no consensus on the components of initial evaluation. The presenting problem is not considered the focus of change, for it symbolically represents unconscious conflicts. Instead, the therapist attempts to assess interactional themes as they relate to the unconscious conflicts. The role of the past and the unconscious is central to treatment; the couple's eventual conscious understanding of unconscious aspects of the marital choice process is considered the vehicle for change. The history of the relationship is important, particularly as it relates to unconscious dynamics, for past conflicts and experiences in the family of origin are considered manifest in the current relationship. The treatment goal consists mainly of change through understanding and a recapitulation within the therapeutic process of earlier experiences. Other goals are increased intimacy, role flexibility and adaptability, improved sexual relationships and gender identity, improved communication and individual self-esteem, and resolution of the presenting problem.

In the therapeutic endeavor, the therapist clarifies comunication, provides rationale for the couple's difficulties through interpretation, encourages expression of feelings, and interprets both feelings and behavior to clarify insight. The role of the therapist is primarily an interpretive one so that the couple gain insight and understanding.

Object-Relations Therapy

Object-relations theory addresses an understanding of the development of the personality, with a special emphasis on the ego, by examining the introjections and projections of earlier interpersonal relationships. Within this conceptualization, much of the self originates by incorporating external objects, i.e., others (Boesky, 1980). The term "object" or "object relation" refers to the individual's introjected representation of the earlier interpersonal relationship (Arlow, 1980), with a special emphasis on the impact of its affective component. Each object relation has a self-representation, an object representation, and an affect component. Thus object relations as an incorporated part of the developing ego include a perceptual experience, affect tone, and a memory component (Kernberg, 1976).

Meissner (1978) attempted to integrate the various outlooks inherent in the object-relations schools of thought as it pertains to the marital relationship. Individual development occurs by internalizing relationships into object relations that possess object constancy. A mature individual, thus, should be able to maintain his or her attachment and regard for the important other and its internal object representation throughout various emotional vicissitudes that include both the gratifying and frustrating experiences of the relationship. A mature individual is thus able to tolerate the inevitable ambivalence experienced with a loved one because of an internal object constancy (Dicks, 1967). The ambivalence is inevitable because disappointment in need fulfillment is inevitable in this less-than-perfect world.

Simultaneous with this ability to remain emotionally connected, there is a requirement that the individual be able to negotiate a separate identity from that of the beloved attachment figure; otherwise the individual lives with a "borrowed identity" (Meissner, 1978, p. 33). Thus the maturational process of attachment/separation is difficult, for it entails conflict, both intrapsychic and interpersonal. Failure to achieve individuation and object constancy results in the individual's interactions with others being characterized by emotional overinvolvement with the family of origin, feelings of often being hurt and rejected by criticism from significant others, and the experience of emotional merging or overidentification with the other's feelings (Meissner, 1978).

Introjection is crucial to the process of individuation. "Introjection is the earliest, most primitive, and basic level in the organization of internalization processes. It is a reproduction . . . of an interaction with the environment" (Kernberg, 1976, p. 46). The child must separate from the infantile symbiosis with the caregiver, establish a separate identity, and then be able to take from the caregiver those wants and needs that are a part of his or her own view of himself or herself. In order to negotiate successfully this individuation process, both the caregiver and the child must be as free as possible from defensive needs, a freedom that rarely, if ever, occurs in actuality. Otherwise, the process results in the child's self becoming organized around pathogenic parental introjects that arise from the symbiotic/separation process. The extent of the pathogenic introjects in the core self will then be projected onto current significant others, e.g., in marriage. These projections will be both positive and negative aspects of the self that the individual has failed to integrate into his or her person. As a result, the transference within the dyad will be determined by the individual's negotiation of the parental introjects (Meissner, 1978).

Other object-relations theorists emphasize additional aspects of the development processes in addition to introjection and projection. These aspects can be classified on a continuum, depending on how closely they adhere to original Freudian concepts of psychosexual development and a closed energy system. For example, Arlow (1980), like Freud, thinks of the pleasure principle as a central theme in development, whereas Bowlby (1969), at the other end of the continuum, stated that attachment behavior is instinctual, rising from man's evolutionary environment of adaptedness rather than as a secondary drive to the pleasure principle. Freudians adhere more to the intrapsychic experience, while others (Bowlby, 1969; Dicks, 1967) emphasize the importance of the interpersonal parameters of individual behavior, including the physical and cultural context of development.

Dicks (1967) discussed the contributions made by Fairbairn and the object-relations theoretical framework. The ego is seen as central to the development of the personality; it is not just a mediator between the inner and the outer worlds. Dicks (1967) paraphrased Fairbairn:

Ego development is furthered by the secure passage through a succession of positions of ambivalence toward objects. It begins with the crude and undifferentiated "good" and "bad" relations . . . and grows toward an integration of ambivalence which can be tolerated both in self and in others without splitting the antithetical components one from the other. In a healthy outcome of this conflictual process, relations with objects will be felt to contain the promise of love and security . . . as the result of a preponderance of "good" results of reality-testing with primary figures . . . there emerges not only a unified central ego . . . but also a stored reservoir of "relational potential" with these figures which are the person's good internal objects (p. 127).

Relational potential refers to the fact that the child can make the good object's feelings his or her own as self-valuations and role models. The child identifies with the good object's characteristics and feelings, and these identifications form his or her inner resources. Through them, children learn adult love by feeling adult loves within themselves. Children tolerate ambivalent feelings within themselves and in others because they have experienced the parents' tolerance of them and of their anger in a loving way (Dicks, 1967, p. 38).

On the other hand, if the objects were experienced as hate-arousing or dangerous, splitting occurs and diminishes the relational potential as well as the central ego. Splitting is a defensive maneuver to preserve the ego, a primitive form of repression (Kernberg, 1976) in which there is an "unconscious defensive fission of parts of its inner world of objects, much

as a lizard sheds its tail to a pursuing enemy" (Dicks, 1967, p. 41). It is not feelings or impulses that are repressed, but the affective relationships between the self and some figure outside the self (Dicks, 1967). The "libidinal ego" refers to the split-off unrequited love need, which may be exceedingly infantile if split off very early in life. The "anti-libidinal ego" is the split-off frustration–rage–dangerous aspects of the rejecting object, which the child internalized out of fear. Such pathological development results in persistent need demands toward primary figures because they were experienced as hate-arousing and frustrating; splitting then occurred, diminishing the relational potential (Dicks, 1967). It is as if the individual cannot be finished with the important object until gratification of those frustrated needs is obtained through *some* relationship.

It is important to note, however, that the central ego can function perfectly well in nonlibidinal activities, even if greatly impoverished by splitting. It is only in emotional matters that the functioning suffers; thus, the often common occurrence of successful businessmen or -women who cannot establish and/or maintain intimate ties (Dicks, 1967).

Various theorists within the object-relations school of thought emphasize different aspects of the marital union, but all agree that unconscious factors related to previous object relations are extremely powerful. Dicks (1967) perceives marriage in its cultural context, as well. He states that marriage is a contract between two persons to play certain roles in ways that will not only satisfy the other as best they can perceive but will also fulfill the requirements of the culture. At a higher level, couples have a need to be seen as a harmonious unit while at a deeper level they are engaged in an old feud (Dicks, 1967, pp. 126–127).

Dicks specified three levels in the marriage:

1. A public level at which the marriage is "the ultimate unit of social structure through whom the continuity and the changes in the culture are transmitted" (Dicks, 1967, p. 181). Kernberg (1980) addresses the issue of the couple's relationship to the larger social group. He maintains that they are mutually dependent upon one another because the couple's stability depends upon establishing autonomy within the group.

The group needs the couple because of its "hope for sexual union and love in the face of potential destructiveness activated by . . . large group processes" (p. 308). The public context of the marriage is significant, for it structures modes of depending in marriage and families. Dicks affirmed that, in the history of the family, our

"desideratum of lasting commitment in marriage . . . requires an unprecedented overcoming of emotional dependence on the family is almost self-liquidating by dispersal, just when in their isolation they need each other the most among the frightening impersonality of modern industry" (Dicks, 1967, p. 29). It is the task of the modern family to grow its children to selfhood "against its own age-long traditional functions and its very existence" (Dicks, 1967, p. 29). There is an emphasis on self-sufficiency so that all the "resources and capacities for making strong and effective emotional commitments have to be carried inside the individual person" (Dicks, 1967, p. 29). Intimacy in marriage is especially difficult to achieve, in that it requires "an established sense of personal identity and ego-strength—with a preservation of the capacity for dependence" (Dicks, 1967, p. 29). In addition, the spouse and a-few-to-no children in the nuclear family are now the primary, if not exclusive, target of our intense human dependent needs.

2. Dicks (1967) delineated a second level within the marriage, which he termed the "personal norms of the central egos" (p. 130). This aspect includes conscious judgments and expectations derived from object-relations as well as from social learning. Interference at this conscious level necessitates looking at the third one:

3. Unconscious forces. These include the object relations, both positive and negative. Dicks stated that it is the mixture of the unconscious object relations that governs the long-term quality of the marriage. These unconscious factors are the most powerful determinants of the marital union.

Dicks (1963) and other theorists insist that marriage is the ultimate adult equivalent to the original parent–child relationship and that

marital success requires the tolerance of regression by the partners, who must make room for their "little needy egos" to emerge in their mutual dependence (Dicks, 1963, p. 127). Bowlby (1969) shares this view, "that attachment behavior in adult life is a straightforward continuation of attachment behavior in childhood" (p. 208). He objects to those psychoanalysts who judge such attachment behavior inappropriate in adults. To do so "is indeed to overlook the vital role that it plays in the life of man from the cradle to the grave" (Bowlby, 1969, p. 208). Furthermore, Bowlby (1969) asserted that no form of behavior arouses stronger feelings than does attachment behavior. Marriage is the

human situation in which the personality structure is most fully challenged, and the object relations can be seen . . . most notably displayed. Not even the trials of war show up the adequacy or insufficiency of maturity and of capacity for sustaining meaningful and satisfying human relations so clearly as marriage and its stresses (Dicks, 1953, p. 182).

Choosing a spouse is a refinding of an old love object, more so than a finding of a new one (Bergmann, 1980). This refinding is a Freudian as well as object-relations theorists' concept. Freud's refinding was that of a person, however, while Berman (1980) suggests the refinding of a lost ego state:

If the original objects were good enough, the refinding process can run more or less smoothly. For those who had unempathetic or neglectful parents, the refinding process will lead to pathological object selection unless the ego intervenes. Thus, an already burdened ego impoverished by splitting is under pressure to direct the choosing of an object in opposition to infantile prototypes (Berman, 1980, p. 69).

Even when the mate is indeed different from the defective parental object, the individual may succeed in eliciting responses from the mate that are characteristic of the parent. If sufficient conflict arises between the ego and the infantile wishes, two objects may be chosen— one, the ego's counterselection and, the other, a dangerous refinding of a pathological object relation. The individual clings to the counterselection for safety and goes to the "dangerous" refound person for gratification (Berman, 1980). Thus this type of conflict often accounts for extramarital affairs.

Dicks (1963) asserted that there are unconscious signals that draw partners together and through which they each recognize the other's "fitness for joint working-through . . . of still unresolved splits or conflicts inside each . . . while . . . paradoxically, also sensing a guarantee that with that person they will not be worked through" (Dicks, 1963, p. 127). The collusion to avoid the working through is an attempt to escape the pain of growth. Implicit in this view is a basic human need for growth and integration.

The refinding of the lost love object associates the bliss of that rediscovery with the fear that the possession of the loved one is unattainable (Bergmann, 1980). Kernberg (1980) believes that in order to fall in love and stay in love, two developmental tasks must have been mastered: (1) the capacity for establishing a total object-relation, rather than partial ones, integrated with the ability to experience sensuous stimulation, and (2) the resolution of Oedipal conflicts.

The theme of mastery of developmental tasks in order to achieve lasting love is a common one in object-relatons theory, as is the distinction between falling in love and the capacity for mature object-relations. Bergman (1980) explains Mahler's position on loving as a function of completing the rapprochement subphase of separation–individuation. Rapprochement occurs when the infant returns to the mother, after ending symbiosis, in hopes of reconnecting with her differently—wanting her at least to tolerate if not approve of his or her individuation:

During the rapproachement subphase the "unspecific cravings" are transmuted into longing. In the state of longing, separateness is experienced for the first time. Longing marks the birth of love. For longing . . . will not be appeased by the need-satisfying object; . . . only . . . by the constant object that is the true love object. Lovers . . . ask . . . "Have you missed me?" There is no loving without missing, and when severe disappointment in the early love object results in an inhibition of longing, love cannot be experienced (Bergmann, 1980, p. 72).

A higher level of maturity is required to *sustain* a love relationship than to fall in love. Arlow (1980), however, cautioned against such a "judgment on the phenomenology of love," maintaining that falling in love is "impossible to reduce . . . to any of the simple basic formulas proposed by several of the proponents of

object-relations theory" (p. 125). He disagreed with Bak (1973) and Bergmann (1980), "who trace the psychology of loving to a specific developmental vicissitude, the wish to re-achieve symbiotic fusion with the mother in order to undo the primordial separation" (Arlow, 1980, p. 122). Arlow cautioned that establishing developmental milestones that must be achieved in order to love results in a simplistic idealizing process:

In other words, it is not just the experience with the object, but what is done with the experience, that is decisive for development. . . . Later experiences in love relationships may modify the effect of earlier object ties (Beres & Obers, 1950). . . . Cultural ambience influences not only how love is expressed, but how it is is experienced. The cultural influence may transcend the specific set of interactions characteristic of the relations with the infantile love object (Arlow, 1980, p. 129).

Arlow did not argue against a developmental interpretation of the ability to love per se, but he did note the dangers of a narrow interpretation that would fix the development of the necessary emotional skills in childhood and ignore the context of experience by focusing too narrowly on intrapsychic processes. He argued for inclusion of later experience and context in the concept of development; i.e., that adults continue to develop. All is not set in concrete in early childhood. Arlow (1980) opted for the expansion rather than elimination of developmental competence. To fail to do so means isolating object relations from their contexts and establishing "an artificial evolution toward a hypothetical stage of mature object-relations" (Arlow, 1980, p. 131).

Kernberg (1980) takes exception to the distinction that is commonly made between romantic love and "marital affection" (p. 315). He flatly states that the romantic element continues in the relationship and is necessary in the couple's establishment of an identity autonomous from that of the group by affording them a private experience and sexual intimacy. The mature couple in Kernberg's (1980) view includes infantile features in its sex life and maintains its separateness from the group. In fact, the more the couple is intruded upon by the group, the less of an emotional marriage there is. Thus Kernberg (1980) disagrees with the popular notion that falling in love and romantic love are discontinuous from more long-lived marital affections.

Bergmann (1980) offers a thoughtful resolution to this split between romance and marriage in his description of the transition between them: "The road from falling in love to enduring love involves the transmutations of the idealization into gratitude for the refinding and for the healing of earlier wounds" (p. 74).

Concerning marital conflict, Kernberg (1980) states: "The couple stands at the crossroads where individual unconscious conflicts intersect with the expression of these conflicts in the external world" (p. 277). Thus unconscious expectations of the partner, which are the result of an individual's object relations, are the primary sources of conflict.

Dicks (1967) claimed that in troubled marriages there is a fear of commitment that is the result of the relational potential still being invested with a "highly ambivalent feeling towards the significant loved figure" (p. 43).

One of the main causes of marital tension is the disappointment in the spouse for not conforming to a built-in fantasy based on early object relations. Problems develop when the disappointed spouse attempts to coerce the partner into fitting the fantasy. Another significant source of tension is attributing to the partner those aspects of the self that are felt to have been lost (Dicks, 1967). These can be either negative or positive attributes. In the case of either, there is significant apprehension about the "lost" aspect of the self or it would not have been split off in the first place. When these aspects are then projected onto the partner, intense ambivalence results, with a persecution of the partner for possessing aspects to which one may have initially been attracted. The aspect has been split off because it was experienced as dangerous or hate-arousing, but it is also longed for as a forsaken part of the self.

There are defenses in the marriage that function to protect the relationship from these conflictual underlying processes. The major defense of marriage is idealization, "the unreal expectation that in their marriage the partners must be 'all in all' to each other, make good all defects and offer perfect gratification of all needs" (Dicks, 1967, p. 71). Some degree of idealization is normal and necessary to mating, but in excess it hinders growth in the marriage and the development of a relation-

ship that can respond to the *real* needs of the *real* persons in it. Dicks (1967) described the process as follows:

> By denying the reality of ambivalent hate or anger, and by the variants of projective identification, one or both spouses attribute to the partner those bad feelings they must own themselves, or else make the partner all good and exalted while themselves taking on the guilt and the badness. . . . Because the other half of the ambivalence is not offered for reality-testing—one is oneself, acting a false part (p. 43).

How do the partners bring about a collusion to avoid the working through of their unresolved individual and joint processes, to avoid their painful growth? Nadelson (1978) believes that marriage serves a defensive rather than growthful purpose when the partners use their interaction to protect themselves from their individual unconscious objects, which are perceived as potentially destructive and, therefore, are disguised, denied, or projected. The marriage can be used to defend against fear of merger, loss of self-identity, depression, or object loss. In these cases, closeness might threaten the ego because it might make available material that has been kept from consciousness because of splitting.

Dicks (1967) described such collusive marriages as having developed a joint ego by which partners attribute to each other their unconsciously shared feelings. He stated that a "folie à deux" occurs when the partners develop a near psychotic or fully psychotic, shared world of fantasy relations in which personalities dovetail in their primitive object needs and anxieties; they can then easily mutually affect one another to such an extent that both individuals' inner worlds become identical and may bear little or no relation to external realities. This folie à deux is a severe case of the joint ego collusive process.

In the collusion, there is a need for unconscious complementarity in which each partner provides part of the qualities for a whole personality. Expressions such as "my other half" or "my better half" reflect this process. On a conscious level, there is the expectation of the ideal union, with the aim of keeping all bad feelings out of the marriage. It requires large amounts of unconscious energy, however, to develop a joint resistance to change, "a smooth facade of 'happiness,' of perpetual sunshine without a shadow" (Dicks, 1967, p. 73). Such unions often endure if there are

inner resources (e.g., secure repression) and living conditions to keep the fiction in being. The tensions generated then often bypass the marital integrate, but may break surface either in psychosomatic form, or a periodic depression; or else they appear as neurotic problems in the children, whose unconscious cannot be cheated (Dicks, 1967, p. 73).

Kernberg (1980) alludes to a similar collusive process in asserting that over time there gradually emerges in a relationship "the hidden presence of ambivalence and aggression" (p. 317). When the couple colludes to deny this powerful aspect of intimacy, they often transform "a deep love relation into a superficial and conventional one that lacks the very essence of love" (Kernberg, 1980, p. 316). Nadelson (1978) adds that problems are intensified when children are born because their neediness may "reactivate infantile disappointment acutely and relentlessly" in the parents. "With each developmental stage of the child, new challenges emerge which must be reconciled with the individual developmental issues of the parents and with the developmental process of the marriage" (Nadelson, 1978, p. 110).

Although there are extensive theoretical object-relations formulations of the marital relationship, the nature of marital therapy is the least clear aspect of object-relations theory. Dicks (1967) made a coherent statement about the goals of the therapy relative to object-relations assumptions, if not to the process: the goals should be to help the partners internalize the parts of themselves that are projected onto the spouse and to help them own more of their previously split-off, guilt-laden libidinal and antilibidinal egos (p. 118). He elaborated this concept by saying that the outcome of therapy should be that the partners are better adapted to inner and outer reality; they should be able "to see themselves more objectively, to project less, and to manage their aggression and ambivalence in a less infantile and destructive way" (p. 118). Furthermore, he admonished the therapist to stay out of the "omnipotent decision-maker's role" and, instead, to focus on "enlarging the couple's shared insight into their tensions" (Dicks, 1967, p. 230). The therapist in this model is not to "save the marriage"

but to facilitate either the couple's getting together in a better way or separating.

Dicks (1967) described various formats within which these therapeutic processes occur: (1) concurrent individual therapy for the partners by different therapists, (2) separate therapy for the partners by the same therapist, (3) joint therapy by one therapist on a co-therapy team. Dicks (1967) maintained that the second choice is the worst because one is treating interaction but keeping the interacting persons separate. One also risks encouraging and/or disclosing "secretive" information between partners. The therapist also risks getting caught in the middle of the marital strife and may be rendered helpless to influence it. Dicks' (1967) preferred model is conjoint therapy with a male-female co-therapy team. Individual sessions may be conducted during the course of diagnosis and treatment but only within the *context* of the ongoing conjoint format. The model consists of the following:

Each partner originally seen and "identified with" by a therapist "of their own," and then the four—or rather—six-way ongoing relationship in which the therapists struggle with the *same* forces as the patient couple, accept and reject one another's insights, can differ, and also accept the patient's shifting transferences towards the two therapists. The difficulty is, of course, that such stable, well-run in-staff partnerships are rare. (Dicks, 1967, p. 252)

Here, he alluded to the therapy team's serving as a *model* of marriage; it is a chance for the marital partners to see a functional relationship "close-up." Not only do the partners get a close-up view, they also tend to use the therapists and the therapists' "marriage" to one another as a shared transitional object to the next (Dicks, 1967, p. 278). Dicks even suggested that perhaps the best therapy team is a married one.

Beyond the goals and format of the therapy, Dicks (1967) is vague about the actual therapy process except to say that it is more active than formal psychoanalysis. The major transference focus is on the ways in which the partners transfer and project onto each other rather than onto the therapists. The technique of interpreting such transference issues is used, but it is more often interpreted in the context of the marriage relationship, not the therapy relationship: The goal of an interpretation is to facilitate the emergence of forgotten, re-pressed, or ignored material and to mobilize those feelings which have been previously denied. Apart from the function as a symbolic object who is then seen as more real, the actual job of the therapist is a repetitive one: "to reinforce the early interpretations by further glosses, by reminders . . . using different words or new variants of the older material" (Dicks, 1967, p. 268). The patient externalizes onto the partner and therapists; the therapists then feed back to him or her as an interpretation. Nadleson (1978) adds,

The ultimate aim of interpretation and working through in psychoanalytically oriented marital therapy is the neutralization and integration of aggressive and libidinal needs so that behavior is motivated more in the service of the ego and less by impulse and intrapsychic conflict (p. 146).

Behaviors and interaction in the therapy session itself are used as material for interpretation as well as for historical data. Therefore there is an added here-and-now focus not often associated with analytically oriented therapy. Dicks (1967) insisted that the therapy sessions should be the arena for the marital tensions so that life at home goes more smoothly. There is also an intensification of the couple's emotional process because the tensions are condensed and keenly focused on within the therapy hour. That the marriage is ultimately the focus in Dicks' (1967) formulations is illustrated by his response to reluctant partners. When there is a partner who is reluctant to enter the therapy process, he interprets the situation so that the attending spouse is working on the marriage for both of them and keeps the invisible presence of the absent partner constantly a part of the context of the therapy.

Nadelson (1978) addresses the issue of the marital therapy process more specifically:

It is important to realize that a theoretical perspective deriving from psychoanalytic theory does not necessarily commit the therapist to psychoanalysis or to psychoanalytically oriented psychotherapy (p. 114).

Nadelson (1978) offers a rationale for using a combination of available techniques from psychoanalytic, role, systems, and learning theories of development and change. Her approach to changing the couple is an integration of the most powerful aspects of each of these methods. In the end, therapists are ultimately pragmatic, focusing on what works, no matter from what theory they choose to take it.

Friedman (1980) believes that psychoanalytic therapy and systems therapy techniques are naturally complementary. Psychoanalytic techniques provide depth while family systems techniques clarify interpersonal transactions rapidly, providing breadth. Friedman (1980) prefers to think of the intrapsychic components of interpersonal relating as providing a map: from the family of origin, each person develops "a model of the personally significant aspects of human experience, including representations of self and other people that become a map of inter- and intrapersonal reality" (p. 64).

Friedman (1980) views the therapist as a guide to experimentation, taking the patient to the edge of his or her mapped (known) world. He elaborates this concept into a new understanding of the unconscious, which means that it does not always involve defensive aspects:

Unconsciousness need not be a matter of repression. Many feeling–action processes are selectively attended or inattended to. Some have no names, or must not be noticed or remarked on. Some are simply not on the map of the known world (Friedman, 1980, p. 66).

The therapist restructures beliefs, using experiences:

Treating the action mode as meaningful allows understanding of the family system as it constitutes the field and context in which the individual develops, i.e., in which affective sequences, notions of what constitutes explanation, and expectations of relationships emerge (p. 66).

The therapist looks at the process models in the patient's relational world, highlights concordance, discrepancy, and omissions in each person's models, and relates them to family constellations and experiences. This function of the therapist requires empathetic skills and an ability to " 'join the dance' . . . like a psychodrama director or auxiliary ego" (p. 68). Friedman (1980) is refreshingly specific about his usage of therapy techniques. Tasks are prescribed in order to "generate new experiences, supplementing verbal clarification of the implicit models of the interpersonal world: the overt acknowledgment of covert processes, the recognition of conflicting loyalties, and the re-opening of unresolved mourning" (p. 75). The "implicit models" to which he alludes and the "map" refer to the internal object-relations. Specific examples of these tasks are (1) pre-scribe the symptom but reverse the roles; (2) use sculpturing/psychodrama techniques, through which scenes from the family of ori-gin or from plausible fiction are reenacted to get at the subjective experience; (3) have the couple explore what a marriage between his father and her mother would be like (and vice versa). Each partner writes the account and does not share it until the therapy session:

One of the pairings is likely to represent, in more extreme form, many of the snarls the couple is in, while the other pairing has more of their harmoni-ous experiences or suggests shifts which would be more satisfying (Friedman, 1980, p. 75).

Friedman's concept of the internal object relations as the individual's map of the exter-nal world is quite a useful concept in linking the internal to the external. The concept that he and Nadelson (1978) propose is that psycho-analytic understanding of a problem does not necessarily imply psychoanalytic treatment as such. It is a wise therapist who can be eclectic, integrating the useful and powerful aspects of several approaches rather than settling for the partial explanations or interventions offered by any single approach.

Bowenian Marital Therapy

Murray Bowen's exploration of family sys-tems began in the 1950s at the National Insti-tute for Mental Health. Bowen trained in a psychoanalytic model and began the change to the systems model by exploring the relation-ships between mothers and their schizophrenic children. His original hypothesis discussed schizophrenia as the product of a symbiotic mother–child relationship. Bowen did not pre-dict how this mother–child dyad operated within the family, however, and repeated ob-servations of nuclear family functioning led him eventually to include fathers in his theoreti-cal formulation of schizophrenia. Continued work by Bowen and his students led them to observe the same relational patterns in fam-ilies with problems other than a schizophrenic child. Bowen's final formulation, which stands today in extended form, was that all symp-toms are manifestations of disorders in emo-tional systems. This basic premise has become the cornerstone of commonality of all family systems theories, whatever the specific in-tervention style (Haley, 1976; Hall, 1981; Minuchin, 1974).

The two basic diagnostic premises of Bowenian therapy are the importance of level of anxiety and level of differentiation in the re-lational system. Bowen proposed that humans operate either from their emotional or their thinking systems. The emotional system is au-tonomic nervous system activity not mediated by cognitive processing, while the thinking sys-tem is rational processing of informational cues. These two systems are important in that they control behavior and, under conditions of anxiety, the two systems tend to fuse so that much of what we perceive as thinking is actu-ally verbal reaction to the emotional system.

Bowenian theory is based on eight concepts that interact to compose the relational system and its patterns. These concepts include dif-ferentiation of self, triangles, nuclear family emotional process, family projection process, multigenerational transmission process, emo-tional cut-offs, sibling position, and societal emotional process.

Bowen views individuals as operating on a continuum of fusion to differentiation. The degree of differentiation is essentially the de-gree of emotional maturity of the individual (Boszormenyi-Nagy & Spark, 1973). The degree of differentiation of individuals in a couple is diagnostically significant, not in terms of pa-thology but in terms of vulnerability to stress. Differentiation can be assessed in a number of areas. Individuals at the low end of the differ-entiation continuum are easily influenced by other people: being either very dependent upon others or very reactive to others. The undiffer-entiated person operates primarily from the emotional rather than the thinking system and is prone to denial or outbursts of uncontrolled emotion. Another diagnostic clue to the level of differentiation is the degree to which the in-dividual either feels responsible for the feel-ings of others or blames others for his or her own feelings. One of the ways in which Bowen has his students become aware of their own levels of differentiation is to ask them to write their important beliefs or values and where they think these values came from (Hall, 1981). The differentiated individual arrives at personal values through an objective look at data and experience, while the individual with low levels of differentiation typically accepts the values of the family, based on emotional loyalty issues (Boszormenyi-Nagy & Sparks, 1973).

Bowen proposed two different types of differentiation: basic and functional. Basic differentiation is the average ability of the individual to operate from a thinking system: taking in all the data and behaving in a goal-directed fashion. Basic differentiation is called the "solid self" and is not likely to change appreciably over time without therapeutic intervention. In contrast, functional differentiation is the everyday shifts in degree of fusion that the individual experiences relative to shifts in anxiety. Functional differentiation is the pseudoself of the person, which is negotiable and reactive to external stressors and life-cycle changes (Carter & McGoldrick, 1980).

Individuals tend to marry those with relatively equal levels of differentiation, so that the individual differentiation parallels the degree of marital differentiation. The most difficulty arises in marriages in which both spouses are at low levels of differentiation. These relationships tend to be based on emotional complementarity involving a dominant and an adaptive member, in which the dominant member gets strength from the adaptive one. The system is fused in this mirror-opposite fashion and is exacerbated by stress. These couples can be characterized by a sense that they can't live without one another but can't live with one another as they move along a closeness-versus-distance continuum in their avoidance of intimacy (L'Abate, 1976). These individuals need closeness to combat the loneliness of being "selfless," and need distance to relieve the intensity of fusion when they become close.

Bowen hypothesized that families have characteristic ways of dealing with surplus anxiety in the relational system. He proposed that there are four options to the process of responding to tension: (1) emotional distancing, (2) marital conflict, (3) spouse dysfunction, and (4) scapegoating. All these options are normal in the process of relationships but become pathological when they are emotionally determined and static. Emotional distancing can be a conscious choice made by a spouse to "cool down" as a first step in dealing with conflict, or it can be reactive and extreme. Marital conflict, when

dealt with in a manner designed to resolve the conflict, is a positive quality of relationships, but becomes pathological when it is constant and unresolved. Spouse dysfunction occurs when one member's sense of self is eroded by the relational system. Dominant–submissive relationship patterns can be complementary and function well but become pathological in the extreme. Scapegoating is the process whereby the couple bands together against something or someone else, usually a child. This process is normal in the relief of tension; however, when the scapegoating process is rigidified in the family system, the child exhibits symptoms and the marital tension is ignored.

Triangles are relatively stable, three-person groups, with shifting emotional forces (Hall, 1981). Bowen proposed that families are composed of a series of overlaping triangles, with the central triangle composed of the married couple and one member or thing, i.e., a job. The theoretical assumption is that dyads are unstable systems because of the closeness–distance conflict. When the anxiety of one member of a couple becomes too high on this issue, the system is stabilized by bringing in a third member. During periods of medium tension, the balance of emotional forces in a triangle can stay relatively fixed and comfortable for all members. Under high tension, however, conflict is overloaded on one leg of the triangle, and under low tension, one member usually feels isolated (Gurman & Kniskern, 1981). The scapegoating process is usually the result of triangulation under high stress.

The family projection process is a Bowenian concept concerning how undifferentiation is transmitted to children. In this process, a parent with a low level of self-differentiation focuses attention on and fuses with a child to avoid loneliness. The child's personaity is defined by the parental emotionality and not by the objective reality of the child's behavior and feelings. This fusion impairs the child's capacity to function in a differentiated, or emotionally mature, manner.

Bowen also proposed that symptoms that are exhibited in the present in a nuclear family system are an end product of the levels of differentiation and subsequent emotional problems of past generations (Bowen, 1978). Therefore there is a multigenerational transmission process.

Guerin and Guerin (1976) have proposed that it takes at least three generations to produce a schizophrenic family member from the projection of lower and lower levels of self-differentiation. The process can be slowed if the undifferentiation of spouses is played out within the marital system rather than being projected onto a child.

Bowen (1978) characterized an emotional cut-off as the ceasing of communication or relating to family-of-origin members. Cutting oneself off from relating is seen as a reactive move to unresolved fusion in the family of origin and is not a resolution of this fusion. The greater the degree of alienation from one's past, the higher the probability of overinvestment of feelings and fusion in future relationships (Hall, 1981).

Bowenian theory also stresses the importance of functioning sibling position in the diagnosis of emotional vulnerability. Sibling position as a factor in marital relationships was first investigated by Toman (1972), who distinguished 10 important categories of sibling positions that impinge upon future relationships: oldest brother of brothers, oldest brother of sisters, oldest sister of sisters, oldest sister of brothers, youngest sister of sisters, youngest sister of brothers, only child, and one of twins. He proposed relational structures that tend to complement one another as well as those that have a high probability of leading to conflict. An example of a high-conflict relationship would be one in which two youngest members of opposite-sex sibling systems are married to one another. The individuals would have little experience in taking a dominant position in decision-making and would probably expect to be taken care of by the spouse. Sex of siblings and sibling order are both seen as important variables.

Bowen (1978) took Toman's work a step further by looking at the sibling position of one's parents and other generations in an attempt to differentiate the toxicity, or emotional vulnerability, of certain positions within a family. Bowen also stressed the importance of exploring the function as well as the order of the sibling. For example, a child might operate as an oldest in terms of responsibility or as a youngest in terms of dependency issues relative to the relationship with parents.

Bowen has recently added the concept of societal emotional process. He proposes that societies operate within a conflict of adaptation versus extinction. During periods of high anxiety, people are pressured to make short-term decisions based on emotionality rather than to exhibit long-term, goal-directed behavior and the ability to solve problems. The level of anxiety within the society as a whole thus influences the level of stress experienced by the nuclear family (Hall, 1981).

Bowenian theory gives a framework for a broad look at marital conflict. Carter and McGoldrick (1980) suggest a framework for diagnosis of family level of anxiety that includes both horizontal and vertical stressors. Horizontal stressors include important life-cycle events, financial pressures, and unpredictable life events. Vertical stressors relate to the level of differentiation of past family members, the level of intensity of the relationship with one's parent of the opposite sex, sibling positions and sex distribution in family of origin, and level of emotional importance attached to certain life-cycle events. Bowenian therapy aims at integrating these two types of stressors and reducing the anxiety resulting from them by improving basic levels of differentiation in the spouses and thus decreasing their emotional reactivity.

In the Bowenian therapy model, the evaluation of couples is aimed at objectively observing behavior and gathering information. A thorough diagnosis includes a history of the presenting problem, a time-line of the marital relationship, and a family history (genogram) from both husband and wife. The goals of therapy include (1) to open communication by allowing the couple access to more information about one another, (2) to improve the functional differentiation and reduce the anxiety level by helping the individuals distinguish between thinking and feeling, and (3) to improve the level of basic differentiation by directing interventions at the individuals' families of origin.

Members of a couple may be seen separately or together to discuss their families of origin. Ideally, the couple is seen together with a therapist who then becomes the third leg of the emotional triangle necessary to stabilize the system. The therapist's goal is to remain emotionally contacted with the couple so that they do not triangulate someone else into the dyadic system, while remaining objective enough to stay detriangulated from the power of the emotional system. The therapist encourages engagement of the couple in conflict into a thinking rather than an emotional system, and thus defuses the anxiety associated with intimacy.

The genogram of each individual is viewed as a map for therapeutic intervention, and the therapist must be aware of a variety of diagnostic implications that can be signaled by the genogram information. Fogharty (1976) has developed a model of relational systems based on a pursuer–distancer polarity. A pursuer is someone who views the solution to anxiety as lying in external action; to a distancer, anxiety comes from the external world and the solution to anxiety is to go away internally and escape. Pursuer and distancer elements can be identified in marital therapy and related to the family of origin from which these patterns were projected. Much information can also be gained from a look at repetitive sequences of behavior used in past generations for coping with anxiety.

Other dimensions important to diagnosis and intervention are the emotional cut-offs in the system, the route of communication through the family system triangles, and the ways in which life events are characteristically handled in the family of origin. All of these factors affect the level of anxiety and emotional fusion in the present relationship.

Therapy, from a Bowenian perspective, operates in two stages. The initial stage involves information-gathering and teaching components. The individual is given a basic overview of Bowenian theory to engage the thinking system. By making the individual aware of triangles, patterns, and toxic issues in the family of origin, a more objective view of the self can be obtained. This initial stage also aims at increasing the individual's sense of flexibility of choices and range of behaviors, which are not instinctually present in the emotional system.

The second stage of therapy engages the individual directly with his or her family of origin in an attempt to change relational patterns and promote basic differentiation. During this stage, when one person begins to function more independently, the system will characteristically become unstable and respond with togetherness-preserving moves (Boszormenyi-Nagy & Spark, 1973). It is the therapist's job to predict these events so that the client can anticipate them and respond rationally. Tension in the system actually promotes differentiation because rigid patterns are unbalanced and no longer operable (Hall, 1981). Differentiation is facilitated when the client becomes involved with members of the extended family in a different behavioral style and maintains an objective stance while watching the family process from an emotional distance, as it were. In this manner, the individual can detriangulate himself or herself from the family emotional process and thus reverberate changes throughout the interlocking triangles in the family system.

Bowenian therapy is the only systems perspective that is based on the past rather than here-and-now interactions (Steinglass, 1978). It attacks the roots of anxiety and lack of boundaries in a marital system rather than simply alleviating the present anxiety. Haley (1972) proposed, from a structural viewpoint, that systems exhibit symptoms when they get "stuck" at a particular life-cycle stage or set of interactions. Bowenian theory is compatible with this view but differs in its level of attack on the "stuckness." Bowenian therapy requires motivation, commitment to a relatively long-term therapy, and cognitive strength. It does not directly address the symptom–resolution task as do structural or behavioral interventions but, instead, focuses on the importance of the individual's past experiences in determining his or her present marital relationship.

Other Marital Therapy Approaches

Transactional Analysis marital therapy. Transactional Analysis (TA) is, for the most part, a derivative of psychoanalysis, with the major difference being a more active role by the therapist.

The presenting problem is viewed as arising from the individual's childhood experiences related to self and other people. Each of the childhood-experience-derived existential positions of "I'm OK—You're OK," "I'm OK—You're Not OK," "I'm not OK—You're OK," and "I'm Not OK—You're Not OK" leads to conflict between people. In the "I'm OK—You're OK" position, conflicts in the relationship are viewed from an orientation of "getting on with it." In the "I'm OK—You're Not OK" position, the individual sees himself or herself as having no responsibility for conflicts with the partner and projects his or her not-OKness onto either the mate or some other source. In the "I'm Not OK—You're OK" position, the individual is helpless, victimized, and feels rejection because of his or her dependency needs. In the "I'm Not OK—You're Not OK" position, there is a sense of helplessness and futility (O'Connor, 1977).

Assessment is not systematic, but the TA therapist attempts to assess the rackets, i.e., a series of transactions in which the function is to maintain a symbiotic relationship (English, 1971), leading to failures to receive strokes (acknowledgment and affirmation).

The past and unconscious are important, for they are viewed as the cause of the presenting problem(s) and the inability of each partner to relate to the other from positions of autonomy. The TA therapist actively intervenes in interpreting the couples' transactions to help them gain insight and change their scripts (lifelong patterns of behavior); the goal of treatment being to have each person in charge of himself or herself and to give up being in charge of the spouse. The TA therapist may also establish autonomy contracts and cooperation contracts with the couple so that end results of therapy are acknowledged and agreed upon at the outset of treatment.

Rational emotive marital therapy. Rational emotive therapy (RET) has been applied to couples by Ellis (1973) since the 1950s. RET is primarily a cognitive therapy based on the belief that the presenting problem, which involves anxiety and hostility, results from each individual's irrational beliefs about himself or herself in the world. Ellis (1973) sees all human beings as subscribing to a series of irrational beliefs that cause panic, self-blame, and self-doubt. These beliefs are as follows:

1. It is a dire necessity for an adult to be loved or approved by virtually every significant person in the community.
2. One should be thoroughly competent, adequate, and achieving in all possible respects if one is to consider oneself worthwhile.
3. Human unhappiness is externally caused and people have little or no ability to control their sorrows and disturbances.
4. One's past history is an all-important determinant of one's present behavior, and because something once strongly affected one's life, it should indefinitely have a similar effect.
5. There is invariably a right, precise, and perfect solution to human problems and it is catastrophic if this perfect solution is not found.
6. If something is or may be dangerous or frightening, one should be terribly concerned about it and should dwell on the possibility of its occurring.
7. Certain people are bad, wicked, or villainous, and they should be severely blamed and punished for their villainy.
8. It is awful and catastrophic when things are not the way one would very much like them to be.
9. It is easier to avoid than to face certain life-difficulties and self-responsibilities.
10. One should become quite upset over other people's problems and disturbances.

To Ellis, the presenting problem is how the individual feels, based on his or her irrational beliefs. Assessment is primarily to ascertain the individual's irrational beliefs about marriage. The role of the past and the unconscious is considered minimal; instead, the focus is on the ways in which the couple maintain their irrational beliefs.

The goal of treatment is to help an individual give up irrational beliefs. Ellis views the therapist as active and directive, verbal, forceful, and didactic in this endeavor to analyze and challenge the negative thinking of the clients. Thoughts rather than feelings are emphasized, for Ellis views behavior in a five-step process consisting of (1) awareness, (2) cognition, (3) emotion, (4) behavior, and (5) consequence of behavior. Ellis states that marital problems result from neurotic disturbances in one or both spouses. People are said to enter marriage with two primary expectations, one related to sexuality, the other to companionship and love. If there is a large gap between the spouses as to these expectations, the marriage is likely to suffer. Therapy, for Ellis, involves clearing the discrepancy between the spouses relative to these expectations (which have usually been exclusively formulated at a cognitive level) and include the irrational beliefs.

The "reality therapy" of Glasser (1965) is similar to RET and will not be elaborated here except to note that marital therapy conducted by the reality therapist is similar to RET. Both therapies are readily adaptable to couples group therapy.

In reviewing the contributions of cognitive therapies to marital therapy, one finds that there is a general agreement that the cognitive therapies modify unrealistic expectations so that the couple may more realistically address their needs (Jacobson & Martin, 1976; Weiss, 1975; Weiss, Hops & Patterson, 1975). There is also a general agreement that cognitive therapies correct faulty attributions, thus providing an avenue for behavior change (Gurman, 1978; Jacobson, 1978; O'Leary & Turkewitz, 1978) and that the use of self-instructional procedures is effective in decreasing destructive interactions (Bockus, 1980; Liberman, Wheeler & Sanders, 1976). Furthermore, the cognitive approaches to marital therapy may primarily be viewed as approaches that change behavior by first changing the perceptual field by which individuals define their reality. Thus, each individual acts and reacts according to his or her definition of reality or perception of the state or event.

CONTEXTUAL APPROACHES

Steinglass (1978) provides both a historical and a theoretical overview of the systemic perspective. At present, the ideas that can best be described as "systemic" in the area of marriage and marital therapy more typically represent a series of loosely connected concepts and ideas rather than a fully integrated theoretical perspective. Some characterize the systemic perspective not as a theory per se, but as a style of thinking about complex relational processes.

The historical roots of the systemic perspective of marriage and marital therapy are provided by general systems theory. The concepts that eventually became unified as part of general systems theory were devised by von Bertalanffy (1968) in an effort to develop an "organismic" approach to biological problems, one that represented a move away from the oversimplified, reductionistic, mechanistic tradition in science. The proposed emphasis was not on cause–effect, stimulus–response equations, but on the examination of the patterns found in nonlinear relationships between living entities. This position stresses the importance of context and the impact that it has on determining the nature of the relationships under investigation. The systems view, which was adapted from general systems theory, has had more appeal for those theorists who are interested in relationships among individuals or groups of individuals (e.g., sociologists, social psychologists, marital and family therapists) and apparently less appeal for theorists and practitioners who have maintained an interest in individually-based phenomena.

The concept of organization is an important one in this perspective, one that is virtually synonymous with the concept of a system. When a system is viewed as a set of units or elements that stand in consistent relationship to each other, the organization of this system (and the elements in it), in terms of a describable, predictable pattern of relationships, is important. There are three basic organizational constructs of interests in the systemic position:

1. *Wholeness*—the proposition that the system cannot be adequately understood or explained with only an examination of the component parts of the system, i.e., the combination of component parts in a system results in an entity that is qualitatively different from and greater than the additive sums of each of the separate parts.
2. *Boundaries*—the spatial or temporal variables that affect the component parts of a system to clarify the pattern of relationships existing between them. From a marital perspective, the concept of boundary has relevance when speaking of the relationship defined by the roles of the husband and wife separately and the husband and wife together as a marital pair. In the latter instance, the boundary between the husband and wife and the external environment (i.e., both in a physical and interrelational sense) is of importance. Boundaries between the component parts of a system (and groupings of component parts, as in the case of a husband and wife) must be rigid enough to protect the component parts on a functional level but also permeable enough to allow a functional exchange with other elements of the system, the external environment, etc.

3. *Hierarchies*—the notion that systems are organized one to another according to a series of hierarchical levels, each system composed of smaller component subsystems but also being a component part of a larger suprasystem. In marriage the husband and wife represent two individual subsystems while, together, they are component parts of a larger family system that, in turn, is part of a community system, etc.

The concept of control is central in the systemic position. Control makes possible the development of highly complex, fluid, interactional relations between the component parts of a system. Relative to control, there are two central concepts: homeostasis and feedback. The former concept refers to processes that regulate the internal environment of a system, in part through the mediation of the system's interplay with the natural or social environment. Relative to the latter, both positive and negative feedback establish a steady-state systemic balance (over time).

A third concept, that of energy, is relevant to a discussion of entropy and negentrophy, the operative processes that determine either the increased organization or randomness of a system. Significantly, information is specified as functionally equivalent to negentrophy in that it provides a means of reducing the level of uncertainty, or randomness, in a system. This provides a logical connection with the theorists who view marriage as an information-processing arrangement and communication as the datum of interest in therapy. Analyses of systems can be along either a spatial (structural) or temporal (process) dimension. There are three primary systemic positions that have had an impact on theories related to marriage: the communications-based work of the Palo Alto group at the Mental Research Institute, the work of Minuchin and Bowen, and the contribution of family sociologists (most notably from a developmental perspective relative to the life-cycle notions of family life).

Moving away from a simple definition of terms, Sluzki (1978) provides a look at the actual clinical application of systems ideas. Generally, the position that Sluzki describes is one that suggests that change in a marital system often must come from outside the system. Oftentimes this change must be patterned so that it forces the husband and wife to depart from their traditional ways of attempting to deal with stress and difficulties in the marriage. The point is made that such traditional attempts are often ineffective simply because they are governed by the same set of systemic rules (i.e., those idiosyncratic to the couple) that led to the pathology in the first place. The systemic therapist must therefore devise ways of disrupting couples' traditional means of dealing with problems by shattering traditional representations of control and role-behavior in the marriage. Within this viewpoint, the communicational sequences between the marital partners are seen as a powerful means of altering both the rules and the resulting pathological behavior commonly observed in a marital system. Changes are considered possible only if conceptualized from a circular rather than a linear reference, for a linear perspective only feeds into the traditional rules that have governed the system and ignores the circularity and cybernetic nature of marital interaction.

Strategic marital therapy. Jay Haley is usually considered the most representative theorist of this approach, which may be described as a combination systems-communication approach. The basic premise of strategic therapy is that reality is defined as one chooses to define it. As people define their reality, their attempted solutions to problems often become the problem. It is hoped that strategic interventions will alter and redefine a more functional solution (Haley, 1976). Dysfunction in the couple or family always leads to the therapist's use of strategic therapy and family structural therapy (Haley, 1976).

Haley does not focus much on diagnosis or history-taking, but attempts to intervene as soon as possible with an emphasis on participation. He stresses that the role of the therapist is one of being in charge, neutral, and involved, with an initial focus on the digital communication of the couple and the presenting problem. The therapist is directive and is considered effective to the extent that he or she enforces a dominant position and controls the relationship.

The essence of therapy is the "technique of interviewing" (Haley, 1976). Change is the focus and is brought about by a system of interaction rather than by insight and interpretation. Change is considered the only valid outcome, with the kind and degree of change determined by the couple, and the focus of change centered on the realignment of alliances. In the initial stage of treatment, the therapist relabels the behavior and the presenting problem, with an emphasis on the positive. He or she narrowly redefines the presenting problem and gets family members to talk with each other about the problem. The therapist encourages the usual behavior and gives paradoxical directives that force the couple to take the initiative to change (Haley, 1976).

A paradox is defined as a message containing a relationship directive that qualifies another directive in a conflicting way, either simultaneously or at a different time. The receiver cannot obey or disobey because of the conflicting nature of the paradox. The person posing the paradox will "win" in controlling the relationship, and the familiar becomes redefined (Minuchin, 1974). The therapy becomes strategic because the clinician is in charge and determines how therapy will proceed (Haley, 1973).

Haley stresses that if one changes behavior, one changes feelings; therefore, feelings are not an essential focus of the therapy. The couple changes by being forced to act in different ways, and the therapist moves the family to new ways of operating. Haley stresses, however, that the degree of change should be determined by the couple. In therapy, the couple is faced with a relationship containing multiple paradoxes, which forces them to abandon old behavior, since the couple can only deal with the relationship or escape from it amicably by undergoing change (Haley, 1969).

Therapy also consists of the therapist as model (Haley, 1963a) and the therapist as metagovernor of the system (Haley, 1973). Although the therapeutic paradox forces the family to take the initiative, the behavior is determined by the therapist (Haley, 1976). Haley states that creative change is the outcome of the struggle for control between the therapist and the family members. The therapist is the agent who produces family change by directions that are ambiguous, emphasizing the positive, and relabeling and encouraging the usual behavior. Therapy is effective when the therapist wins the power struggle

with the family, is in control of the therapy, and produces change in behavior (Haley, 1976).

Finally, Haley describes family and couple therapy as the "art of coalitions" (Haley, 1976). Therapy is directive, active, and specific-problem-oriented, with little emphasis on insight; the only focus of treatment being change in behavior.

Structural marital therapy. Minuchin and his co-workers (Stanton, 1981) have been identified with this therapeutic approach that views marriage as a hierarchical organization.

Like Haley's, Minuchin's approach is strategic, active, and directive, using a systems framework to conceptualize the marital relationship and conduct the marital therapy. Unilike Haley's, Minuchin's approach is more theoretically developed, more comprehensive, and contains several working models. Minuchin is also more of a synthesizer in his approach, using direct verbal confrontations as well as indirect strategic maneuvers. Structural marital therapy is symptom-oriented and context-determined. The target of intervention is the marital subsystem, and problems are defined as symptomatic of current relationships. Past relationships are not explored; the focus is entirely on what is happening in the present. Thus Minuchin strongly differs from Haley in that he will sometimes openly confront and interpret to help the family understand its relationship to any presenting problem (Stanton, 1981).

Overall, Minuchin's approach is more similar to than different from Haley's. However, Minuchin also offers well-developed restructuring operations, categorizations of four different sources of family stress, and some assessment techniques that can be taught prior to therapy. He also advocates teaching theory to trainees.

In the structural approach of Minuchin, the focal point of therapeutic change is realignment of the marital structure via changing dysfunctional subsystem boundaries and transactional patterns. To this end, he has developed a working model for spatially diagramming the marriage's organizational schema. In his model, he notes the flow or sequence of interaction along open and concealed power lines, whether the boundaries across subsystems are diffuse, rigid, or functional, and how conflicts are sequenced (e.g., a parent subsystem may triangulate a child in order to detour around a marital conflict). This model is used to design "balancing" strategies whereby the therapist may temporarily coalign with one member in order to change the structure.

Basic to Minuchin's approach is the view that the context of the individual and the presenting problem is a relational one (the interaction between the "intracerebral" and the "extracerebral"). The goal of therapy is to change the relationship so that the person can have new experiences that will shift his or her position in the family system. Important in the maintenance of change is positive reinforcement. The reinforcement comes from the person's being better able to perform tasks that are functional to the system and from experiencing functional transactional patterns. Changing a dysfunctional transaction pattern (repeating operations of interactions that maintain a system) into a functional one involves clarifying and defining boundaries in a system so that the functions of the system can be carried out without interference. Futhermore, it is the therapist's responsibility to help reinforce the changing system by confirming the strengths of the family.

Minuchin expends more conceptual energy on the boundaries of a system than does Haley. He describes the boundaries as the rules of a system; it is through them that a partner's participation in the marriage is defined to include how, when, and to whom that member will relate. Based on his boundary assumptions, Minuchin derives a linear model of pathology and health. Accordingly, any marital system can be placed on a continuum of boundaries, with rigid boundaries on one end denoting a "disengaged" marriage. In the disengaged marriage, relationships in the system are essentially almost separate from one another, in that stress must be severe before it reverberates through the system. On the other end of the continuum are marriages with diffuse boundaries, or "enmeshed" marriages, in which there is little differentiation of the subsystem, and almost any stress reverberates too quickly throughout the system.

Minuchin's (1974) position on the role of subjective experience is quite succinct. He states, "By changing the position of the system's members, the therapist changes their subjective experience" (p. 14). That is, first he

[the therapist] changes behaviors, and then the members' subjective experience changes; however, changing their subjective experience will not necessarily lead to changing their behavior.

To change the family system, the therapist "joins that system and then uses himself to transform it" (Minuchin, 1974, p. 14). The structural marital therapist takes an active role in changing the family, and his course of action is determined by the situation. It is an action-oriented approach, with the therapist challenging marital roles, rules, and structures. Thus Minuchin strongly indicates that therapy involves more than a teachable skill. It also involves a highly developed, flexible, sensitive, and diversely experienced human being behind the interventions.

Systemic marital therapy. This approach to marital therapy derives from the notion of paradox and counterparadox propagated by the Palo Alto and the Milano Groups (Palazzoli, et al, 1978; Watzlawick, et al, 1974). Both groups rely heavily on the notion of *positive reframing* for the dysfunctional partner or symptom as *protector* of the marital system, *paradoxical injunction* or prescription of the symptom (if the symptom is good because it protects the marital system from change, then it should go on . . .), *systemic linking* to both partners (i.e., the nonsymptomatic partner is to become more active in the maintenance of the symptom) and *ritual prescription*.

The essential basis of this approach, elaborated in greater detail in Weeks and L'Abate (1982), is *control*. Up to the present, the symptom has controlled the marital system, and if the therapist does not watch out, the therapist will be controlled by it and eventually defeated. By reframing positively and prescribing ritually the symptom ("On Mondays, Wednesdays, and Fridays, from 9 to 10, for 30 minutes in the kitchen"), the therapist instead teaches the couple to achieve control of the symptom and, in the process, the therapist, too, achieves control of the symptom.

Positive reframing and prescription of the symptom are now so universally applied by most therapists that their theoretical and historical origins are often forgotten. In combination with strategic and structural approaches, this approach promises a major step toward briefer and more effective marital therapies. Their eventual and inevitable combination with behavioral approaches may add the empirical component that many of these contextual strategies still sorely lack.

For a more elaborate explanation of these and other therapeutic approaches, the interested reader may want to consult Gurman and Kniskern (1981).

THE MARITAL TREATMENT PROCESS

The therapeutic treatment process varies among practitioners, depending on their theoretical orientation and their conceptualization of marital distress. Although a number of practitioners align themselves with the specific approaches discussed in this chapter, for the most part, practitioners are eclectic in orientation, conceptualizing the focus of treatment as the systemic interrelationship of the couple.

Within this general systems orientation, the therapist may actively orchestrate and conduct the therapeutic focus or, instead, may respond to issues presented by the couple, with the therapeutic focus being determined by the couple. Depending upon the theoretical orientation of the therapist, the therapist views the primary component of change as feelings, rationality, or behavior. Humanistic orientations, represented by client-centered, experiential, existential, and Gestalt approaches, stress the importance of the phenomenological determinants of distress, with change consisting of acknowledging, experiencing, and altering one's subjective, feeling interpretation of himself or herself and the external world. Psychoanalytic and object-relations orientations emphasize the importance of past experience and the unconscious as it determines present feelings and behavior, with change consisting of one's awareness and understanding of primarily unconscious phenomena. The Bowenian approach, as well as RET, TA therapy, and reality-oriented therapy, also stress the importance of past experience as a determinant of one's present difficulties in relationships, and that change consists of understanding the past in order to alter the present. Systems orientations, represented by

strategic therapy, general systems theory, structural therapy, and systemic therapies, stress the importance of here-and-now patterns of interrelationships, with change consisting of altering behavior.

The psychoanalytically oriented therapist focuses on the goal of facilitating each individual's awareness of past experiences that underlie projections and distortions (Dicks, 1967). Unconscious choices are stressed, and the therapist helps individuals become aware of how they repeat interactions based on the internalized models of their own parents (Skynner, 1976). Facilitating understanding is the main goal of treatment.

The systems-oriented therapist focuses on the goal of intervening in the established pattern of relating within the dyad so that the cybernetic system, composed of verbal and nonverbal feedback loops, is altered (Bockus, 1975). The ways of interrelating that maintain a dysfunctional relationship are altered within the couple.

The communications-oriented therapist focuses on the verbal and nonverbal patterns of communication that maintain marital dysfunction and dissatisfaction (Bolte, 1970). The goal of treatment is to eliminate contradictions in communication and establish clear communication within the dyad. The behavior in the marital relationship is seen basically as an outcome or function of communicative interaction within a social system, and problems consist of persisting patterns of undesired behavior (Guerin & Guerin, 1976).

Underlying all theoretical rationales is the treatment goal of alleviating the presenting problem of the couple and facilitating growth. The term "growth" is as yet a somewhat nebulous and undefined term, but it incorporates the ideas of greater intimacy, individual autonomy, flexibility, and adaptability.

In practice, the marital therapist may essentially analyze the relationship to facilitate understanding, educate the couple about maladaptive patterns of relating, or actively intervene to help individuals alter their behavior. Because of differing and overlapping theories, however, what is done in actual practice is often difficult to discern.

Other techniques used by marital therapists include the following:

1. *Contracting.* Agreements are arrived at by negotiation and conflict resolution between the therapist and family members (Friedman, 1972).
2. *Affect release and control.* The therapist asks questions, comments on nonverbal behavior, and verbalizes covert feelings in the marital dyad (Bowen, 1978; Kempler, 1971; Satir, 1965).
3. *Restructuring and relabeling.* Physical seating arrangements may be altered (restructuring) and problems are relabeled by the therapist in terms different from those used by the couple (Haley, 1976; Lazarus, 1971; Minuchin, 1972).
4. *Confrontation–feedback.* The therapist feeds back to family members their verbal or nonverbal behavior in relation to themselves or others (Friedman, 1974).
5. *Homework and task assignments.* The therapist assigns or recommends tasks for family members to do, either during or outside the therapy session.
6. *Reversals and prescribing the symptom.* The therapist asks each member to do what the other member is doing, the opposite of that behavior, or reverse roles. The therapist may also ask an individual to exaggerate or do more frequently a current behavior (Haley, 1976).
7. *Negotiation, mediation.* The therapist mediates exchanges between the couple.
8. *Coaching.* The therapist guides or instructs in a behavior skill.
9. *Role-playing.* The therapist and couple play roles other than themselves (i.e., parents, children, alter egos, living or dead figures) (Beels & Ferber, 1972).
10. *Brief therapy with couples groups.* Couples are seen in groups; therapy is highly structured, intensely focused, and directive (Papp, 1976).
11. *Multiple couple therapy.* Couples are treated in group therapy with other couples (Alger, 1976).

Current practice can be defined as consisting of a variety of theories, techniques, and goals, which are stated from the viewpoint of the individual theorist and/or practitioner. Theoretical orientations are still nonintegrated and, as a result, practice approaches appear to be nonintegrated, as well. Practitioners in actual practice may be more similar than their theories or recommended treatment approaches might indicate, however, for there are still few studies indicating the exact nature of the treatment as practiced by the therapist.

Co-Therapy

Marital therapy is almost universally conducted as a conjoint process in which the couple is seen together by one or more therapists, with the focus on treating the marital relationship (Olson, 1978). The rationale for conjoint marital therapy is that the relationship is the focus of treatment and cannot be effectively addressed via one individual in the couple.

Co-therapy (treatment conducted by one or more therapists) has been widely used and espoused as a more effective treatment approach than treatment by one therapist (Holt & Greiner, 1976; Leslie, 1974; MacLennan, 1976). Rationale for co-therapy has been that one therapist is often overwhelmed, that the presence of another therapist checks transference and countertransference reactions, that two therapists re-create the original situation of two parents, and that there is more combined knowledge and expertise. Later studies, however, have found that co-therapy provides no better benefits than does one therapist (Gurman, 1973a; Rabin, 1967); and some have suggested that co-therapy may create more problems due to disagreement between the co-therapists, increased transference and coutertransference issues, and lack of a cohesive working relationship (Rubenstein & Weiner, 1967). Whitaker (Napier & Whitaker, 1972) suggested that co-therapy is merely a convenience for the therapists rather than an increased benefit for the couple.

Aside from specific strutured approaches to marital therapy (strategic therapy, structural therapy, and systemic therapy), it is difficult to describe the actual marital therapy process, for the process is determined by the theoretical orientation of the components of change. As with individual approaches to therapy, the therapy process is also determined by the therapist's personality and style of interrelating.

Assessment and Diagnosis

Diagnosis has received little attention in the field of marital therapy. Marriages have usually been described as functional or dysfunctional, nondisturbed or disturbed, conflicted or nonconflicted, or normal or disturbed (Alsbrook, 1976; Hansen & L'Abate, 1982). Since there is no coherent, unified theory to guide observations, most assessment and diagnosis is conducted in unsystematic and subjective ways, using unspecified criteria that practitioners have found useful in their clinical experiences (Cromwell & Keeney, 1979).

Another difficulty with attempted diagnosis is that existing measures and schemas of classification do not consider a dyadic interaction, but are usually descriptive of the intrapersonal dynamics of one individual. Some researchers and practitioners have attempted to develop methods of assessment for couples; however, there are few validated and reliable measurements (Hurvitz, 1965; Olson, 1970; Phillips, 1973; Smith, 1967), and more promising measurements are either too lengthy or too costly to be used in a clinical setting.

In most cases in which systematic diagnosis is attempted, practitioners have relied on standardized tests used in individual assessment such as the Minnesota Multiphasic Personality Inventory, the Rorschach, and the Thematic Apperception Test. There is no demonstrated relationship between individual assessment and marital interaction assessment, however (Olson, 1969). Most practitioners continue to subjectively evaluate marriages on the dimensions of happiness, stability, and meeting role expectations (Keeney & Cromwell, 1977).

The Role of the Therapist

Depending upon the theoretical orientation of the therapist, the role of the marital therapist can be viewed in several ways. Beels and Ferber (1972) proposed an early classification system for the roles of various therapists. They proposed three types of therapists:

1. "Conductors," who seek to re-educate the family with clear ideas about what is best for the family. Conductors are represented by Bell, Ackerman, Satir, Minuchin, and Bowen.
2. "Reactor analysts," who seek to uncover the potential for growth. Reactor analysts are characterized by Whitaker, Wynne, Framo, Freidman, and Boszormenyi-Nagy.
3. "System purists," who seek to change family rules. System purists are characterized by Haley, Jackson, and Zuk.

This classification system was initially proposed for family therapists but describes, to some extent, the role of the marital therapist. Although a more psychoanalytically oriented marital therapist might, in practice, be viewed as a reactor analyst, a more systems-oriented marital therapist might, in practice, be viewed as a system purist or a conductor. Given the setting of conjoint marital therapy, however, one would, from a practical standpoint, be more a conductor than a reactor because of the necessity to mediate within a dyadic relationship.

Ideally, the marital therapist is an individual who understands marital dynamics and can intervene in the marital dyad so as to assist a couple to better understand or change their marital interaction and attempt to find ways in which their needs can be mutually satisfied so that the growth and development of each partner can be maximized in the relationship (Olson, 1975). Inherent in the understanding of the marital dyad is the understanding of the individual's needs, although individual dynamics are little stressed except perhaps by psychoanalytically oriented marital therapists.

RESEARCH IN MARITAL THERAPY

Although marital therapy as a field is 50 years old, a relatively small amount of literature has been published on treatment and outcome. Gurman (1973a) noted that the literature on marital therapy experienced a major growth spurt after 1960, and that half of all the current publications on marital therapy have appeared since 1967. Most of the articles and books published have been multidisciplinary in nature and have consisted primarily of advocated theory and technique, with accompanying case studies.

In addition to the advocacy of preferred

theoretical orientation and technique, current empirical literature concerning marital therapy may be roughly divided into three categories: (1) characteristics of therapists and individuals who become marital therapists, (2) characteristics of individuals and couples who request or are in need of marital therapy, and (3) treatment outcome studies.

Therapist's Characteristics

Studies on therapists' characteristics have been the fewest and have consisted primarily of self-report and observer ratings. Alexander (1975) mailed questionnaires to members of the American Association of Marriage and Family Counselors. He received a two-thirds response and found that professional affiliation was multidisciplinary, that the types of cases treated were varied, and that the majority (85 percent) of the respondents reported seeing couples conjointly as the primary mode of treatment. Gurman (1975) surveyed research related to co-therapy relationships and found that in some cases therapists in joint interviews were rated as significantly poorer than the individual therapists. Knapp (1975) sent 465 questionnaires to a random sample of the clinical membership of the American Association of Marriage and Family Counselors to assess therapists' attitudes toward affairs, swinging, and open marriage. He indicated that 43 percent of the respondents felt negative toward swinging, that 14 percent felt negative toward extramarital sex, and that most were supportive of sexually open marriages. He concluded that therapist biases concerning sexual behavior are widespread. Phillips (Beck, 1975) attempted to assess the clinical prediction of marital therapists by comparing their ratings of the dimension of power in couple relationships to MMPI profiles. He found significant correlations between therapists ratings and MMPI profiles but no significant correlations to indicate the predictive validity of the MMPI.

In a large-scale study, Beck (1966) reported the results of an open-ended questionnaire administered to 400 caseworkers at 104 different agencies and compiled data on a description of the advantages and limitations of conjoint marital therapy. Lanier (1976) examined 22 articles from the *Journal of Marriage and the Family* and *The Family Coordinator*

to determine whether or not the language of the medical model was evident. In three-fourths of the articles, she found that medical terminology was used by writers who disclaimed association with the medical school.

These studies, although limited by the nature of self-report data, indicate that marital therapists are multidisciplinary in nature, with a preference for conjoint couple therapy. They may work with clients more effectively if they do not use co-therapists, and they are biased about sexual relationships. These studies also indicate that marital therapists may have poor diagnostic skills, and although often defining themselves as practitioners who do not employ the medical model in treatment, they nevertheless employ medical terminology.

One must note, however, that the studies described all have methodological problems. Sampling problems, the nature of self-report data, and the relatively few studies on therapists' characteristics require that no conclusions be made from the data.

Client Characteristics

Client characteristics have been widely reported, and studies investigating client characteristics have consisted primarily of descriptive and self-report data. Kimber (1966) compared referred and nonreferred couples, using MMPI profiles. He found that the MMPI profiles were similar for both groups and that no distinguishing differences could be found. Levitt and Baker (1967) compared 25 patients and spouses, using MMPI profiles, and found that the spouse judged most disturbed by a panel of professional judges was not necessarily the spouse who had initiated treatment. In a descriptive study, Green (1975) described the characteristics of 500 consecutive couples who came to a conciliation court in Los Angeles. He found that the predominant characteristics of the couples were that they were middle-class, had had no previous therapy, and complained primarily about money.

In an attempt to relate marital adjustment test scores to shared personal construct test scores, Weigel, Weigel & Richardson (1973) administered self-report tests to 24 married couples and found no significant differences between marital adjustment scores and shared personal constructs; however, they noted the difficulties with instrumentation in their study. Wills, et al (1974) intensively studied seven couples defined as well adjusted and concluded that marital satisfaction may vary in meaning across the sexes. In their study, men valued instrumental behaviors, while women valued affectional behaviors. Wills, et al (1974) had the seven volunteer couples record instrumental events (i.e., taking out the garbage) and affectional events (i.e., overt displays of affection or love on a daily basis) to determine the behavioral determinants of self-reported marital satisfaction or "happiness." They concluded that instrumental and affectional events were the main contributors to daily satisfaction ratings, but that the ratings were more sensitive to aversive events. That is, couples tended to focus on aversive events as opposed to positive events.

Vincent, et al (1975) compared the problem-solving behaviors of 24 distressed versus nondistressed marrieds. They concluded that the problem-solving skills in distressed marrieds are more deficient and more negative than the problem-solving skills in nondistressed marrieds. In a similar study, Fineberg and Lowman (1975) administered self-report inventories to 10 maritally adjusted couples and 10 maritally nonadjusted couples. They concluded that adjusted marrieds communicate more affection and submission than do maladjusted marrieds. Gottman (1976) studied the communication patterns of distressed versus nondistressed couples on high- and low-conflict tasks and found that there was no significant difference in how couples intended their behavior to be received. He found that the behaviors of the distressed spouses were received more negatively and were more consistent with a communication-deficit explanation of distressed marriages. He concluded, however, that there was only minimal data to support the belief that distressed marriages are characterized by more negative reciprocity than nondistressed marriages.

In a study to compare couples who requested sex counseling with couples who requested marital therapy, Frank, et al (1976) evaluated 29 couples seeking marital therapy and 25 couples seeking sexual therapy. They found that the sex-therapy couples were more antagonistic, less conservative, and more thoughtful in their approach to life and their problems. Thurnher (1976) compared marital relations between newlywed and middle-aged couples across socioeconomic classes and found that the middle-aged individual places a greater emphasis on role performance and that the middle-aged woman gives the least positive evaluations of marriage. In another study related to sex differences, Alsbrook (1976) conducted a three-year study of 40 conflicted versus nonconflicted marriages. He found that in the conflicted marriages, the partners struggle for control and that women in conflicted marriages see themselves less positively than they see their husbands. He also indicated that they show low self-disclosure but higher amounts of information sent and understood.

Kleinke (1977) asked 78 male and 109 female students to rate six conflict areas in their marriages and found that males and females conform to the stereotype of assuming that responsibility for conflict concerning finances is the husband's. He also found that males blamed more problems on their wives, whereas females assigned blame equally. Birchler and Webb (1977) gathered self-reports on 50 "happy" versus 50 "unhappy" couples and concluded that the unhappy couples showed a deficit in problem-solving abilities and less involvement with one another.

Fiore and Swenson (1977) matched 35 functional and 35 dysfunctional married couples on age, social, educational, and occupational strata to compare their expressions of love in the marital relationship. He found little difference in expectations of expression of affection but found that functional couples provided more moral support and encouragement for each other. He also found that functional couples expressed more affection for each other than did dysfunctional couples. Frederickson (1977), in a survey to evaluate couples receiving therapy versus couples not receiving therapy, found that a significant number of those receiving therapy had experienced a greater amount of life-stress events during the 12-month period prior to therapy. Glenn and Weaver (1977) surveyed married college-student couples and found that when intercourse was higher than the rate of arguing, couples were "happy," and that when the rate of arguing was higher than the rate of intercourse, couples were definitely unhappy.

Cronkite (1977) examined the determinants of spouses' normative preferences for family roles and the determinants of changes in these roles. After compiling data collected from 681 family interviews, she found that the most significant background determinants of role preference were ethnic origin and education. She also found that the earnings of wives were related to less traditional preferences of both spouses. She also found that the husbands' preferences did not generally dominate the wives' preferences.

Hawkins, et al (1977) examined the relationship between social class and the style of marital communication among 171 couples. They found that the higher the class level, the more contacting and less conventional were the styles of communication. No overall significant differences in communication were found between classes, however. In a study on violence in the family, Araj (1977) administered a family roles questionnaire to 1,154 married men and women and found that a significantly high number of women are pressured through intimidation or force into having sexual relations with their husbands.

These studies indicate that there are few, if any, distinguishing features between those couples who seek marital therapy and those who do not. These studies also indicate that different individuals define marital satisfaction in different ways and that there are sex differences concerning perceptions of the state of the marriage. Couples may focus on the "bad" more than on the "good," and problem marriages may lack effective problem-solving and communication skills. Problem marriages may also be defined by insecurity and power issues, lack of expressed affection, a reaction to life-stress events, and sexual problems. There are also ethnic and class differences that affect the nature of the marital relationship.

In drawing conclusions from this data, one must keep in mind that the studies described are correlational in nature and do not necessarily indicate a causation of marital problems or marital dysfunction. It appears that different couples vary on different problem dimensions and that a dimension that may cause one couple to seek marital therapy may not cause another couple to do so. There are also methodological problems with most of the studies cited.

Treatment Outcome

Treatment outcome studies have differed on two dimensions: (1) on a structured versus unstructured dimension and (2) on a nonbe-

havioral versus behavioral dimension. Nichols (1974) reported that the most common approach to the measurement of treatment outcome is a questionnaire follow-up of marital therapy cases to investigate the effectiveness of treatment.

Mudd (1957) attempted to review existing outcome research prior to 1957, but at the time found no research to summarize. Nichols (1974) reviewed 200 articles published in the field of marital therapy and found that only 20 of the studies related directly to treatment outcome. Of the 20 studies, all had methodological problems.

Comparative studies have consisted of comparing two types of treatment for marital discord. Dicks (1967) studied 100 consecutive marital therapy cases at the Tavistock Institute and measured treatment outcome by client self-report of affect (i.e., feeling better). His results indicated that 20 percent of the short-term conjoint therapy cases felt better, and that 41 percent of the medium-term conjoint therapy cases felt better, and that 53 percent of the long-term conjoint therapy cases felt better. In comparing conjont therapy cases, he reported that 20 percent of the short-term individual cases felt better, that 65 percent of the medium-term individual cases felt better, and that 82 percent of the long-term individual cases felt better. Therefore individual therapy for marital problems had a higher reported success rate.

Burton and Kaplan (1970) mailed questionnaires to 144 clients who had received group marital therapy as opposed to individual counseling for marriages in which one spouse was alcoholic. Results indicated that 76 percent of those treated in group marital counseling reported that they had gained something, whereas 57 percent of those in individual treatment reported that they had gained something. Hickman and Baldwin (1971) saw 30 consecutive couples in a conciliation court and treated 10 couples with unstructured counseling and 10 couples with programmed instruction to improve their communication. An additional 10 couples received no treatment and served as a control group. They reported a significantly greater number of conciliations in the unstructured counseling group.

Cookerly (1976) compared the outcome of four forms of marital counseling: individual interview, individual treatment in a group, concurrent interviews, and concurrent group marital therapy. Comparisons were made on the basis of judges' ratings of outcome from the case histories of 773 clients over a five-year period. Results indicated that conjoint interviews were most effective for couples staying married and least effective for divorcing couples. Conjoint group therapy was better for those obtaining divorces, while concurrent interviews were least effective for those couples remaining married. Overall, conjoint marital therapy was more effective than concurrent marital therapy.

Pierce (1973) compared insight-oriented, conjoint marital therapy to a structured group communication training program that used Rogerian and behavioral components. Of the couples, eight were assigned to each treatment group, and eight couples were assigned to a no-treatment control group. Results indicate that raters found more communication and self-exploration in the communication training group. Ziegler (1973) compared weekly marital group therapy to marathon marital group therapy: six couples were given 20 weekly one-and-a-half-hour sessions of group therapy, while six couples participated in a single marathon session. Results indicated that the marathon group exhibited a wider range of change, whereas the extended group exhibited more intense changes on several personal inventory scales.

Gurman (1973a) reviewed 26 outcome studies in which a wide range of therapeutic techniques had been employed. Gurman calculated an improvement rate across the studies of 66 percent, but noted that all of the studies had methodological problems. In most of the 26 studies, there was a lack of rigor of design, the author was the treatment person, and the most frequently used criterion was global ratings of change measured by the self-report of the client.

Valle and Marinelli (1975) compared five couples treated in a traditional therapy group with an emphasis on cathartic release and problem-solving to five couples treated in a communication skills course. Self-reports indicated that the couples treated in the communication skills course were significantly improved over the couples treated in the traditional group therapy.

Brady (1977) compared short-term behavioral and interventional therapy in a community mental health center to nonstructured therapy. The 20 consecutive couples were assigned randomly to either treatment group. Results indicate that self-reports of marital satisfaction significantly improved in both treatment groups and that there was no significant difference in self-report between the two treatment groups. In the behavioral group, raters found a significant difference for more positive and mutually supportive verbal and nonverbal behaviors.

Other treatment outcome studies, which have differed on the structured- versus unstructured-treatment-approach dimension, have included self-report and rater report as measures of outcome. One of the first treatment outcome studies was conducted by Ballard and Mudd (1957). At the Marriage Council of Philadelphia, they sampled 54 couples receiving marital counseling. Treatment outcome was measured by judges who reviewed ratings of client self-reports and case records. A global judgment of improvement indicated that judges rated 59 percent of the couples improved, while client self-reports rated 52 percent of the couples improved. In another early study, Whitaker (1958) reported on 30 couples he had treated in conjoint therapy. His self-report of treatment outcome was that, of the 30 couples, 6 withdrew from treatment and 10 ended with no change in one member. Therefore his success rate was less than 50 percent.

Brandreth and Pike (1967) sampled 50 husbands and 50 wives receiving marital counseling at a family counseling service. Treatment outcome was measured by global ratings of improvement made by the clients and the therapists. Their findings indicate that 62 percent of the individuals receiving marital therapy had improved. Bellville, et al (1969) studied the outcome of conjoint short-term therapy for sexual incompatibility. Of the couples, 44 were treated in 16 sessions, and client self-reports were used to indicate success. The results indicate that 27 couples completed the program: 21 reported that treatment was successful. Of the 17 couples not completing treatment, 5 reported that treatment was successful, 12 reported that treatment was not successful, and 7 divorced. Therefore the success rate was 59 percent.

Fitzgerald (1969) evaluated 57 couples

whom he had seen in conjoint therapy. Of the couples, 31 had come for individual treatment and 26 had come for marital conflict. After an average of 26 hours of treatment, outcome was measured 2.5 years after the last treatment session by client self-report and the author's evaluation. Results indicated that three-fourths of the couples in both problem groups were judged improved.

Reid and Shyne (1969) randomly assigned 48 couples in a community counseling center to short-term treatment versus long-term treatment. Treatment outcome was measured by caseworker evaluation and research interviewers' evaluations. Results indicated that research interviewers rated 65 percent improved with short-term therapy and 55 percent improved with long-term therapy. Caseworkers rated 64 percent improved with short-term therapy and 48 percent improved with long-term therapy.

Targow and Zweber (1969) evaluated 13 couples treated in a couples group in a private practice setting. Outcome measure was a global rating scale in a mailed questionnaire. Results indicated that 92 percent of the husbands reported improvement, while 69 percent of the wives reported improvement. Beutler (1971) administered pre- and post-test measures to 10 couples seen conjointly to compare their attitudes with the therapist's attitudes. Results indicated that improvement was correlated with the convergence of attitudes between the two partners but not between the two partners and the therapist.

Beck and Jones (1973) reviewed for the Family Service Association of America the records of 1919 cases with marital problems. Over half (1257) had a marital problem as the presenting problem. Of this group, 58 percent responded to a follow-up global-rating and composite-change questionnaire: counselors and clients were asked independently to rate indicators in the areas of change in presenting problem, the client's approach to problem-solving in the family, the client's approach to individual family members, and family relationships. Results indicated that one-half of the clients reported improvement outside the marriage relationship and two-thirds reported improvement on a global basis. Clients reported improvement more frequently than did counselors. Although this study described

the results of counseling, it is included here because of its large number of subjects and the inability to distinguish the type of treatment used on the basis of therapy versus counseling.

Cadogan (1973) provided marital group therapy to 35 male and 5 female hospitalized alcoholics. Marital group therapy emphasized problem-solving techniques. A six-month follow-up indicated that nine subjects in the group treatment were abstinent, and that for all subjects, relapses occurred within three months of ending hospitalization.

Gurman (1974) studied the convergence of therapist and client attitudes as a variable related to therapy outcome. Using 12 couples in co-therapy, he concluded that patient-attitude convergence is related to positive outcome. Scheinbein (1974) studied the effects of test feedback on the outcome of marital therapy. He divided 30 couples into 3 groups: a nondirective-discussion-of-test-results group, a direct-feedback group, and a control group. His results indicate that the nondirective discussion of the results provided more improved relationship patterns over time.

Watzlawick, Weakland, and Fisch (1974) studied the outcome of brief marital therapy. For a total of 10 sessions, 97 couples were seen, with treatment consisting of interpersonal-directed paradoxical interventions. Results in terms of specific problem resolution as measured by self-report indicate that 40 percent of the cases were treated successfully, that 32 percent of the cases were treated significantly improved, and that 27 percent of the cases were failures. Edelson and Sedman (1975) used videotape versus verbal feedback with 39 college-student couples. On self-report measures of changed perceptions, the results indicated that the videotape altered couples' perceptions more significantly than did verbal feedback, but the changed perceptions applied to self rather than to spouse.

Knox (1975) reported attempting specifically to treat the wife's feelings of being a sex object in the marriage. He treated 10 couples conjointly; after termination, 5 couples reported that they had achieved their goals in treatment. Frank and Kupfer (1976) reported the effects of a marital therapy group on 10 couples seen for marital therapy versus 10 couples seen for sexual dysfunction, and reported that the marital therapy group reported a greater discrepancy in their views of marriage after treatment.

Behavioral studies indicate that behavior-change skills can be taught to couples, with resulting changes in desired behavior, and that no one specific behavior-change model is superior to another. Comparative studies indicate contradictory results for preferred mode of treatment, although there is some evidence to indicate the validity of including communication-skills training for couples in the treatment program. Other treatment outcome studies indicate that the success rate for a variety of treatment modalities rarely exceeds 65 percent, and that results are often contradictory.

It must be noted that, as with studies of therapists' and clients' characteristics, there are numerous methodological problems in the research cited. Virtually none of the current studies meet the criteria for adequate research designs. The major methodological problems consist of self-report or therapist-report data as opposed to objective data, lack of control groups, lack of random sampling procedures, and lack of pre- and post-test measures. Another major problem is that few studies include more than 10 to 20 couples as subjects; therefore it is impossible to generalize treatment outcomes to any specific populations.

DISCUSSION AND COMMENTS

It attempting to assess the current state of marital therapy, it is important that one look at theory, the role of the therapist, treatment, clients served, research, and, finally, values.

Theory

Marital therapy has been criticized as an ill-defined field, lacking an adequate theoretical base (Ackerman, 1972; Allen, 1975; Bowen, 1978; Haley, 1971b; Olson, 1970). In an earlier paper, Manus (1966) described marital therapy as a technique in search of a theory. From the current literature in the field, this criticism appears well-founded. Although theoretical development has increased in the last 10 years, there is still no widely shared language and no comprehensive theoretical foundation (Vines, 1979).

There has been the development of specific comprehensive theories to explain marital distress and dysfunction. These theories, however, tend to stress specific unitary components of behavior rather than more global or more integrated components of dyadic relationships. As has been noted in this chapter, major theories stress altering feelings, altering rationality, or altering behavior, with no theory incorporating all three areas of human functioning. Each major theoretical orientation presupposes that changing one area of functioning (feelings, thoughts, or behavior) will produce changes in the other two areas.

Basic to the lack of a more integrated theory is the lack of a universal definition of a dysfunctional, as opposed to a functional marriage. Although marital satisfaction, growth, and happiness are often stressed as characteristics of a functional marriage, the characteristics of a dysfunctional marriage are not clear. In addition, current therapy may be too simplistic to explain dyadic relationships aside from specific theories and practitioners. Sprenkle and Fisher (1980), in a survey of marital therapists' goals, found the majority of goals to be the improvement of communication skills. Although communication deficits have been found to correlate with marital dissatisfaction, to attribute causality rather than symptomatology to communication skills may ignore the numerous difficulties and issues underlying the marital relationship.

Role of the Therapist

The role of the marital therapist is, like theory, vague and often unclear. The majority of practicing marital therapists are self-taught and from other formal disciplines. There currently exists no consensus on training standards or the components of formal training. Liddle and Halpin (1980) have recently criticized the therapist as becoming more of an activist promoting a new philosophy than a healer focusing on the problem of alleviating distress.

Treatment

Treatment is increasingly focusing on the optimal growth of the individual and the relationship. Increased intimacy is being stressed, as in increased marital satisfaction. These goals may be more philosophically ideal than practical, for there appears to be no evidence that these goals are often, if ever, achieved.

Although conjoint treatment is emphasized as more effective than individual therapy, difficulties for the therapist in conjoint marital therapy are usually ignored. The issue of multiple transference issues operating among and between three or more persons is not addressed, nor is the knowledge of group, in addition to couple, dynamics. Marital therapy may be a much more difficult enterprise than theorists and practitioners currently acknowledge, simply because more persons are involved in the treatment and the nature of the group interaction requires an extensive psychological, sociological, and cultural understanding.

Clients Served

One must acknowledge that, to date, as with individual and other forms of psychotherapy, marital therapy is a treatment developed and practiced primarily with middle-class couples. Whether or not theory and practice are relevant to other, differing dyads remains to be seen.

Research and Evaluation

The current state of research in the field of marital therapy still lacks not only quantity but quality. Although current behavioral research claims valid and often excellent results, it must be noted that behavioral research attempts to measure complex relationships by assessing only a few discrete, concrete variables in the marital relationship (i.e., exhibition of specific behaviors.). The widespread methodological problems include using instrumentation with little or no established validity and reliability, and using self-report data without acknowledging the possibility of improvement reported for any reasons other than real gains (i.e., justifying treatment or pleasing the therapist). Raters are often used without consideration for rater bias, and therapist ratings are often used as the criteria for "improvement." There are relatively few studies that include control groups, and there is a lack of breadth in treatment populations. Therefore outcomes are restricted to relatively small numbers of, usually, middle-class clients.

Other research studies have the same methodological problems as current behavioral research but include lack of specificity of treatment, as well. Their primary methodological problems are lack of pre- and post-test measures, lack of control groups, lack of objective instrumentation, and sampling problems.

The major question about the current state of research in marital therapy concerns its applicability to treatment and practice. Unfortunately, studies have not been replicated with representative samples, nor has treatment always been defined in such a way that it can be replicated. Most studies have not only used middle-class clients but have failed to relate individual differences to outcome.

Finally, criterion measures in most studies related to marital therapy are satisfaction–happiness measures. Satisfaction–happiness criteria are usually ill-defined and may lead researchers to ignore other important and relevant theoretical questions. In addition, marriage is still seen as a closed system, with little data contributed to theory and practice from other fields. Cultural and environmental factors are still relatively ignored as input to the understanding of marital relationships.

Values

Banks (1965) has stated that every therapist is engaged in altering human values. Values concerning human behavior are inherent in any form of therapy. The inherent values of the marital therapist are rarely stated or addressed, even though one may raise questions about the values implied in marital therapies. Coleman (1977) has criticized marital therapists for valuing only marital relationships, excluding other dyadic relationships. Fisher (1975) has also criticized the marital therapists for addressing only marriages, stating that the title "marital therapist" ignores the high divorce rate and the reality that many individuals actually live and relate in a variety of dyadic and group arrangements.

In addition to the failure to address all intimate dyadic relationships per se, current ideas of increased "growth" and intimacy may continue to perpetuate an adjustment model to earlier values concerning a romantic and all-fulfilling relationship. While the public begins to acknowledge the failure of marriages to fulfill these often idealistic expectations, marital therapists may continue to advocate the promise of unrealistic, all-meaningful, and intense relationship.

The marital therapist must also address his or her own values on a number of issues, including the negotiation of roles, various sexual issues and practices, divorce, dual-career couples, and changing societal roles and values. Maladjustment as defined by some marital therapists may merely be a couple's violation of accepted cultural norms and values. Since most literature reports work with traditional couple relationships, one could conclude that only the traditional couple relationship is valued by many practitioners.

Other authors (Blood, 1976; Humphrey, 1975; Wolman, 1976) have criticized marital therapy for ignoring the effect of the women's movement on changing life styles, life goals, value systems, and interpersonal relationships. Laws (1971), in a recent survey of the literature, reports that traditional stereotypic views of women are still held by most authors, who assume that women's roles are nurturing ones while men's roles are instrumental and providing ones.

What the marital therapist specifically values is certainly not known, and only conjectures about the effect of values on practice can be made at this point. It must be acknowledged, however, that the definition of a satisfactory marital relationship will include the therapist's value system.

The development of marital therapies offers a needed alternative treatment approach to what have traditionally been individual approaches that ignore the importance of one's interpersonal environment. Since there are still no clear definitions of marital health or marital dysfunction, however, approaches to marital therapy vary widely and still lack unified concepts and goals. A systemic view of the dyadic relationship is widely acknowledged, improving marital satisfaction is widely acknowledged, and alleviating presenting symptoms is widely acknowledged. Beyond these three aspects, however, there is little integration of theory, goals, and treatment approaches. Jackson (1973) stated that marital therapy is like a Lolita theory because it appears older, wiser, and more complex than it really is. From current literature and practice,

it does indeed appear that marital therapy seems more complex than it really is, for it remains an ill-defined field that lacks any integrated theory or treatment approaches.

THE FUTURE

The current state of marital therapy has numerous implications for future practice, for it is possible that its divergent state may lead to an even greater conglomerate of nonvalidated theories and techniques, which may or may not be relevant to the treatment of marital dysfunction. Therefore several areas deserve consideration for the further development of marital therapy:

1. *Theory and practice considerations.* Theory needs to become more integrated through basic research. The effects of cultural changes, the role of the women's movement, and the role of changing values need to be addressed. Current hypotheses need to be empirically validated as well. Practice is ill-defined and rarely based on theoretical considerations, and future practice needs to be derived from a sound theoretical base.

2. *Therapist value considerations.* Currently unclear, either in literature or in the code of ethics published by the American Association of Marriage and Family Therapists, is the therapists's value system concerninig the definitions of a healthy marriage, divorce, various sexual practices, and alternative life styles. It is implied that the marital therapist values only the marital relationship as a valid dyadic relationship. The question of therapist biases needs to be clarified by a definition of marital therapy that is more detailed than its current global definition.

3. *Client considerations.* The field of marital therapy needs to develop and evidence treatment modalities for those clients who are other than middle-class.

4. *Training considerations.* Currently, marital therapists are multidisciplinary, and few have training directly related to marital therapy. The confused nature of training often leads to the confused nature of practice. It is suggested that training pro-

grams need to be further developed to include theory, research, and practice, with an emphasis on treatment.

5. *Research considerations.* Research is needed to validate and/or invalidate current theories of marital dysfunction and treatment. It is important that the diverse theories and techniques be integrated into viable treatment considerations.

In summary, it must be emphasized that the current state of marital therapy appears somewhat confused in both theory and practice. This statement does not negate the importance of marital therapy nor its effectiveness with many clients under many different conditions. Nevertheless, the field needs to assess its status in relation to effective treatment and begin to integrate its rapid and divergent growth.

REFERENCES

AAMFC board votes to support name change. *AAMFC Newsletter*, May 1978, pp. 1, 7

Ackerman N. Behavior trends and disturbances of the contemporary family. In I Goldston (Ed), *The family in contemporary society*. New York: International University Press, 1958

Ackerman N. The growing edge of family therapy. In C Sager & HS Kaplan (Eds), *Progress in group and family therapy*. New York: Brunner/ Mazel, 1972

Alexander F. The empirical study of the differential influence of self-concept on the professional behavior of marriage counselors. In D Beck (author), Research findings on the outcome of marital counseling, *Social Casework*, 1975, *56*, 53–181

Alger I. Integrating immediate video playback in family therapy. In D Guerin (Ed), *Family therapy: Theory and practice*. New York: Gardner Press, Inc., 1976

Allen T. For our next act . . . an unsystematic prescript to marriage and family counseling. *The Counseling Psychologist*, 1975, *5*, 3–15

Allred G. *How to strengthen your marriage and family*. Provo, UT: Brigham Young University Press, 1976

Alsbrook L. Marital communication and sexism. *Social Casework*, 1976, *57*, 517–522

Araj S. Husbands and wives: Attitude-behavior congruence on family roles. *Journal of Marriage and the Family*, 1977, *39*, 309–320

Ard B. Assumptions underlying marriage counseling. *Marriage Counseling Quarterly*, 1967, *2*, 20–24

Aries P. *Centuries of childhood: A social history of family life*. New York: Vintage Books, 1962

Arlow JA. Object concept and object choice: Symposium on object-relations theory and love. *Psychoanalytic Quarterly*, 1980, *49*, 109–133

Bak R. Being in love and object loss. *International Journal of Psychoanalysis*, 1973, *55*, 1–8

Ballard R, & Mudd E. Some theoretical and practical problems in evaluating effectiveness of counseling. *Social Casework*, 1957, *38*, 533–538

Bandler R, & Grinder J. *The structure of magic: A book about communication and change*. Palo Alto, CA: Behavior Books, 1976

Bandler R, Grinder J, & Satir V. *Changing with families*. Palo Alto, CA: Science and Behavior Books, 1976

Banks S. Psychotherapy: Values in action. In P Regan (Ed), *International Psychiatry Clinics' Behavioral Science Contributions to Psychiatry*, Vol. 2, 1965, *2*, 497–515

Bateson G, Jackson D, Haley J, & Weakland J. Toward a theory of schizophrenia. In D Jackson (Ed), *Communication, family and marriage*. Palo Alto, CA: Science and Behavior Books, 1968

Bayer A. Early dating and early marriage. In B Adams & T Weiroth (Eds), *Readings on the sociology of the family*. Chicago: Markham Publishing Co., 1971

Beck D. Marital conflict: Its course and treatment as seen by caseworkers. *Social Casework*, 1966, *47*, 211–221

Beck D. Research findings on the outcome of marital counseling. *Social Casework*, 1975, *56*, 153–181

Beck D, & Jones MA. *Progress on family problems. A nationwide study of clients' and counselors' views on family agency services*. New York: Family Service Association of America, 1973

Beels C, & Ferber R. What family therapists do. In A Ferber, M Mendelsohn, & A Napier (Eds.), *The book of family therapy*. New York: Science House, 1972

Bell J. Family group therapy—A new treatment method for children. *Family Process*, 1967, *6*, 254–263

Bell J. *Family therapy*. New York: Jason Aronson, 1975

Bellville T, Raths O, & Bellville C. Conjoint marriage therapy with a husband-and-wife team. *American Journal of Orthopsychiatry*, 1969, *39*, 73–83

Beres D, & Obers J. The effects of extreme deprivation in infancy on psychic structure in adolescence: A study in ego development. In

Psychoanalytic study of the child (Vol. 5). New York: International Universities Press, 1950, pp. 212–235

Bergmann MS. On the intrapsychic functions of falling in love. *Psychoanalytic Quarterly*, 1980, *49*, 56–77

Berman MS. On the intrapsychic function of falling in love: Symposium on object-relations theory and love. *Psychoanalytic Quarterly*, 1980, *49*, 56–77

Bertalanffy L von. *General system theory: Foundations, development, applications*. New York: George Braziller, 1968

Beutler L. Attitude similarity in marital therapy. Journal of Consulting and Clinical Psychiatry, 1971, *37*, 298–301

Birchler G, & Webb L. Discriminating interaction behaviors in happy and unhappy marriages. *Journal of Consulting and Clinical Psychology*, 1977, *45*, 494–495

Blood R. Research needs of a family life educator and marriage counselor. *Journal of Marriage and the Family*, 1976, *38*, 7–12

Blood R, & Wolfe D. Husbands and wives. New York: The Free Press, 1960

Bockus F. A systems approach to marital process. *Journal of Marriage and Family Counseling*, 1975, *1*, 251–258

Bockus F. *Couple therapy*. New York: Jason Aronson, 1980

Boerop JL. Marital therapy: An existential approach. *Family Therapy*, 1975, *2*, 269–276

Boesky D. Introduction: Symposium on object-relations theory and love. *Psychoanalytic Quarterly*, 1980, *49*, 49–55

Bolte G. A communications approach to marital counseling. *The Family Coordinator*, 1970, *19*, 32–40

Boszormenyi-Nagy I, & Spark GM. *Invisible loyalties*. New York: Harper & Row, 1973

Boszormenyi-Nagy IA. A theory of relationships: Experiences and transactions. In I Boszormenyi-Nagy & JL Framo (Eds.), *Intensive family therapy*. New York: Hoeber, 1965

Bowen M. Principles and techniques of multiple family therapy. In J Bradt & C Moynihan (Eds), *Systems therapy—selected papers: Theory, technique and research*. Washington, D.C.: Broome Center, 1972

Bowen M. *Family therapy in clinical practice*. New York: Jason Aronson, 1978

Bowlby J. The study and reduction of group tensions in the family. *Human Relations*, 1949, *2*, 123–128

Bowlby J. *Attachment and loss*. New York: Basic Books, 1969

Brady J. An empirical study of behavioral marital therapy in groups. *Behavior Therapy*, 1977, *8*, 512–513

Brandreth A, & Pike R. Assessment of marriage counseling in a small family agency. *Social Work*, 1967, *12*, 34–39

Burgess EW. The family as a unity of interacting personalities. *The Family*, 1926, 7, 3–9

Burton G, & Kaplan HM. Group counseling in conflicted marriages where alcoholism is present: Clients' evaluation of effectiveness. *Journal of Marriage and the Family*, 1970, *30*, 74–79

Cadogan DA. Marital group therapy in the treatment of alcoholism. *Quarterly Journal of Studies on Alcohol*, 1973, *34*(4-A), 1187–1194

Carter EA, & McGoldrick M. The family life cycle and family therapy: An overview. In EA Carter & M McGoldrick (Eds), *The family life cycle*. New York: Gardner Press, 1980

Coleman S. A developmental stage hypothesis for nonmarital dyadic relationships. *Journal of Marriage and Family Counseling*, April 1977, pp. 71–76

Cookerly JR. Evaluating different approaches to marriage counseling. In D Olson (Ed), *Treating relationships*. Lake Mills, IA: Graphic, 1976

Cromwell R, & Keeney B. Diagnosing marital and family systems: A training model. *The Family Coordinator*, 1979, *28*, 101–108

Cronkite R. The determinants of spouse's normative preferences for family roles. *Journal of Marriage and the Family*, 1977, *39*, 575–585

Crosby J. *Illusion and disillusion: The self in love and marriage*. Belmont, CA: Wadsworth Publishing Co., 1976

Crowe MJ. Conjoint marital therapy: Advice or interpretation. *Journal of Psychosomatic Research*, 1973, *17*, 309–315

Dicks HV. Experiences with marital tensions in the psychological clinic. *British Journal of Medical Psychology*, 1953, *26*, 181–196

Dicks HV. Object-relations theory and marital studies. *British Journal of Medical Psychology*, 1963, *36*, 125–129

Dicks HV. *Marital tensions*. New York: Basic Books, 1967

Eckland B. Theories of mate selection. In B Adams & T Weiroth (Eds), *Readings on the sociology of the family*. Chicago: Markham Publishing Co., 1972

Edelson R, & Sedman E. Use of videotaped feedback in altering interpersonal perceptions of married couples: A therapy analogue. *Journal of Consulting and Clinical Psychology*, 1975, *43*, 244–250

Ellis A. *Humanistic psychotherapy: The rational-emotive approach*. New York: The Julian Press, Inc., 1973

English F. The substitution factor: Rackets and real feelings. Part I. *Transactional Analysis Journal*, 1971, *1*, 225

Erikson G, & Hogan T. *Family therapy: An intro-*

duction to theory and technique. Monterey, CA: Brooks/Cole, 1972

Ewing D. Twenty approaches to individual change. *The Personnel and Guidance Journal*, February 1977, pp. 331–338

Fineberg B, & Lowman J. Affect and status dimensions of marital adjustment. *Journal of Marriage and the Family*, 1975, *37*, 155–160

Fiore A, & Swenson C. Analysis of love relationships in functonal and dysfunctional marriages. *Psychological Reports*, 1977, *40*(3, Pt 1), 707–714

Fisher E. Divorce counseling and values. *Journal of Religion and Health*, 1975, *14*, 265–270

Fitzgerald R. Conjoint marital psychotherapy: An outcome and follow-up study. *Family Process*, 1969, *8*, 260–271

Fogharty T. Marital crisis. In PJ Guerin (Ed), *Family therapy, theory and practice*. New York: Gardner Press, 1976

Foley V. *An introduction to family therapy*. New York: Grune & Stratton, 1974

Frank E, Anderson C, & Kupfer D. Profiles of couples seeking sex therapy and marital therapy. *American Journal of Psychiatry*, 1976, *133*, 559–562

Frank E, & Kupfer D. In every marriage there are two marriages. *Journal of Sex and Marital Therapy*, 1976, *2*, 137–143

Frankl VE. *Psychotherapy and existentialism: Selected papers on logotherapy*. New York: Washington Square Press, Inc., 1967

Frederickson CG. Life stress and marital conflict: A pilot study. *Journal of Marriage and Family Counseling*, 1977, *3*, 41–47

Friedman LJ. Integrating psychoanalytic object-relations understanding with family systems intervention in couples therapy. In JK Pearce & LJ Friedman (Eds), *Combining psychodynamic and family systems approaches*. New York: Grune & Stratton, 1980

Friedman P. Personalistic family and marital therapy. In A Lazarus (Ed), *Clinical behavior therapy*. New York: Brunner/Mazel, 1972

Friedman P. Outline (alphabet) of 26 techniques of family and marital therapy A through Z. *Psychotherapy: Theory, Research and Practice*, 1974, *2*, 259–263

Giovacchini P. The treatment of marital disharmonies: The classical approach. In BL Greene (Ed), *The psychotherapies of marital disharmony*. New York: The Free Press, 1965

Glasser W. *Reality therapy*. New York: Harper & Row, 1965

Glenn N, & Weaver C. The marital happiness of remarried divorced persons. *Journal of Marriage and the Family*, 1977, *39*, 331–337

Gottman J. Behavior exchange theory and marital decision making. *Journal of Personality and Social Psychology*, 1976, *34*, 14–23

Goulding M, & Goulding RL. *Changing lives through redecision therapy*. New York: Brunner/Mazel, 1979

Green, BC. Marital disharmony: Concurrent analysis of husband and wife. *Diseases of the Nervous System*, 1975, *21*, 73–83

Green BL (Ed). *The psychotherapies of marital disharmony*. New York: The Free Press, 1965

Guerin PJ, & Guerin KB. Theoretical aspects and clinical relevance of the multi-generational model of family therapy. In PJ Guerin (Ed), *Family therapy, theory and practice*. New York: Gardner Press, 1976

Guerney LF. Filial therapy program. In D Olson (Ed), *Treating relationships*. Lake Mills, IA: Graphics, 1976

Gurin G, Veroff J, & Feld S. *Americans view their mental health*. New York: Basic Books, 1960

Gurman AS. The effects and effectiveness of marital therapy: A review of outcome research. *Family Process*, 1973a, *12*, 145–170

Gurman AS. Marital therapy: Emerging trends in research and practice. *Family Process*, 1973b, *12*, 45–53

Gurman AS. Attitude change in marital co-therapy. *Journal of Family Counseling*, 1974, *2*, 50–51

Gurman AS. Some therapeutic implications of marital therapy research. In AS Gurman & DG Rice (Eds), *Couples in conflict: New directions in marital therapy*. New York: Jason Aronson, 1975, pp. 407–429

Gurman AS. Contemporary marital therapies: A critique and comparative analysis of psychoanalytic, behavioral and systems theory approaches. In TJ Paolino & BS McCrady (Eds), *Marriage and marital therapy: Psychoanalytic, behavioral and systems therapy perspectives*. New York: Brunner/Mazel, Inc., 1978

Gurman AS. Couples' facilitative communication skill as a dimension of marital therapy outcome. *Journal of Marriage and Family Counseling*, 1979, *1*, 5–16

Gurman AS, & Kniskern DP. *Handbook of family therapy*. New York: Brunner/Mazel, 1982

Gurman AS, & Rice D (Eds). *Couples in conflict*. New York: Jason Aronson, 1978

Hale BJ. Gestalt techniques in marriage counseling. *Social Casework*, 1978, *71*, 428–433

Haley J. An interactional description of schizophrenia. *Psychiatry*, 1959, *22*, 321–332

Haley J. Marriage therapy. *Archives of General Psychiatry*, 1963a, *8*, 213–234

Haley J. *Strategies of psychotherapy*. New York: Grune & Stratton, 1963b

Haley J. *The power tactics of Jesus Christ and other essays*. New York: Grossman, 1969

Haley J. *Changing families*. New York: Grune & Stratton, 1971a

Haley J. Family therapy: A radical change. In J Haley (Ed.), *Changing Families*. New York: Grune & Stratton, 1971b

Haley J. Marriage therapy. In GD Erickson & TP Hogan (Eds), *Family therapy: An introduction to theory and technique*. Monterey, CA: Brooks/Cole, 1972

Haley J. *Uncommon therapy*. New York: WW Norton, 1973

Haley J. *Problem-solving therapy*. San Francisco: Jossey-Bass, 1976

Hall CM. *The Bowen family theory and its uses*. New York: Jason Aronson, 1981

Hansen JC, & L'Abate L. *Approaches to family therapy*. New York: Macmillan, 1982

Havens LL. *Approaches to the mind*. Boston: Little, Brown & Co., 1973

Hawkins J, Weisberg C, & Ray D. Marital communication: Style and social class. *Journal of Marriage and the Family*, 1977, *39*, 479–490

Heidegger M. *Existence and being*. Chicago: Henry Regnery, 1949

Hickman ME, & Baldwin BA. Use of programmed instruction to improve communication in marriage. *The Family Coordinator*, 1971, *20*, 121–125

Holt M, & Greiner C. Co-therapy in the treatment of families. In P Guerin (Ed), *Family Therapy: Theory and Practice*. New York: Gardner Press, 1976

Humphrey F. Changing roles for women. Implications for marriage counselors. *Journal of Marriage and Family Counseling*, 1975, *1*, 219–227

Hunt R, & Rydman E. *Creative marriage*. Boston: Holbrook, 1976

Hurvitz N. The marital roles inventory as a counseling instrument. *Journal of Marriage and the Family*, 1965, *27*, 492–501

Jackson D. Marital quid-pro-quid: Family rules. *Archives of General Psychiatry*, 1965, *12*, 589–594

Jackson D. Aspects of conjoint family therapy. In G Zuk & I Boszormenyi-Nagy (Eds), *Family therapy and disturbed families*. Palo Alto, CA: Science and Behavior Books, 1973

Jacobson NS. Specific and nonspecific factors in the effectiveness of a behavioral approach to marital discord. *Journal of Consulting and Clinical Psychology*, 1978, *46*, 442–452

Jacobson NS, & Martin B. Behavioral marriage therapy: Current status. *Psychological Bulletin*, 1976, *83*, 540–566

Jaspers K. *Reason and existence*. New York: Noonday, 1955

Jourard SM. Marriage is for life. In ID Welch, GA Tate, & F Richards (Eds), *Humanistic psychology: A source book*. Buffalo, NY: Prometheus Books, 1978

Kantor D, & Lehr W. *Inside the family: Toward a theory of family process*. New York: Harper & Row, 1975

Kaplan ML, & Kaplan NR. Individual and family growth: A Gestalt approach. *Family Process*, 1978, *17*, 195–205

Kaslow F. Essay review: Marital therapy, monogamy and menages. *Journal of Marital and Family Counseling*, 1975, *1*, 281–287

Keeney B, & Cromwell R. Toward systematic diagnosis. *Family Therapy*, 1977, *4*(3)

Kempler W. Experimental family therapy. In J Haley (Ed), *Changing Families*. New York: Grune & Stratton, 1971

Kempler W. *Principles of Gestalt family therapy*. Costa Mesa, CA: Kempler Institute, 1973

Kernberg OF. *Object-relations theory and clinical psychoanalysis*. New York: Jason Aronson, 1976

Kernberg OF. *Internal world and external reality: Object-relations theory applied*. New York: Jason Aronson, 1980

Kimber J. Referred and unreferred patients: A comparison. *Journal of Marriage and the Family*, 1966, *28*, 293–295

Kleinke C. Assignment of responsibility for marital conflict to husbands and wives: Sex stereotypes or a double standard? *Psychological Reports*, 1977, *41*, 219–222

Knapp J. Some non-monogamous marriage styles and related attitudes and practices of marriage counselors. *The Family Coordinator*, 1975, *24*, 505–514

Knox D. *Marriage happiness: A behavioral approach to counseling*. Champaign, IL: Research Press, 1971

Knox D. Affection vs. intercourse: Or all he wants is my body. *Journal of Family Counseling*, 1975, *3*, 65–66

Koffka K. Gestalt psychology. *Psychological Bulletin*, 1922, *19*, pp. 29–42

Kohler W. *Gestalt psychology*. New York: The New American Library, 1947

L'Abate L. *Understanding and helping the individual in the family*. New York: Grune & Stratton, 1976

L'Abate L, & Frey J, III. The e-r-a model: The role of feelings in family therapy reconsidered: Implications for a classification of theories of family therapy. *Journal of Marital and Family Therapy*, 1981, *42*, 143–150

L'Abate L, Sloan S, Wagner V, & Malone K. The differentiation of resources. *Family Therapy*, 1980, *7*, 237–246

Laing RD *The politics of experience*. New York: Ballantine Books, 1967

Laing RD, & Esterson A. *Sanity, madness and the family*. Baltimore: Penguin Books, Inc., 1973

Lanier M. The medical model, mental illness and metaphoric mystification among marriage and family counselors. *The Family Coordinator,* 1976, *25,* 175–181

Lantz H. *Marital incompatibility and social change in early America.* Beverly Hills: Sage, 1976

Lasswell M, & Lobenz N. *No-fault marriage: The new technique of self-counseling and what it can do to help you.* New York: Doubleday, 1976

Laws JL. A feminist view of marital adjustment literature: The rape of the Locke. *Journal of Marriage and the Family,* 1971, *33,* 483–516

Lazarus A. *Behavior therapy and beyond.* New York: McGraw-Hill, 1971

Lederer W, & Jackson D. *The mirages of marriage.* New York: Norton, 1968

Leichter E. Treatment of married couples in groups. *The Family Coordinator,* 1973, *22,* 31–42

Leslie G. Conjoint therapy in marriage counseling. *Journal of Marriage and the Family,* 1964, *26,* 65–71

Leslie G. Conjoint therapy in marriage counseling. In W Nichols (Ed), *Marriage and family therapy.* Minneapolis: Minneapolis Council on Family Relations, 1974

Levant R. Family therapy: A client-centered perspective. *Journal of Marriage and Family Counseling,* 1978, *4,* 35–42

Levitt H, & Baker R. Relative psychopathology of marital partners. *Family Process,* 1967, *8,* 33–42

Liberman RP, Wheeler E, & Sanders N. Behavioral therapy for marital disharmony: An educational approach. *Journal of Marriage and Family Counseling,* 1976, *2,* 383–395

Liddle H, & Halpin R. Family therapy training and supervision: A comparative review. *Journal of Marriage and Family Counseling,* 1978, *4,* 77–98

Luthman S. The growth model in marital therapy. *Family Therapy,* 1977, *1,* 63–87

Mace D. Marriage as relationship in depth. Some implications for counseling. In HL Silverman (Ed), *Marital therapy.* Springfield, IL: Charles C. Thomas, 1972

MacLennan D. Co-therapy. *International Journal of Group Psychotherapy,* 1976, *15,* 154–165

Mahrer AR. *Experiencing: A humanistic theory of psychology and psychiatry.* New York: Brunner/Mazel, 1978

Manus GI. Marriage counseling: A technique in search of a theory. *Journal of Marriage and the Family,* 1966, *28,* 449–453

Markowitz MF. A short-term analytic treatment of married couples in a group by a therapist couple. In BF Reiss (Ed), *New directions in mental health.* New York: Grune & Stratton, 1968

Maslow AH. *Toward a psychology of being.* New York: Van Nostand, 1962

May R. *Love and Will.* New York: W. W. Norton & Co, 1969

Meissner WW. The conceptualization of marriage and famiily dynamics from a psychoanalytic perspective. In TJ Paolino & BS McCrady (Eds), *Marriage and marital therapy: Psychoanalytic, behavioral and systems theory perspectives.* New York: Brunner/Mazel, 1978

Melville K. *Marriage and family today.* New York: Random House, 1977

Minuchin S. Conflict resolution family therapy. In G Erikson & T Hogan (Eds), *Family therapy: An introduction to theory and technique.* Belmont, CA: Wadsworth, 1972

Minuchin S. *Families and family therapy.* Cambridge: Harvard University Press, 1974

Misiak H, & Sexton VS. *Phenomenological, existential, and humanistic psychologies: A historical survey.* New York: Grune & Stratton, 1973

Mudd EH. Knowns and unknowns in marriage counseling research. *Marriage and Family Living,* 1957, *19,* 75–81

Nadelson CC. Marital therapy from a psychoanalytic perspective. In TJ Paolino & BS McCrady (Eds), *Marriage and marital therapy: Psychoanalytic, behavioral and systems perspectives.* New York: Brunner/Mazel, 1978

Napier A, & Whitaker CA. A conversation about co-therapy. In A Ferber, M Mendolsohn, & A Napier (Eds), *The book of family therapy.* New York: Science House, 1972

Napier AY, & Whitaker CA. *The family crucible.* New York: Harper & Row, 1978

Nichols WC. The field of marriage counseling: A brief overview. In WC Nichols (Ed), *Marriage and family therapy.* Minneapolis: The National Council on Family Relations, 1974

O'Connor W. Some observations on the use of TA in marriage counseling. *Journal of Marriage and Family Counseling,* 1977, *3,* 27–34

O'Leary KD, & Turkewitz H. Marital therapy from a behavioral perspective. In TJ Paolino & BS McCrady (Eds), *Marriage and marital therapy: Psychoanalytic, behavioral and systems theory perspectives.* New York: Brunner/Mazel, 1978

Olson DH. Diagnosing marriage counseling using SIMFAM, MMPIS and therapists. *American Association of Marriage Counselors Newsletter,* 1969, p. 8

Olson D. Marital and family therapy: Integrative review and critique. *Journal of Marriage and the Family,* 1970, *32,* 501–538

Olson DH. Marital and family therapy: A critical overview. In AS Gurman & D Rice (Eds), *Couples in conflict.* New York: Jason Aronson, 1978

Olson D, & Sprenkle D. Emerging trends in treating relationships. *Journal of Marriage and Family Counseling,* 1976, *2,* 317–329

Palazzoli S, Cecchin G, Prata G, & Boscolo L. *Paradox and counterparadox.* New York: Jason Aronson, 1978

Papp P. Brief therapy with couples groups. In P Guerin (Ed), *Family therapy: Theory and practice.* New York: Gardner Press, Inc.; 1976

Patterson CH. *Relationship counseling and psychotherapy.* New York: Harper & Row, 1974

Patterson G, & Hops H. Coercion, a game for two: Intervention techniques for marital conflict. In RE Ulrich & P Mountjoy (Eds), *Experimental analysis of social behavior.* New York: Appleton-Century-Crofts, 1972

Peterson JA (Ed). *Marriage and family counseling: Perspective and prospect.* New York: Association Press, 1968

Phillips CE. Some useful tests for marriage counseling. *The Family Coordinator*, 1973, *22*, 43–53

Pierce R. Training in interpersonal communication skills with the partners of deteriorated marriages. *The Family Coordinator*, 1973, *22*, 223–227

Rabin HM. How does co-therapy compare with regular group therapy? *American Journal of Psychotherapy*, 1967, *21*, 244–255

Rainwater L. *Family design.* Chicago: Aldine Publishing Co., 1965

Rappaport AF. Conjugal relationship enhancement program. In D Olson (Ed), *Treating relationships.* Lake Mills, IA: Graphic, 1976

Reid W, & Shyne A. *Brief and extended casework.* New York: Columbia University Press, 1969

Renne KS. Childlessness, health, and marital satisfaction. *Social Biology*, 1976, *23*, 183–197

Rogers C. *Client-centered therapy. Its current practice, implications, and theory.* Boston: Houghton Mifflin, 1951

Rogers C. *Becoming partners: Marriage and its alternatives.* New York: Delacorte Press, 1972

Rubinstein B, & Weiner D. Co-therapy teamwork relationships in family theory. In G Zuk & I Boszormenyi-Nagy (Eds.), *Family therapy and disturbed families.* Palo Alto, CA: Science and Behavior Books, 1973, pp. 168–182

Ruesch J, & Bateson G. *Communication: The social matrix of society.* New York: Norton, 1951

Russell A, & Russell L. Exorcising the ghosts in the marital system. *Journal of Marriage and Family Counseling*, 1977, *14*, 71–78

Sager CJ, Gundlach R, Kremer M, Lenz R, & Royce JR. The married in treatment. *Archives of General Psychiatry*, 1968, *19*, 205–217

Satir V. Conjoint marital therapy. In B Greene (Ed), *The psychotherapies of maritala disharmony.* New York: The Free Press, 1965

Satir V. *Conjoint family therapy* (2nd ed). Palo Alto, CA: Science and Behavior Books, 1967

Satir V. The family as a treatment unit. In J Haley (Ed), *Changing families.* New York: Grune & Stratton, 1971

Satir V. *Peoplemaking.* Palo Alto, CA: Science and Behavior Books, 1972

Sartre JP. *Existential psychoanalysis.* New York: Philosophical Library, 1953

Saxton L. *The individual, marriage, and the family.* Belmont, CA: Wadsworth Publishing Co., 1968

Scheinbeing M. Feedback in conjoint marital interaction testing. *Family Therapy*, 1974 *1*, 273

Schwartz E, & Leder R. The woman in the family. In HL Silverman (Ed), *Marital therapy.* Springfield, IL: Charles C. Thomas, 1972

Schwartz R, & Schwartz L. *Becoming a couple.* Englewood Cliffs, NJ: Prentice-Hall, 1980

Silverman HL. *Marital therapy: Moral, sociological, and psychological factors.* Springfield, IL: Charles C. Thomas, 1972

Skynner AC. *Systems of family and marital psychotherapy.* New York: Brunner/Mazel, 1976

Sluzki CE. Marital therapy from a systems perspective. In TJ Paolino & BS McCrady (Eds), *Marriage and marital therapy.* New York: Brunner/Mazel, 1978

Smith JR. Suggested scales for prediction of client movement and the duration of marriage counseling. *Sociology and Social Research*, 1967, *52*, 63–71

Sprenkle D, & Fisher B. An empirical assessment of the goals of family therapy. *Journal of Marital and Family Therapy*, 1980, *6*, 131–139

Sprenkle D, & Olson D. Circumplex model of marital systems: An empirical study of clinic and nonclinic couples. *Journal of Marriage and Family Counseling*, 1978, *4*, 59–74

Stanton MD. An integrated structural/strategic approach to family therapy. *Journal of Marital and Family Therapy*, 1981, *7*, 427–480

Steinglass P. The conceptualization of marriage from a family systems perspective. In TJ Paolino & BS McCrady (Eds), *Marriage and marital therapy.* New York: Brunner/Mazel, 1978

Stierlin H. *Psychoanalysis and family therapy.* New York: Jason Aronson, 1977

Stone L. *The family, sex, and marriage in England—1500–1800.* New York: Harper & Row, 1977

Strong J. A marital conflict resolution model redefining conflict to achieve intimacy. *Journal of Marriage and Family Counseling*, 1975, *1*, 269–276

Stuart RB. Operant interpersonal treatment for marital discord. *Journal of Consulting and Clinical Psychology*, 1969a, *33*, 675–682

Stuart R. Token reinforcement in marital treatment. In R Rubin & C Franks (Eds), *Advances in behavior therapy.* New York: Academic Press, 1969b

Targow J, & Zweber R. Participants' reactions to treatment in a married couples group. *International Journal of Group Psychotherapy*, 1969, *19*, 221–225

Thurnher M. Midlife marriage: Sex differences in evaluation and perspectives. *International Journal of Aging and Human Development*, 1976, 7, 129–135

Toman W. *Family constellation*. New York: Springer, 1972

Valle S, & Marinelli R. Training in human relations skills as a preferred mode of treatment for married couples. *Journal of Marriage and Family Counseling*, 1975, 1, 359–365

Vincent JP, Weiss R, & Birchler GR. A behavioral analaysis of problem solving in distressed and nondistressed married and stranger dyads. *Behavior Therapy*, 1975, 6, 475–487

Vines N. Adult unfolding and marital conflict. *Journal of Marital and Famiy Therapy*, 1979, 15, 5–14

Watzlawick P, Weakland JH, & Fisch R. *Change: Principles of problem formation and problem solution*. New York: Norton, 1974

Weakland JH, Fisch R, Watzlawick P, & Bodin AM. Brief therapy: Focused problem resolution. *Family Process*, 1974, 13, 141–168

Weeks GR, & L'Abate L. Paradoxical psychotherapy: Theory and practice with individuals, couples, and families. New York: Brunner/Mazel, 1982

Weigel RG, Weigel VM, & Richardson F. Congruence of spouses' personal constructs and reported marital success: Pitfalls in instrumentation. *Psychological Reports*, 1973, 33, 212–214

Weiss RL. Contracts, cognition, and change: A behavioral approach to marriage therapy. *The Counseling Psychologist*, 1975, 5, 15–26

Weiss RL, Birchler G, & Vincent J. Contractural models for negotiation training in marital dyads. *Journal of Marriage and the Family*, 1974, 36, 321–330

Weiss RL, Hops H, & Patterson GR. A framework for conceptualizing marital conflict: A technology for altering it, some data for evaluating it. In L Hammerlynck, L Handy, & E Marsh (Eds), *Behavior change: Methodology, concepts and practice*. Champaign, IL: Research Press, 1973

Welch IE, Tate GA, & Richards F. *Humanistic psychology: A source book*. Buffalo, NY: Prometheus Books, 1978

Wertheimer M. Gestalt theory. *Social Research*, 1944, 11, pp. 12–42

Whitaker C. Psychotherapy with couples. *American Journal of Psychotherapy*, 1958, 12, 18–23

Whitaker C, Greenberg A, & Greenberg M. Existential marital therapy A synthesis. A subsystem of existential interaction. *Family Therapy*, 1979, 2, 169–200

Willi J. *Couples in collusion*. New York: Jason Aronson, 1982

Wills TA, Weiss RL, & Patterson GR. A behavioral analysis of the determinants of marital satisfaction. *Journal of Consulting and Clinical Psychology*, 1974, 42, 802–811

Wolman R. Women's issues in couples treatment: The view of the male therapist. *Psychiatric Opinion*, 1976, 13, 13–17

Wynne L, Ryckoff I, Day J, & Hirsh S. Pseudomutuality in the family relations of schizophrenics. *Psychiatry*, 1958, 21, 205

Ziegler JS. A comparison of the effect of two forms of group psychotherapy on the treatment of marital discord. *Dissertation Abstracts International*, 1973, 34, 143–144A

SECTION III

Preventing and Dealing with Marital Breakdown: Premarital and Postmarital Interventions

13

Premarital Programs and Counseling

Premarital counseling is usually a structured, short-term intervention, the purpose of which is helping a couple, prior to the legal marriage ceremony, to identify and discuss potential problems in their marital relationship. Although premarital counseling has traditionally been within the domain of religion, it has also existed as a clinical entity since the 1930s, when premarital counseling was initiated at the Merrill-Palmer Institute in Detroit (Bagarozzi & Raven, 1981).

In the past decade, professionals, paraprofessionals, and consumers have shown an increased interest in premarital interventions. This interest stems in part from a resurgence of concern about the quality of family life, but may be traced primarily to a reaction to increasing divorce rates. Thus the concern about the existence or lack of adequate preparation for marriage is a response to the apparent inability of many individuals to sustain long-term relationships. In some churches, including the Catholic Church, premarital counseling has been mandated as a prerequisite to the marriage ceremony.

Thus premarital counseling interventions and preparation programs may be viewed as preventive approaches that attempt to improve, prior to marriage, the quality of the marital relationship and help it become more resilient and resistant to eventual dissolution. Therefore the major goal of premarital interventions may be defined as the prevention of divorce.

There may be a variety of ways to identify premarital interventions. The most traditional approaches, apart from pastoral interventions, however, are family-life education programs, enrichment programs, covenant contracting programs, and counseling (the term *'counseling'* is used to distinguish this intervention from marital therapy in which a couple seeks help on a longer-term basis for individual and dyadic issues that threaten the existence of the marital relationship).

FAMILY LIFE EDUCATION

Family-life education is the oldest and most common premarital intervention (Schumm & Denton, 1979). It is an educational approach consisting of information-giving and teaching about the major areas of concern in a marital relationship (e.g., money, sex, chores, children, in-laws). The underlying philosophical–theoretical assumption of this approach is that providing education and information will be sufficient to help produce positive changes in a relationship. Participants in family-life education approaches are usually passive participants, whose major activity is reading or reading and discussing specific assignments. There is rarely an active experiential component for participants.

Although family-life education has been and continues to be an ongoing and widespread movement, there is little evidence to support its claim for providing preventive education (L'Abate & Rupp, 1981). Currently, no data exist to support the claim that education alone either enhances marital satisfaction or prevents marital dissolution.

ENRICHMENT AND STRUCTURED SKILLS PROGRAMS

In this approach, which has already been reviewed in Chapter 7, there is a high degree of participant activity and subjective experiencing by participants. Each couple must actively respond to questions and attempt to resolve the issues posed to them by the program. Del Monte (L'Abate, 1975) presented two enrichment programs (B & C), entitled "A Problem-Solving Approach to Courtship and Marriage" and "Premarital Problem Solving." Both programs follow a negotiation approach (L'Abate, submitted for publication) based on recognition of a problem, collecting information about the problem, generation of alternative solutions, agreement on a solution that is "best" for both partners; implementation of the solution, evaluation, and reappraisal. Program B contains three lessons: Lesson 1 leads each couple through the actual negotiation process; Lesson 2 develops communication as a resource in problem-solving; and Lesson 3 develops conflict as a resource in problem-solving. This program is essentially an introduction to Program C, in which the previous problem-solving paradigm is applied to five areas of premarital life: (1) dating, (2) loving, (3) sex, (4) alternative stages of the marital life cycle, and (5) mate selection. Both programs are based on the work of Kieren, Henten, and Marotz (1975).

PREMARITAL COMMUNICATION-SKILLS EDUCATION WITH UNIVERSITY STUDENTS

This program uses videotape for modeling and feedback purposes. The program was developed by Van Zoost (1973) in a pilot study with university dating couples, but the author believes that the program can be generalized to other dyads. It involves a structured group process for teaching communication skills.

The objectives of the program are (1) to acquaint participants with the basic principles of communication skills and to have them observe these skills in themselves and others; and (2) to inform participants of ways of handling communication difficulties and to have them practice, both within the group and in their own relationships.

The program is conducted in five sessions. In the pilot study, the participants were six dating couples, ages 19 to 27, with a mean age of 21.6 years. Measures consisted of four paper-and-pencil tests administered pre- and post-treatment: Form C of the Affect Sensitivity Scale (Danish & Kagan, 1971), which uses a videotaped counseling session; the Self-Disclosure Questionnaire (Jourard & Lasakow, 1958); the Interpersonal Communication Inventory (Bienvenu, 1975); and the Communications Knowledge Test (Van Zoost, 1973). During the first session, the pretests were administered, and the couples were assigned to two groups of three couples each, which then met weekly for two hours for a total of four weeks.

In Session 1, each couple met privately with a counselor-teacher and a 10-minute conversation between the partners was videotaped. The tape was then played back, with a three-way discussion of the interaction.

In Session 2, the focus was on nonverbal communication, using a minilecture and videotaped modeling. Small-group discussions followed, with observations of nonverbal behavior. An abbreviated form of Ard's (1967) questionnaire on nonverbal cues was distributed to the participants with instructions to discuss for the next session.

In Session 3, characteristics of good verbal communication were discussed: for example, the function of humor, the necessity of discriminating when, where, and how to make certain comments, the importance of honesty in expressing feelings, and ways to encourage others to speak further. Videotaped illustrations supplemented the discussion. The participants were then asked to do exercises, using different kinds of verbal responses, and finally, at the participants' request, some of the videotapes from Session 1 were played and discussed.

In Session 4, a 14-minute film of handling

marital conflict was shown and discussed, the remainder of Session 1 tapes were played, and two written handouts were distributed for homework: Shostrom's *Man the Manipulator* (1967) and a brief description of Bach and Wyden's (1969) Fair Fight techniques.

In Session 5, the homework was discussed, and the counselor-teacher presented two ways of handling communication difficulties. A feedback exercise that involves repeating the sender's message before responding was explained by the counselor-teacher, shown on videotape, and then performed by the participants. An exercise in role-switching was done, using the same method of presentation. Finally, the participants discussed the program as a whole.

Post-tests and evaluations were done at a later time, and the couples met with the counselor-teacher, if desired, to discuss the test results.

The results indicate that scores on Jourard's Self-Disclosure Questionnaire and the Communication Knowledge Test changed significantly, whereas findings on the other two measures were not significant. The participants significantly increased their knowledge about communication as well as their amount of self-disclosure between partners. A possible explanation for the lack of significant change on the Bienvenu scale (three people obtained lower scores, two remained the same, seven increased) is that a few persons, on becoming aware of communication behaviors, became more critical of their own skills. The videotape playback was evaluated as highly useful.

COMMUNICATION SKILLS-TRAINING PROGRAMS

In designing and implementing social-skills training programs for family populations, it has been suggested that the ineffective communication patterns that trouble many marriages are learned before marriage (Gangsei, 1971). Interactions patterns that later lead to marital conflicts are often begun during dating relationships when couples frequently avoid threatening topics. In order to prevent dysfunctional communication patterns in marriage, Gangsei (1971) and others (e.g., Schauble &

Hill, 1976; Schlein, 1971; Van Zoost, 1973) have suggested that social-skills training programs should be designed for couples prior to marriage. The benefits of training premarital couples in communication skills were perhaps best presented by Schauble and Hill (1976):

This preventive approach comes at a time in the development of the couples' relationship (i.e., "courting") when they can integrate and use the skills to improve caring and establish an honest and straightforward communication process (p. 284).

In an attempt to provide premarital couples with better social-skills training before marriage, a number of educational training programs have been developed. The goals of these programs have ranged from teaching couples basic communication skills to training them in advanced conflict-negotiation procedures. The major research in this area has been conducted with couples communication—CC (e.g., Miller, 1971; Nunnally, 1971; Miller, et al., 1976a, 1976b), relationship enhancement—RE (e.g., Avery, et al. 1980; D'Augelli, et al. 1974; Guerney, 1977; Schlein, 1971), and the Mutual Problem-Solving Skills Program (e.g., Ridley, Avery, Harrell & Haynes, 1978; Ridley, Avery, Harrell, Leslie & O'Connor, 1977).

CC was initially evaluated systematically with a premarital couple population (Miller, 1971; Nunnally, 1971). Training in CC was given to 17 couples, while a control group of 15 couples received no training. Results indicated that the trained couples, compared with the control couples, demonstrated increases in both awareness of their dyadic interaction style and their communication skills.

RE was first applied to premarital dyads by Schlein (1971). The participants, 15 dating couples, received RE training 3 hours per week for 10 weeks, while 27 couples served as a control group and received no training. Results indicated that the trained group, compared with the untrained group, increased their openness, empathy, and perceived rate of improvement in the relationship. Avery, et al. (1979) recently assessed the long-term effects of RE with premarital couples. Results indicated that six months following training, the RE group (19 couples), as compared with a relationship discussion group (18 couples), indicated a significant pretest/post-test increase in self-disclosure and empathy skills.

Ridley, Avery, Dent, and Harrell (1981) compared RE with Ridley's Problem Solving— PS (Ridley, Avery, Harrell, Leslie & Dent, in press)—and with a relationship dimension approach—RD. There were 24, 24, and 26 premarital couples in each group, respectively, seen for a total of 24 hours of treatment in 8 weeks.

The Poberman-Ridley Heterosexual Competency Scale was administered to the three groups on a pre–post test basis. Results indicated that (1) RE-trained couples improved significantly in their perceived heterosexual competence relative to the RD group; (2) PS-trained couples, relative to the RD group, improved in their perceived heterosexual competence, though not significantly; and (3) the RE- and PS-trained couples did not differ significantly from one another in their level of perceived heterosexual competence.

One of the most recent approaches to social skills training for premarital dyads was developed by Ridley, et al. (1977). The authors argue that although basic communication-skills training programs appeared to be highly beneficial and successful for a large percentage of the premarital population, the skills taught may be insufficient to achieve positive relationship change for all couples. The use of effective self-disclosure and empathy skills to solve relationship problems assumes that couples can provide sufficient structure for themselves to deal with essential steps in conflict management such as generating and evaluating alternative solutions, implementing the chosen solution, and evaluating progress. Couples who have already established a pattern of poor communication or simply have difficulty in structuring their communication to cover the essential problem-solving steps may, however, not make satisfactory progress with basic communication-skills training. These couples apparently need the essential self-disclosure and empathy skills, as well as additional training in specific structural components of effective problem-solving.

As a first step in providing problem-solving skills training for premarital couples, Ridley, et al. (1977) developed a 10-step, mutual problem-solving program:

1. Listen carefully and express own feelings.
2. Explore the problem area.
3. Define the problem in relationship terms.
4. Identify how each partner contributes to the problem.
5. State a relationship goal.
6. Generate alternative solutions.
7. Evaluate alternative solutions.
8. Select the best solution.
9. Implement the solution.
10. Evaluate progress.

In the Ridley, et al. (1977) study, 26 experimental couples were trained in the problem-solving paradigm, while 28 couples participated in a relationship discussion group. Results indicated that following training, the experimental group made a significant improvement in all problem-solving steps, whereas no such gain was evidenced by the control group. A six-month assessment of the long-term effects of this program indicate that the problem-solving couples, compared with the relationship discussion couples, demonstrated a significant pretest to follow-up gain on all problem-solving steps (Ridley, et al., 1978).

In another study, Avery, Ridley, Leslie, and Milholland (1980) assessed the effectiveness of the Guerney Relationship Enhancement Program (RE) with premarital couples as compared with a lecture class. Nineteen couples completed the RE Program, and 18 couples completed the lecture program over an eight-week period. Behavioral assessments of their self-disclosure and empathy skills were conducted prior to training, immediately following training, and six months after training.

Results from the pre–post analysis and the pretest to follow-up analysis indicated that the RE Program produced significant changes on self-disclosure and empathy skills compared with a control group.

However, both the empathetic abilities and the self-disclosure skills in the RE groups dropped significantly between the post-test and follow-up evaluation. The reason for the drop in self-disclosure was hypothesized to be the difficulty couples have maintaining the emotional "high" that they experience after a program of this type.

A significant innovation in this study was that half of the couples in the RE program were brought back five months after the training for a "booster training program." In spite of this booster, this group did not do significantly better at follow-up than the group that did not receive the additional training.

Schlein (1971) designed an RE program for premarital couples, called PRIMES—Premarital Relationship Improvement by Maximizing Empathy and Self-Disclosure. Schlein defined PRIMES in the context of an effort toward self-validation within the primary relationship.

The first PRIMES research project employed 27 randomly assigned control couples and 21 treatment couples, divided into six groups. PRIMES group leaders (graduate students) held 2½-hour meetings for 8 to 12 weeks. On self-report measures, PRIMES couples reported using better communication skills patterns at post-test. These results were not significant, however. PRIMES couples did evidence significantly improved abilities to handle relationship problems during the program in comparison with a previous, similar time span; only the PRIMES group members tended to increase their scores on trust and intimacy on self-report measures and saw themselves as more empathic, warm, and genuine at post-test. Both control and experimental group members lowered their ratings of the spouse's empathy, warmth, and genuineness, however. This last finding may reflect the perceived difficulty in opening oneself to another and the belief that "I am surely risking more than you." Internal changes may be more powerfully recognized in the initial stages of a relationship enhancement program, with changes in one's spouse being perceived later.

In another communication skills-oriented program, Markman and Floyd (1980) stressed the importance of empirically derived interventions and the role that communication deficits have in the development and maintenance of marital distress. In accordance with these assumptions, and using data obtained from a previous study (Markman 1979) in which 26 unmarried couples were recruited, before marriage, for a 2½-year study period, a behavioral premarital program was designed.

The Premarital Relationship Enhancement Program (PREP) developed by Markmam and Floyd (1980) is consistent with the communication and problem-solving practices common to other programs (L'Abate, 1981). It involves six group meetings that last approximately three hours each. Training involves the following:

A.   Homework Assignments

B.   Lecturettes
C.   Videotape Feedback
D.   Interaction with Consultants
E.   Cognitive Restructuring, which involves seven aspects:
 1. Learning a language system
 2. Learning the behavioral model
 3. Examining expectations
 4. Learning the concept of "engaging the skills" at conflictual points
 5. Information about couples planning marriage
 6. Information about marital discord
 7. Information about sexual functioning and dysfunction
F.   Skills Acquisition in:
 1. Active listening
 2. Expressive skills
 3. Behavior monitoring skills
 4. Learning which behaviors are pleasing or displeasing to the partners
 5. Making specific requests for behavior change
 6. Contracting skills
 7. Pleasuring skills

The program was used with four couples, each in the experimental and control groups; evaluation consisted of a battery of questionnaires before, during, and after intervention. In spite of subjective claims of satisfaction and improvement by the experimental couples, results failed to show any difference between their test scores and those of the control group.

COVENANT CONTRACTING (CC)

As described in Chapter 4, this approach was originally created to help clinical couples resolve conflicts. However, CC has been used in a preliminary study with premarital nonclinical couples (Caiella, 1982) as an enrichment program.

In this program, eight weekly sessions were conducted, which included six contract-writing sessions and two assessment sessions, one before and one after the contract writing. Evaluation consisted of a battery of self-report and quasi-objective measures. Post-test results were slightly positive, with a slight reduction in dyadic satisfaction and couple self-report of more fighting as well as more awareness of previously ignored marital issues.

Although Sager suggested the use of marriage contracts as a form of premarital counseling (1976, pp. 310–313), to date there have been no systematic attempts to use contracting with premarital couples. The short- and long-term effects of premarital contracts remain to be seen.

PREMARITAL COUNSELING

Premarital counseling is provided by a number of churches, mental health agencies, universities, and private practitioners. Most pastoral programs appear to be didactic in structure; other programs rarely specify goals or focus of treatment. Schumm and Denton (1979) have commented on the failure of a number of premarital counseling programs to investigate the needs of the premarital couple as the couple defines those needs, also noting that there is no consensus on what to teach, how to teach, or when to teach. Concerning what to teach, Rutledge (1966) has provided the most complete list, including health, communication of feelings, expectations, children; whereas other programs (Bienvenu, 1975) have emphasized communication and problem-solving skills-training approaches. Others (Gleason & Prescott, 1977; Miller, Nunnally & Wackman, 1976b) have advocated group approaches to provide a setting in which additional content may be addressed to that which is usually addressed in individual couples counseling, i.e., communication skills and marital preparation.

Premarital counseling programs and approaches are diverse in nature and may be described under one of three categories: (1) instructional counseling, which has traditionally been the province of the pastor, rabbi, or physician (Schumm & Denton, 1979; Trainer, 1979) and which consists of a series of prearranged lessons (similar to some enrichment programs); (2) counseling, which addresses specific issues already being faced by the couple prior to marriage; and (3) premarital therapy, which addresses specific problems existing in the premarital relationship, with an open-ended number of sessions and topics decided primarily by the couple.

Trainer (1979) provides a premarital counseling approach that includes a physical examination. During the first visit, issues related to personality, money, relatives, sex, pregnancy, children, household management, recreation, and religion are addressed with the aid of questionnaires and checklists. Visits 2 and 3 consist of physical examinations and genetic histories of the couple, and consideration of individual issues "not suitable to a joint visit." Visit 4 consists of the gathering of all medical, physical, nutritional, and laboratory information, with recommendations relating to dietary patterns to deal with specific physical problems. Trainer provides a postmarital recheck to address issues that may have appeared 8 to 12 weeks after the wedding, the time Trainer believes is optimal for addressing the issues.

Trainer's attempt to address personality issues is noteworthy, for he offers one of the few premarital counseling programs that does so. He also raised the question of when postmarital "checkups" should be conducted. His only outcome data to date, however, is subjective self-report. Furthermore, his program primarily addresses physical factors and problems that may overshadow the importance of psychological factors in the premarital relationship.

Bagarozzi and Bagarozzi (1982) propose a group workshop approach that uses the concept of developmental tasks, also suggested by Balswick (1979). Participants are asked to consider eight content areas as part of the group process: (1) marital roles and tasks, (2) finances and financial decision-making, (3) sexual relations, (4) in-laws, (5) friends, (6) recreation, (7) religion, and (8) children. To facilitate discussions, couples are initially taught communication skills, and in each area, the couple answers preset questions.

The program format is not as rigidly structured as most enrichment programs. The prearranged sequence of questions for participants is, however, typical of most premarital counseling programs. Bagarozzi and Bagarozzi offer a program that attempts to link premarital interventions with theories of family development, attempts to provide an evaluation and follow-up component, and is structured enough to be replicable by other practitioners. Thus, if further evaluation can discern any significant results, this program offers the potential for an effective premarital intervention.

Showick (1975) described another premarital counseling program, which was mandated by the state of California for individuals under 18 years of age. The program consisted of three weekly group sessions, each lasting four to five hours. The groups were structured and consisted primarily of imparting information on marital issues, areas of marital stress, and health services. Of 1300 couples seen, 80 percent were minority couples. Survey results indicated that couples significantly used resources in their health districts after marriage and that less than 1 percent decided not to marry after the counseling program. More importantly, a significant number of couples came back for further counseling in times of stress after their weddings. These results lead, of course, to speculative conclusions, for there are no data to indicate any preventive effects related to the quality of the participants' marriages.

Ball and Henning (1981) recommend the use of Ellis's rational emotive therapy—RET (Ellis & Grieger, 1977)—as an approach to premarital counseling. RET focuses primarily on the unrealistic expectations and irrational thoughts that precipitate personal and marital conflict, e.g., ideas of unbound love, self-perfection, and always getting one's way. Ball and Henning, however, provided no outcome data to indicate that RET is any better than any other counseling approach.

Bager, et al. (1980) describe the development, implementation, and evaluation of an innovative marriage preparation program based on a small discussion-group format. This program also provides postwedding sessions and emphasizes the importance of communication skills and conflict resolution in four areas: (1) roles, (2) kin, (3) sexuality, and (4) finances. The first five sessions are held about three months prior to the wedding ceremony, while the last three sessions are held about six months after the ceremony. The authors consider this six-month period optimal for the follow-up intervention.

Couples are randomly assigned to either experimental or control groups and interviewed one month before starting the program and one year after marriage. During these two interviews, couples answer various questionnaires and hypothesize marriage conflict situations.

Results suggest that spouses who took part in the marriage preparation program found more constructive solutions to areas of disagreement than did couples in the control group. The experimental group addressed sensitive issues earlier in the marriage and showed an increased ability to resolve hypothetical conflict situations.

Other authors have addressed sexual counseling as a premarital intervention. Although sexual counseling interventions have been discussed in Chapter 10, it is important to stress that knowledge about sexuality and attitudes toward sex are major components of the marital relationship (Herold & Goodwin, 1981).

DISCUSSION

Premarital interventions for couples have been acknowledged as an important and needed preventive component in the field of marital therapy. Peck and Swarts (1976) have reiterated the widespread clinical belief that later marital difficulties can be traced to how a couple addresses their relationship after they decide to marry. In this "premarital impasse" stage, the decisions made and the resolution of various conflicts will dictate the course of the marriage. In addressing the importance of the premarital relationship, Guerney (1977) stated,

In addition to being a source of deep satisfaction in its own right and laying the foundation for future marital happiness, there is every reason to believe that a good premarital relationship can serve as a primary ingredient in the individual psychological well-being and personal growth of each of the partners; even including the remediation of very disturbing emotional difficulties (p. 271).

Nevertheless, the field of premarital interventions for couples remains nebulously defined, the majority of interventions being emotional, information-giving programs. Although widespread, premarital counseling is rarely addressed specifically in the literature, nor is there any outcome data to indicate that premarital interventions have any significant preventive impact on future marital issues and difficulties.

In a significant study, Rubin and Mitchell (1976) raised several questions about the impact of premarital interventions on the couple relationship. Between 1972 and 1974, they conducted a survey of 231 sophomore and junior college students who were "dating" or "going together." During the course of the study, the couples were asked to complete a series of three detailed questionnaires (50 or more pages each) pertaining to a wide range of events, experiences, attitudes, and feelings about their relationships. As the study progressed, Rubin and Mitchell believed that they, as "basic researchers," had been active agents in influencing the relationships of many of the couples they studied: "By asking couples to scrutinize their relationships and prompting them to discuss their relationships with one another, our study played a role in shaping these relationships" (p. 17).

At the end of the 1973 questionnaire, one year after the study began, the respondents were asked to indicate the degree to which participation in the study had affected their relationships. Approximately half of the men and half of the women indicated that the study had had at least a slight impact on their relationships. In their open-ended assessments of the study, especially those provided one year later, many of the participants denied "too loudly" that the study had had any impact at all. Rubin and Mitchell pointed out that these strong denials tended to come from persons whose relationships had broken up, especially from men in such relationships (p. 18).

Rubin and Mitchell identified two major processes by which the study influenced the couples: first, processes of definition and, second, processes of disclosure.

Processes of definition operate primarily on the individual level; as a result of taking part in the study, the individual participant may come to view or to define aspects of the relationship in new ways. Processes of disclosure take place at the dyadic level; as a result of their participation in the study, members of couples may be prompted to exchange feelings about one another and about the relationship, and by doing so, affect the relationship (Rubin & Mitchell, 1976, p. 19).

By the spring of 1974, two years after the initial questionnaire session, 20.4 percent of the couples were married, 35.1 percent were still dating or going together, and 44.6 percent had broken up. Of the participants, 18 percent believed that taking part in the study had caused the couple to become closer than they otherwise would have been, 4 percent that it had caused them to become less close, and the

large majority (78 percent) that the net effect of the study had been neither greater nor lesser closeness. Rubin and Mitchell (1976) concluded that,

The study probably did not lead to many marriages, long-term commitments, or breakups that would not have occurred anyway, but by setting in motion the process of definition and disclosure that we have discussed, the study clearly facilitated and in some cases hastened many couples' movements toward outcomes that otherwise would have taken place with greater difficulty and, perhaps, over a longer period of time (p. 21).

In discussing the ethical implications of their study, Rubin and Mitchell pointed out that the participants freely volunteered to take part in a study of the development of close relationships and that no deception was involved. It may still be asked, however, whether they had sufficiently detailed understanding of the possible "enlightening" effects of their participation at the time they agreed to take part. Although there were a few negative reactions expressed by the participants, at the end of the follow-up questionnaire in 1973, virtually all of the participants—98 percent of the women and 92 percent of the men—indicated that they would be interested in further participation (p. 22).

In providing "informed consent" as indicated by the 1973 APA guidelines for conducting human research, Rubin and Mitchell stated that it might be advisable to go further in discussing the possible negative effects of participation before proceeding to the research. However, extensive discussion might also create a self-fulfilling prophecy for some participants. In terms of responsibility for long-term consequences to the participants, the investigators have the responsibility to "detect and remove or correct these consequences" (APA, 1973, p. 80). This means that the investigators must not only be sensitive to any possible negative consequences, but must also be prepared to provide counseling when appropriate.

Rubin and Mitchell raised important questions related not only to research and evaluation, but to the nature and impact of premarital interventions. No matter what approach is used to address premarital interventions, there can be no way to ask a couple to examine the nature of their future marriage without asking them to examine their relationship. Although it is assumed that asking a couple to examine the relationship will be therapeutic, the question of negative impact is raised. Without clarifying process and outcome evaluation, particularly long-term follow-up of effects, one can only hypothesize the effects of premarital interventions. Thus the steady increase in premarital preparation programs has not been equaled by evidence that would support its hopeful basis. Thus far, there is little, if any, evidence to support the contention that such programs do, in fact, what they claim to do, i.e., improve the quality of marriage and decrease the chances of divorce.

Furthermore, available subjective data offer no significant results. Guldner (1971), in an early study, surveyed couples who had participated in premarital pastoral counseling. The couples believed that the pastoral counselor had been looking for conflict or that the counselor had not used the premarital interview to explore the couple's readiness for marriage. Guldner proposed an agenda for postmarital counseling but found that it broke down with couples who had been married six months because these couples brought their own agendas with them to the counseling session. Guldner thus proposed that an appropriate time for counseling is at least six months after the wedding. Prior to this time, couples are too "starry-eyed" to address relationship issues. Baum (1978) also found that cohabiting and married couples gained more from a marital enrichment program than did engaged couples, a finding that may support Guldner's observation of the "starry-eyed" couple, and tends to reconfirm the idea that premarital programs may be less effective than postwedding intervention. Microys and Bader (1977) found that couples who had participated in counseling both before and after their weddings reported that postwedding sessions were slightly more helpful than those sessions occurring before the wedding. Furthermore, their results indicate that postwedding sessions appeared to improve couples' ability to resolve conflict constructively, whereas premarital sessions did not.

There have been a few more recent studies that have begun to use pre- and post-tests to measure gain scores in premarital counseling, usually in the context of marital enrichment programs. Using such measures, Boike (1977) found no improvement in communica-tion, and Van Zoost (1973) noted positive changes on two of her four measures of communication. Other pre- and post-test designs with experimental and control groups have yielded mixed results, some showing improvement of some aspects of communication and others showing no improvement (Miller, Nunnally & Wackman, 1976a, 1976b; Schlein, 1971).

Thus premarital programs do not appear to improve communication, and, unfortunately, there are no existing studies providing evaluation data to suggest that the impact of a program lasted for a year or more. Even evidence to suggest that short-term counseling is effective is mixed (Baum, 1978; Microys & Bader, 1977).

One of the reasons for lack of evidence to support positive effects of premarital interventions may be the relative lack of theoretical knowledge concerning courtship, decision-making about whether or not to marry, and the dynamics of initial attraction. A great deal of speculation is available (Peck & Swarts, 1976), but hard data are scarce. Without any guiding, empirically derived theory, it is not only difficult to decide what issues may need to be addressed, but interventions are left solely to the discretion of the particular practitioner. Thus, exactly what is addressed in many premarital counseling programs is difficult to define and/or assess. If one addresses the four major types of premarital counseling—(1) family life education, (2) counseling, (3) instructional counseling, and (4) enrichment programs (Schumm & Denton, 1979)—one finds a vast array of designated "relevant" issues addressed by a variety of practitioners with various training backgrounds.

Concerning the training backgrounds of those practitioners engaged in premarital counseling, Schumm and Denton (1979) have cited as a major deficiency the lack of training in both secular and religious graduate programs. Furthermore, there is no unifying guide or up-to-date interdisciplinary text.

Bagarozzi and Raven (1981) criticized the lack of specific goals in many premarital programs (in addition to inadequate empirical standards). They believe that premarital intervention programs should try to achieve at least three goals: (1) to provide spouses with an opportunity to become aware of and discuss the developmental tasks they will face in the early stages of their marriage, (2) to teach couples a variety of behavioral skills that will enable them to resolve successfully these developmental tasks, and (3) to help couples make structural changes in their relationships. They recommended that skills should include, but not be limited to, conflict negotiation, problem-solving, communication training, and positive behavior-change strategies.

Although their critique and recommendations appeared prior to the growth in premarital interventions, the criticisms and recommendations are still timely. The field of premarital interventions and programs continues to grow. Nevertheless, there is still no guiding theory, no specification of treatment, no outcome evaluation, and thus, no modification or improvement of approach.

THE FUTURE

The increase in premarital intervention programs has been paralleled by attempts at improved methodology, instrumentation, and measurement of outcome. As both Schumm and Denton (1979) and Bagarozzi and Raven (1981) have concluded, however, there are no data as yet to support the contention that premarital programs improve the quality of marriage and therefore decrease the risks of divorce.

Premarital intervention programs may be one of the most neglected, as well as one of the most widely practiced, forms of marital intervention. With no data to define what is being addressed or what has changed, however, premarital counseling approaches appear still to fall into the category of approaches that seem, but may not be, worthwhile. Couples may or may not respond to premarital interventions in the same ways that they respond to postmarital interventions; they may even respond negatively.

Thus the future of premarital counseling is dependent on the development of theory and appropriate interventions, adequate problem definition, and long-term follow-up of results. Premarital counseling approaches will not be viable so long as they are based on the assumption that, logically, they are needed.

REFERENCES

American Psychological Association. Ethical principles in the conduct of research with human participants. *American Psychologist*, 1973, *28*, 79–80

Ard P. Assumptions underlying marriage counseling. *Marriage Counseling Quarterly*, 1967, *2*, 20–24

Avery A, Ridley C, Leslie L, & Milholland T. Relationship enhancement with premarital dyads: A six-month follow-up. *American Journal of Family Therapy*, 1980, *8*, 23–31

Bach GR, & Wyden P. *The intimate enemy.* New York: Avon, 1969

Bader E, Microys G, Sinclair C, Willett E, & Conway B. Do marriage preparation programs really work? A Canadian experiment. *Journal of Marital and Family Therapy*, 1980, *6*, 171–179

Bagarozzi DA, & Bagarozzi JI. A theoretically derived model of premarital intervention: The building of a family system. *Clinical Social Work Journal*, 1982, *10*, 52–64

Bagarozzi DA, & Raven P. Premarital Counseling: Appraisal and Status. *American Journal of Family Therapy*, 1981, *9*, 13–30

Ball JD, & Henning LH. Rational suggestions for premarital counseling. *Journal of Marital and Family Therapy*, 1981, *7*, 69–73

Balswick JK. The importance of developmental test achievement to early marital adjustment. *Family Therapy*, 1979, *6*, 145–153

Baum MC. The short-term, long-term, and differential effects of group versus bibliotherapy relationship enhancement programs for couples (Doctoral dissertation, The University of Texas at Austin, 1977). *Dissertation Abstracts International*, 1978, *38*, 6132–B–6133B.

Bienvenu M. A measurement of premarital communication. *The Family Coordinator*, 1975, *24*, 65–68

Boike DE. The impact of a premarital program on communication process, communication facilitativeness and personality trait variables of engaged couples (Doctoral dissertation, Florida State University, 1977). *Dissertation Abstracts International*, 1977, *38*, 3083A–3084A (University Microfilms No. 77–24,740)

Caiella C., & Florez J. *The process and effects of premarital covenant counseling.* Research in progress, Georgia State University, 1982

Danish SJ, & Kagan M. Measurement of affective sensitivity: Toward a valid measure of interpersonal perception. *Journal of Counseling Psychology*, 1971, *71*, 51–54

D'Augelli AR, Deyss CS, Guerney BG, Jr, Hershenberg B, & Sborofsky SL. Interpersonal skill training for dating couples: An evaluation of an educational mental health service. *Journal of Counseling Psychology*, 1974, *21*, 385–389

Ellis A, & Grieger R. *RET: Handbook of rational-emotive therapy*. New York: Springer Publishing Company, 1977

Gangsei LB. *Manual for group premarital counseling*. New York: Association Press, 1971

Gleason J, & Prescott M. Group techniques for premarital preparation. *The Family Coordinator*, 1977, *26*, 272–280

Guerney BG, Jr. (Ed.). *Relationship enhancement: Skill training programs for therapy, problem prevention and enrichment*. San Francisco: Jossey-Bass, 1977

Guldner C. The post-marital: An alternative to premarital counseling. *The Family Coordinator*, 1971, *20*, 115–119

Herold ES, & Goodwin MS. Premarital sexual guilt and contraceptive attitudes and behavior. *Family Relations*, 1981, *30*, 247–253

Jourard SM, & Lasakow P. Some factors in self-disclosure. *Journal of Abnormal and Social Psychology*, 1958, *56*, 91–98

Kieren DJ, Henton J, & Marotz R. *Hers and his: A problem-solving approach to marriage*. Hinsdale, IL: Dryden Press, 1975

L'Abate L. *Manual of Enrichment Programs for the Family Life Cycle*. Atlanta: Georgia State University, 1975

L'Abate L. Skill training programs for couples and families: Clinical and nonclinical applications. In AS Gurman & DP Kniskern (Eds.), *Handbook of family therapy*. New York: Brunner/Mazel, 1981

L'Abate L. *The goals of family therapy: Toward a negotiated life style*. Manuscript submitted for publication, 1982

1..L'Abate L, & Rupp G. *Enrichment: Skill training for family life*. Washington, DC: University Press of America, 1981

Markman, HJ. The application of a behavioral model of marriage in predicting relationship satisfaction of couples planning marriage. *Journal of Consulting and Clinical Psychology*, 1979, *4*, 743–749

Markman HJ, & Floyd F. Possibilities for the prevention of marital discord: A behavioral perspective. *The American Journal of Family Therapy*, 1980, *8*, 29–48

Microys G, & Bader E. *Do marriage programs really help?* Unpublished manuscript, 1977. (Available from Department of Family and Community Medicine, University of Toronto)

Miller SL. The effects of communication training in small groups upon self-disclosure and openness in engaged couples' systems of interaction: A field experiment. (Doctoral dissertation, University of Minnesota, 1971). *Dissertation Abstracts International*, 1971, *32*, 2819 (University Microfilms No. 71–28,263)

Miller S, Nunnally EW, & Wackman DB. A communication training program for couples. *Social Casework*, 1976a, *57*, 9–18

Miller S, Hunnally EW, & Wackman DB. Minnesota Couples Communication Program (MCCP): Premarital and marital group. In DHL Olson (Ed.), *Treating relationships*. Lake Mills, IA: Graphic Publishing, 1976b

Nunnally EW. Effects of communication training upon interaction awareness and empathic accuracy of engaged couples: A field experiment (Doctoral dissertation, University of Minnesota, 1971). Dissertation Abstracts International, 1971, *32*, 4736 (University Microfilms No. 72–5561)

Peck BP, & Swarts F. The premarital impasse. *Family Therapy*, 1976, *4*, 1–10

Ridley CA, Avery AW, Dent J, & Harrell JE. The effects of relationship enhancement and problem-solving program on perceived heterosexual competence. *Family Therapy*, 1981, *8*, 59–66

Ridley CA, Avery AW, Harrell JE, & Haynes L. *Problem-solving training for premarital couples: A six-month follow-up*. Paper presented at the Annual Meeting of the American Psychological Association, Toronto, September, 1978

Ridley CA, Avery AW, Harrell JE, Leslie L, & Dent JA. Conflict management: A premarital training program in mutual problem solving. *American Journal of Family Therapy*, in press

Ridley CA, Avery AW, Harrell JE, Leslie LA, & O'Conner J. *Conflict management: A premarital training program in mutual problem solving*. Paper presented at the Annual Meeting of the American Psychological Association, San Francisco, September, 1977

Rubin Z, & Mitchell C. Couples research as couples counseling: Some unintended effects of studying close relationships. *American Psychologist*, 1976, *31*, 17–25

Rutledge A. *Pre-marital counseling*. Cambridge, MA: Schenkman Publishing Co, 1966

Sager CJ. *Marriage contracts and couple therapy*. New York: Brunner/Mazel, 1976

Schauble PG, & Hill CG. A laboratory approach to treatment in marriage counseling: Training in communication skills. *The Family Coordinator*, 1976, *25*, 277–284

Schlein SR. *Training dating couples in empathic and open communication: An experimental evaluation of a potential preventative mental health program*. Unpublished doctoral dissertation, Pennsylvania State University, 1971

Schumm WR, & Denton W. Trends in premarital

counseling. *Journal of Marital and Family Therapy*, 1979, 5, 23–32

Shostrom EL. *Man, the manipulator.* Nashville, TN: Abingdon Press, 1967

Showick H. Premarital counseling: Three years' experiences of a unique service. *The Family Coordinator*, 1975, 24, 321–324

Trainer JB. Premarital counseling and examination. *Journal of Marital and Family Therapy*, 1979, 5, 61–78

Van Zoost B. Premarital communication skills education with university students. *The Family Coordinator*, 1973, 22, 187–191

14

Divorce Mediation

With the increasing divorce rate currently estimated as one of every two marriages in the United States (U.S. Bureau of the Census, 1977), marital therapists have been forced to address theory, methods, and techniques related to helping couples both dissolve and adjust to the dissolution of their marriages. Weiss (1975) noted that marital separation has become almost a commonplace, if unanticipated and undesired, experience in American lives. Although divorce may ultimately have desirable or undesirable effects on individuals, available data suggest that most individuals experiencing marital dissolution represent a high-risk group for social and psychological maladjustment (Bohannan, 1970; Goode, 1956; Gove, 1972; Gurin, et al., 1960; Weiss, 1975). Therefore, rather than addressing the resolution of issues and the growth of an ongoing marital relationship, marital therapists are now often requested to aid in resolving the social and psychological issues arising from the divorce process.

One unique and pioneering structured intervention is divorce mediation. Divorce mediation, based on the work of Coogler (1977a, 1978), is defined as a process by which a couple agrees that a third, impartial party will use his or her "good offices," not to dictate a resolution, but to help them reach their own agreements concerning the divorce settlement. The concept and techniques of divorce mediation are designed to offer an intervention that reduces or eliminates the adversarial legal sys-

tem approach to marital dispute resolution. The voluntarily accepted boundaries of mediation require that the couple follow rational rather than emotional means of resolving the conflictual issues of the divorce (Coogler, et al., 1979) and negotiate mutual decisions. Mediation, unlike any other form of marriage counseling or therapy, is a binding legal contract whereby couples agree to reach a divorce settlement through mediation or through arbitration if mediation fails to help them arrive at a mutual agreement.

BACKGROUND AND DEVELOPMENT

The background of the development of divorce mediation can be seen in the history of American divorce law. Family law in the United States, in contrast to Western Europe, has always been secular. Marriage was a civil contract (in theory), with two forms of marriage legitimated: the civil ceremony, which had colonial antecedents, and the common-law marriage (Mueller, 1957).

In the colonial period, the South was generally faithful to the English tradition of no judicial divorces. Absolute divorce was unknown, and legal separation was rare. In New England, however, courts and legislatures occasionally granted divorce. In Pennsylvania, spouses were given the right to a Bill of Divorcement if the marriage partner was convicted of adultery.

Eventually, the General Assembly empowered itself to grant divorces. This power was vetoed by the English privy council and was not reinstated until after the Revolution (Blake, 1962).

After American independence, legal divorce remained uncommon. The law was different in different parts of the country, however. In the South, divorce was rare or nonexistent. South Carolina did not grant divorces; Georgia granted occasional legislative divorces. In the North, courtroom divorce became more usual than legislative divorce. Pennsylvania passed a general divorce law in 1785; Massachusetts passed a general divorce law one year later. Every New England state, along with New York, New Jersey, and Tennessee, had a divorce law before 1800. New York's 1787 law permitted absolute divorce only for adultery; Vermont allowed divorce for impotence, adultery, intolerable severity, three years' willful desertion, and long absence with presumption of death. Rhode Island permitted divorce for "gross misbehavior and wickedness in either of the parties, repugnant to and in violation of the marriage covenant"; New Hampshire permitted divorce if a spouse joined the Shaker sect (Friedman, 1973, p. 182).

During the 19th century, divorces were increasingly handled, not through legislative branches of states, but through the judiciary branches. In the light of American political history, this change was only natural, for, initially, the colonial governor and the judiciary, to a certain extent, represented foreign domination. The assemblies, on the other hand, were the voice of local influential persons. Over the course of the years, however, states became somewhat disillusioned with legislative supremacy. Judicial power increased at the legislature's expense, taking the form of judicial review (i.e., review, through private litigation, of acts of other branches of government). This decline of legislative supremacy occurred primarily because influential Americans were more afraid of too much law than too little law (Friedman, 1973). A movement arose to limit the power of the legislatures, thus protecting the public from the wealthy and powerful, who were often the majority of representatives in these assemblies. Rules to control legislation were written into one after another of the states' constitutions. Georgia's constitution (1798) outlawed the practice of legislative divorce unless

the parties had gone to "fair trial before the superior court" and obtained a verdict upon "legal principles" (Friedman, 1973, p. 107). Even then, it took a two-thirds vote of each branch of the legislature to grant a divorce.

As power was removed from legislative branches, the number of easier divorce laws increased. Easier divorce laws grew out of popular demand and the rising divorce rate. Divorce proceedings became simpler than in earlier generations, but never automatic, and in form, divorce remained an adversary proceeding.

By 1880 the legislative divorce had disappeared. What remained were extremely variable general state laws governing divorce. From about 1850 to 1870, many states adopted liberal divorce laws, with vague terms such as "cruelty" and "misconduct" added to the grounds for divorce. After 1850, however, influential moral leaders attacked loose divorce laws (Blake, 1962). Fervent diatribes from the press and the pulpits were delivered by such leaders as Horace Greely, Henry James, Wendell Phillips, and militant feminists who contended that the prevailing restrictions on divorce "were an intolerable burden on unhappy and abused wifes" (Shaffer, 1973, p. 788). Moralists, however, equated the feminists' stance with a desire for free love and violently opposed more liberalized divorce laws.

In 1881, the National League for the Protection of the Family was founded to promote a more restrictive federal divorce law. In 1882, the National Divorce Reform League was formed for the same purpose. The National League convinced Congress in 1887 to conduct its first survey of divorce in the United States. This survey found a large growth in the divorce rate in the post-Civil War period of 1867 to 1886. In 1870 there were 11,000 divorces per 40 million population.

With rising concern over the increasing divorce rate and a national panic about morality, more rigorous divorce laws were once again initiated nationwide. In theory, divorce remained an ordinary action at law, with an attacking plaintiff and a resisting defendant; however, state statutes remained frozen in a hodgepodge of divorce laws because of the prevailing arguments against divorce.

In the 1920s there was a sharp rise in the divorce rate, reflecting post-World War I social changes and the change from Victorian mores. During the Depression, the divorce rate went down, partly because of the expense of obtaining a divorce. After World War II, the divorce rate rose again, presumably because of the outcomes of many hasty prewar and war marriages. The rate dropped again in the 1950s; then, in the 1970s, grew again. Since 1960 the divorce rate has doubled and is now estimated to affect one of every two marriages (U.S. Bureau of the Census, 1977).

The most significant issue in divorce law since the 1870s has been the concern that liberalized divorce laws will produce more divorces. Shoen & Huber (1975) reported that the effect of the California Family Law Act of 1969, which instituted nonadversarial proceedings for divorce, can be misinterpreted on first examination. The act provided for a significant relaxation of requirements for divorce in California by reducing the minimum waiting time and proposing more equal property division. A rapid increase in the divorce rate followed. Analysis of the statistics revealed that the law did not lead to a real increase in divorces or produce significant changes in the population filing for divorce. It only provided an opportunity for those wanting divorces to stay in their own state rather than travel to Nevada or Mexico for the "quickie" divorce. Along with the rise in divorces in California, there was a significant drop in Nevada divorces.

Nevertheless, present-day divorce law in many states still prohibits any agreement by the parties to obtain a divorce. Until the advent of no-fault divorce (now found in some 20 states), the law cnsidered mutual consent agreements contrary to "public policy," and thus void (i.e., mutual consent exists when both husband and wife agree to divorce). Although mutual consent has been acknowledged by the courts, the Canons of Ethics, under which lawyers practice, do not permit an attorney advocate to represent more than one party. Attorneys are prohibited from giving the opposite party any legal advice at all. It is common for a couple to have only one lawyer, although in such cases the lawyer has no obligations at all to the unrepresented party. It can be deduced from these canons that an attorney is still mandated to promote the traditional position of the attacking plaintiff and a resisting defendant. Many states, however, have be-

gun to offer and advocate conciliation services for divorcing couples. Conciliation services for couples came into vogue in the 1960s (MacLean, 1977), but have been dropped in many states because of expense and difficulties with failure (MacLean, 1977).

MAJOR PHILOSOPHY

From his personal disdain for the adversarial system, the late James Coogler (1977b), a lawyer and psychotherapist, created the first divorce mediation program in the United States. He opened the Family Mediation Center in Atlanta, Georgia, after his personal involvement with divorce in the court system:

I am indebted to my former wife and the two attorneys who represented us in our divorce for making me aware of the critical need for a more rational, more civilized way of arranging a parting of the ways. Her life, my life, and our children's lives were unnecessarily embittered by that experience. In my frustration and anger, I kept thinking of something Mahatma Ghandi wrote over half a century ago: "I have learned through bitter experience that one supreme lesson, to conserve my anger, and as heat conserved is transmuted into energy, even so our anger can be transmuted into a power which can move the world." This system of structured mediation is, therefore, my anger transmuted into what I hope is a power to move toward a more humane world for those who find themselves following in my footsteps (Coogler, 1977b, p. 2).

Coogler's rationale for his program was simple. He believed that divorce proceedings should be more humane and less hurtful. He studied the rules of commercial arbitration and tailored them to a process that would entail a third party's facilitating the couple to make their own decisions about a divorce settlement before having to involve a third-party arbitrator who would make the decisions for them. In divorce mediation, an arbitrator is called in only when a settlement cannot be reached.

Since Coogler's initial work, the American Arbitration Association (AAA) has promulgated the "Family Dispute Services," a package of rules and procedures designed to address the four phases of marital disputes—conciliation, mediation, reference, and arbitration. Conciliation is the process of counseling, the goal being for the couple to stay together. Mediation is the process of assisting a couple to arrive amicably at terms for a separation agreement. Reference is the process of referring those items on which the parties cannot agree following mediation to a referee for final and binding determination. Arbitration is the process of dealing with disputes arising from separation agreements.

The AAA is presently working to familiarize lawyers with the Family Dispute Services, as well as to provide and initiate in-depth training for mediators, referees, and arbitrators (Spencer & Zammitt, 1977). There are three new rules under the Family Dispute Services that are different from the commercial arbitration rules. Arbitrators (1) may obtain professional opinions as to the best interests of the child, *with* the parents' consent; (2) may interview the child privately *(in camera)* to ascertain the needs of the child as to custody and visitation (the AAA is clear in stating that the arbitrator should not put the child in a position in which he or she has to choose between parents or reject either of them); and (3) are appointed by a panel sent by the AAA. This means that the divorcing couple is sent a list of possible arbitrators, all of whom are trained as arbitrators but who come from varying disciplines. Extensive biographical material about the arbitrators is sent with the list to help the couple eliminate those they do not want. They then return the list of their choices, and the AAA appoints an arbitrator. The purpose of this lengthy process is to preserve family autonomy by permitting the family to take part in choosing the decision-maker. In the court adversarial system, decisions are left to a judge, who may have a very different value system. The AAA points out that these Family Dispute Service rules "must be recognized by the courts as an adequate substitute for judicial resolution" (Spencer & Zammitt, 1977, p. 116).

THEORY

Two primary theoretical orientations are used in the divorce mediation process: Deutsch's (1973) conflict resolution theory and transactional analysis (Schiff, 1978). Conflict resolution theory centers on identifying types of bargainers and their motivational orientations. The person with a cooperative motivational orientation exhibits a positive interest in others' welfare and has a high need for affiliation. The person with a competitive motivational orientation has a strong need for power and for being "one up" on the other. The individualistic motivational orientation is characterized by a person with a high need for achievement who must maximize his or her own outcomes, regardless of how the other person fares. Deutsch's theories lead to cognizance of the types of interventions that work best with different motivational orientations. Presently, however, there are no research findings available on the most effective interventions with the identified types of bargainers.

Transactional analysis is the major theory used in mediation. Coogler chose TA therapists to staff the Family Mediation Center, believing that the ability to diagnose ego states is essential, primarily because the thrust of the mediation effort is to keep each member of the couple constantly in his or her adult ego state, thereby encouraging rational decision-making.

Coogler outlined six conflicts in which he believed couples are involved. The first is a values conflict involving a parent-to-parent ego-state transaction. Issues of what is best for the children or what ought to happen result in fighting between the two partners. The second conflict is between child-to-child ego states and is a conflict of needs. The third conflict of blame–guilt is between a critical, blaming-parent ego state, which controls a child ego state through guilt. The fourth conflict is an escalation of the blame–guilt conflict, in which each person is fighting to maintain self-worth. The fifth conflict is counterfeit conflict, in which it appears that one or both partners are operating in their adult ego states but are actually conning each other. The sixth conflict style is rational, between two individuals in their adult ego states. They are aware of their own parent values and child needs and have incorporated them into their adult negotiations. This conflict style is considered the most mature, ideal way to resolve conflicts.

Schiff (1978) has contributed a theory of passivity that is also applied in divorce mediation. Schiff stated that there are four passive behaviors: do-nothing, over-adaptation, agitation, and immobility or violence. The passive person enters the negotiations with a great deal of power, either through actions or withholding.

The Role of the Mediator

The role of the mediator is to mediate between the husband and the wife to help them find a new alternative for the resolution of their conflict, specifically concerning the marital dissolution (Coogler, et al., 1979). The mediator also enables both parties to appreciate the financial effects of the divorce and make agreements so that each may ultimately become financially independent. The mediator follows a structured program, with the underlying requirement that he or she be fair and impartial concerning agreements reached. The mediator must have training in the principles and application of Transactional Analysis, as well as in negotiation skills. This training is currently provided by the Family Mediation Association *(The Family Mediator*, 1981).

Coogler stated that the skill of the mediator is measured by his or her sensitivity and ability to deal with shifts on the parts of the negotiating partners. Changes toward resolution will produce stress that will not decrease until the fear is dissipated that the offered change will be perceived as weakness and exploited by the other person. Therefore the mediator must be aware of the conflict styles used by individuals in order to employ appropriate interventions, as well as to deal with the increased stress level leading to or following a change in position by individuals in the mediation process (Coogler, 1977b). Mediators must be sensitive, tactful therapists and negotiaters, in that they must support individuals in a time of emotional stress and crisis while aiding them to make rational decisions and bargains. They also teach partners to negotiate, particularly when passive partners must be more assertive in the negotiation process.

Treatment

The divorce mediation process involves three areas. Couples must decide on property division (i.e., division of all material goods accumulated during the marriage); couples must terminate their dependency on the relationship and make decisions about any ongoing business initiated by the partnership (e.g., making decisions about children); and couples must decide whether or not to become legally divorced.

When couples enter the mediation process, the first step is an orientation in which the "Marital Mediation Rules" are explained. If the couple agrees to continue mediation after the rules are explained, they sign a contract with each other and with the mediator, agreeing to follow the mediation rules. The rules provide for the appointment of a mediator and for the couple's selection of an impartial advisory attorney.

The couple then makes a monetary deposit to cover up to 10 hours of mediation times. An additional amount is also deposited to cover the costs of the advisory attorney. The couple is given detailed budget forms to be completed at home as preparation for the first mediation session.

At the first mediation session, the couple agrees upon arrangements for temporary support and custody in order to stabilize their relationship while they work toward a final settlement. When the couple and the mediator have developed the general form of the settlement, the advisory attorney is called in to provide legal and tax advice. The attorney then drafts the formal settlement agreement. With the legally binding settlement agreement negotiated, either party may then obtain an uncontested no-fault divorce at a nominal cost.

If couples cannot reach an agreement in mediation, they are legally bound by their written contract to go to arbitration. Arbitrators are called in from an approved list of trained individuals of various backgrounds. Both parties can decide to stop the mediation process and remain together, whereupon their initial deposit is refunded. If both parties stop mediation and hire lawyers, however, they forfeit their deposit. For those couples who complete the mediation process, the return of the unused part of their deposit acts as a motivator to help the couple reach an agreement. Most mediation lasts between five and seven sessions, rather than the ten for which the couple has initially deposited money.

Structured mediation is scheduled on a one-hour-per-week basis. This schedule provides for regularly allocated, uninterrupted time for working toward resolution. Initially, the mediator makes it clear that all issues pertaining to a settlement are open in mediation. Nothing is presettled. It is assumed that this provision protects a passive, willing-to-be-manipulated partner who, prior to entering mediation, may have agreed with his or her spouse on several issues concerning property or children. The mediator states that all allocations are to be negotiated in mediation; not only do the couple have to be in agreement about the settlement, but the mediator must also agree that their settlement is fair. The overriding principle by which mediators conduct the interventions is that each partner must take responsibility for his or her own life.

When couples enter the mediation process, they also agree to follow the marital mediation rules, and thereby accept a mutual value system about negotiation. Under the marital mediation rules, issues are clearly defined and limited to those that need resolution for settlement. The marital mediation rules are summarized as follows:

1. Parties sign a contract that they will follow the marital mediation rules to reach a divorce settlement agreement, as well as any postdivorce settlement agreements that might arise in the future.
2. Responsibilities of the Mediation Center are to appoint a trained mediator and to offer a panel of advisory attorneys from which the couple may select one (or the couple may choose their own). The attorney is not involved in negotiating the terms of the settlement, but will translate the agreement into a clear, legal document that maximizes tax advantages for the family.
3. The deposit for 10 hours of mediation and advisory attorney's fees is refunded for the unearned portion when settlement is reached, if the couple reconciles or becomes disabled, or if they reach an impasse and go to arbitration. The deposit will not be refunded if partners drop out.
4. The mediator and advisory attorney will not talk with parties outside sessions except to change appointment times. There is a 24-hour cancellation policy, as well as a confidentiality policy.
5. Impasse may be declared by the mediator, by a negotiating party if the mediator agrees, or by a party without the mediator's agreement if he or she has been in mediation for at least 10 hours.
6. Full disclosure of income and financial

holdings is imperative. Both parties will prepare their own budgets.
7. Children, if old enough, are encouraged to participate in mediation sessions concerning custody and visitation.
8. Parties are not to discuss mediation sessions with each other or anyone else outside the mediation sessions without mutual consent.
9. Temporary custody and support settlement will be agreed upon in the first session and will be legally binding for two months. If an agreement is not reached, the issue will go immediately to arbitration.
10. Division of property includes anything acquired by either party during the marriage—gifts and inheritances excluded.
11. Spousal maintenance is determined according to the support need of the dependent spouse and the ability of the supporting spouse to provide; it is not based on assessment of fault. During an initial period, support may be greater to help the dependent spouse become self-supporting; age, physical condition, and amount of time out of the job market are taken into consideration, but such disabilities are not the sole basis for the decision.
12. Parties are encouraged to share child support responsibilities.
13. Child custody guidelines are the same as those used by the American Arbitration Association.
14. The custodial parent has ultimate power to make decisions concerning the child, although couples are encouraged to reach decisions together.
15. The responsibilities of postdivorce parenting should continue to be shared by both parents. The custodial parent makes agreements about communication with the noncustodial parent (i.e., informing about a child's school play, grades, losing a good friend, a parent's illness, anything that may have a significant effect on the child).
16. Joint custody is an option to consider, and an agreement can be made, although it probably will not be upheld by a court. The mediation center endorses joint custody as a workable option.

17. If controversy over custody is apparent at the first session, each party is to fill out two budgets—one as the custodial parent and another as the noncustodial parent. Prior to determining custody, parties will agree on visitation and support arrangements. This agreement is to avoid making the children financial pawns.

18. The mediator has the power to open and close issues. Once an issue has been resolved, the mediator will close the issue and deem it non-negotiable for future discussion.

19. It is believed that the mediator and the advisory attorney are in the best position, having the most detailed information, to evaluate the feasibility of the settlement agreement. Parties may request an evaluation from them before the settlement is signed. If there are revisions requiring further negotiations, the mediator may offer more mediation sessions or declare an impasse and go to arbitration under the marital arbitration rules.

20. The mediator must agree that the settlement agreement is fair. When the mediator declares nonconcurrence, parties are encouraged to work out a more equitable agreement.

21. If the parties and the mediator are not able to reach an agreement on interpretation of any of the marital mediation rules, the Center will make the final decision (Coogler, 1977b).

These rules are the principles upon which the process of mediation takes place. The couple has entered a legal contract requiring them to reach a resolution on four basic issues: division of marital property, spousal maintenance for the dependent spouse, child support when there are dependent children, and custody and visitation arrangements. The process of divorce mediation addresses only these four issues, and only addresses them by following the marital mediation rules.

In the initial session, the mediation process is explained to the couple and they are presented with a contract to sign, legally binding them to follow mediation to completion unless both agree that they want to terminate mediation before a settlement is reached. They agree that neither will hire a private attorney. The deposit is then prepaid for 10 sessions, which begin within 10 days of the initial meeting.

During the first session, the couple is assisted to work out a temporary support and custody agreement that is legally binding for only two months. These temporary arrangements are considered essential to the mediation process to stabilize the couple so that they may work effectively during mediation. Extensive and detailed financial forms are given out in the first session. The mediator suggests that the husband and wife may help one another with estimated costs with which they are not familiar. For example, the wife may be better able to assess food and laundry costs, and the husband may have a clearer idea of costs of automobile maintenance. This kind of cooperation is encouraged if it appears that the couple can discuss these issues at home without becoming competitive and fighting. The couple can also agree on a third person whom each of them can consult about their needs. This third person needs to be one they both trust. The wife is encouraged to establish credit for herself as a first step in establishing her own financial autonomy.

The second hour is spent on marital property division. The mediator studies the financial forms and proposed budgets that each party has completed. If for some reason the budgets have not been prepared for the second session, the mediator reserves the right to cancel the session and charge the full fee. Stalling is not tolerated. When the budgets are reviewed, the mediator determines whether the combined budgets exceed the family income. The options for resolution are presented: either find more income or reduce the budgets. There is a strong emphasis on each person's taking individual responsibility for tailoring his or her own budget without crossreferencing with the other spouse. The question to each individual is, "How might you decrease *your* budget or increase *your* income?"

The third through sixth sessions deal with resolving property, support, and custody issues. If not resolved, the options are to extend the mediation hours or declare an impasse. A significant observation has been reported: in the first three years' existence of the Family Mediation Center, 250 cases were seen; in none of these cases was an impasse requiring the decision to go to arbitration declared (Coogler,

1978). Many times an extension of mediation hours is granted but seldom goes 3 or 4 hours beyond the 10. An additional deposit is required before the extra hours begin.

If an agreement has been reached, two hours are designated for the seventh session, which includes the advisory attorney. The agreement is presented to the lawyer and legal questions are asked. Discussion about maximizing tax benefits is also included. In the eighth session, the lawyer presents the legal contract to the couple.

The ninth session may be a time to continue resolution of custody and visitation if an agreement has not been reached. The mediator, as stated before, encourages the children's participation in these sessions. The mediator insists that each parent give the children explicit permission to talk in the session.

Participation by the children is considered important for several reasons. First, the reality of the parents' impending divorce is made evident. Since children often try to manipulate their parents to get back together, the mediation process makes clear that this is not a possibility. Second, input from the children about their desires (e.g., to remain in the same school, near the same friends) is valuable information to both mediator and parents in assessing custody and visitation arrangements. It is thought that decisions that are reached by the entire family have a much better change of being carried out effectively postdivorce.

SPECIFIC TECHNIQUES

Specific interventions used during the course of divorce mediation involve primarily those interventions that will enable individuals to maintain an adult ego state during negotiation. If supplying adult information does not work, the mediator approaches each person's child ego state to help him or her get in touch with and understand the underlying feelings. The objective of the mediator's intervention is to cross the transaction so that the discussion may take a new direction. In general, when a couple are angry and fighting, the mediator either shifts to another issue for resolution or terminates the hour. Ventilation of anger is considered unproductive and a hindrance to the goal of mediation (i.e., reaching a settled

agreement rather than resolving differences). Arguing is allowed only when the mediator uses a paradoxical injunction designed to stop the arguing. The mediator prescribes the symptom to the couple by instructing them to continue the argument for the next five minutes while the mediator keeps time.

When conflicts are child–child oriented, interventions are designed so that the mediator uses his or her nurturing parent to care for the sacred child of the individual, allowing him or her to move out of the child ego state into the adult ego state and to resume reasonable negotiations.

When blaming and guilt conflicts occur, the mediator employs his or her parent ego state and tells the critical parent to stop blaming and the child to stop responding to blame. The mediator also sets firm limits on arguing and addresses each person's child ego state about the feelings being experienced underneath the anger.

There are frequent occasions when it becomes clear to the mediator that the couple is stuck on an emotional issue and unable to negotiate effectively. When this occurs, the mediator encourages the couple to be seen in counseling for one or two sessions by another mediator. If couples are in outside counseling, they are encouraged to continue while going through the mediation process.

CLIENTS

Of the divorcing population in Atlanta, one-tenth of one percent have come to the Divorce Mediation Center. They have been, by and large, an upper-middle-class population, with the following characteristics:

1. *Age Range:* 28 to 45, with exceptions tending to fall beyond 45 rather than under 28.
2. *Duration of Marriage:* 6 to 15 years, with exceptions being longer than 15 years.
3. *Family Income Level:* $18,000 to $30,000 annually, with exceptions exceeding $30,000.
4. *Children:* One to three.
5. *Education:* Two to four years' college, with a significant number of professionals having graduate degrees.
6. *Property:* Equity in a residence, two cars, and household furnishings.

7. *Savings:* Vary widely, from an insignificant amount to a range of $5,000 to $10,000 in a variety of forms.
8. *Insurance:* Hospitalization, medical and life insurance on the life of the husband.
9. *Debt:* Mortgage on residence or other real estate owned, credit cards. Outstanding balance, other than real estate or business loans, are about $600 (Coogler, 1977b, p. 8).

Therefore, divorce mediation has so far only served a middle- to upper-middle-class population. No evidence presently exists of the use of divorce mediation by other populations. Coogler, et al. (1979) reported that although divorce mediation is presently a system designed to serve couples of a middle- and upper-income range, mediation techniques are now being adapted to serve lower-income families. Typically, however, couples who have used divorce mediation have been married 6 to 15 years, have 1 to 3 children, an annual income of $17,000 or more, own equity in a home, and have a modest amount of savings.

OTHER DEVELOPMENTS IN DIVORCE MEDIATION

Since Coogler's (1977a) initial work, the process of divorce mediation has become a nationwide service. Coogler founded the Family Mediation Association in Atlanta, Georgia, in 1974. The Family Mediation Association (FMA), however, now has its headquarters in Washington, D.C. It is a nonprofit, educational-research organization dedicated to "enhancing the quality of family life" (Coogler, 1981, p. 3). FMA's primary goal is to focus on how conflicts resulting from marital separation and divorce are resolved and to promote cooperative rather than competitive divorce negotiations.

Several training centers now exist in various regions of the United States. The five-day intensive training workshops focus on the mediation process, therapeutic skills needed to mediate settlements, financial aspects of divorce, and legal aspects of mediation. Didactic presentations and role-playing are used to teach the mediator practical philosophy, communication skills from a viewpoint, tax consequences of divorce, postdivorce budgeting, and legal issues relevant to mediation in various states.

Adaptation of the structured mediation model for use with lower-income populations has been started by Coogler (1978). He defined the target population by seven criteria: (1) limited verbal skills, (2) low family income, (3) erratic employment, (4) lack of job skills, (5) poor reading ability, (6) reliance on extended family, and (7) alienation from society. These "low income" families, he proposed, have fewer financial issues than middle-class couples and a variety of lifestyle issues usually ignored by agencies handling the divorce process because middle-class values permeate their procedures. He prescribed intake and treatment measures that recognize the importance of time and the extended family as primary assets versus money and property. Thus the clients' time is regarded highly in specific, concrete ways, and the extended family is incorporated into the mediation process. The family support system is realigned by including other family members and the services that they contribute to the negotiations. Finally, cultural and procedural elements of the mediation procedure that reinforce these families' reticence to participate are altered. This is done, in part, by enlisting the aid of neutral parties from the family's subculture. Coogler proposed a revision of the rules of mediation, but such a revision is not yet available.

OTHER ORIENTATIONS TO DIVORCE MEDIATION

In addition to Coogler's (1978) work, others have offered a variety of perspectives on the divorce mediation process. A discussion of divorce mediation would be incomplete without an examination of the conceptual and practical alternatives and additions to Coogler's system.

Haynes (1981) offers an alternative mediation style and addresses several interpersonal, emotional, and procedural issues that Coogler neglected. He further integrates his intervention with a model of the adaptation of couples to marital dissolution. The role of therapeutic skills and the proximity of mediation to therapy are incorporated into his approach. Haynes provides a framework within which to mediate divorce, which has much in common with

Coogler's model but is less structured and procedurally specific. In some respects, it is also more complete.

Whereas Coogler accepts the decision to divorce as a given and excludes this from the negotiations, Haynes states that many people entertain the notion of divorce as a gambit to produce change in the relationship or simply decide to litigate before they are ready to actually separate. Thus the mediator must evaluate appropriateness of the couple for mediation. Signs of inappropriate clients are clients who (1) balk at the fee despite knowledge of the cost of adversarial divorce, (2) deny that divorce is the reason for their referral, and (3) refuse to accomplish early task assignments. In these cases, clients should be referred to a marital therapist. One party may resist settlement through refusal to come to final agreement on all issues. Haynes suggests taking time out from mediation to clarify the reasons for the divorce and focus in joint sessions on each partner's needs that were unfulfilled by the marriage. Through articulation of the dissatisfaction by the party who feels rejected, the process of rejection becomes mutual and resistance to separation is overcome.

Haynes proposes a first session that is essentially identical to divorce mediation. The process is described, basic data are collected, and the groundwork for construction of budgets is established. It is, however, unclear how Haynes provides for financial arrangements during the mediation process. The therapeutic goals are building rapport, establishing the mediator's credibility, and beginning to assess the readiness of the couple for divorce. In the remaining sessions of the first phase of mediation, the mediator sees each partner in individual sessions. The mediator assesses the degree of equality of power in the relationship and defines the individual goals of each client in separate interviews. Feelings that are expressed in individual sessions but are not articulated in joint ones are identified, catologued as possible points that may require attention in joint sessions, and drawn out in individual sessions. Settlement goals for each partner are identified, and the degree of disagreement on these issues is assessed. A strategy for dealing with power imbalances is devised.

Negotiations progress in a carefully planned order. Issues on which the partners are in close agreement are raised first. A sense of cooperation and successful movement toward settlement are maintained. More difficult items are the behind-the-scenes negotiations in individual sessions. The mediator trains each person to think in terms of trade-offs. The acceptability of each plan for mutual concessions is tested in individual sessions. These quid pro quos are built into an overall settlement through shuttle diplomacy. Only after the issues have been substantially reduced to solutions are the face-to-face negotiations begun. This preparation results in very short bargaining sessions, with minimal chance of impasse. Emotional items that may block settlement and have been identified are ventilated in joint sessions before the bargaining begins. Unexpected emotional issues are allowed expression to the degree that establishment of a sense of successful movement toward a settlement has been established. The item is removed for later consideration if an impasse seems to be developing, and the cooperative spirit is reintroduced through more easily resolved items. Emotions are shared but only in the context of moving toward resolution of the issues.

Haynes believes that the feelings experienced by divorcees are a normal part of transition. As such, the mediator must know the common emotions that accompany stages in divorce and must encourage ventilation in a carefully arranged atmosphere of movement toward a new lifestyle. When these emotions interfere with negotiations, they are shared with the partner in this context. Otherwise, they are shared with the mediator. Although Haynes does not mention this, this procedure probably aids the parties to begin or continue the emotional separation from the marriage. In addition, Haynes sees emotional reactions as being a product of unequal power relationships or ambivalence about the divorce. Straightforward approaches to rectifying these situations are proposed.

A major goal of Haynes' mediation is to help the clients to set up functional postdivorce lifestyles. The strengths of the individual clients are determined, and weaknesses are bolstered by helping the clients take charge of the challenges arising from divorce. In addition, Haynes sees the clients as having a continuing relationship as parents. Negotiation is aimed at a settlement that not only meets the needs of the parents, but the children's need for access to both parents. This is accomplished largely by fostering open lines of communication between the parents and between each parent and the children. This also is done in a mediation format. A cooperative atmosphere is established, and the issue of "access" rather than "custody" is discussed. The necessity for a permanent cooperative relationship is emphasized. The question of where the children will reside is assumed to be a negotiating tool for one party and a genuine desire for the other. Disputes over custody are resolved by determining the "real" issue for the less committed parent and negotiating a trade-off in individual sessions. Children are included in the negotiations to (1) get and keep them informed about the fact of the divorce, (2) develop the precedent of continuing access to both parents, (3) remove the children's conceptions that they are responsible for the divorce and/or can somehow reconcile the parents, and (4) emphasize that they are not in sessions to choose one parent over another.

The settlement is written, based on the agreements made during the bargaining phase. It is then reviewed by a lawyer and processed under no-fault divorce laws. The settlement provides a basis for continued parenting, property division, child support, and the development of a viable lifestyle for both parties. The settlement may include provisions for the previously dependent spouse to acquire job skills. Post-divorce disputes can be negotiated using skills learned in mediation, or mediation can be renewed.

Coogler and Haynes agree on the relative roles of the mediator and the lawyer. The former serves as mediator and the latter steps in after mediation is completed to adjust the settlement to legal realities. This format rests on the assumption that a therapist's training in interpersonal skills provides him or her with a basis that is superior for mediation to the lawyer's training in advocacy of a client's point of view. It also assumes that knowledge of legal rights of clients is irrelevant in achieving equitable settlements.

Neither this format nor this point of view is universally accepted. Steinberg (1976) suggested that nonadversarial divorce can be achieved through the use of lawyers who ob-

tain training in therapeutic skills or through attorney-therapist teams. In one team approach (Black & Joffe, 1978), the therapist helps the couple to identify emotional issues and communicate about individual and relationship issues; the lawyer focuses the couple on the possible alternatives for settlement and protects the rights of both parties. Differentiation of legal and emotional issues is seen as helpful, and the members of the team work together to move the negotiations toward settlement. Another approach (Wiseman & Fiske, 1980) utilizes the therapist as a consultant to the attorney as a means of dealing with resistance and moving the process through impasses. The therapist may enter the process directly when emotional issues substantially retard the mediation process.

EVALUATION

Questions about the utility and efficacy of divorce mediation can be formulated in several ways: Is mediation effective? If so, by what criteria? Does mediation provide a good alternative to and/or a replacement for adversarial divorce? How widely applicable is it?

To date, there are three available sources of outcome assessment. Reviews of the conciliation court process have shown that results have been disappointing (MacLean, 1977). These studies, however, do not separate counseling aimed at reconciliation from mediation of divorce, and they also utilize reconciled marriages as the criterion of success. These studies are thus useless in evaluating divorce mediation, which sets as its goal less traumatic, completed divorce settlements.

The second source is reports by mediators. Reports of the percentage of settlements reached and the dropout rate estimate success from 40 to 98 percent (Kessler, 1978). The reports cluster around 70 percent. The time investment in many of these cases is substantially lower than that required for adversarial divorces. The major problem with these statistics, however, is that they do not evaluate the quality of the settlements.

Kressel, et al. (1980) have published initial results from the only study that identified the mediation process explicitly (Coogler's system) and focused on qualitative aspects of the process. They generate some interesting, if only suggestive, results. The results can be taken only as suggestive because of acknowledged methodological limitations. Mediators achieved their stated goals only in part 'with virtually all couples. The degree of success appears to have depended on several features of the couples' interactional styles that were consistent over the period during which the decision to divorce was reached and the period of negotiation in mediation. All but one couple achieved a settlement (N = 9). Some degree of dissatisfaction with the settlement, difficulties with implementation of the settlement (e.g., problems with property division), and/or problems with postdivorce adjustment of the children were present for most couples.

Comparison couples who used the adversarial system, however, fared the same or worse (N = 5) in the study. For this reason, mediation does seem to provide a promising alternative to the judicial arbitration. Although it has been recommended that divorce be taken out of the hands of the courts altogether (Davis, 1977), mediation does not seem to provide a basis for doing so. Some of the nonmediated couples in Kressel's study were aware of the availability of mediation but chose not to use it. As an alternative in the sense of a universally preferable alternative to court hearings, the results are inconclusive.

TRAINING IMPLICATIONS FOR MEDIATORS

The Family Mediation Association (Coogler, 1981) has trained a number of professionals to be mediators. Initially, the training program was a year-long, one-evening-per-week design that offered legal, psychological, and experiential input into the process of mediation. Coogler's (1977b) manual was the basic text, each chapter concluding with additional reading assignments on no-fault divorce, legal aspects, conflict resolution, and TA theory. Trainees were familiarized with all the details of Georgia state law, since that was the state of practice. The training included role-playing and increasing the clinical skills of mediation. Each trainee had the opportunity to sit through several actual mediation processes with the trainers. Each trainee was then supervised through at least one couple's entire mediation. All of those trained were required to have at least a master's degree in social work, psychology, pastoral counseling, or law, plus three years of full-time counseling experience. All the trainees returned to the agencies where they had been practicing and used their skills as mediators as an additional intervention.

Currently, training for mediators consists of a five-day, intensive training program that focuses on the mediation process, the resolution of interpersonal conflict and property division, and support and custody issues. There has been no follow-up on trainees after completion of the program, however.

DISCUSSION

Divorce mediation is the only well-developed and conceptualized mediation approach to divorce negotiation (Levinger & Moles, 1979). It also offers an alternative to the adversarial process and can be viewed as a pioneering, creative approach to a more human treatment of the legal divorce process. There are numerous inherent difficulties in structured mediation, however, primarily due to its relatively new and evolving approach.

From a theoretical viewpoint, one can state that intervention is guided by the theoretical approaches of TA and conflict resolution (Coogler, et al., 1979). Both these approaches demand that clients be rational and somewhat objective. The effectiveness of TA and negotiation skills as rational intervention approaches is, however, questionable in what is often a crisis situation. Although the mediator is seen primarily as a facilitator in a structured negotiation process, the mediator is not only called upon to be objective in an often highly stressful, emotional situation, but also needs therapeutic skills in marital crisis intervention. The mediator cannot always follow the structured mediation approach because of the emotional demands of the clients. In addition, the mediator's techniques are crucial when children are included in the sessions. Coogler (1977b) suggested that to clear the air, the mediator should ask the children, "What were you told not to say in here?" Although this recommended intervention does help to establish a policy of openness and the unacceptability of secrets, it could also add to the children's initial feelings that they must side with one or the other parent. It would take a sensitive and skilled mediator to ensure that a child not be put in the middle of a situation in which he or she has to state directly a preference for living with one parent while rejecting living with the other.

Thus two major concerns with the divorce mediation approach are raised. First, it may take a highly skilled therapist/mediator to intervene in the negotiation of the couple's divorce. Second, divorce mediation may be a simplistic, structured approach to a couple's immediate emotional crisis. For example, although cooperation between divorcing partners is stressed, the ultimate designation of one parent as a "custodial parent" still gives that parent the final authority to make decisions about the children. Designating one parent as the ultimate authority figure often leads to years of controversy (Coogler, 1977b).

Unfortunately, as with most marital and divorce interventions, the cost of the service is prohibitive for couples other than those of the middle and upper-middle classes. The Family Mediation Association's statistics confirm that no lower-class families are presently served by the mediation process. Whether it is an intervention suitable only for educated, middle- to upper-middle-class families remains to be seen.

Finally, there currently exists no evaluative research on the effectiveness of structured divorce mediation, and although a humane settlement is desirable, long-term ramifications for participants are unknown. Furthermore, mediation has still received little acceptance. Wood (1978) believes that lawyers will not refer clients because referral diminishes lawyers' own incomes. Mediation is indeed a potentially serious economic threat to family-law attorneys. In addition, few divorcing couples are initially "rational," and they may simply not be receptive to the divorce mediation approach.

FUTURE CONSIDERATIONS

Divorce mediation appears to be useful primarily for middle-class couples who have the following characteristics: They are relatively clear in their decision to divorce. If ambivalence still exists, the couple has made substantial progress toward resolving it since the initial discussion of divorce. Thus the couple is fairly well functioning.

Other mediation strategies have been proposed, varying primarily on the dimensions of structures and specific interventions relative to potential and actual impasses. They are all similar, however, in that they advocate an atmosphere in which couples can negotiate a fair settlement actively and cooperatively. They all emphasize minimizing trauma to children, and they all define the role of the mediator(s) similarly, i.e., to identify issues, equalize power imbalances, diffuse tension, teach negotiation skills, and keep the couple focused on movement toward a mutually agreed upon settlement (Black & Joffe, 1978; Coogler, 1978; Haynes, 1978; Kessler, 1978; Wiseman & Fiske, 1980). Haynes' approach, however, is the only one that heavily emphasizes assessment and the equalization of power relationships, as well as the importance of addressing clients' resistance to negotiate cooperatively. Haynes' proposed model may thus more fully consider the emotional complexities of the divorce process.

Structured mediation appears to be a pioneering, valid, and useful option for pursuing a divorce settlement. The approach needs further theoretical and technical development, however, particularly in the theory and techniques of negotiation styles. Research and evaluation need to be initiated because, currently, divorce mediation can only offer face validity for its potential effectiveness. Furthermore, it is a model that limits participation to middle- and upper-class individuals. Thus its applicability to a broader range of clients needs to be explored.

REFERENCES

Black M, & Joffe W. A lawyer/therapist approach to divorce. *Conciliation Courts Review*, 1978, *16*, 15

Blake NM. *The road to Reno. A history of divorce in the United States.* New York: Jossey-Bass, 1962

Bohannon P. *Divorce and after.* Garden City, NJ: Doubleday, 1970

Coogler OJ. Changing the lawyer's role in matrimonial practice. *Conciliation Courts Review*, 1977a, *15*, 1–8

Coogler OJ. *Structured mediation in divorce settlements*. Atlanta: Family Mediation Association, 1977b

Coogler OJ. *Structured mediation in divorce settlements*. Lexington, MA: Heath, 1978

Coogler OJ. *Marital mediator training*. Bethesda, MD: Family Mediation Association Training Division, 1981

Coogler OJ, Weber R, & McKenry P. Divorce mediation: A means of facilitating divorce and adjustment. *The Family Coordinator*, 1979, *28*, 255–259

Davis JD. Effects of communication about interpersonal process on the evolution of self-disclosure in dyads. *Journal of Personality and Social Psychology*, 1977, *35*, 31–37

Deutsch M. *The resolution conflict*. New Haven: University Press, 1973

The Family Mediator. January 1981 Newsletter. Published by the Family Mediation Association

Friedman LM. *A history of American law*. New York: Simon & Schuster, 1973

Goode WJ. *Women in divorce*. New York: Free Press, 1956

Gove WR. The relationship between sex roles, marital status, and mental illness. *Social Forces*, 1972, *51*, 34–44

Gurin G, Veroff J, & Feld S. *Americans view their mental health. A nationwide study*. New York: Basic Books, 1960

Haynes JM. Divorce mediator: A new role. *Social Work*, 1978, *23*, 5–8

Haynes JM. *Divorce mediation*. New York: Springer, 1981

Kessler S. *Creative conflict resolution: Mediation*. Atlanta: National Institute for Professional Training, 1978

Kressel K, Jaffee N, Tuchman B, Watson C, & Deutsch M. A typology of divorcing couples: Implications for mediation and the divorce process. *Family Process*, 1980, *19*, 101–116

Levinger G, & Moles O (Eds). *Divorce and separation: Context, causes, and consequences*. New York: Basic Books, 1979

MacLean JV. Marriage counseling through the divorce courts—Another look. *South Carolina Law Review*, 1977, *28*, 687–701

Mueller G. Inquiry into the state of a divorceless society: Domestic relations law and morals in England from 1660 to 1857. *University of Pittsburgh Law Review*, 1957, *18*, 545

Schiff J. *An introduction to transactional analysis*. New York: Brunner/Mazel, 1978

Shaffer HB. No fault divorce. *Editorial Research Reports*, 1973, *2*, 779–796

Shoen R, & Huber J. California's experience with non-adversary divorce. *Demography*, 1975, *12*, 223–243

Spencer JM, & Zammitt JP. Reflections on arbitration under the family dispute services. *Arbitration Journal*, 1977, *22*, 111–122

Steinberg JL. The therapeutic potential of the divorce process. *American Bar Association Journal*, 1976, *62*, 617–620

U.S. Bureau of the Census. *Current Population Reports* (Series P-20, No. 306). Washington, DC: U.S. Government Printing Office, 1977

Weiss RS. *Marital separation*. New York: Basic Books, 1975

Wheeler M. *No fault divorce*. Boston: Beacon Press, 1974

Wiseman JM, & Fiske JA. A lawyer-therapist as mediator in a marital crisis. *Social Work*, 1980, *25*, pp. 425–445

Wood J. Personal communication, November 10, 1978

15

Divorce and Postdivorce Interventions*

Traditionally, the institution of marriage was considered a sacred and lifelong bond. The marriage couple made various promises about fealty, love, and honor that were to last "till death do us part." These vows were usually witnessed by family members, friends, the church, and in turn were supported by a variety of social institutions. It has been widely held that societal involvement and concern with marriage stemmed from the essential functions performed by the marriage and family system. That is, marriage was more than just the private concern of the couple since it was intimately related to such basic social functions as replacement of members, status ascription, nurturant socialization, personality formation, and economic cooperation. It may be added that many traditional functions of marriage for economic and procreative reasons have given way to more personal and worthy emotional functions, i.e., self-fulfillment, self-confrontation, and companionship. From these functions, it follows that divorce may take place because of inadequate self-fulfillment, avoidance of self-confrontation, or inadequate companionship.

The importance of marriage is illuminated by traditional attitudes toward divorce. In America, divorce was taboo and regarded as an evil to be avoided. Various segments of society viewed it as an indicator of familial and societal breakdown, deviant behavior, religious

heresy, individual pathology, and a prime cause of juvenile deliquency. In summarizing the traditional prevailing attitudes toward divorce in America, Singer (1975) identified four major categories. The first is "The Moral Deterioration Theory," based on various aspects of the Protestant ethic, which asserts that divorcing couples are irresponsible and lack moral courage. Many adherents of this theory propose that divorce laws be tightened as a means of dealing with the increasing divorce rate. The second category, "The Ignorance Theory," suggests that divorce results when immature and insufficiently prepared young people marry before they are ready. This perspective asserts that what is needed are didactic approaches, such as "preparation for marriage courses," and more premarital counseling. The third, the psychodynamic viewpoint, is based upon psychoanalytic and psychological theory, and it proposes that divorce is the result of intrapsychic conflicts left over from the family of origin. Many proponents of this viewpoint suggest that some form of systematic intervention is needed, since divorced people will tend to repeat over and again with future partners their neurotic patterns of interaction. Finally, "The Divorce is Inevitable" theory is based on the sociological notion that divorce is a mass phenomenon inherent to cultures that allow free choice of marital partner and, therefore, freedom to divorce if one chooses. According to Singer (1975), supporters of this approach do not see divorce as undermining the social fabric, since be-

---

*This chapter was researched by John Blount.

tween 85 and 90 percent of all divorced persons eventually remarry.

These rather rigid and, in some cases, ominous perspectives on divorce have changed radically in recent years. Researchers from a variety of disciplines have documented the changing attitudes toward divorce in the United States. Brown (1976) indicated that since the mid-1960s there has been a pronounced trend toward a more positive view of divorce, the most obvious indicator of change being the adoption by many states of "no-fault" divorce laws. Our society is beginning to accept divorce as a fact of life (and of marriage) or is attempting to learn how to live with it.

A somewhat different line of thought characterizes changing attitudes toward divorce in terms of the traditional labels attributed to divorcing couples. These people were often labeled abnormal, deviant, and neurotic. Fisher (1975), however, suggested that today the divorcing and divorced population is observed as coming from all walks of life, a diversity of cultural backgrounds, and a myriad of life situations. A large proportion are as likely to be "normal" as those who choose to keep their marriages.

Similarly, many mental health professionals see some divorces as flights toward health—a search to escape a living arrangement that is no longer tolerable or fulfilling (Kaslow, 1981). Crosby (1980) supports this view and believes that many divorces are indicative of personal growth and of the continual struggle for personal fulfillment. He goes on to suggest that today there is a change in the social climate, in that many persons are less reluctant to leave a nonproductive, nonrewarding relationship, and that a significantly greater number of persons are divorcing because they are no longer socially stigmatized and/or locked into a destructive relationship.

Sociologists have also described the changing social climate as it relates to increased divorce rates and attitudes toward divorce. Using a macrolevel of analysis, Goetting (1979) pointed to five interrelated components of the social structure that have been contributing factors: (1) the doctrine of individualism, (2) the sexual equality movement, (3) the trend toward acceptance of divorce, (4) increasing systemness, and (5) affluence. Other sociologists have pointed to the effect that social policy may have on the decision to divorce. Nye and Bernardo (1966), Greenfield and Falk (1973), Caplan (1975, 1976), and Bahr (1979) have all suggested that social programs such as Aid to Families with Dependent Children, Food Stamps, and Legal Aid may aggravate the very problems they are supposed to resolve. That is, instead of contributing to family stability, these programs often provide financial incentives that encourage and support divorce among the poor.

Concomitant with the changing attitudes toward divorce, the United States has experienced a steadily increasing divorce rate in the past two decades. Although most demographers and other researchers would agree that there has been an increase, the extent of increase is a matter of considerable debate (e.g., Crosby, 1980; Eshleman, 1978). The problems with interpreting divorce statistics are many: for example, there are six different ways in which divorce rates are calculated, each with its own distinct advantages and disadvantages. Although the problems of calculating and interpreting divorce statistics are acknowledged, one cannot escape the fact that approximately 1,000,000 divorces have been granted each year for the past five years. Furthermore, as Kressel (1980) indicated, however one chooses to regard divorce statistics, one is clearly dealing with a phenomenon of extensive societal and personal significance.

It is in this context of changing attitudes toward divorce and increasing numbers of people affected by it that the new fields of divorce and postdivorce counseling have emerged.

BACKGROUND AND DEVELOPMENT

In a discussion of the origins of divorce counseling, Brown (1976) summarized her findings by stating,

While it is an outgrowth of the social services, it has not developed from either the marital or family therapy fields, or from any one of the helping professions, nor is it an adjunct to the courts or the legal professions. Rather, it is a concrete extension of the changes in societal attitudes toward the family. For the most part, those individuals active in the area of divorce, in any capacity, are those who through personal experience have become aware of the problems and have decided to do something about them (p. 409).

In this brief excerpt, Brown (1976) identified many of the threads that together resulted in the emergence of divorce counseling. However, by emphasizing certain variables, deemphasizing others, and omitting still others, a rather simplistic picture of the genesis of this counseling specialty emerges. It should also be noted that with the exception of Brown's (1976) discussion, little can be found in the literature that traces the historical development of divorce counseling. With these limitations in mind, a more elaborate and holistic perspective about the origins of divorce counseling is attempted here.

The basic assumption used in this analysis is that human organization is systemic. Society and its components are seen as complex networks of interlocking and interdependent social systems that are regulated by a variety of feedback mechanisms. The key concepts here are interlocking, interdependent, and feedback. That is, all the parts of the social system are influenced by and influence the other parts in patterned ways. This perspective, which evolved from functionalism in the biological and social sciences, has proved useful in analyzing such diverse topics as physiology, the economy, families, and marriages. If one accepts its applicability and usefulness in these various areas, it should also prove enlightening when analyzing social movements such as the emergence of clinical interventions and, more specifically, divorce counseling.

What follows is a description of how the field of divorce counseling emerged from the coalescing of many systems within the social sciences. Although a precise model, which might be time-sequenced and evaluated in terms of each component's impact, is beyond the scope of this chapter, a discussion of the predisposing variables and a tentative model about the emergence of this new specialty is presented.

Perhaps the earliest precursor to divorce and postdivorce counseling was research on the divorce process and subsequent adjustments to it. Waller's (1930) *The Old Love and the New* initiated research into this area and, as Rose and Bonham (1973) noted, it provided

an historical backdrop for more contemporary studies. Above and beyond the findings reported and the hypotheses generated, its major contribution was to help strip away the academic and public taboos about divorce and establish it as a legitimate and sorely needed area for future research.

The next benchmark in the history of divorce adjustment was Goode's (1965) study of divorced women in Detroit. Although a multitude of findings and hypotheses were generated by this study, only those that impinge directly on divorce counseling are reviewed. Furthermore, as will become evident later in this chapter, many of these findings have provided the basis for a variety of clinical interventions presently in vogue.

Using a variety of self-reported behavioral indicators, Goode (1956) trichotomized his sample on the level of trauma experienced as a result of divorce. He found high trauma to be associated with (1) an ongoing and strong attachment or emotional involvement with the ex-spouse, (2) feeling ambivalent about obtaining a divorce, (3) personally disapproving of divorce in general, (4) experiencing disapproval of divorce by significant others, (5) being discriminated against as a result of being divorced, (6) having the divorce initiated by one spouse unexpectedly, and (7) a desire to punish the ex-spouse. Conversely, a higher degree of adjustment after divorce was associated with (1) economic stability such as dependable child-support payments and having a full-time job, (2) an attitude of indifference tword the ex-spouse, and (3) having greater opportunities to develop new social relationships through jobs or other social activities.

In their review of divorce adjustment, Rose and Bonham (1973) described another major conclusion of Goode's (1956) research that bears directly on divorce and postdivorce counseling. Similar ideas have been expressed elsewhere by such researchers as Bernard (1956), Hunt (1966), and Bohannon (1969): i.e., although divorce is permitted in our society, postdivorce institutional arrangements for divorced persons are lacking. The societal inadequacies include (1) a lack of prescriptions concerning reaction to divorce, (2) no clear definition of the proper relationship between divorced spouses, and (3) the ambiguous arrangements provided by the kinship structure in such areas as readmission into the kinship structure, proper behavior and emotional attitudes, and material and emotional support. Therefore it seems likely that one of the important variables in the emergence of divorce and postdivorce counseling is the lack of institutionalized norms concerning the roles associated with divorce, resulting in the divorced person's perceiving his or her status as ambiguous and often painful.

Encompassing the research on divorce adjustment and important to the origins of divorce and postdivorce counseling has been the explosion of academic interest and research in the general area of marriage and the family. As early as 1960, Hill and Hansen noted that in the United States alone, research articles numbered more than 200 a year, and the annual production of research findings adds up to a magnitude sufficient to baffle the research librarian. This outpouring of research has not abated but has increased exponentially in the last 20 years. A myriad of private and public organizations have helped fund research in this area and have also been instrumental in providing outlets for the research findings (e.g., NCFR sponsors *The Journal of Marriage and Family* and *Family Relations*, formerly *The Family Coordinator*, and other publications).

Several specialty areas that may be seen as contributors to divorce and postdivorce counseling are (1) parent–child relations, (2) effects of divorce on children, (3) single-parent families, (4) family violence, (5) marital satisfaction, and (6) marital stability. Crucial to the evaluation of divorce and postdivorce counseling has been the clinical practice of and research on marriage and family therapy and counseling. As Brown (1976) suggested, there have always been some marriage and family agencies that provided divorce counseling. These services were not provided on any systematic basis, however, and were not called divorce counseling. Furthermore, when divorce counseling was provided, it was usually as an outgrowth of the work with an individual or couple that had resulted in a decision to divorce. The central point here is that, in the past, divorce and postdivorce counseling interventions usually arose from a clinical desire to provide services for clients in need, even though adequate training and knowledge about the divorce process and treatment approaches were often beyond the expertise of the coun-

selor. This theme is repeated throughout the literature.

Fisher (1975) observed, prior to 1960, the pain and suffering of divorcing persons and the futile efforts at reconciliation and help by human lawyers who were without the benefit of clinical training and knowledge:

Naively, I thought: "Somewhere there must be people who help these persons in their emotional, physical, social, and economic distress." There was no one: no agency, no therapists, no ministers really equipped to help those either in the process of divorcing or already divorced (p. 265).

These sentiments are echoed from a variety of sources: Kessler (1976) described the need for divorce adjustment groups; Morris and Prescott (1976) responded to increasing requests for divorce and postdivorce counseling at a university counseling center; and Wallerstein and Kelly (1977) developed a divorce counseling service in response to the needs of an emerging and rapidly increasing population of children and parents in divorcing families. In a similar vein, Brown (1976) suggested that many of the practitioners of divorce counseling are professionals who have been divorced themselves and have been confronted by the lack of supportive services and by the problems associated with the legal adversary process.

Another major thrust in the emergence of divorce and postdivorce counseling has come from the legal system in the form of conciliation or family courts. Elkin (1977) suggested that with the greater number of family breakdowns, there has been an increasing awareness that the responsibility of the law and the courts should not be limited to the narrow and traditional considerations of the legal grounds for divorce. Furthermore, since a marriage cannot be terminated without recourse to a legal procedure, the judicial system is in an advantageous position to provide marital, divorce, or postdivorce counseling services.

Although conciliation courts have existed since 1939, their acceptance by the public and professionals has been mixed. For example, New York abolished its mandatory conciliation procedures in 1973 because of the expense and lack of success in reconciling broken homes. Data from family courts in other states show no convincing evidence that family courts are any more or less successful than their predecessor courts in promoting family stability while on the other hand, the voluntary conciliation court system in California, particularly in Los Angeles, has been held up as an exemplary model for other courts and claims considerable success (Elkin, 1977). Despite their effectiveness, or lack of it, these court systems have been valuable in that they have been in the forefront in the training and utilization of professional clinicians in the field of divorce and postdivorce counseling.

A final variable to be considered in the origins of divorce and postdivorce counseling is the society-wide increase in specialization, a consequence of what Toffler (1970) called the superindustrial revolution. Specialization in the helping professions is analogous to the process of differentiation in biology, by which embryos develop, forming more and more specialized organs:

The entire march of evolution, from virus to man, displays a relentless advance toward higher and higher degrees of differentiation. There appears to be a seemingly irresistible movement of living beings and social groups from less to more differentiated forms (Toffler, 1970, p. 300).

With increased specialization in the social order itself and the assumption of systemic relationships among the parts, it is not surprising or accidental that parallel trends in diversity should occur in the helping professions.

To summarize, a tentative model is presented that attempts to incorporate the major variables responsible for the emergence of divorce and postdivorce counseling. First, human organization is viewed as systemic and composed of interlocking and interdependent parts. Coupled with this assumption is the notion that the social system is becoming more differentiated, resulting in greater specialization in all spheres of life. Viewed from a macrolevel of analysis, these two observations would in themselves predict greater specialization in the helping professions, including the emergence of new specialties, such as divorce and postdivorce counseling. As we have seen, however, quite a few intervening variables entered the scene to bring this new area of intervention to fruition.

Moving down from assumptions about social organizations, one comes to the societal level and finds changing attitudes toward divorce, an ever-increasing number of persons affected by the divorce process, and a lack of institutional arrangements, or norms, concerning the status and roles for divorcing or divorced persons. This anomic situation in society filters down to the individual level, often resulting in ambiguity, pain, and requests for help from clinicians.

Coinciding with this need and a sincere desire to help are a plethora of clinical, academic, and legal interests in marriage and family life, of which divorce is an integral part. As the research and theory about marriage and the divorce process begins to proliferate, counselors in turn are able to apply these findings in a variety of settings. The stage is set, and the new specialty of divorce and postdivorce counseling begins to emerge.

THE TREATMENT PROCESS

An analysis of the treatment process involved in divorce and postdivorce counseling requires an exploration of several intimately related issues, including rationale (i.e., definitions, purposes, and goals of divorce and postdivorce counseling), the role of the counselor, and intervention techniques. Since a growing number of persons in the helping professions differentiate between divorce and postdivorce interventions, they are discussed separately.

Divorce counseling is generally seen as beginning during the decision-making process to sever the relationship and ends with the divorce decree. Postdivorce counseling begins at some point after the final legal processes and progresses through the adjustment period as the individuals struggle with the new identity of being single and its attendant problems. Although this dichotomy may be esthetically pleasing, a note of caution is warranted. The counselor involved with clients in the divorce process often finds no clear demarcation between these phases. This is because issues and problems that arose in the marital system before divorce often linger or reemerge long after the final decree. This is particularly frequent when children are involved; property settlement, child support, or alimony are issues; one of the spouses opposed the divorce and continues to press for reconciliation; and/or the couple remains emotionally enmeshed after divorce. With an understanding that the two stages often overlap, this discussion will attempt to identify the processes involved with each.

DIVORCE COUNSELING

Definition and Goals

Fisher (1975) defined divorce counseling as an answer to the cultural and individual needs of the divorcing population. It is a process in which the individual who is experiencing pain and doubt can be helped toward personal adjustment and growth. Unlike marriage counseling, which focuses on the potential for rehabilitation of the marital relationship, divorce counseling focuses on the diminution and final dissolution of the marital relationship, with concern for the intrapsychic needs of the individual spouse(s).

Brown (1976) described divorce counseling similarly by suggesting that it is a process that aids the couple in assessing whether their needs can be met in the marriage and, if not, assists them as they carry out a decision to divorce. Brown also differentiated marriage and divorce counseling and suggested that in some ways they are opposites. That is, while marriage counseling focuses on the individuals adjusting to the relationship and on increasing the functioning of that relationship, divorce counseling is concerned with saving the individual and decreasing the functions of the marriage, with the goal of eventual dissolution. It implies acceptance of the fact of divorce, rather than opposition to it, and focuses on helping the individuals understand their roles in the marital breakdown while encouraging personal growth and individuation.

In a discussion of psychotherapy during marital dissolution, Defazio and Klenbort (1975) view the decision to divorce as a crucial point on which the therapist and patient can focus. They see this period as an especially appropriate opportunity to focus on characteriologic traits and issues of individuation, separation, and dependency. It can be viewed as a time of growth and the attainment of maturity, as well as a time of self-confrontation and reassessment. They warn, however, that

if either the therapist or client simply views the situation as a failure in the life of the client, the opportunity for positive growth may be missed.

One also finds considerable agreement in the literature concerning more specific purposes and goals of divorce counseling (e.g., Brown, 1976; Fisher, 1975; Kaslow, 1981; Kressel & Deutsch, 1980). A prevalent metaphor found in this literature is that counseling sessions provide a battleground for the warring combatants. It is in this setting that the disturbed couple thrash out their disagreements over feelings about each other, their children, custody and visitation rights, and financial support. Here, in the counselor's office, one can ventilate feelings, needs, and desires more productively and safely than in the lawyer's office or the courtroom. Paradoxically, although the counseling session may serve as a battlefield, a central goal of the clinician is to alter conflict patterns and develop a setting in which sensible and reasonable agreements can emerge. As Fisher (1975) suggested, divorce counseling aims to help the couple, who were unable to agree in marriage, to agree to disagree and develop a measure of trust and faith that had been lost.

Another concern during divorce counseling is the impact the process has on the children and parent–child relationships. The family therapy literature is replete with examples of how children bear the burden (e.g., by becoming identified patients) of parental conflict or manifest a variety of acting-out behaviors in order to divert the attention from marital disharmony onto themselves. Whether this is a conscious or unconscious maneuver, the effect is often to solidify the suffering marital relationship for the well-being of the child. Also, as Kaslow (1981) suggests, some parents draw the children into the divorce process, expecting them to take sides and/or using them as a bond to keep the relationship together. In such situations, the child may be used as a go-between, pleading the case of one parent and attempting to prevent the parent who is pressing for divorce from leaving the system.

When confronted with these destructive patterns, it is often the goal of the counselor to extricate the child from the triangle. The agenda becomes (1) straightforward dialogue between parents and children about the impending divorce, (2) a consideration of the child's needs in the process, (3) facilitating the children's understanding that they are not responsible for the divorce or for getting the parents back together, and (4) helping the parents understand how they may be manipulating the child for individual gains at the child's psychological expense.

Brown (1976) pointed out that since our legal system encourages custody battles, some advocates of divorce reform are recommending that children be represented by an attorney, while others suggest providing a nonlegal advocate for the child during divorce proceedings. Although calling for additional research on the matter, Brown sees some form of family counseling as the most therapeutic approach. The goals are a consideration of the needs and emotions of all family members when making decisions on custody, visitation, and related matters.

In a discussion of intervention with children of divorcing families in a community mental health center, Kelly and Wallerstein (1977) identified the following goals, which seem to summarize counselors' concerns for children involved in the divorce process: (1) reduction in suffering, with suffering defined as intense anxiety, fearfulness, depression, anger, longing, or other symptoms causing distress; (2) reduction in the cognitive confusion as it relates to the divorce and its sequelae; (3) increasing psychological distance between the divorcing situation and the child, or between a parent and the child when the child has become directly involved in the parental conflict; and (4) successful resolution of various idiosyncratic issues of the family system.

Role of the Counselor

Kressel and Deutsch (1980) pointed out that research on the role of the counselor in divorce is the most underrepresented area in the literature on the divorce process and its consequences. In their description of the strategies and tactics used by experienced therapists, however, three general perspectives on the role of the divorce counselor can be gleaned.

In reflexive strategies, the role of the counselor is to orient himself or herself to the marital conflict and establish a framework on which

later activities can be built. Here the focus is on the counselor rather than the couple, with the goal of making the counselor the most effective possible instrument of intervention, given the circumstances.

On the other hand, in contextual interventions, the counselor's role is to affect the climate surrounding the marital conflict and establish the ground rules of interaction. In this situation, the counselor is the instrument for assisting in decision-making and negotiation of the divorce settlement.

Finally, in substantive strategies, the counselor's role involves taking active and direct responsibility for promoting specific agreements on matters of substance. The implication is that the counselor understands the dynamics underlying the marital conflict, knows what should be done to resolve it, and attempts directly to pressure or manipulate the divorcing couple into resolving their conflicts over substantive issues.

In the process of describing the stages of marital dissolution, Defazio and Klenbort (1975) also delineated several aspects of the role of the divorce counselor. Frequently, in the initial stage of divorce, one or both spouses entertain fantasies about reconciliation and the resumption of life as normal. The counselor's role is to focus on the fantasy, which may involve a great deal of denial and rationalization, in order to expedite the divorce process and/or the blocking of appropriate affect.

During the first stage, the client is also likely to experience anxiety and rage at being abandoned and left alone in the world (Defazio & Klenbort, 1975). At this juncture in treatment, the client often seeks authority, support, and nurturance in an effort to magically put his or her life back in order. The counselor is often tempted to provide the magic by giving aid, suggestions, and soothing words. The authors suggested that by assuming a supportive role, the counselor blocks the client's rage and avoids becoming its target.

Rice (1977) concentrated on the narcissistic injury resulting from the process of separation that may or may not lead to divorce. According to him, one of the main therapeutic tasks involves getting beneath "ego-preserving" resistances by concentrating on underlying infantile fantasies of grandiose self-importance and unconditional valuing by others. Rice suggested that the therapist's "ego" be used for support and help in restoring lost narcissistic gratifications. The therapist needs to help both partners become more aware of their needs for intimacy and the need to disclose their own vulnerability without risk of rejection.

Kressel and Deutsch (1980) interviewed 21 highly experienced therapists on the criteria of a constructive divorce, including the obstacles in advising such a divorce, and the strategies and tactics of divorce therapy. They found that the primary criterion for a constructive divorce is the successful completion of the process of "psychic" separation and the protection of the welfare of minor children. Therapy, then, needs to focus on the decision to obtain a divorce, with a parallel negotiation of the terms for a divorce settlement.

Kressel and Deutsch were able to identify three different types of therapeutic strategies: (1) reflexive interventions at the beginning of therapy when the therapist becomes oriented to the nature of the marital problems and attempts to gain the trust and confidence of the partners; (2) contextual interventions, by which the therapist attempts to present a climate that would be conducive to decision-making; and (3) substantive interventions intended to produce resolutions in terms of the dissolution of the marriage, which the therapist has found or has come to believe inevitable and necessary.

In addition to these strategies, Kressel and Deutsch commented on (1) the "nascent state" of divorce therapy as an area of specialization; (2) the problem of diagnostic criteria for divorce, which was addressed in a subsequent publication (Kressel, et al., 1980); (3) the relationship between therapists and lawyers, which can be found in a more recent compendium edited by L'Abate, 1982 (for further comments on legal issues, see Kargman, 1973; Robbins 1973, 1974); (4) the course and consequence of therapeutic impartiality; and (5) the degree to which therapists should validate the terms of divorce, an issue that is considered in detail in the next chapter.

POSTDIVORCE INTERVENTIONS

The literature on this process has grown by leaps and bounds in the last decade. It would be impossible to review all of it. Consequently, this section is selective and organized around (1) issues of postdivorce adjustment, (2) interventions based on individual approaches, (3) interventions based on group approaches, and (4) interventions with children of divorce.

Issues of Postdivorce Adjustment

Theory

Most of the theoretical models of postdivorce adjustment have been reviewed by Kaslow (1981) in a chapter that stands out as a landmark review in this field. She presented a dialectic model of stages in the divorce process, based on three broad stages: (1) predivorce deliberation period, (2) during-divorce litigation period, and (3) re-equilibration during postdivorce. These three stages are accompanied by at least six identifiable clusters of feelings: (1) disillusionment, dissatisfaction, and alienation; (2) dread, anguish, ambivalence, shock, emptiness, chaos, inadequacy, and low self-esteem; (3) depression, detachment, anger, hopelessness, and self-pity; (4) confusion, fury, sadness, loneliness, and relief; (5) optimism, resignation, excitement, animosity, and regret; and (6) acceptance, self-confidence, energy, self-worth, wholeness, exhilaration, independence, and autonomy.

The feelings are also paralleled by six other sequential clusters of requiste actions and tasks: (1) confronting partner, quarreling, seeking therapy, and denial; (2) physical and emotional withdrawal, pretending all is okay, and attempting to win back affection; (3) bargaining, screaming, threatening, attempting suicide, and mourning; (4) physical separation, filing for legal divorce, considering economic and custody arrangements, grieving and mourning, and making the divorce public through telling relatives and friends; (5) finalizing the divorce, reaching out for new friends, undertaking new activities, stabilizing the new lifestyle, and keeping up daily routines with self and children; and (6) resolution of identity, completing the psychic divorce, seeking new love-object and making a commitment to some permanency, becoming comfortable with new lifestyle and friends, and helping children accept finality of the divorce and their continuing relationship with both parents.

Laner (1978) presented a theory of marital dissolution based on a systems perspective and derived from propositions found in the relevant literature. The theory is made up of eight configurations representing positive and negative permutations of three levels—the societal, the dyadic, and the individual. Three of the eight configurations predict marital dissolution, two predict idiosyncratic outcomes, either dissolution or nondissolution, while the three remaining configurations predict marital nondissolution. Laner implied that this theory has implications for therapeutic interventions in each of the eight configurations. Unfortunately, the author failed to give diagnostic guidelines or criteria whereby each profile could be derived validly and reliably. As far as can be determined, no test of this theory has been published.

Information

For a sketchy and simple description of legal and tax consequences of divorce in the various states, with an excellent sample of a separation agreement, the reader should consult a monograph edited by L'Abate (1982). Albrecht (1980) compared the divorce experiences of 500 males and females drawn from eight Rocky Mountain states. Contrary to some early suggestions, Albrecht found that the experiences of males and females were quite different, particularly in such areas as stress associated with the divorce, property settlement, changes in social participation, and effects on income.

De Frain and Erick (1981) studied 33 divorced single-parent fathers and 38 divorced single-parent mothers, who showed almost no statistically significant differences on a large number of demographic measures, suggesting that the two groups were matched. Fathers had a slight edge over the mothers in income, education, and the tendency not to move from home and community after the divorce. In responding to 63 questions concerning (1) history of the divorce process, (2) feelings as a single parent, (3) childbearing issues, (4) children, feelings and behaviors, (5) relations with the ex-spouse, and (6) forming new social relationships, both groups differed significantly only on one question. Nearly a third of the fathers encouraged the children to take sides with them against the ex-spouse, while only one mother fostered such an approach. Consequently the authors of this study concluded that "the divorced single-parent life style for both men and women is very similar."

Individual Approaches

It is difficult, sometimes, to surmise when an individual approach has been followed or, indeed, if it was followed. Most reports on this issue are very generic and vague. Lazarus (1981), for example, maintained that divorce, if properly conducted by a trained therapist, can be a freeing experience that promotes family solidarity. He considered especially the role of "emotional blackmail" and other coercive maneuvers in unhappy marriages. This incompatibility should be identified to show more clearly its limits and its outcomes. In this regard, Lazarus used mental imagery as one therapeutic approach.

Goldman and Coane (1977), on the other hand, suggested therapy with the whole family because the parenting function continues even though the parents are by now divorced. They described a four-part model of intervention: (1) redefining the family as existentially including all members, (2) firming up generational boundaries to reduce parentification, (3) replaying the marriage history to correct developmental distortions and offer a chance to mourn the loss of the intact family, and (4) facilitating an emotional divorce—a task much more difficult than that of obtaining a physical or legal divorce.

Vaughn (1981) presents a model of divorce adjustment therapy based on specific techniques for each area and phase of the divorce process, i.e., emotional concerns, parent–child relationships, dating and remarriage, establishment of a new identity, and financial and legal concerns.

Among other therapeutic approaches, one finds the use of transactional analysis (Morris & Prescott, 1976), developmental psychoanalytic psychology (Singer, 1975), or Bowenian systems therapy (Cristofori, 1977). Dreyfus (1979) reported on his experiences in counseling with divorced fathers. He divided this process into four phases: (1) dealing with the immediate crisis that brought the father for counseling, (2) examining various losses and dependency needs, (3) focusing on beliefs, values, and social realities, and (4) focusing on issues of being an unmarried parent. Each of these phases, according to Dreyfus, has its own unique set of issues indigenous to the divorced father; in this sense, countertransference by male therapists is discussed.

Finally, Walker and Messinger (1979) considered remarriage after divorce as the dissolution and reconstruction of family boundaries and roles. In comparing nuclear and remarriage family models, Walker and Messinger begin with the formation of the first-marriage nuclear family and end with the formation of a second-marriage family conceptualized in terms of changing family boundaries and roles.

Group Approaches

A variety of group approaches differing in ideology, techniques, and emphases are available in the literature. Some representative reports are considered here.

Granvold and Welch (1977) used what they called "The Treatment Seminar," in which cognitive-behavioral treatment methodologies are applied to various postdivorce adjustment problems. The seminar follows a structured format of seven weekly meetings, three hours per meeting, with each session devoted to a new topic. The sessions begin with a 15 to 30-minute didactic introduction to the content to be considered that evening. Common dilemmas, factors influencing individual adjustment, and new ways of viewing the experience of separation and divorce are identified. After this introduction, participants are divided into smaller groups to facilitate interaction through group dimension, problem-solving, modeling, role rehearsal, and cognitive restructuring following RET of Albert Ellis.

Morris and Prescott (1976), developed what they called "transition groups" in a university counseling center to deal with individuals who had undergone male–female partnership failures (not necessarily divorces). According to these authors, groups can potentially offer support, companionship, and the opportunity for individuals to help each other with the adjustment process by sharing insights and experiences.

Elkin (1977) described the pioneering postdivorce counseling service of the Conciliation Court of the Superior Court of Los Angeles County. The author discussed the rationale for the program, its goals and procedures, clinical questions generated by postdivorce counseling, and the psychodynamics of postdivorce conflicts.

Kessler (1976) is one of the few writers in this field to have conducted some research using groups differing in degree of structure, i.e., structured, unstructured, and control. As criterion measures, she used preselected subscales of the Tennessee Self-Concept Scale, the Self-Description Inventory, and a Self-Report Questionnaire. The results on these measures show significantly higher mean scores on the subtests of the Tennessee Self-Concept Scale and the Self-Desdription Inventory for the structured groups over the unstructured and control groups. The Self-Report Questionnaire only gave some support for the level of satisfaction with the group process. Her conclusions suggest that skill-building exercises found in most preventive approaches (see Chapters 1 to 10) may add an important therapeutic dimension to the therapeutic process of those adjusting to divorce. Kessler is also responsible for giving a phase-sequence of postdivorce adjustment that is incorporated into Kaslow's (1981) model, previously reviewed.

DISCUSSION

One of the major features of divorce and postdivorce intervention is inadequate research and specification of who profits by what approach at what price—an issue that can be found in most unstructured approaches. One of the major issues of consumer satisfaction was addressed by Brown and Mavela (1974), who reviewed the experiences of 429 men and women in a court-related marriage and divorce counseling service. These authors found significant gender and race differences in how the clients perceived this agency and whether or not it was helpful to them. Most respondents felt that the service helped them in (1) gaining better perspective and understanding, (2) developing more helpful expression of feelings, (3) providing emotional support, (4) giving them concrete aid or advice, (5) helping them to better communicate. Those who considered counseling not helpful attributed that to insufficient contact with the agency, dissatisfaction with the counselor, or discrepancies between the client's and the counselor's expectations and goals for the outcome of counseling. These findings have implications for agencies that need to provide a broad spectrum of therapeutic strategies to meet and match the various needs of their clients. In addition, counselors need to be sensitive to the stage the client is experiencing in the process of marital dissolution— different stages requiring different emphases. Of course, no agency can be all things to all people, and realistic limitations need to be faced up front by the staff before involving energy and effort in nonproductive outcomes. The fact that 75 percent of this sample considered this service "helpful" indicates that agencies of this kind can perform a useful societal function.

THE FUTURE

One can safely predict that as the field of marital intervention becomes more and more differentiated from other therapies, the specialty of divorce and postdivorce interventions will become more and more one facet of this field. Again, there will be a need for specific training, specific techniques, and—more in this field than in any other specialization of marital interventions—better research. A great deal of progress has been made; more progress needs to be made.

REFERENCES

Albrecht SL. Reactions and adjustments to divorce: Differences in the experiences of males and females. *Family Relations*, 1980, *29*, 59–68

Bahr S. The effects of welfare on marital stability and remarriage. *Journal of Marriage*, 1979, *41*, 553–560

Bernard J. *Remarriage: A study of marriage*. New York: Dryden Press, 1956

Bohannon P. *Love, sex, and being human*. New York: Doubleday, 1969

Brown EM. Divorce counseling. In DHL Olson (Ed), *Treating relationships*. Lake Mills, IA: Graphic, 1976

Brown P, & Mavela R. Client satisfaction with marital and divorce counseling. *The Family Coordinator*, 1977, *26*, 294–303

Cristofori RH. Modification of loss in divorce: A report from clinical practice. *The Family*, 1977, *5*, 25–30

Crosby JF. A critique of divorce statistics and their interpretation. *Family Relations*, 1980, *29*, 51–58

Defazio VJ, & Klenbort I. A note on the dynamics of psychotherapy during marital dissolution. *Psychotherapy: Theory, Research and Practice*, 1975, *12*, 101–104

Defrain J, & Erick R. Coping as divorced single parents: A comparative study of fathers and mothers. *Family Relations*, 1981, *30*, 265–274

Dreyfus EA. Counseling the divorced father. *Journal of Marital and Family Therapy*, 1979, *5*, 79–85

Elkin M. Postdivorce counseling in a conciliation court. *Journal of Divorce*, 1977, *1*, 55–65

Eshleman J. Here to stay—American families in the 20th century. *Journal of Marriage*, 1978, *40*, 847–848

Fisher EO. Divorce counseling and values. *Journal of Religion and Health*, 1975, pp. 165–170

Goetting A. Some societal level explanations for the rising divorce rate. Family Therapy, 1979, *6*, 71–87

Goldman J, & Coane J. Family therapy after the divorce: Developing a strategy. *Family Process*, 1977, *16*, pp. 357–362

Good W. *Women in divorce*. New York: Free Press, 1965

Granvold DK, & Welch GJ. Intervention for postdivorce adjustment problems: The treatment seminar. *Journal of Divorce*, 1977, *1*, 81–91

Greenfield L, & Falk M. Welfare grant reductions and family breakup among the working poor. *Public Welfare*, 1973, *31*, 26–31

Hill R, & Hansen DA. The identification of conceptual frameworks utilized in family study. *Marriage and Family Living*, 1960, *22*, 299–311

Hunt M. *The world of the formerly married*. New York: McGraw-Hill, 1966

Kaplan H. Sex is psychosomatic. *Journal of Sex and Marital Therapy*, 1975, *1*, 275–276

Kaplan H. Towards a rational classification of sexual dysfunctions. *Journal of Sex and Marital Therapy*, 1976, *2*, 83

Kargman MW. There ought to be a law: The revolution in divorce law. *The Family Coordinator*, 1973, *22*, pp. 245–248

Kaslow F. Divorce and divorce therapy. In A Gurman & D Kniskern (Eds.), *Handbook of family therapy*. New York: Brunner/Mazel, 1981, pp. 662–696

Kelly JB, & Wallerstein SS. Brief interventions with children in divorcing families. *American Journal of Orthopsychiatry*, 1977, *47*, 25–39

Kessler S. Divorce adjustment groups. *Personnel and Guidance Journal*, 1976, *54*, pp. 250–255

Kessler S. Building skills in divorce adjustment groups. *Journal of Divorce*, 1978, *3*, pp. 209–216

Kressel K. Patterns of coping in divorce and some implications for clinical practice. *Family Relations*, 1980, *29*, 234–240

Kressel K, & Deutsch M. Divorce therapy: An in-depth survey of therapists' views. *Family Process*, 1980, *19*, 413–443

Kressel K, Jaffe N, Tuchman B, Watson C, & Deutsch

M. A typology of divorcing couples: Implications for mediation and the divorce process. *Family Process*, 1980, *19*, 101–116

L'Abate L (Ed.). Values, ethics, legalities and the family therapist. Rockville, MD: Aspen Systems, 1982

Laner MR. Saving sinking ships: Implications from a theory of marital dissolution. *Journal of Marriage and Family Counseling*, 1978, *4*, 51–57

Lazarus AA. Divorce counseling or marriage therapy? A therapeutic option. *Journal of Marital and Family Therapy*, 1981, *7*, 15–22

Morris JD, & Prescott MR. Adjustment to divorce through transactional analysis. *Journal of Family Counseling*, 1976, *4*, 66–69

Nye FI, & Bernardo F. Emerging conceptual frameworks in family analysis. New York: Macmillan, 1966

Rice DG. Psychotherapeutic treatment of narcissistic injury in mutual separation and divorce. *Journal of Divorce*, 1977, *1*, 119–127

Robbins NN. Have we found fault in no fault divorce? *The Family Coordinator*, 1973, *22*, 359–360

Robbins NN. End of divorce—beginning of legal problems. *The Family Coordinator*, 1974, *23*, 185–188

Rose VL, & Bonham SP. Divorce adjustment: A woman's problem. *The Family Coordinator*, 1973, *22*, 291–297

Singer TJ. Divorce and the single life: Divorce as development. *Journal of Sex and Marital Therapy*, 1975, *1*, 254–262

Toffler A. *Future Shock*. New York, Random House, 1970

Vaughan FK. A model of divorce adjustment therapy. *Family Therapy*, 1981, *8*, 121–128

Walker KN, & Messinger L. Remarriage after divorce: Dissolution and reconstruction of family boundaries. *Family Process*, 1979, *18*, 185–192

Waller W. The old love and the new: Divorce and readjustment. New York: Liverwright, 1930

Wallerstein JS, & Kelly JB. Divorce counseling: A community service for families in the midst of divorce. *American Journal of Orthopsychiatry*, 1977, *47*, 4–22

SECTION IV

Issues in Marital Intervention

16

Marital Interaction Theories and Research*

An index of the extent to which marital therapy is becoming a formalized profession is the increasing emphasis on the empirical validation of both outcome theory and treatment.[1] This emphasis on validation is also an index of the extent to which the mental health professions are directing their attention to finding viable solutions to the problems of marital dysfunction and dissatisfaction. The empirical investigation of theory and outcome is a relatively new phenomenon, even though conjoint couples therapy was practiced as early as 1932 in England (Olson, 1970). Prior to 1960 there were no relevant outcome studies on marital therapy other than subjective case reports (Gurman 1973b), and there were few investigations of theoretical constructs.

This almost complete absence of objective study can be traced to three independent historical foci (Gurman & Kniskern, 1978b). First, the autonomy of several independent professional disciplines actively committed to family study (i.e., psychiatry, clinical psychology, social work, family sociology, and the ministry) has resulted in parallel but unrelated developments of marital and family therapy (Olson, 1970). Second, marital therapy was "born" in child-guidance and family-service agency treatment settings; psychology, typically the discipline most active in psychotherapy research, was absent and made relatively no impact on the field (Gurman, 1971). Third, there was a general devaluing of the idea of treating family systems directly and a related devaluing of psychological treatment by nonphysicians. This devaluation led to little interprofessional collaboration as well as little interest in the evaluation of outcome.

Since the early 1970s, due to the increased interest in marital therapy as a distinct and needed discipline, a number of empirical investigations have been directed toward further delineating both the nature of marital interaction and the outcome of marital interventions. This chapter briefly reviews a number of those empirical investigations.

TREATMENT OUTCOME

Enough substantive empirical study has been conducted to support several critical reviews of the research literature (Beck, 1976; Gurman, 1971, 1973a, 1973b; Gurman & Kniskern, 1978b; Lebedun, 1970). All of these reviews have concurred in a cautious optimism about the efficacy of marital and family therapy and found marital and family therapy's gross improvement rates to be similar to those

---

*Research assistance was provided by Edgar Jessee, Jackie Johnson, Mary R. Register, Gary Rupp, J. W. Thompson, Donna Ulrici, Kay Watson, and R. W. Wildman, II.

[1]For more complete reviews of the literature on marital evaluation and interaction, the reader should also consult Bagarozzi and L'Abate (in preparation); Olson, Sprenkle and Russell (1980); and Spanier and Lewis (1980).

reported for individual therapy (Bergin & Garfield, 1971). All of these reviews, however, also repeat the continuing need for controlled investigation, multidimensional change measures, and treatment specificity.

In addition, since most reviews of outcome studies report gross improvement rates, results are concluded from a number of studies that are not comparable in subjects, treatment, design, or methodology. Although it is suggested that marital therapy as a whole is effective, there are not enough empirical data representing all orientations to allow meaningful comparisons among differing types of approaches nor among differing types of couples. Thus it is not known which general orientations, much less which specific techniques, are effective in treating marital problems. It is not possible to relate specific changes in "marital happiness" to specific procedures. Furthermore, there are little comparison data to suggest spontaneous remission, recovery, or the effects of social treatment or history. Even with these noted difficulties, however, a number of studies point to the general efficacy of marital therapy as a treatment intervention for those couples reporting that their marriages are unsatisfactory or distressed.

Gurman (1973a) reported the summary of the results of 77 studies of marital (N = 36) and family (N = 41) therapy reporting gross improvement rates. The studies included a mixture of client types and problems, with a majority of both marital (89 percent) and family (74 percent) therapies conducted in outpatient settings. The marital studies were of couples with undifferentiated difficulties; outcome was based on measures varying from highly objective (e.g., weight gain) to highly subjective (e.g., satisfaction with treatment), and included a wide range of rating sources. The modal study used only one evaluative perspective, usually that of the therapist or client(s) and a single index change of global change or marital satisfaction. Overall results were that marital therapies seemed to produce positive change in almost two-thirds of clients, whereas individual therapies for marital problems yielded improvement in only 48 percent of clients.

In another review, Gurman (1978) noted that 36 studies that addressed deterioration effects reported worsening effects in half of the studies and deterioration effects in 42 per-

cent. On the whole, it appears that 5 to 10 percent of marital therapy clients' relationships worsen as a result of treatment (Gurman & Kniskern, 1978b).

The results of comparative marital studies are consistent with the results of single-group studies. Conjoint marital therapy is found to be superior to alternative treatments in 70 percent of the comparisons and inferior in only 5 percent. When marital therapies are compared with no-treatment control groups marital therapy is found to be superior in half of the studies. Behavioral marital therapy studies, as compared with nonbehavioral marital therapy studies, yield few results to indicate clearly the superiority of behavior therapy over no treatment or other treatments. Cumulative data, however, suggest a 64 percent rate of superiority over control conditions (similar to 66 percent superiority rate of nonbehavioral marital therapies (Gurman, 1978).

In summarizing overall conclusions for marital therapy studies, Gurman and Kniskern (1978b) note that:

1. Individual therapy for marital problems is an ineffective treatment strategy and one that appears to produce more negative effects than alternative approaches.
2. Couples benefit most from treatment when both partners are involved in therapy, especially when they are seen conjointly.
3. Behavioral marital therapy offers insufficient research support to justify the training of therapists in this approach alone.
4. Short-term therapies appear to be at least as effective as treatment of longer duration.
5. Several enrichment programs appear to have promise as useful preventive strategies in family living.
6. Deterioration is as common in marital therapy as it is in individual psychotherapies.
7. Therapist relationships skills have major impact on the outcome of marital-family treatment, regardless of the "school" orientation of the clinician (pp. 883–884).

These cumulative results are based on a generalization of a number of studies that differ on varying dimensions. Although results indicating that marital therapy causes improvement are encouraging, the nature of the improvement is not delineated. What is not known about the outcome of marital therapy is similar to the difficulties in defining the impact of individual therapies. The delineation of which treatment for which clients under what circumstances remains to be refined further.

DEVELOPMENTAL THEORIES OF MARITAL INTERACTION

There are three widespread developmental perspectives that have been applied to the evaluation and understanding of the marital relationship. These perspectives are birth order theory, cognitive development theory, and family lifecycle theories. While other theoretical orientations have also been applied to the study of marital choice and marital adjustment, i.e., psychoanalytic theory, ego psychology theory, and systems theory, these three have been the most thoroughly elaborated.

Birth Order

Since Adler first introduced into formal psychology the concept of the influence of birth order on personality organization, its theoretical impact has increased steadily (Forer, 1969; Harris, 1964; Konig, 1973). The most recent example of this approach to the study of personality is by Wilson and Edington (1981), who have developed personality descriptions for the major birth orders by evaluating their clients' experiences.

In spite of widespread interest, birth order as a research variable is still surrounded by tentative and inconclusive findings; yet this variable is ubiquitous in psychological research (Forer, 1977; Miley, 1969; Vockell, et al, 1973). The attitudes toward birth-order research and its value to psychology cover a broad continuum, ranging from positive and hopeful (Breland, 1973) to extremely negative and doubtful (Schooler, 1972). All work related to the effects of birth order, however, remains essentially in agreement with Adler's early theoretical formulations. The only difference has been a semantic one: current researchers stress birth order's *determining* personality as compared with Adler's hypothesis that it is one's *perceptions* of one's position and role and conclusions about them, rather than the position itself, that determine personality organization

(Shulman & Mosak, 1977). In other words, the current emphasis on the determination of personality characteristics by the ordinal birth position is contrary to Adler's idea of creative choice. Nevertheless, from a theoretical viewpoint, the outcome on personality development remains the same.

Adler's understanding of human nature was basically a social one. He considered man capable of creating his own way of being in the world (Leibin, 1981), with much of this creativity taking place in the family. Adler (1927) said that, "before we can judge a human being, we must know the situation in which he grew up. An important aspect of the situation is the position which a child occupied in his family constellation" (p. 149). Adler's theoretical assumptions about this position were:

Assumption one. Children never develop in the same family. That is, the family situation is never the same for children in a particular family constellation. For example, the firstborn of a two-child family experiences his or her situation as that of the elder with a younger sibling. The young sibling obviously experiences the same family in a quite different way (Adler, 1927).

Assumption two. Each birth-order position has common demands that affect the child's view of his or her family and of life, and "increase the likelihood of the child's developing attitudes and styles of behavior in correspondence with his/her perceived position" (Manaster, 1977, p. 4).

Assumption three. Children in same or similar birth-order positions perceive common challenges to their being in the family and develop similar personality characteristics to adapt to the circumstances. Therefore, similarities are found among persons of same or similar birth order, and differences are found among persons of different birth-order positions.

For the most part, it is these three assumptions that have stimulated birth-order research. One of the more consistent findings about birth order is that firstborns are characterized by greater educational achievement (usually measured by achievement test scores and college attendance; Adams, 1972; Wark, swanson & Mack, 1980). Several investigators (Belmont & Marolla, 1973; Belmont, et al, 1978; Zajonc, 1976; Zajonc & Marcus, 1975) have studied large numbers of subjects (400,000 to 800,000) and have found in their aggregate data clear and stable trends for achievement. These general trends are that (1) ability and achievement decrease as birth-order positions increase and (2) ability and achievement decrease as spacing between siblings decreases (Cicirelli, 1978). These findings, however, have also been explained by the socioeconomic status of families. Colleges are attended by a higher proportion of firstborns from middle- and upper-class families (Cicirelli, 1978). In commenting on these general findings, Price and Hare (1969) have noted a failure to study long-term population trends in birth rates. In a population with a large number of new families, there will be a higher proportion of firstborns. On the other hand, a population limiting births will show an increase in lastborns. If these populations are compared, findings may suggest a difference in birth order when, in fact, they are merely reflecting a trend in birth rates. Hayes and Bronzaft (1979) controlled for population trends in their study of 850 members of Phi Beta Kappa and found that this group of academic achievers represented all of the birth-order positions, as well as all family sizes, thus lending strong support to Price and Hare's hypothesis.

Other studies have been characterized by concern with the emotional developmental aspects of birth order. Croake and Olson (1977) discovered that firstborn and youngest males "scored significantly higher on most MMPI scales than did middleborn males" (p. 15). These differences were found to be the greatest on the scales that measure hypochondriasis, masculinity–feminity, and paranoia. These results support a previous study by Weiner (1973), which reported that firstborns consistently seek out college health services more frequently than the other birth positions. McDonough (1978) reported that "twice as many first children were identified as problem children by their parents than any other category. Youngest children have the second largest proportion, with 'second' and 'middle' being third" (p. 68). A recent study (Lahey, et al, 1980) substantiated McDonogugh's findings by concluding that

firstborns are referred for pyschological help at a significantly higher rate than secondborns. Shrader and Leventhal (1968) also had found the same results earlier in evaluating cases referred to a child-guidance center.

Delameter, et al (1981) compared a group of hyperactive (HA) learning-disabled children with a group of nonconduct-problem children, i.e., nonhyperactive learning-disabled children (NHA). The two groups did not differ on age, sex, family income, education of parents, race, perinatal factors, or family history of psychiatric illness. The HA group was found to have a significantly higher number of firstborns than the NHA group. Interestingly, the HA group also had a larger amount of psychosocial stress (e.g., parental separation, divorce, child abuse). Overall, these findings suggest that firstborns and lastborns seem to be at a higher risk for maladjustment than their middleborn siblings. To add to this data, Murphy (1972) found that middle children had the most positive self-reported attitudes toward others.

Looking at other personality characteristics, Hornbostel and McCall (1980) found that firstborns show higher need-achievement (dependence) than do secondborns. They note, however, that this finding is reversed when the secondborn was of the opposite sex. Several authors have also reported a correlation of birth order and vocational choices (Burnand, 1973; Farley, et al, 1974; Herrell, 1972; Rule & Comer, 1979).

Birth-order findings are confounded by other studies that address similar variables but find different results (Greene & Clark, 1970). For instance, Farley (1975) administered the Eysenck Personality Inventory to female subjects and found that the characteristics of extroversion–introversion and neuroticism were not correlated with birth ordinal position. Likewise, no birth-order effects were found for dogmatism and authoritarianism (Fakouri, 1974; Wisdom & Walsh, 1975), need for affiliation (DeAvila, 1970), creativity (Wilks & Thompson, 1979), or behavioral and academic adjustment (Sprowls, 1979). A number of studies have also failed to find any relationship between birth order and self-concept (Irvin, 1974; Nystal, 1974; Watkins & Astilla, 1980).

Schacter's (1959) theory "has been the foundation for more ongoing birth-order research than any other viewpoint" (Adams, 1972,

p. 415). His theory can be categorized as the indulgent–anxious parent view. He asserted that firstborns are generally the focus of a worried, overly concerned mother who offers more attention than necessary to meet the child's needs. As births in the family increase, this parental anxiety lessens. To support this idea somewhat, several recent studies have found that the mother–child interaction is significantly different among birth-order positions. Unfortunately for Schacter, these differences have not been linked to anxiety or indulgence (Cohen & Beckwith, 1977; Jacobs & Moss, 1976; Lewis & Kreitzberg, 1979). In fact, Sigman, et al (1981) have found that firstborn, preterm infants are more competent than later borns, an opposite conclusion from Schacter's prediction.

Bayer (1967) claimed that family economics can account for birth-order differences such as college attendance. Elder (1962) found that firstborns benefit most from their ordinal position in high-SES families; whereas in low-SES families, it is the lastborn who seems privileged. This theory, however, seems to explain only the discrepancy among birth orders in college attendance and is too narrow to be an adequate explanation of other birth-order effects.

Undoubtedly the most exhaustive research conducted on birth order is Toman's work (1959, 1969, 1976). He started with the "assumption that a person's family represents the most influential context of his life, and that it exerts its influence more regularly, more exclusively, and earlier in a person's life than do any other life contexts" (1976, p. 5). With this as his guiding construct, Toman delineated the psychological consequences of birth order and its effects on marital choices, adjustment, parenting, sibling interactions, friendships, and even vocational choices. He concluded that "other things being equal, new social relationships are more enduring and successful, the more they resemble the earlier and earliest (intrafamilial) social relationship of the persons involved" (1976, p. 80). This "duplication theorem" is fairly well documented in Toman's research, although Birtchnell and Mayhew (1977), Ortiz (1981), and Levinger and Sonnheim (1965) have had difficulty substantiating it in their studies.

As a theoretical approach to the understanding of marital choice and marital adjustment, assumptions about the effects of birth order essentially dictate how two individuals of differing or same birth orders will relate. For example, firstborn children will relate in a more complementary way to lastborn children because of early role definitions related to their ordinal positions in their families of origin. Individuals of the same birth order will be more competitive because of similar achievement needs (Toman, 1976).

However, Adlerian assumptions about birth order (Adler, 1927, 1935) have been shown to be neither valid nor invalid by the many research studies that include this family structure variable. The vast majority of these studies are methodologically flawed and often ignore data from previous research (Adams, 1972; Breland, 1973; Schooler, 1972). In addition, although the study of birth-order effects is based on an attempt to understand the effects of family of origin dynamics, most studies address only outcome variables rather than actual family dynamics.

Cognitive Theory

Cognitive theories related to the attempted understanding of marital choice and marital adjustment can be classified as (1) moral development and (2) structural-descriptive (perspective-taking). Although moral issues have been considered primarily within the scope of philosophy and religion, investigators of the psychological aspects of human nature have been interested in morality as it affects behavior, emotion, and judgment. The major theorists of the effects of moral development on human behavior have been Piaget and Kohlberg.

Moral Development

The cognitive-developmental view of morality set forth by Piaget (1948) paralleled his general theory of the development of the child's conception of the world (Piaget, 1928). According to Piaget, moral development involves both a cognitive capacity for defining situations in terms of a social-moral framework and an emotional empathic capacity learned through role-taking. In order to empathize with others and to conceptualize the results that his or her actions will have on another, the child must have developed the capacity to "play" the role of the other. Only when he or she has reached the cognitive development normally attained around age eight does the child attain the capacity for reciprocity, or the ability to recognize his or her position relative to the position of another.

Until this stage of development, the child tends to judge actions only in terms of their consequences to himself or herself or in terms of the extent of damage resulting from his or her behavior. The young child views an act as either totally right or totally wrong and expects everyone to agree with him or her since, without reciprocity, the child cannot consider diversity of viewpoints. The child's definition of good or bad behavior comes primarily from the presence or absence of punishment associated with that behavior, and the child expects that behavior so labeled will remain consistent, regardless of the situation. Moral norms are not internalized but are determined by how the child interprets the given situation.

Before eight years of age, the child operates from this "heteronomous" kind of moral judgment, based on an unquestioning respect for adult authority and power. As this stage is replaced by the "autonomous" type of morality, the child begins to govern himself or herself by internal principles of reciprocal justice aimed at maintaining social relationships. According to Piaget, this tremendous change in the child's concept of morality is achieved mainly through interaction with peers. The child's view becomes horizontal or equalitarian, having equal but relative rights and responsibilities to peers. This view is opposed to the child's earlier vertical viewpoint in which adults were considered superior and infallible.

Elaborating and expanding Piaget's theory, Kohlberg (1963a, 1963b, 1964, 1968, 1969b) developed a theory of moral judgment defining six distinct stages of moral development. His theory is based on a cognitive-structural model that stresses change in cognitive structure rather than content. In contradistinction to Freud's theory of psychosexual development, which postulated a series of stages differentiated on the basis of content, Kohlberg's stages depend upon sequential change in the structure of cognitive processes, or an advancing hierarchy of mental processes by which one's moral judgments are made. Similar to Freud's theory, individuals may retain remnants of each past moral developmental stage and

carry fixations of primitive cognitive structures into adulthood.

In a sequence that Kohlberg (1968) believes to be universal, each stage is dependent upon the development of previous stages. Although the content of moral decisions differs from culture to culture, the cognitive structure underlying each stage remains constant. Kohlberg investigated this question by comparing the process of moral development in children in Great Britain, Canada, Taiwan, Mexico, and Turkey, as well as in various socioeconomic subcultures within the United States. His studies suggested that in these cultures all movement through this developmental process was progressively forward in sequence, without skipping stages. Children move through these stages at varying speeds, may be found half in and half out of a particular stage, or become fixated at any given stage and at any age. If the child continues to move, however, he or she moves in accord with these steps.

Each step of development represents a more complex cognitive organization than the one before it. Each step takes into account everything present in the previous stage but also makes new distinctions and organizes them into a more comprehensive or more equilibrated structure. The higher stages seem to involve reorganization and displacement of lower stages. An individual's use of higher stages demonstrates the tendency to avoid using the lower stages: i.e., higher stages are not simply added to lower stages but are structurally different from them and preferable to them (Kohlberg, 1963a).

In one series of studies, Turiel (1966) showed that children and adolescents comprehended all stages up to and including their own, but not more than one stage beyond their own. Furthermore, they consistently prefer arguments based on the structure of the higher stage.

Blatt and Kohlberg (1969) conducted experimental moral discussion classes that showed that the child at an earlier stage of development moved forward when confronted by the views of a child one stage above his or her own. For example, in an argument between a Stage 3 and a Stage 4 child, the child in the third stage tended to move toward or into Stage 4, while the Stage 4 child understood but did not accept the arguments of the Stage 3 child. The implications are that forward development is engendered through peer interaction or an intellectual challenge presented to the child in the cognitive form of the next higher stage rather than through exposure of the child to instruction based on orientations representative of stages two or more steps above his or her own.

Kohlberg's (1964) typology of moral development consists of three distinct levels of moral thinking, parallel to Piaget's levels of cognitive development. He differs from Piaget's stages of moral development, however, by seeing a more direct relationship between cognitive processes and moral judgment. Each of Kohlberg's three levels—preconventional, conventional, and postconventional—contain two related stages. These levels and stages may be considered separate moral philosophies, or distinct views of the sociomoral world. They are characterized by increasing differentiation and integration of data pertaining to conflicts between roles, personal and social values, and man's structure of social order.

At the preconventional level, the child is concerned with cultural labels of good and bad, but the child interprets these labels either in terms of their physical consequences (punishment or reward) or the physical power of those who enforce the rules, or label things as good or bad. Although chronological age is not a determining factor in the assigning of children to a given level, this period normally extends from about age 4 to age 10. Prior to this age, the child is considered amoral. The end of this period and the beginning of development toward the second level coincides with the movement of the child from Piaget's preoperational to concrete operational periods.

Children above Level 1 are able to pass Piaget's test of logical reciprocity or reversibility, being able to reverse perspective. For example, they know that a person facing them would have a right hand counterposed to their left hands. Children (Level 1) who fail these tasks in logical reciprocity think that bad acts will and should be followed by bad events or punishment and than an act eliciting punishment must be bad. They do not define "justice" as reciprocal, equal exchanges between persons. The power and prestige of a person's status, not equality or reciprocity, determine what he or she may do or have.

There are two Stages within Level 1. At Stage 1, the child defines the sociomoral order in terms of relative amounts of power and possessions. The positive actions, or "principles," that are seen as maintaining the social order are obedience to the strong by the weak and punishment by the strong of those who deviate. For example, a Stage 1 child would say that a son should give his father some money he has earned because, "It's his father, he owns him; he has to do what he says," or that a "troublemaker" should be the one sent on a suicide mission in the army, "because he's bad and he has to do what the captain says" (Kohlberg, 1973, p. 36). In other words, the physical consequences of an action determine its goodness or badness, without any consideration of its meaning in terms of human feelings or values.

In contrast, Stage 2 individual have a clear sense of fairness as quantitative equality in exchange and distribution between individuals. The positive actions or principles of the sociomoral order are acts of primitive reciprocity, conceived of as the equal exchanges of favors or blows, or as acts of cooperation in terms of a goal of which each person gets an equal share. "You shouldn't hurt or interfere with me, and I shouldn't hurt or interfere with you." When social or moral action requires more than positive exchange or negative noninterference, it becomes either a matter of selfish whim or an inappropriate expression of individual exchange and equality. For example, Stage 2 children frequently say that one should steal a drug to save a friend's life, "because you may need him to do the same for you someday." The Stage 2 perspective is that right action consists of that which instrumentally satisfies one's own needs and, occasionally, the needs of others. Although elements of fairness, reciprocity, and equal sharing are present, they are interpreted in a physical or pragmatic way. Reciprocity is a matter of "you scratch my back and I'll scratch yours"—not of loyalty, gratitude, or justice.

The second, or "conventional," level (made up of Stages 3 and 4) can be described as "conformist." Maintaining the expectations and rules of the individual's family, group, or nation is perceived as valuable in its own right. There is a concern not only with conforming to the individual's social order but in maintaining, supporting, and justifying that order.

With ideal reciprocity now at his or her disposal, the Stage 3 individual can take the role of another and anticipate how this "other" will act upon him or her. In this way, the Stage 3 sense of justice is broadened by something like empathy and goes beyond the physical, instrumental domains of Stages 1 and 2. The reciprocity that was practiced in the actions of the Stage 2 child has become a part of his or her thinking. Piaget would say that the behavior has been changed from within, its form acting upon its content until the principle of the action has become conscious. Characteristically, then, the Stage 3 conception of justice is integrated with a conception of good (positive and stable) interpersonal relationships. The sociomoral order is conceived of as primarily composed of dyadic relations of mutual role-taking, mutual affection, gratitude, and concern for one another's approval. It is primarily a "good-boy" or "good-girl" orientation. Good behavior is that which pleases or helps others and is approved by them. There is much conformity to stereotypical images of what is majority or "natural" behavior. Behavior is often judged by intention; "he means well' becomes important for the first time and is overused. One seeks approval by being "nice."

The limitation of a Stage 3 orientation as reciprocal role-taking is that it cannot easily be extended outside concrete dyadic interpersonal relationships. It is logically difficult to extend because it is cognitively indeterminate as to who should take whose role and to what extent. It is also difficult to extend to a larger society because it rests on positive personal sentiments and relationships that become weak outside the dyad.

Stage 4 overcomes the limitations of Stage 3 by defining justice in terms of a system, or a social order, or roles and rules that are shared and accepted by the entire community and that constitute the community. Accordingly, justice is no longer a matter of real or ideal reciprocity or equality between individuals, but a matter of the relations between each individual and the system. Questions of positive reciprocity are questions of the relation of individual work and merit to the rewards of the system, "a good day's work for a good day's pay." Not only should merit be rewarded by the system, but every individual must pay his or her dues to society by contributing in some way. Stage 4 positive reciprocity is exchange of reward for effort or merit, not interpersonal exchange of

goods or service. Negative reciprocity is even more clearly centered on the social system, since vengeance is the right of society, not the individual victim. Such vengeance is conceived not as vengeance but as "paying your debt to society." Stage 4 represents an orientation toward authority, fixed rules, and the maintenance of the social order. Right behavior consists of doing one's duty, showing respect for authority, and maintaining the given social order for its own sake.

In every society studied by Kohlberg, Stage 4 was the most frequent mode of moral judgment found in adults. His data indicated that since Stage 4 is an advanced sequential stage emergent from prior stages quite unlike it, it is neither a direct reflection or internalization of current adult collective roles and beliefs, nor is it a primitive internalization of parental taboos and authority.

Most individuals reach a point of fixation either at or below Stage 4. The higher stages, on the postconventional level, are characterized by a major thrust toward autonomous moral principles, which have validity and application apart from authority or the groups or persons who hold them, and apart from the individual's identification with those persons or groups.

Stage 5 is a social-contract orientation, generally with legalistic and utilitarian overtones. Moral action is defined in terms of general rights and of standards that have been critically examined and agreed upon by the whole society. There is a clear awareness of the relativism of personal values and opinions, and a corresponding emphasis upon procedural rules for reaching consensus. Aside from what is constitutionally and democratically agreed upon, right or wrong is a matter of personal "values" and "opinion." The result is an emphasis upon the "legal point of view," but with the possibility of changing the law in terms of rational consideration of social utility, rather than freezing it in the terms of Stage 4 "law and order." Outside the legal realm, free agreement and contract are the binding elements of obligation. This is the "official" morality of the American government and is rooted in the thought of the writers of the Constitution.

Stage 6 is an orientation toward the decisions of conscience and toward self-chosen ethical principles that appeal to logical comprehensiveness, universality, and consistency. Stage 6 principles are abstract and ethical rather than concrete moral rules, i.e., the Ten Commandments. They are universal principles of justice, of the reciprocity and equality of human rights, and of respect for the dignity of human beings as individual persons. Kohlberg (1968) cited Socrates, Thoreau, Lincoln, and Martin Luther King as examples of Stage 6 morality. Although the majority of individuals never develop to this stage of moral judgment, it is possible for an individual to achieve this final stage by his or her early 20s. Rate of advancement through the stages shows considerable individual differences and is affected by sociocultural differences.

Kohlberg (1969a) believes that after age 21 the adult tends to become more consistent, or stable, in the use of his or her predominant stage, and typically shows greater consistency between his or her moral judgment and moral behavior. He or she may become more consistently dishonest, or conforming, or more honest, or innovative, in thinking. There is some indication that adult stabilization often represents a regression to a lower stage (Kohlberg, 1969b), serving to stabilize the individual in the stage that best serves his or her cultural and sex-role identity.

Adult stabilization of moral judgment is achieved through the resolution of conflicts between one's personal view and social reality. Adaptation to adult responsibilities may require the abandonment of youth's lofty ideals; maintenance of one's self-esteem may require that an individual adopt a value perspective consonant with the demands that everyday living places upon him or her. In adulthood, moral development may align itself with ego development and become more closely related to personality functioning than to cognitive development alone.

Concerning marital adjustment and marital satisfaction, Kohlberg's theory states that by the time an individual reaches adulthood, he or she has probably become solidified at one or another of the moral stages, depending on the extent of his or her development. The individual will base most decisions in the structural context of his or her predominant stage. As a result, an individual will reject arguments based on stages less developmentally mature than his or her own and will be unable to comprehend fully the arguments from orientations more than one stage beyond his or her own. An individual's maximum potential for understanding and sharing moral views, then, would be limited to those views proposed by individuals at the same or the next higher stage of development. In turn, individuals at the next lower stage would be morally incompatible.

Register (1976) tested Kohlberg's assumption that moral judgment in two individuals at nonsimilar and nonadjacent stages of development would not agree with each other's reasoning in moral dilemma situations. She compared two sets of stage pairings of married couples, with an assessment of their marital satisfaction. Stage level of moral judgment was determined by the Kohlberg Moral Maturity Scale. Marital satisfaction was defined by the Locke-Wallace Short Marital Adjustment Test and a modified form of the Barrett-Lennard Relationship Inventory. The hypothesis that partners at the same stage or adjacent stages of moral development would be more satisfied with their marriages than partners at nonsimilar or nonadjacent stages was supported at the 0.05 level of significance by only the Barrett-Lennard Relationship Inventory. One scale of the Relationship Inventory, however, the "Willingness to be Known" scale, discriminated the two groups at the 0.01 level of significance.

Structural–Descriptive

Researchers in the past 20 years have investigated numerous aspects of marital interaction, e.g., power hierarchies, problem-solving abilities, marital cohesion, and communication skills. These studies have generally looked at actual behavioral practices or reports of behavioral practices and correlated this information with some measure of marital stability or satisfaction/happiness (Blood & Wolfe, 1960; Kahn, 1970; Ravent & Rodrigues, 1971; Russell, 1979).

The study of individuals' conceptions of marital issues has been limited to attitudinal studies. These studies have investigated concepts concerning different aspects of marriage, such as mate selection or sexual practices, to determine "what" people think" about different marital dimensions (Hudson & Henze, 1972; Mace, 1972). Little attention, however, has been given to the structural dimensions of individuals' conceptions of marital relations, i.e., how they organize their thoughts about a marriage relationship. Fundamental questions concerning the development of mature marital concepts and how underlying cognitive variables affect marital behavior have not been addressed.

Recent research by Bernal and Baker (1979, 1980) suggests that there are qualitatively different levels of couples' communication. They have identified five levels by which couples' communications can take place; these interactional levels increase progressively in abstraction, with higher levels subsuming lower levels. This progression suggests involvement of underlying cognitive processes. That is, the qualitatively different levels of interaction denote structurally different modes of conceptualization. Also, it appears that couples' abilities to utilize all different levels of interactional process would require that individuals have the cognitive ability to conceptualize at all levels of abstraction. In other words, the ability to understand cognitive concepts about the marital relationship may be a prerequisite for the use of different interactional levels.

Cognitive-developmental theorists have conducted considerable investigation that verifies a structural-developmental progression in various domains of social cognition (e.g., moral development, social role-taking, friendship relations), but the dimensions of one's cognitions about marital relationships have not been addressed by developmental research. Nevertheless, theoretical conceptualizations have been hypothesized to provide a structural-developmental analysis of the stages of one's cognitions about marriage.

Tamashiro (1978) proposed four stages of marital interaction, based on the structural-developmental theories of ego development (Loevinger, Wessler & Redmore, 1970), moral reasoning (Kohlberg, 1964), ego ideal (Von der Daele, 1968), and self-knowledge (Tamashiro, 1975). His initial stage is described as the magical stage in which an illogical way of thinking about marriage links simple ideas to observable actions and things. It is a fairy-tale notion of marriage, which is nonsequential and somewhat supernatural. Marriage is viewed from only one perspective; there is no awareness of how one person's actions affect another. There is also an inability to define the relation-

ship beyond observable actions and events. Stage 2 is described as idealized conventional, which emphasizes getting along well together, maintaining similar opinions and feelings, and following rules in give-and-take interactions. Stage 3 is described as individualistic, in which the emphasis is on personally defined values and emotions, and individual identity; there is also a concern for mutual companionship. Stage 4 is described as a stage of affirmation, a stage in which there is an interdependent relationship.

Bernal and Baker (1979, 1980) have looked at actual dialogues between couples and described levels of interaction. Level I is object-oriented. Transactions at this level are focused on an issue (e.g., finances, in-laws). Problems are seen concretely, as being the objects discussed. There is a focus on the objective consequences of interaction or results that can be qualified by the lack of agreement about surface events.

Level II of couples' interaction is "individualistic." At this level, the content is focused on one of the individuals in the interaction. There is an either-or-position. Interactions at this level include mutual accusations and blaming. Level III is "transactional," involving a change to a focus on patterns of interaction and couples' acknowledgment of a connection between their behaviors (e.g., recognizing vicous circles). There is not yet a focus on the relationship itself, however. Both Levels II and III of interaction denote a limitation of thinking about marital interactions. In Stage 2 there is an awareness that what one does affects the other, but the object of giving to the other is to receive for the self. Persons at this stage have difficulty seeing the marriage as an entity in itself.

Level IV is relationship-oriented. Issues are discussed, not in terms of how they affect the individual, but how they affect the relationship. Individuals can remove themselves from momentary conflict and abstractly view their marital system.

Level V is described as "contextual." This level is the most advanced position and is distinguished by the concern for the context that sets the current relationship. Larger sociocultural influences as well as deeper psychological variables that affect the individual and the marriage are addressed.

Bernal and Baker proposed that their levels of couples' communication may be viewed as a metaphor with pragmatic value for understanding and growth in a couple's interaction. The framework can be a helpful schema by which to follow transactional processes and develop intervention strategies. For example, a therapist may attempt to synchornize a couple's level or try to move them from one level to another. Change in a couple's ability to use different levels of interaction may also be used as a measure of progress.

Striking similarities between Bernal and Baker's levels of couples' communication and independently derived marital stages suggest that the quality of understanding in a marriage relationship may be related to the quality of interaction. The extent to which partners' perceptions of their marriage affect their interaction remains an empirical questions. One could hypothesize, however, that the quality of interaction between a couple is correlated with how the couple perceives the marriage.

Jurkovic and Ulrici (1980) developed a hierarchy of stages to hypothesize the structural and developmental characteristics of marital awareness. These stages closely follow the empirically validated structural-developmental analysis of friendship understanding formulated by Selman (1980; Selmand & Jaquette, 1977), i.e., formation, trust, reciprocity, autonomy, jealousy, conflict resolution, intimacy, and termination. Each marital stage is described as follows:

Stage 0: marriage as a momentary-physicalistic interaction. At this stage, young children's thinking about marital relations is limited by two cognitive characteristics: (1) their failure to differentiate the internal processes of people (i.e., how they think and feel) from the physicalistic qualities a person displays; (2) their inability to define relationships beyond the momentary experience or repeated incidences of physical interaction between two people.

The importance of marriage is limited to the momentary experience of pleasing the self (Why do people marry? "So they have a place to live"). The selection of one's partner is based on proximity and availability (e.g., someone who lives close, goes to the same school,) and on surface physical traits such as gender identity (boys marry girls, girls marry boys). An ideal mate is one who pleases and does not harm the partner. (What kind of person makes a good partner? "One who would not hit you, who it pretty"; "One who buys you presents.")

There is the idea that the marriage relationship is defined by a momentary physical experience. (Are you going to marry? "I'm married. . . . I had a tea party with Sally.") Intimacy and closeness are synonymous with physical proximity. Marital couples have a close relationship because they "kiss each other," or "walk next to each other." Separation and independence in marriage are seen as a result of physical barriers (e.g., "not enough room to sit next to each other"; "not enough money for both to go"). Jealousy is a momentary and immediate experience that results from not having something that the partner is seen to have, or not doing something another is seen to do (e.g., not sharing ice cream, not getting to play a specific game).

Trust is determined by what one sees the other do, and it is based on what one is physically capable of doing, e.g., carrying groceries, cooking dinner. There is no comprehension of give-and-take; reciprocity is equated with getting what one wants and includes some recognition that one also gives, but giving and taking are not yet coordinated.

Marital conflict is understood only in terms of one's being physically blocked from what each spouse wants to do or have (e.g., both wanting to use the car at the same time). Resolution is through physical power and coercion ("just taking what you want") or physical withdrawal from the scene. Leaving, however, is not seen as a part of the solution or a step in renegotiation; rather, it is the total solution: one moves to another place so the problem will go away. At Stage 0, marital termination is not understood in terms of conflict but in terms of physical harm and physical separation. (When should people divorce? "When one hits you"; "If one goes away and doesn't come back.")

Stage 1: marriage as a one-sided relationship. At this stage, there is an awareness of the motives, thoughts, and feelings that serve to influence the observable actions of others and an awareness that these aspects of self and others need to be considered in understanding relationships. Conceptions tend to be one way, however; that is, focused on one person's subjective perspective of a marriage. The other person's motives, thoughts, and feelings are judged in terms of what one does with and for another (i.e., objective consequences of interaction or results that can be quantified).

Thus the value of marriage is seen in terms of overt benefits for the self (e.g., having children; having someone to help you, to live with you). A good marriage partner is someone who will care for and do things for the other. There is a sense that the quality of a relationship is based on the number of activities the couple does together and the extent to which they show physical caring for each other. Independence of activities threatens the relationship. Jealousy is hurt feelings from being denied objects and excluded from activities.

As in later stages, there is an emphasis on dependability of one's words and actions as a basis for love and trust in a relationship. What is absent, however, is a sense of reciprocity of feelings. There is only concern for one perspective. One shares with and gives to another, not because of how the other might feel, but because of the consequences (i.e., one shares a secret because the other might find out and be mad).

Lack of agreement focuses on surface events as the root of all interpersonal conflicts. Conflicts are solved by an emphasis on good intentions (i.e., try hard, help if one can). A concern for a satisfactory resolution is not expressed, however. There is no awareness of working out conflicts together. Therefore, arguments and not getting along with people are criteria for termination.

Stage 2: marriage as a two-way partnership. At this stage, the individual is aware that interpersonal perspectives may differ and has the ability to see how they are reciprocally related, i.e., each person is seen as capable of taking into account a perspective of self. As a result of this awareness, there is concern that marital partners have a meetings of minds, that both be happy and satisfied. There are two basic limitations at this level. One is that the individual sees the purpose of this reciprocal awareness as serving each partner's need rather than supporting mutual concerns of the marriage. Second, there is a static conceptualization of persons and relationships that focuses on the stability of individual characteristics and resolution of specific incidents and issues. There is no consideration for the changing aspects of the personalities involved or the dynamic processes that underlie the partner's interactions.

At Stage 2, an interpersonal orientation to the importance of marriage emerges. Marriage is significant, not only for the objective benefit, but also for the emotional needs of the individuals involved (to love and be loved). With the awareness that another can view the self, a paramount quality of a good partner is willingness to see another's point of view, i.e., work toward a satisfactory agreement. Due to the assumption that one's interpersonal dimensions are basically static, the most important consideration in choosing a marriage partner is the matching of goals, interests, and activities ("both enjoy the same recreational activities").

In this stage, intimacy is developed through sharing thoughts and feelings with another and meeting each other's needs, both emotionally and physically. There are, however, fair-weather aspects of sharing and caring, because they are viewed as important in that they provide for individual needs and personal satisfaction. Sexuality is important as an activity to share with one's partner. A good sexual relationship, like a good marriage, is based on the individual feelings of satisfaction expressed by each partner.

Reciprocity toward one's partner takes into consideration the other person's needs, but the objective of giving to another is to receive for oneself (e.g., love is a two-way street; you get out what you put in). Trust becomes more than just keeping one's word on specific issues; it is based on the predictability and consistency of the other's behavior toward self. There is a concern for the dependability of fulfilling one's agreements (e.g., I stand by you; you stand by me).

Individuals at this level have difficulty understanding marriage as a system that transcends specific events and feelings. Independence from one's marriage partner is conceptualized as a total separation from the marital relationship, i.e., standing on one's own, a total forgetting of responsibilities to the other). Decisions about autonomous actions take into account the needs of both partners, and there is a concern to establish a balance between things done apart and things done together in order to prevent a conflict of demands and feelings of jealousy (e.g., if I do what I want alone, then I'm willing to go somewhere my wife likes). There is an awareness that jealousy can emerge as a result of being excluded from the interpersonal activities of another (i.e., choosing another person or activity over the self), and this jealousy is considered in determining the degree of autonomy one can have.

Conflicts are seen as developing over differences in opinion and feelings, rather than differences in personality or in the quality of the interpersonal interaction. Viewed in this way, resolving conflicts becomes critical to the couple to reestablish the relationship. At this level, there is little room for differences of opinion if the relationship is to continue. Resolution comes through logical solutions and appeals to another person's perspective. The concern is to ensure that both benefit from the agreement.

Stage 3: marriage as mutual sharing. At this stage, individuals can abstractly remove themselves from the marital relationship and view it as an ongoing, stable system. Thus the focus shifts from the concerns of each individual separately to the concerns of the relationship itself. There is a notion of collaboration of resources and a mutual sharing of benefits.

The importance of marriage is viewed as providing a foundation for a mutually sharing unit—a committed relationship, for better or worse—in which individuals work together to accomplish mutual goals. There is a feeling that each is part of the other. A good marriage partnership is one in which the individuals have a common set of values, ideals, and beliefs that will support their relationship during troublesome periods.

Intimacy is discussed in terms of sharing intrapersonal emotions and interpersonal experiences. There is an emphasis on the importance of communication to ensure that (1) each understands the other and (2) the other can benefit from one's experience. Time spent together becomes important because of the mutual experiences that are shared. Sex is seen as important for more than just an activity of satisfaction; it is also seen as a way of being one with one's partner in an experience of mutual bonding.

Trust in one's marriage develops through sharing personal problems and helping each other with emotional needs. Trust is based more on the couple's ability to communicate and the integrity of the individual's personality than on a reciprocal, binding agreement to which both partners must adhere equally. At this stage, reciprocity is not seen in terms of fairness or balance, but as taking of what one is part of (i.e., one belongs to the other). Giving and getting are not differentiated. One gains from giving to the other, not because the other will reciprocate, but because the marriage will benefit.

Autonomy is discussed in terms of the effect of independence and dependence on the marriage relationship, and the varying needs of the partners. Independence and individual identity are no longer equated with "making it alone" but are seen as mutually agreed areas of separation within the larger context of a marriage relationship (e.g., even by yourself, you always have the other person's feelings to consider). Feelings of jealousy are evoked if activities or persons threaten the quality of the marriage relationship, i.e., there is possessiveness in the relationship due to fear of loss. Jealousy is seen as an individual trait as well as a state.

At this stage there is an awareness that conflicts can develop not only because of discordance of attitudes and opinions, but also because of basic personality differences. Conflict about different issues is not viewed as a threat to the relationship but as a natural part of living together. Resolution of specific disagreements is seen within the context of the total marriage relationship. The bond of the relationship works to solve conflicts. Solutions to conflicts take into consideration the mutual needs and long-term goals of the marital relationship. Termination is not a result of disagreements over specific opinions and events, but is based on a disagreement about how to relate to each other, i.e., the quality of interpersonal relating.

Stage 4: marriage as an interdependent relationship. At this stage, the individual can not only view the marital relationship as an ongoing, stable system, but is also able to see how each individual affects and is affected by this system, i.e., the interdependent processes that regulate the marriage system. Larger sociocultural influences on the individual and on the marriage can be taken into account in assessing the dynamics of the marital interaction. In addition, there is an awareness of the deeper psychological variables that may consciously or unconsciously affect one's personality, expression, and development.

At this stage, the importance of marriage is seen from several perspectives. There is an awareness that the experience of a committed marital relationship can increase the quality of one's life, provide a meaningful social unit, and enable support for individual growth and psychological well-being. A good marriage partner is one who shows intra- and interpersonal sensitivity and expresses concern for the partner's growth. Selection of a good mate emphasizes a matching of the couple's unique needs and mutual acceptance of each other's personality flaws.

Intimacy at this stage is an ethical commitment as well as a personal experience. There is a sense of obligation and responsibility that bonds the relationship. Respect for one's partner as an individual and support for his or her social and psychological growth are an integral part of the experience of intimacy. The sexual relationship is seen as having both concrete and symbolic significance. It is an expression of commitment to each other, but it is also a concrete expression of closeness that can serve to balance other, conflictual aspects of the marriage.

Reciprocity in the relationship is defined on the basis of "from each according to his abilities, to each according to his needs." There is concern for balancing the individual's needs for growth and for maintaining the quality of the relationship. Spouses serve the role of reciprocal therapists, providing psychological support for each other's growth. Trust in marriage is based on a belief that one can be independent and grow but still remain loyal to the relationship. There is trust in oneself as a good marital partner and trust in the quality of the relationship that is shared.

Autonomy is seen as necessary for the growth of the individual as well as the development of the marriage. Jealousy is assumed to be a natural part of a close relationship. It shows an admiration for the meaningfulness of the relationship, i.e., a desire to protect that which is valued. There is an awareness that too much independence may threaten the stability of the marital relationship. Balancing autonomy takes into consideration the psychological needs of each individual as well as the needs of the marital system.

At Stage 4, marriage has a more dynamic quality. The relationship is seen as being in a constant process of change and reformulation, with conflict playing a natural role. Termination results when communication breaks down and partners do not make an effort to share their experiences of growth.

A pilot investigation (Jurkovic & Ulrici, 1980) attempted to discern empirically whether children's and adults' thinking about marital understanding moves through the qualitatively different stages previously described. Specific questions of interest were: Can Selman's stage-descriptive approach to the understanding of friendship issues be adapted to the study of marital conceptions? If so, do differences in thinking in this area relate to age, sex, or marital status?

To answer these questions, an interview was developed based on Piaget's clinical method of investigation. A marital dilemma was presented to stimulate conversation, followed by a series of open-ended questions related both to the dilemma and to the individual's own marital experiences. In the case of children, questions were asked about their understanding of their parents' marriage. The following is a synopsis of the marital dilemma and interview questions presented.

Jack and Susan have been married for 6 years and have a 4-year-old child. They had an intense courtship and married after having known each other for a few months. In the first year of their marriage, problems emerged. For example, Susan disliked the extent to which Jack was away from home. Although the birth of their child helped to bring them closer together, they continued to have difficulties. Then a crisis developed. Jack was offered a big promotion in the home office of his company, which he wanted to accept, but Susan did not want to move for various reasons, including the fact that she had a highly rewarding teaching position.

Formation

1. Do you think Jack and Susan had a good basis for getting married? Why or why not? Why do people get married anyway?

2. What kind of person makes a good marriage parnter? Why?

Autonomy and Jealousy

3. Why do you think Susan began to resent Jack's time away from the family? To what extent should marital partners be independent of each other? What factors need to be considered in deciding their independence?

4. Do you think Susan should go along with Jack's desire to move? Why or why not? If she does, will he owe her something?

Trust and Reciprocity

5. What does give-and-take mean in a marriage relationship?

6. Do you think trust is important in order to remain together? What is trust in marriage?

Intimacy

7. Do you think Jack and Susan have a close marriage? Why or why not? What makes a close marriage?

Conflict Resolution

8. Why do you suppose Jack and Susan had so many conflicts? How do conflicts develop in marriage?

9. What are important factors in Jack and Susan's decision to move? How should arguments in marriage be settled? Why?

Termination

10. Why do marriages break up? What holds marriages together?

Participants in the study included 22 women and 18 men, ranging in age from 18 to 53 years, and 12 children, ranging in age from 3 to 17 years. The adults attended a large urban university. Children were drawn from an upper-middle-class neighborhood.

The interviews were scored with an adaptation of Selman's (1980) manual for coding friendship understanding. Following this system, the individual's understanding of each previously noted issue was assigned a stage score. The weighted average of his or her issue scores was then calculated and converted to a number ranging from 0 to 400 (0 = pure Stage 0; 400 = pure Stage 4).

If the stages described earlier form a hierarchically organized developmental sequence, they should co-vary with age. To test this

hypothesis, a Spearman rank-order correlation was conducted. As expected, rankings on age and scores on the marital understanding interview were significantly related [rho = 0.55, $z = 3.93, p > 0.0001$]. The scores ranged from one extreme (0) to the other (400). Predictably, the preschoolers showed little evidence of movement beyond Stage 0. By middle childhood, however, the developmental level of most of the younger participants in the study had reached Stages 1 and 2. A few of the adolescents, surprisingly, reasoned at Stage 3, although the majority were still at Stage 2. The adults varied in their understanding from Stages 2 to 4. Approximately 35 percent of the adults (18 years and older) exhibited a major Stage 2 orientation, 50 percent relied more heavily on Stage 3, and 15 percent attained a Stage 4 level. These age trends were fairly consistent for both sexes. A direct comparison between the adjusted mean stage scores for males $(M = 254.90)$ and females $(M = 259.90)$ revealed no significant difference.

Jurkovic and Ulrici (1980) were also interested in whether marital status of the adult participants related to maturity of marital understanding. Three groups were formed: single adults who had never been married $(N = 12)$, adults in their first marriage $(N = 15)$, and adults who were either divorced or remarried $(N = 13)$. An analysis of covariance of the scores of these two groups was performed. Age was the covariate. A significant overall F of 6.17 $(df = 2/36, p > .025)$ was obtained. Supplemental analyses indicated that the adjusted mean of the single adults $(M = 253.56)$ did not differ from that of the divorced/remarried group $(M = 271.91)$ but was significantly lower than the mean of the married adults $(M = 322.77)$. The last group of participants also earned significantly higher scores than the divorced/remarried sample.

Jurkovic and Ulrici discussed several conclusions. One is that young children, not unlike adults, think about marital issues in an organized, albeit immature, concrete fashion. It was also found that the thinking of both children and adults reflected underlying structural patterns that followed a developmental sequence similar to sociocognitive growth in other domains. In particular, Selman's levels of friendship understanding proved to be a useful framework for describing qualitative differences in reasoning about marital issues. Although only preliminary, this research lends further support to the validity of Selman's model.

In contrast to indications that age and level of marital understanding are positively related, observed differences between the various groups as a function of marital status should be interpreted with caution. The sample sizes were small; thus the groups may have greatly misrepresented the popultion from which they were drawn. Yet, if reliable, the findings are interesting. They suggest, for example, that for many people the experience of being married facilitates their movement to sophisticated levels of marital understanding. It is not clear, however, why the divorced/remarried group scored lower than their once-married counterparts. Sampling problems notwithstanding, one possibility is that limitations in their thinking about these issues figured in the marital conflict that led to divorce. Alternatively, attitudinal and affective factors may have influenced them to reason during the interview in ways that did not reflect their true capabilities.

In summary, the various developmental and cognitive views of marriage and marital relationships can be compared (Table 16-1) to illustrate some degree of consequence among the major representatives of this viewpoint.

THE FAMILY LIFECYCLE

The concept of the family lifecycle emerged from the field of sociology. Pioneer work by sociologists Hill and Rodgers (1964) began to look at the interdependence among the developmental tasks of family members. In 1957, Duvall published her landmark work that broke the family lifecycle into eight stages and subsequently outlined the developmental tasks at each stage. Although there have been many variations of Duvall's eight stages, all encompass the modal events related to the coming and going of family members: marriage, birth, raising children, departure of children, retirement, and death. Sociological theory presents the successive stages of the family lifecycle as heirarchically related. That is, successful completion of early tasks facilitates successful completion of later tasks; whereas failure to complete early stages leads to difficulties with later ones.

Baltes and Schaie (1973), in their discussion of life-span development, noted that different stages in the family lifecycle actually produce different roles, role expectations, and different activities for the individual. Based on research in the area of adult development, Neugarten (1976) proposed that coping with lifecycle tasks creates changes in self-concept and in sense of identity. Coping marks the incorporation of new social and emotional roles and precipitates intrapersonal adaptations.

Understanding and evaluating stages of family lifecycles has been deemed central to clinical work with distressed families (Carter & McGoldrick, 1980; Haley, 1973; Minuchin, 1974). Explicit reference to the family lifecycle and its clinical implications did not appear in family literature until the 1970s, however. In *Uncommon Therapy* (1973), Haley discussed the ideas of Milton Erickson and described the family lifecycle in six stages. He stated his belief that family stress is highest at the transition points from one stage to the next. Symptoms are most likely to appear in a family member if there is an interruption or derailment in advancement from one stage to the next. Thus treatment efforts from this perspective are directed toward mobilizing the lifecycle transitions so that normal development can continue.

Some family therapists have theorized about the change processes involved in the family lifecycle (Hughes, et al, 1978; Weeks & Wright, 1979). They have built on Watzlawick, et al's (1974) concepts of change, and view lifecycle transitions as requiring "second order change" or systems change. First-order change is seen as a rebalancing of the family within its present organization, whereas second-order change is discontinuous and requires quantum leaps that change the system itself, i.e., a structural reorganization. Carter and McGoldrick (1980) went on to relate that there are changes in the individual family members that correspond to these structural reorganizations. They hypothesized that the emotional task to be fulfilled by the family system at each phase of its life cycle requires a change in the states of the individual family members, and that these changing states involve a complex emotional process.

Table 16-1
Marriage and Marital Relationships from Cognitive
Developmental Viewpoints

Authors	Stages			
	1	2	3	4
Tamashiro (1978)	Magical	Idealized, conventional	Individualistic	Affirmation
Bernal & Baker (1979)	Object-oriented	Individualistic	Transactional	Relationship
Jurkovic & Ulrici (1980)	One-sided	Two-way partnership	Mutual sharing	Interdependency

CLASSIFICATIONS OF MARRIAGE AND MARITAL QUALITY

There are a variety of ways to classify marriages structurally, i.e., by characteristics present and observable at the time of evaluation. Most of the classifications available thus far have had clinical-impressionistic bases. For example, Sager (1981) identified seven different types of marital partners, which he described in detail: (1) equal, (2) romantic, (3) parental, (4) child-like, (5) rational, (6) compassionate, and (7) parallel. From these seven profiles, he derived a variety of partner contributions based on matched or mismatched characteristics.

Sluzki and Beavin (1965) developed seven types of couples based on symmetrical or repetitive sameness or complementary–polarized relationships. These seven types are (1) stable symmetry, (2) stable complementarity, (3) symmetrical competition toward one-up, (4) symmetrical competition toward one-down, (5) assymetrical competition toward one-up and symmetry, (6) assymetrical competition toward one-down and symmetry, and (7) fluid.

Lederer and Jackson (1968) developed a fourfold classification of couples, each with two subtypes: (1) stable-satisfactory (heavenly twins and collaborative geniuses, (2) unstable and satisfactory (spare-time battlers and pawnbrokers), (3) unstable-unsatisfactory (weary wranglers and psychosomatic avoiders), and (4) stable-unsatisfactory (gruesome twosome and paranoid predators).

Martin (1976) also used a fourfold classification that applies only to dysfunctional couples: (1) the "love-sick" wife and the "cold-sick" husband, (2) an "in-search-of-a-mother" marriage, (3) the "double-parasite marriage" (hysterical-hysterical or dependent-dependent), and (4) the paranoid marriage.

Symmetry, Complementarity, and Parallelism

The constructs of symmetry, complementarity, and parallelism are used in a diversity of theories, i.e., interpersonal attraction, political systems, and the dialectic (contrast of opposites), among others. The constructs related to parallel relationships have been more elusive

than the other two constructs; nonetheless they have provided a means of integrating symmetrical and complementary patterns of behavior that are viewed as incomplete by themselves. Historically, these three constructs can be traced to Bateson's (1936) anthropolgical work, which he later applied to a family communication theory.

Bateson (1936) formulated two conceptually clear types of relationships for describing the differentiated categories of cultural groups. First, he described the differentiated group as individuals who have the same aspirations and behavior patterns, e.g., keeping up with the Joneses, armament races. Second, he described the complementary differentiated group as individuals who have opposite behavior patterns, e.g., dominance-submission, sadism-masochism. Bateson asserted that there are elements in both groups that may lead to "progressive differentiation" or "schismogenesis" (1972, p. 68)). In the case of symmetrical schismogenesis, the groups drive each other to excessive emphasis of same behaviors, and if the process is not restrained, it will lead to more and more rivalry, and finally to the breakdown of the system. Similarly, in complementary schismogenesis, the groups escalate their opposite behaviors (e.g., as the submissive group becomes more submissive, the dominant one becomes more dominant) until the members' personalities in both groups become distorted. If the process is not restrained, the pattern leads to hostility between both groups and, ultimately, breakdown of the system. Bateson believed that most relationships could be categorized as either complementary or symmetrical. However, he proffered the possibility that no healthy relationship is of either pure type and that every relationship contains elements of both types in order to control schismogenesis. To this end, he postulated a third type of relationship, which he called "mixed" or "reciprocal."

The reciprocal relationship is a balanced relationship and does not tend toward schismogenesis. Bateson (1972) added two ideas; (1) symmetrical and complementary relationships are logical opposites of each other and, thus, antithetical; (2) the reciprocal relationship is more complex than the other two types and of a higher logical type.

Haley (1963) incorporated both symmetrical and complementary types of relationships into his theory on marital relationships. Accordingly, he viewed all marriages as rule-governed. The process of working out rules for living together is the same as the process of defining the relationship:

Any rule established by a couple defines a certain type of relationship. A rule that a husband is to comfort his wife when she is in distress defines a relationship as complementary. Similarly, an agreement that the wife is to have equal say about the budget is a mutual definition of a symmetrical relationship in that area (Haley, 1963, p. 124).

Haley believed that marital conflict can center on disagreements about the mutual definition of the relationship, disagreements about which spouse is to set the rules, and attempts to enforce incompatible rules. He proposed that past training in symmetrical and complementary relationships in the spouses' families of origin is a prominent factor in the cause of marital conflict. For example, "if a wife has been disappointed in complementary relationships with her parents," she will have difficulty responding "to her husband's attempts to take care of her" (1963, p. 125). Haley did not delineate a third type of relationship comparable to Bateson's reciprocal relationship. He did, however, state that a reasonably successful marriage consists of establishing both complementary and symmetrical relationships in various areas of the marriage and that the "inability to accept a range of types of relationships creates a marriage which is to some extent a depriving situation for both spouses" (p. 125).

Sluzki and Beavin, who were inspired by Bateson's research group and the Mental Research Institute, published an article in Spanish in 1965 (not published in the United States until 1977), operationalizing symmetry and complementarity. Essentially, Sluzki and Beavin (1977) tried to address what they considered to be a flaw in symmetry and complementarity, the concepts of "pseudosymmetry (when the partner in the one-up position allows the other to appear as an equal) and of metacomplementarity (when both partners agree, symmetrically, that one of them will be in the one-up, complementary position)" (p. 70). Sluzki and Beavin devised seven variations or types based on symmetry and complementarity. With the exception of the "fluid" type

(similar to parallel) and a "stable complementarity" type, the other types encompassed dyads in some form of symmetry, e.g., one-up and one-down in symmetrical competition. Despite their analysis of the metacommunicative aspects of symmetry, their typology can still be compared and divided along the three interactional types of symmetrical, complementary, and parallel.

Lederer and Jackson (1968) were the next family communication theorists to employ symmetrical and complementary interactions in defining relationships. Also, they were the first theorists to use the term "parallel relationship." Essentially, their conception of symmetrical and complementary relationships is similar to that of Haley, except that Lederer and Jackson believe the symmetrical relationship has become the most problematic type in our egalitarian culture because of the blurring of male–female roles. Conversely, in cultures where there are well-defined sex roles, competition between the sexes is lessened and relationships tend to be complementary.

Lederer and Jackson (1968) also added to Haley's ideas on the etiology of symmetrical runaway or the struggle between the spouses to prove their equality. They stated that these spouses often come from emotionally lopsided families in which "one parent was overtly dominent and the other tried to maintain some sense of equality by undermining . . . the efforts of the dominant spouse" (1968, p. 168). Furthermore, once symmetrical runaway begins, a spiraling effect occurs in which each spouse is caught in a game of trying to prove that he or she is as good as the other. Lederer and Jackson (1968) advocated that one solution is for the spouses to divide the area of responsibility. Then, the relationship may "change to a complementary, interdependent one" (p. 169) in which the spouses' behaviors are mutually enhancing. The best solution for our culture, however, is a parallel relationship in which the "spouses alternate between symmetrical and complementary relationships, in response to changing situations" (p. 161). The parallel relationship, however, does not preclude a conflict-free marriage. Lederer and Jackson (1968) wrote,

There may be episodes of conflict concerning particular areas, but since the spouses feel equal to each other, they can be both supportive and competitive without fear, knowing that neither will win all issues at the expense of the other. . . . The ability to be honest and open in regard to both agreement and disagreement makes for trust, since each spouse knows where he stands in relation to the other (p. 161).

From the preceding, the obvious implication is that the parallel relationship is not only more functional but of a higher logical level than either a symmetrical or a complementary relationship because it is a shift, or change, out of both of these types. This line of thought, which can be traced to Bateson, has recently been adopted by Scoresby (1976) and his colleagues (Harper, Scoresby & Boyce, 1977).

Like the communication theorists already mentioned, Scoresby derived his typology of relationships from the types of messages exchanged between spouses. He proposed that an interaction, or exchange, is created by both partners, a point frequently disregarded by both. Consistent, too, with the preceding theorists, Scoresby (1977) defined symmetrical and complementary relationships similarly, and he believed that all marriages contain some behaviors of all three types. His definition of a predominantly parallel relationship is more clearly presented than those of the other communication theorists. Scoresby (1977) defined the parallel relationship as follows:

Two people exhibit greater variation in their actions. At the time when a husband is discouraged, for example, a wife may be calm (not opposite). . . . Parallel behavior is neither opposite nor identical; that is, rather than interlocking with or mirroring the partner's behavior, it takes shape alongside the partner's behavior in somewhat independent fashion. Thus there is no set pattern of "oppositeness" or "identicalness." People in parallel interaction are generally flexible and cooperative (p. 29).

Additionally, he said that each person tends to be perceived according to his or her unique personal attributes, and although perceptions will vary according to different situations, both persons are viewed as having weaknesses that are acceptable, as being caring, concerned, and cooperative. In contrast, Scoresby argued that the predominant complementary relationships lead to such perceptions as one spouse's viewing the other as passive and less knowledgeable, whereas the other spouse views the first spouse

as controlling and difficult. Similarly, the symmetrical relationship leads to each spouse's viewing the other as competitive, argumentative, and unwilling to listen.

To date, the only two published research studies using the symmetrical, complementary, and parallel constructs have been conducted by Scoresby and others (Scoresby & Christensen, 1976; Harper, et al, 1977). In the first study, Scoresby and Christensen (1976) compared the interactional styles of clinical and nonclinical families as units and as dyads, using father–mother, father–adolescent, and mother–adolescent combinations. Based on the theory of interaction classes, the researchers hypothesized that clinical families would report more complementary and symmetrical interaction than nonclinical families, and that nonclinical families would report more parallel interaction.

To assess the interactional styles of each dyadic combination, Christensen and Scoresby (1975b) developed the Relationship Styles Inventory (RSI), a paper-and-pencil questionnaire that measures how each family member perceives his or her interaction style for every relationship in which each is involved. The RSI assesses the three styles of interaction—symmetrical, complementary, and parallel—by which each member of the dyad indicates whether he or she exchanges opposite, identical, or different behaviors in the four categories of (1) decision-making, (2) control and use of power, (3) change-stability, and (4) information-processing.

Results from this study indicate that when considered as family units, clinical and nonclinical families differ significantly in terms of parallel and symmetrical interaction but not in complementary interaction. As predicted, more parallel interaction was found in nonclinical families. Furthermore, when each dyad in each group was considered separately, results showed that there are significantly more complementary interactions in the clinical mother–father dyads than in the same nonclinical dyads, thus substantiating part of their hypothesis.

It is not surprising that Scoresby and Christensen did not find significant differences in the direction predicted in the complementary interaction classes across the parent–adolescent dyads when one considers developmental influences on the relationship of the adolescent to parents. That is, adolescents as a whole could be expected to perceive their relationship to parents as more symmetrical than complementary, in that adolescents are in the stage of mastering skills necessary for asserting their own autonomy or symmetry to their parents. Thus, whenever the interactional typology is used, one must consider the stage of the lifecycle of the subject and the nature of the relationship examined. Haley (1963) remarked on this idea when he said that relationships can "shift in nature either rapidly, as when people take turns teaching each other, or more slowly over time" (p. 11). Specifically, Haley (1963) referred to the parent–child relationship as one in which the child in growing up shifts from a complementary toward a symmetrical relationship with his or her parents as the child becomes an adult.

The second study using symmetrical, complementary, and parallel constructs was performed by Harper, et al (1977). According to the Theory of Logical Types, these researchers postulated that the parallel interaction class is of a higher logical order than symmetrical and complementary interaction classes, which are of the same logical type. Using Venn diagrams and set theory, Harper, et al conceptualized three possible models of logical orders for the interaction classes. In their model, they viewed (1) parallel as a combination of symmetrical and complementary but of the same logical type; (2) parallel as a separate, nonoverlapping class but of the same logical type; (3) parallel as a higher logical type subsuming symmetrical and complementary. Parallel is depicted as a higher logical type or class containing the symmetrical and complementary members; therefore parallel can be neither symmetrical nor complementary. Conversely, symmetrical and complementary members cannot be parallel because members cannot be a class. Their rationale for arguing that the parallel interaction class is of a higher type is that, in most situations, a predominantly symmetrical relationship would habitually employ symmetrical rules for exchanging behavior, and a predominantly complementary relationship would habitually employ complementary rules for exchanging behavior. In both instances, the pattern of exchange becomes rigid, with structured rules that are redundantly followed (adapted from Haley's 1963 theory that rela-

tionships are rule-governed). In contrast, a predominantly parallel relationship is more flexible and can accommodate to a wide range of rules appropriate to the situation, including symmetrical and complementary rules. Thus the parallel interaction class or relationship is more than a combination of symmetrical and complementary, and constitutes a change to a higher logical type. If symmetrical and complementary interactions are of the same logical type and subsumed under the parallel class, then,

Neither should be capable of accommodating rules outside the limits of their own class. In other words, people engaged in habitual symmetrical interaction cannot accommodate complementary rules, neither can people with a predominance of complementary exchanges accommodate symmetrical rules, but individuals engaged in a high frequency of parallel interaction adjust to either condition (Harper, et al, 1977, pp. 202–203).

Harper, et al tested their hypotheses on father–mother, father–adolescent, and mother–adolescent dyads of 48 families (intact and single-parent), who were categorized into symmetrical, complementary, and parallel, using the RSI, Revised Edition (Scoresby, 1976). Each of the dyads in these three interaction classes was randomly assigned to one of two experimental conditions—one comprising complementary rules and the other comprising symmetrical rules—in which they jointly resolved a moral dilemma task adapted from Rest's (1975) Defining Issues Test. Task solution time and paper-and-pencil measures of each dyadic member's perceived level of task satisfaction and difficulty were used as the dependent variables. The researchers predicted that (1) parallel dyads would accommodate to both symmetrical and complementary rule conditions in rapid completion in both conditions; (2) complementary and symmetrical dyads would each accommodate to their respective rule conditions in rapid completion of tasks, with little reported difficulty and high satisfaction because the rules fit their redundant patterns; and (3) complementary dyads in symmetrical rule conditions, and vice versa, would not accommodate to the rule conditions as evidenced in long task-completion time, reported difficulty, and high dissatisfaction because the rules do not fit their redundant patterns.

All of the predictions were supported by the results of this study. The parallel dyads were not significantly different from the symmetrical and complementary dyads in rule conditions on time or difficulty and satisfaction. Thus the flexibility of parallel interaction in different contexts was supported. The complementary and symmetrical dyads were significantly different from the parallel dyads in the directions predicted on all measures. It was found that symmetrical and complementary classes were positively correlated, but both were negatively correlated with parallel scores. This last finding was interpreted as lending further support to the idea that symmetrical and complementary interactions are of the same logical type.

Since Harper, et al (1977), one or more of the three interactional classes have been employed in clinical theory and interventions but sometimes under different linguistics. For example, Madanes' (1981) term, "incongruous hierarchy," is used to describe one marital solution to balancing a power struggle whereby one spouse becomes symptomatic in order to control the definition of the relationship. In an incongruous hierarchy, the nonsymptomatic spouse, if he or she assumes the role of helper, ostensibly appears to be in the superior position in relationship to the symptomatic spouse, who appears to be in the inferior position. If the nonsymptomatic spouse fails to change the symptomatic spouse, then the symptomatic spouse is in the superior position. According to Madanes (1981), the power struggle results in an "unfortunate solution" whereby "the couple become restricted to a situation where one behavior defines simultaneously an inferior and a superior position of each spouse in relation to the other" (p. 31). Thus the couple is caught in an interaction that is an example of a schismogenetic, symmetrical relationship. Madanes' (1981) solution to working with such couples is to devise a means to change the symptom, the metaphor for the power struggle, by creating a congruous hierarchy.

Another example using symmetrical interactions comes from Palazzoli, et al (1978). The Palazzoli group employ "hidden symmetry" to describe a family in schizophrenic transaction in which each family member cooperates in refusing to define his or her relationship with others because of the dangerous threat of rejection.

In contrast, the Palazzoli group describe "open symmetry" as a relationship in which each partner "rejects the definition of the relationship made by the other," but the "rejection is foreseen" and each partner "boldly exposes" self to the other (pp. 21–22). Furthermore, the exposition can escalate into a game that can last forever, "but it can also run the risk of schismatic process: abandonment of the field by one of the couple" (p. 22). Simply stated, "hidden symmetry" denotes denial of conflict over control of the relationship, and "open symmetry" denotes acceptance of and/or reluctance to give up conflict over control of the relationship.

Thus the three interactional classes—symmetrical, complementary, and parallel interaction—are viable and logically interrelated constructs that still need empirical validation to integrate their theoretical and clinical usage. Ostensibly, the three interactional classes appear to be a heuristically useful typology of all dyadic interactions. Further refinement by other theorists, however, offers permutations of one or more of the basic types.

Marital Classifications According to Psychopathology

Historically, the most common method of classifying marital difficulties has been by definition of the symptomatology of one spouse. This spouse has usually been defined by both the couple and the therapist as the identified patient. Although marital therapists currently define the marital relationship as the identified patient, there still exist common marital classifications based on the overt pathology of one partner in the couple. The commonly used classifications are as follows:

Abuse and violent partners. There has recently been an increase in the literature concerning physically abusive spouses. An individual viewpoint (Coleman, 1981) saw the violent spouse as reenacting violent behavior learned in the family of origin, whereas interactional and systems viewpoints (Saunders, 1977) focus on the sadistic/masochistic interaction of the couple.

Alcoholic couples. A large amount of data has been obtained about this kind of marriage since the mid-1970s (Paolino & McCrady, 1977). Rae (1972) was one of the first investigators reporting empirical MMPI data supporting a successful discrimination of the couples who did not benefit from psychoterhapy from those who did benefit from psychotherapy. Gorad (1971) found that (1) alcoholics may use a style of communication characterized by responsibility avoidance when interacting with their wives; (2) their wives use a more direct, responsibility-accepting style of communication than their husbands; (3) the interaction between an alcoholic and his wife is marked by an inability to function as a unit for mutual benefit. Steinglass, Davis, and Berenson (1977) reported on inpatient experiences of couples admitted together as patients, even though only one was the admitted alcoholic. During hospitalization, these couples were encouraged to reproduce as closely as possible their usual drinking patterns and interactional behavior. Therapists used observations of interactional behavior during intoxication and sobriety to formulate central issues to be confronted by each couple. On the basis of these observations, these authors developed an interactional model to explain alcoholic maintenance through the family system.

Scott and Manaugh (1976) treated alcoholic couples in group therapy through the strong emphasis on building spatial boundaries between thoughts, feelings, and behaviors within or outside the individual.

Psychosomatic marriages. Although some investigators are beginning to address the psychosomatic marriage (Marshall and Neill, 1977), Minuchin (1974) has developed a conceptual approach to the "psychosomatogenic family" (p. 241), whereby there is a family organization characterized by enmeshment, overprotectiveness, loose boundaries, lack of autonomy, and physiological vulnerability. Although his model primarily addresses the child in the family, it also theoretically addresses the spouse subsystem of the family whereby the psychosomatic partner responds to dependency/lack-of-autonomy binds by becoming sick. Marshall and Neill (1977) have provided empirical data on the psychosomatic spouse in a study of patients undergoing intestinal bypass surgery for extreme obesity. Their findings show that these patients had issues primarily related to sexuality, independence, and dependence in the marital relationship.

Physical disability in marriage. Peterson (1979) reviewed most of the available literature on marital adjustment among couples in whom a physical disability was present. Extreme stress was found in marriages with a physical disability, the most relevant variable for a successful adjustment being role flexibility. Individuals who had a severely handicapped spouse were found to become biased by the disability, altering appreciably the content of the marriage.

Depression in marriage. More has been written on the depressed spouse than any other specific variable (Feldman, 1976; Green, Lee & Lustig, 1975; L'Abate & Goodrich, 1980; Madanes, 1981).

In Heins' (1978) review, most statistical surveys and other studies have shown that the majority of depressed patients are currently married or have been married and that depression is the most common at ages when marital satisfaction is the least. Couples with a depressed spouse were found to have (1) reduced general affective involvement, (2) reduced expression of affection, (3) increased criticism, (4) increased husband domination, and (5) a marked struggle for interpersonal control.

Paykel, et al (1969) found that marital difficulties are the major presenting problem prior to onset of depression in women. Weissman and Paykel (1974) found that depressed women are more likely to have marital relationships typified by friction and hostility.

Overall (1979) examined the relationship between symptom patterns and marital status in over 2000 subjects and found that depressive mood and guilt were much more likely to be found in the married and once-divorced group. Rounsaville, et al (1979) reported that women involved in active marital disputes have a poorer prognosis than those without mates or with happy marriages. Yet women who were able to improve their marriages were also more likely to recover from their depression. Thus depressed women most often report marital difficulties and only have a good chance of recovering from their depression if their relationships are treated.

The nature of the depressive marital relationship has been commented on by various authors. Overall (1971), Rubinstein and Timmins (1978), and Hinchliffe, et al (1978) delineated several factors that may relate to marital dysfunction, ultimately manifesting itself as depression. In addition to the importance of the male role, i.e., the male's feeling adequate and fulfilling his expected role (Barry, 1970), they maintain that the marital system must be flexible enough to respond effectively to stress events. The relationship prone to depression is inflexible because of a dependent mode of functioning. Neither partner has achieved a proper sense of mastery in the situation; consequently, they both are vulnerable to actual or threatened loss because they tend to increase their dependency demands during stress. Hinchliffe, et al maintained that this relationship pattern is counterproductive because it does not allow the couple to support each other successfully in threatening situations and, ultimately, one spouse responds with depression.

Paranoia in marriage. Williams, et al (1981) have described what they called the "paranoid wife syndrome," a term originally used by D. C. Carter and other contributors to this topic, who are reviewed by these authors. Carter (1968, 1970) originally used the terms "paranoid wife syndrome" and "husband's paranoidism" to condense the picture of wives who present a paranoid delusional system of thought, supposedly to make up for their feelings of failure as women and their inability to deal with their husbands' unpleasant characters. Williams, et al used the same term to describe a marital dyad made up of an actively aggressive wife and a rather passive–aggressive husband.

Obsessive-hysterical marriages. The obsessive–hysterical marriage is recognized clinically as one of the most common types of marital pairs. Although it is viewed as complementary, it is also viewed as having numerous inherent difficulties and issues.

Bergner (1976) reviewed his experiences with 16 couples, of whom one partner, usually the woman, had been diagnosed as hysterical on the basis of denial of responsibility for one's beliefs, histrionic self-presentation, labile and extreme but shallow emotionality, manipulativeness, feigned helplessness, and/or dependent demandingness. Typically, these women select husbands who avoid taking disagreeable stands on any issue and who enjoy playing the role of helpers and caretakers for their wives.

Bergner (1976) and Boszormenyi-Nagy (1967) observed marriages in which the hysteric seemed to have married an obsessional individual. For both individuals, the central focus of the marriage is avoidance of intimacy. This impass could be described in the roles of the *rescuer, distancer,* and *distance-regulator* (Berne, 1964). Each member of the couple alternately takes on the role of the emotional pursuer or the emotional distancer. The couple's degree of intimacy, however, never changes.

Workaholic husbands. L'Abate and L'Abate (1981) have described the marriages of workaholic husbands in terms of the polarization between dream and reality. They pursue "The Great American Dream," forcing their wives to pursue "The Petty Realities of Life." This polarization is related to other polarities in which husbands present nice, reasonable, pleasant facades, while their wives present themselves as bitchy, angry, and/or depressed. In this polarization, both partners justify their lack of intimacy in terms of the other's shortcomings, i.e., overinvolvement with work in the husband's case and depression and/or anger in the wife's.

EMPIRICAL EVALUATION

With the growth of interest in the empirical validation of marital therapies, there have also been increasing attempts to study and define the salient features of marital interaction. These attempts are typically based on the use of one instrument, usually a paper-and-pencil questionnaire administered pre- and/or post-intervention. These questionnaire measurements usually lack validity and reliability, and at best can only recommend subjectively reported trends and/or outcomes.

Recently, however, Gottman (1979) has presented an impressive attempt to integrate the many approaches to research on marital interaction. He has attempted to construct empirical and conceptual schema by integrating the four prominent orientations to the study of marriage (i.e., sociological, family systems, information theory, and behavioral and developmental) and has also made use of recent advances in observational and sequential analyses methodology.

Gottman's approach, developed from an idea first proposed by Haley (1964), uses as the unit of study the marital dyad's interactive sequence, or exchange of behaviors. This approach to the study of the marital dyad is broader, for it focuses on the concept of an ongoing interactive unit rather than a specific behavior and its rate of occurrence. Gottman, in effect, focused on the fact that behavior occurs, not in a vacuum, but in an interactive context.

Gottman also emphasized detailed description, based on objective observations of behavior. He stated that the social and behavioral sciences have suffered from premature theorizing based on insufficient objective, descriptive data. Thus he advocated an approach to theory and therapy based on model construction. Models are derived from descriptive data and are then tested and refined in basic and applied research.

Gottman proposed a structural model of marital interaction aimed at differentiating distressed from nondistressed couples, based either on marital satisfaction scores, requests for professional help, or both. The three dimensions of his model are positiveness, reciprocity, and dominance, with an emphasis on searching for interaction patterns among the three variables.

In order to address his proposed research emphasis, Gottman proposed four hypotheses:

Ho_1. Distressed couples will show more patterning and structure in interaction than nondistressed couples (patterning refers to immediate sequences of interaction in a chain of interactions, by which one can predict later behaviors from earlier ones). Conditional (contingent) probabilities will significantly exceed unconditional (base rate) probabilities for distressed couples.

Ho_2. Distressed couples will be more negative and less positive toward each other than nondistressed couples. The difference will be greater for negative than for positive behaviors and greater for nonverbal (affect) than for verbal (agreement and disagreement) behaviors.

Ho_3. Distressed couples will show more reciprocity of negative behaviors than nondistressed couples.

Ho_4. Distressed couples will show a greater dominance patterning (not specific to either sex) than nondistressed couples. (Dominance is defined as asymmetry between husband and wife in predictability of behaviors, with one spouse's behavior contingent on the behavior of the other spouse.)

Gottman developed the Couples Interaction Scoring System (CISS), which addresses verbal and nonverbal behaviors (context codes and affect codes). The coding system is used to code listener affect as well as speaker affect. Videotapes are made of couples' interactions and transcribed. The transcription of the videotapes is then divided into thought units (speech acts or utterances). Coders code both the transcription and the videotape according to each verbal and nonverbal speaking unit as well as the simultaneous listening nonverbal unit. In his initial development of the coding system, Gottman's criterion for a trained coder was 70 percent coder agreement for each unit. Separate coders recorded the affect and content codes of all units, and all coders were blind to whether a couple was in a distressed or a nondistressed group and whether or not the couple had participated in any of the clinical intervention sessions designed by Gottman.

The eight content codes of the CISS are agreement, disagreement, communication talk, mind-reading, problem-solving/information exchange, summarizing self, summarizing other, and expressing feelings about a problem. Affect codes are based on facial expression, voice tone, and body cues. The affect codes are positive, neutral, and negative. Reliability of coders' performance was assessed in several separate studies, and the results indicate that coders achieved impressive levels of interrater agreement.

Gottman emphasized Jacobsen's (1978) findings that of the 57 research studies he reviewed, which all involved hypotheses based on patterns of family interaction, none actually addressed interaction itself in the analyses of the data. Rather, measures of behavioral rates and rate correlations across couples or families were used to generalize inappropriately to questions or contingencies. Often, these behavioral unit rates were not even controlled for total amount of interaction. Gottman's purpose is to firmly establish a precedent for the use of *changes* in probabilities of certain interactive behaviors (rather than rates or rate-based probabilities alone) as a function of the same or other interaction behaviors, given that these have occurred.

According to Gottman, patterns emerge in marital interaction when any given behavior by one member of the marital pair reduces the observer's uncertainty, that is, increases the probability beyond a base or random rate, of what the other spouse's next behavior will be, which in turn increases the probability of the first spouse's reply, and so on. In his analysis, Gottman utilized the concept of time-lag to calculate the probabilities for whole sequences. For example, given that wife emits behavior A and husband responds with behavior B (lag-2), what is the probability that the wife will respond to B with A, C, or D at lag-3? If she responds with C, what is the probability that the husband will respond at lag-4 conditional probability with A, B, C, or D? As long as conditional probabilities significantly exceed base-rate probabilities, a sequence or chain can be said to exist. Gottman presented the statistical equations needed to calculate these contingency-based probabilities.

Gottman's use of sequential analysis is unique in that it points the way toward increased use of complex statistical analyses and detailed description of marital and family interaction. His work also reflects concentrated focus on methodological detail and rigor.

For analysis of verbal behavior, Gottman calculated the ratio of agreements to agreements-plus-disagreements (in order to avoid divisions by zero) for distressed versus nondistressed couples. This variable significantly differentiated both husbands and wives across the distress–nondistress factor. For analysis of nonverbal behavior, Gottman summed positive, neutral, and negative affect (nonverbal behavior) across all content (verbal behavior) codes. There were no significant effects for the husband–wife factor, or the interaction between the husband–wife, and distress–nondistress factors. There was a significant main effect for the distress–nondistress factor that could be accounted for by the negative and neutral, but not positive, codes. Distressed cou-

ples were significantly more negative and less neutral nonverbally than nondistressed couples, but the two groups did not differ overall on the proportion of positive affect.

The *F*-ratios were larger for nonverbal than for verbal behaviors, leading to the conclusion that nonverbal behaviors discriminate better than verbal behaviors between distressed and nondistressed couples along the positive–negative dimension.

In providing more detailed description of the data, Gottman noted that distressed couples were more likely than nondistressed couples to exhibit negative affect when expressing feelings about a problem, mind-reading, and disagreeing. In fact, the negative-affect code accounted for 78 percent of the variance between distressed and nondistressed couples for the content category of expressing feelings about a problem.

Thus the hypothesis that distressed couples are more negative and less positive than nondistressed couples was given support, and the findings suggest that these differences are more pronounced for negative than positive behavior and for nonverbal than verbal behavior.

Gottman used detailed sequential analyses on the data from 18 couples to explore the results on reciprocity. He studied 14 clinical couples versus 14 nonclinical couples instead of the initial 5 distressed (clinical) and 5 nondistressed (nonclinical) couples used in analyzing the data on positiveness. The distress–nondistress factor was defined by marital satisfaction scores and by the couples' having presented themselves as having a problematic marriage.

Calculating the probability of negative affect cycles, Gottman found higher conditional probabilities for clinical than for nonclinical couples for both husband and wife initiations. For positive affect cycles, Gottman reported slightly greater probabilities for positive affect reciprocity for clinical couples during the early stages (lags).

These findings supported the hypothesis that clinical couples show more rigid patterning in the form of higher conditional probabilities in interaction than nonclinical couples. The tendency to reciprocate negative affect was greater than for positive affect, and negative reciprocity was a better discriminator of clinical from nonclinical couples than was positive reciprocity.

Gottman defined dominance as asymmetry in predictability of affect between husband and wife so that one spouse's affect is dependent upon the other's, more than vice versa. He employed a two-oscillation component model within a bivariate, crosscorrelational time-series analysis to investigate the concept of dominance in marital interaction. The time-series analysis allowed a crosscorrelation that was a measure of the extent to which one spouse's changes in affect predict (lead) or are predicted by (lag) changes in the other spouse's affect. The measure is determined by the slope of the correlation function, either positive or negative. The two-oscillation component model allows analysis of a rapid oscillation component (expressive) separate from the slow oscillation component (mood).

Gottman reported that the most likely pattern for nonclinical couples was equalitarian for both the expressive component and the mood component. When asymmetry did exist for nonclinical couples, affect was as likely to be wife- as husband-led for both components.

For clinical couples, however, the picture was different. For the mood component, the equalitarian pattern was more common; when asymmetry did exist for clinical couples, it was more likely to be wife-led. For the expressive component, the most likely pattern among clinical couples was husband-led, and clinical couples were far more likely than nonclinical couples to show asymmetry in the expressive component.

These findings held for high-conflict tasks only. For a low-conflict task, asymmetry for both components for both groups was unlikely.

Thus the data for the high-conflict task/expressive component supported the hypothesis that clinical couples show more asymmetry in predictability or dominance than do nonclinical couples. Gottman's definition of dominance as asymmetry in predictability of affect is in keeping with an interactive view, suggesting a process rather than content orientation. He noted that the partner who dominates the affective component of the interaction is, by this definition, the one who is less emotionally reactive.

Using the content codes from the CISS, Gottman tabulated the respective rates, across all couples, within three equal time-segments of the total interaction. The first segment he called the agenda-building phase, this process involving the expression of feelings about the

problem and mind-reading. This phase sets the stage for subsequent discussion by bringing out which aspects of the problem will be dealt with. The second stage, called the arguing phase, is marked primarily by the disagreement and summarizing-self codes. The third stage is most likely to involve problem-solving/information exchange, agreement, communication talk, and summarizing the other. This last phase is called negotiation.

For nonclinical couples, Gottman reported that the most likely sequence involved expressions of feelings about the problem with neutral affect by either spouse, followed by a chain that was interspersed with agreement by the wife. She thus validated and brought out her husband's expressions. Gottman called this the validation sequence. For clinical couples, however, the most likely chain in this phase involved a continuous exchange of feelings about the problem, without agreements, a pattern labeled the crosscomplaining sequence. Although mind-reading codes were less frequent, the same pattern was evident. A nonclinical husband's mindreading was followed by the wife's agreement, and the nonclinical couples showed a pattern of the wife's mind-reading followed by husband's agreement, which was not likely for clinical couples. Gottman also reported that clinical couples showed a common sequence during this phase of negative affect following an expression by either spouse of feelings about the problem. Once these sequences were begun, they tended to become self-perpetuating.

In the arguing phase, both clinical and nonclinical couples showed short sequences of disagreement followed by agreement. In the negotiation phase, counterproposal strings, involving one spouse's problem-solving followed by the other's alternative problem-solving, were equally likely for clinical and nonclinical couples. For clinical couples, however, problem-solving was as likely to lead back into arguing as to lead toward agreement. Contract strings ending in agreement were more likely for nonclinical than for clinical couples. Also, for clinical couples, communication talk increased the probability of more communication talk, resulting in a self-perpetuating chain. For nonclinical couples, however, communication talk chains tended to be brief even though the two groups did not differ in terms of frequency of communication talk codes.

Concerning the effects of the listener's nonverbal behavior, Gottman reported that the clinical wives and husbands were more likely to be negative listeners than the nonclinical wives and husbands, respectively. Clinical husbands were more often negative listeners than were their wives.

Clinical and nonclinical husbands were equally likely to be negative speakers after being negative listeners, whereas clinical wives were more likely than nonclinical wives to show this pattern.

The Rausch, et al (1974) data were made available to Gottman, who had the audiotapes recoded according to the CISS system. By comparing agreement with agreement-plus-disagreement ratios, Gottman placed Rausch, et al's 13 newlywed couples in the distressed range, although Rausch, et al had divided subjects into discordant and harmonious groups, based on a complex factor analysis. In any case, the discordant couples differed from the harmonious couples in the same way that Gottman's distressed group differed from the nondistressed group.

Discordant couples were more likely to engage in negative affect chains than harmonious couples. The differences in incidence of positive, neutral, and negative affect for discordant versus harmonious groups closely resembled the trends in the data for Gottman's distressed versus nondistressed groups. It is interesting to note that the Rausch, et al discordant couples showed the same pattern of positive reciprocity as clinical couples in Gottmans study; that is, these couples showed greater likelihood of reciprocity of positive affect at early stages of discussion than did harmonious couples.

Both discordant and harmonious couples showed evidence of unproductive crosscomplaining chains, whereas this feature discriminated Gottman's distressed from nondistressed groups. Despite important procedural and sampling differences between the two studies, the results from both revealed quite similar patterns.

Gottman presented the results of a study designed to test the generalizability of his original findings on positiveness and reciprocity across a variety of improvised conflict resolution tasks and a nonconflict task. The study was conducted by a student of Gottman's as a doc-

toral dissertation; it required each of 38 couples (19 clinical and 19 nonclinical) to role-play themselves in six standard improved conflict situations. The six situations were sharing events of the day, money, sex, in-laws, decision to have children, and discipline of children. The nonconflict task involved discussing a fun deck of cards containing reference to enjoyable couple activities.

In general, the findings were similar to those of Gottman's earlier study. For positiveness, agreement to agreement-plus-disagreement ratios discriminated the distressed from the nondistressed spouses even on the fun deck. Also, positive affect and negative affect significantly discriminated the two groups for five of the six improvisations.

Analyzing the sex improvisation codes related to reciprocity of affect, Gottman reported that clinical couples showed greater reciprocity of negative affect. Although clinical couples were, again, more likely than nonclinical couples to reciprocate positive affect early in a sequence, nonclinical couples in this study were more likely to reciprocate positive affect at later lags in the sequences. Clinical couples were more likely to use crosscomplaining chains, while nonclinical couples were more likely to use validating sequences in response to expressions of feelings about a problem.

Overall, clinical couples were more negative, less positive, and more likely to reciprocate negative affect than were nonclinical couples. These findings generally held up across all six conflict tasks. In addition, the fun-deck task revealed greater likelihood of the clinical group's expressing feelings about a problem (even on this nonconflict task), less likelihood of agreeing with spouse, and greater likelihood of reciprocating negative affect.

Gottman, Markman, and Notarius (1977) developed a scaling of selected CISS content and affect codes, which are summed across a given time period, called a "floor switch." These sums are plotted cumulatively across floor switches to indicate graphically a kind of affect bank account. By studying these cumulative point graphs for the couples used in the initial study and the dissertation study, Gottman tentatively identified five clinical and one nonclinical curve shapes. His goal was to provide a less global, stylistically oriented, and more specific behavioral description of the interaction styles of couples, especially clinical couples.

The typical nonclinical pattern for both spouses was a gradual increase in the plot of affect in the direction of continued positiveness.

The clinical pattern showing the most positive interaction, called the J-curve, was a positively accelerated increasing plot. A second clinical pattern, called the "flat beginning," indicated a greater likelihood of crosscomplaining than validation sequences in the agenda-building phase, but more use of contracting than counterproposal sequences in the negotiation phase. A third group, the flat-end pattern, showed the reverse pattern; they were more likely to use validation over crosscomplaining in the beginning phase and more likely to engage in counterproposal than contracting during the last phase. The fourth pattern, the asymmetrical, involved opposite curves for husband and wife; that is, one spouse generally used positive behaviors and the other negative. This group was more likely than the other groups to use both crosscomplaining and counterproposal sequences. The fifth clinical pattern had continuously decreasing negative curves for both spouses, but it occurred too infrequently for the use of sequential analyses needed for more specific descriptions.

The Talk Table Studies

Gottman discussed the lack of a connection in the research literature and in personality theory between people's perception of their own interaction and the perception and recording of their behavior by objective observers. At the same time, he sought to construct a bridge between the couples' evaluative perception of their relationship overall and their immediate perceptions of each other in the process of interacting.

Toward these ends, Gottman constructed the talk table, at which the couple sits facing each other. As they interact, each presses buttons to indicate, to the observers only, the intended impact of the verbal message delivered and the impact of the message received. The buttons comprise a five-point scale ranging from super-positive to super-negative. Meanwhile, the interaction is videotaped for separate coding and later analysis.

Gottman summarized the results of the intent–impact data (Gottman, Notarius, Markman, et al, 1976), using a principle-components analysis to identify a major affective component accounting for approximately half of the total variance, with high loadings by three of the five impact codes (super-negative, negative, and positive) and a questionnaire of marital satisfaction. Distressed and nondistressed couples could not be distinguished on the basis of intended-impact codes, whereas impact codes were significantly more positive and less negative for nondistressed than distressed couples. The authors concluded that these findings supported both an impact model and a communication model, in which the *discrepancy* between impact and intended impact distinguishes distressed and nondistressed groups.

In a further analysis of data from the talk table, sequential analysis procedures were used, which had not been available when the first analysis was made. Analysis of the observational data from the coding of the videotapes showed support for the negative reciprocity of affect hypothesis. These results indicated greater reciprocity of negative affect for distressed couples. Thus the data from couples' perceptions of their interaction and the data based on observers' codings were consistent.

Analysis of a second study originally reported by Gottman, et al (1976) revealed an interaction between the distress–nondistress factor and the level of conflict induced by the task factor. In other words, it was easier to discriminate distressed from nondistressed couples on the high-conflict task than on the low-conflict task. This interaction was not found in the second study reported by Gottman, et al (1976).

Gottman noted that the couples in the first study averaged 24.95 years of age and 3.22 years of marriage, whereas the couples in the second study averaged 32.5 years of age and 9.44 years of marriage. To determine whether length of marriage or procedural changes between the two studies influenced results, two of Gottman's students replicated the procedures in Study 2, using a sample matched in length of marriage to the sample of Study 1. The results were consistent with those of Study 1, and there was no distress by conflict-level interaction. Gottmann thus argued that stable but unhappily married couples have learned over time to keep their interaction positive in low-conflict situations (unlike unhappily married couples in earlier stages of marriage), but that this positiveness is lost in high-conflict situations.

Gottman noted the consistent lack of findings of positive reciprocity in the interaction of nondistressed marriages. Nondistressed couples generally exhibit more positive behaviors in their interaction than distressed couples do, but these behaviors do not occur contingently. Gottman favors a bank-account model as opposed to a reciprocity or quid-pro-quo model of satisfactory marriages. Nondistressed couples continue to make positive deposits rather than many negative withdrawals in a context of lack of contingency on the other spouse's behavior.

Gottman reported the results of a dissertation study conducted in his laborator (Markman, 1977), in which talk-table impact data were gathered on unmarried couples who were planning to marry. This procedure successfully predicted differences between low-satisfaction and high-satisfaction groups 2.5 years after the study was begun. Impact ratings discriminated the two groups on both future impact ratings and on relationship satisfaction. The correlations were higher (0.60) than usually found in the mate selection research despite lack of common method variance, which tends to elevate correlations. Talk-table impact variables did not correlate with actual personality similarity or value similarity, but did correlate with male-perceived similarity as measured during the courtship stage. Markman's data suggest that the impact codes themselves, but not the intent–impact discrepancy, reflect a dimension that includes perceived similarity as an early predictor of later marital satisfaction.

The Private Message System

Through a long chain of inferences and speculations, Gottman hypothesized that happily married couples will show more of a private message system, especially nonverbally, than the unhappily married. Comparing objective coders' ratings with the listening spouse's impact ratings, Gottman found that observers' codes were less likely to agree with those of a nondistressed spouse listener than with those of a distressed spouse listener. According to Gottman, this relative lack of a private message system among distressed couples allows for the large distortion found when there is a noticeable intent–impact discrepancy. Gottman interpreted this in light of his speculation that distressed couples have a need for greater interpersonal distance in marriage. He cited research indicating that negative reciprocity (negative symmetrical mirroring of behaviors) in animals is involved in territorial disputes and is aimed at increasing distance.

Gottman reported the results of a comparison of audiotapes made by couples interacting with tapes made by other couples in the laboratory. The groups did not differ significantly in marital-satisfaction scores, both falling in the range between distressed and nondistressed. The results indicated a greater proportion of agreements to agreements-plus-disagreements, less negative and more positive affect, and less negative affect reciprocity for couples in the laboratory. Also, interaction at home was less likely to involve validation and contracting sequences and more likely to involve crosscomplaining and counterproposal sequences. Based on a series of detailed anlayses, Gottman concluded that high- and low-satisfaction groups were more easily distinguished, based on codings of tapes made at home. The confidence of the laboratory findings in Gottman's studies is thus increased.

Gottman presented the results of a three-phase model-testing and intervention-assessment study. He argued that clinical treatment programs should be based on descriptive empirical findings and refined through feedback from detailed process–outcome assessment.

The clinical intervention results are complex and offer only tentative support of Gottman's proposed couple-training package. This package includes training in the following social skills:

1. *Listening and validating* is aimed at reducing intent–impact discrepancy and summarizing-self sequences, and increasing validation sequences.
2. *Leveling* is aimed at reducing mind-reading behaviors by using more specific and fewer general statements.
3. *Editing* is aimed at increasing politeness

as a method of de-escalating self-perpetuating quarrel sequences.

4. *Negotiation* teaches couples to identify the segments of a conflict resolution and encourages contracting sequences.
5. *Hidden agenda identification* helps couples identify and discuss unstated issues (i.e., issues of intimacy, responsiveness to each other, couple status), that, if not made overt, cause couples to spin their wheels discussing irrelevant issues.

Phase One of Gottman's clinical intervention program involved administration of process and outcome assessments of the empirically derived program. Phase Two tested a refined version of the procedure and circumvented the waiting-list drop-out and deterioration problems of the time-lagged control design. This was done by applying two pre-workshop testing sessions. Phase Three assessed the differential effectiveness of the program according to couple differences, based on pretraining assessments, and it also involved further procedural refinements.

In Phase One, Gottman analyzed the extent to which changes in the three structural model variables (negative affect, negative affect reciprocity, and dominance) predicted changes in marital satisfaction scores after clinical intervention. Decreases in the wife's negative affect were significantly correlated with increases in the couple's marital satisfaction. The Phase One intervention introduced significant increases, compared with a control waiting-list group, in marital satisfaction, but only for husbands. Part of this differential was due to a decrease in marital satisfaction in the waiting-list group, and the increase in marital satisfaction for the experimental group of husbands was very small (from 89.9 to 92.3).

The Phase Two procedure eliminated the decrease in marital satisfaction in the waiting-list group by using two pretest sessions. Marital satisfaction increased after the clinical intervention workshops for only one of the two groups in this phase. Using tapes made by couples at home, Gottman found that negative affect decreased immediately after the workshop intervention but tended to increase again over time, as measured in a later follow-up. This suggests a problem of decrement in the effects over time of the workshop intervention. In addition,

Gottman found evidence of a decrease in negative affect between the two preassessments, before the workshops, in the waiting-list group. These findings make it difficult to determine any specific effectiveness of the intervention package itself in terms of long-lasting changes. The potential benefits, on a very short-term basis, of the couple's act of presenting themselves to professionals must be considered.

In Phase Three, Gottman again ran into the problem of maintenance of change from post-test to follow-up. Also in this phase, Gottman grouped couples at pretest according to the classification system derived from analyses of the point graphs in his earlier research (J-curve, flat end, flat beginning). This group failed to predict differential change in marital satisfaction among the participants. In other words, it appears that the benefits of participating in the workshops were not related to initial assessments of levels of social (i.e., marital) skills.

Gottman did tentatively identify a profile of the kind of couple who most benefited from the workshops. This hypothetical couple had a wife initially high in negative affect but low in reciprocating her husband's negative affect, and a husband initially as emotionally responsive as his wife and initially low in negative affect. Intuitively, it seems plausible that such a couple might be experiencing a situational stress rather than a fundamental interactive disturbance.

Despite Gottman's optimism for his empirically derived clinical intervention package, these results are not very impressive, especially in light of the great effort required by researchers, coders, and participating couples.

Gottman must be credited for his research rigor, his commitment to empirical testing and to empirically derived models and interventions, and for his willingness to report his findings candidly and in detail. The greatest difficulty, however, lies in the lack of success in uncovering, by means of intense methodological focus, measures that increase understanding at a genotypical versus phenotypical level (L'Abate, 1976) of the processes involved in fundamental change. Nevertheless, Gottman's work raises numerous theoretical questions related to the current state of theory and practice in marital therapy. From his findings, one can question numerous commonly held clinical beliefs about the nature of marital interaction. Gottman's work implies the following:

1. Reciprocity may not be a viable concept by which to define a satisfactory marriage, for distressed couples reciprocate negative as well as positive behaviors in what can potentially be a vicious cycle. Behavioral exchanges may not be related to degree of distress.
2. Affect may be the most important component of the marital relationship, with the variables determining positive affect and intimacy currently unknown.
3. Increased communication may not correlate with marital satisfaction or problem-solving ability.
4. Closeness–distance issues may be a crucial determinant of distressed versus nondistressed couples. Variables related to increasing closeness–distance are unknown, however.
5. The phenomenon of complementarity may lead to more distress rather than to a balance in the marital relationship. Equalitarian marriages may provide the most functional relationship for satisfactory interaction. Spouses who are dependent on each other to provide specific complementary role functions show greater distress.

In addressing the nature and understanding of marital interaction, Gottman's body of work cogently focused on a number of theoretical assumptions that to some extent have become accepted clinical lore for marital therapists. His work is cited here in some detail to point to the need to explore further and understand dyadic interactional phenomena.

MARITAL EVALUATION

Evaluation is an effort to obtain whole and systematic samples of certain types of verbal, perceived, and motor behavior in the framework of a standardized situation. Traditionally, psychological tests have measured differences between individuals or between the reaction times of the same individual on different occasions (Anastasi, 1976). The evaluation and diagnosis derived from these tests have usually consisted of the analysis and description of individual personalities who are having some kind of difficulty in adaptation. The assessment of the individual personality has then presumably been used to assist in planning beneficial treatment (Rappaport, et al, 1978).

With the advent and growing popularity of family and marital therapies, the question of assessment has become one not only of attempting to analyze and describe the individual personality systematically, but of attempting to analyze and describe the individual personality as he or she interacts with another individual. It is, therefore, the task of the marital evaluator to integrate intra- and interpersonal dynamics into the paradigm of clinical prediction so that assessment describes a relationship and is predictive of specific criterion variables such as marital adjustment and maladjustment.

Historically, family diagnosis and family assessment have been based on single-concept notions related to marital adjustment and satisfaction (Fisher, 1976). Early literature focused on husband-power versus wife-power (Ryder & Goodrich, 1966), whereas later studies focused on independent variables such as occupation, income, and education (Glenn & Weaver, 1978).

Currently, most family-assessment strategies are single-concept notions, theoretical notions, broadly based clinical lists, and a few empirically derived approaches (Fisher, 1976), with marital "adjustment" the most frequently studied dependent variable (Spanier, 1976). Phillips (1973) classified the major types of marital assessment into four categories:

1. *True–false.* Self-reports related to how one sees self or marriage.
2. *Interpersonal relationship tests.* Self-reports of how one views his or her behavior with, toward, about, and around others.
3. *Item-by-item reports.* Self-reports of specific problems.
4. *Projective.* That is, Rorschach Sentence Completion Tests, Thematic Apperception Test.

Cromwell, et al (1976) described the major ways to assess marital problems: (1) assessment of the character of individuals, with an emphasis on personality and affect; (2) assessment of the group structure, primarily looking at discrepancies in role perceptions; (3) assessment of interchanges in communication; (4) observation of the dyad working on an analogue task.

Phillips (1973) presented the most frequently used tests in marital counseling. Among the true–false, paper-and-pencil tests, he noted the Taylor-Johnson Temperament Analysis, Edwards Personal Preference Schedule, MMPI, Leary's Interpersonal Checklist, and the Sex Knowledge Inventory—Form X. Among sentence-completion tests, he noted Manson and Lerner's Marriage Adjustment Sentence Completion Survey and the tests published by Western Psychological Services: (1) Multiphasic Marital Inventory, (2) Marital Roles Inventory, (3) California Marriage Readiness Evaluation, (4) Sexual Development Scale for Females, and (5) Male Impotence Test.

Most tests currently used in assessment and evaluation of marriage and marital therapy lack sufficient predictive criteria, validity, and reliability, however. Although a number of tests purporting to measure primarily marital satisfaction–distress have been developed since the early 1970s, most continue to be subjective self-report measures.

DISCUSSION

In the last decade, there has been a significant increase in interest in the empirical study and evaluation of marital interaction. As can be seen from the areas reviewed in this chapter, investigators are beginning to attempt to validate empirically a number of theoretical propositions as well as treatment interventions.

These interventions still offer little for an understanding of the exact nature and dynamics of the marital relationship, however. Each focuses on specific aspects of the individual or the relationship, with a lack of ability to integrate the numerous levels of dyadic interaction existing at any given moment.

Treatment outcome studies indicate that marital therapies are at least comparable to individual therapies in overall improvement rates. Improvement, however, is usually defined as increased marital satisfaction/happiness measured by either subjects' or therapists' self-reports. The criterion for change is not objectively or concretely defined; neither is the treatment intervention. Therefore, defining what has changed or improved is difficult when there is evidence of improvement. In addition, since there are few long-term outcome studies available, deterioration effects are still unknown.

Developmental approaches, primarily birth-order theory and cognitive-development theories, describe the effects of early experiences within the family of origin on the personality organization of the adult individual. It is hypothesized that if one can predict individual adult psychodynamics, one can also predict dyadic adult interactions based on personality organization. Although some specific variables are recognized as determinants of later individual personality organizations, the possible interactions of specified variables are not only not clearly specified, but potentially myriad.

Structural developmental approaches are primarily descriptive ones, which in essence catalogue observed correlations between specific (usually one) variables and behavior. Like developmental approaches, however, the specification of the interaction of a number of variables as a criterion for predicting and describing marital interaction is still nonexistent.

Psychopathological descriptive approaches remain ones that catalogue and describe overt symptomatic behaviors. Underlying dynamics are hypothesized but as yet unverified. One of the few attempts at a detailed understanding of sequences of interactions in a couple relationship has been made by Gottman (1979). His data, however, leads one to conclude that specific marital interactions cannot be predicted from specific variables. Couples have unique and sometimes varying responses to the same variables. In addition, the role of affect in marital interaction cannot be clearly described, i.e., some couples who express numerous conflict issues report satisfactory marriages while other couples who express numerous conflict issues report unsatisfactory marriages.

Assessment has the same inherent difficulties as other empirical attempts to describe marital interaction. Criterion is usually subjective and nebulous (i.e., satisfaction), and most assessment instruments have little validity other than face validity. The major inherent difficulty with marital assessment procedures is that there is little to no empirical clarification of what is being measured. Thus the investigation of both theory and outcome consists primarily of the description of numerous variables and concepts, with little ability to integrate them into a dynamic understanding of dyadic interaction.

THE FUTURE

There are numerous difficulties and deficits in the existing empirical approaches to studying marital interaction and marital therapy outcome. In spite of these difficulties, however, it must be noted that there is an increasing interest in empirical validation as well as an increasing growth of available data on marital interaction.

The next step remains one of refining research techniques, employing measures of interaction rather than individual dynamics of characteristics, employing long-term developmental change studies, and further clarifying the complex nature of dyadic interaction. Furthermore, theoretical assumptions that have been accepted as valid in the field of marital therapy (i.e., reciprocity, communication skills, the role of conflict) need to be reexamined, as well. These assumptions may be valid in some couples' relationships but not in others.

REFERENCES

Adams BN. Birth order: A critical review. *Sociometry*, 1972, *35*(3), 411–439

Adler A. *Understanding human nature*. New York: Greenberg Publisher, 1927

Adler A. Introduction: The fundamental views of individual psychology. *International Journal of Individual Psychology*, 1935, 1, 5–8

Anastasi A. *Psychological testing*. New York: Macmillan, 1976

Bagarozzi DA, & L'Abate L. *Family evaluation*. Manuscript in preparation, 1982

Baltes PB, & Schaie KW. On life-span developmental research paradigms: Retrojects and prospects. In PB Baltes & KW Schaie (Eds), *Life-span developmental psychology: Personality and organization*. New York: Academic Press, 1973

Bateson G. *Naven* (1st ed). Stanford: Stanford University Press, 1936

Bateson G. *Steps to an ecology of mind*. San Francisco: Chandler Publishing, 1972

Bayer AE. Birth order and attainment of the doctorate: A test of economic hypotheses. *American Journal of Sociology*, 1967, 72, 540–550

Belmont L, & Marolla FA. Birth order and intelligence. *Science*, 1973, *182*, 1096–1101

Belmont L, Stein Z, & Zybert P. Child-spacing and birth order: Effect on intellectual ability in two-child families. *Science*, 1978, *202*, 995–996

Bergin AE, & Garfield SL. Introduction. In SL Garfield & AE Bergin (Eds), *Handbook of psychotherapy and behavior change* (1st ed.). New York: Wiley, 1971, pp. i–viii

Bergner RM. The marital system of the hysterical individual. *Family Process*, 1976, *15*, 85–95

Bernal G, & Baker J. Toward a metacommunication framework of couples' interaction. *Family Process*, 1979, *18*, 292–302

Bernal G, & Baker J. Multilevel couple therapy. Applying a metacommunication framework of couples' interaction. *Family Process*, 1980, *19*, 367–376

Berne E. *Games people play*. New York: Grove Press, 1964

Birtchnell J, & Mayhew J. Toman's theory: Tested for mate selection and friendship formation. *Journal of Individual Psychology*, 1977, *33*, 18–36

Blatt MM, & Kohlberg L. The effects of classroom moral discussion upon children's level of moral judgment. *Merrill-Palmer Quarterly*, September 1969

Blood RO, & Wolfe DM. *Husbands and wives: The dynamics of married living*. Glencoe, IL: The Free Press, 1960

Boszormenyi-Nagy IA. A theory of relationships: Experiences and transactions. In I Boszormenyi-Nagy & JL Framo (Eds), Intensive family therapy. New York: Hoeber, 1965, pp. 118–136

Breland HM. Birth-order effects: A reply to Schooler. *Psychological Bulletin*, 1973, *80*, 210–212

Burnand G. Birth order and autobiography. *Journal of Individual Psychology*, 1973, *29*, 35–38

Carter DC. Paranoid wife syndrome. *Minnesota Medicine*, 1968, *51*, 307–310

Carter DC. The diagnosis and treatment of husband paranoidism. *West Virginia Medical Journal*, October 1970, pp. 365–368

Carter EA, & McGoldrick M. *The family life cycle: A framework for family therapy*. New York: Gardener Press, Inc., 1980

Christensen B, & Scoresby AL. *The measurement of complementary, symmetrical, and parallel interactions in family dyads*. Unpublished manuscript, Brigham Young University, 1975a

Christensen B, & Scoresby AL. *Relationship style inventory*. Provo, UT: Brigham Young University, 1975b

Cicirelli VG. The relationship of sibling structure to intellectual abilities and achievement. *Review of Educational Research*, 1978, *48*, 365–379

Cohen SE, & Beckwith L. Caregiving behavior and early cognitive development as related to ordinal position in preterm infants. *Child Development*, 1977, *48*, 152–157

Coleman KH. Conjugal violence: What 33 men report. *Journal of Marital and Family Therapy*, 1981, *6*, 207–213

Croake JW, & Olson TD. Family constellation and personality. *Journal of Individual Psychology*, 1977, *33*, 9–17

Cromwell RE, Olson DHL, & Fournier DG. Tools and techniques for diagnosis and evaluation in marital and family therapy. *Family Process*, 1976, *15*, 1–49

DeAvila BEH. Birth order differences: An attempt to isolate conditions under which they occur. *Dissertation Abstracts International*, 1970, 4547-A

Delamater AM, Lahey BB, & Drake L. Toward an empirical sub-classification of "learning disabilities": A psychophysiological comparison of "hyperactive" and "nonhyperactive" subgroups. *Journal of Abnormal Child Psychology*, 1981, *9*, 65–77

Duvall E. *Family Development*. Chicago: Lippincott, 1957

Elder GH. *Adolescent achievement and mobility aspirations*. Chapel Hill, NC: Institute for Research in Social Sciences, 1962

Fakouri ME. Relationship of birth order, dogmatism and achievement motivation. *Journal of Individual Psychology*, 1974, *30*, 216–220

Farley FH. Birth order and a two-dimensional assessment of personality. *Journal of Personality Assessment*, 1975, *39*, 151–153

Farley FH, Smart KL, & Brittain CV. Birth order, rank, and branch of service in the military. *Journal of Individual Psychology*, 1974, *30*, 227–231

Feldman LB. Depression and marital interaction. *Family Process*, 1976, *15*, 389–395

Fisher L. Dimensions of family assessment: A critical review. *Journal of Marriage and Family Counseling*, 1976, *2*(4), 367–382

Forer LK *Birth order and life roles*. Springfield, IL: Charles C. Thomas, 1969

Forer LK. Bibliography of birth order literature in the 70's. *Journal of Individual Psychology*, 1977, *33*, 122–141

Glenn ND, & Weaver AN. A multivariate, multisurvey study of marital happiness. *Journal of Marriage and the Family*, 1978, *40*, 269–282

Gorad SL. Communicational styles and interaction of alcoholics and their wives. *Family Process*, 1971, *10*, 475–489

Gottman J. *Marital interaction: Experimental investigations*. New York: Academic Press, 1979

Gottman J, Markman H, & Notarius C. The topography of marital conflict: A study of verbal and nonverbal behavior. *Journal of Marriage and the Family*, 1977, *39*, 461–477

Gottman J, Notarius C, Markman H, Bank S, Yoppi B, & Rubin M. Behavior exchange theory and marital decision making. *Journal of Personality and Social Psychology*, 1976, *34*, 14–23

Greene BL, Lee R, & Lustig N. Treatment of marital disharmony where one spouse has a primary affective disorder (manic depressive illness). I. General overview—100 couples. *Journal of Marriage and Family Counseling*, 1975, *1*, 39–50

Greene RI, & Clark JR. Adler's theory of birth order. *Psychological Reports*, 1970, *26*, 387–390

Gurman AS. Group marital therapy: Clinical and empirical implications for outcome research. *International Journal of Group Psychotherapy*, 1971, *21*, 176–189

Gurman AS. The effects and effectiveness of marital therapy: A review of outcome research. *Family Process*, 1973a, *12*, 145–170

Gurman AS. Marital therapy: Emerging trends in research and practice. *Family Process*, 1973b, *12*, 45–54

Gurman AS. Contemporary marital therapies: A critique and comparative analysis of psychoanalytic, behavioral and systems theory approaches. In TJ Paolino, Jr, & BS McCrady (Eds), *Marriage and marital therapy*. New York: Brunner/Mazel, 1978

Gurman AS, & Kniskern DP. Deterioration in marital and family therapy: Empirical, clinical and conceptual issues. *Family Process*, 1978a, *17*, 3–20

Gurman AS, & Kniskern DP. Research in marital and family therapy: Progress, perspective and prospect. In SL Garfield & AE Bergin (Eds), *Handbook of psychotherapy and behavior change*. New York: Wiley, 1978b

Haley J. *Strategies of psychotherapy*. New York: Grune & Stratton, 1963

Haley J. Research on family patterns: An instrument measurement. *Family Process*, 1964, *3*, 41–65

Haley J. *Uncommon therapy: The psychiatric techniques of Milton Erickson*. New York: Norton, 1973

Harper JM, Scoresby AL, & Boyce WD. The logical levels of complementary, symmetrical, and parallel interaction classes in family dyads. *Family Process*, 1977, *16*, 199–209

Harris ID. *The promised seed*. London: The Free Press of Glencoe, 1964

Hayes RF, & Bronzaft AL. Birth order and related variables in an academically elite sample.

Journal of Individual Psychology, 1979, *35*, 213–224

Heins T. Marital interaction in depression. *Australian and New Zealand Journal of Psychiatry*, 1978, *12*, 269–275

Herrell JM. Birth order and the military: A review from an Adlerian perspective. *Journal of Individual Psychology*, 1972, *28*, 38–44

Hill R, & Rodgers RH. The developmental approach. In HT Christensen (Ed), *Handbook of marriage and the family*. Chicago: Rand McNally, 1964, pp. 98–123

Hinchliffe MK, Hooper D, & Roberts FJ. *The melancholy marriage*. New York: Wiley, 1978

Hornbostel LK, & McCall JN. Sibling differences in need-achievement associated with birth order, child-spacing, sex and siblings' sex. *Journal of Individual Psychology*, 1980, *36*, 36–43

Hudson J, & Henze LF. Values in mate selection: A replication. In RE Albrecht and EW Bock (Eds), *Encounter: Love, marriage and family*. Boston: Holbrook, 1972

Hughes SF, Berger M, & Wright L. The family life cycle and clinical intervention. *Journal of Marriage and Family Counseling*, 1978, *4*, 33–40

Irvin MG. Self, mother, and teacher perceptions of the child as related to academic readiness, sex, and sibling position in the family. *Dissertation Abstracts International*, 1974, 7046-A

Jacobs BA, & Moss HA. Birth order and sex of sibling as determinants of mother–infant interaction. *Child Development*, 1976, *47*, 315–322

Jacobsen NS. A review of the research on the effectiveness of marital therapy. In T Paolino & B McCrady (Eds) *Marriage and Marital Therapy*, New York: Brunner/Mazel, 1978

Jurkovic GJ, & Ulrici DK. *Developing conceptions of marital issues: A cognitive-developmental analysis*. Paper read at the meeting of the American Association of Psychiatric Services for Children, New Orleans, November, 1980

Kahn M. Nonverbal communication and marital satisfaction. *Family Process*, 1970, *9*, 449–456

Kohlberg L. The development of children's orientations toward a moral order: 1. Sequence in the development of moral thought. *Vita Humana*, 1963a, *6*, 11–33

Kohlberg L. Moral development and identification. In H Stevenson (Ed), *Child psychology. 62nd yearbook. Natural Social Studies in Educ.* Chicago: University of Chicago Press, 1963b

Kohlberg L. Development of moral character and moral ideology. In ML Hoffman and LW Hoffman (Eds), *Review of child development research* (Vol 1). New York: Russell Sage Foundation, 1964

Kohlberg L. The child as a moral philosopher. *Psychology Today*, September 1968, pp. 98–107

Kohlberg L. Continuities and discontinuities in childhood and adult moral development. *Human Development*, 1969a, *12*, 93–120

Kohlberg L. Stage and sequence: The cognitive-developmental approach to socialization. In DA Goslin (Ed), *Handbook of socialization theory and research*. Chicago: Rand McNally, 1969b

Kohlberg L. A cognitive-developmental approach to moral education. In L Kohlberg, *Collected papers on moral development and moral education*. Unpublished manuscript, Harvard University, 1973

Konig K. *Brothers and sisters*. Blauvelt, NY: St. George Books, 1973

L'Abate L. *Understanding and helping the individual in the family*. New York: Grune & Stratton, 1976

L'Abate L, & Goodrich ME. Marital Adjustment. In RH Woody (Ed), *Encyclopedia of Clinical Assessment*. San Francisco: Jossey-Bass, 1980

L'Abate L, & L'Abate BL. Marriage: The dream and the reality. *Family Relations*, 1981, *30*, 131–136

Lahey BB, Hammer D, Crumrine PL, & Forehand RL. Birth order × sex interactions in child behavior problems. *Developmental Psychology*, 1980, *16*, 608–615

Lebedun M. Measuring involvement in group marital counseling. *Social Casework*, 1970, *51*, 35–43

Lederer W, & Jackson D. *The mirages of marriage*. New York: Norton, 1968

Leibin VM. Adler's concept of man. *Journal of Individual Psychology*, 1981, *37*, 3–4

Levinger G, & Sonnheim M. Complementarity in marital adjustment: Reconsidering Toman's family constellation hypothesis. *Journal of Individual Psychology*, 1965, *21*, 137–145

Lewis M, & Kreitzberg VS. Effects of birth order and spacing on mother–infant interactions. *Developmental Psychology*, 1979, *15*, 617–625

Loevinger J, Wessler R, & Redmore C. *Measuring ego development* (Vols 1 & 2). San Francisco: Jossey-Bass, 1970

Mace DR. Competing issues in marriage. In RE Albrecht & EW Bock (Ed), *Encounters: Love, marriage and the family*. Boston: Holbrook, 1972

Madanes C. *Strategic family therapy*. San Francisco: Jossey-Bass, 1981

Manaster GJ. Birth order: An overview. *Journal of Individual Psychology*, 1977, *33*, 3–8

Markman H. *A behavior exchange model applied to the longitudinal study of couples planning to marry*. Unpublished doctoral dissertation, Indiana University at Bloomington, 1977

Marshall JR, & Neill J. *The removal of a psychosomatic symptom: Effects on the marriage. Family Process*, 1977, *16*, 273–280

Martin PA. *A marital therapy manual*. New York: Brunner/Mazel, 1976

McDonough JJ. Sibling ordinal position and family

education. *International Journal of Family Counseling*, 1978, *6*, 62–69

Miley CS. Birth order research 1963–1967: Bibliography and index. *Journal of Individual Psychology*, 1969, *25*, 64–70

Minuchin S. *Families and family therapy*. Cambridge: Harvard University Press, 1974

Minuchin S, Rosman B, & Baker L. *Psychosomatic families: Anorexia nervosa in context*. Cambridge: Harvard University Press, 1978

Murphy ME. Behavioral, self-report and projective factors related to birth order. *Dissertation Abstracts International*, 1972, 6037-B

Neugarten B. Adaptation and the life cycle. *The Counseling Psychologist*, 1976, *6*, 1–

Nystal MS. The effects of birth order and sex on self-concept. *Journal of Individual Psychology*, 1974, *30*, 211–215

Olson DH. Marital and family therapy: Integrative review and critique. *Journal of Marriage and the Family*, 1970, *32*, 501–538

Olson D, Sprenkle D, & Russell C. Circumplex model of marital and family systems: I. Cohesion and adaptability dimensions, family types, and clinical applications. *Family Process*, 1980, *18*, 3–28

Ortiz BE. Birth order and marital satisfaction: A review of the literature. *Family Therapy*, 1981, *8*, 29–32

Overall J. Association between marital history and the nature of manifest psychopathology. *Journal of Abnormal Psychology*, 1971, *78*, 213–221

Palazzoli MS, Cecchin G, Prata G, & Boscolo L. *Paradox and counterparadox*. New York: Jason Aronson, Inc., 1978

Paolino TJ, Jr, & McCrady BS. *The alcoholic marriage: Alternative perspectives*. New York: Grune & Stratton, 1977

Paykel ES, Myers JK, Dienfelt MN, & Klerman GL. Life events and depression: A controlled study. *Archives of General Psychiatry*, 1969, *21*, 753–760

Peterson Y. The impact of physical disability on marital adjustment: A literature review. *The Family Coordinator*, 1979, *24*, 47–51

Phillips CE. Some useful tests for marriage counseling. *The Family Coordinator*, 1973, *22*, 43–53

Piaget J. *The child's conception of the world*. London: Routledge, Kagan Paul, 1928

Piaget J. The moral judgment of the child. Glencoe, IL: Free Press, 1948 (Originally published, 1932)

Price JS, & Hare EH. Birth order studies: Some sources of bias. *British Journal of Psychiatry*, 1969, *115*, 633–646

Rae JB. The influence of the wives on the treatment outcome of alcoholics: A follow-up study at two years. *British Journal of Psychiatry*, 1972, *120*, 601–613

Rappaport D, Gill MM, & Schafer R. *Diagnostic psychological testing*. Chicago: Yearbook Publisher, 1978

Rausch H, Barry W, Hertel R, & Swain M. *Communication, conflict, and marriage*. San Francisco: Jossey-Bass, 1974

Ravent R, & Rodrigues BH. Conjugal power structure: A re-examination. *American Sociological Review*, 1971, *36*, 264–278

Register MC. Moral compatibility in married couples: A study of marital satisfaction as related to stage of moral development of spouses. *Dissertation Abstracts International*, 1976, *36*(8-B)

Rest JR. Longitudinal study of defining issues: Test of moral judgment—strategy for analyzing developmental change. *Developmental Psychology*, 1975, *11*, 738–748

Rounsaville BJ, Weissman MM, Prusoff BA, & Herceg-Baron R. Process of psychotherapy among depressed women with marital disputes. *American Journal of Ortho Psychiatry*, 1979, *49*, 505–510

Rubinstein D, & Timmins J. Depressive dyadic and triadic relationships. *Journal of Marriage and Family Counseling*, 1978, *9*, 13–23

Rule WR, & Comer AT. Family constellation and birth order variables related to vocational choice of dentistry. *Psychological Reports*, 1979, *45*, 883–890

Russell C. Circumplex model of marital and family systems: Empirical investigations with families. *Family Process*, 1979, *18*, 29–45

Ryder R, & Goodrich D. Married couples' responses to disagreement. *Family Process*, 1966, *5*, 30–42

Sager CJ. Couples therapy and marriage contracts. In AS Gurman & DP Kniskern (Eds), *Handbook of family therapy*. New York: Brunner/Mazel, 1981

Saunders DG. Marital violence: Dimensions of the problem and modes of intervention. *Journal of Marriage and Family Counseling*, 1977, *3*, 43–52

Schachter S. *The psychology of affiliation*. Stanford, CA: Stanford University Press, 1959

Schooler C. Birth order defects: Not here, not now! *Psychological Bulletin*, 1972, *78*, 161–175

Scoresby AL. *Relationship style inventory* (rev ed). Provo, UT: Brigham Young University, 1976

Scoresby AL. *The marriage dialogue*. Reading, MA: Addison-Wesley, 1977

Scoresby AL, & Christensen B. Differences in interaction and environmental conditions of clinic and nonclinic families: Implications for counselors. *Journal of Marriage and Family Counseling*, 1976, *1*, 63–71

Scott EM, & Manaugh TS. Territorial struggles in the marriages of alcoholics. *Journal of Marriage and Family Counseling*, 1976, *2*, 341–345

Selman R. *Growth of interpersonal understanding: A developmental and clinical analysis*. New York: Academic Press, 1980

Selman R, & Jaquette D. Stability and oscillation in ineterpersonal awareness: A clinical developmental analysis. *Nebraska Symposium on Motivation*, 1977, *25*, 261–304

Shrader WK, & Leventhal T. Birth order of children and parental reports of problems. *Child Development*, 1968, *39*, 1165–1175

Shulman B, & Mosak H. Birth order and ordinal position: Two Adlerian views. *Journal of Individual Psychology*, 1977, *33*, 114–121

Sigman M, Cohen SE, Beckwith L, & Parmelee AH. Social and familial influences on the development of preterm infants. *Journal of Pediatric Psychology*, 1981, *6*, 1–13

Sluzki C, & Beavin J. Symmetry and complementarity: An operational definition and a typology of dyads. In P Watzlawick & J Weakland (Eds), *The interactional view: Studies at the MRI 1965–1974*. New York: Norton, 1977. (Also in *Acta Psiquitrica y psicologica de America Latina*, 1965, *11*, 321–330)

Spanier GB. Measuring dyadic adjustment: New scales for assessing the quality of marriage and similar dyads. *Journal of Marriage and the Family*, 1976, *38*, 15–28

Spanier GB, & Lewis RA. Marital quality: A review of research in the seventies. *Journal of Marriage and the Family*, 1980, *42*, 825–839

Sprowls FS. A study of the relationships among birth order, family size, and sibship constellation and high school behavioral and academic adjustment. *Dissertation Abstracts International*, 1979, *3483-A*

Steinglass P, Davis DI, & Berenson D. Observation of conjointly hospitalized "alcoholic couples" during sobriety and intoxication. *Family Process*, 1977, *16*, 1–16

Tamashiro RT. *Measuring self-knowledge development: Construction of a preliminary scoring manual*. Unpublished doctoral dissertation, University of Massachusetts, 1975

Tamashiro RT. Developmental stages in the conceptualization of marriage. *The Family Coordinator*, July 1978, pp. 237–244

Toman W. Family constellation as a basic personality determinant. *Journal of Individual Psychology*, 1959, *15*, 199–211

Toman W. *Family constellation* (2nd ed). New York: Springer, 1969

Toman W. *Family constellation* (3rd ed). New York: Springer, 1976

Turiel E. An experimental test of the sequentiality of developmental stages in the child's moral judgments. *Journal of Personality and Social Psychology*, 1966, *3*, 611–618

Vockell EL, Felker DW, & Miley CH. Birth order literature 1967–1971: Bibliography and index. *Journal of Individual Psychology*, 1973, *29*, 39–53

Von der Daele LA. A developmental study of the ego ideal. *Genetic Psychology Monographs*, 1968, *78*, 191–256

Wark DM, Swanson EO, & Mack J. More on birth order: Intelligence and college plans. *Journal of Individual Psychology*, 1980, *137*, 221–226

Watkins D, & Astilla E. Birth order, family size and self-esteem: A Filipino study. *The Journal of Genetic Psychology*, 1980, *137*, 297–298

Watzlawick P, Weakland JH, & Fisch R. *Change: Principles of problem formation and problem resoltuion*. New York: Norton, 1974

Weeks GR, & Wright L. Dialectics of the family life cycle. *American Journal of Family Therapy*, 1979, *7*, 85–91

Weiner H. Birth order and illness behavior. *Journal of Individual Psychology*, 1973, *29*, 173–175

Weissman MM, & Paykel ES. *The depressed woman: A study of social relationships*. Chicago: University of Chicago Press, 1974

Wells RA, Dickes T, & Trivello N. The results of family therapy: A critical review of the literature. *Family Process*, 1972, *7*, 188–207

Wilks L, & Thompson P. Birth order and creativity in young children. *Psychological Reports*, 1979, *45*, 443–449

Williams AR, Frick OL, & Fromm RA. The paranoid wife syndrome: Diagnosis and treatment. *Journal of Marital and Family Therapy*, 1981, *7*, 75–79

Wilson B, & Edington G. *First child, second child. . . .* New York: McGraw-Hill, 1981

Wisdom G, & Walsh R. Dogmatism and birth order. *Journal of Individual Psychology*, 1975, *31*, 32–36

Zajonc RB. Family configuration and intelligence. *Science*, 1976, *192*, 227–236

Zajonc RB, & Marcus GB. Birth order and intellectual development. *Psychological Review*, 1975, *82*, 74–88

17

The Training of Marital Therapists

The field of marital therapy continues to be differentiated into a number of growing specialties, i.e., therapy versus social-skills training versus treatments for specific dysfunctions (e.g., assertion, sexual dysfunction). This differentiation of treatments has resulted in a number of practitioners whose primary identities, allegiances, and loyalties are to their chosen form of treatment or intervention. In actual practice, however, the marital therapist must still be a generalist as well as a specialist. He or she is a generalist in the sense that treatment must address the interaction of a number of complex issues and problems, and a specialist in that treatment must address specific interpersonal symptoms, problems, and issues. As a result of both the differentiation of the field and the variety of issues seen in practice, marital therapy has, instead of becoming a more integrated approach, become a collection of diverse marital therapies with no cohesive body of theory and technique.

This current state of the art of marital therapy leads to the historical problem of what constitutes the training of the professional marital therapist. Traditionally, practitioners of marital therapies have come from varied backgrounds, with little or no formal and/or specific training in marital therapy. Marital therapists have been and continue to be clergy, psychologists, psychiatrists, social workers, and lawyers. Current societal trends, however, have led to demands not only for training credentials, but also for displayed and, often, measurable competencies by practioners in the mental health field.

Thus numerous questions are raised about the nature of training programs for marital therapists. Given the ill-defined, hodgepodge nature of the profession, the lack of systemic theories and treatments, and the demonstrated inability to evaluate treatment sufficiently, there are certainly no guidelines for a successful and appropriate marital-therapy training program. The resultant issues that must then be addressed in training are the following:

1. What kind of curricula should be offered and by whom?
2. What constitutes appropriate credentials and length of training (i.e., B.A., M.A., Ph.D., or post-Ph.D.)?
3. How are competencies defined and assessed, including those in the philosophical, personal, and professional areas?
4. Is certification or licensing needed and, if so, what levels and types are needed?
5. What criteria should determine those individuals selected for training?
6. How many individuals should be trained?
7. What should the cost of training be?

Concerning proposed curricula, one can only point out that in order for a trainee to be cognizant of the numerous theories and methodologies in current practice, an eclectic and general curriculum is at present the only practical option. One can, however, become so much of a generalist that one lacks basic therapeutic skills and/or may be incapable of being a specialist when the need arises.

Concerning credentials, there is no existing literature to indicate which kind of degree or length of training program is related to practice and outcome. Therefore the specification of the appropriate degree is left to subjective bias and preference. Certainly minimal degree requirements are necessary, but the nature of the degree requirements cannot be objectively based on objective data of what a competent marital therapist is, or which skills and variables constitute competence. Therefore indices of competency are left, as choice of degree, to mostly subjective judgment.

Concerning certification and licensing, there are no outcome measures comparing noncertified and nonlicensed therapists with those who are certified and/or licensed. Certification and licensing can at best only protect the profession from those wishing to enter it, rather than protecting the consumer seeking an effective therapist.

As to who would be trained, again, subjective bias based on subjective experience can be the only guidelines, for there is no evidence that specific personal qualities can guarantee a competent marital therapist. Perhaps the only issue that can be easily addressed in terms of training is that there is definitely a need, as indicated by current demands, for trained, knowledgeable, and competent marital therapists. Exactly what skills these therapists possess is at present unclear and debatable.

Another difficulty in defining and/or assessing what should constitute a marital-therapy training program is that training programs still do not differentiate between marriage and family therapy. Most curricula fail to distinguish between the task characteristics and demands that make these two forms of intervention different (other than to define marital therapy as treating a marriage issue and family therapy as treating a family issue). Although there is certainly an overlap in dynamic theories and treatment, techniques related to marriage and family marital therapy could conceivably be a separate training specialty.

It is proposed that training in marital *interventions* (the term 'interventions' is stressed to cover a wider range of treatment possibilities than does therapy) address five different areas: (1) academic curriculum, (2) experiential methods, (3) clinical experiences, (4) supervision, and (5) research.

ACADEMIC CURRICULUM

Based on current theories and differing treatment practices, a curriculum in marital therapy should minimally contain the following courses:

1. Historical and crosscultural perspectives on marriage.
2. Personality development in marriage or the developmental lifecycle of marriage from premarital stages through parenthood.
3. General survey introduction course on theories of marital intervention.
4. The assessment of marital interaction.
5. Structured skill-training methods of intervention.
6. Ethical and legal issues in marital intervention.
7. Behavioral methods.
8. Existential, cognitive, and contextual therapeutic techniques.
9. Treatment of sexual dysfunctions.
10. Divorce mediation and counseling.
11. Research methodology in marriage (assuming previous statistical knowledge).

Winkle, et al (1981) suggested courses in eight different areas, including: individual and group psychotherapy; normal/abnormal human growth and development/lifecycle theories, specific theories and techniques of marriage and family therapy, topics related to marriage and family therapy, topics related to marriage and family relationships (sexuality, alternative lifestyles), supervised clinical practice, topics related to ethics and professional development, and competencies in statistics and research methodologies.

Their suggested list of courses was obtained from 20 AAMFT-approved supervisors and 25 training directors of graduate-level marriage and family therapy programs, using the Delphi technique to refine group opinion. Thus the suggested courses were based on opinions and suggestions of advanced professionals in the field. Learning structured preventive skill-training programs was excluded from the final list because "panelists did not endorse preventive/developmental psychoeducational strategies, such as marriage enrichment and parent education, highly enough for inclusion" (Winkle, et al, 1981, p. 208).

This omisson in part supports the contention made in this book that there is a distinct value difference between skill training-oriented interveners and therapy-oriented professionals. This distinction, however, may not apply to behavior-oriented therapists, who combine both approaches.

EXPERIENTIAL CURRICULUM

Little has been written (Springer & Springer, 1978) about the nature and use of experiential learning in marital therapy training programs. However, the model used by the Family Studies Center is outlined here in order to present a suggested experiential sequence that requires different skills at different levels.

1. Conducting structured enrichment role-playing of a near-functional couple. This experience takes place between pairs of graduate students who reverse roles of mock couples and enrichers (Jessee & L'Abate, 1981).
2. Conducting structured programs with a near-functional couple drawn from volunteer undergraduates attending introductory psychology courses (L'Abate, 1980).
3. Conducting structured enrichment programs with clinical couples or couples with a substantive degree of dysfunctionality but who are not chaotic or in crisis.
4. Conducting covenant contracting programs (as described in Chapter 4 and Appendix C) with volunteers and clinical couples.
5. Conducting intimacy workshops. Although previous experiences were usually with single couples on a weekly basis for a total of 8 to 10 hours, this workshop format is one entire day and has 3 to 5 couple participants, giving students the experience of working with groups of couples.
6. Marriage therapy with clinical but mildly disturbed couples (within the confines of the University Family Study Center), with supervision.
7. Marriage therapy with clinical couples, with supervision, in a clinical agency where the degree of disturbance is greater than that usually found in university population.
8. Internship. To this point, all experiences have been part-time and parallel to the academic curriculum. The internship consists of working full-time, with supervision, in a clinical setting away from and outside the range of control of the University.

SOLO VERSUS CO-THERAPY PRACTICE

One issue in training has pertained to treatment practice performed by one or two therapists (same or opposite sex). Arguments pro and con have abounded, with Haley (1976), Bowen (1976), and Guerin and Guerin (1976) taking the stand for individual therapy practice versus Neill and Kniskern (1982), Duhl and Duhl (1981), and others in favor of co-therapy teams (Cornwell & Pearson, 1981; Epstein, Jayne-Lazarus & DeGiovanni, 1979). The usual objections to co-therapy are the lack of evidence that the outcome is any better than with an individual therapy and that costs are necessarily higher.

What this controversy overlooks, as Whitaker (1967) has noted, is the comfort of the therapist, i.e., whether he or she is more comfortable practicing alone or with a co-therapist. Treatment problems arise whether one is an individual therapist or a co-therapist. Therefore the ultimate judge may need to be the therapist. He or she should be given the experience of both models in training so that the final choice is made on the basis of personal experience rather than on the experience of someone else.

SUPERVISION

A great deal has been written about the crucial role of supervision in the training of marriage and family therapists (Liddle & Halpin, 1978; Liddle, 1981; Mead & Crane, 1978; O'Hare, et al, 1975; Stier & Goldenberg, 1975; Tucker, et al, 1976), not without controversy and disagreements.

Liddle and Halpin (1978) reviewed most

of the literature on family therapy training and supervision. Their review covered six major areas: (1) goals of training and supervision, and skills of the supervisor; (2) training and supervision techniques; (3) supervisor–supervisee relationship; (4) personal therapy for trainees; (5) politics of family therapy training; and (6) evaluation of training.

The skills of the supervisors will depend on the theoretical orientation of the program and of the individual supervisor. If the orientation is humanistic (emotionality), emphasis will be on "growth" and the affective sensitivity of the trainee to the affective experiences of the couple. If the orientation is psychodynamic (rationality), emphasis will be on how the trainer is able to conceptualize his or her experiences with the couple and how the couple "thinks." If the orientation is behavioral (activity), patterns of reinforcement between the couple and what the trainee can do to have the couple change their behaviors will be stressed. If the orientation is contextual, whether systemic (Watzlawick, et al, 1974; Selvini-Palazzoli, 1978), structural (Minuchin, 1974), or strategic (Haley, 1976), the emphasis will be on the relational give-and-take of the couple. The degree of active intervention will increase from a rather laissez-faire position in the humanistic approach to more active and intrusive intervention in the behavioral and contextual approaches.

Techniques in supervision vary: (1) bug-in-the-ear of the trainee, with the supervisor watching through a one-way mirror; (2) telephone in the therapy room, by which the supervisor, watching through a one-way mirror, can call the trainee; (3) actual supervisor, again watching through a one-way mirror, enters the therapy room and tells the trainee what to do; (4) the trainee leaves the therapy room to confer with the supervisor, who has been watching, and then comes back to deliver an argument or conclude the therapy session; (5) videotapes and audiotapes of trainees' sesions and supervision of trainees' verbal or written reports of sessions. Supervision can take place with groups of trainees or with one trainee and the supervisor alone. Pros and cons for each of these techniques can be found in Liddle and Halpin's (1978) review as well as in the papers cited at the beginning of this section. Each program and each supervisor has a preferred technique,

and it may suffice to say that the trainee should be given the opportunity to experience as many modes of supervision as are feasible and possible.

The supervisor–trainee relationship, like goals and techniques of supervision, is a function of the theoretical biases of the supervisor. Most psychodynamically and behaviorally oriented supervisors may tend to take a strongly directive position, while more humanistically and contextually oriented supervisors may tend to take a more egalitarian and democratic position. Whereas the former emphasizes the trainee's personal family history and the need for his or her personal therapy, the latter stresses present competencies, considering personal therapy either irrelevant or a waste of time. Liddle and Halpin (1978) have summarized:

> A continuum emerges with some believing in an equal, personal, and more process-focused definition, while at the opposite pole a more task, skills, and goal-oriented philosophy exists, eschewing the assumption that a non-hierarchial structure to any trainer–trainee is possible (p. 86).

Another mode of supervision, which by definition ceases to fit into the mold of the supervisor–supervisee relationship, is *peer consultation*, in which the roles are reversed from time to time, as in the case of the Milano Group, who switch positions from watching through a mirror to sitting in the therapy room. A variation on this theme is the practice of cotherapy, in which the two therapists debrief each other before and at the end of each session (O'Hare, et al, 1975).

Mead and Crane (1978) have suggested an empirical approach to supervision that is behaviorally derived. They point out six steps in the process of supervision: (1) observation, (2) specification of the problem, (3) hypothesis formulation, (4) testing of the hypothesis, (5) evaluation of results, and (6) going on to the next problem without delay. These authors suggested that the trainee's behavior is influenced by at least six possible factors: (1) setting, (2) trainee personal history and theoretical perspective, (3) the supervisor's personal history and theoretical orientation, (4) administrative influences, (5) the couple's behavior, and (6) the supervisor's behavior. Most of these interactions are viewed from a simplistic reward/

punishment framework that may be useful at the beginning stages of training.

Stier and Goldenberg (1975) raised the issue of the feasibility of training paraprofessionals in therapeutic techniques; they object to such training. These authors see the issue in a different light, however. Rather than a simple dichotomy of approval versus rejection of paraprofessional therapists, it has been demonstrated that therapists can supervise paraprofessionals in the use of clearly defined social-skills training approaches, with the therapist in charge of the treatment of the couple and ready to intervene therapeutically if and when necessary (L'Abate, 1973). It is also conceivable that a graduate curriculum could include student supervision of paraprofessionals, with a professional conducting final supervision of both the paraprofessional and the student.

THERAPIST COMPETENCIES

The Colgary group (Tomm & Wright, 1979) has recommended competencies in what they define as executive functions. Their tripartite model of skills is an input–throughput–output model that focuses on perceptual input (focusing on emotionality), conceptual throughput (focusing on rationality), and executive output (focusing on activity). Their model, however, is a conductor rather than a reactor model for therapists. Therapists who react to what is presented by the couple rather than conducting what is to be addressed by the couple would not fit this model. Furthermore, defining the competencies needed in each proposed category is difficult because of the subjective nature of definition. Tomm and Wright (1979) do, however, provide an attempt to begin to delineate the competencies needed.

In addition to the work of the Colgary

group, Liddle and Saba (1982) discriminate among necessary, if insufficient, perceptual, cognitive, and executive skills. This framework can serve as a base from which to start a functional evaluation of available and lacking skills in each trainee, making training more appropriate for the individual needs of each trainee. Nevertheless, no empirical attempts have been made to delineate further those competencies that are correlated with successful outcome of treatment interventions.

CONCLUSION

Nichols (1979a, 1979b) has described the current trends in the training of marriage and family therapists. These trends are (1) from service to training to education; (2) from trial-and-error, or extrapolation, to specialized knowledge, i.e., from an individual-only approach to a relationship-only approach; (3) from offering a variety of courses to offering sequential education and training; and (4) from generalization to specialization in curriculum.

Even though training programs are becoming more defined and more rigorous, there is still no consensus on which training experiences produce a professional marital therapist. Until the field of marital therapy is more empirically defined, training will, by necessity, be general and vary from program to program.

Nichols' (1979a) final conclusion is worth repeating:

Training therapists in techniques without reference to the substantive knowledge of the field in which they are practicing is a shortsighted way of preparing practitioners. Educating therapists so that not only are they acquainted with such materials in depth, but also so that they are equipped to remain in touch with research and theory in the marriage and family field in their subsequent careers is a major need (p. 27).

REFERENCES

Bowen M. Theory in the practice of psychotherapy. In PE Guerin, Jr. (Ed), *Family therapy: Theory and practice.* New York: Gardner Press, 1976

Cornwell M, & Pearson R. Co-therapy teams and one-way screen in family therapy practice and training. *Family Process*, 1981, *20*, 199–200

Duhl BS, & Duhl FJ. Integrative family therapy. In

AS Gurman & DP Kniskern (Eds), *Handbook of family therapy.* New York: Brunner/Mazel, 1981

Epstein N, Jayne-Lazarus C, & De Giovanni IS. Cotrainers as models of relationships: Effects of the outcome of couples therapy. *Journal of Marital and Family Therapy*, 1979, *5*, 53–60

Guerin PE, Jr., & Guerin KB. Theoretical aspects and

clinical relevance of the multi-generational model of family therapy. In PE Guerin, Jr. (Ed), *Family therapy: Theory and practice.* New York: Gardner Press, 1976

Haley J. *Problem-solving therapy.* San Francisco: Jossey-Bass, 1976

Jessee E, & L'Abate L. Enrichment role playing as a step in family therapy training. *Journal of Marital and Family Therapy*, 1981, *7*, 507–514

L'Abate L. The laboratory method in clinical child psychology: Three applications. *Journal of Clinical Child Psychology*, 1973, *2*, 8–10

L'Abate L. Toward a theory and technology for social skills training: Suggestions for curriculum development. *Academic Psychology Bulletin*, 1980, *2*, 207–228

Liddle HA. On teaching a contextual or systemic therapy: Training content, goals and methods. *American Journal of Family Therapy*, 1981, *8*, 58–69

Liddle H, & Halpin R. Family therapy training and supervision: A comparative review. *Journal of Marriage and Family Counseling*, 1978, *4*, 77–98

Liddle HA, & Saba GW. Teaching family therapy at the introductory level: A conceptual model emphasizing a pattern which connects training and therapy. *Journal of Marital and Family Therapy*, 1982, *18*, 63–72

Mead E, & Crane PR. An empirical approach to supervision and training of relationship therapists. *Journal of Marital and Family Counseling*, 1978, *4*, 67–75

Minuchin S. *Families and family therapy.* Cambridge, MA: Harvard University Press, 1974

Neill JR, & Kniskern DP. (Eds). *From psyche to system: The evolving therapy of Carl Whitaker.* New York: Guilford, 1982

Nichols WC. Education of marriage and family therapists: Some trends and implications. *Journal of Marital and Family Therapy*, 1979a, *6*, 19–28

Nichols WC (Ed). Special issue: Education and training in marital and family therapy. *Journal of Marital and Family Therapy*, 1979b, *5*, 3–105

O'Hare G, Heinrich AG, Kirschner NN, Oberstone AV, & Ritz MG. Group training in family therapy—A student's perspective. *Journal of Marriage and Family Counseling*, 1975, *2*, 157–162

Selvini-Palazzoli M, Cecchin G, Prata G, & Boscolo L. *Paradox and counterparadox.* New York: Jason Aronson, 1978

Springer J, & Springer S. *Experimental methods for teaching about marriage.* New York: The Free Press, 1978

Stier S, & Goldenberg I. Training issues in family therapy. *Journal of Marriage and Family Counseling*, 1975, *1*, 63–68

Tomm KM, & Wright LM. Training in family therapy: Perceptual, conceptual, and executive skills. *Family Process*, 1979, *18*, 227–250

Tucker BZ, Hart G, & Liddle HA. Supervision in family therapy: A developmental perspective. *Journal of Marriage and Family Counseling*, 1976, *3*, 269–276

Watzlawick P, Weakland J, & Fisch R. Change: Principles of problem formation and problem resolution. New York: W. W. Norton, 1974

Whitaker CA. The growing edge of techniques of family therapy. In J Haley & L Hoffman (Eds), *Techniques of family therapy.* New York: Basic Books, 1967, pp. 265–360

Winkle CW, Pierce FP, & Haverstadt AJ. A curriculum for graduate level marriage and family therapy education. *Journal of Marital and Family Therapy*, 1981, *8*, 201–210

Conclusion

18

Conclusions: Current Issues in Methods of Marital Intervention

Marriage counseling, which formerly consisted primarily of educational and advice-giving interventions, evolved rapidly in the 1970s to include a variety of divergent theoretical and treatment stances. There is no doubt that the field of marital interventions and marital therapy now constitutes a specialty area within and, at times, outside the field of family therapy. Yet, like any rapidly growing specialty, numerous issues have both evolved and been raised about theory, techniques, goals, and the efficacy of treatment. Throughout this book, these issues have been presented as they relate to specific theories, methods, and techniques. However, most of the issues raised and discussed about one specific form of intervention are applicable to the current state of the art of the entire field of marital interventions.

This final chapter reviews and summarizes the issues already presented throughout the book, as well as presenting other issues relevant to the current status and future of the field of marital therapies. In order to delineate clearly specific concerns related to the practice of marital interventions, this chapter specifically addresses the areas of theory, treatment, the role of the therapist/intervener, the kind of clients treated, evaluation, the role of values, the cultural nature of marriage in our society, and future needs.

THEORY

Historically, marital therapy developed in the early 1920s from a social demand for practitioners to address marital problems (Olson,

1974, 1978). Both theory and treatment were contained in an adjustment model by which marital difficulties were assumed to result from individual maladaptations to prescribed roles. Treatment thus focused on helping an individual adjust to those marital roles prescribed by the culture as healthy and appropriate (Burgess, 1926; Mudd, 1951). As a result, treatment was primarily educational and oriented toward intervening in individual dynamics rather than intervening in dyadic dynamics (Broderick & Schrader, 1981). Beginning in the late 1950s and influenced primarily by the field of family therapy, general systems theory and communications theory began to influence and ultimately dominate the pervading theoretical assumptions about the nature of the marital relationship. As a result, treatment began to add to its educational model an attempt to understand the interpersonal dynamics of the couple dyad and to alter these interactions that seemingly contributed to marital dissatisfaction. During the 1970s, influenced primarily by social demands for shorter term and more cost-efficient treatments, a resurgence in educational treatment models occurred. As in the earlier treatment orientation of the 1920s, the majority of these models stressed the importance of role adaptation (Bosco, 1973; Garland, 1978; Guerney, 1977; Harrell & Guerney, 1976; Otto, 1976), with an added emphasis on successful role negotiation (Patterson, et al, 1973). These two factors were often seen as both the cause and the effect of marital satisfaction. Thus there are currently four divergent but interrelated major theoretical orientations to marital therapy. The predominant one, general systems theory, views the marital dyad as an ongoing interrelationship in which the actions and reactions of one individual influence the actions and reactions of another individual. This theoretical orientation addresses the complexities of the relationship by no longer hypothesizing a linear, individual cause–effect explanation of marital distress. Instead, marital interaction is viewed as an ongoing interrelationship in which cause and effect are nonlinear and, often, circular. The second major theoretical orientation, communications theory, hypothesizes marital distress as the result of a failure in dyadic communication. It is assumed that ineffective communication causes a breakdown in the satisfaction levels within the dyad, for needs cannot be adequately conveyed or responded to without effective communication. The third major theoretical orientation, behavioral marital therapy, hypothesizes the nature of the marital relationship as one in which reciprocity and behavioral exchange are the determinants of marital satisfaction (Patterson & Reid, 1970). That is, within the dyad, there is an exchange of positive and rewarding behaviors between the two partners. This exchange must be mutual and equivalent for marital satisfaction to exist. The fourth and final major theoretical orientation is an educational model in which marital distress is hypothesized as occurring as a result of lack of appropriate education in the skills required to interact within an intimate dyad.

Although these four theoretical stances are divergent in nature, they do have the underlying similarities of stressing the importance of communication, both verbal and nonverbal, and behavioral exchange, negotiated overtly and covertly. Marital distress is hypothesized in a general way as resulting from the inability of the partners in the dyad to successfully negotiate ways by which to meet their needs.

These four major theoretical orientations point to variables in a dyadic relationship that influence the nature of that relationship. There are, however, numerous deficits related to the conceptualization of these variables that ultimately limit both the understanding and the treatment of marital distress. First, although effective communication and behavioral negotiation are emphasized as predictors of the cri-

terion of marital satisfaction or functionality, there is a lack of specific definition of these concepts. The exact nature of what is being communicated or negotiated under which specific conditions is not clear. For example, communication theorists stress the importance of the ability of spouses to discuss conflict issues. Gottman (1979), however, found that clinical couples who engaged in communication talk tended to increase the communication talk, resulting in a self-perpetuating chain. Nonclinical couples displayed brief communication talk chains. Therefore nonclinical couples were found to communicate verbally less than clinical couples their feelings, needs, and wants concerning conflict issues. Gottman (1978) also found that rate of behavioral exchanges (reciprocity) was not necessarily predictive of marital distress.

Gottman's work points to a second deficit in theory. There is an inability to provide constructs for predictable dyadic issues. Although developmental studies offer concrete categories of external stress that will influence the marital relationship over its life span (i.e., birth of children, loss of job, retirement), the interaction of these external stresses with specific marital constellations is unknown. All couples do not react in the same predictable ways to the same stress events. Current work by theoreticians influenced by ego psychology does offer a potential ability to clarify further the nature of dyadic relationships (Schwartz & Schwartz, 1980). Their work stresses the integration of both the conscious and unconscious individual variables that influence and determine that individual's relational approach to his or her partner. While promising a potential clarity of the integration of numerous intra- and interpersonal variables, there is, however, still a lack of specific understanding of the ongoing conscious and unconscious interpersonal dynamics that determine the affect nature of the relationship. Couples with similar psychodynamics vary in their reports of distress versus nondistress.

This inability to specify the causal factors of self-reported distress and nondistress relates to a third theoretical issue. There is little to no agreement concerning diagnostic criteria for marital relationships, other than self-report by the couple. These self-report criteria are usually defined in terms of distress, disharmony, disturbance, dissatisfaction, and satisfaction or happiness. The typical couple beginning any form of treatment usually presents the problems of dissatisfaction, distress, communication difficulties, and inability to renegotiate behavior. Marital therapists, as a result, must attempt a treatment guided by little, if any, empirically derived theory. The marital therapist must help a couple become "satisfied," with a decided inability to specify the exact nature of "dissatisfaction."

Systems theorists attempt to alter interactions to alleviate the presenting problem, while the communications theorists attempt to alter communication patterns. The behavioral theorists attempt to alter behavioral exchanges, and the educationally oriented theorists attempt to teach new forms of interaction. Thus no distinction is made between the symptom and the cause (Ables & Brandsma, 1977). The cause becomes the symptoms, defined in terms of poor versus good communication and/or positive, or effective, behavior versus negative, or ineffective, behavior. Nevertheless, the question remains: What specific issues underlie the presenting difficulties that are being treated? For example, do communication difficulties cause the distress or does the distress resulting from other factors cause the communication difficulties? Furthermore, how, except through a qualitive contextual analysis, can one objectively define good, or effective, versus poor, or ineffective, behavior?

A fourth problem stemming from the inability to define adequately the relevant diagnostic constructs is that there are few, if any, validated and reliable tests that measure and confirm hypothetical constructs. Intrapersonal measures (usually self-report) are still used to diagnose interpersonal problems (Cromwell & Keeney, 1979). As a result, systematic objective diagnosis is nonexistent.

Since no theory addressing marital interaction has been systematically developed, there is no comprehensive theory to explain the numerous complexities of the dyadic relationship. Terms used are vague (i.e., distress, dissatisfaction), and there is an inability to quantify these terms. As a result, it is difficult, if not impossible, to validate those hypotheses that purport to explain and understand the presenting problem of marital distress.

It is somewhat ironic that marital theory explains extensively the dynamics of individual behavior by a number of various theories and acknowledges them to be complex. Yet a marital relationship, which is composed of the interaction of two complex individuals, is explained by theories that are simplistic, usually linear in attempting to determine etiology, and rarely cognizant of the complex individual dynamics that contribute to the nature of the interaction of the relationship.

Ideally, theory dictates goals, and those goals dictate treatment. The effects of the treatment may be systematically evaluated. Then, systematic evaluation modifies theory and practice (Patterson, et al, 1973). Since the practitioner of marital therapies has no comprehensive theory, however, the goals and techniques of treatment become highly individualistic and are left, for the most part, to the subjective judgment of the practitioner.

TREATMENT

In earlier criticisms of marital therapy, Manus (1966) described treatment as a "technique in search of a theory," with no integrated, comprehensive approach. Olson (1970, 1978), in later criticisms, stated that practice had outrun theory even though efforts were being made to develop more comprehensive theories, with treatments logically related to those theories. Both criticisms are still valid as we face a plethora of both old and new treatment methods and techniques. Currently, the vast array of marital interventions and treatments largely focuses on the general goals of happiness/satisfaction and increased intimacy, with the inherent or overt promise that these goals can be reached with somewhat short-term and, often, simplistic interventions. These general goals of most treatments, as well as the interventions related to them, raise further questions about the nature of theory and treatment.

Since the late 1960s, American society has experienced a major cultural shift in expectations of intimate dyadic relationships (Melville, 1977). As Lasch (1979) has aptly hypothesized, a growing solution to the problems of marital and societal strain has become a "cult of intimacy." This "cult of intimacy" stresses personal emotional fulfillment, with the emphasis on personal fulfillment increasing both the individual's and the couple's goals and expectations of marriage and, thus, often leading to the request that the practitioner help the couple achieve goals of happiness, fulfillment, and intimacy.

From both a theoretical and a treatment perspective, this cultural emphasis on intimacy raises the question of the extent to which marital therapists' treatment goals are merely a response to shifts in cultural phenomena and values. Compounding the influence of the culture's stressing increased intimacy is the cultural value of quick solutions and remedies to difficulties. Long-term or time-consuming solutions are thought to be ineffective; therefore a number of relatively simple treatments and interventions appear to have been created in the wake of the demand for faster "cures." Since little research has been conducted on the nature of marital satisfaction, happiness, or intimacy, there is still no evidence to indicate that these goals are realistic, possible, or attainable if they are possible. Theory and practice create the ironic treatment situation of providing short-term, simple treatments for complex, abstract, and ill-defined issues.

The general goal of treatment becomes one of alleviating distress and increasing satisfaction and intimacy when there is no understanding of the interrelationship of factors underlying the etiology of marital satisfaction and intimacy. Therefore marital therapies currently treat a problem that is ill defined, in hopes of achieving a goal that is also ill defined.

As a result of overriding cultural values (increased intimacy), current treatment interventions may in essence be a continuation of the historical emphasis on an adjustment model of marital health. Instead of attempting treatment aimed at facilitating individual adjustment to valued prescribed roles, marital therapists may now be attempting treatment aimed at facilitating individual and dyadic adjustment to the valuation of one's ability to relate with increasing intimacy and self-fulfillment.

In addition to the problem of ill-defined and perhaps questionable, goals of treatment, it is difficult to ascertain the nature of most marital interventions. Although current educational/preventive models of treatment offer what are often detailed descriptions of treatment interventions (i.e., marital enrichment programs, marital communication programs), most do not delineate or describe their treatment approaches. In part, this lack of delineation of treatment technique may result from the fact that there are still few training programs; those training programs that exist often disagree as to which techniques constitute treatment. This lack of delineation of treatment techniques may also result from the fact that most marital therapists have been trained in other disciplines, deriving their approaches to marital therapy from their own experiences in attempting to treat marital difficulties. The ultimate influence on the current inability to define treatment technique, however, results from the absence of an integrated theory to guide treatment goals or techniques.

THE ROLE OF THE THERAPIST/INTERVENER

As a result of the still ill-defined nature of theory and treatment, the role of the marital therapist/intervener varies according to differing orientations to treatment. The therapist/intervener may take the role of a psychodynamically oriented therapist, an advice-giving counselor, an educator/trainer, or a technician. He or she may respond experientially to that which is presented by the couple, structure and conduct the topics and issues to be addressed by the couple, or teach programmed courses on various facets of the marital relationship. Treatment goals may range from adjustment to growth and further actualization, or from renegotiation of roles to negotiation of divorce.

Theoretically, marital therapists/interveners align themselves with a variety of orientations, including those who have traditionally addressed individual dynamics (i.e., psychoanalytic, Gestalt, TA, Rogerian client-centered therapy).

Most practitioners of marital therapies, however, do not align themselves with any school of thought and are eclectic. In a survey of 310 clinical members of the American Association for Marriage and Family Therapy, Sprenkle and Fisher (1980) found through member self-reports that the eight highest-rated goals of treatment were (1) listening attentively; (2) differentiation; (3) negotiation; (4) valuing the sender, the message, and the self; (5) flexibility; (6) speaking for self; (7) expressing feelings; and (8) supportiveness. Of the top eight goals, four related to communication skills, two related to cohesion, and two related to adaptability. Thus communications theory and its goals dominated the focus of treatment, although systems theory and adjustment theories were also important. Therefore the role of the therapist/intervener is subjectively reported to be one of skills, closeness, and adaptability.

The prevailing mode of the structure of treatment, regardless of theoretical orientation, is conjoint couples therapy in which couples are seen together by one or more therapists (more recent educational programs are conducted in conjoint couples groups). In addition, there has been an increased emphasis on the use of co-therapists, with some therapists claiming that the ideal marital therapist/intervener is a husband and wife co-therapy team. Although co-therapy appears to be gaining in popularity among marital therapists, there is, however, no evidence to indicate that co-therapy is more effective than the use of a single therapist (Russell & Russell, 1979). The use of co-therapists may also present further issues that must be addressed in the therapeutic setting. These issues are the negotiation of a working relationship between the co-therapists, additional transference and countertransference problems, and the increased cost of treatment. In the case of the husband and wife co-therapist team, there is the further possibility that the therapists' own marital issues may interfere with the ability to discern objectively the marital issues of the couple in treatment.

Although one may claim that the variety of marital therapists/interveners is sufficient to present ample choices to the consumer or client, it must be remembered that the therapist/intervener's role is still ill defined due to the predominant eclectic approaches to treatment and the lack of any systematic theory and treatment goals. Because the nature of marital health and marital distress is not clear, the role of the therapist remains unclear. Those aspects of the marital therapist/intervener's role that may be crucial to successful treatment cannot be defined or systematically evaluated as long as those factors constituting successful treatment cannot be defined.

THE NATURE OF CLIENTS TREATED

The majority of clients treated by the various marital therapies and interventions, consistent with the majority of clients seen by individual therapists, are white, educated, middle-class couples. For the most part, they are motivated to seek some therapeutic experience and have the basic intellectual and social skills (primarily verbal communication) necessary for treatment. This predominance of middle-class couples in treatment leads to several questions and issues concerning the nature of clients treated.

First, is the white, middle-class client the only client responsive to treatment, or can current treatments only address the issues of white, middle-class clients? Second, do practitioners discourage other social classes or ethnic groups from seeking marital therapies, or is there an immediate failure rate with clients from other social classes or ethnic groups who do seek treatment? Jones (1974) has criticized marital therapists as working with and believing that they can only work with middle-class clients. He stated that the reason for the prevalence of literature related to middle-class clients is that therapists are biased against the lower classes and prefer to work with middle-class clients. Third, if it may be true that the white, middle-class client is more motivated for treatment, how do marital therapists/interveners address the issues and needs of unmotivated couples? Fourth, little attention is paid to the treatment needs of the more severely disturbed couple. For example, it would be difficult to imagine that a couple with one psychotic spouse would benefit from a communications theory approach or a marital enrichment group.

Unfortunately, most marital therapies demand that the client be fairly well educated, rational, and able to benefit from insight or further education. One could conclude that the qualities needed in couples beginning treatment are those very qualities that treatment purports to improve. Thus couples who may need treatment the most will also be the most unable to benefit from treatment, if there is a benefit to be derived.

It must be concluded that current marital therapies and interventions address only one segment of the population, a segment that may already be functioning at a higher psychosocial level than others. While treatments focus on improved communication, enhancement, and optimal forms of growth, other more serious issues, such as physical abuse, drug and polydrug abuse, psychosis, or more crippling forms of emotional functioning, may be ignored.

EVALUATION AND ASSESSMENT

The evaluation of marital therapies may be viewed as still in its infancy. Gurman (1973) noted that the literature on marital therapy experienced a major growth after 1960. Over half of the evaluation studies have appeared since the early 1970s, however. Of the evaluation studies conducted to date, studies of therapist characteristics have been the fewest in number; studies evaluating client characteristics have been the second highest in number; and studies evaluating treatment outcomes have been the highest number published. For the most part, however, the majority of these studies are designed to advocate various theories and techniques. Therefore, there still exists a relatively small number of empirical outcome studies.

Unfortunately, few conclusions can be drawn from existing outcome studies because of the numerous methodological problems inherent in the research. Sampling problems in marital therapy literature usually relate to the fact that samples are neither random nor sufficiently large to be representative of the studied population. The use of control groups has been minimal, and clients studied have been white, middle-class clients.

As for the hypotheses and questions posed in outcome research, there has been no coherent theory to guide observations. Questions asked about outcome have often been simplistic and, at times, irrelevant to the enterprise of therapy. Without theory, it is difficult to conduct research, for one is never sure of the question that one is asking. Another problem with the formation of hypotheses is that practitioners and researchers are often isolated in their endeavors. Whereas a researcher might pose one question, a practitioner might pose an entirely different one, with the practitioner's questions being more relevant to treatment issues.

Methodological problems are numerous. Data are usually self-reports, which introduces the problem of subjective bias. Furthermore, the most common criterion measures have been self-reports of marital satisfaction, with few pretests. Thus initial level of satisfaction is unknown. Whether self-report of the feeling state of satisfaction is indicative of successful treatment outcome remains to be discerned. There is also a difficulty in both treatment and study when one spouse initially presents the problem of dissatisfaction while the other does not.

In addition to the problem of self-report measures, those objective measures that have been used usually consist of tests initially constructed to assess individual dynamics. Thus numerous individual measures have been used to assess an interactional dyadic relationship. Furthermore, in addition to inadequate measurement constructs, those measures most commonly used have little to no established validity or reliability. Observer ratings have been used in addition to other measures. The use of observer ratings, however, presents additional problems concerning an adequate definition of what is being observed, as well as the problem of the raters' own subjectivity in assessment.

In marital therapy research, there have been few multiple criterion measures. Without the use of multiple criterion measures, it is difficult to assess the complexity of issues being addressed by treatment. For example, there are few outcome studies on the impact of the treatment on both the dyad and on each individual in the dyad. Without assessing both individuals in addition to their dyadic functioning, one is faced with the question of what effect altering dyadic interaction has on individual functioning. Behavioral marital therapy (BMT) does assess the individual–marital feeling and behavioral states, claiming valid and, often, excellent results. Behavioral research, however, faces the problem of attempting to measure complex relationships by assessing only a few discrete, concrete variables in the marital relationship (i.e., exhibition of specific behaviors taken at face value and reports of positive or negative reward).

Fortunately, there has been a recent increase in the systematic study of treatment programs. This increase is characterized by the increase in multimethod evaluation, using multidimensional measures of outcome and treatment objectives (Gurman & Kniskern, 1978b). Although little can as yet be concluded from more comprehensive studies, it is significant that the field of marital therapy is beginning to seek a more valid assessment of its theory and practice.

The state of the art of evaluation in marital therapy, however, still faces the ongoing problem of adequate methodologies. Adequate research designs are still needed, as is specificity of theory as it relates to treatment and outcome. Evaluation research has unfortunately contributed to the field's continuing use of ill-defined and nonintegrated approaches, for its main conclusions are that some ill-defined marital treatments, in some cases, increase self-reports of marital satisfaction.

VALUES IN MARITAL THERAPY/INTERVENTION

The marital therapist/intervener is faced with a number of value issues raised by the presenting problems of the clients. These issues are subjective in nature, with no clear-cut guidelines for the practitioner. Because a marital therapist is titled as such, the practitioner is immediately confronted by his or her title with the question of how much and to what extent the marital relationship is valued. Fisher (1975) has criticized the marital therapist's position, stating that the title "marital therapist" ignores the fact of the high divorce rate. Furthermore, the title implies that a goal of treatment is that marriages will stay intact. Not only does this implied value ill prepare marital therapists to deal with their failures (dissolutions of marriages), but it also requires that marital therapists define their value systems as to when, how, and if couples should divorce as a solution to marital issues. The title, marital therapist, also inherently ignores other forms of intimate relationships. The marital therapist must decide if he or she sees the legal marriage relationship as the most viable and acceptable form of dyadic relationships or whether other forms of dyadic relationships

(i.e., living together without marriage, homosexual relationships) are viable and acceptable, as well. Additionally, what value does the marital therapist place on individuals who live alone or live in other forms of nondyadic relationships (i.e., group relationships)?

Currently, literature in marital therapy addresses only the study of the marriage relationship and treatment aimed primarily at improving it. Thus one may conclude that there is a distinct value system implying that marriage is the only valued form of intimate dyadic relationships or lifestyles. There is, however, the possibility that comparative study of alternative lifestyles might yield data to indicate that this value may not be supported by reality.

In treating relationships, the marital therapist must also address presenting problems that are value-laden by society, i.e., parenthood, abortion, childlessness, sexual issues such as sexual functioning, extramarital affairs, issues of sexual as well as physical abuse. Given that these topics are value-laden by society, one must assume that the marital therapist will have previously formed values and must acknowledge them as they relate to treatment issues. Furthermore, the issues of the therapist may also relate to ethical considerations of the therapeutic treatment. For example, a therapist who views abortion as unacceptable might discourage (overtly or covertly) a couple from deciding to choose abortion, thus potentially violating the couple's freedom to negotiate their own decision. A therapist who negatively views extramarital affairs might deny treatment to a couple of which one member is having an extramarital affair, thus denying treatment when treatment might be beneficial.

It is important that the marital therapist recognize his or her values concerning the marital relationship, primarily because values affect treatment goals. For example, it must be remembered that marital therapy has historically been an adjustment-to-roles model, and in some forms of treatment, adjustment is still stressed, with the potential of continuing to value traditional male and female roles. Behavioral marital therapy stresses adjustment by increasing positive reciprocal behavior exchanges. In this adjustment model, in an early, often called "pioneering" study, Stuart (1969a) had husbands exchange tokens for sex.

These tokens were earned as positive rewards for behaviors requested by their wives. One can easily see in this work a traditional adjustment-to-roles model whereby the female dispenses sexual pleasures as a bargaining tool for other behaviors. The view of women as sexual objects is not only perpetuated by this model of treatment, but the centuries-old, exchange-of-goods model of marriage is perpetuated, as well.

One can also look at the goals of other forms of marital intervention as value-laden. Treatments with goals of enhancement and enrichment stress current cultural values of increased personal fulfillment within the marital relationship, while "marriage encounter" clearly derives its goals from religious values.

Treatments such as fair fighting, problem-solving, and contracting may be seen to derive from the value placed on rationality and problem-solving skills, while the numerous forms of treatments for sexual dysfunctions may derive from the increased cultural emphasis on the value of sexuality and increased sexual pleasure. Since these varied goals have not been empirically derived or validated, the marital therapist must ask whether he or she is ascribing to achievable treatment goals for the alleviation of distress or ascribing, for the most part, to a philosophical system based on cultural values and shifting mores.

These cultural shifts raise other value-laden treatment questions for the marital therapist. First, the marital therapist must address changing cultural definitions of a "good" or "healthy" marriage. Since there is still no guiding theory or research, the therapist must decide for himself or herself whether the current emphasis on intimacy, "growth," and self-fulfillment is viable. Second, the marital therapist must also address the impact of the Women's Movement, not only on assumptions about women's roles, but on changing assumptions about the psychology of women, as well. Theory and treatments developed for the traditional nuclear family, in which the husband has been viewed as more cognitive, less emotional, and more independent and the wife has been viewed as more nurturing, warm, and emotional (Blood & Wolfe, 1960; Komarovsky, 1962; Parsons & Bales, 1955), have been widely criticized. Major criticisms have centered on the existence of negative sex-role stereotyping by which traditional male roles are valued more than traditional female roles (Abramowitz & Dokecki, 1977; Abrams, 1976; Davidson & Abramowitz, 1980). Since major modes of marital treatment address the impact of roles and role behavior on the marital relationship (Olson, 1978), the question of potential negative sex-role stereotyping must be addressed as an issue related to values in treatment.

The changing roles of women have led to changes in the traditional marital and family structure. Childrearing practices are being redefined as more families become dual-career families; lifestyles are changing in the time couples spend together and in the lack of organization of social networks. Theory and values must address these changes.

Sexual mores have become more permissive in the last decade. Thus the marital therapist, called upon to address a variety of sexual issues and sexual dysfunctions, must make some judgment on the value and feasibility of those goals presented by clients. Furthermore, the therapist must address alternate lifestyles. Various couple lifestyles do not fit the current definition of marital dyad, i.e., two heterosexuals who are legally married.

As the culture continues to change rapidly, the marital therapist will be further faced with changing values and changing lifestyles. He or she will thus be forced to confront his or her own value system. The major question concerning values and treatment is whether or not beneficial treatment results from attempting to help a couple achieve what is currently valued in the couple's society. The possibility exists that by ascribing to current social values for a healthy dyadic relationship, the marital therapist imposes on clients unrealistic and rigid definitions of marital health.

THE NATURE OF MARRIAGE AS IT RELATES TO THE FUTURE OF MARITAL THERAPY

Marriage as a social institution continues to undergo radical changes in its structure, values, and expectations. Since the mid-1960s, there has been a shift from the traditional marriage to various alternative lifestyles, changing roles and expectations of and for women, changing values and mores about divorce and sexuality, and the growth of the dual-career couple, the childless couple, and the unmarried couple. Expectations of marriage have changed from adjustment to increased intimacy and self-fulfillment; individuals both expect and demand more from their marriage.

The marital therapist not only must react and adapt to societal changes and issues, but must make some judgment as to what constitutes the nature of marriage and marital distress and health. Currently the marital therapist works in an ill-defined field that appears to react continually to specific cultural issues while the culture moves headlong into new issues and values. At times, marital therapy appears to be one step behind those issues that are of most concern.

For example, numerous therapies now focus on self-actualizing marriages while the culture is beginning to question the goal of self-actualization in a marriage relationship as unrealistic and too idealistic. While marital therapies continue to focus on the marriage relationship per se, other segments of the population are now raising the issue of the importance of the support of social networks and communities for individuals, and while marital therapists see significant relationships as dyads, other fields such as sociology, cultural psychology, and family therapy are now studying the effects of larger systems on the mental health and well-being of the individual.

The need for marital interventions is evident based on the interest and demand of the consumer. In order to become an effective response to marital distress, however, the field of marital therapy and marital intervention must begin to address the broader issues inherent in its assumptions. Primarily, the field cannot define marital health, which is what it purports to address. Therefore, without further research into more significant questions of marital mental health and well-being, the field will remain a vast array of simplistic and untested solutions to complex and crucial issues that are constantly being raised by the society as a whole.

THE FUTURE

The field of marital interventions now offers a broad and diverse array of both theory and practice. Marital therapies have evolved from treatments that have addressed primarily dysfunctional couples to include a variety of social skills programs aimed not only at educational, preventive marital interventions, but also at enhancing what may be described as an already functional marital relationships. As one can easily discern, however, the nature of the field remains in a state similar to that described by Mudd (1957, p. 79), "we have not verified or refuted many of our constantly applied assertions and theories"; by Manus (1966, p. 453), marital theory appears to be "a technique in search of a theory . . . there is a clear picture of inconsistency, contradiction, and lack of coherent theory"; and by Mace (1967, p. 159), "It can be said without fear of contradiction that marriage counseling is a field in which practice has far outrun theory." Theory has been derived from practical and subjective experience rather than from empirical investigation, and treatment has been derived from primarily subjective theories. Thus a large body of practice is based on clinical lore. For example, three widely accepted beliefs in the field of marital therapy are that better communication improves marriages, that positive reciprocity of behavior improves marriages, and that education can improve marriages. None of these widely held beliefs/theories have been validated in practice, however.

Because theory and treatment are not empirically based or at times clear, the role of the therapist/intervener, as well as the training of the therapist/intervener, is also unclear. Thus whether the therapist/intervener should provide a conductive structured role, a reactive/experiential role, or an educational/teacher role is a moot question.

Clients remain primarily well-educated, motivated, middle-class persons, with little emphasis, investigation, or treatment of other populations. Thus any efficacy claimed by marital interventions relates only to one specific segment of the population. Unfortunately, little efficacy can be claimed because of the numerous methodological flaws in existing research. Treatment outcome studies are marred by the same difficulties as research, investigating theories: hypotheses are not clearly defined nor is outcome criteria; subjects are few in number and rarely comparable; measurements lack validity and reliability; and there have been few efforts to study interactive (dyadic) versus intrapersonal (individual) phenomena.

Finally, the institution of marriage continues to evolve and change as it reacts to numerous societal forces and changes. The "given" nature of marital relationships is no longer clear. Couples no longer expect their marriages to be similar in structure to their parents', grandparents', or, often, to their peers'. Therefore treatment must constantly address a changing institution.

It is recommended, as a concluding remark about the theories, methods, techniques, and treatments presented in this book, that future theorists and practitioners need to address a number of questions and issues:

1. Further research needs to address the empirical validation of commonly held clinical assumptions, i.e., communication skills as both cause and cure of marital distress, reciprocity of behavior correlating with reciprocity of affect, marital distress hypothesized as resulting from an educational deficit.

2. Theory must not only be empirically validated, but must also be further integrated with treatment.

3. Evaluation of outcome studies needs to be refined to address numerous methodological problems that currently invalidate most conclusions.

4. Assessment must be objective, with diagnostic criteria derived from empirically derived variables.

5. There is a need for integration of treatments with further specification of what type of clients will benefit from what type of treatment. Some integration of theory per se and social-skills training

programs needs to be made so that clients more likely to benefit from therapy will receive therapy and clients more likely to benefit from social-skills training programs will receive short-term educational treatment.

6. Marital interventions must be provided for those clients who are other than highly motivated, white, educated, and middle-class.

7. The issue of the therapist's values as they relate to treatment goals must be questioned further.

8. Further research must address "failures" as well as successes.

9. Treating couples' relationships must also involve dyadic relationships that are not legal marriages.

10. The nature of interaction in marriage must be investigated by including the individual's and couple's interaction with the society as a whole. The impact of the societal system must be included in the delineation of intrapersonal and interpersonal systems.

ALthough the field of marital interventions has grown tremendously since the early 1970s, it remains ill defined and nonintegrated. In some ways, marital interventions have become defined as a specialty within or apart from family therapy. Until theory and practice become empirically based, however, the field may remain a vast array of methods and techniques, with little or no clinical organization.

REFERENCES

Ables B, & Brandsma J. *Therapy for couples.* San Francisco: Jossey-Bass, Inc., 1977

Abramowitz C, & Dokecki PR. The politics of clinical judgement. Early empirical returns. *Psychological Bulletin,* 1977, *84,* 460–474

Abrams C. Counselors' perceptions of career images of women. *Journal of Vocational Behavior,* 1976, *8,* 197–207

Blood RE, & Wolfe DM. *Husbands and wives: The dynamics of married living.* Glencoe, IL: Free Press, 1960

Bosco A. *Marriage encounter: Rediscovery of love.* St. Meinrad, IN: Abbey Press, 1973

Broderick CB, & Schrader SS. The history of profes-

sional marriage and family therapy—Review. In A Gurman & D Kniskern (Eds), *Handbook of family therapy.* New York: Brunner/Mazel, 1981, pp. 5–35

Burgess E. The family as a unity of interacting personalities. *The Family,* 1926, *7,* 3–9

Cromwell R, & Keeney B. Diagnosing marital and family systems: A training model. *The Family Coordinator,* 1979, *28,* 101–108

Davidson C, & Abramowitz S. Sex bias in clinical judgment: Later empirical returns. *Psychology of Women Quarterly,* 1980, *4,* 377–393

Fisher E. Divorce counseling and values. *Journal of Religion and Health,* 1975, *14,* 265–270

Garland DR. *Couples communication and negotiation skills.* New York: Family Service Association of America, 1978

Gottman JM. *Marital intervention.* New York: Academic Press, 1979

Guerney BG, Jr. *Relationship enhancement.* San Francisco: Jossey-Bass, 1977

Gurman A. The effects and effectiveness of marital therapy: A review of outcome research research. *Family Process*, 1973, *6*, 145–170

Gurman A, & Kniskern D. Enriching research on marital enrichment programs. *Journal of Marriage and Family Counseling*, 1978a, *13*, 3–11

Gurman AS, & Kniskern D. Research on marital and family therapy: Progress, perspective, and prospect. In S Garfield & E Bergin, *Handbook of psychotherapy and behavior change: An empirical analysis.* New York: John Wiley & Sons, 1978b

Harrell J, & Guerney BG, Jr. Training married couples in conflict negotiation skills. In DH Olson (Ed), *Treating relationships.* Lake Mills, IA: Graphic Publishing Co., 1976

Jones E. Social class and psychotherapy: A critical review of research. *Psychiatry*, 1974, *37*, 307–320

Komarovsky M. *Blue-collar marriage.* New York: Random House, 1962

Lasch C. *The culture of narcissism: American life in an age of diminishing expectations.* New York: W. W. Norton & Co., Inc., 1979

Mace DR. Introduction. In HL Silverman (Ed), *Marital counseling.* Springfield, IL: Charles C. Thomas, 1967

Manus GI. Marriage counseling: A technique in search of a theory. *Journal of Marriage and the Family*, 1966, *28*, 449–453

Melville K. *Marriage and family today.* New York: Random House, 1977

Mudd E. *The practice of marriage counseling.* New York: Associated Press, 1951

Mudd EH. Knowns and unknowns in marriage counseling research. *Marriage and Family Living*, 1957, *19*, 75–81

Olson DH. Marital and family therapy: Integrative review and critique. *Journal of Marriage and the Family*, 1970, *32*, 501–538

Olson DH. Marital and family therapy: Integrative review and technique. In W Nichols, Jr. (Ed), *Marriage and family therapy.* Minneapolis: National Council on Family Relations, 1974

Olson DH. A critical overview. In A. Gurman & D. Rice (Eds.), *Couples in conflict.* New York: Jason Aronson 1978.

Otto HA (Ed). *Marriage and family enrichment: New perspectives and programs.* Nashville: Abington, 1976

Parsons T, & Bales R. *Family socialization and interaction process.* Glencoe, IL: Free Press, 1955

Patterson GR, Hops H, & Weiss RL. A social learning approach to reducing rates of marital conflict. In R Stuart, R Liberman & S Wilder (Eds), *Advances in behavior therapy.* New York: Academic Press, 1973

Patterson GR, & Reid J. Reciprocity and coercion: Two facets of social systems. In C Neuringer & J Michael (Eds), *Behavior modification in clinical psychology.* New York: Appleton-Century-Crofts, 1970

Russell A, & Russell L. The uses and abuses of co-therapy. *Journal of Marital and Family Therapy*, 1979, *5*, 39–46

Schwartz R, & Schwartz L. *Becoming a couple.* Englewood Cliffs, NJ: Prentice-Hall, Inc., 1980

Sprenkle D, & Fisher B. An empirical assessment of the goals of family therapy. *Journal of Marital and Family Therapy*, 1980, *6*, 131–139

Stuart R. Operant-interpersonal treatment for marital discord. *Journal of Consulting and Clinical Psychology*, 1969a, *33*, 675–682

Appendixes

Appendix A: The Assessment of Assertive Behavior— Selected References

It is not the purpose of this Appendix to review all of the instruments or methods to assess presence, absence, or degree of assertiveness. To do so would duplicate other relevant and extensive publications (Buros, 1978). Furthermore, it would be useless to review all of the available measures of assertion because most of the available measures define assertiveness *outside* rather than *inside* the martial context. Consequently, most measures of assertiveness view assertiveness as an *individual* rather than a *marital* and bidirectional phenomenon. Some references in this area may, however, be useful to the reader who wants to explore further the area of assertiveness in couples.

Existing empirical evidence suggests a strong confounding of assertiveness and aggressiveness in each of these inventories (Galassi, et al, 1974; Galassi & Galassi, 1975; Gay, et al, 1975; Hollandsworth, et al, 1977; Rathus, 1973). In their review of the assertion literature, Galassi and Galassi (1978) found 13 paper-and-pencil measures of assertion, of which 6 had adequate reliability and some validational evidence to warrant their use.

Lehman-Olson (1976) suggested the use of the Man–Women Interaction Game to measure assertive and aggressive behaviors. This measure uses a competitive game format with high motivation to win in order to assess just how assertively or agggressively the client will behave. Using blocking cards to win is considered assertive; using blocking cards to keep one's opponent from winning is considered aggressive. Assertive and aggressive scores are derived from the number of blocking cards used by the client.

To date, however, Eisler's observational method of measurement appears to be the most reliable measure of assertive behaviors between couples. Concerning instruments and measures used in studies of assertiveness training, the behavioral recording procedures of Eisler, et al (1973) had a reliability of over 90 percent. Their procedures have subsequently been used to study marital communication (Alberti & Emmons, 1976; Blau, 1978; Simon, 1975).

Rich and Schroeder (1973), in a review of 17 self-report measures of assertiveness, found most of those measures to be inadequate psychometrically. These reviewers noted that the development of many inventories had been accompanied by little investigation or demonstration of validity; a major problem was also that none of the inventories that were reviewed were designed for the assessment of subdimensions of assertiveness. A third problem noted by Rich and Schroeder (1973) was that research on all 17 inventories had been developed using college populations exclusively, and their applicability for other populations had not been explored. The three inventories described next are among those deficient in all areas.

Constriction Scale. Bates and Zimmerman (1971) developed the Constriction Scale (CS) for the selection of nonassertive ("constrictive") candidates for assertiveness training. The CS is a 37-item, self-report inventory; the higher the subject's score on the CS, the more nonassertive the subject is assumed to be. The CS was one of the first inventories developed for assessing levels of assertiveness and the only one existing that is (purportedly) a measure of nonassertiveness per se. When information on the CS was published, Bates and Zimmerman (1971) explained its development on the grounds that "although a brief, objective, paper-and-pencil measure of nonassertiveness of known psychometric properties which is designed to screen subjects for assertiveness training would offer the clinician considerable practical advantages, no such instrument has been available" (p. 100). The "known psychometric properties" of the CS, however, are known only for a single sample of middle-class college students, and there is little evidence of validity for the instrument. Aside from CS correlations with the Adjective Check List, Bates and Zimmerman (1971) offer only CS correlations with brief neuroticism scales and a comparison of high and low CS scorers' grade-point averages as evidence for the validity of the inventory. The relationship between CS scores and students' grade-point averages was investigated (with reference to the "predictive validity" of the inventory) on the assumption that nonassertive subjects being more compliant, would study harder and be more reliable in completing assignments. The predicted relationship between CS scores and grade-point averages was found, but its relevance to the validity of the CS is dubious. Rich and Schroeder (1976) concluded that "the usefulness and validity of the Constriction Scale are very much in doubt" (p. 1083).

College Self-Expression Scale. Galassi, et al (1974) developed the College Self-Expression Scale (CSES) as an assertiveness inventory to be used with college students. The CSES is a 50-item inventory with a 5-point Likert item format. The inventory is used frequently in the screening of candidates for assertiveness training, but validity data for the instrument are meager. Correlations of the CSES with Adjective Check List scales were presented by Galassi, et al (1974) as evidence for the construct validity of the inventory. Beyond this, data concerning the validity of the CSES are

limited in scope and not convincing. Mixed results were obtained in several attempts to discriminate populations presumed to differ in assertiveness. Concurrent validity was assessed by examining correlations of CSES scores with ratings of overall assertiveness made by independent judges. The correlation of 0.19, although statistically significant, was completely unimpressive. In a further attempt at concurrent validation (Galassi & Galassi, 1974), a significant but small correlation (0.33) was found between CSES scores of dormitory residents and ratings of assertiveness by residence hall counselors.

Adult Self-Expression Scale. The Adult Self-Expression Scale (ASES) is an adaptation of the CSES. On the assumption that certain CSES items were too complex and/or irrelevant for noncollege populations, Gay, et al (1975) developed the ASES for use with the general adult population. The ASES is a 48-item, self-report format used in the CSES. In content, the two tests are quite similar. The ASES includes 33 items from the CSES (in original form or rewritten to reduce item complexity) and 15 items that do not appear in the CSES. Since the test was designed for noncollege subjects, it seems paradoxical that validity data for the ASES were gathered in a study of community college students. Correlations of the ASES with the Adjective Check List were examined; like the developers of the CSES, Gay, et al (1975) presented these results as their primary evidence for the validity of the inventory. Gay, et al (1975) also found that high scorers on the ASES attained significantly lower scores on the Taylor Manifest Anxiety Scale than did low ASES scorers, and that subjects seeking personal adjustment counseling at the college counseling center obtained significantly lower ASES scores than did members of the subject sample not seeking such help. These data were construed by the test developers as supporting the validity of the ASES. The relevance of anxiety level or interest in adjustment counseling to the validity of an assertiveness measure is questionable at best, however, and no further data concerning the validity of the ASES have been presented.

The emphasis placed by Galassi, et al (1974) and Gay, et al (1975) on aspects of their findings that conform to their own assumptions about the nature of assertiveness appears related to the fact that their studies were investigations of the construct validity of the inventories.

INTERPERSONAL BEHAVIOR SURVEY

The Interpersonal Behavior Survey (Mauger & Adkinson, 1980) has significant advantages over the inventories described earlier in a number of areas. The development of the IBS and research on its psychometric properties have involved a wide variety of subject samples, in contrast to the uniform focus on college students seen in development and research on the assertivenesss inventories already mentioned. The instrument was designed not only for assessment of general assertiveness but for the assessment of subdimensions of assertiveness (and of aggressiveness, as well). It will be recalled that one of the major criticisms that Rich and Schroeder (1973) raised about all of the assertiveness inventories they reviewed was the failure of test developers to address the multidimensionality of assertiveness in this way. The same criticism has been made in a review by Cochrane (1975) concerning scales of aggressiveness. Also, two of the inventories of assertiveness described previously, the CSES and the ASES, are ones in which a confounding of assertiveness and aggressiveness has been identified empirically.

Several years of research have been devoted to the development of the IBS as an inventory for the assessment of assertiveness and aggressiveness as distinct phenomena. The IBS is a self-report instrument containing 136 items, written in the first person, describing interpersonal behaviors, attitudes, preferences, and emotional tendencies. To each item, the subject responds either True (if he or she believes the item to be self-descriptive) or False (if he or she does not). Administration time is approximately 20 to 30 minutes for normal subjects. IBS scale scores can be obtained on a variety of scales of three basic types: validity scales, scales of general assertiveness and aggressiveness, and scales of subdimensions of assertiveness and aggressiveness. In the course of research on the IBS, a number of scales of each type have been, and continue to be,

developed. Those selected for use in the present study will be described.

The IBS is unique among assertiveness and aggressiveness measures in its inclusion of validity scales. These scales are used in detecting those instances in which the inventory may have been completed inappropriately by the subject. The Denial (DE) validity scale is composed of items referring to attributes that, though mildly undesirable, are normally admitted by most subjects to be self-descriptive. A sample DE item (and the scoreable response) is "Sometimes I feel like swearing" (false). A subject who attains an elevated score on this scale (by denying a high number of such attributes) can be assumed to have presented an unusually favorable picture of himself or herself in responses to the inventory.

The Infrequency (IF) validity scale of the IBS was designed for the detection of highly atypical patterns of responding to IBS items. The IF scale is composed of items related to assertiveness or aggressiveness endorsed by less than 10 percent of a college-student normative group; examples are "I enjoy making people angry" (true), and "I often imagine myself beating or killing a person or animal" (true). Thus an elevated IF score indicates a deviant response pattern. Moderately high elevations may reflect authentic admission of adjustment problems rather than profile invalidity. A markedly high score on the IF scale, however, indicates an extremely deviant response set that is more likely to be associated with profile invalidity; this can result from one or more factors, including reading comprehension problems, insufficient attention to the task, "random" or careless responding, or the subject's attempt to fake or exaggerate problems.

The IBS scales used as measures of general assertiveness and aggressiveness in the study were General Assertion, Rationally Derived (SGT) and General Aggression, Rationally Derived (GGR). In the construction of SGR and GGR, items were composed and assigned to the scales on the basis of their apparent relevance to the construct being measured (assertiveness and aggressiveness, respectively). In order to minimize effects of social desirability bias on responding, items showing significant correlations with the DE scales were eliminated from the item pool.

Subsequently, the internal consistency of each scale was improved by eliminating items not possessing substantial correlations with the appropriate total scale score. A study of the relationship between these scales was then performed, using a sample of 201 male and 201 female community residents (the "General Reference Norm Group" used in much of the early development of IBS scales); correlations of -0.05 and -0.04 were found in the male and female samples, respectively (Mauger & Simpson, 1978). As Mauger, et al (1979) reported, minimal correlations between these scales have subsequently been found in studies of 30 different groups; the highest correlation yet obtained between these scales is 0.26.

In his analysis of IBS item intercorrelations from a large university sample, Hook (1977) identified six nonoverlapping item clusters that are now used as factor scales of the IBS. These scales were used as measures of subdimensions of assertiveness and aggressiveness in the present study. The two aggressiveness factor scales, labeled Hostile Stance and Expression of Anger, correlated 0.90 and 0.70, respectively, with GGR, and negligibly with SGR in Hook's sample. The correlations of the four assertiveness factor scales with SGR were as follows: Self-Confidence (0.79), Initiating Assertion (0.74), Defending Assertion (0.63), and Frankness (0.68); near-zero correlations were found between these assertiveness factor scales and GGR. All items in the asssertiveness factor scales were component items of the SGR scale, and all items in the aggressiveness subscales were component items of the GGR scale (i.e., Hook's cluster analysis showed no items to be misplaced with regard to the assertiveness–agressiveness dichotomy).

The Hostile Stance (HS) aggressiveness factor scale contains items reflecting an antagonistic and hostile orientation toward others, and a view of aggression as a justifiable means of attaining goals or expressing hurt or anger. The HS scale contains items such as "I think that you can get ahead in the world without having to step on others" (false), and "When a friend does something which hurts me deeply, I would rather get even than let him or her know of my deep hurt" (true). The Expression of Anger (EA) scale is a measure of the inclination to lose one's temper and express anger in uncontrolled ways such as abusive speech or physical violence. EA scale items include "Some people think I have a violent temper" (true), and "Sometimes I say nasty things when people don't understand what I'm trying to say" (true).

The Self-Confidence (SC) assertiveness factor scale is a measure of the *lack* of such qualities as negative attitudes toward the self, inability to accept praise, uneasiness in social situations, and resultant avoidance of direct communication with others. SC scale items include "I often avoid members of the opposite sex because I fear doing or saying the wrong thing" (true), and "I am afraid to refuse to do favors for friends for fear that they will not like me" (true). The Initiating Assertiveness (IA) factor scale is a measure of tendencies toward exercising leadership, showing initiative, and taking an ascendant role in relating to others. Content tapped by the IA scale includes tendencies to voice opinions, make suggestions, influence or persuade others in dyadic or group situations, and to enjoy and occupy roles in which leadership and advice-giving are central. IA scale items include "I tend to help many of my friends make decisions" (true), "I usually do not speak until spoken to by others" (false), and "I have seldom taken the lead in organizing projects" (false). The Defending Assertiveness (DA) factor scale is a measure of the capacity to stand up for one's rights. The DA scale taps such abilities as asking persons who are annoying one to stop, refusing inappropriate requests, reminding people to return one's borrowed items, saying no to salespersons when necessary, and expressing dissatisfaction with purchased products or services; at a general level, the DA scale is a measure of the extent to which one expresses rights rather than placating others when treated unfairly. The DA scale includes items such as "If a friend of mine damaged some of my best records, I would ask him or her to replace them" (true), and "I would hesitate to return food in a restaurant, even if it were burnt" (false). The Frankness (FR) factor scale is a measure of the tendency to express forthrightly to friends, relatives, or respected others one's opinions, preferences, and feelings of anger, hurt or annoyance, even when such expression may be difficult. FR scale items include "When a close and respected relative annoys me, I usually hide my true feelings" (false) and "I would state what I think is right, even if someone I respect had just said something different" (true).

Validity of the IBS

In contrast to the paucity of work directed toward examining the scales of assertiveness mentioned previously, much effort has been devoted to investigating the validity of the IBS scales discussed earlier, as well as other scales of the IBS developed for research purposes. A number of standard approaches have been taken in examining the validity of IBS scales (group comparisons, studies of IBS scale correlations with other inventories, etc.), and results are promising. Other data gathered in the course of IBS research have a bearing on the validity of the inventory. For example, two IBS scales of general assertiveness and aggressiveness (not mentioned previously) were developed using an "empirical" approach to scale construction (Edwards, 1970; Wiggins, 1973) as opposed to the "rational" method used in constructing SGR and GGR: these scales are called General Assertion, Empirically Derived (SGE) and General Aggression, Empirically Derived (GGE). These scales are composed of items found to be correlated with independent ratings of assertiveness and aggressiveness made by friends of persons who completed an early version of the IBS (Hernandez, 1976). SGE and GGE were found to be highly correlated (0.73 and 0.83) with the rationally derived scales SGR and GGR, respectively (Mauger & Simpson, 1978). These high correlations between scales constructed by different strategies support the generality of the dimensions of assertiveness ad aggressiveness, and the meaningfulness of the SGR and GGR scales as related to measures based on behavioral ratings of these constructs.

Much of the investigation of the validity of IBS scales has been performed through examination of correlatons of IBS measures of assertiveness and aggressiveness (and subdimensions of these constructs) with other self-report inventories. Patterns of correlations of IBS scales with other assertiveness and aggressiveness measures have provided empirical support for the validity and independence of IBS measures of assertiveness and aggressivene: Additionally, in a variety of subject samples, examinations have been made of IBS correla-

tions with seven wideband personality inventories such as the California Psychological Inventory (Megargee, 1973), the Leary Interpersonal Checklist (LaForge & Suczek, 1955), and the Minnesota Multiphasic Personality Inventory. Information from these studies also provided considerable support for the construct validity of IBS scales (Mauger & Adkinson, 1980). It has been applied to white (Hebblewhite, 1979; Hebblewhite, et al, 1981) and black (Mouzon, 1980) couples.

In his study, Dunne (1980) obtained data relevant to the construct validity of the Interpersonal Behavior Survey (IBS). The IBS and the Personality Research Form (PRF) were administered to a large and varied psychiatric sample composed of male patients selected from four treatment units within a Veterans Administration Medical Center. Correlations obtained between IBS scales and selected PRF measures conformed to expectations and were interpreted as supporting the convergent and discriminant validity of IBS scales in a psychiatric sample. The importance of these findings was discussed in relation to deficiencies prevalent in other inventories of assertiveness and aggressiveness, which include confounding of these constructs and attempts at construct validation that have been unimpressive and limited to investigation within normal samples.

The study also included a general exploration of the PRF personality correlates of various dimensions of assertiveness and aggressiveness among these patients. The design of the IBS allows assessment of aggressiveness and assertiveness as multidimensional constructs, and the PRF correlates of three dimensions of aggressiveness and five dimensions of assertiveness were examined in the patient sample in the interest of expanding and delineating the empirical definitions of these construct dimensions within the framework of the psychology of personality. Findings from the study were compared with previous similar studies involving normal samples. Although some degree of concordance was seen in the results of these studies on normals and results from this study on psychiatric patients, many differences were identified in the personality correlates associated with measures of assertiveness and aggressiveness (and subdimensions of each) in comparing findings from the different sample types. It was concluded that assertiveness and aggressiveness are concepts best characterized as having empirical definitions that are relative to the type of sample being considered, and that measures of aggressiveness and assertiveness (including the IBS) cannot be assumed to measure the same constructs in psychiatric and normal samples (nor even in different types of normal samples). Findings from the study were also interpreted as supporting the usefulness of a multidimensional approach in the self-report assessment of assertiveness and aggressiveness.

Contributions of the study to existing literature were examined in the context of a discusson of the current lack of empirical information concerning assertiveness and aggressiveness among psychiatric patients and the present rather primitive state of affairs in defining these constructs conceptually,

operationally, and empirically within the field of psychology.

Findings from the study included substantial correlations of assertiveness and aggressiveness scales with social desirability response set measures. The implications of these findings as related to impression management tendencies and characterological dimensions associated with self-reported aggressiveness and assertiveness are discussed, and similarities are noted between these findings and those obtained in normal samples using a variety of measures of assertiveness and aggressiveness. The need is stressed for routine examination, in different sample types, of the relationships of such response set measures with self-report inventories of aggressiveness and assertiveness.

REFERENCES

Alberti RE, & Emmons MR. Assertion training in marital counseling. *Journal of Marriage and Family Counseling,* 1976, *2,* 49–54

Bates H, & Zimmerman S. Toward the development of a screening scale for assertive training. *Psychological Reports,* 1971, *28,* 99–107

Blau J. *Changes in assertiveness and marital satisfaction after participation in an assertiveness training group* (Order #7812186). Philadelphia: Temple University, 1978

Buros O (Ed). *The eighth mental measurements yearbook.* Highland Park, NJ: Gryphon Press, 1978

Cochrane N. Assessing the aggressive component of personality. *British Journal of Medical Psychology,* 1975, *48,* 9–14

Dunne EE. *An examination of the measurement and personality correlates of aggressiveness and assertiveness among psychiatric patients.* Unpublished doctoral dissertation, Georgia State University, 1980

Edwards A. *The measurement of personality traits by scales and inventories.* New York: Holt, Rinehart & Winston, 1970

Eisler RM, Miller PM, & Hersen M. Components of aggressive behavior. *Journal of Clinical Psychology,* 1973, *29,* 295–299

Galassi J, DeLo J, Galassi M, & Bastien S. The college self-expression scale: A measure of assertiveness. *Behavior Therapy,* 1974, *5,* 165–171

Galassi J, & Galassi M. Validity of a measure of assertiveness. *Journal of Counseling Psychology,* 1974, *21,* 248–250

Galassi J, & Galassi M. Relationship between assertiveness and aggressiveness. *Psychological Reports,* 1975, *36,* 352–354

Galassi J, & Galassi M. Assertion: A critical review. *Psychotherapy: Theory, Research, and Practice,* 1978, *10,* 16–29

Gay M, Hollandsworth J, & Galassi J. An assertiveness inventory for adults. *Journal of Counseling Psychology,* 1975, *22,* 340–344

Hebblewhite MC. *Assertiveness and aggressiveness of couples as variables in couple adjustment.* Unpublished master's thesis, Georgia State University, 1979

Hebblewhite M, Mauger P, & Holland D. *The assertiveness and aggressiveness of spouses and the adjustment of their marriage.* Paper read at the 98th Meeting of American Psychological Association, Montreal, Canada, September, 1980

Hernandez S. *Assertion, aggression, and Eysenck's personality variables.* Unpublished master's thesis, University of South Florida, Tampa, 1976

Hook J. *Factor scales of the interpersonal behavior survey.* Unpublished master's thesis, University of South Florida, Tampa, 1977

LaForge R, & Suczek R. The interpersonal check list. *Journal of Personality,* 1955, *24,* 94–112

Lehman-Olson D. Assertiveness training: Theoretical and clinical implications. In DHL Olson (Ed), *Treating relationships.* Lake Mills, IA: Graphic Publishing, 1976

Mauger P, & Adkinson PR. *Interpersonal behavior survey (IBS manual).* Los Angeles: Western Psychological Services, 1980

Mauger P, Adkinson D, Hook D, & Hernandez S. *Mapping the domains of assertive and aggressive behavior classees.* Unpublished manuscript, 1979 (available from Paul A Mauger, Department of Psychology, Georgia State University, University Plaza, Atlanta, GA 30303)

Mauger P, & Simpson D. *The interpersonal behavior survey: A manual.* Unpublished manuscript, 1978 (available from Paul A Mauger, Department of Psychology, Georgia State University, University Plaza, Atlanta, GA 30303)

Megargee E. *The California Psychological Inventory handbook.* San Francisco: Jossey-Bass, 1972

Mouzon R. *Assertiveness and aggressiveness and their relatonships to marital adjustment in black couples.* Unpublished master's thesis, Georgia State University, 1980

Rathus S. A 30-item schedule for assessing assertive behavior. *Behavior Therapy*, 1973, *4*, 398–406

Rich AR, & Schroeder HE. Research issues in assertiveness training. *Psychological Bulletin*, 1973, *83*, 1081–1096

Simon SJ. An assertiveness enrichment program. In L L'Abate and Collaborators, Manual: Enrichment program for the family life cycle. Atlanta: Social Research Laboratories, 1975

Wiggins J. *Personality and predicton: Principles of personality assessment.* Reading, MA: Addison-Wesley, 1973

Appendix B: The Measurement of Communication in Couples*

This appendix outlines some of the methods and uses of measurement of communicaton in assessing marital communication.

Navran (1967) used the Primary Communication Inventory (PCI) to study the relationship between marital adjustment and communication by comparing the results with an early version of the Locke-Wallace Marital Adjustment Scale (Locke & Wallace, 1959). The scales were administered to distressed and nondistressed couples. The hypothesis was that couples who make a good or "happy" adjustment to marriage are those whose communication skills have been expanded to deal effectively with problems inherent in marriage. The PCI was developed to measure communication in marriage and requires each spouse to rate the quality of different aspects of communication in marriage, including verbal and nonverbal components. The two groups were not only discriminated by the PCI, but a high intercorrelation of PCI and LW scores suggested a positive relationship between communication and marital adjustment.

Kahn (1970) demonstrated a positive relationship between accurate nonverbal communication and marital satisfaction. He used the PCI along with the Marital Communication Scale (MCS), a behavioral measure of nonverbal communication, to compare nonverbal communication with marital satisfaction. Well-adjusted couples performed significantly better on a nonverbal interaction task than poorly adjusted couples, thus replicating Navran's findings.

Bienvenu (1970) developed the Marital Communication Inventory (MCI), which measured, not content, but the process of communication as an element of marital interaction. The scale contains 46 items that are concerned with patterns and styles of communication such as listening, comprehension, ability to express self, and verbal and nonverbal elements. The scale is a self-report inventory and significantly discriminated between groups of distressed and nondistressed couples.

Murphy and Mendelson (1973) further validated the MCI by comparing the MCI with the Locke Marital Adjustment Scale. A positive correlation resulted between scores on the two instruments. They also observed that couples scoring low on marital adjustment either became involved on a relationship rather than a content level or tended to handle the research task (developing stories from TAT cards) as though each spouse were alone.

The conclusion from these studies is that there appears to be a significant relationship between marital communication and marital satisfaction.

With progress in technology, a number of objective behavioral observation methods have been developed for analyzing in vivo samples of couples' marital communication. These have

*This appendix was prepared by Stephanie Ezust.

included audiotaped recording, videotape recording, electromechanical recording devices, and live observers (the last is not a product of technology).

Carter, Thomas, and Gambrill combined the use of audiotape recordings with an innovative electromechanical device to assess and modify couples' marital communication and verbal problem-solving behavior (Carter & Thomas, 1973; Thomas, et al, 1971).

Miller, Nunnally, and Wackman (1976a, 1976b), and Pierce (1973), have all used audiotapes and typescripts to study problem-related marital communication.

The talk table devised by Gottman, et al (1976) was described earlier. A similar procedure is described by Margolin and Weiss (1978) in which a button-press procedure is used in both asessment and treatment of marital communication skill deficits. In the case study presented, spouses independently rated their "helpfulness" as senders and receivers while coding videotaped samples of their own previous problem-solving negotiations. Additional training procedures utilized electromechanical cueing devices. This technique also follows Gottman in using the couple as their own observers rather than using outside observers.

Videotaping systems have enabled investigators to analyze both verbal and nonverbal aspects of marital communication. In assessing the reliability and validity of videotaping versus existing alternatives, studies indicated that (1) the percentages of inter-rater agreement were significantly higher using videotaped communication samples than typescripts prepared for audiotapes (Murphy & Mendelson, 1973); (2) a positive relationship was found between coders' observations from videotapes and couples' self-reports of their communication process (Murphy & Mendelson, 1973); (3) reliabilities in scoring discrete, material, interaction behaviors such as "looking" and "smiling" were found to be as high for videotape analysis as for live observation and scoring (Eisler, Herson & Agras, 1973).

Weiss, Patterson, and their associates (Hops, et al 1971) have employed videotape technology in the development of the Marital Interaction Coding System (MICS).

A recently developed scale that discriminates among communication skills has been presented by Boyd and Roach (1977). Derived from a review of the literature, 25 statements representing specific communication skills were arranged as two scales, Interpersonal Communication Skills Inventory-Self (ICSI-Self) and Interpersonal Communication Skills Inventory-Spouse (ICSI-Spouse). Four instruments were completed by 111 married couples: Locke and Wallace's MAT, Bienvenu's MCI, and the two new scales. The scores on the MAT were used to identify criterion groups as most satisfied (28 couples) and least satisfied (21 couples). A multiple discriminant analysis indicated that 14 of the 25 ICSI-Self items and 17 of the 25 ICSI-Spouse items differentiated the two criterion groups at the 0.05 level or better. The items are divided into three major groups, or clusters: (1) 8 items—sending direct, clear messages; (2) 5 items—active listening or receiving messages; (3) 4 items—verbal expressions of esteem or respect for spouse. The conclusion of the study is that the scales may be effective to marital counselors, especially since the scales measure observable behaviors.

The six studies described next have examined various aspects of the impact of CC. Of the studies, two (Campbell, 1974; Dillon, 1976) were among the eight studies mentioned earlier and are presented here in further detail.

The Campbell study (1974) was designed to determine whether CC would have a statistically significant effect on the dyadic interaction of married couples in the childrearing years when communication often tends to focus on topics outside the dyadic relationship.

The participating 30 couples were randomly assigned to experimental and control groups. A post-test-only design was used. Analysis of the post-test results for the two groups revealed significant differences in self-disclosure, communication effectiveness, and communication "work patterns." There was no significant correlation between self-disclosure and years of marriage. There was a positive correlation between self-rated willingness to self-disclose and communication effectiveness in both groups, and a negative correlation between the couples' perceptions of their communication effectiveness and evaluator-rated effectiveness, also for both groups. Apparently, the communication skill-training component of the program was relatively effective, while the awareness training component was not.

Larsen's (1974) study attempted to determine whether participation in CC would result in significant changes in marital communication and in self and mate perceptions. The participants were 16 couples, and a pre- and post-test and six-week structured follow-up interview design was used. The MCI was used to measure communication, and the Interpersonal Check List to measure perceptions of self and mate.

High scores on the MCI pretest did not change significantly on post-test, but low scores increased more than 20 points on post-testing. CC was believed to benefit the latter group. The data suggested that for those couples who changed, there was a tendency to work toward a companion-type marriage. Similar perceptions of ideal-self and ideal-mate appear to be an important part of marital adjustment.

The purpose of Fleming's (1976) study was to evaluate specific skills learned in CC, overall use of self-disclosure, expression of feelings and intentions, and use of "work styles" of communication.

In the Fleming study, 15 couples were used; no control group was used. Data were collected four times: three weeks prior to the program, immediately before, immediately after, and three weeks after the program ended. The participants increased significantly in the use of four of the five program skills: overall self-disclosure, feeling statements, work styles, and work-pattern communication. The fifth skill, use of intention statements, decreased, but not significantly.

Larson's (1976) study evaluated CC's effectiveness on specific relationship dimensions. The 19 couples were divided into two groups, experimental and wait-list control. A pre- and post-test design was used, employing three measures. The subjects' perceptions of marital adjustment increased significantly on postmeasures compared with the controls. There were no significant differences on the measurements of self-disclosure and caring.

Dillon's (1976) study was designed to determine whether CC would result in significant increases in self-esteem for the participants, and whether there would be correspondingly significant increases in communication and self-esteem and between communication and marital adjustment for married couples. Of 37 volunteer couples, 16 were assigned to an experimental group and 21 to a no-treatment

control group. A pre- and post-test design was used, measuring self-esteem, communication, and marital adjustment. Post-tests were conducted immediately after the program and 10 weeks later.

There were four major results: experimental subjects significantly increased in self-esteem, controls did not; no significant positive correlations between self-esteem and communication were found for the experimental group, but there were two signiificant correlations for the control group; there were two significant positive correlations between communication and marital adjustment for the experimental group, and none for the control group; one significant positive correlation was found between self-esteem and marital adjustment for the experimental group and three for the control group.

Wampler and Sprenkle (1980) are currently examining the relationship between participants' level of ego development and the learning and retention of skills taught by CC. Long-term retention has not yet been documented (other than the survey study already mentioned), and there is little evidence to date that the communication skills learned affect the couple's overall marital satisfaction. Only one study (Dillon, 1976) found that CC had a positive effect on marital satisfaction. Sprenkle, et al used the stages of ego development as defined by Loevinger (1976) as criterion levels for their study: Autistic, Impulsive, Self-Protective, Conformist, Conscientious, Autonomous, Integrated. Their expectation was that CC would affect the relationship of the couples and that higher-ego-development couples would evidence higher scores on the Relationship Inventory.

Three hypotheses were to be examined:

1. At the pretest, couples beyond the conformist level of ego development would use higher amounts of work-style communication and have higher scores on the Relationship Inventory than couples at the conformist level or below.

2. Regardless of level of ego development, couples completing CC would use a significantly higher amount of work-style communication and show an increase in the Relationship Inventory immediately after the program, as compared with pre-

program levels; the contrast group and no-treatment control groups would not change in the amount of work-style communication or in scores on the Relationship Inventory.
3. At the delayed post-test, those couples beyond the conformist level of ego development would continue to evidence a greater amount of work-style communication and a higher level on the Relationship Inventory, while couples at the Conformist level or below would have returned to pre-CC levels on these measures. No change was predicted for the contrast group or no-treatment group.

Two additional studies that deal with distressed couples, neither of which used CC training, are Cassidy (1973) and Henry (1971).

Cassidy's (1973) study was designed to develop, for married couples with verbal communication problems, a treatment mode to develop measures for assessing treatment-related changes and to develop a formal experimental test of all procedures and instruments.

A pilot study was run, which developed three criterion measures through formulative evaluation techniques. The resulting cross section of observations allowed a differentiation of attitudes and behaviors associated with successful and unsuccessful communication between spouses. Instruments measuring general communication difficulties, as well as pre- and post-treatment attitude, were designed. The experimental test of the program was conducted using a treatment and a control group. The treatment was a composite of diverse verbal techniques described as successful both in the literature and by pilot informants. The mode was written as a verbal communication instruction program aimed at teaching specific skills involving direct feedback, and supervised and unsupervised practice periods. The treatment mode was effective in reducing both specific (target) and general problem communication behavior and in increasing positive attitudes.

Henry's (1976) study evaluated the effects of a group treatment program for married couples, based on the systems-communications theoretical approach and focused on helping distressed couples experientially learn improved communication behavior. The 14 dis-

tressed couples were randomly assigned to experimental or waiting control groups.

The experimental group was broken into small groups of 3 to 4 couples who met once a week for eight weeks and participated in communication facilitation exercises and techniques. The control group received no treatment. A pre- and post-test design was used; a multidimensional assessment approach was implemented, involving both self-report and direct observational measures. Scores were obtained on self-reported marital satisfaction and marital communication, on directly observed clarity, relationship quality, and agreement and acknowledgment in marital communication.

The communication group was found to be effective in improving marital communication. The results were signiificant on both self-report and observation measures.

The last group of studies are four studies that compared two programs. Hickman and Baldwin (1971) compared a programmed communications text with a no-treatment and a conventional counseling approach to improving communication in marriage. Glisson (1977) compared reciprocity counseling with communication training. Witkin (1977) used two communication training programs, Communication Skills Workshop (CSW) and Couples Communication (CC), as well as a wait-list control group.

Hickman and Baldwin (1971) compared the use of a programmed text emphasizing communication skills with a no-treatment and conventional counseling approach to improving communication in marriage. The 30 couples who had indicated their primary problem was "lack of communication" were randomly assigned to each of three groups: control, programmed text, and counseled group.

The programmed test used was *Improving Communication in Marriage* (Human Development Institute, 1967), which consists of eight programmed lessons, each requiring approximately one hour. The focus of the program is on cognitive material about the communication processes: understanding personal feelings, the two-way nature of communication, expression and suppression of feelings, having feelings versus acting on them, direct, indirect, and accusative expression of feelings, and communication as a developmental process. At intervals, the spouses are required to "interact in various ways to emphasize the affective component of communication" (p. 58). The Semantic Differential (Osgood, et al, 1957) was used to assess changes in meaning four concepts related to the marriage relationship: (1) communication, (2) understanding, (3) my relationship to my spouse, (4) my spouse's relationship to me. A decision on reconciliation was obtained from the couples after treatment to corroborate the measured attitude changes on the Semantic Differential.

After assignment to a treatment group, each couple was pretested and interviewed. Post-tests and conciliation decisions were obtained four weeks later, after treatment. The control group received no treatment in the four-week interval between pre- and post-test. Those in the programmed-text group met one hour twice a week for four weeks. The couples essentially worked alone, under nominal supervision of a counselor. The counseled group met with a counselor for one hour twice a week for four weeks to resolve their communication difficulties. The counselor provided direction in the counseling sessions and intervened when necessary to facilitate the communication process.

The results were statistically significant between the control group and the counseled group. The programmed-text group changed more than the control group but less than the counseled group. More couples in the programmed-text group reconciled following treatment, but the difference was not statistically significant.

The authors concluded that since the use of the programmed text was more effective than no treatment but less effective than counseling, the human factor apparently remains a most important element in resolving communication difficulties in marriage. A balance between cognitive and affective elements is necessary in any effective communication between persons. The programmed texts may be effective as an ancillary technique in marriage counseling but not as an alternative.

Glisson's (1977) study attempted to evaluate the relative and combined effects of communication training and reciprocity counseling on groups of marital dyads. The nine couples were randomly divided into three treatment groups: (1) behavioral training, then commu-

nication training; (2) communication training, then behavioral training; and (3) extended behavioral training that included a sexual enrichment component. All treatments were administered by the same male and female, co-therapist team.

Reciprocity counseling (behavioral training) was based on Epstein and Williams (1981), Azrin, et al (1973), and Weiss, et al (1973). Communication training was based on CC (Miller, et al, 1976a, 1976b). The research was aimed at assessing the effects of these treatments on couples' marital satisfaction and marital communication.

After four weeks of one treatment, none of the treatment groups improved significantly with respect to marital satisfaction, and no between-group treatment differences were found. With respect to communication effectiveness, nonsignificant declines in all three groups were reported after one treatment. When the combination of treatments was compared to either the behavioral training or communication training alone, Group 2 couples (communication, then behavioral) were found to have made significant improvements in communication effectiveness over what they had reported after only communication training. Similar improvements were *not* observed in Groups 1 and 3. No between-group treatment difference or order-of-treatment difference was found. Marital communication was found to be positively correlated with marital satisfaction.

The author alluded to several methodological weaknesses in the abstract but did not specify. It would certainly seem that the complicated nature of the design as well as the small sample would create several of the problems. In order to compensate for the weaknesses, individual changes were evaluated, and significant positive findings resulted on 13 of the 18 individuals' attitudinal and/or behavioral satisfaction measures. Of the 14 persons who evidenced problems, 10 reported significant improvements in satisfaction. No association was observed between individual positive outcome and particular group membership.

Glisson tentatively concluded that communication training should not be used as therapy in and of itself. The "getting worse" phenomenon observed for some subjects after four weeks of treatment was attributed to the questionable validity of self-report methods and the possibility of a "deviation amplifying feedback" effect (Wender, 1971). All treatment conditions helped to increase reported marital satisfaction for subjects characterized as problematic and nonproblematic, which suggested that the treatments could be successfully used for marital discord and marital enrichment purposes. There were some indications that the sexual enhancement component had a positive effect on the couples' communication effectiveness. Marital satisfaction may lead to better couple communication, but the reverse is not always true. The pleasurable and displeasurable dimensions of behaviorally assessed marital satisfaction were independent.

Witkin (1977) compared two communication training programs, CSW and CC, and a wait-list control group on measures of communication effectiveness, problem-solving, and relationship satisfaction. The study used 54 volunteer couples and randomly assigned them to the conditions; highly distressed couples or those seeking marital therapy were excluded. All training was done in groups utilizing male and female co-trainers.

Communication Skills Workshop (CSW) is "behaviorally oriented," deriving its conceptual base from social-learning frameworks (Birchler, et al, 1975; Patterson & Hops, 1972) and communication theorists (e.g., Haley, 1959; Miller, 1975; Satir, 1965), and drawing upon the intervention strategies of the Oregon group (e.g., Patterson, et al, 1972; Epstein & Williams, 1981; Weiss, et al, 1973). The emphasis is on learning specific communication skills (e.g., specificity, feedback, and nonaversive requests) and applying these skills to relationship-solving. The program is conducted in six two-hour sessions with at-home assignments, including readings, between sessions.

The other communication training program was CC (see earlier description).

All subjects participated in a pretraining assessment session with information on the training and completion of the Locke Marital Adjustment Questionnaire. Couples meeting the criteria were assigned to the three groups. The control group subjects completed all evaluation measures and received training following completion of the study. All subjects were evaluated approximately one week (post-test) and seven weeks (follow-up) after completion of the training program.

Subjects in both programs were trained in groups of three to five couples. The CC leaders were older, had more years of education, and significantly more experience leading groups than the CSW leaders.

In assessing the results of the measurement instruments, Witkin concluded that when attempting to resolve relationship conflicts, the CC couples tended to exchange more positive and fewer negative nonverbal behaviors than the CSW couples. Both training programs were successful in decreasing verbal negative messages relative to the control group. The difference between the group leaders should be taken into account in assessing the results of the study.

Witkin (1977) concluded:

Ironically, it seems possible that "poor communication" between behavioral and non-behavioral investigators may have led to a perception of differences that is more apparent (or semantic) than real. For example, CC procedures to increase awareness might be found in a behavioral training program under the label of "cognitive restructuring." Assuming even the partial validity of this notion, the differences between the CSW and CC outcomes may be less substantive and more related to variables associated with group leadership and presentation of learning material ("marketing style") (pp. 9–10).

REFERENCES

Azrin NH, Naster BJ, & Jones R. Reciprocity counseling: A rapid learning-based procedure for marital counseling. *Behavior Research and Therapy*, 1973, *11*, 365–383

Bienvenu MJ. Measurement of marital communication. *The Family Coordinator*, 1970, *19*, 26–31

Birchler GR, Weiss RC, & Vincent JB. A multimethod analysis of social reinforcement exchange between maritally distressed and non-distressed spouse and stranger dyads. *Journal of Personality and Social Psychology*, 1975, *31*, 349–360

Boyd LA, & Roach AJ. Interpersonal communication skills differentiating more satisfying marital relationships. *Journal of Counseling Psychology*, 1977, *24*, 540–542

Campbell EE. The effect of couple communication training on married couples in the child-rearing years: A field experiment. *Dissertation Abstracts International*, 1974, *35*, 1942–1943A

Carter R, & Thomas EJ. Modification of problematic marital communication using corrective feedback and instruction. *Behavior Therapy*, 1973, *4*, 100–109

Cassidy MJ. Communication training for marital pairs. *Dissertation Abstracts International*, 1973, *34*, 3054A

Dillon JD. Marital communication and its relation to self-esteem. *Dissertation Abstracts International*, 1976, *37*, 5862B

Eisler RM, Hersen M, & Agras WS. Effects on videotape and instructional feedback on nonverbal marital interaction: An analog study. *Behavior Therapy*, 1973, *4*, 556–558

Epstein N, & Williams AM. Behavioral approaches to the treatment of marital discord. In GP Sholevar (Ed), *Handbook of marriage and family therapy*. New York: SP Medical and Scientific Books, 1981

Fleming MJ. An evaluation of a study program designed to teach communication skills and concepts to couples: A field study (Doctoral dissertation, Florida State University, 1976). *Dissertation Abstracts International*, 1977, *37*, 7633A–7634A (University Microfilms No. 77-13,315)

Glisson DH. A comparison of reciprocity counseling and communication training in the treatment of marital discord. *Dissertation and Abstracts International*, 1977, *37*, 7973A

Gottman J, Notarius C, Gonso J, & Markham H. *A couple's guide to communication*. Champaign, IL: Research Press, 1976

Henry J. *Pathways to madness*. New York: Random House, 1971

Hickman ME, & Baldwin BA. Use of programmed instruction to improve communication in marriage. *Family Coordinator*, 1971, *20*, 121–125

Hops H, Wills T, Weiss RL, & Patterson G. *Marital interaction coding system*. Unpublished manuscript, 1971 (available from Department of Psychology, University of Oregon, Eugene, OR)

Human Development Institute. *Improving communication in marriage*. Palo Alto, CA: Human Development Institute, 1967

Kahn M. Nonverbal communication and marital satisfaction. *Family Process*, 1970, *9*, 449–456

Larsen GR. An evaluation of the Minnesota Couple Communications Training Program's influence on marital communication and self and mate perceptions. *Dissertation Abstracts International*, 1974, *35*(5-A), 2627–2628

Larson KB. The effects of communication training in small groups upon self-disclosure, marital adjustment, and emotional attachment in marriage. *Dissertation Abstracts International*, 1977, *37*, 5328–5329B

Locke HJ, & Wallace KM. Short-term marital adjustment and prediction tests: Their reliability and validity. *Journal of Marriage and Family Living*, 1959, *21*, 251–255

Loevinger J. *Ego development*. San Francisco: Jossey-Bass, 1976

Margolin G, & Weiss RL. Communication training and assessment: A case of behavioral marital enrichment. *Behavior Therapy*, 1978, *9*, 508–520

Miller S (Ed). *Marriages and families: Enrichment through communication*. Beverly Hills: Sage Publications, 1975

Miller S, Nunnally EW, & Wackman DB. A communication training program for couples. *Social Casework*, 1976a, *57*, 9–18

Miller S, Nunnally EW, & Wackman DB. Minnesota Couples Communication Program (MCCP): Premarital and marital groups. In EHL Olson (Ed), *Treating relationships*. Lake Mills, IA: Graphic Publishing Co., 1976b

Murphy PC, & Mendelson LA. Communication and adjustment in marriage: Investigating the relationship. *Family Process*, 1973, *12*, 317–326

Navran L. Communication and adjustment in marriage. *Family Process*, 1967, *6*, 173–184

Osgood CE, Suci GJ, & Tannenbaum PH. *The measurement of meaning*. Urbana: University of Illinois Press, 1957

Patterson GR, & Hops H. Coercion, a game for two: Intervention techniques for marital conflict. In RE Ulrich & P Mountjoy (Eds), *The experimental analysis of social behavior*. New York: Appleton-Century-Crofts, 1972

Patterson GR, Hops H, & Weiss RL. A social learning approach to reducing rates of marital conflict. Paper read at the Sixth Annual Meeting of the Association for the Advancement of Behavior Therapy, New York, October 1972

Pierce RM. Training in interpersonal communication skills with partners of deteriorated marriages. *The Family Coordinator*, 1973, *22*, 223–227

Satir V. Conjoint marital therapy. In B Greene (Ed), *The psychotherapies of marital disharmony*. New York: The Free Press, 1965

Thomas EJ, Carter RD, & Gambrill ED. Some possibilities of behavioral modification with marital problems using "SAM" (signal system for the assessment and modification of behavior. In RD Rubin, H Fensterheim, AH Lazarus & CM Franks (Eds), *Advances in behavior therapy*. New York: Academic Press, 1971

Wampler KS, & Sprenkle DS. The Minnesota Couple Communication Program: A follow-up study. *Journal of Marriage and the Family*, 1980, *42*, 577–584

Weiss RL, Hops H, & Patterson GR. A framework for conceptualizing marital conflict: A technology for altering it, some data for evaluating it. In LA Hamerlynck, LC Handy, & EJ Mash (Eds), *Behavior change: Methodology, concepts, and practice*. Champaign, IL: Research Press, 1973

Wender PH. Vicious and virtuous circles: The role of deviation amplifying feedback in the origin and perpetuation of behavior. In HH Barten (Ed), *Brief therapies*. New York: Behavioral Publications, 1971

Witkin SL. The development and evaluation of a group training program in communication skills for couples. *Dissertation Abstracts International*, 1977, *37*, 5362A

Appendix C: Guidelines for Covenant Writing with Couples*

The guidelines presented in this Appendix were developed at the Family Studies Center of Georgia State University for use with more functional, or normal, couples, and are based on adaptations from Sager's (1976) use of marital contracts as a therapeutic intervention. Covenant writing, as described in this Appendix, is an intermediate intervention between highly structured marital enrichment programs and the less structured therapeutic interventions outlined by Sager.

The underlying rationale is identical to Sager's. Marital partners bring to the relationship their own personal set of expectations about marriages in general and their own marriage in particular. Marital disharmony arises when each partner functions in the relationship as if the other is in agreement with his or her particular expectations about marriage. When these expectations are not upheld, each partner is usually of the impression that the other has violated these agreed-upon marital expectations when, in fact, the expectations of each have typically neither been articulated nor agreed upon. Thus covenant writing attempts to help couples explore the rational expectations of each partner and to negotiate changes in the behavior of each, relative to these expectations. Potential benefits of this process include an increased awareness of formerly unarticulated areas of conflict or avoidance in the relationship, as well as an active resolution of some of the problematic issues.

In this covenant-writing approach, sessions are numbered and limited to eight. Interventions are open-ended so that couples may present issues pertinent to them and so that they will take responsibility for the process. The therapist/intervener serves as a facilitator of change in the couple's process, rather than as an active agent who directs change. Covenant writing becomes the process as well as the goal.

The eight-session process is as follows, with a description of the tasks and activities to be completed by the couple and the therapist(s).

Initial session. For most couples, this session represents the first direct contact that the therapist has with them. As is true of the initial phases of all clinical interventions, a central task during this session is for the therapist to begin to establish rapport with the couple. This also is the time during which a general explanation of the covenant-writing process is provided. A basic description of the distinction between individual and joint covenants is included, as well as a brief overview of what can be expected of the covenant-writing process in subsequent sessions.

The couple is presented the pretest portion of the GSU (Georgia State University) Couples Battery (see Appendix E) and an explanation of its use. The measures in the battery are then completed at home by the couple, in the fol-

---
*Contributors: Hilary Buzas, Cindy Caiella, Debbie Daniels, David Karan, David Kearns, Jim Kochalka, Linda Talmadge.

lowing order: (1) Information Sheet, (2) Social Readjustment Scale, (3) Dyadic Adjustment Scale (Spaniers, 1976), and (4) Feelings Questionnaire (O'Leary & Turkewitz, 1978). These completed materials are returned at the next session. The therapist(s) also inform(s) the couple that they will be required to complete the Marital Satisfaction Scale (MSS) on a daily basis throughout the course of the covenant-writing process and that they will be asked to complete a follow-up questionnaire on their experience of this process three months after its completion.

When covenant writing is conducted by students, the couple is informed that the information from the initial session and subsequent sessions is subject to a regular review as part of the facilitators' clinical supervision. Beyond supervision, however, the specifics of sessions are held in strict confidence. Based on the overview provided, the couple is given the option of either continuing or not continuing with the covenant-writing process. An agreement to continue is finalized with the signing of a consent form by each spouse. The initial session is concluded after the co-facilitators gain specific information as to the relational history of the couple.

Session I. The first session of the covenant-writing process begins with the collection of the pretest evaluation battery. If necessary, part of this session may be used by the therapist(s) to make further inquiries into the couple's relational history. History-taking may also be supplemented by the completion of family genograms and/or the exploration of the perceived quality and dynamics of the marriages of the parents of the couple.

Each partner is then given a copy of the Reminder List for the Marriage Covenant of Each Partner (adapted from Sager, 1976). Each partner uses this list as a guide as they individually complete as homework a listing of individual expectations of marriage (Sager's Category 1). Each partner is told to complete the task in writing, using a format that includes (1) their expectations of marriage before they were married (past expectations); (2) their current individual expectations of marriage (present reality), and (3) the individual goals of each partner, relative to marriage (future goals). Each spouse is also asked to specify in

writing what he or she is willing to offer in exchange for the goals specified in Part 3 of his or her list (What I Will Give in Exchange). The couple is asked to bring this information to the next scheduled session, along with the MSS forms to be completed daily.

Session II. Each partner is encouraged to read aloud the results of the homework, i.e., information relative to the individual expectations of marriage. The therapist(s) encourage(s) the couple to discuss and make inquiries of each other about this information.

The completion of this initial phase of covenant writing (prejoint-covenant) is followed by the assignment of a homework task to specify relational information associated with the individual, psychological, and biological needs of each partner. Using the Reminder List as a guide, each partner is instructed to specify in writing what he or she wants from the mate (relative to the psychological and biological needs outlined in the Reminder List) and what each is willing to give in exchange.

Session III. As in the previous session, the therapist(s) ask(s) each partner to read aloud the completed homework task, setting the stage for an open discussion of the meeting of needs within the context of the relationship. The task of the therapist(s) during this part of the session is to focus the couple's interaction so that there is a thorough discussion of the psychological and biological needs that each partner expects and desires to have met within the marital relationship, as well as what each is willing to trade off in exchange for a meeting of these expectations.

Once this is completed, the third homework assignment is given. This assignment is a specification of what each partner wants from his or her mate in terms of externalized foci relative to the marriage (e.g., expectations in terms of communication, children, friends, home responsibilities) and what will be considered in exchange for what is desired (Sager's Category 3). Again, the Reminder List is suggested as a guideline for the written homework assignment.

Session IV. The homework assignment is the focus of discussion between the partners for a portion of the time in this session. Once the expectations and ideas of exchange of each spouse, relative to Category 3, have been discussed, the therapist(s) shift(s) the discussion to a reexamination of the major issues previously outlined in the individual covenants of each partner. This focus is considered a necessary first step toward working on the couple's joint marital covenant.

The couple is asked to review the specifics of each individual covenant, reexamining the expectations and potential trade-offs that were written relative to Categories 1, 2, and 3. The therapist(s) then has the couple negotiate between themselves (with assistance, if necessary) a prioritized list of issues from the three categories, which they agree should be included in their joint marital covenant. The couple is given the homework task of working together on a single contract, with the focus on the quid pro quo negotiation of tradeoffs between them (e.g., I would like _____ from my spouse and am willng to give _____ in order to get it), which will allow a meeting of agreed-upon individual needs within the context of the relationship.

Session V. The construction of the joint marital covenant of the couple remains the focus of this session, with the task of the therapist(s) largely that of clarifying issues and answering questions that may have arisen while the couple jointly performed the homework task. If more work is needed on the contract, the couple is asked to complete the writing of the joint contract as homework and bring it back to the next session for a final review. If the contract was completed when brought to this session, the therapist(s) ask(s) the couple to take the contract home with them and to give thought to possible modifications or additions in content.

Session VI. The final contract is the focus of this session. Emphasis is placed not only on the expectations and trade-offs that have been included, but also on the actual process of negotiation by which these were agreed upon. The post-test portion of the GSU Battery is given as homework, to be collected during the feedback session.

Feedback session. During this session, the therapist(s) consider(s) possible future format changes in the covenant-writing process. The feedback provided to the couple centers on several kinds of information. First and foremost, the therapist(s) address(es) the strengths that were seen in the couple—their areas of competence both on an individual and a marital level. With some couples, the therapist(s) may make suggestions about areas in the relationship that may warrant further effort. These may include issues that were not successfully (or totally) negotiated as part of the covenant-writing process, as well as others that may not have been addressed at all, especially if they surfaced late in the covenant-writing process. In these cases, recommendations are made by the therapist(s) as to the format that would most appropriately address these issues (e.g., marital therapy, enrichment). If the couple expresses an interest in these recommendations, the therapist(s) make(s) specific recommendations about how and where the services may be received.

The couple is again reminded at the end of the session that after three months, they will receive through the mail a follow-up questionnaire that they are to complete and return.

REFERENCES

O'Leary KD, & Turkewitz H. Marital therapy from a behavioral perspective. In TJ Paolino & BS McCrady (Eds), *Marriage and marital therapy: Psychoanalytic, behavioral, and systems theory perspectives.* New York: Brunner/Mazel, 1978

Sager CJ. *Marriage contracts and couple therapy.* New York: Brunner/Mazel, 1976

Spanier GB. Measuring dyadic adjustment: New scales for assessing the quality of marriage and similar dyads. *Journal of Marriage and the Family,* 1976, *38,* 15–28

Appendix D: Intimacy Enrichment Program

After introductions, say: "This program was designed to increase intimacy. What does the word intimacy mean to you?" *Let them answer; then say:* In the course of this program, we will have a chance to think about what this word means."

LESSON 1: SEEING THE GOOD

Exercise 1: Definitions

"Today (tonight) we are going to talk about 'seeing the good' and what it means to this couple. What do you think it means to see the good in yourself and your partner?" *Allow each member to offer his or her own meaning for "seeing the good." Also, encourage the family members to discuss the similarities and differences among each other's proposed meanings.* "I wonder if we could agree that 'seeing the good' means playing up the positive side, the good side, of those we love. When we love someone, we accept the bad things about them as things that are overshadowed by the good in them. What do you think of that?" *Allow the couple to discuss this definition of seeing the good.*

Exercise 2: Interferences

"How do you show that you see the good in yourselves and in each other?" *Make certain that everyone attempts to answer this question. If someone has difficulty with this,* say: "What is it about this couple that makes it hard for you to see the good in each other?" *Pause for answers.*

Exercise 3: Practicing Good

(a) "I want each of you, in turn, to say something good about each other. Look your partner right in the face and tell him or her about a good trait or quality that he or she possesses." *Make certain that everyone does this.*

(b) "How did it feel to tell your partner about the good in him or her?" *Make certain everyone answers.*

(c) "How did it feel to be told good things about yourself?" *Make certain that everyone answers.*

(d) "Were you surprised to hear how much good there is in this marriage?" *Wait for answers.*

Exercise 4: Both Sides of a Coin

"Now, I'd like each of you to tell about a situation that has both good and bad aspects." *Let them think and answer.*

(a) "Is it better to work and think about mainly the good or the bad aspects of this situation?" *Let them answer.*

(b) "Why?" *(This question may be redundant.)*

(c) "Do you see any relationship between what you have told me and the old story about the optimist and the pessimist looking at the half-filled glass? Remember that the optimist said the glass was half-full, while the pessimist said it was half-empty." *Explain, if necessary. Let them react.*

Exercise 5: Seeing Good Better

"How could you do a better job of seeing the good in yourselves and each other?" *Make sure that everyone answers this question. Encourage the couple to respond to and discuss each other's answers.*

Homework

"During the next week, I'd like each of you to make it a point to tell each other that you recognize something good in that person." *Other appropriate homework assignments may be given at this point.*

LESSON 2: CARING

Check the homework assignment carefully.

Exercise 1: Definition

"Today (tonight), we are going to talk about 'care' and what it means to this marriage. What does it mean to someone?" *Allow each member to offer his or her own meaning for "care." Also, encourage partners to discuss the similarities and differences among each other's proposed meanings.* "I wonder if we could agree that care is the understanding of the importance of one's self and the selves of one's family. In other words, if you care for someone, you see both yourself and that person as being important. What do you think about that?" *Allow the couple to discuss this definition of care.*

Exercise 2: Showing Care

"How do you show that you care for each other? I'd like each one of you to tell one way in which someone shows that he or she cares for you." *If a member cannot think of a way in which someone shows care for him or her, allow another person to remind the member*

---

*Whenever a question is asked by the Trainer, the lack of specific instructions still means that answers and responses by the family are expected.

of possible ways. When appropriate, say: "I can see that there is a lot of care in this marriage." *If some family members show care in a destructive manner, ask the family for their reactions to that way of showing care.*

Exercise 3: Self-Care

(a) "I want each of you, in turn, to stand up and say: 'I am a person and I am important.' Then go up to your partner and say: 'I care for you and you are important to me,' or any other similar comment you feel like making."

(b) *After this has been done, say:* "How did it feel to tell someone that you care? How did it feel to have him or her say that he or she cares for you?" *Wait for answers.*

Exercise 4: Caring

"Now, each of you do something that shows you care for your partner. You might kiss, shake his or her hand, scratch his or her back, or just anything that feels right to you." *Take detailed notes during this exercise.*

Exercise 5: Caring Better

"How could each of you do a better job of letting the other know that you care for him or her?" *Make sure that everyone answers this question. Encourage the couple to respond to and discuss each other's answers.*

Homework

"During the next week, think of all the ways you care for and show care for your partner. Everyday, tell him or her that you care for him or her and do something to show this." *Other appropriate homework assignments may be given at this time.*

"Well, that's the end of Lesson 2. How do you feel about the exercises we did today?" *Ask about specific problems, if necessary. Take notes. Set up the next appointment, and in a manner that shows your respect for the couple, say good-bye to them.*

LESSON 3: DIRECT FEELINGS

Inquire as to how much the couple has practiced telling each other about the care. If they have not practiced, comment to the effect that, "If you do not take outside what we learn here, I am afraid that you may not learn very much." *Then, go on:* "Today you are going to learn how to deal with feelings more directly than you may have done in the past. OK?" *If someone asks what feelings are, name a few positive and a few negative ones.*

Exercise 1: Feeling Good

"I want you to start thinking of one or two things that the other one could do to make you feel good about yourself. What could each of you do that would feel good to you? Think of it and then, in turn, say it." *Pause, and as soon as someone seems ready, allow him or her to start, making sure that each member tells every member what he or she can do that would feel good to him or her.*

Exercise 2: Feedback

"I want each of you to answer back what you heard from your partner. Start a sentence such as, 'I understand you to say that if I did . . . it would make you feel good. Is that right?' Or 'I hear you saying that if I do . . . you will feel good. Is that correct?' " *The answer or reflection may be a paraphrase, a condensation, or a summary of what each family member has said. Make sure that the answer is correct on the basis of its acceptance by the individual who first made the initial request in the previous exercise.*

Exercise 3: Feeling Hurt

"We are going to repeat the same exercise as before. However, this time I want each of you to tell what it is that your partner does that makes you feel bad and hurts you. You can start a sentence by saying to each other, 'It hurts me very much when you . . .' Or, 'It would hurt me a great deal if you were to . . .' Who would like to begin?"

Exercise 4: Feedback

"Now that each of you has talked about what would hurt, I want each of you to answer back what you heard. Start a sentence saying, 'I understand', or 'I hear', or 'Are you saying that if I were to . . . it would hurt you?' or 'It would hurt you if or when I . . .?' " *Make sure*

that the reflection or rephrasing is acceptable to the one who made the original statement in the previous exercise.

Exercise 5: Sharing Secrets

"Now that you have learned to express good and bad feelings, I would like each of you to share a secret with each other. Is there something that you have kept hidden within yourself that you can open up and share with your partner without fear of reprisal? Take the risk of presenting a thought, a feeling, or a memory that you can share with each other. Who will start?"

In closing, say: "Well, we have finished our third lesson about learning to express and accept our feelings and those of others. Make sure now to go home and practice what you have learned today. I'll see you next time. Good-bye."

LESSON 4: SPEAKING WITHOUT FEAR

After greeting both, let them seat themselves and then ask: "Anybody want to say anything about the lesson we had last time?" *Let each answer as best he or she can, then thank him or her for whatever reactions he or she may have expressed:* "Thank you. I appreciate your speaking up. Now, today's lesson consists of exercises that should help you to speak without fear that the other one will hurt you or harm you. In other words, we would like to teach each of you to stand on your own feet and speak up. If you don't learn to stand up and speak up in this marriage, where will you learn?" *Wait for any answer or comment, nodding your acceptance of whatever each member says; then pass to the first exercise.*

Exercise 1: Saying Yes or No

"In this exercise, we will learn how to say yes or no. I want each of you to ask something of one another. Whoever is asked answers either yes or no. Who wants to be first?" *Let each person ask one question of everyone else and let them answer. After they are all finished, ask generally,* "How did it feel to say yes?" *Let some discussion take place.* "How did it feel to say no?" *Let everybody answer to the best of their abilities.*

Exercise 2: Expressing Feelings

"Now we are going to practice to express feelings without hurting the feelings of others. This time, I want each of you to order and demand something of one another. However, each of you should answer nastily and refuse to follow the order. Think of the worst possible way you would answer such an order." *The sequence should be (a) order and (b) spiteful answer. See that everybody gets an order and gets to answer spitefully. Let each have a turn in ordering everybody around and also in answering.*

After they have finished, ask, "How did it feel to give an order to someone you love?" *After they answer the best they can, ask,* "How does it feel to answer nastily?" *Let each answer to the best of his or her ability, then ask,* "What do you get by being mean to each other?" *Ask the same question again, and let the family answer to the best of their abilities; then say,* "Do you like yourself when you answer nastily?" *Wait for individual answers.*

Exercise 3: Empathy

"After being mean to each other, we want to learn how to take someone else's place by talking rather than by doing." *Pause for any comments or answers, nodding acceptingly; then say,* "I want each of you to complete a sentence directed to each other: 'If I were you, I would . . .'" *Let both have a chance to complete a sentence. After both have finished, ask,* "How did it feel to be told something like this?" *Let the couple discuss how they felt when they were addressed.*

Exercise 4: Pretending

"Now that we have practiced how to stand up and speak, let's see if we can start doing something new. I would like for each of you to make up either a mask or a statue. Either way, I want each of you to think now of what mask or statue you could make. Does each of you know what you want to do? OK, go ahead and do it. You can stand up if you want." *After each member has executed his or her stance, say,* OK, very good. Now, I want you to keep that position as you have it. Now, in turn, tell each other what kind of mask or statue you have

made." *Allow each in turn to explain. After each of them has answered your question, ask,* "Do you know why he or she has made that mask or statue? Does that mask or statue have any meaning to you?" *Let everyone answer to the limit of their abilities.*

Exercise 5: Making Up

"In the last exercise of this lesson, we want to start learning how to feel free to talk without any limits. I would like each of you to close your eyes and start making up a tall tale. Feel free to make up the tallest, wildest, biggest tale you have ever made up. Close your eyes and think. I'll give you two minutes to make . . . OK. The two (five) minutes are up. Who will start?" *Let each of them feel free to expand at will. Try to allow up to five minutes, but cut it short by saying,* "You have been going on for four (five) minutes now, and in order to give both of you a chance to talk, you will need to wind up your tale in one minute."

After finishing this exercise, ask, "Well, what did you think of the work we did today?" *Let each member answer and if one does not, encourage him or her to speak up. After each has expressed his or her opinion about the lesson, finish up by telling them you will see them "next time."*

LESSON 5: SHARING OF HURT FEELINGS

Exercise 1: Definition

"Today (tonight) we are going to talk about the 'sharing of hurt feelings' and what it means to this marriage. What does it mean to share your hurt feelings with someone?" *Allow each member to offer his or her own meaning for "sharing of hurt feelings." Also, encourage them to discuss the similarities and differences among each other's proposed meanings:* "I wonder if we could agree that sharing of hurt feelings means telling the people you are close to, not only about your victories and happiness, but also about your pain and defeats. We share victories with anybody, but our defeats belong to the family. What do you think of that?" *Allow the couple to discuss this definition of "sharing of hurt feelings."*

Exercise 2. How is it done?

"How do you share your hurt feelings with each other? I'd like each of you to tell us how you talk about your pains and defeats. Does it make you feel better to share your hurt feelings with each other?" *If one or both report that sharing of hurt does not take place in the marriage or does not make him or her feel better, say,* "What do you think it means that you don't share your hurt (or that sharing your hurt doesn't make you feel better)?"

Exercise 3: Practicing

(a) "Each of you, in turn, please share with us something that is hurting you at this moment." *Make sure you include both.*

(b) "How did it feel to tell your partner about your pains and defeats?"

(c) "How did it feel to hear about the hurt of your partner?"

Exercise 4: Feeling Sharing

"Now I want each of you to touch the other and say, 'I am glad that you are willing to share your hurt with me. I want to know about your defeats and pains because I care about you and hope that I can do something to make things better with you.' You may also say anything else that feels right to you."

Exercise 5: Sharing Hurt Feelings

(a) "How could each of you do a better job of sharing your hurt with each other?"

(b) "How could this marriage better use the sharing of hurt to make both of you happier and stronger?" *Make sure that both answer this question. Encourage them to respond to and discuss each other's answers. Take detailed notes.*

Homework

"During the next week, think of how you share your hurt with each other. Everyday, tell each other about something that hurts you. When someone tells you about his or her hurt, try to respond as you would want him or her to respond to your hurt." *Other appropriate homework assignments may be given at this time.*

"Well, that's the end of Lesson 5. How do you feel about the exercises we did today? How is our work coming along?" *Ask about specific problems if necessary. Take notes. Set up the next appointment, and in a manner that shows your respect for the family, say good-bye to them.*

LESSON 6: SHARING HERE AND NOW

"Have you practiced expressing and accepting each other's hurt feelings?" *If they have done so, compliment and congratulate them. If not, say,* "If you are unable to express and accept each other's hurt feelings, you may not be able to accept each other as full partners." *Then go on,* "The purpose of today's lesson is to teach you to share how each of you sees things in the here-and-now."

Exercise 1: Feelings

"I want each of you to tell everybody how you feel here and now. How does each of you feel here and now?" *Let them express themselves fully.*

Exercise 2: Mutuality

"Now I want each of you to tell how you feel toward each other here and now. How does each of you feel toward everybody else (i.e., the trainer(s) here and now?" *Let them respond fully.*

Exercise 3: Sharing Excitement

"Now I want each of you to tell each other an idea or thought that is exciting to you. What is exciting to you here and now? Share it with each other here and now." *Let them respond fully.*

Exercise 4: Taking Risks

"Now we are going to start something harder. I want each of you to say something that is hard for you to say. What is it that is hard for each of you to day?" *Encourage each to say it.*

Exercise 5: Difficulties

"Now I want you to talk about ways and means that make it hard for your feelings to be expressed openly and freely. Some families don't allow anger, some families don't allow hurt and pain, some families don't allow fear. What feelings does this couple not allow?" *Give five to ten minutes of free discussion and encourage openness to the extent permissible by the couple.*

Say good-bye to the couple by giving them a home assignment: "During all next week, I want each of you to express your feelings and to accept those of others in the family without restraints. OK? See you next time."

LESSON 7 (OPTIONAL): TALKING ABOUT ONE'S SELF

"Have you been able to express and accept feelings more?" *Let them answer. If the answer is generally positive, congratulate them. If the answer is negative, explore what possible blocks exist that make it hard for the couple to express themselves.* "Why is it so hard for this couple to feel free about their feelings?" *Let them answer; then go on:* "One way of learning more about feelings is to look at one's self and use one's self and one's feelings as an important source of direction. Today we want to learn to talk about our own feelings without blaming others, or trying to please them, or arguing and doing whatever does not pay off and hurts this marriage."

Exercise 1: Beginning

"To begin with, I want each of you to tell everybody else how you feel about your own self. What is it that you like about yourself and what is it that you don't like? Who will be first?" *Push, if necessary, to have someone start. If they stress what they like, ask what it is they don't like about themselves. If they stress what they don't like, ask what it is that*

they like. If someone tends to polarize in either direction, denying the other side (like or dislike), **force** *him or her to find something he or she likes or dislikes, even if small or seemingly irrelevant.*

Exercise 2: Wanting Change

"Now that each of you has told what you like and dislike about your own self, talk about what you would like to do to change into a better person. If each of you wants to change, the marriage may change. However, if you don't want to change, you cannot expect your partner to do what you can't or don't want to do. What are you going to do to change into a better person?" *Let them struggle with this even if there is a lengthy pause.*

Exercise 3: Goals

"In order to change yourselves, you need to wish or plan what it is that you want to become. I want each of you to tell what it is that you wish or want to become. Go ahead." *Let them pursue this point fully and openly. Encourage if and when it is necessary.*

Exercise 4: Reaching Goals

"Each of you has talked about how you want to change. Now I want each of you to tell, in greater detail, what goals you want to reach and what steps you are going to take to reach the goals you seek."

Exercise 5: Fantasy and Reality

"Now I want each of you to look at your wishes and plans and the steps you have outlined to fulfill the wishes or reach the goals. How close (realistic, practical, reasonable) are your plans in relationship to your wishes?"

Close the program by saying, "I have enjoyed working with you. We will get together in a week to evaluate what we have learned. Thank you for your help."

Appendix E: Selected Annotated References

ATTITUDES TOWARD HOMOSEXUALITY SCALE

A. P. MacDonald, Jr.

The Attitudes toward Homosexuality Scale is a self-report scale that measures subjects' attitudes toward homosexuality without regard for their own sexual orientation. The scale contains 28 items with a 9-scale position for each item, i.e., ranging from "strongly agree" to "strong disagree." It is available in three forms and is intended for use with a wide variety of populations.

MacDonald AP, Jr, & Games RG. Some characteristics of those who hold positive and negative attitudes toward homosexuals. *Journal of Homosexuality*, 1974, *1*, 9–27

MacDonald AP, Jr, Huggins J, Young S, Swanson RA. Attitudes toward homosexuality: Preservation of sex morality or the double standard? *Journal of Consulting and Clinical Psychology*, 1973, *40*, 161–164

BODY ATTITUDE SCALE

R. Kurz and M. Hirt

The Body Attitude Scale is a self-report instrument that measures global attitudes toward the outward form of a person's body on three primary attitude dimensions. Thirty different body parts are rated through use of a modified Osgood semantic differential. Ratings are made on a 7-point bipolar adjective scale sampling three dimensions of the Osgoods' semantic differential: good–bad, strong–weak, active–passive. Scoring is conducted with a 7-point scale. The three adjectival scales for each dimension are then summed to obtain an item score for each concept on each dimension. These item scores are then summed across the 30 body concepts to obtain a composite global body-attitude score.

This scale is intended for use with adult subjects of various ages and backgrounds. Evidence for internal consistency of the body attitude measures has been reported. Generalizability coefficients for males and females have ranged from 0.93 to 0.98 on the three dimensions, indicating that attitudes could be inferred adequately from their specific attitudes toward individual body aspects.

Kurtz R, & Hirt M. Body attitude and physical health. *Journal of Clinical Psychology*, 1960, *26*, 149–152

BODY CONTACT QUESTIONNAIRE

M. H. Hollender

The Body Contact Questionnaire is a self-report instrument that measures the desire for body contact through 12 items scored on a 5-point Likert Scale. Sample question: "If you have trouble falling asleep, it is helpful to have someone hold you." Scoring ranges from "never" to "always." No validity information and only minimal reliability data have been reported.

Hollender MH, Luborsky L, Scavamella TJ. Body contact and sexual excitement. *Archives of General Psychiatry*, 1969, *20*, 188–194
Hollender MH, & Mercer AJ. Wish to be held and wish to hold in men and women. *Archives of General Psychiatry*, 1976, *33*, 49–55

DEROGATIS SEXUAL FUNCTION INVENTORY

Leonard R. Derogatis

The Derogatis Sexual Function Inventory (DSFI) is a self-report scale designed to measure an individual's current sexual functioning via the assessment of the following domains of sexual functioning: I. Information; II. Experience; III. Drive; IV. Attitudes; V. Symptoms; VI. Affect; VII. Gender Role Definition; VIII. Fantasy; IX. Body Image; and X. Satisfaction. The 245 separate items may be completed in 30 to 40 minutes. Additionally, there are two subtests, the Brief Symptom Inventory and Affect Balance Scale. A 9-point Global Satisfaction Index also provides a measure of the subject's self-rating of his or her present level of sexual functioning. Provisional norms are being developed and updated for the DFSI.

Derogatis LR, Meyer JK, Gallant BW. Distinctions between male and female invested partners in sexual disorders. *American Journal of Psychiatry*, 1977, *134*, 385–394
Derogatis LR, Meyer JK, Vazquez N. A psychological profile of the transsexual: 1. The male. *Journal of Nervous and Mental Disease*, 1978, *166*, 234–238

HETEROSEXUAL BEHAVIOR ASSESSMENTS

P.M. Bentler

Two forms of the Heterosexual Behavior Assessments are available to assess male and female heterosexual behaviors. It is a self-report instrument, and the items consist of 21 classes of heterosexual behaviors arranged in a hierarchical manner. A total score results from the number of items endorsed by the subject.

Internal consistency and scalability have been demonstrated with a college-educated population. A short, 10-item form, which correlates 0.98 with a total scale, is available.

Bentler PM. Heterosexual behavior assessments. I. Males. *Behavior Research and Theory*, 1968, *6*, 21–26
Bentler PM. Heterosexual behavior assessment. II. Females. *Behavior Research and Theory*, 1968, *6*, 27–32

HETEROSEXUAL BEHAVIOR INVENTORIES

C. H. Robinson and J. S. Annon

The Heterosexual Behavior Inventories is a checklist that assesses the ranges and frequency of an individual's heterosexual behavior repertoire. Statements include solitary and partner-directed behavior in male and female forms. This inventory contains 77 items that include self-observation and observation of a partner, interpersonal sexual behavior, and a wide range of direct sexual behavior. This instrument is intended for patients with sexual dysfunction.

No reliability studies have been conducted, and only face validity presently exists.

Annon JS. *The behavioral treatment of sexual problems, vol. 2. Intensive therapy.* Honolulu: Enabling Systems, 1976

INDEX OF SEXUAL SATISFACTION

W. W. Hudson

The Index of Sexual Satisfaction is a short self-rated scale that measures the degree of discord or dissatisfaction that partners perceive exists with the sexual component of their relationship. It is an adult clinical tool with 25 items that are both positively and negatively worded, e.g., "My sex life is very exciting," or "My partner does not want sex when I do." Neither reliability nor validity data are provided.

Hudson WW, & Glisson D. *A short-form scale to measure sexual dissatisfaction.* Honolulu: University of Hawaii School of Social Work, 1976

THE MALE IMPOTENCE TEST

A. El Senoussi

The Male Impotence Test, a self-report test, is, according to the author, able to discriminate among psychogenically impotent men, organically impotent men, and nonimpotent individuals. The questionnaire reveals five scores: (1) reaction to female rejection, (2) flight from male role, (3) reaction to male inadequacy, (4) an organic factor, and (5) total score.

No reliability data are provided. The test has received criticism for its inability to differentially diagnose organic versus psychogenic impotence.

Beutler LE, Johnson D, Neville C, Elkins D, & Jobe A. MMPI and MIT discriminators of biogenic and psychogenic impotence. *Journal of Consulting and Clinical Psychology,* 1975, *43*, 90–91
Ellis A. The male impotence test. In OK Buros (Ed), *The seventh mental measurement yearbook.* Highland Park, NJ: Gryphon Press, 1972

NEGATIVE ATTITUDES TOWARD MASTURBATION SCALE

P. R. Abramson and D. L. Mosher

The Negative Attitudes toward Masturbation Scale is a self-report instrument that is intended to assess attitudes toward masturbation through 30 items that are rated on a 5-point scale that ranges from "strongly agree" to "strongly disagree." Example: "When I masturbate, I am disgusted with myself." Factor analysis reveals three factors: (1) positive attitude toward masturbation, (2) false beliefs about the harmful nature of masturbation, and (3) personally experienced negative effects associated with masturbation.

Split-half reliability data are available. Validational evidence is based on correlations between this measure and the average of masturbation per month for males and females.

Mosher DL, & Abramson PR. Subjective sexual arousal to films of masturbation. *Journal of Consulting and Clinical Psychology,* 1977, *45*, 796–799

A QUESTIONNAIRE MEASURE OF SEXUAL INTEREST

J. J. M. Harbison, P. J. Graham, J. T. Quinn, H. McAllister, and R. Woodward

The purpose of the Questionnaire Measure of Sexual Interest, a self-report questionnaire, is to measure the degree of interest the male or female indicates in social situations that might be of either a homosexual or a heterosexual nature. It may be used to assess differences in sexual interest between clinical and normal groups or to monitor the response of patients to treatment.

The questionnaire contains 140 items set out in random order, with the respondent marking the adjectival statement that best describes his or her response to the sexual situation in question. Data are provided on internal consistency, test–retest reliability, and validity.

No Reference Available

REISS PREMARITAL SEXUAL PERMISSIVENESS SCALES

I. L. Reiss

The Reiss Premarital Sexual Permissiveness Scale is a self-report instrument that has been used with persons 16 years and older as an indicator of premarital sexual attitudes. It is concerned with acceptance of three categories of premarital physical acts: kissing, petting, and coitus, with each behavior considered in the context of different conditions of affection. The conditions of affection are divided into the four categories of engagement, love, strong affection, and no affection. Each of the three physical conditions is qualified by each of the four affection-related states, making a total of 12 statements with which the respondent is asked to agree or disagree, "strongly," "moderately," or "slightly."

There are 12 items on which a respondent

can be rated in two ways: (1) how he or she responds to the scale statements of his or her own sex, and (2) how he or she responds to scale statements using the opposite sex as the referent. Evidence of reliability and validity of the scale has been provided by both the author and independent investigators.

Hampe GD, & Ruppel HJ. The measurement of premarital sexual permissiveness: A comparison of two Guttman scales. *Journal of Marriage and Family*, 1974, *36*, 451–459

SEMANTIC DIFFERENTIAL AS MEASURE OF SEXUAL ATTITUDES

I. M. Marks and N. H. Sartorius

The Semantic Differential as Measure of Sexual Attitudes is an adult self-report scale devised for assessing attitudinal change during treatment for sexual deviation. Test items are 20 sexual and nonsexual concepts rated on 13 bipolar semantic differential scales (e.g., pleasant–unpleasant, repulsive–seductive, bad–good).

Adequate stability on test–retest within 24 hours was demonstrated. The instrument has been determined useful in the follow-up of sexual deviants over two years after treatment.

Marks IM. *Behavioral psychotherapy for neurosis.* London: Royal College of Nursing, 1977

SEXUAL ANXIETY SCALE

M. Obler

The Sexual Anxiety Scale is an adult self-report scale that measures social and sexual anxieties that are cognitively experienced. Content of the 22 items ranges from anxiety experienced during contact with a member of the opposite sex to intravaginal penetration.

The author reports a 0.92 reliability coefficient and a 0.62 validity coefficient with intensity of sexual dysfunction.

Obler M. Systematic desensitization in sexual disorders. *Journal of Behavioral Therapy and Experimental Psychiatry*, 1973, *4*, 93–103

SEXUAL AROUSABILITY INVENTORY (FEMALE FORM)

E. F. Hoon, P. W. Hoon, and J. P. Wincze

The Sexual Arousability Inventory (Female Form) is a female self-report inventory that measures sexual arousability for women. The inventory consists of 28 descriptions of sexual activities and situations, e.g., "When a loved one undresses you . . ." The respondent rates each on a 7-point Likert scale based on how sexually arousing the described activity is to her. The authors report data showing that the instrument has adequate stability and internal consistency.

Hoon EJ, Hoon PW, Wincze JP. An inventory for the measurement of female sexual arousability: The SAI. *Archives of Sexual Behavior*, 1976, *5*, 291–300

SEXUAL ATTITUDES AND BELIEFS INVENTORY

D. Wallace

The Sexual Attitudes and Beliefs Inventory is a 250-item adult self-report inventory that is a scale concerned with the attitudes and information about sexual behaviors of the reporting individuals. Information concerning sexual experience is also elicited.

The author reports test–retest coefficients between 0.75 and 0.85 with a 4-week separation on a population of medical students. No validity information is available.

No Reference Available

SEXUAL COMPATIBILITY TEST

A. L. Foster

The Sexual Compatibility Test is a self-administered test that is used for couples presenting with sexual problems in the assessment of sexual attitudes, activity, responsiveness, and satisfaction. The test consists of 64 items, each of which questions specific sexual activity involving the couple and demands answers along six separate dimensions. A further

37 items require single responses to each specific question. Scoring can be computerized. Several scales are utilized, including a scale with cut-off scores, predicting the likelihood of success in treating a couple's sexual problem. Neither reliability nor validity studies have been published.

Foster AL. The sexual compatibility test. *Journal of Consulting and Clinical Psychology*, 1977, *45*, 332–340

SEXUAL DEVELOPMENT SCALE FOR FEMALES

A. El Senoussi

The Sexual Development Scale for Females is a self-report scale for adult females that attempts to measure the "relative degree of sexual frigidity" and identify aspects or causative factors involved.

The scale consists of 177 items with seven factors scores: lack of feminine identity, free-floating anxiety, unpleasant sexual encounter, passive sex aversion, flight into sex, insufficiency, and early negative conditioning. No validity data are available, and reliability is limited to total scores.

Ellis A. In OK Buros (Ed), *The seventh mental measurement yearbook*. Highland Park, NJ: Gryphon Press, 1972 (a critical examination is included)

SEXUAL INTERACTION INVENTORY

J. LoPiccolo and J. C. Steger

The Sexual Interaction Inventory is a self-report inventory that is used in the assessment of sexual adjustment and sexual satisfaction of heterosexual couples. The inventory consists of 17 items covering a wide range of heterosexual behaviors. For each behavior, both husband and wife answer independently six questions on a 6-point rating scale. The totals from each member of the couple are used to derive an 11-scale profile. The scales assess (1) degree of satisfaction with the frequency and range of sexual behaviors for the male and female, respectively, (2) self-acceptance concerning the pleasure derived from engaging in

sexual activities, (3) pleasure obtained from sexual activity, (4) accuracy of knowledge of partner's preferred sexual activities, and (5) degree of acceptance of partner. A computer scoring programs is available.

Test–retest reliability values range from 0.67 to 0.90 for the 11 scales. The convergent and discriminant validity of the instrument has been assessed. This inventory discriminated between couples suffering from sexual dysfunction and sexually satisfied couples. Longitudinal data are reported indicating that all 11 scales of the Sexual Interaction Inventory reflect changes induced by therapy in a group of patients suffering from sexual dysfunction.

LoPiccolo J, & Steger JC. The sexual interaction inventory: A new instrument for assessment of sexual dysfunction. *Archives of Sexual Behavior*, 1974, *3*, 585–590
McGovern KB, Stewart RC, & LoPiccolo J. Secondary orgasmic dysfunction. 1. Analysis and strategies for treatment. *Archives of Sexual Behavior*, 1975, *4*, 265–275

THE SEXUAL ORIENTATION METHOD

M. P. Feldman, M. J. MacCulloch, V. Mellor, and J. M. Pinschof

The Sexual Orientation Method is a questionnaire that is aimed at assessing the relative degree of homo- and heteroerotic orientation of men who show homosexual behavior. The questonnaire may be used to evaluate the response of homosexual patients to treatment, but it is not intended to detect homosexuality in subjects who are not known to have homosexual characteristics.

The questions are presented at random in pairs, with a total of 120 pairs. Pairs 1 to 60 concern attitudes to males, and 60 to 120 concern attitudes to women. Subjects are asked to respond wth one of six adjectives (interesting, attractive, handsome, hot, pleasurable, and exciting) to two concepts: "Men are sexually to me . . ." and "Women are sexually . . ." For each adjective, five scale positions are used for each adjective, e.g., (1) very attractive, (2) quite attractive, (3) neither attractive nor unattractive, (4) quite attractive, and (5) very unattractive.

Test–retest reliability in samples of control subjects ranged between 0.80 and 0.94. Pretreatment mean scores of homosexual patients were found to be significantly different from control groups. Scores following aversion therapy for homosexuality were significantly related to independent assessment of clinical improvement.

Sambrooks JE, & MacCulloch MJ. A modification of the sexual orientation method and automated technique for presentation and scoring. *British Journal of Social and Clinical Psychology*, 1973, *12*, 163–170 (a revision of the Sexual Orientation Method)

SEXUAL PLEASURE INVENTORY

J. S. Annon

The Sexual Pleasure Inventory is a self-administered instrument that is a checklist of people, objects, and behaviors that are likely to lead to pleasure. The inventory was developed to assess the relative degree of arousal or other pleasant feelings a patient may associate with sexually related activities and experiences. A wide range of activities is covered for both sexes, from the normally expected to the more rare. The instrument may serve as a prime assessment measure for identifying and ordering specific sexual areas for therapeutic intervention.

Separate male and female forms are available and consist of 30 items. There are 5 possible responses for each item, from "not at all" to "very much." No information is available concerning reliability, and only face validity exists.

Annon JS. *The behavioral treatment of sexual problems*, vol. 2. *Intensive therapy*. Honolulu, Enabling Systems, 1976

SEXUAL RESPONSE PROFILE

R. J. Pion

The Sexual Response Profile is a self-administered questionnaire covering knowledge, attitudes, and past and present practices in sexual areas. The items were chosen through an analysis of suggested questions offered by a sample of physicians seeing couples with sexual and marital problems. It is intended to be useful in pinpointing problem areas related to the patient's sexual history.

The questionnaire contains 80 items. Each item is scored according to the content of the subject; the scores, therefore, range from yes/no responses, through checkmarks, to scaled items. No overall scoring system exists for the entire inventory. No reports of reliability are available, and the questionnaire only shows face validity.

Annon JS. *The behavioral treatment of sexual problems*, vol 2. *Intensive therapy*. Honolulu: Enabling Systems, 1976

SEXUALITY EXPERIENCE SCALES

J. Frenken

The Sexuality Experience Scales is a group research inventory that was developed for use in different kinds of research, e.g., survey studies on sexual behavior and attitudes, marriage research, and as an outcome instrument in research in sexual dysfunction therapy. This inventory is based on a hypothesized basic dimension of sexual experience: acceptance versus rejection of sexuality. This hypothesis was operationalized and administered to a pilot group from which three factors were determined: traditional restrictive sex morals (acceptance versus rejection), psychosexual stimulaton (seeking, allowing/avoidance, rejection), and sexual motivation (appetitive versus aversive).

The inventory contains 83 multiformulated questions, e.g., "Some women have very little need of intercourse. Others have a strong need. How often would you prefer to have intercourse? (1) less than once a month; (2) once a month; (3) 2 to 3 times a month; (4) once a week; (5) 2 to 3 times a week; and (6) 4 or more times a week."

Reliability for each of the scales varies from 0.86 to 0.92. Internal consistency of the scales was found to be adequate. The SES is reported to be useful in intake interviews with patients when exact value of the score is not stressed. The scales give some insight on specific problems in sex matters by looking at answers on individual items.

Frenken J. *Sexuality experience scales.* Amsterdam: Swets and Zeitlinger, in press

SEX ATTITUDE QUESTIONNAIRE

B. Fretz

The Sex Attitude Questionnaire is a self-report instrument that is intended to measure attitudes toward behaviors and situations construed as sexual in our society. It can be used to measure the degree of positive or negative regard for sexual behaviors among specific populations and to assess the effects of pertinent communication, such as sex education on attitude change.

Long and short forms are available. The long form consists of 30 concepts each, with 17 bipolar dimensions, for a total of 510 responses. The short form includes 12 concepts, each evaluated on seven bipolar dimensions. Evaluative dimensions include good–bad, valuable–worthless, kind–cruel. Understanding dimensions include understandable–mysterious and familiar–strange. Dynamic dimensions include active–passive and fast–slow. Items can be scored on a scale from 1 to 7.

Retest reliabiliity of the short form on bipolar dimensions ranged from 0.78 to 0.52. Test–retest reliability by concept ranged from 0.35 for homosexual to 0.67 for the oral and/or anal intercourse concept.

Evidence of internal validity has been provided in studies using one instrument to evaluate the effects of sex education programs, revealing significant pre–post treatment changes.

Bekander I. Semantic description of complex and meaningful stimulus material. *Perception and Motor Skills,* 1966, *22,* 201–207

Fretz BR. *An attitude measure of sexual behaviors.* Paper presented at the American Psychological Association, 1974

SEX ATTITUDE SCALE

G. Rotter

The Sex Attitude Scale is an attitude scale concerning a number of sexual issues such as sex roles, sex education, sexual intercourse, and marital relationships. The items are to be rated on a Likert scale of seven degrees of agreement, from totally agree to totally disagree.

There are 100 items scored on a 7-point scale from + 30 to − 3, indicating agreement or disagreement with the statement.

No reliability data have been reported. In terms of validity, in one study a number of items achieved statistical significance from raters' assignment into sexually adjusted and maladjusted categories.

Rotter GS. *Clinician perspectives of adjusted and maladjusted sex attitudes.* (Unpublished manuscript available from the author)

Rotter GS. *Genital and socio-sexual attitudes of college students.* Paper presented at the Eastern Psychological Association, Washington, DC, 1973

A SEX ATTITUDE SURVEY AND PROFILE

G. McHugh and T. G. McHugh

A Sex Attitude Survey and Profile is currently published in a preliminary edition. It is an adult self-report instrument. Its aim is to register individual responses to stated attitudes, beliefs, and values concerning a wide variety of sexual feelings, activities, and practices.

There are 107 items to which the individuals indicate their degree of agreement or disagreement by circling the appropriate response. No information is available concerning reliability and validity.

No Reference Available

SEX EXPERIENCE SCALES FOR MALES AND FEMALES

M. Zuckerman

The Sex Experience Scales for Males and Females is a self-report instrument that was developed on college undergraduates, and consists of a list of sexual behaviors people have engaged in, from the most basic (e.g., kissing) to various coital positions and oral–genital contact. Separate scales for males and females have been arranged in a hierarchy from most endorsed to least endorsed by the population on whom they were developed. There are 12 items requiring forced-choice responses of whether or not the subject has had that experience. Coefficient of reproducibility and rank-order correlations between males and females are available.

Zuckerman M. Scales of sex experience for males and females. *Journal of Consulting and Clinical Psychology*, 1973, *41*, 27–35

THE SEX INVENTORY

F. C. Thorne

The Sex Inventory is an empirically developed inventory comprising nine scales designated as follows: sex drive and interest, sexual maladjustment and frustration, neurotic conflict associated with sex, sexual fixation and cathexes, repression of sexuality, loss of sex controls, homosexuality, sex-role confidence, and promiscuity. This instrument has been used in the study of sexual attitudes and behaviors of adult men in several normal and clinical groups. The self-report inventory may be supplemented by interview and observational verification. The instrument is intended to measure "state" phenomena, which may be in constant flux, or change. There are 200 questions requiring a true or false answer.

Data are available on test–retest reliability of scale scores and on the factorial characteristics of the instrument.

Thorne FC. The sex inventory. *Journal of Clinical Psychology*, 1966, *22*, 367–373
Thorne FC. A grand research design for measuring psychological states. *Journal of Clinical Psychology*, 1976a, *32*, 209–220
Thorne FC. A new approach to psychopathology. *Journal of Clinical Psychology*, 1976b, *32*, 221–226

SEX KNOWLEDGE AND ATTITUDE TEST

H. I. Lief and D. M. Reed

The Sex Knowledge and Attitude Test (SKAT) is an adult self-report scale oriented toward the gathering of information about sex-ual attitudes, sexual knowledge, and the level of experience in sexual activities. A certain amount of demographic and biographical data are also collected. It is an omnibus-type scale designed to function as both a teaching and a research instrument in human sexuality. The SKAT comprises 149 multiple-choice items in four distinct areas: attitudes, knowledge, demography, and sexual experiences.

Internal consistency coefficients in the 1970s and 1980s, and test–retest coefficients in the 1980s are reported. A number of validity studies are reported in the manual.

Buros OK (Ed). *The seventh mental measurement yearbook.* Highland Park, NJ: Gryphon Press, 1972 (a review of SKI included)

SEX KNOWLEDGE INVENTORIES

G. McHugh

The Sex Knowledge Inventories are designed to assess individual levels of sex knowledge. There are two tests, labeled forms X and Y. The SKI form X is aimed at adults. The SKI form Y is aimed at youth groups and for sex-education classes at the high-school level. Form X contains 80 multiple-choice questions. Form Y contains 100 items. No information is reported for reliability and validity.

No Reference Available

SEX ROLE INVENTORY

S. L. Bem

The Sex Role Inventory (SRI) is an adult self-report scale focused on the measurement of gender role definition by characterizing a person on two independent dimensions of masculinity and femininity. It also includes a social desirability scale. Masculinity and femininity scores reveal the degree of endorsement of typical masculine and feminine personality characteristics as self-descriptive. An androgeny score indicates the relative amount of masculinity and femininity that the person includes in his or her self-description.

Items include 60 descriptive personality

characteristics rated on 7-point Likert scales. Test–retest and internal consistency reliability have been reported. Validation studies are reported in reference publications.

Bem S. The measurement of psychological androgyny. *Journal of Consulting and Clinical Psychology*, 1974, *42*, 155–158

Bem S. Sex-role adaptability: One consequence of psychological androgyny. *Journal of Personality and Social Psychology*, 1975, *31*, 634–639

SEX QUESTIONNAIRE

M. Zuckerman

The Sex Questionnaire is an adult self-report questionnaire that is a scale designed to provide an evaluation of sexual attitudes and behaviors. It comprises 10 subscales that vary in length from several one-item scales to the Heterosexual Experience Scale of 14 items.

The 91 items are rated along 5-point scales. The instrument is composed of the following subscales: heterosexual experience, attitudes toward heterosexual behavior, parental attitudes, homosexual experience, orgasmic experience, masturbatory experience, number of heterosexual partners, and desire to view erotic movies. Test–retest reliabilities are available. No validity information is reported.

Zuckerman M, Tushup R, & Finner F. Sexual attitudes and experiences: Attitudes and personality correlates and changes produced by a course in human sexuality. *Journal of Consulting and Clinical Psychology*, 1976, *44*, 7–13

SEX QUESTIONNAIRE FOR COLLEGE STUDENTS

R. Shipley

The Sex Questionnaire for College Students is a self-report questionnaire that covers areas such as information and attitudes toward contraception, physiology and anatomy, sex-role behaviors, marriage, and childrearing.

There are 156 true–false items, multiple-choice items, and Likert Scale. The author reports an internal consistency reliability coefficient of 0.74. No validity information is available.

No Reference Available

SEX-ROLE SURVEY

A. P. MacDonald, Jr.

The Sex-Role Survey is a self-report scale that measures subjects' attitudes toward sex roles and was developed on subjects ranging in age from 14 to 73. There are 53 items, with a 20-item short form available. Each item is scored by the subject on a 9-point scale of agreement ranging from "I agree very much" through "I disagree very much." Scores yield a total score and four factors: (1) equality in business and the profession, (2) sex-role appropriate behavior, (3) equal involvement in social and domestic work, and (4) power in the home.

Reliability data have been reported. On a study of 317 males and 322 females, ranging in age from 14 to 73, alpha coefficients on the four factors and total score were obtained as follows: (1) business and the profession = 0.94; (2) sex-role appropriate behavior = 0.85; (3) social and domestic work = 0.85; (4) power in the home = 0.85; SRS total = 0.96. Normative data and information on validity are available.

MacDonald AP, Jr, & Games RG. Some characteristics of those who hold positive and negative attitudes toward homosexuals. *Journal of Homosexuality*, 1974, *1*, 9–27

MacDonald AP, Jr. Identification and measurement of multidimensional attitudes toward equality between the sexes. *Journal of Homosexuality*, 1974, *1*, 165–178

Appendix F: Some Experimental Marriage Assessment Procedures*

*These scales are presented as information and their use must be kept strictly on an experimental basis.

Family Information

	Very Dissatisfied									Very Satisfied
1. Your present occupation	1	2	3	4	5	6	7	8	9	10
2. Your occupational progress	1	2	3	4	5	6	7	8	9	10
3. Your present relationship with close relatives	1	2	3	4	5	6	7	8	9	10
4. Your present religious participation	1	2	3	4	5	6	7	8	9	10
5. Your personal time	1	2	3	4	5	6	7	8	9	10
6. Your physical health	1	2	3	4	5	6	7	8	9	10
7. Your emotional satisfaction	1	2	3	4	5	6	7	8	9	10
8. Marriage	1	2	3	4	5	6	7	8	9	10
9. Parenthood	1	2	3	4	5	6	7	8	9	10
10. Today my spouse is listening to me	1	2	3	4	5	6	7	8	9	10
11. Today my spouse understands me	1	2	3	4	5	6	7	8	9	10
12. Today my spouse loves me	1	2	3	4	5	6	7	8	9	10
13. Today things are peaceful in this home	1	2	3	4	5	6	7	8	9	10
14. Today I learned something about my spouse	1	2	3	4	5	6	7	8	9	10
15. Today I feel welcome in this family	1	2	3	4	5	6	7	8	9	10
16. Today there is less tension in this home	1	2	3	4	5	6	7	8	9	10
17. Today I am happy with this family	1	2	3	4	5	6	7	8	9	10
18. Today I feel this marriage has potential	1	2	3	4	5	6	7	8	9	10

Family Study Center Description

Name _____ Sex _____ Date _____

Write here term to be defined: Marriage (or any other term). Check that position on each of the scales below that best represents the direction and intensity of your judgment of the term noted above.

Good	____ ,	____ ,	____ ,	____ ,	____ ,	____ ,	____	Bad
Useful	____ ,	____ ,	____ ,	____ ,	____ ,	____ ,	____	Useless
Superior	____ ,	____ ,	____ ,	____ ,	____ ,	____ ,	____	Inferior
Smart	____ ,	____ ,	____ ,	____ ,	____ ,	____ ,	____	Stupid
Square	____ ,	____ ,	____ ,	____ ,	____ ,	____ ,	____	Cool
Selfish	____ ,	____ ,	____ ,	____ ,	____ ,	____ ,	____	Unselfish
Tough	____ ,	____ ,	____ ,	____ ,	____ ,	____ ,	____	Soft
Friendly	____ ,	____ ,	____ ,	____ ,	____ ,	____ ,	____	Unfriendly
Kind	____ ,	____ ,	____ ,	____ ,	____ ,	____ ,	____	Cruel
Important	____ ,	____ ,	____ ,	____ ,	____ ,	____ ,	____	Unimportant
Small	____ ,	____ ,	____ ,	____ ,	____ ,	____ ,	____	Big
Slow	____ ,	____ ,	____ ,	____ ,	____ ,	____ ,	____	Fast
Helpless	____ ,	____ ,	____ ,	____ ,	____ ,	____ ,	____	Helpful
Aggressive	____ ,	____ ,	____ ,	____ ,	____ ,	____ ,	____	Passive
Dangerous	____ ,	____ ,	____ ,	____ ,	____ ,	____ ,	____	Harmless
Powerless	____ ,	____ ,	____ ,	____ ,	____ ,	____ ,	____	Powerful
Pleasant	____ ,	____ ,	____ ,	____ ,	____ ,	____ ,	____	Unpleasant
Strong	____ ,	____ ,	____ ,	____ ,	____ ,	____ ,	____	Weak
Quiet	____ ,	____ ,	____ ,	____ ,	____ ,	____ ,	____	Noisy
Dependent	____ ,	____ ,	____ ,	____ ,	____ ,	____ ,	____	Independent

Thank you for your help.

Measure of Affectionate Behavior*

Couples exchange various types of affectionate behavior. You will be asked to indicate which of the behaviors listed below you have recently engaged in. Please read and carefully follow the directions.

During the designated time period, did you engage in any of the listed behaviors? If you mark "yes" by any behavior, indicate approximately how many times during the designated time period the behavior occurred.

During the past _____ , did you:

			No. of times
1. Say "I Love You" to your intimate?	yes ____	no ____	_____
2. Kiss your intimate?	yes ____	no ____	_____
3. Hug your intimate?	yes ____	no ____	_____
4. Gently touch your intimate?	yes ____	no ____	_____
5. Sit close to your intimate?	yes ____	no ____	_____
6. Telephone your intimate for no special reason?	yes ____	no ____	_____
7. Give a present to your intimate?	yes ____	no ____	_____
8. Wear something special for your intimate?	yes ____	no ____	_____
9. Think fondly about your intimate?	yes ____	no ____	_____
10. Compliment your intimate on his or her appearance?	yes ____	no ____	_____
11. Make something for your intimate?	yes ____	no ____	_____
12. Do a favor for your intimate?	yes ____	no ____	_____
13. Write a love note to your intimate?	yes ____	no ____	_____
14. Share a laugh with your intimate?	yes ____	no ____	_____
15. Cook a special meal for your intimate?	yes ____	no ____	_____

*Developed by Juan Florez and reprinted with his permission.

Family Study Center

Some people have trouble starting sentences with an "I" pronoun. The following stems have been found helpful to start making "I" statements. Please complete these sentences and start thinking about other possible completions of these sentences.

I wish _____ .

I would _____ .

I hate _____ .

I want _____ .

I feel _____ .

If I were _____ .

If I could _____ .

I love _____ .

I can _____ .

I could _____ .

I should _____ .

I ought _____ .

I enjoy _____ .

I must _____ .

I need _____ .

I like _____ .

It pleases me when _____ .

I understand _____ .

I see _____ .

I remember _____ .

I fear _____ _____ .

It pleases me if _____ .

I am _____ .

I trust _____ .

I hurt _____ .

I think _____ .

I do not like _____ .

I complain _____ .

It scares me when _____ .

I blame _____ .

I try _____ .

I work _____ .

It hurts me if _____ .

I look _____ .

I do not want _____ .

Make up three stems on your own and complete them.

1. _____ .

2. _____ .

3. _____ .

Family Study Center Georgia State University Family Adjustment Inventory

Complete columns A through D.

A	B	C	D	E
List three general areas of satisfaction/dissatisfaction in your life, your marriage, or your family.	For each area, specify further concrete behaviors that are pleasing/displeasing and satisfactory/unsatisfactory to you.	Now rank which of these behaviors (1–10) needs closest attention. 10 is top priority; 1 is lowest priority.	Rate each behavior on a scale of -5 (very negative) to $+5$ (very positive). Do not use 0.	(Ratings × Rankings) Scores
1.	1. 2. 3.			
2.	4. 5. 6.			
3.	7. 8. 9.			
4. List on the side any behavior not listed above.	10.			
				Total

It is important that 10 specific behaviors be listed.

Spouse Abuse Questionnaire*

Rate the following statements.	+2 Strongly agree	+1 Agree	0 Can't say	−1 Disagree	−2 Strongly disagree
1. A man who hits his wife enough to leave bruises should be removed from the home by the police.	___	___	___	___	___
2. The best approach to counseling with abusive spouses is couples therapy.	___	___	___	___	___
3. When a woman gets hit by her husband, she probably has it coming.	___	___	___	___	___
4. Men who abuse their wives should probably get out of the marriage.	___	___	___	___	___
5. A man who cannot stop himself from hitting his wife has never learned self-control.	___	___	___	___	___
6. The underlying cause of spouse abuse today is the rise of the women's movement.	___	___	___	___	___
7. No real progress in spouse abuse can be made until more widespread social changes are made in our attitude toward violence in general.	___	___	___	___	___
8. The real culprit in spouse abuse is alcohol abuse.	___	___	___	___	___
9. Men who were abused as children will tend to be spouse abusers.	___	___	___	___	___
10. The wives of batterers are as pathologically ill or more so than the men they relate to.	___	___	___	___	___
11. Men who physically abuse their wives are sociopathic.	___	___	___	___	___
12. Men who physically abuse their wives are psychotic.	___	___	___	___	___
13. Men who physically abuse their wives are neurotically dependent.	___	___	___	___	___
14. Battered wives are mostly innocent victims.	___	___	___	___	___
15. Insane jealousy on the part of the batterer is the main cause of his physically abusing his spouse.	___	___	___	___	___
16. It is useless to attempt to do therapy with a spouse abuser unless his compliance is totally voluntary.	___	___	___	___	___
17. If a man hits his wife on one occasion, a reconciliation should be attempted; if it recurs a second time, she should leave him.	___	___	___	___	___
18. As therapists, we should refuse to deal with spouse abusers unless they admit they are wrong.	___	___	___	___	___
19. Attempting to change the behaviors of batterers without altering underlying psychological structures is only bandaid therapy and will not have a lasting value in stopping spouse abuse.	___	___	___	___	___

*Developed by Frank J. Ostrowski and reprinted with his permission. Unlike many of the other questionnaires, respondents are requested *not* to sign this questionnaire.

Rate the following statements.	+2 Strongly agree	+1 Agree	0 Can't say	−1 Disagree	−2 Strongly disagree

20. Spouse abusers are also child abusers.

    _____ _____ _____ _____ _____

21. Since some violence of males toward their mates has gone on in all times and cultures, a bit of it is to be expected and allowed for.

    _____ _____ _____ _____ _____

22. Most men who might come for counseling on spouse abuse are really too proud to look at their own shortcomings and make any changes.

    _____ _____ _____ _____ _____

23. Most men who batter have an extremely poor self-image.

    _____ _____ _____ _____ _____

Tally Sheet

	Strongly agree	Agree	Can't say	Disagree	Strongly disagree
I. Characteristics of the women					
3. . . . probably have it coming . . .	———	———	———	———	———
6. . . . women's movement . . .	———	———	———	———	———
10. . . . wives . . . pathologically ill . . .	———	———	———	———	———
14. . . . wives . . . innocent victims . . .	———	———	———	———	———
II. Characteristics of the men					
5. . . . no self-control . . .	———	———	———	———	———
8. . . . alcohol abuse . . .	———	———	———	———	———
9. . . . abused as children . . .	———	———	———	———	———
11. . . . sociopathic . . .	———	———	———	———	———
12. . . . psychotic . . .	———	———	———	———	———
13. . . . neurotically dependent . . .	———	———	———	———	———
15. . . . insanely jealous . . .	———	———	———	———	———
20. . . . child abusers . . .	———	———	———	———	———
23. . . . poor self-image . . .	———	———	———	———	———
III. Social causes					
7. . . . attitude toward violence . . .	———	———	———	———	———
21. . . . all times and all cultures . . .	———	———	———	———	———
IV. Civil action					
1. . . . removal by police . . .	———	———	———	———	———
4. . . . man get out . . .	———	———	———	———	———
17. . . . woman leave after 2nd time . . .	———	———	———	———	———
V. Therapy with batterer					
A. *Therapy of choice*					
2. . . . couples . . .	———	———	———	———	———
16. . . . voluntary . . .	———	———	———	———	———
19. . . . depth . . .	———	———	———	———	———
B. *Barriers to change*					
18. . . . must admit are wrong . . .	———	———	———	———	———
22. . . . too proud . . .	———	———	———	———	———

Index

a
b
3 c
4 d
5 e
6 f
7 g
8 h
9 i
8 0 j